THE NEW COMPLETE BOOK OF
COOKERY

THE NEW COMPLETE BOOK OF
COOKERY

ONTARIO·CANADA

CONTENTS

FOREWORD

When you open this book and turn over the pages—over 500 of them—one of the first things you will notice is that the many sections are written by a large number of different authors. The reason is that this book represents the combined efforts of a unique group of top cookery writers and journalists, chefs, restauranteurs, wine and food connoisseurs, and home economists from many different specialist areas. Widely traveled and unchallenged experts in their own fields, these contributors have given us an exciting cookbook which breaks new ground in cookbook writing, and which, because of its size and the varied experience of the contributors, has an enormous scope and variety.

A most noticeable thing about all the contributors was their enthusiasm for the sort of fresh foods which are available to everyone. They have all exploited to the full the flavors and potential of such ingredients as good meat and fish, dairy produce, and fresh fruits and vegetables, and the result is to give the reader a new viewpoint on cooking both for every day and for company meals.

I would like to express my sincere thanks to all the contributors for their helpful co-operation with the photography for this book, to Ben Ericksson, the photographer, for his patience and skill, to Babette Hayes, the designer, for her artistic talent, and to Alison Burt for her willing assistance. I hope you will enjoy reading and using this book as much as I enjoyed preparing it, and I am sure that whether you are housewife and mother, experienced cook, young bride, complete beginner, or gourmet you will find it of inspiration and use.

THE EDITOR

INTRODUCTION

Food and Flavor

START WITH BUTTER AND OIL

Butter, margarine, and all cooking oils should be of good quality to give a good flavor to your food.

Many delicious dishes owe their special taste to butter: asparagus au beurre, baked potatoes, new potatoes served hot with butter, smooth creamy white sauces, fish cooked à la meunière, tender fillets of beef, veal, and pork fried in butter, the flavor of fried mushrooms, mouth-watering rich pie crusts, cakes, shortbread, and delicious hot buttered toast.

Margarine gives good texture, color, and flavor to cakes, pastries, and cookies. The margarines made from vegetable oils are low in cholesterol, which makes them valuable in certain diets.

Vegetable oil mixed with equal quantities of butter is ideal for shallow frying or sautéing of meat, fish, and vegetables. The oil prevents the butter from browning.

Olive oil gives a rich flavor to French dressing and mayonnaise.

Lard, drippings, and chicken and goose fats are used for authentic regional dishes and kosher cookery.

THE ONION FAMILY

The pungent onion family, which includes garlic and scallions, is an essential basic flavoring in all dishes where flavour is developed. Onions add to the flavor of meat, poultry, fish, and vegetables. The onion is one of the most valuable and versatile ingredients. If onions are fried until a golden 'honey brown' to caramelize their sugar content, they give a rich brown color to stews and casseroles, which looks appetizing, apart from tasting delicious. Onions studded with cloves give flavor to stock, sauces, boiled ham, or poultry. Onions are used in stuffings, soups, and flans. They are delicious in their own right, baked, boiled, fried, or pickled.

Garlic is a strong pungent bulb which is an essential ingredient in Mediterranean cookery. It can be used to give a hint of garlic flavor or a strong taste to casseroles, pasta sauces, soups, roast meat, and salads.

The cloves of garlic should be used crushed or finely chopped to release their flavor.

Shallots are tiny, delicate, violet-tinted bulb onions. They are usually sautéed in butter and oil as a flavoring in casseroles, stews, and sauces served with game and poultry. Finely chopped shallots sautéed in butter add a delicious flavor to sautéed meat, fish, and poultry.

Scallions are long tender young white onions which add flavor to salads. They are also chopped and sautéed and served in rich wine sauces with meat and poultry. They are an indispensable ingredient in oriental cookery.

Chives have a delicate flavor. Finely chopped chives add a subtle taste to omelets, soufflés and salads, and a sprinkling of chopped chives is a useful garnish on delicately flavored soups and hors d'oeuvres.

SALT AND PEPPER

Salt and pepper are necessary ingredients to bring out the flavor of foods.

Coarse salt gives a better flavor when used in cooked food than ordinary table salt. It can be used for the table in a salt grinder.

Freshly cracked black pepper gives a freshly seasoned flavor to food. This can also be used for the table in a grinder. White pepper is used in delicately colored foods.

HERBS AND SPICES

Herbs and spices give their own special flavor to food (see chapter on Herbs and Spices).

TAKE STOCK

Stock is a liquid which contains the flavors, nutrients, and extracts of bones, meat or fish, and vegetables. It is used to enrich the flavor of soups, sauces, gravies, and casseroles. Many dishes rely on rich beef or chicken stock for their flavor. Home-made stock is still made in some kitchens where serious cooking is done, but commerical bouillon cubes are equally successful and more convenient for most recipes.

USE WINE ADVENTUROUSLY

The flavor of good wine adds unequaled richness to good food and the same wine should be served with the food to complement the flavor of the dish. It is best used in slowly-cooked casseroles with meat or poultry. The slow, careful cooking gives a uniquely delicious flavor. The alcohol content of wine is evaporated during cooking, leaving only the distinctive taste. Use it for basting roast meat or for blending ingredients into a casserole. Use it to marinate meat to tenderize the tissues as well as to add flavor. A little sherry adds flavor to a simple clear soup and makes gravy taste delicious.

THE RICH ONES

Egg yolks and cream are the ingredients which add the quality of richness to well-flavored food.

Egg yolks are used to enrich and thicken. They add flavor and color to fricassées, cream soups, soufflés, rich sauces, desserts, and pastry.

Cream is a luxurious complement to high class cookery. It is used mainly in sauces, soups, soufflés, fricassées, and desserts to create a smooth texture and rich flavor.

The Store Cupboard

A good cook always has the basic ingredients in stock, for these are essential for the development of good flavors in food.

Staples:	*Have a good supply of:*
flour	eggs
sugar	milk
rice	cream
cornstarch	cheese
spaghetti or macaroni	
gelatin	

To give flavor:	*Add to these:*
butter	fresh meat
vegetable oil	fresh fish
olive oil	fresh vegetables
bacon	fresh salad greens
onions	fresh fruit
garlic	
salt	
freshly ground pepper	
herbs	
spices	
stock or bouillon cubes	
wine	
tomato paste	
wine vinegar	

Marketing Hints

1. Make a list and keep to it as far as possible but be flexible enough to take advantage of good bargains.
2. Buy ahead, with your menu plans for several days or a week in mind.
3. Buy groceries and dry goods once a week. Perishable foods need only be bought about twice a week, if stored in a refrigerator.
4. Shop for value for money. Cheap cuts of meat can be good value if they are cooked correctly. Expensive cuts of meat can be better value for money than cheap cuts which contain a large proportion of fat and bone.
5. Buy food in season when it is reasonably priced and of good flavor.
6. Buy in bulk or in large sizes when possible. It works out cheaper.
7. Remember that fish is nutritious and some varieties are excellent value for money.
8. Cheese, weight for weight, is more nutritious than meat, quicker to prepare, just as versatile, and much cheaper.
9. Read the labels on cereal foods, bread, and cookies, for 'restored', 'enriched', 'fortified', and the ingredient lists on canned and convenience foods. Know what you are buying!

Marketing Guide

Your list should be based on these groups:
Meat, fish, and poultry
Diary produce and eggs
Fresh fruit, vegetables, and salad
Bread and baked goods
Frozen food
Staple ingredients—such as flour and sugar
Packaged, canned, and bottled groceries.
The following is a guide to the average amounts of uncooked foods to allow per person when planning a main meal. It will help with your marketing list.

Meat:	
Raw meat	$\frac{1}{4}$-$\frac{1}{3}$ lb.
	with bone $\frac{1}{2}$-$\frac{3}{4}$ lb.
Chops	$\frac{1}{3}$-$\frac{1}{2}$ lb.
Rump steak or tenderloin	$\frac{1}{4}$-$\frac{1}{3}$ lb.
Liver or kidneys	$\frac{1}{4}$ lb.
Chicken	piece $\frac{1}{3}$-$\frac{1}{2}$ lb.
Bacon	slices 3
Cooked meats	2-3 oz.

Fish:	
White fish	$\frac{1}{3}$-$\frac{1}{2}$ lb.
Mullet	$\frac{1}{2}$ lb.
Kippers	$\frac{1}{3}$-$\frac{1}{2}$ lb.
Prawns or shrimp with shell	$\frac{1}{4}$-$\frac{1}{3}$ lb.
Lobster or crab with shell	$\frac{1}{2}$-$\frac{3}{4}$ lb.

Eggs:
2 per person per main course

Cheese:	1/6 lb.

Vegetables:	*Servings per lb.*
Potatoes	3-4
New potatoes	4-5
Broccoli	3-4
Brussels sprouts	4-5
Cabbage	4-5
Cauliflower	3
Green beans	4
Lima beans	in pod 2
Peas	in pod 2
Root vegetables: pumpkin, turnips	3
Spinach	2-3
Frozen vegetables	4

Soup:	$\frac{3}{4}$ cup

Rice and Pasta:	2 oz.

Milk puddings:	$\frac{2}{3}$ cup

Emergency Meals

A tremendous variety of prepared and partially prepared food stuffs help you produce attractive meals quickly and cope with the problem of unexpected guests to feed. There is a wide range of convenience foods available in the shops today: quick frozen, canned, powdered, dehydrated, and accelerated freeze dried. Certain foods should be kept on hand for emergencies—the egg is a supreme standby!

For Your Emergency Shelf

Soup—keep a variety of meat and vegetable soups and a good quality consommé or exotic game soup.
Canned fish—salmon, tuna, sardines, smoked oysters.
Canned ham.
Canned vegetables—tomatoes, sweet corn, champignons, asparagus, and artichoke hearts, to serve as an hors d'oeuvre or vegetable.
Canned fruits—have a variety handy for desserts and relishes.
Pasta and rice—good substitutes for potatoes and quicker to prepare.
Bouillon cubes—always useful.
Dried or canned milk.
Instant coffee powder.

Meal Planning

When planning meals it is important to include food which is essential to good health.

Start with the main dish of meat, fish, eggs, or cheese and build the rest of the meal around it, remembering to keep a balance of flavor, color, and texture.

Plan a weekly menu. It will make your shopping and organization of cooking much easier. Be adventurous, but introduce new dishes and new flavors to the family gradually, along with well-tried family favorites.

Do's

Plan 2 to 3 days' menu in advance.

Vary the food and cooking methods.

Avoid serving the same sort of food in different courses.

Avoid repeating a cooking method in a meal.

Vary the color of the food in your menu.

Plan attractive appetizing meals.

Serve something to bite and something to chew in every meal.

Cook simple dishes that are quick to prepare on busy days.

Serve light refreshing meals in hot weather.

Serve soup and substantial hot dishes in cold weather.

Follow hot spicy foods and rich flavors with light refreshing food.

Make imaginative and tasty dishes with cheap food by adding tasty ingredients.

Make tasty dishes with leftovers (see page 131).

Plan a meal which uses your oven sensibly—cook more than one dish in it at a time.

Don'ts

Plan only 1 meal ahead.

Serve broiled chops 3 times in a row.

Serve a fruit hors d'oeuvre and fruit dessert, or rice pilaff followed by a rice pudding.

Follow a meat stew with stewed fruit or steak and kidney dumpling with a steamed sponge pudding.

Serve potato soup, followed by chicken with white sauce, creamed potatoes, and vanilla ice cream.

Forget garnish or overgarnish.

Serve only a cheese soufflé followed by a fruit mousse, and forget the crisp salad.

Try to make skilful creations during the week if you are a working wife.

Serve hot rich heavy food in hot weather.

Serve chilled light dishes only in cold weather.

Serve a rich chocolate mousse with cream after a rich beef stroganoff with sour cream.

Buy expensive cuts of meat for every meal.

Waste leftovers.

Waste fuel and oven space unnecessarily.

Basic Cooking Methods

ROASTING

Now that many of us have freestanding, open broiler units or cookers with built-in spits, the roasting of meat in its true sense is once again possible. If the meat is cooked in an oven, baking would be a far better description. The roast on a spit, on the contrary, cooks in a dry atmosphere and retains its own particular flavor. Roasting (or baking) is a simple operation and needs little attention other than frequent basting during the cooking process to keep the meat from drying out. Tender joints of meat, game, and poultry are suitable for roasting.

An oven roast should be placed on a grid in a roasting pan in a 400° to 450° oven for 15 to 30 minutes to seal it. The heat is reduced to 325° to 350° and the meat continues to cook until done. Meat is basted frequently with fat, whether it is cooked on the spit or in the oven, beginning about 45 minutes after the meat has started to cook.

Roast beef can be tested with a sharp kitchen fork or skewer. Blood-red juice means the meat is very rare, pink, that it is medium done, and a clear liquid indicates the meat is well cooked. For pork or veal, the juices that run out should be perfectly clear. For lamb, the liquid should be clear or lightly touched with pink.

BROILING

Broiling is a popular and quick method of cooking tender, good-quality food over a red hot charcoal fire or under a red hot electric or gas broiler. The metal grid should always be hot and greased when the food is placed on it, to avoid sticking. A minute on one side and a minute on the other side initially, under a fierce heat, when broiling meat and fish, will seal the surface and preserve the flavor of the natural juices. Cooking is continued at a more moderate heat to allow gradual penetration into the thick juicy center. Thicker cuts should be cooked further from the heat, thinner cuts near the heat.

FRYING

Frying is cooking food in very hot fat or oil. The term refers to shallow frying, deep frying, dry frying. It also extends to oven frying and has come to mean the same as sautéing.

SHALLOW FRYING

A quick method of cooking food in a shallow layer of fat or oil in a skillet. Butter or margarine with a little oil to prevent it from browning is used to fry meat, fish, and vegetables. Finely chopped parsley, lemon juice, or slivered almonds are sometimes added to the sauce obtained.

Only very tender foods are suitable for pan-frying: fish, young chicken, chops, liver, beef tenderloin, and some vegetables. Thick slices of meat cannot be shallow fried successfully. Do not crowd food in the pan and do not cover the pan when frying because the steam thus held in will moisten and destroy the surface crispness of the food.

DEEP FRYING

A method of cooking food immersed in very hot oil or fat. Vegetable oil is good for all deep frying. Rendered beef fat is good for meat and less delicate foods. Butter, margarine, and chicken fat are unsuitable because they brown at a low temperature. The correct heat is important. If you do not have an automatically controlled electric skillet, use the bread test: drop a 1-inch cube of day-old bread in the hot oil; if the bread browns on one side in about 30 seconds, the temperature is right for deep frying. It must be hot enough to set the coating on the food, to prevent the oil from penetrating, and to conserve the juices and shape of the food. Do not allow the oil to smoke and make sure food to be cooked is as dry as possible. Keep the temperature invariable during cooking and drain food well on paper towels before serving.

DRY FRYING

Foods containing fat, such as bacon and sausages, are placed in a hot frying pan and fried gently in their own fat.

OVEN FRYING

This process is a very useful method of cooking fish or chicken. Heat the oven to 400°. Use enough oil, or oil and butter, to cover the bottom of a shallow baking dish. Heat the dish in the oven and then put in the food which you have first rolled in bread crumbs and basted with melted butter.

SAUTÉING

Originally sautéing was to fry food gently, in a small amount of fat or oil, in a covered sauté pan, until the food had absorbed all the fat. It was used to develop flavor in soups, sauces, and stews. Nowadays it is associated with shallow frying.

STEWING

A long slow method of cooking in a vessel with a tightly fitting lid. Usually used to make tough meats tender and tasty. Vegetables and meat are usually sautéed first in a mixture of fat and oil to develop flavor, then covered with a well-flavored stock, water, or wine and simmered, covered, until the meat is tender. The tough connective tissues of meat turn into gelatin with long slow moist cooking, but if overcooked the meat fibers tend to fall to shreds. Stewed fruit is a term associated with poached fruit.

BRAISING

Braising is simply a combination of roasting, stewing, and steaming. The meat to be braised is sometimes larded, often marinated, always browned in fat, and then cooked gently, covered, in a little liquid to preserve juices and flavor. In the classic French method, the casserole is lined with a mirepoix, a layer of sautéed or sliced vegetables, before slow simmering begins.

In general, meat, poultry, and fish to be braised is not cut up, but is braised in the piece. Cook until tender, basting from time to time to keep the top of the meat moist. Before serving, correct seasoning, and thicken the sauce, if necessary, with a beurre manié (equal quantities of flour and butter kneaded together). Vegetables as well as meats, poultry, and fish may be braised in this way with excellent results.

Any casserole may be used for braising provided it is thick enough to prevent scorching during the long cooking process and has a tightly fitting lid.

BOILING

The food is usually covered by liquid in a covered vessel and when the water comes to a boil the heat is regulated to keep it at the boiling point—212° at sea level—until the food is tender. The lid prevents steaming up the kitchen, saves fuel, and in some cases helps retain valuable vitamins which would otherwise be lost.

Many foods may be cooked in boiling water, but care is still essential to preserve and develop flavor. Vegetables are cooked in boiling, salted water, but these may be improved by adding 2 tablespoons butter, a little wine or vinegar, onion, sprigs of herbs, bay leaf, and peppercorns. Chicken and ham are delicious boiled in water with beer or cider or a dry white wine, herbs, and vegetables. Pasta takes on an aromatic flavor with crushed garlic, olive oil, and lemon juice added to a light stock.

POACHING

A slow, gentle method of cooking in a small amount of liquid, not necessarily water, where the surface of the liquid bubbles gently. The term 'poach' applies to fish, large and small, chicken pieces, vegetables, and fruit, as well as to eggs.

STEAMING

Food is cooked in steam rising from boiling water. A special steamer consists of a double saucepan with a perforated bottom, which allows the steam to rise to the upper container. A metal trivet under the dish holding the food to be cooked, in a large pan, with boiling liquid to come half way up the dish, is equally successful if you have no steamer. Thin cuts of fish or meat are steamed successfully on a covered heatproof plate, placed over a pan of boiling water.

Steaming is a most effective method of cooking for preserving the maximum of original taste. It also tenderizes tough tissues in meat and poultry. The water must be boiling when the food is placed over it and must be kept at a constant rapid boil with steam rising. A very tight lid is essential to prevent steam escaping and a further supply of boiling water at hand is a good idea for refills as the water evaporates.

Poultry steamed over boiling stock is delicious, the flavor adding to the juices. Steamed vegetables retain their original flavor. Valuable vitamins are not lost in water. Served with attractive dressings of butter, parsley, sautéed almonds, crisp fried bacon, or buttered bread crumbs, they are quite delicious. Well-made steamed puddings are light and flavorsome.

Basic Kitchen Tools and Utensils

For preparing ingredients

Essential	Desirable
1 carving knife	1 apple corer
1 French cook's knife	1 bean slicer
1 grater	1 cherry pitter
1 lemon squeezer	1 egg slicer
1 pair kitchen scissors	1 filleting knife
1 paring knife	1 grapefruit knife
1 utility knife .	1 grinder
1 vegetable peeler	1 melon baller
	1 meat chopper or cleaver
	1 parsley/mint cutter
	1 pastry crimper/butter curler
	1 potato masher
	1 rotary cheese grater
	1 slicing knife
	1 utility knife with serrated edge
	1 pair kitchen shears

For measuring and weighing

Essential	Desirable
1 liquid measuring cup, glass	1 measuring jug, 1-pint or 1-quart
1 set measuring cups	1 set kitchen scales
1 set measuring spoons	

For mixing and beating

Essential	Desirable
1 flour sifter	1 electric blender
1 household fork	1 electric mixer
1 mixing bowl, large	1 mixing bowl, very large
1 mixing bowl, medium	1 wire whisk
1 mixing bowl, small	
1 pastry blender	
1 rotary beater	
1 spoon, medium wooden	
1 spoon, small wooden	

For surface cooking

Essential	Desirable
1 deep fat fryer	1 candy thermometer
1 double boiler	1 coffee grinder
1 fish kettle	1 coffee percolator or dripolator
1 kettle	1 electric deep frier
1 lipped milk saucepan	1 electric skillet
1 omelet pan	1 pressure cooker
1 saucepan and lid, large	1 saucepan and lid, very large

1 saucepan and lid, medium
1 saucepan and lid, small
1 skillet and lid

For oven cooking

Essential	Desirable
2 baking sheets	1 cake pan, large, round or square
1 casserole and lid, oblong	6 custard cups
1 casserole and lid, round	1 flan ring
1 jelly roll pan	1 meat thermometer
1 loaf pan	1 soufflé dish
1 pair 7-inch layer pans	
1 pair 8-inch layer pans	
1 muffin or cup cake pan	
1 pie dish	
1 pie plate or pan	
1 roasting pan	
1 spring form pan, medium	
1 spring form pan, small	

For miscellaneous uses

Essential	Desirable
1 bottle opener	1 cookie press
1 can opener	1 Chinese hat or conical strainer
1 chopping board	1 fish scaler
1 colander	1 funnel
1 corkscrew	icing tips
1 flour dredger	1 jello mold
1 fork, long handle	6 individual jello molds
1 ladle	1 knife sharpener
1 pair kitchen tongs	1 marble slab
1 pancake turner	1 pepper grinder
1 pastry board	1 mortar and pastle
1 pastry brush	1 pastry bag with star and plain nozzles
1 perforated spoon, long handle	1 pudding bowl
1 plastic scraper or spatula	1 ring mold or baba mold
1 rolling pin	1 salt grinder
1 set cookie cutters plain round	1 set cookie cutters, fancy shapes
1 set salt and pepper shakers	1 set cookie cutters, fluted round
1 set skewers	1 set trussing needles
1 spoon, long handle	
1 strainer, medium	
1 strainer, small	
1 sugar dredger	
1 vegetable brush	

Helpful Facts and Figures

MEASURES

The cup and spoon measures used in this book refer to the United States Standard Measuring Cups and Spoons. The following tables give their capacity.

3 teaspoons	= 1 tablespoon	= $\frac{1}{2}$ fluid ounce
2 tablespoons	= $\frac{1}{8}$ cup	= 1 fluid ounce
4 tablespoons	= $\frac{1}{4}$ cup	= 2 fluid ounces
$5\frac{1}{3}$ tablespoons	= $\frac{1}{3}$ cup	= $3\frac{1}{3}$ fluid ounces
8 tablespoons	= $\frac{1}{2}$ cup	= 4 fluid ounces
		= $\frac{1}{4}$ pint
12 tablespoons	= $\frac{3}{4}$ cup	= 6 fluid ounces
16 tablespoons	= 1 cup	= 8 fluid ounces
		= $\frac{1}{2}$ pint
32 tablespoons	= 2 cups	= 16 fluid ounces
		= 1 pint
2 pints	= 1 quart	
4 quarts	= 1 gallon	

BAKING POWDER

All references to baking powder in this book are to American double-acting baking powder. Should you run out of double-acting baking powder you may substitute a mixture of cream of tartar and baking soda, allowing 1 teaspoon cream of tartar and $\frac{1}{2}$ teaspoon baking soda for every 1 cup flour.

FLOUR

All the baking and pie crust recipes in this book have been tested using all-purpose flour, and excellent results will be obtained using this flour. If you wish, you may substitute cake flour, using 1 cup plus 2 tablespoons cake flour to every 1 cup all-purpose flour called for in the recipe.

USING CUP AND SPOON MEASURES

Dry ingredients, e.g., flour, granulated sugar, confectioners' sugar, should be spooned lightly into the measuring cup and then leveled off with a knife, *without shaking the cup or packing down the contents.* Flour and sugars should be sifted first if they are at all lumpy, and confectioners' sugar is always measured sifted. Brown sugar should be firmly packed into the cup so that it will hold its shape like a miniature mud-pie when it is turned out of the cup. If you follow these directions when measuring you will get accurate quantities; accuracy is particularly important with cakes, pastry, and baking recipes.

When measuring fats, remember that they weigh the same melted or solid. You may find it helpful when measuring quantities of less than 1 cup to use the displacement method. This is as follows: Subtract the amount you wish to measure from 1 cup, then fill the cup with the difference in water. Then add enough butter or other fat to bring the water level to the top of the cup. This will give you the required quantity of fat. For example, if your recipe calls for $\frac{1}{4}$ cup butter, put $\frac{3}{4}$ cup water in the measuring cup and add butter until the water level rises to the top of the cup. Drain off the water and you are left with $\frac{1}{4}$ cup butter.

A list of common ingredients and their weights appears opposite.

Table of Equivalents

Food	Quantity	Yield
Almonds—whole shelled	5 oz.	1 cup
—ground	4 oz.	1 cup
Apples	1 medium-sized	1 cup sliced
Breadcrumbs	3-4 slices bread	1 cup dry crumbs
	1 slice bread	$\frac{3}{4}$ soft crumbs
Cabbage	1 lb.	4 cups shredded
Cheese	4 oz.	1 cup shredded
Clear honey, molasses	12 oz.	1 cup
Cocoa	1 oz.	$\frac{1}{4}$ cup
Cornstarch	1 oz.	$\frac{1}{4}$ cup
Cream (whipping)	1 cup	2 cups whipped
Currants, raisins	1 lb.	3 cups seedless
Dates	1 lb.	$2\frac{1}{2}$ cups pitted
Dry beans, Lima	1 cup	$2\frac{1}{2}$ cups cooked
Flour	1 lb.	4 cups
Graham crackers	9 squares	1 cup coarse crumbs
Lemon	1	2-3 tablespoons juice
Lentils	1 lb.	2 cups
Onion	1 medium	$\frac{1}{2}$ cup chopped
Orange	1 large	$\frac{1}{3}$-$\frac{1}{2}$ cup juice
Rice	1 lb.	$2\frac{1}{4}$ cups
	1 cup.	$3\frac{1}{2}$ cups cooked
Pasta—macaroni, noodles, spaghetti	8 oz.	4 cups cooked
Peanuts, shelled	7 oz.	1 cup
Sugar—brown (moist)	8 oz.	1 cup, firmly packed
—sifted confectioners'	1 lb.	$3\frac{1}{2}$ cups
—granulated	1 lb.	2 cups plus 2 tablespoons
—granulated	1 oz.	2 tablespoons
Walnuts—chopped	4 oz.	1 cup
—halved	4 oz.	1 cup

Table of Substitutions

Ingredient	Quantity	Substitute
Cooking chocolate, unsweetened	1 oz. (1 square)	3 tablespoons cocoa plus 1 tablespoon butter
Eggs	1 whole egg	2 egg yolks
Herbs	1 tablespoon fresh	1 teaspoon dried
Honey	1 cup	1 cup granulated sugar plus $\frac{1}{4}$ cup water
Milk	1 cup milk	$\frac{1}{2}$ cup evaporated milk plus $\frac{1}{2}$ cup water or 1 cup reconstituted non-fat dry milk plus $\frac{1}{2}$ oz. butter
	1 cup sour milk	2 tablespoons lemon juice or vinegar plus fresh milk to make 1 cup
Sour cream	1 cup	2 tablespoons lemon juice or white vinegar plus fresh cream to make 1 cup
Yeast	1 cake compressed yeast (1 oz.)	1 package active dry yeast ($\frac{1}{2}$ oz.)

Freezing

- A carefully planned and well-stocked home freezer provides a variety of foods, regardless of season, ready for selection when planning meals.
- Home freezing is a safe method of preservation when carried out correctly using quality foods prepared under hygienic conditions.
- A wide variety of home-frozen foods available for immediate use adds pleasure to entertaining and provides a ready welcome to unexpected guests.
- A half animal carcase may be purchased, already jointed, prepared, and stored at one time if the freezer capacity is large enough.

TYPES OF FREEZERS

Choose a freezer with sufficient capacity for your needs. An approximate guide to size suggests 3 cubic feet for each member of the family. There are two main types of freezers for domestic use, the upright type and the chest type. Combination models of refrigerator with freezer are also available.

EMERGENCIES

Before sending for the service man check the following points:
1. Is the main switch on?
2. Is the electric plug loose or pulled out?
3. Is the thermostat turned off?
4. Has the fuse blown out?
5. Is there a power break in the area?
   A well stocked freezer will keep its contents safely frozen for about 24 hours in the event of a power break, provided the freezer is kept tightly closed.
   Dry ice placed in the freezer will keep frozen foods in good condition for much longer than 24 hours.

THAWED FOOD

Food which becomes accidentally thawed must not be refrozen. It should be used within 24 hours if kept at refrigerator temperature (35° to 40°) or discarded.

SELECTION AND PREPARATION OF FOOD

1. Select only those foods which are of good quality.
2. All foods should be prepared and frozen when fresh; shortly after harvesting, soon after killing, or immediately after preparation in the case of cooked dishes.
3. Pack all foods in moisture-vapor-proof materials, in the quantities expected to be used at one time— one package can comprise a family-sized serving for one meal.
4. Put food into the freezer only when the package is cold.

FOODS UNSUITABLE FOR FREEZING

Cooked, fried meats—the outside crispness is lost. Milk sauces, non-egg custards, cream-pie fillings, gravy, and mayonnaise—these tend to separate and give a curdled appearance. Some sandwich fillings, such as lettuce, tomato, and jelly, seep into the bread and make it soft. Herb and spice flavorings—salt, chili, and pepper —loose their flavor after a few weeks, so it is best to add these when the food is reheated.

PACKAGING AND WRAPPING

The packaging material should keep moisture in and air out of the package to prevent desiccation or 'freezer-burn'. The material should prevent the development of off-flavors, or the transference of flavors between foods, and the tainting of air in the freezer. The packaging material must be strong enough to avoid tearing by irregular-shaped food, for example poultry. Containers should be transparent or opaque and stackable. The label should describe the contents of the package, the amount, and the date of preparation for storing:–

Cheese and celery sandwiches, 1 lunch, 10/21/72.

HELPFUL HINTS

Bread

Unbaked: Allow the dough to rise once, then knead once, pack, and freeze. Before cooking, defrost the dough completely and allow time for it to rise and 'prove' before baking.

Baked: Allow to cool completely, then pack and freeze.

Cookies

Unbaked: Make the dough and form to a roll like a fat sausage; then wrap and freeze. Thin circles may be sliced from the frozen roll, placed on a baking sheet, and cooked immediately.

Baked: Allow to cool completely, then pack and freeze.

Cakes (excluding sponges)

Unbaked: Put the cake batter into prepared greased pans, or muffin molds. Wrap and seal, then freeze, or freeze in containers and remove when solid, wrap separately, and return to the freezer.

Baked: Allow to cool thoroughly, seal, and freeze.

Pie crusts

Unbaked: Make the dough, and either wrap and freeze as a whole or roll to the shape desired (for example, a pie shell), then wrap and freeze. Dough frozen unshaped must be completely thawed and rolled out before use. Pie shells do not require defrosting before baking.

Baked: Allow the pie shell to cool, then wrap, seal, and freeze.

Soups and Stocks

Prepare and cook until a considerable amount of liquid has been evaporated, then allow to cool, package, seal, and freeze. To defrost, turn out and heat gently over low heat, add water or milk to dilute, reheat, and serve.

Stews

Prepare stews, etc., but do not over-cook. Allow to cool, package, seal, and freeze. Before serving, remove from the package, reheat gently, season if necessary, and serve.

Guide to Freezing Times

Food	Recommended Storage Period at 0°F.
Meat	
Beef	10-12 months
Beef—ground	4- 6 months
Ham—uncured	3- 4 months
Lamb	10-12 months
Liver—beef	3- 4 months
—poultry	2- 3 months
Mutton	4- 6 months
Pork—fresh	10-12 months
—cured	4- 6 months
—ground or sausage meat	3- 4 months
—sausage, cooked	2- 3 months
Poultry	Preferably 6 months but not more than 1 year
Poultry—giblets	2- 3 months
Rabbit	8-12 months
Veal	4- 6 months
Game birds	8-12 months
Fish	
Oily—salmon, trout, herring	3- 4 months
White—lean	6- 8 months
Shellfish	1- 2 months
Dairy Foods	
Butter—salted	5- 6 months
—unsalted	10-12 months
Cream—pasteurized	2- 3 months
Cottage cheese—dry and unsalted	2- 3 months
Cheese—Cheddar type	3- 4 months
Eggs—separated and beaten	8-12 months
Garden Produce	
Fruits	12-15 months
Vegetables	8-12 months
Baked Foods	
Bread—yeast, unbaked	2- 3 months
—yeast, baked	3- 6 months
—non-yeast, unbaked	2- 4 months
—non-yeast, baked	2 months
Cookies—uncooked or cooked	6-12 months
Cakes—uncooked	2 months
—baked, not iced	2- 4 months
—baked, iced	3- 4 weeks
Fruit cake	12 months or more
Sponge or angel cake	12 months
Pies—unbaked, fruit-filled, with double crust	2- 3 months
—baked, fruit-filled, with double crust	2- 3 months
chiffon, etc., with no top crust	2- 3 months
Pancakes, waffles	1- 2 months
Biscuits—unbaked	1 months
—baked	3 months
Sandwiches and fillings	2-20 weeks—depending on the fillings
Foods cooked as completed dishes	**2-4 months**

Timing Your Cooking

At the beginning of the 18th century it was not unusual for the housewife to spend six hours preparing one dish, and for special occasions, two or three days would be allowed for the preparation of the meal. Today there are more demands on our time and many homemakers are working wives or career women, or are involved in community activities. The food and appliance industries have come to our rescue with nutritious and convenient foods easily prepared in a shorter time, and home freezers, automatic cookers, mixers, and other time and labor saving devices. But the question of how to organize the preparation and service of a meal on time remains a worry for many wives, mothers, and hostesses.

Planning ahead is the answer:
1. Start with simple meals.
2. Plan your menu ahead.
3. If you are entertaining use recipes you have already tried with success.
4. Check recipes for time involved in preparation and cooking time.
5. Plan meals with some dishes that can be prepared in advance to avoid too many last-minute processes.
6. Dovetail each course into the next.

The following meal plans are guides to help you with your time and schedules.

Guests for Sunday lunch after Church

Grapefruit Cups

Roast Leg of Lamb
Roast Potatoes and Pumpkin
Green Beans

Apricot Cheesecake

Day Before:
Make Apricot Cheesecake.

Sunday Before Church:
Prepare potatoes and pumpkin and cover with cold water.
Prepare beans.
Prepare Grapefruit Cups and chill.
Place lamb in oven.

After Church:
Cook potatoes and pumpkin.
Cook beans.
Set table.
Make gravy.
Serve lunch.

Mid-week dinner party for the parents given by the newly married wife

Seafood Cocktail

Crown Roast of Pork
Château Potatoes
Peas

Apricot Flan

Night Before:
Make Apricot Flan.
Peel and shape Chateau Potatoes.
Shell peas and refrigerate.

TIMETABLE

6.00 p.m.
Put pork in oven.
Prepare lettuce and seafood and chill in refrigerator.
Prepare sauce for cocktail.
Set table.

7.00 p.m.
Place potatoes around meat to roast.
Cook peas.

7.20 p.m.
Drain peas, toss in butter, cover with foil, and keep hot.
Make gravy and keep meat warm.

7.30 p.m.
Join guests for a drink.

7.45 p.m.
Pour cocktail sauce over seafood and serve dinner.

Family lunch on a busy Saturday

Brampton Burgers
Sautéed Cabbage
Brown Bread and Butter

Speedy Coffee Cream

TIMETABLE

12.30 p.m.
Prepare pudding, cool, and chill.

12.35 p.m.
Shred cabbage.

12.40 p.m.
Grill hamburgers, prepare sauce, and simmer.

12.50 p.m.
Sauté cabbage

1.00 p.m.
Serve lunch, finish dessert when changing plates.

Mid-week summer dinner party for four given by the working wife

Mushrooms à la Grecque

Mango Chicken
New Potatoes
Green Salad

Chocolate Mousse

Night Before:
Prepare and joint chicken; make chicken stock.
Scrub new potatoes and cover with cold water.
Make Chocolate Mousse.

TIMETABLE

6.00 p.m.
Prepare Mango Chicken and place in oven.
Make Mushrooms à la Grecque.
Prepare salad.
Set table.

7.00 p.m.
Boil potatoes.
Complete Mango Chicken; cover with foil and keep hot.
Toss potatoes in butter; cover with foil and keep hot.

7.30 p.m.
Join guests for a drink.

7.45 p.m.
Serve dinner.
Salad is dressed at the last minute just before serving.

Saturday night supper after a day at the beach

Lasagne Napoli
Green Salad

Fresh Fruit

TIMETABLE

6.00 p.m.
Boil pasta for 20 minutes.
Make sauce and allow to simmer.

6.30 p.m.
Assemble Lasagne Napoli in a baking dish and place in oven. Wash and dry salad greens and make French dressing.

7.10 p.m.
Cover Lasagne Napoli with cheese and cook until brown.
Prepare fresh fruit.

7.30 p.m.
Toss salad and serve supper.

Mid-week winter dinner party for four given by the working wife

French Onion Soup

Melba Toast
Coq au Vin
Rice
Broccoli
Glazed Carrots

Quick Cherry Strudel

Night Before:
Prepare basic stock for French Onion Soup, add sautéed onions, and simmer for 1 hour.
Prepare and joint chicken.
Scrape carrots and cover with cold water.
Make Quick Cherry Strudel.

TIMETABLE

6.00 p.m.
Prepare Coq au Vin, simmer for 40 minutes.
Make Melba Toast.
Set table.

7.00 p.m.
Boil rice and broccoli and cook glazed carrots.
Pour soup over Melba Toast and cheese in a casserole.

7.20 p.m.
Test Coq au Vin.
Drain rice, toss broccoli in butter, serve carrots, cover with foil, and keep hot.
Warm Strudel.

7.30 p.m.
Place soup in oven to brown cheese.
Join guests for a drink.

7.45 p.m.
Serve dinner.

HORS D'OEUVRE

Babette Hayes

Babette Hayes, born of French parents, learnt the art of French cuisine from her grandmother.

Every meal should have a beginning, a gentle introduction, a first course, an hors d'oeuvre. The words 'hors d'oeuvre' literally mean 'outside the main work', so do not make this course too large, filling, or heavy. Remember there is a main course to follow. If the hors d'oeuvre course is the beginning of a long dinner, do choose dishes which are light and delicate. With a luncheon, where fewer courses are served, the first course may be more substantial and nourishing; in fact if a selection of dishes is served, it could form the entire meal.

By the addition of an hors d'oeuvre to the menu, one can make a comparatively simple meal into a dinner party. Foods such as smoked salmon, rollmops, salami, and stuffed olives may be bought, ready to serve, from a delicatessen. Other dishes may be prepared easily at home. Hors d'oeuvre dishes are not necessarily always served cold—some are served hot. They can vary from a simple platter of thinly sliced dry sausages with shiny olives, tiny tomatoes, or crisp radishes, to fresh oysters or shrimp served on crushed ice. If cold hors d'oeuvres are being served, make sure they are well chilled, fresh, and crisp. Hot hors d'oeuvres may consist of small dishes such as stuffed pancakes and pasta, or slices of a delicious quiche, garnished with fresh or fried parsley, lemon, or watercress according to the nature of the dish. A suitable sauce may be served in a separate bowl.

Many interesting hors d'oeuvres can be made from the foods you keep in your store cupboard. Always keep a good stock and you will be able to prepare a surprisingly large number of first course dishes from your shelves. Keep a jar of French dressing and one of mayonnaise in your refrigerator so that dishes may be served in minimum time and with very little effort.

If offering a selection of dishes (hors d'oeuvres variés), always choose two or three 'straight' dishes—olives, sliced salami, or fillets of anchovy—together with two or three raw or cooked vegetable salads tossed in mayonnaise or vinaigrette dressing. Hors d'oeuvres variés are usually served in a selection of small dishes, assembled on a large platter or tray. An important fact to remember is that if small amounts of this type of hors d'oeuvres are left after a meal they may be covered and kept satisfactorily in the refrigerator for a few days.

Try to select foods which will give a contrast in texture, color, and taste. A dish may be made bland or sharp by the addition of different dressings and seasonings. One feasts on the colors and smells before even starting to eat. This course should give guests a foretaste of the meal to follow.

I have given you a simple selection of light and refreshing hors d'oeuvre dishes, bearing in mind that you will find recipes in other sections of this book for dishes which may be served as a more filling first course. The following recipes are some of my favorites.

Vegetable Hors d'Oeuvre, Shellfish
Platter, and Mayonnaise (see Sauces)

ARTICHOKE HORS D'OEUVRE

4 globe artichokes
¼ cup butter

¼ cup lemon juice or
½ cup French dressing

Serves: 4

Trim the artichokes and wash under cold running water. Cook in boiling, salted water to cover for 25 to 60 minutes (depending on size), or until tender.

Drain the artichokes and serve hot with the melted butter and lemon juice mixed together, or chill and serve with French dressing.

How to eat artichokes: Pull each leaf away from the artichoke with the fingers and dip into the dressing. The fleshy part of the leaves only is eaten.

Variation: Artichokes Vinaigrette: Cook the artichokes as above and serve chilled, marinated in vinaigrette dressing (see page 177).

STUFFED ARTICHOKES

4 globe artichokes
juice of 1 lemon
1 onion, finely chopped
1 cup fresh bread crumbs

7 tablespoons Parmesan cheese
½ cup olive oil
½ cup white wine
1 teaspoon salt

Cooking time: 1 hour
Temperature: 300°
Serves: 4

Remove the tough outer leaves from the artichokes, cut off the top halves, and scoop out the chokes (the hairy part), so the hearts and the juicy fat leaves remain. Cover with cold water and the lemon juice to prevent them from turning brown. Mix the chopped onion with

the bread crumbs and cheese. Drain the artichokes and fill each with stuffing. Place in a casserole and add the olive oil, wine, and salt. Cover and place on the middle shelf of a 300° oven for 1 hour, or until tender. Serve hot.

AVOCADOS WITH ORANGE

3 avocados
French dressing

3 oranges
lettuce for serving

Serves: 6

Cut the avocados in half lengthwise and remove the seeds. Keeping the skins whole, remove the flesh with a melon baller or cut into dice. Coat with French dressing (see page 177) to prevent discoloration. Peel the oranges and cut into segments, removing all the skin and pith.

Mix the avocado balls and orange segments together with enough French dressing to moisten. Pile into the avocado shells. Place lettuce leaves on a serving plate and arrange the filled avocados on top.

AVOCADOS WITH PRAWNS

⅔ cup oil
¼ cup white wine vinegar
1 clove garlic, crushed

salt and pepper
2 cups shelled prawns
3 avocados

Serves: 6

Beat the oil, vinegar, garlic, and seasonings together well in a bowl. Add the prawns and place in the refrigerator until chilled.

Cut the avocados in half lengthwise and remove the seeds. Place the prawns in the cavities, making sure the dressing covers the whole cut area of the avocados to prevent discoloration.

Variations: Other shellfish may be substituted for the prawns, e.g., rock lobster tails, crab, or a mixture of shellfish. The avocados may also be served alone with the dressing covering the whole cut area, and an extra spoonful in the cavity.

STUFFED EGGS WITH MUSHROOMS

14 eggs
2 cups button mushrooms
⅔ cup mayonnaise
6 anchovy fillets, chopped
2 tablespoons finely chopped
   scallions

salt and pepper
½ cup red caviar for garnish
   (optional)

Serves: 6

Hard-cook the eggs for 15 minutes, stirring occasionally to keep the yolks in the center. Plunge at once into cold water and shell when cold. Poach the mushrooms in salted water for 5 minutes. Drain and cool. Reserve 12 mushrooms of good shape for decoration. Chop the remaining mushrooms finely. Cut 12 of the eggs in half lengthwise and carefully remove the yolks. Chop the 2 remaining eggs finely. Mix the egg yolks, chopped eggs, mayonnaise (see page 55), anchovies, scallions, chopped mushrooms, and salt and pepper to taste. Spoon the mixture into the egg halves. Place the stuffed eggs on a serving platter and top with the reserved mushrooms. Garnish with the caviar, if desired, and serve.

Note: Canned mushrooms may be used instead of fresh button mushrooms.

STUFFED EGGPLANTS

A recipe from Morocco

4 medium-sized eggplants
½ cup olive oil
2 onions, thinly sliced
2 cloves garlic, crushed
3 tomatoes, skinned and sliced
½ cup pine nuts

1 teaspoon coriander seeds,
   crushed
salt and pepper
mint leaves for garnish
radishes

Serves: 8

Wash and dry the eggplants. Remove the stalks and cut the fruit in half lengthwise. Heat the olive oil in a large heavy-bottomed skillet and gently fry the eggplants, cut side down, for 5 minutes. Turn over and fry for a further 5 minutes. Remove from the skillet. Gently fry the onions, garlic, and tomatoes. Scoop out the flesh from the eggplants, combine in a saucepan with the onion mixture, pine nuts, coriander seeds, salt, and pepper, and cook gently for 5 minutes. Place the eggplant shells on a serving platter and fill with the mixture. Allow to cool before serving. Garnish with mint leaves and serve with crisp radishes.

Note: Avoid chilling in the refrigerator if possible, as the flavor develops and improves if the dish is allowed to stand for a few hours at room temperature.

FISH FRITTERS
(FRITTO MISTO DI MARE)

A delicious Italian hors d'oeuvre.

½ lb. fish fillets (oily or white)
1 cup green prawns
1 cup shrimp

all-purpose flour
oil for frying
2 lemons

Serves: 4

Skin the fish fillets (see page 85) and cut into small finger-length strips. Dry well on paper towels. Shell the prawns and shrimp. Dip the fish strips and shellfish into the flour. Deep fry the fish in hot oil until golden brown and cooked.

Drain well on paper towels. Serve immediately, piled high on a serving plate, accompanied by wedges of lemon.

HAM CORNETS

2 cups mixed, cooked, diced
    vegetables (green beans,
    potatoes, carrots, zucchini)
1 cup mayonnaise
1 teaspoon French mustard

$\frac{1}{4}$ cup lemon juice
8 thin slices lean cooked ham
julienne strips of red sweet
    pepper for garnish

Serves: 4

Combine the mixed vegetables with the mayonnaise, French mustard, and lemon juice. Divide the mixture and place some on each slice of ham; roll into cornets.

Place the ham cornets close together on a serving dish and garnish with julienne strips of sweet pepper.

SMOKED HAM WITH FRESH FRUIT

The delicate combination of smoked ham with perfumed fruit is quite delicious, and very refreshing.

$\frac{1}{2}$ lb. parma ham or prosciutto,
    thinly sliced

1 small melon
8 figs

Serves: 4

Ask your delicatessen to slice the smoked ham wafer-thin. Peel and slice the melon and peel the figs just before serving. Serve the ham and prepared fruit on a large platter or on individual serving plates.

Variation: Peaches and juicy pears may be used instead of melon and figs. If it is obtainable papaya makes a delicious and unusual alternative.

RUSSIAN HERRING

8 fillets pickled herring or
    mullet
$\frac{1}{2}$ cup finely chopped onion
1 large dill pickle

1 cup mayonnaise
scant $\frac{1}{2}$ cup lemon juice
2 tablespoons tomato paste
$\frac{1}{4}$ cup black caviar

Serves: 4

Place the fillets of pickled herring on a board with the skin sides down. Put 1 tablespoon of the chopped onion on each fillet and roll up tightly. Slice the dill pickle into 8 thick slices. Place a rolled fillet of herring on each

slice of dill pickle and put onto a serving dish. Mix the mayonnaise (see page 55) with the lemon juice and tomato paste, and spoon over each rolled fillet. Top with caviar and chill before serving.

MUSHROOMS À LA GRECQUE

2 cups button mushrooms
    cup olive oil
2 tablespoons lemon juice
1 large tomato, skinned and
    chopped

1 bay leaf
sprig thyme
1 teaspoon coriander seeds,
    crushed
salt and pepper

Serves: 4

Wash and dry the mushrooms. Slice them if large. Place all the ingredients except the mushrooms into a saucepan and bring to a boil. Add the mushrooms and simmer

for 6 to 7 minutes. Place in a shallow serving dish, allow to cool, chill, and serve.

Stuffed Eggs and Mushrooms, Ripe Olives, Anchovies, Salt Pork
Vinaigrette, Tomatoes, and Prawns with Coarse Salt (see Shellfish Platter)

MUSHROOM TIMBALE

This is a tasty baked custard served with a mushroom sauce.

4 eggs
2½ cups milk
1 cup grated Cheddar cheese
salt and pepper

1¼ cups white sauce
1 cup thinly sliced raw
   mushrooms

Cooking time: 1 hour
Temperature: 350°
Serves: 6

Beat the eggs lightly. Heat the milk, pour onto the beaten eggs, and mix well. Season with salt and pepper. Stir in the grated cheese. Pour into a soufflé dish and place in a roasting pan of water, so that there is 1 inch of water around the base of the dish. Place on the bottom shelf of a 350° oven and bake for 1 hour, or until set. Make the sauce (see page 50), stir in the sliced mushrooms, and season to taste.

Turn the egg custard out onto a heated serving platter, and serve hot accompanied by the mushroom sauce. *Note:* The custard may be baked in individual custard cups.

RUSSIAN OYSTERS

12 oysters
⅓ cup finely chopped onion or
   chives

1 hard-cooked egg
½ cup black caviar

Serves: 1

Oysters must be absolutely fresh. Arrange the oysters on a bed of ice. Sprinkle with the chopped onion or chives. Separate the egg white from the yolk. Finely chop the white, sieve the yolk, and sprinkle both over the oysters. Top with the black caviar and serve immediately.

STUFFED SWEET PEPPERS

8 sweet peppers
1 cup canned tuna
½ cup ripe pitted olives
⅓ cup finely chopped onion

⅓ cup capers
2 anchovy fillets, finely chopped
½ cup olive oil

Serves: 8

Broil the whole peppers until the skin turns black. When cool, remove the skins, stalks, seeds, and pith and spread the peppers out flat. Mix together the remaining ingredients, except the olive oil. Divide the mixture among the peppers. Roll the peppers up and place in a shallow serving dish in tightly packed rows. Pour the olive oil over and marinate for 3 to 4 hours. Serve chilled.

SALT PORK VINAIGRETTE

A cheap hors d'oeuvre to prepare at home.

1 lb. lean salt pork
1 bay leaf
6 peppercorns
1 teaspoon allspice
sprig parsley

½ cup French dressing
2 tablespoons finely chopped
   scallions
¼ cup chopped parsley
vinegar (optional)

Cooking time: 40 minutes
Serves: 4

Place the salt pork in a saucepan with water to cover. Add the bay leaf, peppercorns, allspice, and parsley. Bring to a boil, reduce the heat, and simmer for 40 minutes, or until tender. Drain and while still hot cut into 1-inch cubes. Marinate in the French dressing (see page 177) with the chopped scallions, and parsley. Chill before serving accompanied by a selection of vegetable hors d'oeuvres. Add a little vinegar if the pork is very fatty.

RATATOUILLE

I make a large quantity of Ratatouille and serve half hot as a vegetable; the remainder, I chill and serve as an hors d'oeuvre.

3 red or green sweet peppers
3 eggplants
6 zucchini
3 large tomatoes, skinned and chopped

⅔ cup olive oil
1 clove garlic, crushed
3 large onions, thinly sliced
salt and pepper

Cooking time: 45 minutes
Serves: 12

Wash the peppers, remove the seeds and membranes, and slice the flesh into rings. Wash the eggplants and zucchini and cut into ½-inch slices. Heat the oil with the garlic in a heavy skillet or flameproof casserole, add the peppers, eggplants, zucchini, and onions, cover, and simmer gently for 30 minutes. Add the tomatoes and salt and pepper to taste and stew gently for a further 15 minutes, without a lid. The oil should be absorbed entirely by the vegetables. Serve cold, with French crusty bread to mop up the juices.

Variation: Egg Ratatouille: Place about ⅓ cup hot Ratatouille into individual earthenware or soufflé dishes. Make a well in the middle of each and break an egg carefully into it. Bake in a 350 oven until the eggs are just set and the yolks soft. Serve immediately.

SALAMI PLATTER

For 4 servings allow ½ lb. salami.

Serve a variety of thinly sliced salami and other dry sausages attractively arranged on a platter. Accompany with fresh crisp radishes, stuffed olives, and a selection of vegetable hors d'oeuvres.

SARDINE HORS D'OEUVRE

Sardine hors d'oeuvre is usually served as part of the popular mixed hors d'oeuvre, or hors d'oeuvres varies, but is also delicious served on its own.

2 (3¾ oz.) cans sardines
1 onion
2 hard-cooked eggs

2 teaspoons capers
1 lemon

Serves: 4

Arrange the sardines on a shallow serving dish. Slice the onion into thin rings. Chop the hard-cooked eggs coarsely. Sprinkle the onion rings, chopped eggs, and capers over the sardines. Serve with wedges of lemon.

SEAFOOD COCKTAIL

For cocktail sauce:
½ cup mayonnaise
cup tomato paste
1 teaspoon Worcestershire sauce
1 teaspoon lemon juice

few drops Tabasco sauce
dash paprika
½ cup whipping cream

Serves: 6

2 cups mixed shelled shellfish, shrimp, rock lobster tails, oysters, and crab

lemon for garnish
lettuce

To make the cocktail sauce: Mix the mayonnaise, tomato paste, Worcestershire sauce, lemon juice, Tabasco sauce, and paprika. Whip the cream lightly and fold into the sauce. Shred the lettuce very finely and put into serving glasses. Combine the shellfish lightly with the sauce and pile onto the lettuce. Garnish each glass with a small slice of lemon.

SHELLFISH PLATTER

Arrange an assortment of freshly caught, freshly cooked shrimp and other shellfish on a large platter. Serve shellfish if possible on a bed of crushed ice or coarse salt, with wedges of lemon and a bowl of rich mayonnaise (see page 55). The variety of shellfish very much depends on what is available at the time; small pink shrimp, fat juicy prawns, freshly opened oysters, and clams are all good served in this way.

CORN ON THE COB

| 6 ears corn | freshly cracked black pepper | Serves: 6 |
| salt | butter | |

Remove the husks from the corn and strip away all the silk. Place in a large saucepan with boiling water to cover and simmer for 5 to 10 minutes, until tender. Drain. Season and serve with salt, pepper, and melted butter.

STUFFED ZUCCHINI

1 lb. zucchini	2 tablespoons lemon juice	Serves: 4
¾ cup French dressing	2 tomatoes, skinned	
4 cloves garlic, finely chopped	chopped parsley and chives	
1 onion, thinly sliced	for garnish	
1 cup mayonnaise		

Wash the zucchini and remove the stalks. Boil in salted water for 15 minutes, or until tender. Drain, slice lengthwise, and place cut side up on a serving platter. Pour over the French dressing (see page 177), and sprinkle with chopped garlic and slices of onion. Cover tightly with aluminum foil and marinate in the refrigerator for 5 to 6 hours. Drain off any excess dressing. Mix the mayonnaise (see page 55) with the lemon juice and spoon onto each zucchini. Decorate with segments of tomato, sprinkle with chopped parsley and chives, and serve.

VEGETABLE HORS D'OEUVRES

Raw vegetables served as an hors d'oeuvre provide a refreshing contrast in texture and flavor. They need only the lightest of dressings. Toss in a French dressing (see page 177) made with lemon juice instead of vinegar. The following suggestions for vegetable hors d'oeuvres serve 4.

Carrot: Grate 4 carrots coarsely. Use the orange part only and discard the hard yellow core. Mix with 2 finely chopped scallions, toss in dressing, and serve chilled.

Celery: Wash 6 stalks celery, remove the coarse strings, and slice thinly. Add a clove of garlic, crushed, a few sliced radishes, the segments of an orange, or ¼ cup chopped cucumber. Mix with dressing and serve chilled, sprinkled with 1 teaspoon crushed coriander or cumin seed.

Cucumber: Peel 1 cucumber and slice thinly. Sprinkle with salt and allow to stand for 30 minutes, then drain. Mix with dressing, chill, and serve sprinkled with 1 teaspoon cumin seed and chopped parsley or chives. Prepared cucumber may also be mixed in a dressing of sour cream.

Mushrooms: Wash 2 cups button mushrooms or wipe with a damp cloth. Mix with dressing and 1 thinly sliced onion. If desired, mix in 6 chopped anchovy fillets or 2 teaspoons capers or 1 clove garlic, crushed. Serve chilled, sprinkled with chopped parsley or mint.

Cooked vegetables are mixed with a French dressing (see page 177) while still hot. Use olive oil and wine vinegar in the dressing and add French mustard, finely chopped onion, chives, garlic, or fresh herbs to taste.

Beans: Top and tail 1 lb. green beans and remove the strings. Boil in salted water for 10 to 15 minutes, until just tender. Drain and arrange in a serving dish. Cover with the dressing and sprinkle with 1 teaspoon freshly grated nutmeg.

Beets: Boil 1 lb. beets for 40 to 50 minutes, or until tender. Peel and slice thinly while still hot. Cover with dressing, chill, and serve.

Leeks: Wash 4 medium-sized leeks thoroughly and boil in salted water for 20 minutes, or until tender. Marinate in dressing while still hot. Serve chilled, sprinkled with 3 to 4 tablespoons finely chopped scallions.

Potato: Boil 1 lb. small potatoes in their skins for 15 to 20 minutes, or until just tender. Peel, slice, and dress while hot. Mix with 1 chopped hard-cooked egg, and serve chilled.

Zucchini: Wash 1 lb. zucchini and cut into ½-inch slices. Boil in salted water for 5 to 10 minutes. Mix with French dressing while hot. Serve chilled, sprinkled with chopped parsley or chives.

Russian Herring, Sardine Hors d'Oeuvre, and Celery Hors d'Oeuvre

SOUPS

Ted Moloney

Ted Moloney's love for and skill in French cooking inspired his first cookbook *Oh For A French Wife*.

Soup: I am the greatest enthusiast for soups. I am sure that I could live through an entire winter on soups. Big, hearty soups such as French onion, bortsch, pea, and minestrone. All of these and dozens of other body-warming, engery-giving soups are easily made. When summer comes chilled soups take over and then I tend more toward creamed soups such as the incomparable Vichyssoise on which I play many themes and variations. How I love soup.

STOCK

In the following recipes you may use beef bouillon cubes, chicken bouillon cubes, or any other short cuts to making stock unless the recipe indicates otherwise. Important soups do deserve home-made stock. This is especially essential for consommé. Its flavor should not need bolstering up with sherry as so often happens in restaurants, even though sherry is the best of wines to drink with soup. Ideally a supply of stock to start your soup should always be at the ready in your refrigerator. Keep building it up with boiling water poured from beans, peas, carrots, spinach, and potatoes and strengthen it by simmering for the primary stock.

SERVICE OF SOUP

Soup plates—every bride who makes out a gift list should ask for two types of soup plates. First of all she needs bouillon cups (or soup cups) with handles for dinner party soups which are not served in large portions. She also needs big old-fashioned soup plates for family soups which can be a meal in themselves. The serving of soup becomes so much more of an occasion, either for a formal dinner or a family meal, when the tureen is brought to the table and the soup served there. A large casserole is a good substitute for a soup tureen.

ACCOMPANIMENTS

Croûtons are the most frequent accompaniment to soup. These are $\frac{1}{4}$-inch cubes of bread, best fried in butter or oil although croûtons fried in drippings are delicious with pea soup. Drain well and sprinkle lightly with salt before serving. Serve in a small bowl with a spoon. Guests help themselves and sprinkle croutons over the soup. Profiteroles stuffed with a light pâté are served with consommé. Make profiteroles with Choux Paste (see page 291) and drop a little blob no larger than a pea onto a greased baking sheet, then put into a 375° oven for 10 minutes. Cool before filling with pâté. Serve floating on the soup.

Piroshki are served with bortsch. These are tiny puff paste turnovers filled with chopped hard-cooked egg, cooked rice, finely shredded lettuce and salt and pepper, or chopped bacon and onion. Serve warm as an accompaniment to hot soup.

BEEF STOCK (BROWN)

2 lb. beef shank
7½ pints water
1 carrot
1 parsnip
1 turnip

1 onion
2 stalks celery
1 large tomato
¼ cup butter
salt and pepper

Cooking time: 2½-3 hours

Slice the beef finely and place in a large saucepan, cover with the cold water, and bring to a boil. Cover and simmer for 30 minutes. Chill. Remove the surface fat, skim off floating particles, and strain. Prepare the vegetables and cut into thin slices. Sauté the vegetables in butter in a large saucepan over medium heat for 10 minutes, being careful not to let the onion burn. Add the strained liquor, salt, and pepper, and bring to a boil. Simmer, covered, for 2 hours. Strain the stock off the meat and vegetables, cool, and keep in the refrigerator for future use.

If the stock is to be used for consommé, reheat with 2 crushed eggshells and the lightly beaten white of 1 egg, stirring until the liquid boils. Simmer gently for 10 minutes. This helps to gather up all the floating particles. Strain through a sieve lined with cheesecloth. *Note:* When watercress is available I use a whole bunch in making brown stock. This gives a subtle flavor to your soup. The watercress should be well washed and any bruised leaves and stalks removed. Also add an extra 2½ cups water.

CHICKEN STOCK (LIGHT)

1 3½-lb. stewing chicken
7½ pints water
1 carrot
1 parsnip
4 stalks celery

1 white onion
¼ cup butter
6 sprigs parsley
salt and pepper

Cooking time: 2½-3 hours

Place the cleaned chicken in a large saucepan, cover with cold water, and bring to a boil. Cover and simmer for 30 minutes. Chill. (Fowl fat does not set hard like beef fat but the chilling makes it easier to lift off.) Remove the surface fat and strain the stock. Rinse the semi-cooked carcass, inside and out, with warm water. Prepare the vegetables and cut into ¼-inch slices. Sauté the vegetables in the butter in a large saucepan over

medium heat for 10 minutes, being careful not to let the onion burn. Add the strained liquor together with the chicken and parsley. Simmer, covered, for 2 hours with 2 crushed eggshells, skimming the surface occasionally. Add salt and pepper. Remove the chicken, strain the stock, cool, and keep in the refrigerator.
Note: The well-washed giblets may be added with the parsley, but will darken the stock.

BORTSCH

Both Russia and Poland claim Bortsch as their national soup. This is Ukrainian Bortsch and is a meal in itself.

2 large Spanish onions, sliced	2 large carrots	Cooking time: 4 hours
6 tablespoons beef drippings	1 leek	Serves: 8
4 lb. beef foreshank	1 turnip	
salt and pepper	1 medium-sized head cabbage	
good dash mixed herbs	4 large tomatoes, skinned and	
1 bay leaf	chopped	
sprig thyme	3 large fresh raw beets	
½ cup butter	⅔ cup sour cream	

Brown the sliced onions in the beef drippings in a large saucepan. Cut the beef into 2-inch cubes, discarding as much fat as possible. Add the beef to the browned onions and quickly sear on all sides, adding a little more drippings if necessary (try to use as little fat as possible). Add the salt, pepper, mixed herbs, bay leaf, and thyme. Cover with water to about ½ inch above the meat. Simmer for 2 hours, or until the meat is tender.

Melt the butter in another large saucepan. Cut the carrots, leek, and turnip into ¼-inch slices and throw into the sizzling butter. Stir with a wooden spoon for 2 minutes and then add the cabbage, cut into fairly coarse shreds, and the tomatoes. Simmer, uncovered, for 10 minutes. Lift the cooked meat out of the stock and add to the fried vegetables. Strain the stock and add to the meat and vegetables. Simmer for 2 hours.

Shred the beets with a coarse grater, add 3 minutes before you are ready to serve the soup, and reheat. That's long enough for your soup to go ruby red. Taste, and adjust the seasoning if necessary. Add the sour cream and serve hot, with an additional fluff of sour cream if desired.

Note: To make Bortsch consommé, strain the soup before adding the grated beets.

COCK-A-LEEKIE

1 5-lb. stewing chicken	1 cup rice	Cooking time: 1¼ hours
7½ pints cold water	salt and pepper	Serves: 8
8 large leeks, washed and sliced		

Cut the fowl into 8 or 10 pieces. Place in a large pan with the water. Cover, bring to a boil, reduce the heat, and simmer for 30 minutes, or until the chicken is tender. Remove the chicken, separate the meat from the bone, and cut the meat into ½-inch dice. Add the sliced leeks to the chicken stock and cook for 15 minutes. Boil the rice in 4 cups water for 5 minutes, drain and add to the chicken stock, and cook for a further 15 minutes. Add salt and pepper to taste. Return the chicken to the pan and simmer for 5 minutes before serving.

Variations: Although it is not traditional, I like to stir in ¼ cup butter or ⅔ cup cream just before serving.

PEA SOUP DUTCH TOUCH

In Holland, pea soup is so thick that slices of dill pickle sit on top of it without sinking.

2 cups split dried peas	2 frankfurters	Cooking time: 3 hours
2 lb. ham bones	1 tablespoon white vinegar	Serves: 8
5 pints chicken stock or water	sour dill pickle and croûtons,	
and chicken bouillon cubes	for serving	

Soak the peas overnight. Drain off the water. Add the peas and ham bones to the stock or water, bring to a boil, and simmer for 2½ hours. (Simmer an hour longer for a thicker soup.) Cool. Remove the bones, scrape the meat off, and return the meat to the soup.

Cook the frankfurters in boiling water for 3 minutes. Cool. Peel and cut into ¼-inch slices; add to the soup with the white vinegar. Reheat the soup and serve with 3 or 4 slices of sour dill pickle on each helping, accompanied by croûtons (see page 32).

CREOLE SOUP

½ cup ground pork
vegetable oil
few drops chili sauce or dash
   chili powder
1 small green sweet pepper,
   chopped
1 small white onion, chopped
2 tablespoons butter or

vegetable oil
¼ cup all-purpose flour
3¾ cups chicken stock or water
   and chicken bouillon cubes
1 (12 oz.) can tomatoes
1 cup cooked rice
salt

Cooking time: 35 minutes
Serves: 8

Sauté the ground pork in a small pan in its own fat for 5 minutes—add a few drops of oil if necessary. (This is almost dry frying.) Drain off any surplus fat. Add the chili sauce or chili powder. Fry the pepper and onion in the butter or oil in a large saucepan for 5 minutes.

Stir in the flour until smooth. Blend in the heated stock, combined with the tomatoes. Add the ground pork and simmer over low heat for 20 minutes. Add the cooked rice and simmer for a further 5 minutes. Taste and adjust the seasoning. Serve hot.

HUNGARIAN SOUP

4 small onions
2 tablespoons butter or oil
2 lb. beef foreshank
1 tablespoon paprika
3 large ripe tomatoes, skinned
   and quartered

5 pints beef stock or water and
   bouillon beef cubes
¼ lb. pickled red cabbage
salt and pepper
¼ lb. lean smoked sausage

Cooking time: 2½ hours
Serves: 8

Peel the onions, slice thinly, and push into rings. Fry the onion rings in the butter or oil in a large saucepan until lightly golden but not mushy. (Throughout the making of this soup, try to keep the shape of the onion rings.) Cut the beef into ½-inch cubes, add to the pan, and sear the meat pieces on all sides. Add the paprika, tomatoes, beef stock, and red cabbage. Add salt and

pepper to taste. Simmer, covered, for 2 hours.

Smoked sausage requires different cooking times according to type. Check with your delicatessen on timing and add the skinned, sliced sausage to the soup, allowing time to cook before serving. Serve with pumpernickel.

FRENCH ONION SOUP

4 lb. beef foreshank
7½ pints water
2 Spanish onions
½ head celery, coarsely chopped
salt and pepper
½ cup butter

1½ lb. Bermuda onions, thinly
   sliced
melba toast
3 cups freshly grated Cheddar
   cheese

Cooking time: Stock: 4 hours
                  Soup: 1½ hours
Temperature: 350°
Serves.   8

Remove as much fat as possible from the beef and place in a large covered kettle with the cold water. Bring to a boil, reduce the heat, and simmer continuously for 1 hour. Cool and leave in the refrigerator until the fat sets on top. Remove the surface fat and strain the stock. Return to the pan, add the sliced Spanish onions, celery, salt, and pepper, and simmer for a further 3 hours. Strain the stock, discard the vegetables, and return to a clean pan.

Melt the butter in a saucepan, add the sliced Bermuda onions, cover, and sauté over low heat until the onions become soft and golden. Stir occasionally with a wooden spoon to prevent catching, as there must not be the

tiniest hint of burn. Add the sautéed onions to the stock and simmer continuously for 1 hour.

Cover the base of a large white enamel baking dish, or a casserole, with the thinnest possible slices of melba toast. Sprinkle half the freshly grated cheese over the toast. Pour the soup carefully into the baking dish, so the cheese-covered toast floats gently to the surface. Sprinkle the remaining cheese over the soup. Place in a 350° oven for 10 minutes, or until the cheese turns to a deep golden crust without burning. Serve piping hot. *Note:* To make melba toast, slice white bread very thinly and dry in a 300° oven until crisp and golden.

VEGETABLE MINESTRONE

Minestrone, a hearty peasant soup, is not always as hearty as you may think. Back in sunny Italy meat is expensive, not an everyday item. I have seen recipes where the only meat in the stock was $\frac{1}{4}$ lb. salt pork. The soup gets its body from vegetables and pasta.

Vegetable soups are all the better for some minestrone influence. The addition of beans, salt pork, tomato paste, and even spaghetti adds new flavors and interest. So does that final, generous sprinkle with Parmesan cheese.

generous $\frac{1}{4}$ cup red kidney beans
2 lb. beef shank cross cuts, on the bone
10 pints water
1 large onion, sliced
12 peppercorns
salt
2 large tomatoes, skinned
1 tablespoon olive oil
1 stalk celery, sliced

1 carrot, chopped
1 clove garlic, crushed
$\frac{1}{4}$ lb. lean salt pork, diced
2 tablespoons tomato paste
$\frac{1}{4}$ lb. white cauliflower
pepper
2 oz. fine spaghetti
Parmesan cheese, for serving

Cooking time: 3 hours
Serves: 8

Soak the red kidney beans in cold water overnight. Put the beef in a large kettle with the water. Simmer, covered, for 2 hours, with the onion, peppercorns, drained kidney beans, and 2 teaspoons salt. Skim occasionally to clear the soup. The meat should come off the bone easily when the cooking is complete. Chill. Remove the surface fat and the onion. Discard the bones and return the meat to the stock.

Cut the tomatoes in quarters and sauté in the oil over medium heat, together with the celery, carrot, and garlic, for 10 minutes. (You may have to add a little more oil.) Transfer the vegetables to the stock and add the diced salt pork, tomato paste, and cauliflower (broken into flowerets and any coarse pieces of stalk discarded). Add salt and pepper to taste. Simmer for 40 minutes.

Add the spaghetti 15 minutes before the cooking is completed. Sprinkle each serving with grated Parmesan cheese.

MY OXTAIL SOUP

I say 'my oxtail' because I use red wine in the stock, and at the end I add a few pickled walnuts, because their sharpness adds 'bite' which I think this rich soup needs.

1 oxtail, disjointed
$\frac{1}{4}$ cup drippings
$7\frac{1}{2}$ cups hot water
$1\frac{2}{3}$ cups dry red wine
salt and pepper
2 bay leaves
1 stalk celery, chopped
1 onion, chopped

1 carrot, chopped
dash mixed herbs
12 peppercorns
3 cloves
1 tablespoon all-purpose flour
$\frac{1}{2}$ teaspoon Worcestershire sauce
3 pickled walnuts, chopped

Cooking time: $4\frac{1}{2}$ hours
Serves: 8

Brown the oxtail joints in the drippings in a large pan for 10 minutes. Skim off the fat. Add the hot water, wine, salt, a little pepper, and the bay leaves. Cover and simmer gently for 3 hours. Skim off the fat globules, bring back to a boil, and strain the stock into a bowl, using a fine strainer. Remove the meat from the bones and cut into $\frac{1}{4}$-inch dice. Return the stock to a clean saucepan and add the celery, onion, carrot, mixed herbs,

peppercorns, and cloves. Taste, and adjust the seasoning. Simmer for 1 hour. Strain. Return the liquor to the saucepan and discard the vegetables. Blend the flour to a smooth paste with a little cold water, add to the stock, and bring to a vigorous boil. Add 1 cup oxtail meat, the Worcestershire sauce, and the pickled walnuts. Reheat gently, and serve hot with pumpernickel.

PHILADELPHIA PEPPER POT

After your trial run you may decide to use more or less peppercorns next time. I like to use double quantity. Please yourself!

¾ lb. honeycomb tripe
⅓ cup chopped celery
3 tablespoons chopped sweet
   pepper
3 tablespoons chopped onion
½ cup butter

¼ cup all-purpose flour
5 cups home-made chicken stock
2 large potatoes, diced
12 peppercorns, crushed
salt to taste
⅔ cup cream

Cooking time: 1¾ hours
Serves: 8

Cook the tripe in salted milk and water for 30 to 45 minutes, or until about half tender. Drain. Cut into 1-inch squares. Simmer the vegetables in three fourths of the butter in a covered soup pan or large kettle for 10 minutes. Stir in the flour until well blended. Gradually add the chicken stock, stirring constantly. Add the tripe, diced potatoes, peppercorns, and salt. Cover and simmer gently for 1 hour.

Blend ½ cup of the hot soup with the cream and stir into the soup.

Taste, and adjust the seasoning if necessary. Stir in the remaining butter and serve hot.

PUMPKIN SOUP

¼ cup butter
1 large onion, finely chopped
2½ cups chicken stock or water
   and chicken bouillon cube
1 lb. pumpkin

2½ cups hot milk
dash allspice
salt and pepper
chopped parsley, for garnish
croûtons, for service

Cooking time: 1 hour
Serves: 8

Melt half the butter in a large pan and gently fry the onion for 10 minutes, or until soft. Add the chicken stock and bring to a boil. Peel the pumpkin and cut into 2-inch chunks; add to the stock and simmer until tender (about 30 minutes). Cool. Rub through a sieve or purée in a blender. Return to the pan, add the hot milk, allspice, and salt and pepper to taste, and heat gently. Serve in a tureen with the remaining butter stirred in at the last minute, and lightly sprinkled with chopped parsley. Serve with croûtons (see page 32).

TOMATO SOUP

Make this easy, delicious home-made soup when tomatoes are plentiful.

¼ cup butter
2 tablespoons each finely
   chopped celery, onion, and
   carrot
¼ clove garlic, crushed
¼ cup all-purpose flour
½ teaspoon mixed herbs
6 peppercorns

½ bay leaf
5 cups beef stock, or canned
   consommé, or water and beef
   bouillon cubes
1 lb. tomatoes, skinned and
   chopped
3 cloves
salt and pepper

Cooking time: 1¼ hours
Serves: 8

Melt the butter in a large pan, add the celery, onion, carrot, and garlic, and sauté, covered, over medium heat for 5 minutes. Stir in the flour. Add the mixed herbs, peppercorns, and bay leaf. Cover and cook gently for a further 5 minutes. Add the stock, diced tomatoes, and cloves. Cover and simmer gently for 1 hour. Add salt and pepper to taste. Serve hot.

Variations: Add ½ cup cooked rice, or 2 tablespoons tomato paste, or ½ cup cooked, chopped ham, during the last 10 minutes. Transform this to Cream of Tomato Soup by stirring in ⅔ cup cream before serving.

CREAM OF ALMOND SOUP

1 cup blanched almonds
3¼ cups milk
1 stalk celery, thinly sliced
1 onion, finely chopped
2 tablespoons butter
¼ cup all-purpose flour

1¼ cups chicken stock or water
    and chicken bouillon cube
⅔ cup cream
dash mace
juice of ½ lemon
salt and pepper

Cooking time: 45 minutes
Serves: 4-6

Pour boiling water over the almonds and allow to stand for 10 minutes. Drain, halve the almonds, and crush with a rolling pin or pulverize in an electric blender. Place the almonds in a large saucepan with the milk, celery, and onion, and simmer over low heat for 30 minutes, stirring occasionally. Melt the butter in a heavy saucepan, stir in the flour, cook for about 1 minute, then add half the hot milk stock. Stir until smooth, then stir into the remaining milk stock. Add the chicken stock, warmed cream, mace, lemon juice, salt, and pepper and heat gently. Serve hot.

CREAM OF CARROT SOUP

1 lb. young carrots
5 cups chicken stock or water
    and chicken bouillon cubes
3 cloves garlic, crushed

⅔ cup cream
salt and pepper
chopped parsley, for garnish
croûtons, for serving

Cooking time: 30 minutes
Serves: 8

Buy very young carrots with smooth skins. Cut off the carrot tops if green and remove any rough bumps on the skin. Wash the carrots well but do not scrape as the skin gives both color and flavor to the soup. Slice the carrots ½ inch thick, place in a large saucepan with the chicken stock, bring to a boil, reduce the heat, and simmer for 20 minutes. Cool. Add the garlic and rub the soup through a sieve or purée in an electric blender. Reheat. Stir a cup of warm soup into the cream and combine with the remaining soup. Bring to the simmering point. Avoid boiling, for the cream may curdle. Add salt and pepper to taste. Serve hot, sprinkled with chopped parsley and accompanied by croûtons (see page 32).

CREAM OF LETTUCE SOUP

2 medium-sized heads young
    lettuce
5 cups milk
3 thick slices onion
3 sprigs parsley
1 clove
1 bay leaf
6 tablespoons butter

1 tablespoon all-purpose flour
dash nutmeg
salt and pepper
2 egg yolks
⅔ cup cream
chopped parsley, for garnish
croûtons, for serving

Cooking time: 1½ hours
Serves: 6-8

Remove the coarse outer leaves from the lettuce. Use only the crisp inner parts. Shred the lettuce finely and rinse in a colander under running cold water. Shake off the excess water and pat dry with clean dish towels. Heat the milk slowly to just below the boiling point with the onion, parsley, clove, and bay leaf. This should take about 20 minutes. Strain and discard the flavorings. Melt ¼ cup of the butter in a large heavy pan, stir in the flour, and cook for about 1 minute, then add the strained milk, gradually stirring all the time over medium heat until just below the boiling point. Add the shredded lettuce and simmer gently over very low heat for 30 minutes, or until very tender. Stand the soup on an asbestos mat to avoid burning. Add the nutmeg and salt and pepper to taste. Rub the soup through a sieve or purée in an electric blender. Return the purée to a clean pan, place over moderate heat, and bring almost to a boil. Simmer for 10 minutes, stirring occasionally. Beat the egg yolks with the cream. Stir and add with the remaining butter to the simmering purée, stirring continuously. Taste the soup and adjust the seasoning if necessary. Serve garnished with chopped parsley and accompanied by croûtons (see page 32).

Variations: Cream of Celery Soup: Use 1½ lb. celery, well washed and chopped, instead of lettuce.
Cream of Cauliflower Soup: Use 1½ lb. cauliflower, well washed and broken into small flowerets, instead of lettuce.

Pumpkin Soup, Cream of Mushroom Soup, Cream of Carrot Soup, and Cream of Lettuce Soup

CREAM OF CHICKEN SOUP

Make home-made chicken stock for this soup (see page 34) and use the chicken breast in the soup. Alternatively, boil chicken bouillon cubes with the chicken breast.

5 cups chicken stock
1 chicken breast
¼ cup butter
½ cup all-purpose flour
2½ cups scalded milk (or ½ milk and ½ cream)

1 small stalk celery, finely chopped
few drops Tabasco sauce
salt and pepper
2 egg yolks

Cooking time: 40 minutes
Serves: 8

Prepare the chicken stock and cut the chicken breast into ¼-inch pieces. Melt the butter in a large heavy pan, stir in the flour, and cook for about 1 minute, then add half the chicken stock. Stir continuously over medium heat until boiling. Add the remaining stock, scalded milk, chicken breast, celery, Tabasco sauce, and salt and pepper to taste and bring to a boil. Reduce the heat and simmer, covered, for 5 minutes. Beat the egg yolks well with a fork and pour into a heated tureen. Pour the soup very slowly over the egg yolks, stirring all the time with a wooden spoon. Serve immediately.

CREAM OF MUSHROOM SOUP

½ lb. mushrooms
½ cup butter
freshly cracked pepper
salt
3 cloves garlic, finely chopped

5 cups chicken stock or water and chicken bouillon cubes
few drops Tabasco sauce
cup cream
croûtons, for serving

Cooking time: 15 minutes
Serves: 8

Before cooking the mushrooms select some of the smallest ones and take a slice from the center of each so you have the outline of the mushroom. Put these aside for garnishing.

Wash the mushrooms (do not peel them) and chop coarsely. Fry the mushrooms in sizzling butter with a good grind of fresh pepper and ½ teaspoon salt. Cool, then press through a sieve, or purée in an electric blender, with the garlic and 1 cup of the stock. Add the purée to the remaining stock in a large pan and bring to the simmering point. Add the Tabasco. Stir in the cream at room temperature. Add the reserved mushroom slices and simmer for 5 minutes. Taste and adjust the seasoning if necessary. Serve hot with croûtons.

WATERCRESS SOUP

(POTAGE SANTÉ)

Why do the French call this delightful soup of subtle flavor Potage Santé, which translated is Health Soup? The reason is that a whole bunch of watercress is used to make it, and watercress is rich in vitamins and iron, so has much health-giving quality.

1 large bunch watercress
2 lb. potatoes, peeled and sliced
5 pints chicken stock or water and chicken bouillon cubes

salt and pepper
4 egg yolks
⅔ cup cream
croûtons, for serving

Cooking time: 2½ hours
Serves: 8

Remove any bruised leaves and stalks from the watercress. Wash in cold water and shake off the excess water. Chop the watercress finely and place in a large saucepan with the potatoes and chicken stock. Cover, bring to a boil, reduce the heat, and simmer for 2 hours. Press through a coarse sieve, return to the pan, add salt and pepper, and reheat for 10 minutes. Drop the egg yolks into the warmed soup tureen, beat quickly with a fork, add the warmed cream, and beat to combine with the egg yolks. Pour the hot soup into the tureen gradually, stirring until smooth. Taste, and adjust seasoning if necessary. Serve hot with croûtons (see page 32).

BOUILLABAISSE

Bouillabaisse provides two courses from the one pot, first the broth, then the fish!

For fish stock:
1 lb. haddock or mullet	1 large tomato, chopped	Cooking time:	Stock: 1 hour
fish heads (snapper and whiting)	2 cloves garlic, crushed		Soup: 20 minutes
rock lobster shell and claws	2 bay leaves	Serves:	8
prawn shells	12 peppercorns		
9 pints cold water	3 teaspoons salt		

For soup:
2 onions, chopped	1 lb. whiting
4 tomatoes, skinned with seeds removed	1 lb. green prawns or jumbo shrimp
4 cloves garlic, crushed	$\frac{1}{2}$ cup olive oil
4-inch strip orange rind	1 teaspoon saffron
sprig fennel	cup cream
3 sprigs parsley	salt and pepper
3 lb. rock lobster tails	French bread, for serving
1 lb. snapper	

To make the fish stock: Wash the fish, fish heads, claws, and shells thoroughly. Place in a large saucepan with the remaining ingredients, cover, and bring to a boil. Reduce the heat to moderate and simmer for 1 hour. Strain before using.

To make the soup: Cover the bottom of a heavy soup kettle or pan with the onion, tomato, garlic, orange rind (remove the bitter inner white pith), fennel, and parsley and allow to stand for 2 days. Prepare the fish and cut the rock lobster tails, snapper, and whiting into 2-inch pieces. Cover the ingredients in the soup kettle with the rock lobster, snapper, and prawns and sprinkle with the olive oil and saffron. Add the hot fish stock and boil for 6 to 8 minutes to cook the rock lobster. Add the whiting and continue to cook for 5 minutes. Stir in the cream. Add salt and pepper to taste. Reheat before serving.

To serve: Firstly, place a slice of crusty French bread, a day old, in the center of each big soup plate and ladle the fish broth over the bread. When this portion has been eaten, the fish pieces are piled onto each plate with more broth, to form a second course.

SCALLOP SOUP

For fish stock:
2 fish heads	1 onion, chopped	Cooking time:	25 minutes
$2\frac{1}{2}$ cups water	salt and pepper	Serves:	8

For soup:
1 lb. scallops	$\frac{2}{3}$ cup cream
$\frac{1}{4}$ cup butter	salt and pepper
$2\frac{1}{2}$ cups milk	paprika
2 cups fish stock	chopped parsley, for garnish
	crackers for serving

To make the fish stock: Simmer the fish heads in a large covered saucepan with the water, onion, salt, and pepper. Reduce slowly until there are 2 cups fish stock after straining.

To make the soup: Separate the coral from the white meat of the scallops. Melt the butter in a large pan until bubbling gently and add both the coral and white of the scallops. Fry the scallops for 5 minutes, turning over gently, so they absorb some of the butter. Add the warmed milk and fish stock, blending the butter in well. Simmer over low heat for 15 minutes. Blend a little of the hot soup with the cream and stir into the soup in the pan. Add salt and pepper to taste. Serve hot, with a sprinkling of paprika and garnish of chopped parsley on each serving, accompanied by crackers. The crackers are broken up over the soup.

Note: Dry white wine may be substituted for water when making the stock.

LOBSTER BISQUE

1 1½-lb. lobster, cooked
1½ cups chicken stock or water
   and chicken bouillon cube
¼ cup butter

¼ cup all-purpose flour
2½ cups milk
⅔ cup cream
salt and cayenne pepper

Cooking time: 30 minutes
Serves: 8

Remove the lobster meat from the shell and claws. Place the pieces of shell, together with any coral found inside the crustacean, in a saucepan with the chicken stock. Cover, bring to a boil, and simmer for 15 minutes. Line a colander with cheesecloth and strain the stock through this to remove the rough shell fragments. Melt the butter in a large saucepan, add the flour, and stir over medium heat for 3 minutes. Add the stock and bring to a boil, stirring continuously.

Chop one fourth of the lobster meat very finely, using up the bits and pieces. Add the chopped lobster to the milk and scald by heating in a saucepan to just below the boiling point, then reducing the heat and simmering for 5 minutes. Combine the scalded milk with the stock. Add the remaining lobster meat cut into ½-inch dice. Warm the cream and stir into the soup. Add salt and cayenne pepper to taste. Simmer for 5 minutes and serve hot.

OYSTER SOUP

The best oysters to use for this soup, which is really a stew, are big oysters in the shell which are opened in your own kitchen and dropped with all their briny fluid straight into your soup. Allow 6 oysters per portion.

For fish stock:
2 fish heads
1 onion, chopped
2½ cups water

salt and pepper
1 bay leaf

Cooking time: 20 minutes
Serves: 8

For soup:
10 cups milk
48 oysters
scant 2 cups fish stock
6 tablespoons butter
paprika

celery salt
freshly cracked black pepper
⅔ cup cream
fresh dill or chopped parsley,
   for garnish

To make the fish stock: Simmer the fish heads in a large covered saucepan with the chopped onion, water, salt, pepper, and bay leaf. Reduce slowly until there are 2 cups stock after straining.

To make the soup: Scald the milk (see previous recipe) with 12 oysters in a large saucepan. Add the fish stock, bring to a gentle simmer, then drop in the remaining oysters with the butter and a dash of paprika. Stir until the butter melts. Add celery salt and freshly cracked black pepper to taste. Stir in the cream and reheat gently. Serve garnished with a little fresh dill or finely chopped parsley, accompanied by crackers or brown bread and butter.

GREEK FISH SOUP

1 lb. cheap white fish
2 large fish heads (snapper
   or cod)
5 pints water
1 onion, chopped
1 teaspoon dried oregano

⅔ cup long-grain rice
2 egg yolks
juice of 2 lemons
grated zest of 1 lemon
salt and pepper

Cooking time: 1 hour
Serves: 8

Put the fish, fish heads, and water (together with any extra fish pieces you can coax out of the storekeeper) into a large saucepan. Add the chopped onion and dried herbs. Bring to a boil and simmer, covered, for 30 minutes. Strain off the stock, squeezing the fish pieces to obtain the utmost possible amount of juice before discarding. Reheat the stock and add the rice. Simmer

for 20 minutes. Beat the egg yolks well, then gradually add the lemon juice, stirring with a fork until well blended. Spoon some of the hot soup into the egg and lemon mixture, then stir into the gently simmering soup. Add half the lemon zest and simmer for a further 5 minutes. Add salt and pepper to taste. Serve with a light sprinkling of lemon zest on each portion.

Scallop Soup

Chilled Soups

CONSOMMÉ MADRILÈNE

The classic consommé double is simply a clarified rich stock. This basic consommé may be flavored in various ways and served hot or cold. It really has worthwhile flavor. Cold Consommé Madrilène is one of the most delicious of the many variations on the basic consommé.

2 envelopes gelatin
5 pints home-made chicken
   stock
1 (12 oz.) can tomato juice
2 large ripe tomatoes, skinned
   with seeds removed

salt and pepper
2 egg whites with shells
lemon slices and watercress
   sprigs, for garnish

Cooking time: 30 minutes
Serves: 8

Dissolve the gelatin in a little cold water and add to the warm stock (see page 34). Add the tomato juice and tomatoes. Add salt and pepper to taste. Stir in the beaten egg whites with the shells and bring very slowly to the boiling point, stirring continuously. Boil rapidly for 5 minutes and remove any scum from the surface or bits adhering to the sides of the saucepan. Reduce to a slow simmer for 20 minutes, then skim the surface clear, using a perforated spoon. Cool and strain through a sieve lined with cheesecloth. Chill thoroughly. Serve in soup cups, garnished with thin lemon slices and tiny sprigs of watercress.

CHILLED AVOCADO PURÉE

2 large avocados
few drops Tabasco sauce
2½ cups chicken stock or water
   and chicken bouillon cube
⅔ cup cream

salt and pepper
⅔ cup cream, whipped
1 avocado and paprika for
   garnish

Cooking time: 30 minutes
Serves: 4

Cut the avocados in half, remove the seeds, scoop out the pulp, and sprinkle with Tabasco sauce. Heat ½ cup of the chicken stock, add to the avocado, and purée in an electric blender. Heat the remaining stock in a double boiler until just on the point of simmering and add the puréed avocado, 1 tablespoon at a time, beating with a rotary beater between each spoonful. Warm the cream and beat into the soup gradually. Add salt and pepper to taste. Cool, then chill thoroughly. Serve topped with whipped cream, sprinkled with tiny cubes of avocado and paprika.
Note: If your double boiler is too small, substitute a medium-sized saucepan inside a large pan of hot water.

CHILLED CURRY SOUP

1 large onion, finely chopped
1 green apple, peeled, cored, and
   finely chopped
¼ cup butter
1 large banana, peeled and sliced
¼ cup curry powder
5 cups chicken stock or water
   and chicken bouillon cubes

6 cardamon pods
juice of ½ lemon
2 tablespoons Indian mango
   chutney
salt

Cooking time: 30 minutes
Serves: 6-8

Sauté the onion and apple in the butter in a large covered saucepan for 5 minutes, until soft and golden. Add the banana and cook gently for 5 minutes, stirring with a wooden spoon. Stir in the curry powder and cook for 1 minute, then stir in the chicken stock. Shell the cardamom pods, crush the black seeds, and add to the soup with the lemon juice and chutney. Simmer for 20 minutes. Add salt, taste the soup, and adjust the flavor if necessary. Stir in more curry powder for a hotter soup. Cool. Chill thoroughly before serving.
Note: Cardamom pods are obtainable at delicatessens and natural food stores.
   A dry white wine may be used to replace half of the chicken stock.

GAZPACHO

For soup:
1 large ripe tomato, skinned
1 cucumber, peeled
1 medium-sized green sweet
   pepper
½ cup olive oil

For garlic-flavored croutons:
4 slices white bread
vegetable oil, for frying

¼ cup white vinegar
salt and pepper
3 scallions, thinly sliced
7½ cups consommé

2 cloves garlic, crushed
salt

Serves: 8

To make the soup: Remove the seeds from the tomato and cucumber and cut the flesh into ¼-inch cubes. Remove the seeds and bitter white center from the pepper and cut into ¼-inch cubes.

Mix the oil and vinegar with salt and pepper to taste and combine with the tomato, cucumber, green pepper, and sliced scallions. Allow to stand for 1 hour, stirring occasionally so the vegetable absorb the dressing.

Strain the vegetables well and combine with the consommé. Chill thoroughly before serving with garlic-flavored croûtons.

To make the croûtons: Cut the bread in ¼-inch thick slices and remove the crusts. Cut the bread into ¼-inch cubes. Fry in hot oil with the garlic until golden. Drain well and sprinkle with salt before serving.

VICHYSSOISE

4 leeks
1 large white onion
½ cup butter
5 cups chicken stock or water
   and chicken bouillon cubes
2 medium-sized potatoes, peeled
   and sliced

3 tablespoons chopped parsley
1 stalk celery, finely chopped
salt and pepper
1¼ cups whipping cream, chilled
finely chopped chives, for
   garnish

Cooking time: 50-60 minutes
Serves: 8

Cut the leeks into ¼-inch slices, using the white part plus about 1 inch of the lightest green part. Chop the onion finely. Melt the butter in a large heavy pan and sauté the leeks and onion, covered, over moderate heat until soft (about 10 minutes). Avoid burning. Add the chicken stock, sliced potatoes, parsley, celery stalk, salt, and pepper. Simmer until the potato is tender (about 30 minutes). Cool. Rub through a sieve, or pureé

in an electric blender. Reheat until just below the boiling point. Taste and adjust the seasoning if necessary. Transfer to a soup tureen and chill thoroughly. Chill the soup cups.

Just before serving stir in the very cold cream. Serve at table from the chilled tureen. Sprinkle a scant teaspoon of very finely chopped chives on top of each serving.

APPLE SOUP

4 large tart dessert apples
2½ cups water
½ teaspoon cinnamon
1 teaspoon grated ginger root
2 tablespoons fresh white bread
   crumbs

rind and juice of 1 lemon
2 tablespoons red currant jelly
2 tablespoons sugar
salt
1⅔ cups Moselle wine

Cooking time: 20 minutes
Serves: 6-8

Peel, core, and slice the apples and place them in a heavy saucepan with the water. Add the cinnamon, ginger root, bread crumbs, and finely grated lemon rind. Bring to a boil, reduce the heat, and simmer for 10 minutes. Add the lemon juice, red currant jelly, and sugar and stir until the sugar dissolves. Cool. Press

through a sieve or pureé in an electric blender. Add salt to taste and the Moselle wine. Serve chilled, sprinkled with thin shreds of lemon rind and extra cinnamon.
Note: Moselle is a light, slightly fruity wine and, although not sparkling, has a liveliness which enhances this soup.

SAUCES

Neville Baker

Neville Baker's love of entertaining persuaded him to set out on a course to learn about cookery. Neville has been the Foodmaster of The Wine and Food Society of New South Wales for 10 years, is a member of the Escoffier Society, and is also a restauranteur. He writes a regular cookery column and cookery articles.

It is a widely held belief that the French, who are the world's acknowledged experts in sauces, developed their sauces in order to cover poor materials, and that sauces are only served when the cook lacks confidence in the flavor or quality of the ingredients being used in a dish. This is not so. The high point of the development of sauces was during the reign of Louis XIV, who was one of the world's great eaters. The kitchens in many of the great palaces were sometimes up to a quarter of a mile away from the banquet rooms and at large feasts the food often arrived cold. In order to distract from the chill of the meal, elegant and flavorsome sauces were developed. Some of the chefs went to incredible trouble to prepare their sauces. The story is told of the chef in the service of Prince Condé who requisitioned fifty hams for a luncheon for twenty people. When his master questioned the requisition, saying, 'I am only entertaining my friends, not my troops,' the chef replied, 'My lord, only one ham is for the luncheon, forty-nine are for the sauces!'

Many of the sauces that are accepted today as commonplace, such as Béchamel Sauce, created by Louis de Béchamel, Lord Steward of the household of Louis XIV, were created during this period, and over the centuries their methods of making have been simplified, so they can be enjoyed by households throughout the world.

As one has to eat at least twice a day it is my philosophy that each meal should be made interesting. The flavor of a piece of beef or fresh fish, cooked simply, is excellent, but simple food may become boring, and the correct use of a sauce adds interest to the plainest dish.

French housewives make excellent sauces with very little equipment. However, correct equipment makes the preparation of sauces simpler and quicker. I recommend that you should have the following in your kitchen:
1. A double boiler. These are sold in various sizes. A 1½-quart size is ideal.
2. A fine strainer. The best strainer is the one known as a Chinese hat or conical strainer, which is, as its name implies, conical in shape.
3. Wooden spoons. Always use wooden spoons in making sauces as metal spoons can taint the flavor, scratch the saucepan, and burn your hand.
4. An asbestos mat. Most useful for keeping prepared sauces warm, or as a substitute for a double boiler for the slow cooking of a sauce.

TYPES OF SAUCES

Sauces fall into categories according to the method of making them:
1. Roux sauces—white and brown
2. Egg-thickened sauces (butter sauces)
3. Mayonnaise
4. Sweet sauces.

Béchamel Sauce

Roux Sauces

A roux is flour gently cooked in fat over heat. The cooking time of the roux, and the ingredients added to it, make the difference to the sauce.

The roux can be cooked to three stages, white for white and cream sauces, pale straw color for velouté sauce, and brown for brown sauces. Brown is a misnomer, as it should not be allowed to become darker than sand.

The essential thing in making a roux, no matter what color, is to cook it so the starch grains, contained in the flour, burst and absorb the butter completely, so there is no raw starch taste. Care must be taken to ensure the roux is well combined and cooked over a gentle heat before the liquid and flavorings are added. A good tip is to cook the finished sauce in a double boiler over low heat for at least 30 minutes. This achieves greater flavor and silkiness of texture. However, it is not always possible to spend this time, and it is quite simple to make a good, everyday white sauce quickly. This sauce has many uses as it may accompany most vegetables, fish, and white meats and many of the variety meats, and is used in some pasta dishes.

White Roux Sauces

WHITE SAUCE

¼ cup butter
½ cup all-purpose flour

salt and pepper
2½ cups milk

In a heavy saucepan melt the butter, then stir in the flour and add salt and pepper to taste. Cook over gentle heat, stirring constantly, for 1 to 2 minutes, or until the flour has absorbed all the butter. The roux should not be allowed to color. When the roux has a granular appearance, pour in the milk, all at once, and bring to a boil over medium heat, stirring constantly. Reduce the heat and simmer for 1 to 2 minutes. Taste, and add more salt and pepper if necessary.

BÉCHAMEL SAUCE

½ onion, finely chopped
½ carrot, finely chopped
½ stalk celery, finely chopped
½ cup butter
½ cup all-purpose flour

2½ cups milk
¼ lb. veal, chopped
2-3 thyme leaves
dash white pepper
dash grated nutmeg

Sauté the onion, carrot, and celery in half the butter in a heavy saucepan until soft and golden. Stir in the flour and cook over low heat for 3 minutes, until the roux is granular. Gradually add the milk, stirring constantly until boiling.

Sauté the veal in the remaining butter over very low heat. Add the thyme leaves, pepper, and nutmeg. Cook for 5 minutes, stirring frequently. Do not allow to brown. Drain and stir the veal into the sauce.

Cook the sauce in a double boiler over hot water for 30 minutes, stirring occasionally. Strain through a fine sieve, pressing the vegetables to extract all the flavor. Reheat and adjust the seasoning before serving. If not serving immediately, dot with butter to prevent a skin forming, or pour over a small amount of milk to cover the top of the sauce completely. Beat the butter or milk into the sauce just before serving.

Variation: For a richer Béchamel Sauce, remove the saucepan from the stove and beat in 2 egg yolks; do not return to the heat as the sauce may curdle.

Note: This sauce may be kept for up to 2 days in a jar in the refrigerator. Pour melted butter over the top of the sauce to seal it.

BÉCHAMEL SAUCE

(SIMPLE METHOD)

1¼ cups milk
1 onion, quartered
1 stalk celery, chopped
1 carrot, chopped
6 peppercorns
dash or 1 blade mace

1 bay leaf
2 cloves
2 tablespoons butter
¼ cup all-purpose flour
salt and pepper

Place the milk, onion, celery, carrot, peppercorns, mace, bay leaf, and cloves in the top of a double boiler over gently boiling water, cover the pan, and heat very slowly for 30 minutes. Strain the milk. Melt the butter in a heavy saucepan, stir in the flour, and cook for 1 minute over medium heat. Add the milk and heat, stirring constantly until boiling, then reduce the heat to low and cook for 2 minutes. Season with salt and pepper.

VARIATIONS ON BÉCHAMEL SAUCE

Here are some quick and easy methods of making sauces, using 1¼ cups Béchamel Sauce as a base.

Aurore Sauce: Add 2 tablespoons tomato paste. Excellent with eggs, shellfish, and stewed chicken.
Caper Sauce: Add ⅓ cup chopped capers.
Celery Sauce: Add ⅓ cup chopped cooked celery.
Cheese Sauce: Add 1 cup grated cheese to the sauce over hot water and stir until well blended. Season to taste with mustard and paprika.
Mornay Sauce: Add ⅔ cup cream and boil to reduce by one third. Add ½ cup mixed grated Gruyère and Parmesan cheese and 6 tablespoons butter and mix well.
Mushroom Sauce: Add 1 cup chopped or sliced cooked mushrooms.

Oyster Sauce: Heat 2½ cups small oysters in their own liquor to the boiling point, cook for ½ minute, remove from the heat, and combine with the sauce.
Parsley Sauce: Add 7 tablespoons chopped parsley.
Soubise Sauce: Blanch ½ lb. chopped onions in ⅔ cup beef stock, drain, and sauté in 2 tablespoons butter until soft. Sieve into the sauce.
Tomato Cream Sauce: Cook together ½ lb. fresh or 1 cup canned tomatoes, 1 stalk celery, 1 slice onion, ½ teaspoon salt, and a little pepper for 20 minutes. Press through a sieve. Add to the Béchamel Sauce gradually, stirring constantly.

VELOUTÉ SAUCE

This is the most elegant of all the white sauces. Make it with half chicken stock and half white wine (the white wine may be omitted). If you do not have home-made chicken stock prepared (see page 34), stock made from bouillon cubes may be substituted.

¼ cup butter
½ cup all-purpose flour
2½ cups chicken stock, or
    1¼ cups chicken stock and
    1¼ cups white wine

salt
white pepper
mushroom peelings or stalks
few drops lemon juice

Melt the butter in a heavy saucepan, add the flour, and cook gently until the roux is a pale straw color (8 to 10 minutes). Add the warm stock, salt, and pepper and bring to a boil, stirring continuously with a wooden spoon. Add the mushroom peelings or stalks, reduce the heat, and simmer gently, stirring occasionally and skimming frequently, until the sauce is reduced by one third and is thick but light and creamy. Flavor with lemon, juice, salt, and pepper to taste. Strain quickly through a conical strainer and use as required. It is ideal with chicken.
Variation: To make Fish Velouté Sauce, proceed as above, but substitute fish stock (see page 43) for the chicken stock, and omit the mushroom peelings or stalks.

Brown Roux Sauces

The most common of all the brown sauces is gravy, which is made in most households week after week. Though gravy is not recognized as a classical sauce, it is my opinion that if made the way my mother used to make it, gravy has the flavor and texture of any of the great sauces. When she was cooking a roast dinner she would parboil the potatoes and place them around the joint of meat, retaining the water in which she had boiled them. She would then drop a bouillon cube into this water and cook the other vegetables in it. After draining, the vegetable water was retained, and the vegetables were reheated just before serving by tossing them in butter. When the joint and potatoes were cooked she removed them from the roasting pan, drained off most of the fat, leaving about $\frac{1}{4}$ cup, sprinkled $\frac{1}{2}$ cup all-purpose flour into the pan, and then cooked it over high heat, stirring constantly, and scraping in the brown bits from the sides of the pan. When the roux was a nutty brown color she would add the warm vegetable water, all at once, and stir constantly until the gravy came to a boil. If necessary, she would season with a little salt and pepper, then strain through a sieve.

I have followed this method throughout my cooking career, except that now I add a little red wine to give extra flavor.

The making of a classical brown sauce is not quite as simple as making a white sauce. Espagnole Sauce is the basis for most brown sauces. To achieve a rich, flavorsome sauce, short cuts are not advisable. As the sauce will keep for some time in the refrigerator, in a covered jar, it is worthwhile going to the trouble of making beef stock (see page 34), and using this when making a brown sauce. A beef bouillon cube may be substituted, but will never achieve the flavor of home-made stock.

ESPAGNOLE SAUCE

The basis for most brown sauces. Some chefs specify a demi-glacé or basic brown sauce, but Espagnole Sauce is no more difficult to make.

$\frac{1}{4}$ cup butter or drippings	$2\frac{1}{2}$ cups beef stock
3 slices bacon, chopped	4 mushrooms, sliced
1 carrot, chopped	$\frac{1}{4}$ cup tomato paste
1 stalk celery, chopped	1 bouquet garni
1 onion, sliced	salt and pepper
$\frac{1}{4}$ cup all-purpose flour	about $\frac{1}{4}$ cup sherry

Heat the butter or drippings in a heavy saucepan, add the bacon, carrot, celery, and onion, and cook gently until the vegetables are golden brown—they must not burn. Add the flour and stir well. Cook over gentle heat until the roux is a deep golden brown (12 to 15 minutes). Do not allow to burn. Add the stock and bring to a boil, stirring continuously. Add the mushrooms, tomato paste, bouquet garni, salt, and pepper and simmer gently for at least 1 hour, stirring frequently and skimming if necessary. Strain through a fine conical strainer. Add the sherry, taste, and adjust the flavor if necessary before serving.

BORDELAISE SAUCE

2 scallions, finely chopped	salt and pepper
1 clove garlic, crushed	1 teaspoon finely chopped
$\frac{3}{4}$ cup red wine	parsley
$1\frac{1}{4}$ cups Espagnole Sauce	lemon juice

Simmer the scallions and garlic in a saucepan with the red wine. Add the bay leaf and reduce by half. Add the Espagnole Sauce and simmer for 20 minutes. Skim, strain, and return to the saucepan. Add the parsley, a squeeze of lemon juice, and salt and pepper to taste.

Serve with beef.

Note: To make this sauce in the classical method, add finely sliced beef bone marrow that has been simmered in salted water for 5 minutes.

Straining Espagnole Sauce

BIGARADE SAUCE

½ onion, finely chopped
1 tablespoon butter
¾ cup red wine
1 bay leaf

1 orange
1 teaspoon lemon juice
1¼ cups Espagnole Sauce

Cook the onion in the butter, in a small saucepan, for 1 minute. Add the red wine, bay leaf, orange juice, and thinly pared rind of ½ orange, and simmer until reduced by one fourth. Strain into the Espagnole Sauce. Cut the remaining orange rind into thin shreds, removing as much white pith as possible. Blanch in boiling water for 5 minutes and drain. Add the shredded orange rind and the lemon juice to the sauce and simmer for 5 minutes before serving. Serve with duck or pork.

CHASSEUR SAUCE

6 mushrooms, finely sliced
1 scallion, chopped
1 tablespoon butter

½ cup white wine
1¼ cups Espagnole Sauce

Cook the mushrooms and scallion in the butter for 3 minutes, then add the white wine. Reduce by two thirds and add the Espagnole Sauce.

FINES HERBES SAUCE

¼ cup butter
1 scallion, finely chopped
¾ cup dry white wine
1¼ cups Espagnole Sauce
2 tablespoons finely chopped
   parsley

½ teaspoon dried tarragon
½ teaspoon dried chervil
juice of 1 lemon

Melt half the butter in a saucepan, add the scallion, and cook until golden. Add the white wine and reduce by half. Add the Espagnole Sauce and simmer for 10 minutes. Add the herbs and lemon juice. Remove from the heat and whisk in the remaining butter before serving. Serve with eggs.

ITALIENNE SAUCE

½ cup finely chopped mushrooms
1 tablespoon butter
2 tomatoes, skinned with seeds
   removed
1 teaspoon chopped onion
¾ cup dry Marsala wine

1¼ cups Espagnole Sauce
¼ cup cooked ham, finely
   chopped
salt and pepper
few drops lemon juice
1 teaspoon chopped parsley

Cook the mushrooms in the butter until soft. Chop the tomatoes and cook with the onion in the wine until soft. Allow the mixture to reduce by half. Add the Espagnole Sauce, together with the mushrooms, ham, salt, pepper, and lemon juice. Simmer for 5 minutes, add the chopped parsley, and serve hot. This is excellent with pasta dishes or fried liver.

MADEIRA SAUCE

2½ cups Espagnole Sauce
¼ cup Madeira

Reduce the Espagnole Sauce by half, then add the Madeira. Reheat without allowing to boil, otherwise the flavor of the Madeira is lost. Serve with meat, game, or ham.

Variation: For Armagnac Sauce substitute Armagnac or another very good brandy for the wine.

Mayonnaise

Home-made mayonnaise is so much better than any commercial variety that it is worth going to the trouble to make your own. It will keep very well in the refrigerator for over two weeks.

MAYONNAISE

1-2 egg yolks
1 teaspoon white wine vinegar
½ teaspoon salt
½ teaspoon dry mustard

dash white pepper
⅔ cup olive oil
few drops lemon juice

Make sure your mixing bowl is well washed and dried. In it, beat the egg yolk, vinegar, salt, dry mustard, and pepper with an egg beater. Add the olive oil, drop by drop, beating continuously, until about ¼ cup has been added. Add a few drops of lemon juice, to bring to the consistency of cream. Add the remaining oil in a thin steady stream, beating continuously, stopping the addition of the oil from time to time to make sure the mixture is combining well. When all the oil has been added and the mayonnaise is thick, add extra lemon juice to taste. Adjust seasoning. The mayonnaise when completed should be stiff enough to support its own trail. Use as required, or serve with lobster, prawns, or salad.

Note: Should the mixture curdle, wash the beater, beat 1 egg yolk in another bowl, and very slowly add the curdled mayonnaise to the fresh egg yolk, beating continuously. If an electric mixer is used set it at medium speed.

BLENDER MAYONNAISE

1 egg
½ teaspoon dry mustard
½ teaspoon salt

¼ cup white wine vinegar
½ cup olive oil

Place the egg, mustard, salt, and vinegar in a blender together with half the oil. Cover the blender and blend at a low speed for 2 seconds. Remove the lid, pour in the remaining oil in a steady stream, and mix for a further 15 seconds. Turn to high speed and blend for a further 5 seconds.

VARIATIONS ON MAYONNAISE

Use ⅔ cup Mayonnaise as a base:

Aioli Mayonnaise: Add 4 cloves garlic, finely chopped and crushed, and blend well. This is not a sauce for the faint-hearted. Excellent with summer salads.

Chive Mayonnaise: Add about ¼ cup chopped chives and 2 teaspoons lemon juice. Serve with vegetable or potato salads.

Cucumber Mayonnaise: Add about 1 cup finely chopped cucumber and 1 teaspoon finely chopped mint leaves. Delicious with fish mousse.

Horseradish Mayonnaise: Add ¼ cup horseradish relish, the finely grated rind of ½ lemon, and salt and pepper to taste. Serve with cold roast beef.

Pink Mayonnaise: Add ¼ cup tomato paste, the juice and finely grated rind of 1 lemon, and salt and pepper to taste. Serve with eggs or fish salads.

TARTAR SAUCE

⅔ cup mayonnaise
1 teaspoon chopped capers
1 teaspoon chopped gherkin
1 teaspoon freshly chopped
　parsley

½ teaspoon dried tarragon
½ teaspoon dried chervil
dash sugar
salt and pepper

Combine all the ingredients and add salt and pepper to taste. Delicious served with oysters, or prawns that have been deep fried in batter; also with deep-fried fillets of fish.

Egg-thickened Sauces

Egg-thickened sauces are a mixture of eggs and butter and have a rich but delicate flavor. Often called butter sauces, they are served lukewarm rather than hot.

When making a sauce of this type it is an advantage to use clarified butter. It is prepared as follows:

Clarified Butter: Place the butter in a heatproof cup and stand the cup in a saucepan of hot water over low heat. When the butter has melted, pour off the oiled butter from the top and discard the milky sediment. Use the clarified butter as required.

Clarified butter may be purchased from delicatessen stores.

HOLLANDAISE SAUCE

The most elegant of egg-thickened (butter) sauces.

½ cup clarified butter
4 egg yolks

2 teaspoons lemon juice
salt and pepper

Place 2 tablespoons of the butter and the egg yolks in the top of a double boiler. Place over hot, but not boiling water and stir quickly and constantly with a wooden spoon until the butter and eggs are well combined. Slowly add the remaining butter, beating the mixture constantly until the sauce is well mixed and thickened. Remove the top of the double boiler from the heat and beat the sauce well for 2 minutes. Add the lemon juice, salt, and pepper, place over hot water, and beat for a further 2 minutes. Serve with salmon or asparagus.

Note: Should the sauce curdle add 2 to 3 tablespoons cold water and beat well until smooth.

FIAGARO SAUCE

⅓ cup stewed, puréed tomatoes
2 tablespoons tomato paste
scant 2 cups Hollandaise Sauce

2 tablespoons finely chopped
    parsley
salt and pepper

Add the puréed tomatoes and tomato paste to the Hollandaise Sauce, off the heat, beating constantly.

Stir in the parsley, reheat gently, and add salt and pepper to taste. Serve with fish or steak.

MALTAISE SAUCE

scant 2 cups Hollandaise Sauce
⅓ cup orange juice

1 teaspoon finely grated orange
    rind

Combine the hot Hollandaise Sauce with the orange juice and rind, beating constantly. This is excellent with vegetables, especially with asparagus and beans.

PRAWNS IN PERNOD SAUCE

My favorite way of using Hollandaise Sauce.

½ lb. green prawns or jumbo
    shrimp
¼ cup white wine

2 tablespoons tomato paste
2 tablespoons Pernod
⅔ cup Hollandaise Sauce

Place the prawns in a small pan together with the white wine and cook for 5 minutes. Add the tomato paste and blend well. Add the Pernod, heat for a few seconds, then ignite and burn off all the alcohol. Remove from the heat and stir in the Hollandaise Sauce. Serve immediately.

Béarnaise Sauce

SAUCE VERTE

scant 2 cups Hollandaise Sauce
½ cup finely chopped cooked
 spinach

salt and pepper

Combine the Hollandaise Sauce and spinach away from the heat, beating constantly. Reheat gently. Add salt and pepper to taste. This sauce is a lovely green color, and is delicious with any seafood.

BÉARNAISE SAUCE

Another well-known egg-thickened sauce, this was created for Henry IV of France by one of his chefs. It is a versatile sauce which may be served with broiled meats, fish, and certain vegetables. It is very rich and piquant and a sauce that I always enjoy.

¾ cup white wine
2 tablespoons tarragon vinegar
2 tablespoons finely chopped
 onion
½ teaspoon dried tarragon
1 teaspoon finely chopped
 parsley

2 peppercorns, crushed
3 egg yolks
1 cup clarified butter
pepper

Combine the white wine, vinegar, onion, tarragon, parsley, and peppercorns in a small saucepan and boil until reduced to one third of the original quantity. Cool. Mix the egg yolks together in the top of a double boiler, place over gently simmering water, and add the strained vinegar and wine, stirring constantly. Gradually add the clarified butter (see page 56), stirring continuously until the sauce has consistency of whipped cream. Add pepper to taste.
Note: Should the sauce curdle add 2 to 3 tablespoons cold water and beat to re-emulsify (the sauce becomes smooth).

SAUCE CHORON

1¼ cups Béarnaise Sauce

2 tablespoons tomato paste

Make the Béarnaise Sauce as above. Just before finishing whisk in the tomato paste. This sauce is a lovely pink color and is delicious with any fish, particularly salmon.

SAUCE VALOIS

1¼ cups Béarnaise Sauce

juices from roasting pan

Remove the meat from the roasting pan, pour off the fat, and deglaze the pan with a little water. Reduce the liquid and add to the Béarnaise Sauce just before completion. This sauce is a light brown color and is excellent with chicken, veal, or pork.

Miscellaneous Sauces

APPLESAUCE

4 large cooking apples, peeled
 and sliced
¼ cup sugar

3 cloves
2 tablespoons butter

Cooking time: 30 minutes
Temperature: 350°

Place the apples in an ovenproof dish, sprinkle with the sugar, and add the cloves. Cover and place in a 350° oven for about 30 minutes, or until the apple is soft. Remove the cloves, stir until pulpy, then add the butter in small pieces and leave to cool. Serve warm or cold with roast goose, pork, or duck.

Note: Cook in the oven along with the roast meat.

BREAD SAUCE

1 small onion, chopped
1 cup milk
1 blade mace

approximately 1 cup soft white
   bread crumbs
salt and pepper to taste

Place the onion, milk, and mace in a small heavy saucepan. Simmer with the lid on until the onion is tender, then strain the milk. Stir enough bread crumbs into the milk to make a thick mixture. Season with salt and pepper and place over a very low heat for about 10 minutes. Stir frequently. Serve with roast poultry.

MINT SAUCE

½ cup finely chopped fresh mint
1 tablespoon sugar

salt and pepper
2 tablespoons hot water
vinegar

Serves: 6

Stir the mint into the sugar with salt and pepper to taste. Add the hot water and sufficient vinegar to mix to the desired consistency.

TOMATO SAUCE

4 large tomatoes
1 small onion, finely chopped
½ tablespoon butter
2½ cups stock or water and
   bouillon cube

2 slices bacon
salt
pepper
3 tablespoons cornstarch

Cooking time: 30 minutes
Serves: 6

Chop the bacon. Wash the tomatoes and cut up roughly. Sauté the onion with the bacon in the butter until the onion is soft but not browned. Add the tomatoes and cook for 5 minutes. Then add the stock, salt, and pepper and simmer for 25 minutes. Press the mixture through a sieve, or purée in an electric blender. Blend the cornstarch with a little cold water, add to the sauce, stir well, and cook for 2 minutes.

PARSLEY BUTTER

¼ cup butter
1 teaspoon finely chopped
   parsley

2 teaspoons lemon juice

Beat the butter until light and creamy. Beat in the parsley and lemon juice. Chill well before serving.

BEURRE MANIÉ

2 tablespoons butter

¼ cup all-purpose flour

Beat the butter and flour together. Stir small pieces gradually into cooked stews and casseroles, until thickened as desired.

Sweet Sauces

A selection of favorite sweet sauces. Most can be made and stored in the refrigerator for future use. Allow ¼ cup sweet sauce per person, as they are rich and concentrated in flavor.

ZABAGLIONE

6 egg yolks
½ cup sugar

¼ cup dry Marsala wine or dry
  sherry
¼ cup brandy

Beat the egg yolks with the sugar in the top of a double boiler until foaming and pale in color. Place over gently boiling water and slowly add the Marsala and brandy, beating continuously until the mixture thickens and becomes foamy. Do not over-cook. Remove from the heat, pour into glasses, and serve immediately with ladyfingers or cream wafers. Zabaglione may also be served as a sauce with a hot fruit pudding.

Variation: Strawberry Sabayon is Zabaglione with fresh strawberries added just before serving.

Note: Sabayon is a French corruption of the Italian Zabaglione.

CHOCOLATE SAUCE

2 squares unsweetened cooking
  chocolate
⅔ cup water
1 cup sugar

2 tablespoons cornstarch
¼ cup butter
¼ cup brandy or rum (optional)

Roughly chop the chocolate and add to the simmering water. Heat gently until the chocolate melts and the mixture is smooth. Add the sugar, then the cornstarch, previously mixed to a smooth paste with ¼ cup cold water. Bring to a boil, stirring continuously until the sugar is dissolved and the sauce has thickened. Simmer for 3 minutes, then stir in the butter, and the brandy or rum if desired.

STRAWBERRY OR RASPBERRY SAUCE

This sauce may be made of either fruit, or a mixture of both.

½ cup strawberry or raspberry
  juice

2 tablespoons red currant jelly
1 teaspoon cornstarch

Place the juice in a saucepan, reserving 2 tablespoons, add the warmed red currant jelly, and bring to a boil. Blend the cornstarch to a paste with the reserved juice. Pour the hot juice onto the blended mixture, stirring continuously with a wooden spoon. Return to the saucepan and boil, stirring continuously, until the sauce is clear and thickened.

VANILLA CUSTARD SAUCE

1¼ cups milk
½ teaspoon vanilla extract

6 tablespoons sugar
3 egg yolks

Heat the milk gently to body temperature over low heat and add the vanilla extract. Blend the sugar and egg yolks in a mixing bowl, mixing until smooth. Add a little of the warmed milk, stirring constantly, then add the remaining milk. Return to a low heat and cook, stirring constantly, until the mixture thickens and has the consistency of cream (it should coat the back of a metal spoon). Serve warm with ice cream, baked and steamed puddings, or fruit puddings.

Zabaglione

EGGS AND CHEESE

Phyllis Wright

Phyllis Wright studied cookery at the Cordon Bleu School of Cookery in London and has also taught at the same school. She now has a cookery school where she passes on to others her 'joy and love of cooking'.

Eggs, Omelets, and Pancakes

Eggs: 'An egg,' Oscar Wilde once declared, 'is always an adventure.' To a cook, it should be 'a way of life'.

Eggs are among the most versatile of foods and from the basic methods—boiling, poaching, scrambling, and frying—attractive egg dishes of the simple or sophisticated kind are easy to create. Fresh herbs, finely chopped sautéed mushrooms, slices of skinned tomato, sautéed onion, chopped bacon, grated cheese, and asparagus are but a few possible additions, without taking into account the host of suitable sauces ready and waiting to be used—a creamy Béchamel, to which one may add flavorsome tidbits, or a tasty sauce made from chicken stock.

Many egg dishes may be made beforehand and heated later. To the busy homemaker or the working cook they should be invaluable. An egg dish carefully prepared should have a kind of elegance which sets it apart from any other type of food.

The egg provides the source of food for the developing chicken embryo, and contains the essential food nutrients. Protein, water, and mineral salts are obtained from the yolk and the white, and fats and vitamins from the yolk only. Carbohydrate is not present in an egg, but even without this, it must be considered as a valuable source of protein and a valuable ingredient for the daily diet of every growing child.

The egg, so fragile to the touch, and yet so versatile and far-reaching in its effect, is indeed a wonder ingredient.

TEST FOR FRESHNESS

To test for freshness, place the egg in a basin of cold water; it should sink if fresh. When the egg is cracked, the white should be thick, not watery, and the yolk clear yellow in color and well formed.

STORAGE OF EGGS

If eggs are stored in the refrigerator, care must be taken to bring them to room temperature before using. This method of storing is not necessary if the supply of eggs is being replenished constantly—a cool closet, or a shelf in the kitchen away from the heat, is satisfactory. Egg whites keep well for several weeks if stored in a scrupulously clean screw-top jar and placed in the refrigerator, or they can be kept in the freezer.

SCRAMBLED EGGS

8 eggs
salt and pepper
2 tablespoons finely chopped
   herbs

$\frac{1}{4}$ cup butter

Serves: 4

Beat the eggs with salt and pepper. Add the finely chopped fresh herbs if desired. A small amount of herbs may be kept for garnishing. Place one fourth of the butter in a skillet and heat gently over low heat. Pour in the egg mixture and, using a broad wooden spatula, move the egg slowly across the pan as it thickens. When almost the thickness desired, remove from the heat and add the remaining butter. Turn onto a hot plate, sprinkle with herbs, and serve at once.
Variation: Finely grated cheese may be added with the final butter.

POACHED EGGS WITH SPINACH AND CHEESE

Serves: 4

1 (10 oz.) package frozen
   spinach or 1$\frac{1}{3}$ cups chopped
   cooked spinach
1 tablespoon butter
salt and pepper
dash nutmeg
1 tablespoon vinegar

4 eggs
4 slices bread
French mustard
2 tablespoons grated Parmesan
   cheese

Cook the frozen spinach as directed. Drain between 2 plates, chop if necessary, then return to the saucepan and toss with the butter, salt and pepper, and nutmeg. Keep hot.
To poach the eggs: Heat about 2 inches water in a skillet. Add the vinegar; this helps the eggs to keep their shape. Break an egg into a saucer, swirl the water with a wooden spoon, and slide the egg very carefully into the center of the 'swirl'. Immediately lift the white over the yolk 2 or 3 times. Add the other eggs in the same manner. After 4 minutes, the white should appear just set. Remove the eggs carefully with a perforated spoon and transfer to a bowl of cold water, to release any vinegar and prevent further cooking. Toast the bread and cut with a cookie cutter to a size to hold the egg. Spread lightly with French mustard. Arrange the spinach on the toast, make slight cavities to hold the poached eggs, and place the drained eggs in the hollows. Sprinkle with Parmesan cheese and place under a hot broiler until the cheese is golden. Serve at once.
Note: Eggs for poaching should be very fresh. This simple dish can be very attractive if the eggs and spinach are drained well, and it is served piping hot from under the broiler.

SCOTCH EGGS

4 medium-sized eggs
3 tablespoons butter
salt and pepper
2 tablespoons fresh mixed herbs,
   finely chopped
1 cup sausage meat

seasoned flour
egg and bread crumbs, for
   coating
vegetable oil, for frying
chopped parsley, for garnish

Serves: 4

Put enough water to cover the eggs in a saucepan and bring to a boil. Remove from the heat and lower the eggs into the water, using a tablespoon. Return the pan to the heat, and when the boiling point is reached again, cook for exactly 10 minutes. When the eggs are cooked, remove them from the saucepan and place in a bowl of cold water to prevent discoloring around the yolks. When cool enough to handle, remove the shells carefully. Dry each egg and cut in half lengthwise. Remove the yolks and press through a sieve. Cream the butter, add the sieved yolks, salt, pepper, and chopped herbs, and bind well. Press this filling into each yolk cavity and level with a spatula. Fit the halves together again and cover with sausage meat, allowing $\frac{1}{4}$ cup for each egg. Dip in seasoned flour, shake off any excess, brush with beaten egg, and toss in dry bread crumbs. Press the crumbs on firmly, then lower the eggs into deep, hot oil and fry for 10 to 12 minutes. Drain on paper towels and serve sprinkled with finely chopped parsley.
Note: Scotch Eggs are excellent served cold with a salad.

The Omelet

No-one comes into this world as an instinctive maker of omelets. The omelet needs much more than the breaking of eggs and the application of heat—it can be the easiest, and also the most tricky process. The choice of pan, of eggs, of fat must be considered, and these essentials must be teamed with the time and desire to practise, and more than a soupcon of patience.

An omelet may be varied by the addition of a filling. It must. be remembered that the filling adds interest, but plays the minor role in the cooking process.

THE OMELET PAN

It is a good idea to have one skillet which can be reserved for omelets only—various omelet-makers like different kinds of pans. My choice is a French iron skillet with a bottom diameter of 7 inches, and sloping sides. This size is ideal for the 2- or 3-egg omelet. If larger omelets are desired, the correct size of skillet must be used. A larger omelet is more difficult to cook evenly, and as a perfect omelet cooks quickly, it is perhaps easier to cook several of a smaller size. When a new skillet is bought, it should be thoroughly washed, patted dry, and heated slowly with a small quantity of oil. As the warmth increases, move the skillet gently now and again to coat the whole surface with warm oil. Remove from the heat, allow to stand overnight, and pour off the oil. Dry lightly with a soft dish towel, and your omelet pan is ready to use. Should it become dirty, or show signs of sticking, rub with coarse salt and a little warm oil to clean it.

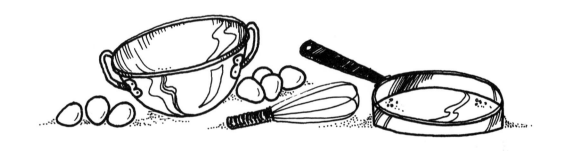

THE BASIC OMELET

Allow 3 eggs per person.

Place the skillet low heat to warm slowly. Meanwhile break 3 large eggs into a bowl and add pepper and salt and 2 tablespoons water, to lighten, for every 3 eggs. Beat these ingredients with a large fork to mix well, and no more. Over-beaten eggs can become watery. Raise the heat under the skillet, add a generous tablespoon butter, and when this begins to show a faint brown color, pour the eggs in. Using a fork, and holding the skillet with your left hand, stir the mixture in the center a few times. This enables any uncooked liquid to run to the sides and cook more easily. As soon as the underside is light golden brown and the center creamy, lift the edge of the omelet nearest the skillet handle, fold in half, and gently roll the omelet towards the edge. To turn out, hold the omelet pan with the left hand underneath the handle, turn over with a quick flick of the wrist, and slide the omelet onto a warmed plate. If a filling is to be added, make this beforehand and keep hot, and spread over half the cooked surface (at right angles to the handle of the pan) when the omelet is ready to fold. In some cases, as with chopped herbs, the filling is cooked with the egg mixture.

OMELET FILLINGS

Potato: Cook a small potato until just tender. Drain well, slice, and fry golden in hot butter. Place the potato slices, lightly seasoned, on the omelet, just before folding.

Asparagus and Bacon: Cut a cooked asparagus spear into small pieces. Warm in butter, season lightly, and use as above. Try also crisp bacon, diced, with the asparagus. Beware of too much salt.

Spinach, Rice, and Cheese: Heat 2 tablespoons cooked, chopped spinach in a little butter. Add the same quantity of cooked rice. Season, add a squeeze of lemon juice, and add to the omelet with 2 tablespoons grated cheese.

Mushroom, Tomato, and Ham (or Chicken): Try this for an omelet with a little more to it. Sauté 2 sliced mushrooms, 2 slices skinned tomato, and $\frac{1}{4}$ cup diced cooked ham, or $\frac{1}{4}$ cup diced cooked chicken. Season lightly and add to the omelet.

Cheese: Add about $\frac{1}{4}$ cup finely grated cheese before folding.

SPANISH OMELET

For omelet:
3 eggs
salt and pepper

2 tablespoons water
1 tablespoon butter

Serves: 2

For filling:
3 tablespoons butter
$\frac{1}{3}$ cup chopped green sweet
   peppers
$\frac{1}{3}$ cup chopped red sweet
   peppers

1 onion, chopped
1 stalk celery, chopped
salt
freshly cracked black pepper

To make the omelet: Beat the eggs, salt, pepper, and water as described previously (see page 65). Heat the butter in the skillet, and when it bubbles gently transfer the cooked filling to the omelet pan. Shake to level over the bottom, then pour the egg mixture on top. Shake the skillet gently as the eggs cook. When set, loosen the edges and run a knife underneath. Ease and slide the omelet to the edge of the skillet (without folding) and turn the omelet over, bottom side up, to display the vegetables, onto a hot plate. Serve at once.

To make the filling: Melt the butter in a small saucepan, add the prepared vegetables and salt and pepper to taste, and cook slowly without coloring. Keep hot.

OMELET ARNOLD BENNETT

$\frac{1}{2}$ lb. smoked cod
milk and water
$\frac{1}{2}$ quantity White Sauce
3 eggs
salt and pepper

$\frac{1}{2}$ cup grated cheese
$\frac{1}{2}$ teaspoon French mustard
2 tablespoons grated cheese,
   for broiling

Serves: 2

Put the fish in an ovenproof dish and barely cover with a mixture of milk and water. Place on the middle shelf in a 350° oven and cook for 15 to 20 minutes, or until it yields easily to a fork. Drain well. (This liquid is too salty for the sauce.) Flake the fish finely with a fork, and remove any bones or skin. Set aside.

Make the White Sauce (see page 50), pour into a bowl, and cover the surface with a circle of damp wax paper, to prevent a skin forming. Stand the bowl in a saucepan of warm water and place over low heat.

Warm the skillet; beat the eggs with salt and pepper and combine with the flaked fish. Cook the omelet as usual. When just set, do not fold, but slide on to a hot plate and place in a 200° oven for a few minutes to keep warm. Remove the sauce from the heat and beat in the grated cheese. Add the French mustard, blend well, and spoon the sauce over the omelet, sprinkle with the remaining cheese and brown quickly under a hot broiler. Serve piping hot.

Omelets, Fillings, and Scotch Eggs

Pancakes and Crêpes

Where would a 'Pancake Tour' round the world lead us? In every country where grain products are a staple of the diet, pancakes are made. At Olney in England, a historic 'Pancake Race' has been held for hundreds of years. On Shrove Tuesday, the pancakes are tossed to church, as the competitors run. San Francisco is proud of its 'silver dollar' pancakes, just over an inch in diameter, while in Germany we find the enormous 'table-top'. Sweden offers the 'plättar', Russia the 'sirniki', Italy 'cannelloni', Israel 'blintzes', and Holland 'flenjses'. France is renowned for the lacy delicate 'crêpe', which is undoubtedly regarded by cooks all over the world as the ultimate in pancake making.

Pancakes began life many years ago, when man first mixed flour and water to make a batter. They were originally baked over a hearth, and were thus 'hearth cakes'. Much has happened since then. We know that crêpes can be made well in advance and filled and reheated as desired. Treated thus, the crêpe holds an enviable place in any menu. It can add a wealth of color to a meal with an attractive filling or accompanying sauce. The cook-hostess, serene and gracious, may be with her guests, knowing that the crêpes can be left to serve when she wishes, or popped under a broiler before being presented. It all sounds so easy, and it is! Recipes for sweet pancakes will be found in the chapter on Desserts.

THE PANCAKE PAN

Various types of pancake pans are available, but, without doubt, the heavy cast-iron skillet is the ideal. When the pan is new, hold it under running hot water for a few minutes, pat dry, fill with oil, and allow to stand overnight. Pour off the oil, dry lightly, and put away ready to use.

TO REHEAT PANCAKES

If they are not to be used within a short time, a very good method of reheating is as follows:

Pack the finished pancakes on an enamel plate, standing over a pan of hot water. Cover with a heatproof mixing bowl or aluminium foil and place over low heat to warm through.

When filled and arranged in an ovenproof dish, put in a 200° oven to keep warm.

PANCAKE BATTER

Makes 12 to 15 small pancakes or crêpes.

1 cup all-purpose flour
dash salt
1 egg

2 tablespoons oil
1 cup plus 2 tablespoons milk,
    mixed with 2 tablespoons
    water

Sift the flour and salt into a mixing bowl. Make a well in the center, drop in the whole egg and the egg yolk, and add the oil. Using a wooden spoon, stir rapidly from the center to blend the egg and oil with a little flour. As this mixture thickens, add the milk by degrees, stirring from the center and making bigger circular movements as more flour is incorporated. When all the flour is blended, beat well and add the remaining milk, reserving 2 tablespoons. The resulting batter should be the consistency of coffee cream. Strain, cover, and allow to stand for at least 30 minutes, to enable the starch cells in the flour to swell and soften. When ready to use, beat in the reserved milk.

PANCAKES

(CRÊPES)

Makes 12 to 15 small pancakes or crêpes.

1 quantity Pancake Batter clarified butter or oil, for cooking

Heat the skillet slightly and add sufficient clarified butter or oil to cover the bottom liberally. As the skillet heats, tilt to allow the butter or oil to run all over the surface. Drain off the superfluous oil, leaving just a film in the skillet. Pour in sufficient batter to run all over the bottom of the skillet—about 2 tablespoons for a pan 5½ to 6 inches across. Replace over the heat and cook until the upper surface appears bubbly. Run a round-bladed knife around to loosen the edges, then slide the knife under and turn or toss the pancake over. The side cooked first is served as the outer side. Turn the finished pancakes onto a cooling rack covered with a clean dish towel. Stack slightly overlapping and wrap to keep warm.

Serve hot filled with an appropriate mixture.

CROÛTON PANCAKES

1 quantity Pancake Batter clarified butter or oil Serves: 4

For filling:
3 tablespoons butter
2 onions, thinly sliced
3 tablespoons all-purpose flour

⅔ cup milk
salt and pepper
3 slices stale bread
oil for frying

To make the filling: Melt the butter in a small saucepan, add the onion, cover, and allow to cook slowly without coloring. Draw aside and stir in the flour. Return the pan to the heat, cook for a few minutes, then add the warmed milk and stir until boiling. Season well with salt and pepper to taste. Keep warm. Remove the crusts from the bread and cut the bread into ¼-inch cubes (croûtons). Fry these in hot oil until golden, drain on absorbent paper, sprinkle with salt, and keep warm.

To make the pancakes: Cook the pancakes as directed above. Spread the onion sauce over half of each pancake, sprinkle some croûtons on top, and fold the other half over. When filled, arrange overlapping on a long ovenproof dish. Sprinkle over any remaining croûtons and keep warm in the bottom of a 200° oven until ready to serve. Serve hot.

SPINACH PANCAKES

2 quantities Pancake Batter clarified butter or oil

Cooking time: 15-20 minutes
Temperature: 300°
Serves: 4

For filling:
2 (10 oz.) package frozen
 spinach or 2⅔ cups chopped
 cooked spinach
salt and pepper
lemon juice

1 teaspoon butter
scant 2 cups Mornay Sauce
10 slices bacon
½ cup grated cheese

To make the filling: Cook the frozen spinach as directed on the package. Drain very thoroughly and season with salt, black pepper, and lemon juice. Add the butter and heat gently. Beat ¼ cup of the Mornay Sauce (see page 51) into the prepared spinach and set aside.

Dice the bacon and fry until crisp. Drain.

Cook the crêpes and spread a little spinach mixture over one. Transfer to a round ovenproof serving dish and sprinkle with bacon. Cover with the second crêpe, and continue to layer in this fashion to form a cake. About 8 to 10 layers are necessary. Coat with the remaining Mornay Sauce, sprinkle with the grated cheese, heat carefully in a 300° oven for 15 to 20 minutes, and brown under a hot broiler before serving.

Note: Use a sharp cheese in the Mornay Sauce and add 1 teaspoon French mustard for additional flavor.

CRÊPES À MA FAÇON

1 quantity Pancake Batter

clarified butter or oil

Serves: 4

For filling:
⅔ cup cold cooked chicken and
   ham, chopped
2 teaspoons chopped mixed
   herbs
salt and pepper
1½ tablespoons butter

3 tablespoons all-purpose flour
1¼ cups chicken stock or water
   and chicken bouillon cube
2 tablespoons sherry
tomato and toasted slivered
   almonds, for garnish

To make the filling: Mix the chicken and ham with the herbs and season lightly with salt and pepper. Melt the butter in a saucepan, add the flour, and, working off the heat, mix to a smooth paste. Warm the stock and add gradually. Blend well, return to the heat, and bring to the boiling point, stirring continuously. Add the sherry. Add sufficient sauce to the chicken mixture to give a spreading consistency.

To make the crêpes: Cook the crêpes as directed on page 69. Spread the filling over the crêpes, roll up, and arrange on a serving dish. Serve hot, garnished with skinned lightly cooked tomato segments and scattered with toasted almonds.

KIDNEY PANCAKES

1 quantity Pancake Batter

clarifed butter or oil

Serves: 4

For filling:
3 lamb kidneys
6 slices bacon
1 onion, thinly sliced
2 tablespoons all-purpose flour
1¼ cups beef stock or water and
   beef bouillon cube

salt
freshly cracked black pepper
1 teaspoon tomato paste
2 tablespoons sherry
finely chopped parsley, for
   garnish

To make the filling: Skin the kidneys, cut in half lengthwise, remove the core, using scissors, and slice thinly. Chop 4 of the bacon slices into small pieces. Heat the skillet, add the bacon pieces, and brown quickly. Remove, add the sliced kidney, fry quickly, and remove from the skillet. A little extra bacon fat or oil may be needed as the cooking proceeds. Fry the onion until golden, sprinkle with the flour, stir, and continue cooking for a few minutes. Remove from the heat, add the stock, salt, pepper, and tomato paste, and blend well. Return to the heat, stir continuously until boiling, then add the bacon, kidneys, and sherry, cover, and allow to simmer for 20 minutes.

To make the pancakes: Cook the pancakes as directed on page 69. Cut the remaining bacon slices into small lengths, roll up tightly, thread on a skewer, and broil. Spread the filling on the cooked pancakes, roll up, and arrange on an ovenproof serving dish around the bacon rolls. Serve hot, garnished with finely chopped parsley.

Eve Knottenbelt

Eve Knottenbelt runs a cookery school and writes cookery articles for *The Epicurean* magazine. She has a Certificate of Home Management and Catering and has studied at the Cordon Bleu Schools in London and Paris.

Soufflés and Savory Flans

Over the years a mystique seems to have grown up around soufflés. No awe-inspiring creations of classic haute cuisine, they are easy to make, delicious, and impressive, and a hostess's reputation is assured when she produces one. These light as air concoctions are basically a sauce enriched with egg yolks, flavored with fish, meat, or vegetables. Sweet soufflés are flavored with chocolate, vanilla, or a subtle liqueur. Soufflés are perfect for a light luncheon or supper and superb as an entrée for a dinner party. A sweet soufflé makes a wonderful dessert, accompanied by a glass of champagne. Recipes for hot sweet soufflés will be found in the chapter on Desserts.

POINTS FOR SUCCESS

Soufflés are usually cooked in a round, straight-sided ovenproof dish. A well-buttered collar of paper is tied round a shallow souffle dish to support the rising soufflé. Soufflés may also be made in individual dishes, and these are most effective for a dinner party.

The first essential for a soufflé is a smooth Béchamel Sauce, to which the appropriate flavorings are added, after the egg yolks have been beaten in separately. A tablespoon of the stiffly beaten egg whites is then added to the mixture to soften it slightly before folding in the remaining whites.

The beating of the egg whites is most important as it is this which lightens the soufflé and gives it its special character. Egg white should be beaten in a spotlessly clean bowl, as any moisture or grease adhering to the bowl, or any specks of egg yolk, will inhibit the egg whites from beating up to to a stiff airy mass. If you are lucky enough to possess an unlined copper bowl and a balloon whisk, use them. You will be thrilled with the extra volume and better texture of the egg whites, which will not collapse the minute you stop beating. This is due to the slight acidity of the copper which stabilizes the beaten egg whites.

The basic mixture can be made beforehand and stored in the refrigerator. All you need do before baking is warm the mixture, fold in the beaten egg whites, cook, and serve with a flourish. It must be remembered, however, that a soufflé will not wait, and for perfection the diners should be ready and waiting for it when it comes out of the oven.

CHEESE SOUFFLÉ

1 tablespoon butter, for greasing
2 tablespoons fresh white bread
   crumbs
generous $\frac{1}{2}$ cup grated Parmesan
   cheese
3 tablespoons butter
6 tablespoons all-purpose flour
1 cup plus 2 tablespoons milk
4 egg yolks

5 egg whites
$\frac{3}{4}$ teaspoon salt
$\frac{1}{4}$ teaspoon freshly cracked black
   pepper
dash cayenne pepper
$\frac{1}{4}$ teaspoon paprika
$\frac{1}{4}$ cup grated Gruyère cheese

Cooking time: 35-40 minutes
Temperature: 400°
Serves: 4

Grease the inside of a 6-inch soufflé dish with butter, then sprinkle with the bread crumbs and one tablespoon of the Parmesan cheese. Cut a band of wax paper about 7 inches wide and long enough to go around the outside of the dish with a 2-inch overlap, fold in half lengthwise, butter the top half of one side of the paper, and tie round the soufflé dish with string. Melt the butter in a saucepan, stir in the flour, and cook over gentle heat for about 1 minute. Add the milk and stir continuously over medium heat until the mixture thickens and boils.

Simmer for 5 seconds. Remove from the heat and add the egg yolks one at a time, beating well. Add seasonings, the remaining Parmesan, and the Gruyère cheese.

Beat the egg whites until stiff, firm peaks are formed. Stir 2 tablespoons of the beaten egg white into the sauce to lighten it, then, with a spatula, lightly fold in the remaining egg whites. Gently pour the soufflé mixture into the prepared soufflé dish. Bake on the middle shelf of a 400° oven for 35 to 40 minutes. Serve immediately.

VARIATIONS ON CHEESE SOUFFLÉ

Mushroom Soufflé
$1\frac{1}{2}$ cups finely chopped raw
   mushrooms
1 tablespoon finely chopped
   onion
1 tablespoon butter
6 tablespoons grated Parmesan
   cheese
1 teaspoon lemon juice
dash freshly grated nutmeg

Sauté the mushrooms and onion in the butter until soft. Make the soufflé as directed above, omitting the grated Parmesan and Gruyère cheese. Instead add the sautéed mushrooms and onion, grated Parmesan cheese, lemon juice, and nutmeg.

Spinach Soufflé
$\frac{3}{4}$ cup cooked spinach, chopped
2 tablespoons finely chopped
   onion
$\frac{1}{2}$ cup grated Gruyère cheese
$\frac{1}{4}$ teaspoon grated nutmeg
2 slices cooked ham, finely
   chopped

Make as for Cheese Soufflé, omitting the bread crumbs, cheese, paprika, and cayenne pepper, and substituting the above ingredients.

Chicken Soufflé
$\frac{3}{4}$ cup finely chopped cooked
   chicken
$\frac{1}{4}$ cup finely chopped cooked
   ham
$\frac{1}{2}$ teaspoon mustard
2 tablespoons chopped parsley
$\frac{1}{4}$ teaspoon grated nutmeg
2 tablespoons brandy

Omit the cheese and bread crumbs from the Cheese Souffle recipe, and add the above ingredients in place of the grated cheese.

Shellfish Soufflé
$\frac{2}{3}$ cup cooked shellfish, flaked
   or finely chopped
$\frac{1}{2}$ cup grated Parmesan cheese
2 teaspoons lemon juice
2 tablespoons brandy

Omit the cheese, bread crumbs, and paprika from the Cheese Soufflé, and substitute the above ingredients.

Soufflé Omelets

In the preparation of this type of omelet the yolks and whites of the eggs are prepared separately. The yolks are mixed with the seasonings or, for a sweet omelet, are creamed with sugar, flavorings, and other ingredients. Care must be taken to ensure that the beaten egg whites reach the 'soft peak' stage only, and are not too firm to combine easily and smoothly with the egg yolk mixture. The greater part of the cooking is done in the oven. Some recipes call for the final stage under the broiler, and some sweet recipes have heated rum or brandy poured around and lit.

SOUFFLÉ OMELET

3 eggs	2 tablespoons cream	Cooking time:	6 minutes
salt and pepper	1 tablespoon butter	Temperature:	375°
		Serves:	3

Separate the yolks from the whites of the eggs. Mix the yolks with the salt, pepper, and cream. Beat the whites until soft peaks are formed, and combine the mixtures lightly and quickly. Heat the skillet, add the butter, and when sizzling pour in the egg mixture. Shake the skillet gently once or twice, and after 1 minute, when the bottom of the soufflé omelet should be set and lightly browned, transfer the pan to a 375° oven and cook for about 6 minutes. Remove from the oven, cover with the chosen filling (described below), fold over in half, using a knife, slide onto a hot plate, and serve immediately.

Suggested fillings:

Spinach and Cheese: Slice a medium-sized onion, cook gently in 2 tablespoons butter, add 1 cup cooked, chopped spinach, season with salt and pepper, add a dash of nutmeg, and bind with a little hot cheese or Mornay Sauce (see page 51).

Extra cheese or Mornay Sauce may be served separately, or poured over the omelet and browned under a hot broiler.

Chicken or Veal: Use leftover chicken or veal, sliced into small pieces to which diced cooked ham or crisp bacon, sautéed mushrooms, or chopped herbs, may be added. Bind the chosen ingredients with a little Béchamel Sauce (see page 51), and warm before adding to the cooked omelet.

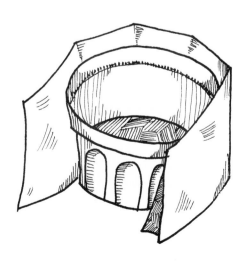

Cheese Souffle

Savory Flans

Stretching back to antiquity, the French flan, or flamiche, oublie, quiche, or galette, has evolved from an open pie made from bread dough with simple fillings, mostly of cheese and eggs, to the present day pies of diverse fillings in rich short crust.

The French claim these pies as their own and give us endless variations, each province using to advantage the local food peculiar to that region.

These flans made excellent appetizers, served hot or cold. They may be the main course for a light luncheon, served with a chilled white wine and followed by a salad; and tiny individual ones may be offered with pre-dinner drinks.

The pie shell is usually baked blind, which means it is half-cooked with a lining of greased wax paper and filled with dried beans, to hold the bottom down and the sides up, until it is set, then wax paper and beans are removed and the filling is added and the pie returned to the oven to finish cooking.

Ideally, these flans are cooked in a loose-bottomed French flan pan, or in a flan ring, placed on a baking sheet. These can be removed before serving, which adds greatly to the flan's appearance. They may be made in an ordinary pie plate or pan, however. Serve flans hot or cold, depending on the occasion.

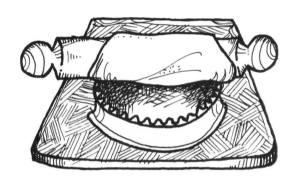

QUICHE LORRAINE

For pieshell:
1 cup all-purpose flour
¼ cup butter
1 egg yolk

squeeze lemon juice
2-3 teaspoons cold water
½ teaspoon salt

Cooking time: 40-50 minutes
Temperature: 400°,
  reducing to 375°
Serves: 4-6

For filling:
¼ lb. bacon
1 teaspoon butter
2 eggs
1¼ cups cream

salt
freshly cracked black pepper
freshly grated nutmeg
2 oz. Gruyère cheese, sliced

To make the pie crust: Sift the flour into a mixing bowl. Rub the butter into the flour with the fingertips until the mixture resembles bread crumbs. Mix the egg yolk, lemon juice, water, and salt together, add to the flour, and mix with a round-bladed knife until the mixture holds together. Allow to stand in the refrigerator for 30 minutes. Roll out thinly on a lightly floured board or marble slab, to fit an 8-inch layer cake pan or flan ring standing on a baking sheet. Roll the dough over the rolling pin and lift and unroll into the pan or flan ring. Press the pastry into the bottom and around the sides, being careful not to stretch it. Roll the pin firmly over the rim of the pan to trim off excess dough. Prick the bottom of the shell and line the inside with a circle of greased wax paper. Sprinkle with dried beans or peas.

Bake on the middle shelf of a 400° oven for 15 to 20 minutes. The shell should not brown. Remove the paper and beans.

To make the filling and finish the flan: Cut the bacon into 1-inch squares and fry in the butter until crisp. Cool. Beat the eggs with a fork, add the heated cream, salt, pepper, and nutmeg, and mix well. Place the bacon in the bottom of the pie shell, cover with the cheese, and pour over the warm egg mixture. Wait until the cheese melts, and then bake on the middle shelf of a 375° oven for about 20 to 30 minutes, or until the top is golden and the mixture is set (a knife inserted comes out clean). Serve immediately, while still slightly puffed up.

76

HAM AND ONION FLAN

1 8-inch pastry flan shell

For filling:
3 large onions, thinly sliced
1½ cups finely sliced mushrooms
2 tablespoons butter
2 tablespoons all-purpose flour
⅔ cup milk
⅔ cup cream
2 egg yolks

salt
freshly cracked black pepper
freshly grated nutmeg
¾ cup cooked ham, sliced
6-8 medium-sized mushrooms,
    for garnish
¼ cup grated Gruyère cheese
extra butter

Cooking time: 25 minutes
Temperature: 400°,
    reducing to 375°
Serves: 4-6

Prepare the pie shell as for Quiche Lorraine (see page 76) and bake blind on the middle shelf of a 400° oven for 15 to 20 minutes, until the shell is set in shape. Remove the paper and beans.

To make the filling and finish the flan: Sauté the onions and mushrooms in the butter in a covered saucepan until soft. Add the flour and stir over medium heat for 1 to 2 minutes, until golden brown. Add the milk and stir continuously until the mixture boils, then simmer for 5 minutes. Remove from the heat and stir in the cream, egg yolks, salt, pepper, and nutmeg. Spread enough ham in the bottom of the pie shell to cover. Pour the onion and mushroom mixture over. Sauté the whole mushrooms in a little extra butter until tender. Arrange the remaining ham and the whole mushrooms attractively on top of the flan. Sprinkle with the cheese and bake on the middle shelf of a 375° oven for 15 to 20 minutes, or until the filling is set. Serve hot.

LEEK FLAN

1 8-inch pastry flan shell

For filling:
1 lb. white part of leeks, thinly
    sliced
¾ cup cream
1 egg
1 egg yolk

salt, pepper, nutmeg, and
    cayenne pepper
¼ cup grated Swiss cheese
1 teaspoon butter

Cooking time: 30-40 minutes
Temperature: 400°,
    reducing to 375°
Serves: 4-6

Make the cheese pastry flan shell as for Quiche Lorraine (see page 76), adding 2 tablespoons grated Parmesan cheese before binding the flour with the liquid. Bake blind on the middle shelf of a 400° oven for 15 to 20 minutes. Remove the paper and beans.

To make the filling and finish the flan: Cook the leeks in as little water as possible until tender. Strain. Beat the cream, egg, egg yolk and seasonings and stir in the leeks. Pour the mixture into the flan shell and sprinkle the cheese on top. Dot with butter. Bake on the middle shelf of a 375° oven for 20 to 25 minutes, or until the mixture is set and the top is golden brown.

SPINACH FLAN

1 8-inch cheese pastry flan shell

For filling:
2 cups cooked spinach
⅔ cup cream
2 eggs
2 tablespoons butter, melted

¼ teaspoon grated nutmeg
freshly cracked black pepper
½ teaspoon sugar
½ cup grated Gruyère cheese

Cooking time: 25-30 minutes
Temperature: 400°,
    reducing to 375°
Serves: 4-6

Prepare a flan shell as for Quiche Lorraine (see page 76). Bake blind on the middle shelf of a 400° oven for 15 to 20 minutes. Remove the paper and beans.

To make the filling and finish the flan: Beat all the ingredients together except the cheese, pour into the flan shell, and sprinkle with the grated cheese. Bake on the middle shelf of a 375° oven for 8 to 10 minutes, or until the cheese is golden.

SHELLFISH FLAN

For pie crust:
1 cup all-purpose flour
¼ teaspoon salt
pinch cayenne pepper
freshly cracked black pepper

¼ cup butter
1 egg yolk
1 teaspoon lemon juice
2-3 teaspoons cold water

Cooking time: 40-45 minutes
Temperature: 400°,
    reducing to 375°
Serves: 4-6

For filling:
¾ cup cream
⅔ cup well-flavored fish stock
3 eggs
1 teaspoon brandy
squeeze lemon juice
1 tablespoon finely chopped
   parsley

12 oysters
⅔ cup chopped lobster, crab, and
   scallops, mixed
salt
freshly cracked black pepper
cayenne pepper
freshly grated nutmeg

To make the pie crust: Sift the flour, salt, and peppers into a mixing bowl. Rub the butter into the flour with the fingertips until the mixture resembles bread crumbs. Mix together the egg yolk, lemon juice, and water, add to the flour, and mix with a round-bladed knife to a stiff dough. Stand in the refrigerator for 30 minutes. Roll out and line an 8-inch flan ring or pie pan. Prick the bottom of the flan, line the inside with a circle of greased wax paper, and sprinkle with dried beans or peas. Bake on the middle shelf of a 400° oven for 15 to 20 minutes. Do not allow to brown. Remove the wax paper and beans.

To make the filling and finish the flan: Beat the cream, fish stock (see method, page 43), and eggs together. Add the remaining ingredients and salt, peppers, and nutmeg to taste; pour into the partly-cooked pie shell. Bake on the middle shelf of a 375° oven for 25 to 30 minutes, or until the mixture is set. Serve hot.

TARTE NIÇOISE

1 8-inch pastry flan shell

Cooking time: 45-50 minutes
Temperature: Pie shell: 400°
    Custard: 375°
    reducing to 300
Serves: 4-6

For filling:
6 small tomatoes
½ cup grated sharp cheese
¼ cup fresh white bread crumbs
2 tablespoons chopped fresh
   basil, or 1 teaspoon dried basil

salt and pepper
grated nutmeg
cayenne pepper
2 tablespoons butter
6 black olives

For custard:
1 egg
1 egg yolk
⅔ cup cream

grated nutmeg
salt
freshly cracked black pepper

Prepare a flan shell as directed for Quiche Lorraine (see page 76), adding ¼ teaspoon grated nutmeg and ¼ teaspoon freshly cracked black pepper. Bake blind on the middle shelf of a 400° oven for 15 to 20 minutes. Remove the wax paper and beans.

To make the filling and finish the flan: Cut the tomatoes in half and, using a teaspoon and squeezing gently, remove all the seeds and juice. Mix together the cheese, bread crumbs, basil, salt, pepper, nutmeg, and cayenne pepper and press into the tomato halves. Place in the cooked flan shell and dot with butter. Make the custard by beating all the ingredients together. Pour the custard into the flan shell around the tomatoes and arrange the olives in the custard. Bake on the middle shelf of a 375° oven for 30 to 35 minutes, or until the custard is set, reducing the heat if necessary to 300°. Serve hot.

Janet Lillie

Cheese

Janet Lillie is a home economist in industry. She has a Diploma of Foods and Cookery and has experience both at home and abroad in food preparation.

Cheese, whether served with crusty fresh bread as an informal lunch, used in cooking, or eaten with fruit at the end of a formal meal, is one of the most versatile and varied of foods. Cheeses of different kinds are made all over the world and are a staple food in many countries. They may be made from cows', goats', or ewes' milk, and range from fresh, unsalted cream cheese to the hard, aged, Italian Parmesan.

When serving cheese at the end of a meal arrange the cheese attractively on a board. For a dinner party of six to eight guests make a colorful selection of four or five varieties of cheese, for example, a mellow-flavored Samsoe, Gouda, or Port Salut, a sharper-tasting matured Cheddar, soft, ripened Brie or Camembert, salty sweet Feta, and a strongly flavored Stilton or Gorgonzola. For formal occasions for large numbers of imaginative gourmets, serve a selection of at least seven varieties including cheeses of varied flavors and different textures and shapes. Present the cheese in pieces of about half a pound in weight, or whole if small cheeses. Serve three or four plain crackers or saltines for each guest.

What of the garnish? Salad vegetables are popular. Introduce a little flair and imagination with fresh raw seasonal fruits—succulent strawberries with Feta, pineapple wedges with blue cheese, pears and red-skinned apples, sliced and soaked in lemon, bunches of grapes, and orange and grapefruit segments with the mild cheeses, and stuffed olives, walnut halves, and dried fruits for a perfect accompaniment to Cheddar.

Just as there is a cheese for every palate, so there is a wine to accompany it. Full-bodied Burgundies and clarets go with strong cheeses and light, well-chilled Chablis, Riesling, or Graves complement and contrast with milder cheeses.

Cheese provides infinite variety for the daily menu and one may travel the world with international cheeses.

A Guide to some Cheeses of the World

Austrian Smoked	A solid, pale yellow cheese with a brown waxy covering, smooth firm texture, and pleasant, mild, smoky flavor.
Brie	Large flat wheel-shaped cheese with a white rind. Creamy, rich flavor; eaten when ripe and very soft.
Camembert	Small, round, flat, yellowy white cheese which when ripe is soft and has a creamy rich flavor. Like Brie, originates in France, but has many imitators.
Cheddar	An English cheese, Cheddar is now made by all the English-speaking nations such as America, Canada, Australia, and New Zealand. Varies from mild to sharp in flavor, with a smooth firm texture. Color pale yellow to reddish according to style.
Cheshire	Firm, pale yellow, English cheese, milder and crumblier in texture than Cheddar.
Danish Blue	A white, blue-veined cheese with sharp flavor and creamy texture.
Edam	A Dutch skim-milk cheese with a smooth, firm texture and yellow color. Made in round balls with a red wax skin.
Emmenthal	A Swiss cheese rather similar to Gruyère but with very large eyes and a sweeter, more fatty flavor. Emmenthal and Gruyère may be interchanged in recipes calling for either one of them.
Feta	A ewes' milk cheese made in Greece. White, soft, and crumbly in texture, pickled in brine.
Gorgonzola	A creamy, naturally veined blue cheese, made in Italy. Its strong flavor sharpens with age.
Gouda	A flattened wheel shape with a yellow wax skin, this whole milk Dutch cheese is similar in texture and flavor to Edam.
Gruyère	A Swiss cheese with small eyes, smooth firm texture, and a slightly sweet, nutty taste.
Mozzarella	A semi-soft Italian cheese, with mild flavor and resilient texture. Eaten very fresh.
Parmesan	A deep yellow in color, with a granular texture and a full, piquant flavor, this famous Italian cheese is invaluable in cooking. Parmesan is matured for 3 or more years; the older it is the better, and the dearer.
Pecorino	Another hard grating cheese from Italy. Made from ewes' milk, it has a granular texture and a strong, pungent taste. Pecorino Romano is the most famous, Pecorino Sardo is made in Sardinia.
Petit Suisse	A fresh, unsalted cream cheese made in France and sold in

tiny 1-inch high cylinders. Eaten with sugar, jam, or fruit as a dessert.

Port Salut	Creamy yellow and firm, with a mildly ripe flavor and a bright orange rind. Originally made by Trappist monks in France, now widely imitated.
Provolone	A southern Italian cheese with a firm, smooth, white flesh and a thin yellow rind. Robust flavor; comes in a variety of shapes and sizes—pear, sausage, flask—tied in cords for hanging.
Ricotta	A soft, unsalted, moist, white, Italian cheese, made from whey from ewes' milk.
Rocquefort	A ewes' milk cheese, pungent and salty in flavor, green veined with a crumbly texture. Made in France and ripened in special caves where the even humidity and temperature encourages the distinctive mold.
Samsoe	Made in Denmark, this cheese has a firm, buttery texture and a good flavor.
Stilton	A famous English veined cheese, white in color with veins and a hard, greyish rind. Strong flavored, it is best at 6 to 9 months old.
Tome de Savoie	A French cheese with a solid texture and milky flavor, ripened in a mixture of grape seeds and skins, which give it a distinctive appearance and flavor.

A Cheese Board

FISH

Michel Ray

Michel Ray has a wealth of knowledge about fish and has cooked over 60 tons of it in eleven years as a chef-restauranteur. Born in France, he first learned to cook from his grandmother and later studied food technology.

Nowadays the fish plays a very important part in many menus, for with modern methods of freezing, packaging, and transportation it is no longer necessary to live beside the ocean to enjoy all kinds of delicious fish and shellfish. Many of the more exotic varieties of fish are now available, as well as many more common types. Fish has a nutritional value equal to the best cuts of meat and in some cases superior. It is not always the large fish that has the best flavor; many of the smaller and less expensive varieties offer excellent flavor and more satisfaction. Fish may be cooked in a very short time, and blends perfectly with wine, and with the addition of a few herbs the most ordinary fish may be transformed into a company dish.

BUYING FISH

When buying fish look for these points. The skin should be brilliant, the eyes bright and clear, and the gills bright red. When buying fish fillets the color should be pinkish white with no gluey appearance and the flesh should be firm with a fresh salty smell.

The best results are obtained by purchasing the fish just before you want to cook it. When stored in a refrigerator the ideal temperature is between 28° and 32°. Before placing the fish in the refrigerator coat it with vegetable oil and wrap in aluminum foil, or cover with dry white wine and add a finely chopped onion, two or three bay leaves, and a dash of mixed herbs. It is important to remember that the fish should always be covered in liquid until used.

CLEANING FISH

Place the fish on a flat surface, tail toward you. Hold the fish firmly by the tail and scrape with a knife from the tail toward the head, using a circular motion to remove all of the scales. Cut off the fins and head if not required. Cut down the middle of the underside of the fish from the tail to the head. Remove the intestines and gills. With the point of the knife scrape the bone on the inside of the fish to remove the blood and remove any that remains by rubbing with salt. Wash the fish under cold running water.

TO FILLET FISH

Round fish such as mackerel are filleted as follows: Lay the fish on a board. With a sharp filleting knife make a clean cut from the back of the head to the tail, with the point of the knife on the backbone. Cut with clean strokes between the flesh and the bones to remove the fillet. Turn the fish over and detach the second fillet as above.

Flat fish are filleted as follows:

Lay the fish on a board with the tail toward you. Make a cut down the backbone from head to tail. Start from the head on the left fillet and cut with a sharp filleting knife between the bone and flesh and remove the fillet. Turn the fish around and remove the second fillet, working from tail to head. Turn the fish over and remove the other two fillets.

TO SKIN FISH

Skinning is necessary for certain fish, particularly when frying them. To remove the skin from fish fillets, place the fish on a flat board with the skin side down, tail toward you, and, using a sharp knife, cut the flesh from the skin at the base of the tail. Pull the skin toward you with the left hand and push the knife along the fillet using a slight zig-zag motion to remove the skin.

Flat fish may be skinned before filleting. Make a cut at the tail and run the thumbs between the skin and the flesh around the fins to loosen the skin. Dip the finger and thumb in salt and rip the skin off quickly from the tail. Turn the fish over and remove the skin on other side.

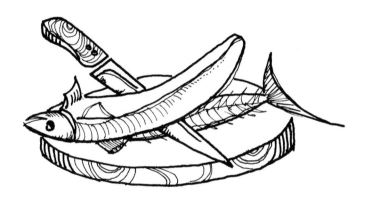

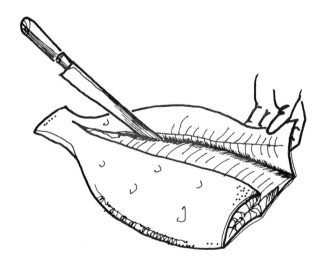

BROILED FISH

A suitable method for small whole fish such as mullet, herring, or whiting, and fish steaks. To prepare whole fish for broiling gently cut the flesh diagonally with a sharp knife so that you have a quilted effect; the spaces between each cut should be $\frac{1}{2}$ inch apart. Brush the fish on each side with melted butter and sprinkle with salt and pepper before placing under a hot broiler. Cook until the flesh is a clear white and flakes easily (about 15 to 20 minutes). Turn once during broiling and watch the fish constantly to avoid burning. Serve hot, garnished with lemon wedges.

DEEP FRIED FISH

Use fillets of fish and cover with a suitable coating before frying.

For coating, use one of the following:
Seasoned flour, for sardines and anchovies
Milk and seasoned flour, for fish fillets
Seasoned flour, beaten egg, and dry bread crumbs, for prawns

Batter (see Pancake Batter page 68), for fish fillets
Pastry dough, for large fish fillets.

For pastry dough:
2 cups all-purpose flour
$\frac{1}{2}$ teaspoon salt
1 egg yolk
$\frac{3}{4}$ cup cold water
salt and pepper

To make the pastry dough: Sieve the flour and salt into a mixing bowl. Add the egg yolk and water and mix to a dough; knead well for 5 minutes. Cover and allow to stand for at least 50 minutes. Roll the dough out on a lightly floured surface to $\frac{1}{8}$ inch thickness. Brush with cold water, sprinkle with salt and pepper, and roll around the fish, previously sprinkled with finely chopped onion, shallot, or garlic. Seal well and deep fry.

To deep fry fish: Heat sufficient oil to cover the fish in a deep skillet or electric skillet. Test by putting in a 1-inch cube of bread which should brown in 1 minute if the oil is at the correct temperature. Place the coated fish in the oil, avoiding contact between each piece. Cook for 2 to 3 minutes. Drain well on absorbent paper towels. Serve piping hot with lemon wedges, French fried potatoes, and Tartare Sauce (see page 55).

FRIED SCALLOPS

1 lb. scallops
seasoned flour
batter

paprika pepper
oil for frying
parsley sprigs

Serves: 4

Roll the scallops in seasoned flour, dip in batter (see page 68), and sprinkle with paprika pepper. Deep fry in hot oil for 1 minute or until the batter is golden.

Drain the scallops and keep hot. Fry parsley sprigs in the hot oil until crisp, drain, and serve with the fried scallops as an entrée.

FRIED OYSTERS

12 oysters
salt and pepper
1 egg yolk
$\frac{1}{4}$ cup milk

dry bread crumbs
oil for frying
lemon wedges
chopped parsley for garnish

Serves: 1-2

Remove the oysters from their shells and season with salt and pepper. Mix the egg yolk with the milk, dip the oysters in the mixture, drain, and roll in the bread crumbs. Deep fry in hot oil for 2 minutes. Heat the shells in the oven and place the fried oysters in hot shells. Serve hot with lemon wedges and sprinkled with parsley.

SAVORY POACHED FISH

Poaching is suitable for large whole fish such as snapper and salmon, small whole fish such as mullet and whiting, and fish fillets and fish steaks.

1 large fish, 3-4 lb. (snapper),
   or 4 small whole fish (mullet)
court bouillon

lemon slices, parsley sprigs,
   and olives for garnish

Serves: 4

For sauce:
½ cup butter
2 teaspoons finely chopped
   scallions

1 teaspoon finely chopped
   parsley
½ teaspoon crushed garlic

Place the prepared fish in a large poacher and cover with court bouillon (see recipe below). Simmer gently until the flesh is white. With large fish check regularly to avoid the flesh breaking up. Drain the fish well.
To make the sauce: Melt the butter in a heavy saucepan and add the scallions and parsley. Add the garlic just before required, and pour over the fish before serving. Garnish with lemon slices, parsley sprigs, and olives.

Note: Allow the following times:
Large whole fish up to 6 lb.:   8-10 minutes per lb.
Small whole fish: 15-20 minutes
Fish fillets: 8-12 minutes
Fish steaks: 10-15 minutes

COURT BOUILLON

Court bouillon is a liquid used for poaching fish. Ideally, use a fish poacher, a large receptacle at least 6 inches high and about 15 inches long. In the bottom, it has a perforated tray with handles to lift the fish out in one piece from the liquid. Alternatively, use a large saucepan.

7½ pints cold water
⅔ cup vinegar
1 onion, thinly sliced
2 tablespoons salt

1 teaspoon white pepper
dash mixed herbs or dried
   bouquet garni

Mix all the ingredients together, bring to a boil, reduce the heat, and simmer gently for 45 minutes. Use as required.

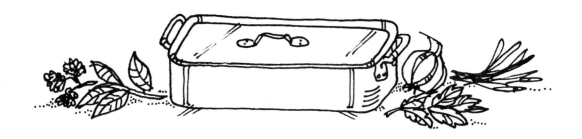

Savory Poached Fish

POACHED FISH IN WHITE WINE SAUCE

This method is suitable for fish fillets, sole, or trout.

1½-2 lb. fish fillets
1½ cups dry white wine
dash tarragon
1 small onion, finely chopped

1½ cups court bouillon
3 egg yolks
⅓ cup cream
salt and pepper

Serves: 4

Prepare the fish and poach in court bouillon (see page 89); drain well and keep hot. Place the wine, tarragon, and onion in a saucepan and bring to a boil. Add the court bouillon and boil continuously until reduced by half. Beat the egg yolks with the cream, add to the cooled liquid, and reheat gently without boiling. Add salt and pepper to taste, pour over the poached fish fillets, and serve hot.

POACHED FISH IN WINE

This is suitable for whole deep sea or river fish, less than 1 lb. in weight, or for fish fillets. Soak whole fish in salted water (1 tablespoon salt to 2½ cups cold water) for 5 minutes, to remove the blood. Wash under cold running water before poaching.

4 small whole fish
2 tablespoons butter
1 onion, thinly sliced
2½ cups white wine

salt and pepper
lemon slices and parsley sprigs
   for garnish

Cooking time: 15 minutes
Temperature: 350°
Serves: 4

Place the prepared fish in a greased ovenproof dish. Add the butter, onion, wine, salt, and pepper and cover tightly with greased aluminum foil. Cook in a 350° oven for 15 minutes. Drain and serve immediately, garnished with slices of lemon and parsley sprigs.

SEA TROUT MEUNIERE

1 1-lb. sea trout
seasoned flour
¼ cup butter

4 slices lemon
2 teaspoons lemon juice
chopped parsley for garnish

Serves: 1

Prepare the sea trout and roll in seasoned flour. Melt the butter in a skillet and fry the lemon slices gently on both sides. Remove from the skillet. Place the fish in the skillet and fry gently for 8 to 9 minutes on both sides, or until the fish is a delicate golden brown. Drain the fish and add the lemon juice to the skillet. Serve the fish on a hot plate, pour the hot butter and lemon juice over, garnish with the fried lemon slices, and sprinkle with chopped parsley.

Note: Small whole fish and fish fillets such as flounder, sole, and whitting may be cooked *à la meunière.* Place 1½ lb. fish fillets in the skillet with the skin side facing upward, fry until golden, and turn to cook the other side.

MARINATED HALIBUT

1 lb. halibut
1 onion, thinly sliced
½ lemon, thinly sliced
1 clove garlic, crushed

salt and pepper
1 tablespoon olive oil
¾ cup dry white wine
¼ cup cream

Cooking time: 15 minutes
Temperature: 300°
Serves: 2

Cut the fish into 1-inch slices and place in an ovenproof dish. Arrange the onion and lemon on top. Sprinkle with the garlic, salt, and pepper and pour over the olive oil and wine. Cover with aluminum foil. Place in the refrigerator and and allow to marinate overnight. Cook in a 300° oven for 15 minutes. Stir in the cream before serving.

Note: This recipe is also suitable for any oily-fleshed fish such as mullet, mackerel, pilchards, or fresh tuna.

Coquilles Saint Jacques à la Crème

OYSTERS NATURAL

12 oysters

lemon wedges

Serves: 1-2

For cocktail sauce:
$\frac{1}{4}$ cup tomato catsup
1 teaspoon Worcestershire sauce

2 teaspoons cream
freshly ground black pepper

Arrange the oysters on a bed of ice with the lemon wedges. Serve with chilled cocktail sauce in the center of the plate.

To make the cocktail sauce: Mix all the ingredients together until blended.

OYSTERS MORNAY

12 oysters
salt and pepper

$\frac{2}{3}$ cup Mornay Sauce
Parmesan cheese

Cooking time: 5-10 minutes.
Temperature: 400°
Serves: 1-2

Choose large flat oysters. Sprinkle with salt and pepper and place under a hot broiler for 1 minute. Spread over each oyster sufficient Mornay Sauce (see page 51) to cover. Sprinkle with Parmesan cheese and bake in a 400° oven for 5-10 minutes or until golden brown. Serve immediately.

OYSTERS MICHELENE

12 oysters
$\frac{2}{3}$ cup peeled prawns

2 tablespoons butter
cayenne pepper

Cooking time: 3 minutes
Temperature: 400°
Serves: 1-2

Remove the oysters from the shells, mix with the prawns, and chop finely. Mix with the butter and cayenne pepper to taste. Replace the mixture in the oyster shells and cook in a 400° oven for 3 minutes. Serve immediately.

OYSTERS SURPRISE

24 oysters
12 snails
2 scallions, finely chopped

2 tablespoons butter
salt and pepper

Cooking time: 3 minutes
Temperature: 400°
Serves: 3-4

Remove the oysters from the shells. Mix with the snails, scallions, and butter and season with salt and pepper. Replace the mixture in the oyster shells and cook in a 400° oven for 3 minutes. Serve immediately.

ROCK LOBSTER MAYONNAISE

Buy rock lobster live for a lobster salad. Frozen lobster, although good for cooked dishes, does not have sufficient flavor to serve cold. When purchasing a live lobster, make sure it is heavy. Place the lobster in a bucket of cold water with a weight on top until it stops moving. Cook covered with Court Bouillon (see page 89) in a saucepan. It should be brought to the boiling point quickly and simmered for 7 minutes for small lobsters, 10 minutes for medium-sized lobsters. Add 6 tablespoons brown sugar to $7\frac{1}{2}$ pints court bouillon to give added flavor. When cold cut the lobster in half lengthwise. Hold the lobster with a cloth, insert a sharp pointed knife into the center of the head, and cut from head to tail, Turn over and cut the other side. Remove the bag in the head and the intestine, which is a thin gray/black line running down through the tail meat. Cut the meat into $\frac{1}{2}$-inch cubes and replace in the half shells. Serve with a fresh crisp salad and Mayonnaise (see page 55). *Note:* A 2-lb. rock lobster should give approximately $\frac{3}{4}$ lb. lobster meat.

ROCK LOBSTER TAILS MORNAY

2 rock lobster tails or
  1 2-lb. lobster
1 scallion, finely chopped
salt and pepper
cayenne pepper

paprika pepper
2 tablespoons butter
$\frac{2}{3}$ cup mornay sauce
parsley sprigs for garnish

Serves: 2

Prepare the lobster tails and remove the meat from the shells. Place the shells in a 400° oven until bright red in color. Cut the meat into $\frac{1}{2}$-inch cubes and add the scallion, salt, pepper, and a dash cayenne pepper. Place in the hot shells, sprinkle with paprika pepper, dot with butter, and place under a hot broiler until the meat becomes clear white and loses its transparent appearance. Coat with hot Mornay Sauce (see page 51) and replace under the hot broiler until golden. Overcooking will toughen the meat. Serve garnished with parsley sprigs and accompanied by French fried potatoes and sautéed mushrooms.

LOBSTER PAELLA À LA MICHEL

2 rock lobster tails or
  1 2-lb. lobster
$\frac{1}{4}$ cup olive oil
2 tomatoes, chopped
1 onion, thinly sliced

$\frac{1}{2}$ teaspoon crushed garlic
1$\frac{1}{2}$ cups dry white wine
$\frac{3}{4}$ cup cream
1 teaspoon paprika pepper

Serves: 2-4

Prepare the lobster and cut the meat into $\frac{1}{2}$-inch thick slices. Heat the olive oil in a large skillet and fry the lobster over high heat for 1 minute on both sides. Add the tomato, onion, garlic, wine, cream, and paprika pepper. Cook over a low heat for a further 15 minutes. Serve hot with Saffron Rice (see page 205).

COQUILLES SAINT JACQUES À LA CRÈME

(SCALLOPS WITH CREAM)

2 tablespoons butter
$\frac{1}{4}$ cup button mushrooms, sliced
$\frac{1}{4}$ cup dry white wine
$\frac{1}{4}$ lb. shelled scallops, with coral
$\frac{1}{4}$ cup cream

dash cayenne pepper
salt and pepper
$\frac{1}{4}$ cup grated Parmesan cheese
lemon slices and parsley sprigs
  for garnish

Serves: 2-4

Melt the butter in a clean saucepan, add the mushrooms and wine, and cook until the wine is reduced by half. Add the scallops and simmer for 2 minutes. Add the cream, cayenne pepper, and salt and pepper to taste. Reheat gently, and place in scallop shells. Sprinkle with Parmesan cheese and place under a hot broiler until golden brown. Serve immediately as an entrèe garnished with lemon and parlsey sprigs.

Note: Allow 2 scallops per person. If scallop shells are not available, other attractive sea shells or individual heat proof dishes may be used.

MUSSELS MARINIÈRE

12 mussels (about 2'' long)
1 small onion, thinly sliced
$\frac{3}{4}$ cup dry white wine
2 tablespoons butter
$\frac{1}{2}$ teaspoon crushed garlic

dash white pepper
2 tablespoons coarse bread
  crumbs
2 tablespoons chopped parsley

Serves: 1-2

Place the well-scrubbed mussels in a saucepan with the onion, wine, butter, garlic, and pepper. Cover and cook quickly over high heat until the mussels open (about 3 minutes). When they are all open add the bread crumbs and heat for 1 minute. Serve in a hot soup plate sprinkled with chopped parsley.

Tui Flower

In New Zealand, Tui Flower is undoubtedly a doyen of cookery. Tui gained her Diploma of Home Science at the University of Otago, Dunedin and has studied cookery at the École Hotelière de Paris. She is home economist and organizer of *N.Z. Woman's Weekly* test kitchen and her magazine recipes, as well as those in her book *Tui Flower's Cookbook*, are universally popular.

More Fish

Although the waters around and in New Zealand abound with many varieties of fish, the selection available commercially is small, no doubt because the population is primarily a meat eating people. The native fish include several which are famous worldwide. The trout which lures fishermen from all over the world to New Zealand's streams and lakes is one. The elusive toheroa, a shellfish with distinctive green coloring, is the other. Neither of these fish can be bought in the local fish shops. Trout fishermen must have a licence and fish during the season. To gather toheroas, enthusiasts must dig at the water's edge in the strict and brief season permitted to avoid depleting the beds. Small quantities of tinned toheroas are available.

A New Zealand fish delicacy that can be bought is the minute whitebait. Netted at river mouths this fish is eaten whole, most frequently in fritters.

The main export fish is rock lobster, the frozen tails being of particularly high quality. Other shellfish to sample are oysters; rock, Stewart Island and cultivated ones. Scallops and mussels are also well liked and as with oysters, commercially available. But those with a taste for pipis and pauas must gather their own! The latter shellfish not only makes an unusual dark delicacy but the beautiful shell is polished and made into jewellery.

The most widely used wet fish are snapper, tarakihi, cod, gurnard, hapuka, flounder and trevally, several of which are sold smoked as well as fresh.

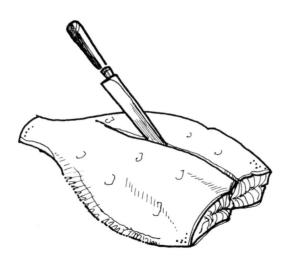

Whitebait Fritters

SMOKED HADDOCK FRITTERS

1 egg
½ cup milk
⅔ cup all-purpose flour
salt and pepper

1 cup cooked smoked haddock
oil for frying
lemon for garnish

Yield: 12

Beat the egg and blend with the milk. Sift the flour with the salt and pepper into a mixing bowl. Stir the liquid into the flour to form a smooth batter. It should be the consistency of whipping cream. (The quantity of flour or milk may be adjusted slightly to get the required consistency.) Cover the batter and allow to stand for 10 minutes. Flake the haddock finely and mix with the batter when ready to cook. Heat the oil in a skillet until very hot. Drop the mixture from a tablespoon into the hot fat and cook quickly until golden, then turn and cook the other side. Drain on paper towels and keep warm while cooking the remainder of the mixture. Serve hot with slices of lemon. These fritters may be served as a first or as a main course.

MUSSELS

2 tablespoons butter
1 onion, finely chopped
2 tomatoes, skinned and chopped
¼ cup white wine

¾ lb. cooked mussels
freshly ground black pepper
chopped parsley

Serves: 3

In a saucepan heat the butter and sauté the onion until clear and tender. Add the tomatoes and cook for 1 minute. Add the wine, cover, and cook for 3 minutes. Add the mussels and heat through, but do not boil. If the mussels are large, cut in half. Season with pepper to taste and serve immediately sprinkled with chopped parsley. Serve with crusty French bread.

BAKED OYSTERS

Serve 4 to 6 oysters per portion for an hors d'oeuvre.

24 oysters
⅓ cup oil
⅓ cup lemon juice
½ teaspoon salt
freshly ground black pepper

1 teaspoon dry mustard
½ teaspoon curry powder
2 tablespoons butter
1 cup soft white bread crumbs

Cooking time: 20 minutes
Temperature: 400°
Serves: 4-6

Drain the oysters well. Mix the oil, lemon juice, and seasonings in a shallow dish and put the oysters in this marinade. Leave for 30 minutes, turning once. Melt the butter in a small pan and stir in the bread crumbs. Cook until lightly colored. Remove the oysters from the marinade and drain on paper towels. Roll each oyster in the prepared crumbs and place in a single layer on a baking sheet. Bake in a 400° oven for about 20 minutes, or until lightly browned and crisp.

Smoked Fish Salad

BROILED SALMON WITH LEMON BUTTER

4 salmon steaks
salt and pepper

butter

Serves: 4

For lemon butter:
½ cup butter
¼ teaspoon finely grated lemon
   rind
2 tablespoons lemon juice

1 teaspoon chopped parsley
salt
freshly ground pepper
cayenne pepper

Heat the broiler. Trim and wipe the steaks and rub with salt and pepper. Brush the broiler rack with butter and place the steaks on it. Brush the tops of the steaks with butter. Broil quickly far enough from the source of heat to cook without scorching. Turn the fish steaks once, using a turner and spatula to avoid breaking the fish. Brush the second side with butter and broil until cooked. Do not overcook. The time will depend on the thickness of the steaks, but will be about 5 minutes on each side. Serve immediately with lemon butter.
To make the lemon butter: Cream the butter and blend into it the flavorings, taste, and adjust the flavor as preferred. Shape the lemon butter into a block or into pats and chill until ready to use.

BRAISED FISH

2 slices bacon
1 onion
2 stalks celery

½ green sweet pepper
4 halibut steaks
salt and pepper

Cooking time: 20 minutes
Temperature: 350°
Serves: 4

Chop the bacon and vegetables finely. Heat an electric skillet and fry the bacon. In the bacon drippings fry the vegetables, pushing the bacon to one side of the skillet to avoid over-cooking. When the vegetables are cooked, mix with the bacon. Spread half the mixture over the center of the skillet to cover an area about the size of the fish steaks.

Trim the fish using scissors to remove any central bone. Rub the fish with salt and pepper and place on the vegetables. Spoon the remainder of the vegetable mixture over the fish. Season with a little more salt and pepper. Cover with the lid, close the vent, and cook for about 15 to 20 minutes. Serve hot.

BAKED SNAPPER

1 whole snapper
1 onion
1½ lb. potatoes
2 tablespoons butter
2 tomatoes, thinly sliced
1 teaspoon salt

1 teaspoon flour
1 teaspoon paprika pepper
½ cup milk or coffee cream
1 teaspoon lemon juice
parsley sprig or lemon slice
   for garnish

Cooking time: 1¼ hours
Temperature: 350°
Serves: 4-6

Make sure that the fish is free of scales and trim off the fins. Do not remove the head. Wash and dry the fish. Peel the onion and potatoes and cut into ¼-inch slices. Arrange in an ovenproof dish and dot with half the butter. Place the tomatoes on top of the potatoes and sprinkle with salt. Place in a 350° oven for 30 minutes, or until the vegetables are half cooked. Put the fish on top of the vegetables and sprinkle with the flour and paprika pepper mixed together. Dot with the remaining butter. Return to the oven for 10 minutes. Mix the milk or cream and the lemon juice together, pour over the fish, and bake for a further 30 minutes, or until tender. Serve from the dish, garnishing the eye with a sprig of parsley or a slice of lemon.

HERB BAKED TROUT

1 trout, 2½-3 lb.
salt
pepper
1 onion, thinly sliced

dash sage or 2 fresh leaves
dash thyme or 1 fresh sprig
2-3 slices bacon

Cooking time: 1 hour
Temperature: 350°
Serves: 4-6

Clean the trout and sprinkle the cavity with salt and pepper. Place the onion, sage, and thyme inside the cavity. Arrange the bacon slices over the fish and place on a piece of greased aluminum foil. Wrap up the fish and place in an ovenproof dish large enough to hold it easily. Bake in a 350° oven for 45 to 60 minutes. To serve, remove the foil and place the fish on a warm serving plate.

SOUSED TROUT

1 3-lb. trout
4 cups water
6 peppercorns
1 teaspoon salt
1 bay leaf
1 sprig parsley
1 sprig thyme

1 stalk celery
1 onion, thinly sliced
1 carrot, thinly sliced
1 cup vinegar
lemon slices and parsley
    sprigs for garnish

Cooking time: 1½ hours
Temperature: 300°
Serves: 6-8

Cut the fish into steaks and place in a large casserole or baking dish. Cover with the water and add the remaining ingredients, tying the bay leaf, parsley, thyme, and celery together. Cover with the lid or aluminum foil and cook in a 300° oven for 1½ hours. Cool, then chill in the refrigerator. When completely cold, lift the fish onto a plate, and garnish with slices of lemon and parsley sprigs.
Note: The liquid will jell if given sufficient cooking and cooling time.

SMOKED FISH SALAD

1 small smoked fish (about ¾ lb. trimmed)
1 small cucumber
6 radishes

4 stalks celery
2 scallions
½ cup mayonnaise
lettuce leaves

Serves: 4

Trim the fish and remove the bones and skin. Break the flesh into chunky pieces. Dice the unpeeled cucumber. Slice the radishes into thin circles. Trim the celery and cut into chunky pieces. Chop the scallions finely. Mix the fish and vegetables in a bowl. Add the mayonnaise and mix gently. Pile into a salad bowl lined with crisp lettuce leaves.

CREAMED ROCK LOBSTER TAIL IN THE HALF-SHELL

1 medium-sized rock lobster tail, cooked
6 tablespoons butter
2 scallions, finely chopped
¼ cup all-purpose flour

¼ cup milk
½ cup cream
¼ cup sherry
salt and pepper
¼ cup fine white bread crumbs

Cooking time: 10 minutes
Temperature: 400°
Serves: 2

Cut the tails in half lengthwise. Discard the intestine. Remove the meat from the shell and cut into cubes. Retain the shell. In a saucepan heat two thirds of the butter and sauté the scallions without browning. Stir in the flour. Cook for 1 minute, then gradually add the milk. Stir continuously over medium heat until the sauce boils and thickens. Add the cream, sherry, and lobster meat and season with salt and pepper to taste. Spoon into the shells, sprinkle with bread crumbs, and dot with small pieces of the remaining butter. Place in a 400° oven for about 10 minutes, or until the crumbs are golden.

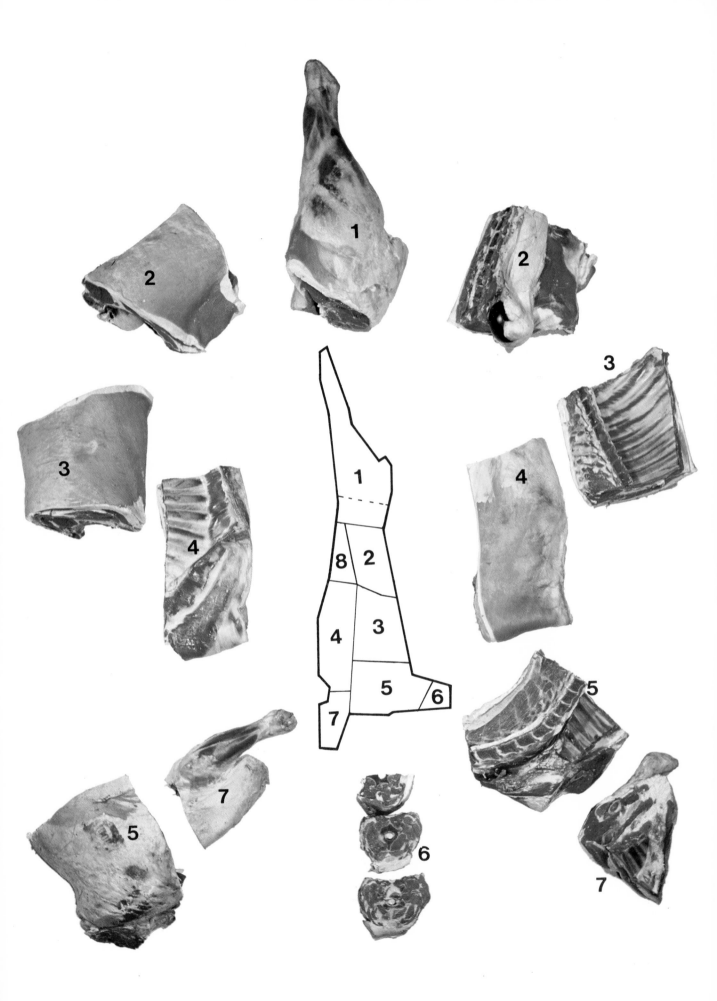

MEAT

Cuts of Meat

LAMB

Lamb is the young animal of the sheep (ovine) family and is classified according to age.

Hothouse lamb is slaughtered between six and ten weeks old. It is reared indoors and is expensive and in small supply. It is milk-fed and has light pink lean.

Spring lamb is killed in spring and early summer, aged three to five months. It has a slightly deeper pink lean and smooth, waxy, white fat, and the bones are porous and red. The meat is very tender.

Lamb, sometimes called spring lamb as well, is under 12 months when killed and is marketed in the fall and winter. It has pinkish-red lean and although not quite as tender as genuine spring lamb has a richer flavor.

Yearling lamb or yearling mutton is between 15 and 20 months old when it is slaughtered. It has light to medium red meat and is relatively tender with a rich pleasant flavor. The 'break' joint (where the foot is removed from the leg) is a reliable indication of the age of lamb. In young lamb there are 4 well-defined ridges which are moist, porous, and red. In older lamb the ridges are hard and white, and in mutton the foot cannot be removed here at all but has to be broken at the real foot joint, lower down the leg.

Mutton is the meat of a mature or adult sheep over 20 months. It comes from wethers (castrated when lambs) or ewes, and is a darker red meat with a coarser grain.

The lamb is cut up in different ways depending on how it is to be prepared. The photograph shows leg, loin, hotel rack (rib section), and breast and flank for stewing.

The photograph and diagram show the basic retail cuts. The leg (1) very often has the sirloin removed (indicated by the dotted line on the central diagram). The complete sirloin may be boned and rolled as a boneless sirloin roast (this roast has *both* sides of the animal in it). The leg roast may be Frenched, i.e., the shank meat is removed and the bone exposed. Protect the end with foil while roasting and tie a paper frill around the bone for serving. Another common way of preparing a leg roast is the American leg, where the shank bone is removed. Leg chops or steaks are slices cut from the leg like beef round steak; they may be broiled or pan fried, or braised. The sirloin also yields chops, which may be cooked as any lamb chop.

The loin (2) may be used as a loin roast, when it is half the animal, split down the back bone, or a complete cross-section may be boned and rolled as a rolled loin roast. Both cuts yield chops, loin chops with the bone, and English chop slices from the rolled roast, and these are excellent for broiling or pan frying. The loin in the photograph shows the kidney, which is removed and sold separately.

The hotel rack, or ribs (3), contains eight or nine ribs and may be used as a rib roast, crown roast, or cut into rib chops for broiling and frying.

The breast (4) is a cheaper cut which when trimmed, boned, stuffed, and rolled makes a good roasting or braising cut. It may also be used as stew meat, or cut into riblets for stewing. The flank (8) is often discarded, or may be ground or used for stew meat. The square-cut shoulder (5) contains three or four ribs. It may be roasted as it is, but is much easier to deal with prepared as a cushion shoulder or a rolled shoulder. Arm chops are cut from the leg side of the shoulder and blade chops from the rib side. Both may be sautéed. Boneless chops are cut from the rolled shoulder. Neck slices (6) are rounds cut from the neck and should be braised slowly.

The shank (7) may be braised slowly. There is a lot of bone in this cut and you should allow one shank per person.

Beef comes from cattle especially raised for their meat. Most beef comes from steers, heifers, and cows, and the first two are generally the most popular. High-grade beef comes mostly from animals between one and three years old and weighing in the region of 1000 pounds. In buying beef you should look for a reasonable covering of firm, creamy white fat over the lean, a certain amount of marbling (loin, rib, and chuck well-marbled, round and rump a little less) throughout the meat tissue for tenderness and flavor, and a good red color. This varies from light to deep red depending on the age of the animal, but the meat should always have a firm texture and fine grain.

The beef carcase is divided lengthwise into 2 sides. The photograph and diagram show a complete side divided into the wholesale cuts, and some of the retail cuts made from them. The round or hind leg is divided up into several retail cuts. The hind shank (1) is half bone, which makes a very rich soupbone. It contains the heel of round or heel pot roast, which is a triangular piece of lean behind the shank bone. This may be braised but is more usually cut up as stew or ground meat. Round steak (2) is cut in thick slices either right across or as top or bottom round steaks. These are all used for braising.

The rump (3) may either be used as it is as a standing rump roast or boned and rolled. If the beef is of good grade these cuts may be roasted like a standing rib, otherwise they should be braised.

Sirloin tip (4) is a roast cut from the bottom round and the lower sirloin. Like rump, it can be roasted if of high grade, but is excellent for braising. The sirloin (5) lies between the rump and the short loin and yields sirloin steaks—pin bone, wedge bone, and flat bone—which may be broiled or pan fried.

The short loin contains the backbone and sometimes the last rib. This is the cut which contains the best steaks—porterhouse and T-bone (shown in the photograph). Sometimes the tenderloin muscle, which begins in the sirloin and ends at the rib end of the short loin, is removed in one piece. This is the least used by the animal and therefore most tender muscle in beef and from it come filets mignons or sliced tenderloin. All these are best sautéing or broiling steaks. The top (rib) end of the loin is sometimes removed as a roast, or club steaks are cut from it—this piece is shown in the photograph between the round (2) and the standing rib (7).

The standing rib (7) is the best roasting cut. An average standing rib roast contains two or more ribs. Alternatively, the bones may be removed to give a rolled rib roast. Rib steaks for broiling or sauteing like club steaks are cut from this. The bottom of the rib section and the top of the plate (12) are cut off to give short ribs for braising or stew meat.

The chuck (8) is the equivalent of the lamb square cut shoulder and contains the top five ribs, the arm and the blade bones, and the neck bone. There are various ways of cutting up the shoulder, but all cuts should be braised or stewed. The boneless shoulder (9) is normally rolled and may be pot roasted or braised. Blade steaks, rolled neck, arm steaks, and boneless chuck pot roast are some names which indicate shoulder cuts.

The brisket (10) may be marketed fresh or corned. The cut is usually boned and should be simmered long and slowly in liquid. It is a very flavorful cut. The foreshank (11) is a very bony piece of beef. Round slices from the shank—shank cross cuts—may be braised or used as soup meat.

Underneath the rib section is the plate (12). This is a rather fatty cut which may be boned and rolled for braising. The meat is also ground for hamburgers. The flank (13), not photographed, contains a high percentage of fat. Flank steak is the main edible part of this and is usually sold scored crisscross fashion to tenderize the fibers. It is very lean and tough but if stuffed and rolled makes a good braising cut. Small slices of flank steak are rolled and held with wooden toothpicks, and marketed as flank steak fillets. These too should be braised. The remainder of the flank is ground and used for hamburgers, etc.

PORK AND BACON

Pork and bacon are the meat of the porcine family and most of the meat sold is from young hogs between five and seven months old. For this reason it is usually tender. Fresh pork should be firm and fine grained, the lean well marbled and with a covering of firm white fat. Cured pork should be a healthy pink color with a good layer of white fat and plenty of marbling.

The ham or leg (1) of the hog may be sold fresh or cured. A fresh ham may be divided into butt half and shank half or it may be boned and rolled. Occasionally a whole fresh ham may be marketed but this a very large roast (about 12 pounds) and usually there is not much demand for it. All these fresh cuts make good roasts. There are various methods of curing pork, and smoking it. A whole

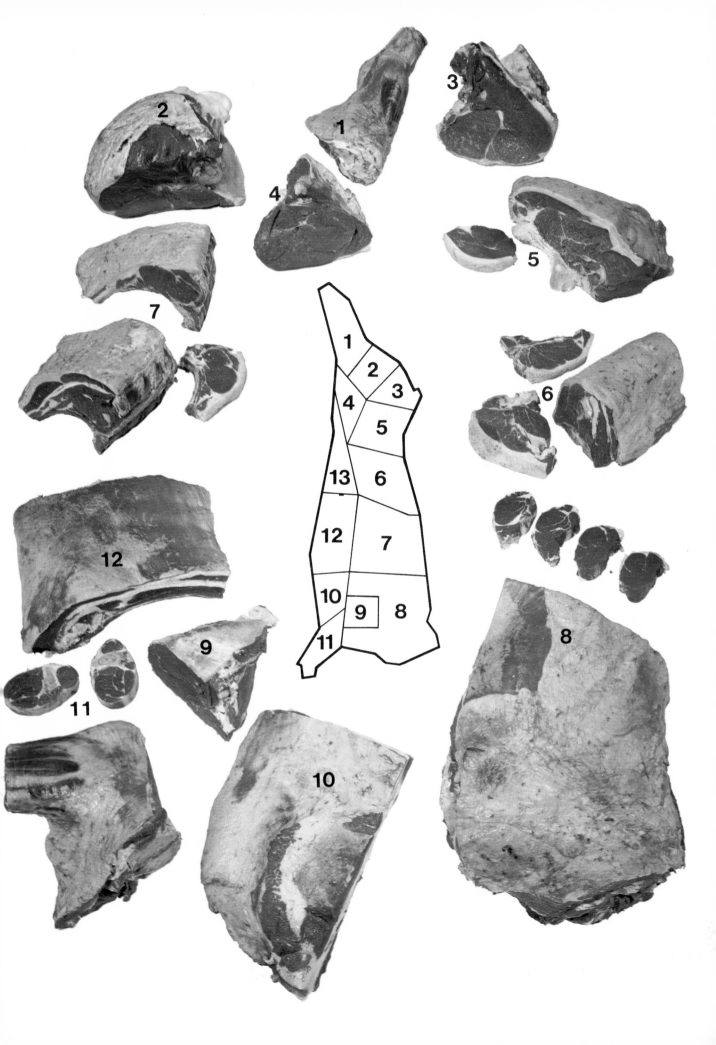

ham weighs anything between 8 and 18 pounds and may be divided into shank and butt half like a fresh ham. Hams produced by national packing houses are generally mild cure, as opposed to aged or country-cured hams, such as Virginia, Smithfield, etc. The mild cure hams may be uncooked or pre-cooked, and very often they are wrapped and clearly labeled with cooking instructions. In general hams may be cooked in liquid or baked in the oven. The aged ones should be soaked overnight and scrubbed well, mild cure need no soaking. Ham slices may be cut from the butt or shank half for broiling or pan frying.

The loin (2) contains the whole back of the animal and is prepared in many ways. The tenderloin (shown above the loin in the photograph) weighs about one pound and is an expensive but very tender cut. It is excellent stuffed and roasted. Slices may be broiled or sautéed. The sirloin, nearest to the ham, may be sold on the bone as a roast or boned and rolled. Both these cuts may be roasted like a fresh ham. Next comes the loin roast center cut which is the choice pork roast. The tenderloin muscle is contained in this cut. Loin chops are cut from this for braising or pan frying. The center loin may also be boned and rolled. The shoulder end of the loin gives another roast which may be prepared as a crown roast (with enough of the ribs to form a circle), and rib chops, which contain no tenderloin. A crown roast has the ends of the ribs Frenched, and rib chops may also be Frenched and served with paper frills. From the loin nearest the shoulder comes blade loin roast which is not such a desirable cut as it contains blade bone, back bone, and ribs which makes it difficult to carve.

Canadian-style bacon comes from the loin. It may be roasted or boiled instead of ham, or cut in thin slices and pan fried.

The butt (3) or shoulder, like the ham, may be cured or fresh. Fresh Boston butt, whole or boned and rolled, makes a flavorful roast. Blade steaks are cut from the Boston cut and may be cooked like chops. Smoked shoulder butt is a boneless roll with a generous amount of intermingled fat which is good for simmering. Slices may be pan broiled like Canadian-style bacon.

The pig's foot (4) is considered by some people a delicacy and should be cooked slowly in liquid. Allow one per serving as they are very bony.

The jowl (5) gives the jowl bacon square which is a cured, very fatty cut. It may be cooked whole or in slices, pan fried, braised, or boiled.

The picnic (6) includes the lower part of shoulder and the foreleg. The lower part of the foreleg may be removed and marketed as hocks, which should be cooked in the same way as the foot. The remainder of the picnic may be sold whole as a roast, or boned and rolled. The arm section may be boned and made into a cushion picnic shoulder which may be stuffed and roasted. Arm steaks are cut from the picnic and are cooked as chops. The picnic shoulder is also cured and smoked like a ham. It is usually cheaper than ham since it is coarser and contains more bone and tough tissue. It can be baked but is better simmered in water.

The underside of the pig is divided into spareribs (7) and side (8). The spareribs may be roasted, barbecued, or simmered and have a very good flavor. The side is cured to make bacon (for broiling and pan frying) and salt pork, which is very fatty and is used for larding and to add flavor to many dishes. Many European recipes call for this as a flavoring. The fat back (9), which is not photographed, is the fat removed from the top of the loin. It is usually rendered down to produce lard.

How to Carve Meat

John Goodman Jones

Well-cooked meat dishes are especially stimulating to the appetite, but their ultimate presentation at the table is also most important. The more attractive the appearance of the dish, the more appetizing it will be. To obtain an attractive appearance it is essential that a joint of meat is carved properly. By doing so, one not only ensures personal achievement but also derives the maximum possible yield from each joint.

To many, carving is a laborious task. This need not be so if the correct knives are used. An extensive range of utensils is not essential, but the task is made easier when they are of correct size and shape for the specific purpose and are kept razor sharp. However tender a joint may be, a blunt blade will merely break the fibers and give an ugly torn appearance. It is essential, therefore, that the cutting edges of all carving knives are ground and stoned regularly and are then steeled and trued before actual use.

Before beginning to carve the following points should be noted:
1. Always 'true' your knife blade on a steel before beginning.
2. Hold the knife firmly and, making use of the full length of the blade, use a slicing action and not a sawing one. Allow the blade to follow through gently with each slice.

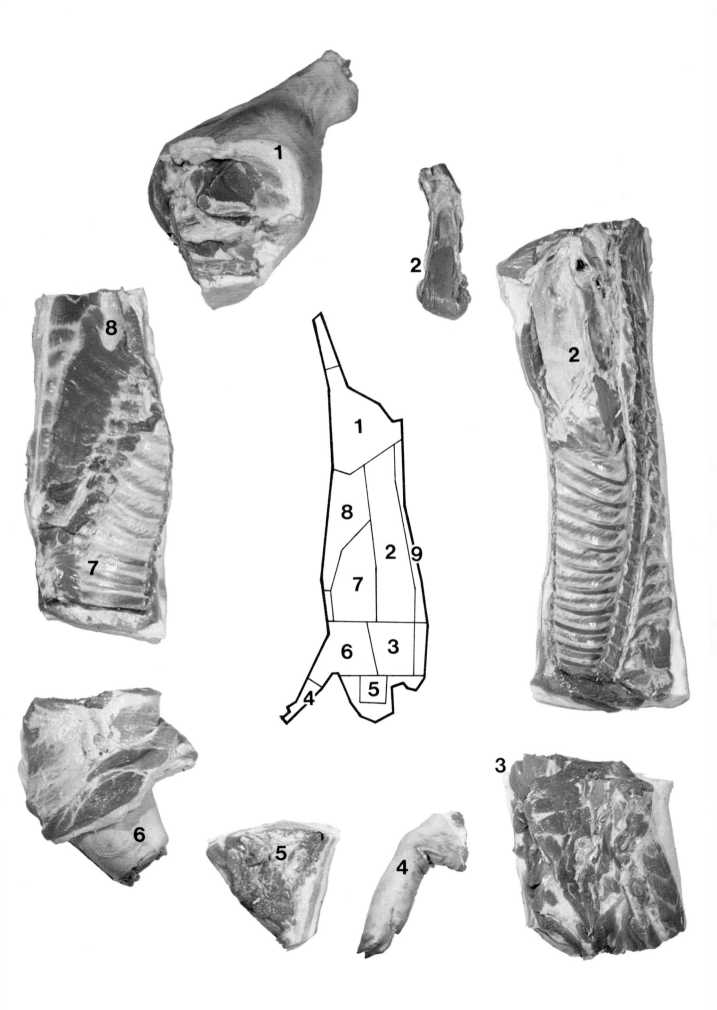

3. Apply only sufficient pressure to cut the meat fibers—too much pressure will only tear and spoil the appearance of the meat surface. A sharp knife will do the cutting if guided correctly.

4. Always carve across the grain of the meat, shortening the meat fibers to the thickness of the slice only. The slice will then fall apart readily when eaten. Carving with the grain of the meat produces long thin fibers which will give the meat a stringy appearance and make it tough to chew.

CARVING A RIB ROAST

1. The joint should be held firmly with a fork, fat side up and the thickest part of the meat away from you. The back chinebone should have been removed by the butcher before cooking.

2. Use a slicing or ham knife with a 10-inch blade. The knife should first be worked along the upper side of the bone making a penetration of not more than 2 inches. The action separates enough of the meat from the bone structure to allow carving to begin.

3. Hold the joint firmly and begin to slice the meat downward across the grain and toward the bone. The slices should be approximately one fourth of an inch thick and should fall away freely if the first cut along the bone is effective.

CARVING A ROLLED RIB OR SIRLOIN OF BEEF

There are two methods suitable for carving a rolled rib or sirloin of beef.

Method I

1. The joint should be held firmly on its side with a carving fork on a wooden carving board.

2. Using a slightly longer slicing or ham knife (14-inch preferably), slice toward the board in a downward direction. Care should be taken to guide the knife straight down and not at an angle. If the knife is sharp and the full length of the blade is used, very little pressure will be required to produce neat even slices.

Note: When carving in a downward direction it is not necessary to use a fork with a safety guard.

Method II

1. The joint should be laid flat and held firmly with a fork stuck into the side. It is advisable to use a fork with a safety guard in this method as the slicing knife will be worked across the top of the joint toward the fork.

2. The knife should be laid flat and, using the full length of the blade, worked smoothly across the top without twisting the wrist or knife in any way. Full

sized round, thin slices will then be obtained.

CARVING A LEG OF LAMB

There are numerous ways in which a leg of lamb may be carved, none of which could truly be called superior to the other. The simple method described here is recommended however, as it gives a higher yield of sliced meat and results in slices of an appetizing appearance.

1. Wrap a clean cloth around the 'handle' of the leg and hold the joint at an angle of approximately 45° with the bottom resting on a carving board.

2. Taking a slicing or ham knife with at least a 10-inch blade, hold it firmly in your hand with your thumb firmly on top of the handle or blade. Do not place your index finger along the back of the blade as this lessens effective control.

3. Make the first cut about half way along the leg slicing toward the handle.

4. Using the full length of the blade and guiding it in an easy sweep (a sharp knife will do the cutting without exerting any great pressure) continue to slice the meat in $\frac{1}{4}$-inch slices until the leg bone is reached.

5. Turn the leg over and repeat the process. In this manner, almost the entire leg may be carved into neat slices, leaving very little on the bone.

Note: The same method of carving may be used for all legs of meat.

CARVING A SHOULDER OF LAMB

1. As there is no protruding bone on the shoulder it is not possible to form a handle as with the leg. It is necessary, therefore, to use a carving fork. The fork should be inserted into the joint at the leg end far enough to provide a firm grip. The meatiest side of the shoulder should be toward the carver.

2. A slicing or ham knife with a 10-inch blade should be used. Hold the joint in the same manner as for the leg, i.e. at an angle of 45° with the bottom resting on a carving board.

3. Begin to slice the meatiest side of the joint about halfway along. Cut the slices about one fourth of an inch thick toward the fork.

4. Continue to carve the slices as large as possible until the formation of the bone is reached. Rotate the shoulder and carve slices from the smaller spine of the blade.

5. Turn over the shoulder completely and insert the fork in the upper leg end and continue slicing toward the fork. The last pieces will be quite small but sweet and palatable.

Osso bucco

Meat Cookery

Graham Latham

The aim of cooking meat is to improve its appearance and make it more palatable, digestible, and tender.

The methods of cooking meat fall into two categories, dry and moist methods. The dry methods are roasting, broiling, and frying (shallow and deep). These methods are suitable for best quality tender meat. The moist methods are stewing, braising, pot roasting, boiling, and steaming. These methods are suitable for the tougher cuts of meat (see page 12).

RACK OF LAMB

Allow 20 minutes cooking time per lb. plus 20 minutes extra.

1 lamb rib roast containing 6 ribs	salt mint jelly or mint sauce	Cooking time: 45 minutes Temperature: 325° Serves: 3

Ask your meat cutter to French the ribs of lamb. Trim the meat and rub with salt. Place on a rack in a roasting pan and cook in a 325° oven for approximately 45 minutes. Carve on a board into 6 chops. Serve 2 drops per person with frills placed on each bone. Serve with mint jelly or mint sauce (see page 59).

Note: Ask your meat cutter to saw between each joint for ease of carving. Ensure that he does not cut into the meat section as this can lead to loss of juices.

MIXED GRILL

4 lamb chops 4 $\frac{1}{4}$-lb. steaks 4 lamb kidneys 4 breakfast sausages 2 tomatoes	melted butter 4 slices bacon shoestring potatoes watercress parsley butter	Cooking time: 15 minutes Serves: 4

Trim the excess fat from the chops and steaks. Skin the kidneys, cut in half and open out flat without cutting right through. Remove the cores. Blanch the sausages by placing in cold water and bringing slowly to a boil. Drain well. Remove the cores from the tomatoes, trim a very fine slice off the ends so the tomatoes will sit flat, and cut in half. Brush food to be grilled with melted butter and cook under a hot broiler in the following order: kidneys and sausages (15 minutes), cutlets and steaks (8 to 10 minutes), tomatoes and bacon (3 to 5 minutes), turning with tongs when necessary throughout cooking. Serve garnished with shoestring potatoes (see page 173), watercress, and parsley butter (see page 59).

BROILED LAMB CUTLETS

2 thick lamb rib chops salt	freshly ground black pepper oil	Cooking time: 15 minutes Serves: 2

Trim the chops of excess fat and season well on each side. Put on a rack in the broiler pan and brush with oil. Place under a preheated very hot broiler for 2 minutes to sear the meat, turn, and sear the other side for 2 minutes. Reduce the heat and broil for approximately 10 minutes more (turning once after 5 minutes), or until cooked. Serve with glazed carrots (see page 167), spinach, and French fried potatoes (see page 173).

Grilled Lamb Cutlets

LAMB KEBABS

(SHASHLIK)

1 4-lb. leg of lamb
1 lb. small onions
1 green sweet pepper
3 slices bacon
6-12 button mushrooms

6 small tomatoes
bay leaves (optional)
salt and pepper
oil or melted butter

Cooking time: 20-25 minutes
Serves: 6

Cut the lamb in 1-inch cubes. Peel the onions and blanch in boiling water; drain. Cut the pepper and bacon into 1-inch pieces. Thread the lamb onto 6 skewers alternately with onions, mushrooms, pepper, bacon, and tomatoes. Small bay leaves may be added if desired. Season with salt and pepper and brush with oil or melted butter. Broil gently, turning and brushing with oil if necessary, for 20 to 25 minutes, or until the meat is cooked. Serve on a bed of Rice Pilaff (see page 203).

LAMB STEW

(NAVARIN OF LAMB)

2 lb. shoulder of lamb, boned
$\frac{1}{4}$ cup drippings or oil
1 lb. onions, chopped
1 lb. carrots, chopped
$\frac{1}{2}$ cup browned flour
2 tablespoons tomato paste

$2\frac{1}{2}$ cups beef stock or water and
   beef bouillon cube
1 bouquet garni
1 clove garlic, crushed
salt and pepper
chopped parsley

Cooking time: 1-1$\frac{1}{2}$ hours
Serves: 6-8

Cut the meat into 1-inch cubes and fry in the drippings until browned on all sides. Add the onions and carrots and fry until the onion is soft. Stir in the browned flour and cook for a few minutes over low heat. Add the tomato paste and stock and bring to a boil stirring continuously. Add the bouquet garni, garlic, and salt and pepper to taste. Cover and simmer over low heat for 1 to 1$\frac{1}{2}$ hours, or until the meat is tender. Serve sprinkled with chopped parsley.

To brown flour: Spread a quantity of all-purpose flour on a baking sheet and place in a 375° oven until lightly browned. Remove, break up with a rolling pin, and sieve. Do not force small lumps through as they will cause lumps in the sauce. Use as required to thicken and color sauces. It gives a slight nuttiness to the flavor.

Variations: Add a mixture of spring vegetables (1 to 2 lb.) with the stock to make Navarin à la Printanière.
   Substitute $\frac{1}{2}$ lb. haricot beans for 1 lb. onions to make Haricot Stew.

MOUSSAKA

2 onions, finely chopped
2 cloves garlic, crushed
7 tablespoons olive oil
1 lb. ground lamb
1$\frac{1}{2}$ cups chopped mushrooms
1 lb. tomatoes, skinned, seeded
   and chopped
$\frac{1}{4}$ cup tomato paste
$\frac{2}{3}$ cup beef stock or water and
   beef bouillon cube

2 medium-sized eggplants
1 cup all-purpose flour
salt and pepper
2 tablespoons chopped parsley
$\frac{3}{4}$ cup grated Parmesan cheese

Cooking time: 1 hour
Temperature: 375°
Serves: 6

Sauté the onion and garlic in 2 tablespoons olive oil in a saucepan until soft, without coloring. Add the lamb and fry until lightly browned. Add the mushrooms and tomato and cook for 5 minutes. Add the tomato paste and stock and cook for a further 5 minutes. Cut the eggplants in $\frac{1}{2}$-inch slices, roll in flour, and fry in the remaining olive oil on both sides. Drain on paper towels.

Line an ovenproof casserole with slices of eggplant, spread with the lamb mixture, season with salt and pepper, and sprinkle with chopped parsley. Cover with another layer of eggplant and repeat the layers until the casserole is full, finishing with a layer of eggplant. Sprinkle with Parmesan cheese and cook in a 375° oven until brown. Serve sprinkled with chopped parsley.

STANDING RIB ROAST OF BEEF WITH YORKSHIRE PUDDING

Allow 15-20 minutes cooking time per lb. plus 20 minutes extra.

1 10-lb. standing rib roast beef
salt

For Yorkshire Pudding:
2 cups all-purpose flour
salt
2 eggs

1 bunch watercress
½ cup horseradish sauce

2½ cups milk
¼ cup drippings

Cooking time: 3 hours
Temperature: Meat: 325°
Pudding: 400°
Serves: 12-15

Have the meat cutter remove the spinal cord, chine, and shoulder bone. Rub the beef with salt and place in a roasting pan. Place in a 325° oven and cook for 3 hours, or approximately 20 minutes per lb. Remove from the oven and allow to set in a warm place for 30 minutes. The process of setting helps retain the juices and makes the meat easier to carve. While the meat is setting prepare the gravy (see page 52) and bake the Yorkshire Pudding.
To make the Yorkshire Pudding:

Sieve the flour and salt into a bowl. Make a well in the center and add the eggs and three fourths of the milk. Mix with a wooden spoon to a smooth paste. Allow to stand for 30 minutes. Stir in the remaining milk. Melt the drippings in hot muffin pans or a roasting pan, pour in the batter, and bake in a 400° oven for 15 to 20 minutes until puffed and golden brown.

Carve the meat, garnish with watercress, and serve hot with horseradish sauce, Yorkshire Pudding, and gravy.

BEEF OLIVES

For stuffing:
1 cup fresh white bread crumbs
1 teaspoon chopped parsley
dash thyme
½ egg
2 tablespoons margarine

1 lb. chuck steak
3 tablespoons drippings
2 carrots, chopped
2 onions, chopped
¼ cup browned flour (see page 110)

¾ cup finely chopped cooked onion
salt and pepper
meat trimmings, finely chopped

2 tablespoons tomato paste
3¾ cups beef stock or water and beef bouillon cubes
salt and pepper
bouquet garni

Cooking time: 1½-2 hours
Temperature: 300°
Serves: 4

To make the stuffing: Mix all the ingredients together. To make the Beef Olives: Cut the meat into thin slices across the grain, flatten with a meat mallet to ¼-inch thickness, and cut into 4-inch squares. (Chop the trimmings finely and add to the stuffing.) Spread the stuffing on the squares of meat, roll up neatly, and tie with string. Melt the drippings in a heavy saucepan and fry the meat rolls until lightly browned. Add the carrot and onion and cook until golden. Place the meat and vegetables in an ovenproof casserole. Stir the flour

into the fat in the saucepan and cook over low heat for 1 minute. Add the tomato paste and cook for 3 minutes. Add the stock and bring to a boil stirring continuously. Add, salt and pepper to taste and pour over the meat and vegetables. Add the bouquet garni, cover with the lid, and braise in a 300° oven for 1½ to 2 hours, or until the meat is tender. Remove the string from the olives and adjust the consistency and flavor of the sauce if necessary before serving.

BROILED SIRLOIN STEAK WITH METROPOLIS SAUCE

4 sirloin steaks, about ¾ lb. each
2 tablespoons oil

For Metropolis Sauce:
¼ cup dry sherry
1¼ cups Espagnole Sauce

1 bunch watercress for garnish
parsley butter
¼ cup cream
2 tablespoons butter

Serves: 4

Trim the steaks and cut the fat at 1-inch intervals. Brush the steaks with oil and broil under a hot broiler, 3 minutes each side for rare steak, 5 minutes each side for medium-rare steak, 8 minutes each side for well-done steak. Serve immediately, garnished with watercress and parsley butter (see page 59) and accompanied by grilled tomatoes, French fried potatoes (see page 173), and Metropolis Sauce.

To make the sauce: Heat the sherry in a small saucepan until reduced by half. Add the Espagnole Sauce (see page 52) and reduce by one third. Add the cream and gradually stir in the butter. Reheat without boiling before serving.

BEEF BOURGUIGNONNE

2 lb. stew beef, chuck, blade, or shank
6 tablespoons lard
¼ cup browned flour (see page 110)
2 tablespoons tomato paste
2 cloves garlic, crushed
scant 2 cups burgundy

2½ cups beef stock or water and beef bouillon cube
salt and pepper
bouquet garni
¼ cup lean salt pork or bacon, diced
12 very small onions
12 button mushrooms
chopped parsley for garnish

Cooking time: 2½-3 hours
Temperature: 325°
Serves: 6

Cut the meat into large cubes. Fry the cubes in the lard in a flameproof casserole, sprinkle with the browned flour, and cook for 5 minutes. Add the tomato paste and garlic and cook a further 5 minutes. Add the burgundy and stock, season lightly with salt and pepper, and add the bouquet garni. Cover and cook in a 325° oven for 2½ to 3 hours, or until tender.

Fry the salt pork or bacon lightly, add the onions, and cook over moderate heat until evenly browned. Add to the casserole. Approximately 15 minutes before cooking is finished add the mushrooms. Adjust the consistency and seasoning if necessary and serve hot, sprinkled with chopped parsley.

Note: The traditional recipe has ¼ cup brandy added in the final stage.

BOILED BEEF

2 lb. corned beef
¾ lb. small carrots

¾ lb. small onions

Cooking time: 2½ hours
Serves: 4-6

For dumplings:
1 cup all-purpose flour, sifted with 1 teaspoon baking powder
pinch salt

6 tablespoons finely chopped suet
2-3 tablespoons cold water

Soak the corned beef in cold water for 2 hours to remove excess brine. Place in a saucepan and cover with fresh cold water, bring to the boil and skim. Add prepared carrots and onions and simmer gently for 2 hours approximately. Add the dumplings and simmer for a further 15 to 20 minutes. Remove the meat, drain, and carve across the grain. Serve hot with carrots, onions, and dumplings. Moisten the meat with a little of the cooking liquor.

To make the dumplings: Sieve the flour, baking powder, and salt into a mixing bowl. Mix in the suet. Make a well in the center, add the water, and mix to a smooth paste. Roll into little balls the size of a walnut and cook as above.

*Broiled Sirloin Steak
with Metropolis Sauce*

ROAST LOIN OF VEAL

Allow 25 minutes cooking time per lb. plus 25 minutes extra.

1 3-lb. veal loin roast
1 sprig rosemary, finely chopped
2 cloves garlic, crushed
salt and pepper
$\frac{1}{4}$ cup butter

1$\frac{1}{4}$ cups chicken stock or white wine
2 tablespoons cornstarch or arrowroot

Cooking time: 1$\frac{3}{4}$ hours
Temperature: 325°
Serves: 6

Have your meat cutter bone and roll the loin of veal. Mix the rosemary, garlic, and salt and pepper with the softened butter and spread over the loin of veal. Roast in a 325° oven for 1$\frac{3}{4}$ hours. Baste occasionally during the cooking. When cooked remove from the roasting pan and keep warm. Pour the excess fat from the roasting pan leaving 2 tablespoons, add the stock or white wine, stir in the sediment, place over heat, and bring to a boil. Stir in the cornstarch blended to a smooth paste with a little cold water and bring back to the boil point. Season to taste. Serve with the veal.

ROAST STUFFED BREAST OF VEAL

1 3-lb. breast of veal
1 lb. sausage meat
$\frac{1}{2}$ teaspoon mixed herbs
1 egg
1 onion, finely chopped
salt and pepper

2 tablespoons lard
1 large onion, sliced
1 large carrot, sliced
2$\frac{1}{2}$ cups chicken stock or water and chicken bouillon cube
2 tablespoons cornstarch

Cooking time: 2 hours
Temperature: 350°
Serves: 6

Have your meat cutter bone the breast of veal and cut a pocket in the middle. Mix the sausage meat, herbs, egg, finely chopped onion, and salt and pepper together. Place in the pocket of the veal, roll up, and tie securely. Grease a roasting pan with melted lard and fry the sliced onion and carrot until golden. Place the meat on top and brush with lard. Brown the meat in a 350° oven for 30 minutes. When well colored add stock and cook for a further 1$\frac{1}{2}$ hours, basting every 30 minutes. When cooked remove meat from the roasting pan and keep warm. Skim the fat from the stock, add the cornstarch blended with a little cold water, and bring to a boil, stirring continuously. Season to taste with salt and pepper. Serve the sauce over the veal.

VEAL CUTLETS NAPLES STYLE

4 veal cutlets, cut from the leg
$\frac{1}{3}$ cup oil
6 tablespoons clarified butter
1 egg yolk
$\frac{1}{2}$ cup grated Parmesan cheese
1$\frac{1}{4}$ cups Béchamel Sauce
1 egg, beaten

1 cup dry white bread crumbs
$\frac{1}{4}$ lb. spaghetti
1 tomato
1$\frac{1}{4}$ cups Tomato Sauce
salt and pepper
chopped parsley for garnish

Serves: 4

Trim the cutlets and fry to a light brown in half the oil and clarified butter. Drain on paper towels. Stir the egg yolk and half the cheese into the Béchamel Sauce (see page 50). Spread the sauce on a lightly greased plate and place in the refrigerator until cold. When cold, spread over the cutlets and coat with egg and bread crumbs. Press the crumbs on firmly and fry in the remaining oil and butter for 2 minutes on each side to a light brown.
Cook the spaghetti in boiling salted water for approx-imately 15 minutes until 'al dente' (see page 192), or just firm in the center. Drain. Remove the core from the tomato, dip into boiling water for 1 minute, place under running cold water, and remove the skin. Scoop out the seeds and chop the flesh up roughly. Mix the spaghetti with the tomato, Tomato Sauce (see page 59), and salt and pepper to taste. Reheat and serve the cutlets on a bed of 'spaghetti napolitaine'. Sprinkle with chopped parsley and the remaining cheese.

FRICASSÉE OF VEAL WITH MUSHROOMS

1½ lb. veal shoulder or breast, boned
3 tablespoons butter
¼ cup all-purpose flour
2½ cups veal or chicken stock or water and chicken bouillon cube

salt and pepper
8 small onions
8 button mushrooms
1 egg yolk
¼ cup cream
few drops lemon juice
chopped parsley for garnish

Cooking time: 1½ hours
Serves: 4

Cut the veal into 1-inch cubes and fry slowly in the butter without coloring. Stir in the flour and cook over a low heat for 5 minutes. Add the stock slowly, stirring continuously, and bring to a boil. Season lightly, cover, and simmer gently for 30 minutes. Remove the veal with a slotted spoon. Adjust the consistency and flavor of the sauce if necessary and strain into a clean saucepan.

Add the veal and onions and simmer for 15 minutes, then add the mushrooms and cook for a further 15 minutes, or until the vegetables are tender. Mix the egg yolk with the cream and stir into the fricassée over low heat, or preferably shake the pan gently until thoroughly mixed. Do not boil. Stir in the lemon juice and serve sprinkled with chopped parsley.

WIENER SCHNITZEL

(ESCALOPE OF VEAL VIENNESE STYLE)

4 veal escalopes, about ⅓ lb. each
1 cup all-purpose flour
salt and pepper
1 egg
2 cups dry white bread crumbs
½ cup oil
½ cup butter
1 lemon, thinly sliced

4 pitted olives
4 anchovy fillets
1 egg, hard-cooked
chopped capers
chopped parsley
¼ cup clarified butter
1 teaspoon lemon juice

Serves: 4

Trim the escalopes and flatten with a meat mallet until ¼ inch thick, being careful not to break the meat. Dip into seasoned flour, then into beaten egg, and finally into bread crumbs. Press the bread crumbs on very firmly. Heat the oil and butter in a skillet and fry the veal until golden brown, approximately 5 minutes on each side. Drain and serve each escalope garnished

with a thin slice of lemon and a pitted olive wrapped around with an anchovy fillet, and sprinkled with chopped hard-cooked egg, chopped capers, and parsley.

Brown the clarified butter in a saucepan, add the lemon juice, and pour over escalopes. This is known as beurre noisette.

OSSO BUCCO

2½ lb. shin bones of veal
1 onion, chopped
2 stalks celery, chopped
4 slices bacon, diced
2 tablespoons butter
⅔ cup dry white wine
dash thyme
1 bay leaf

2 cloves garlic, crushed
1 lb. ripe tomatoes, skinned seeded, and chopped
½ cup all-purpose flour
salt and pepper
2 tablespoons oil
grated rind of ½ lemon
chopped parsley for garnish

Cooking time: 2 hours
Temperature: 325°
Serves: 4

Have your meat cutter saw the shins into 2-inch rounds across the leg bone. Sauté the onion, celery, and bacon in the butter, add the wine, thyme, and bay leaf, and cook slowly for 20 minutes. Add the garlic and tomatoes and cook for a further 5 minutes. Roll the veal in the seasoned flour and fry in the oil until light brown.

Place the fried veal in an ovenproof casserole with the vegetables and stock. Cook in a 325° oven for 1½ hours. Just before serving add the lemon rind. Sprinkle with chopped parsley and serve with Rice Pilaff (see page 203) or Saffron Rice (see page 205).

ROAST PORK

Allow 30 minutes cooking time per lb. plus 30 minutes extra.

1 5-lb. fresh ham	stock or water and chicken	Cooking time: 3 hours
2 tablespoons oil	bouillon cube	Temperature: 450°
salt	pepper	reducing to 325°
2 tablespoons all-purpose flour	watercress for garnish	Serves: 8
2½ cups chicken or vegetable		

Prepare the ham for roasting. Score the skin with a sharp pointed knife in either parallel lines ¼-inch apart, or diamonds. Rub all over with oil and salt. Place on a rack in a roasting pan. Roast in a 450° oven for 30 minutes to crispen the crackling, then reduce to 325° and roast for 2½ hours approximately, until cooked through. Remove and keep warm.

To make the gravy, drain off all but 2 tablespoons of the fat in the pan, stir in the flour, and brown well over medium heat. Add the stock, salt, and pepper and stir until the mixture boils and thickens. Simmer for 1 minute and strain into a sauce boat.

Remove the crackling from the pork and carve. Serve hot with the crackling, garnished with watercress and accompanied by gravy, Applesauce (see page 59), and sage and onion stuffing (see page 152).

CROWN ROAST OF PORK

Your meat cutter will prepare this joint for you. Two rib squares are sawn carefully to allow shaping, tied together, and formed into a crown shape.

1 crown roast of pork (12 chops)	Cooking time: 1-1½ hours
	Temperature: 400°
	Serves: 6

Cover the bare rib bones with aluminum foil to prevent burning. Place on a rack in a roasting pan and roast in a 400° oven for 1 to 1½ hours. Remove the pork, place on a carving platter, and keep warm. Make the gravy (see above recipe). Remove the aluminum foil and place a frill on each bone. Carve by cutting between each chop. Serve with the gravy, Applesauce (see page 59), roast potatoes and pumpkin, and a green vegetable. *Note:* The center of the crown roast may be stuffed with sage and onion stuffing (see page 152).

SWEET AND SOUR PORK

1¼ lb. blade steak pork	2 tablespoons oil	Cooking time: 15-30 minutes
2 tablespoons sugar	¾ cup pineapple juice	Serves: 4
⅓ cup soy sauce	¼ cup white vinegar	
2 tablespoons dry sherry	2 tablespoons tomato catsup	
dash monosodium glutamate	1 teaspoon finely chopped green	
(optional)	ginger	
1 onion	2 tablespoons cornstarch	
1 carrot	1 egg	
¼ green sweet pepper	1 cup cornstarch for coating	
3 stalks celery, chopped	oil for frying	
½ cup chopped fresh pineapple		

Remove the bone from the steaks and cut the meat into ¾ to 1 inch dice. Marinate in a mixture of the sugar, soy sauce, sherry and monosodium glutamate for 20 minutes.

Prepare the vegetables, cut into julienne strips, and sauté quickly with the pineapple in the oil for 5 minutes. Combine the pineapple juice, vinegar, tomato catsup and green ginger in a saucepan and bring to a boil.

Add the cornstarch blended with ⅓ cup cold water and cook, stirring, until the mixture boils and thickens. Add the vegetables.

Drain the pork, coat it in the beaten egg, and roll it in the cornstarch. Fry in deep hot oil (350°), until cooked and golden. Drain well and serve coated with the hot sauce, accompanied by boiled rice.

116

*Crown Roast of Pork
prepared for roasting*

PORK TENDERLOIN HUNGARIAN STYLE

1½ lb. pork tenderloin
¼ cup butter

For sauce:
3 tablespoons butter
1 onion, chopped

2 tablespoons paprika pepper
6 tablespoons all-purpose flour
2½ cups chicken stock or water
   and chicken bouillon cube
salt and pepper
2 tablespoons cream

Serves: 4

Carefully trim the tenderloins and if large, slice obliquely into pieces ¾ inch thick. Fry in the butter until well cooked.

To make the sauce: Melt the butter in a saucepan and fry the onion until soft without coloring. Stir in the paprika pepper and flour and cook for 1 minute over very low heat. Add the stock slowly, stirring continuously. Bring to a boil, stirring, lower the heat, and simmer, covered, for 15 minutes. Add salt and pepper to taste and stir in the cream.

Reheat the sauce and ladle over the cooked pork tenderloin. Serve accompanied by buttered noodles or boiled potatoes.

PICKLED PORK WITH SAUTÉED CABBAGE

1½ lb. lean salt pork
7 slices bacon
2 tablespoons oil

1 large head white cabbage,
   finely shredded

Cooking time: 1¾ hours
Serves: 4

Wash the pork in cold water. Place in a large saucepan with cold water to cover, bring to a boil, reduce the heat, and simmer for 1¼ to 1½ hours until cooked. Test with a skewer or fork which should come out easily.

Meanwhile finely dice 3 of the bacon slices. Sauté in the oil in a large saucepan. Add the cabbage, cover, and cook very slowly for 20 minutes, stirring occasionally.

Carve the pork into slices. Broil the remaining bacon slices. Serve the pork on a bed of sautéed cabbage and garnish with the bacon rashers.

Note: Carrot, onion, and peppercorns are usually added to the boiling liquid for salt pork.

BOILED PICNIC SHOULDER WITH CABBAGE

Allow 25 minutes cooking time per lb. plus 25 minutes extra.

2 lb. smoked boned picnic
   shoulder
1 lb. small carrots

1 lb. onions
1 head cabbage, cut into 6
   wedges

Cooking time: 1¼ hours
Serves: 6

Soak the picnic shoulder in cold water for 24 hours. Drain off the water, cover with fresh cold water in a large saucepan, and bring to a boil. Skim, add the prepared carrots and onions, and simmer gently for 1¼ hours, or until cooked. Allow to cool in the liquid. Drain the bacon, remove the rind and outside brown skin, and carve into thin slices.

Boil the cabbage separately in a small amount of boiling, salted water for 5 to 10 minutes, until tender but slightly crisp. Drain well. Serve the picnic shoulder on wedges of cabbage, garnished with carrots and onions and accompanied by boiled potatoes and Parsley Sauce (see page 51).

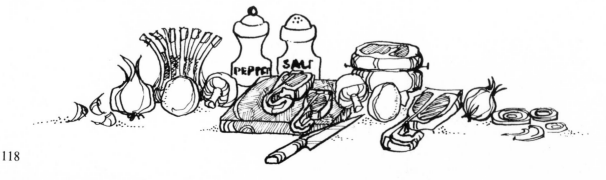

118

Variety Meats

Variety meats are the edible organs of beef cattle, calves, pigs, and sheep.

Dishes made with variety meats are popular throughout the world. A few favorites are lamb fries, steak and kidney pie, and oxtail stew. The food value is very high, for they have a high mineral and vitamin content and are second only to beef and veal in protein content. Variety meats such as brains and sweetbreads are easily digested and therefore very suitable for convalescent and older persons' diets. Variety meats can be divided into two groups:

1. White—brains, sweetbreads, tripe
2. Red—tongue, kidneys, liver, oxtail, heart.

Brains—calf, lamb, pork, beef; can be poached, pan fried, and deep fried. Calf brains are the most popular. They are grayish white and soft with a delicate flavor.

Preparation: Soak in cold water, remove the membrane or skin, and wash well to remove all blood.

Note: Brains can be prepared in advance and stored in cold, salted water until required.

Sweetbread—calf, lamb, beef; can be braised, fried, and broiled. There are two types of sweetbread used in cookery, the pancreas, and the thymus gland.

Preparation: Soak, blanch, and rinse in cold water.

Tripe—beef; can be stewed, boiled and braised. Tripe is the muscular lining of beef stomach. Honeycomb tripe from the second stomach, is the most tender. Tripe is always sold partially cooked.

Preparation: Wash well, blanch, and rinse in cold water.

Tongue—beef, calf, pork, lamb; can be boiled and braised. Tongues may be purchased fresh, pickled or smoked.

Preparation: Cook first, then cool slightly, remove bone and gristle from the root end, and skin; larger tongues (beef) are secured into a neat shape either on a board or in a container and pressed.

Kidneys—beef, lamb, veal, and pork; can be broiled, stewed, and fried. Beef kidney is strongly flavored and tougher than lamb and veal kidney. Pork kidneys are not as acceptable as other kidneys, mainly because of a strong odor.

Preparation: Remove the fat and skin and cut down the center lengthwise. Remove the tubes and cut in half or dice.

Liver—beef, lamb, calf, pork; can be fried, broiled, and braised. Beef liver is less tender than the others, lamb and calf liver is milder in flavor than pork and beef.

Preparation: Skin if possible, remove gristle and tubes, and cut into thin slices.

Oxtail—ox; can be stewed, braised and used for soup.

Preparation: Trim off excess fat and cut between natural joints.

Heart—beef (whole or sliced), veal; can be braised and roasted.

Preparation: Soak in salted cold water for 1 hour. Remove tubes, gristle, and excess fat. Stuff and secure the opening with a small skewer or sew up with fine string.

CALF BRAINS WITH BLACK BUTTER

4 sets calf brains
¼ cup clarified butter
2 tablespoons chopped parsley

2 tablespoons capers, chopped
few drops vinegar

Cooking time: 20 minutes
Serves: 4

Soak the brains in cold water to remove the blood. Wash, trim, and remove the thin covering skin. Poach in a court bouillon (see page 89), allow to cool, and cut into thick slices. Fry quickly in a skillet, in 2 tablespoons clarified butter, on bother sides and place on a warm serving dish. Clean the skillet, add the remaining clarified butter, and heat until it becomes a dark brown color. Do not burn. Add the parsley, capers, and vinegar and serve hot, poured over the brains.

SAUTÉ OF KIDNEYS

4 veal kidneys
¼ cup oil
1¼ cups Espagnole Sauce

salt and pepper
chopped parsley for garnish

Cooking time: 20 minutes
Serves: 4

Slice the kidneys crosswise, removing all the white core. Fry in the oil in a skillet for 4 to 5 minutes. Drain well and season with salt and pepper. Add to the Espagnole Sauce (see page 52). Reheat and serve on a slice of toast sprinkled with chopped parsley.

Variation: For Kidneys Sauté Turbigo, fry 1 cup button mushrooms in butter and broil or fry 4 thin breakfast sausages; arrange on top of the Sauté of Kidneys.

SWEETBREADS WITH CREAM

2 pairs calf sweetbreads
salt and pepper
1 large carrot, chopped
1 large onion, chopped
scant 2 cups chicken stock or
    water and chicken bouillon
    cube

2 teaspoons arrowroot or
    cornstarch
½ cup cream

Cooking time: 1 hour
Temperature: 325°
Serves: 4

Wash the sweetbreads well, blanch, rinse in cold water, and trim. Season and place in an ovenproof casserole on a bed of carrot and onion. Add the stock and cover with buttered wax paper and the lid. Cook in a 325° oven for 1 hour. Strain off the cooking liquor into a saucepan and thicken with the arrowroot blended to a smooth paste with cold water. Add the cream and reheat without boiling. Serve the sweetbreads coated with the sauce.

BRAISED LAMB TONGUES

2 carrots, chopped
2 onions, chopped
2 tablespoons drippings or lard
8 lamb tongues
scant 2 cups Espagnole Sauce

scant 2 cups beef stock or water
    and beef bouillon cube
2 tablespoons tomato paste
bouquet garni

Cooking time: 1½ hours
Temperature: 350°
Serves: 4

Fry the carrot and onion until golden in the drippings in a flameproof casserole. Add the prepared tongues (washed, trimmed, blanched, and rinsed) with the remaining ingredients. Bring to a boil and skim. Cover and simmer in a 350° oven for 1½ hours. Remove and skin the tongues. Cut into long slices. Strain the Espagnole Sauce (see page 52) and adjust the consistency and flavor if necessary. Serve the tongues on a warm serving dish, coated with the sauce.

BEEF TONGUE WITH SPINACH

1 4-lb. beef tongue, pickled
    or smoked
2 carrots
2 onions
1 stalk celery, chopped

bouquet garni
pepper
small bunch spinach
2½ cups Madeira Sauce
chopped parsley for garnish

Cooking time: 3-4 hours
Serves: 6

Wash the tongue, place in a saucepan, and cover with cold water. Add the prepared carrots and onions, celery, bouquet garni, and pepper and bring to a boil, skim, simmer for 3-4 hours. Cool slightly, remove the skin, and trim off the root. Wash the spinach and cook in a saucepan with a tightly fitting lid for 5 minutes, using only the water adhering to the leaves. Drain and chop the spinach finely. Make the Madeira Sauce (see page 54). Slice the tongue and arrange on a bed of spinach. Serve coated with Madeira Sauce and sprinkled with chopped parsley.

LAMB FRY AND BACON

¾ lb. lamb fries
½ cup all-purpose flour
salt and pepper

oil and frying
4 slices bacon
parsley sprigs for garnish

Cooking time: 10 minutes
Serves: 4

Slice the lamb fries thinly. Dip in seasoned flour and fry on both sides in oil. Broil the bacon. Serve the fries with the broiled bacon, garnished with parsley sprigs and accompanied by broiled tomatoes and shoestring potatoes (see page 173).

Kidneys Sauté Turbigo

Nancy Carr

Meat Cookery

Nancy Carr graduated with a Bachelor of Home Science degree. She later studied Foods and Nutrition at the Pennsylvania State University, U.S.A. and became a lecturer in Foods at the university's School of Home Science.

Because of the increasingly high price of meat it is important to use cheaper cuts and to utilize meat left over from a previous meal. Casseroles are delicious and ideal for the busy housewife, especially during the cold winter months. They may take longer to prepare, but they can then be stored in the refrigerator until required. They are also ideal for entertaining and on the day of the party you can concentrate on other dishes and your casserole will improve in flavor when reheated. Cook casseroled meat slowly for a long time and you will find the cheaper meats become tender and delicious to eat.

There are many cuts of meat suitable for broiling and these may be marinated or served with a topping to add extra flavor.

Different types of variety meats should appear on the menu at regular intervals. Nutritionally they are invaluable. Try cooking Liver Loaf or Brain Fritters, your family will love them.

When serving meat which has already been cooked, heat through gently for the meat fibers will toughen if allowed to cook for too long at a high temperature.

Stuffed Pork Tenderloin in preparation

MARINATED ROAST LAMB

2 teaspoons salt
3 cloves garlic, chopped
1 teaspoon oregano
1 teaspoon rosemary

1 teaspoon paprika pepper
½ cup oil
2 tablespoons lemon juice
1 4-lb. leg of lamb

Cooking time: 1½-2 hours
Temperature: 350°
Serves: 6

Crush the salt and garlic to a paste on a plate. Scrape into a small bowl, then stir in the oregano, rosemary, paprika, oil, and lemon juice. Place the meat in a roasting pan and completely coat it with the marinade, rubbing it into the cut surface. Leave to stand for 2 to 3 hours, turning the meat occasionally. Roast in a 350° oven for 20 to 25 minutes per lb. plus 20 to 25 minutes extra.

SPICED LAMB STEAKS

6 lamb leg steaks
¼ cup brown sugar
¼ cup all-purpose flour
¼ cup vinegar
¼ cup tomato catsup
¼ teaspoon ginger
½ teaspoon curry powder

½ teaspoon dry mustard
½ teaspoon mixed spice
1 teaspoon salt
dash pepper
1½ cups water
¼ cup sherry (optional)

Cooking time: 2 hours
Temperature: 325°
Serves: 4-6

Trim off the fat and place the steaks in a casserole. Mix the remaining ingredients together and pour over the steaks. Leave to marinate for 2 to 3 hours. Cover the casserole and bake in a 325° oven for 2 hours.

BAKED SHANKS

4 lamb shanks
1 package onion or mushroom
   soup

2 tablespoons butter

Cooking time: 2-3 hours.
Temperature: 375°
Serves: 4

Place each shank on a piece of aluminum foil large enough to cover it completely. Sprinkle one fourth of the soup over each shank. Divide the butter into 4 and place a piece on each shank. Wrap the foil around the meat, folding the edges to seal the packages. Place the packages in a roasting pan or shallow casserole. Bake in a 375° oven for 2 to 3 hours, until tender.
Note: Small lamb shanks may be cooked in under 2 hours, larger ones may require 3 hours.

STUFFED FRESH PORK ARM ROAST

3½-4 lb. fresh pork arm roast,
   boned

drippings

Cooking time: 3-3½ hours
Temperature: 350°
Serves: 6

For stuffing:
1 onion, chopped
3 tablespoons butter
2 cups fresh soft bread crumbs

1-1½ teaspoons mixed herbs
juice of 1 lemon
salt and pepper

Have the meat cutter leave one side of the roast unsewed to make a pocket for the stuffing.
To make the stuffing: Cook the onion in the butter until tender and lightly browned. Combine the bread crumbs and herbs in a bowl, add the onion and butter, and mix well. Mix in the lemon juice and season to taste with salt and pepper. Place the stuffing in the prepared pocket and secure the opening with skewers or wooden toothpicks. Melt the drippings in a roasting pan, then cook the meat in a 350° oven for 35 to 40 minutes per lb. Serve hot with gravy, Applesauce (see page 59), and vegetables, or cold with salad.

HAM SLICES WITH CHEESE TOPPING

4 ham slices
oil
½ cup grated sharp cheese

¼ cup butter, softened
dash cayenne pepper
2 tablespoons chopped chives

Cooking time: 25-30 minutes
Serve: 4

Cut the fat around the edges of the ham slices to prevent them from curling. Brush the slices with a little oil and broil for 10 to 15 minutes on each side. Transfer the slices to a shallow ovenproof dish. Combine the cheese, butter, cayenne pepper, and chives and mix well. Spread the chops with the cheese mixture and broil under a hot broiler for 2 to 3 minutes, until the cheese is lightly browned.

STUFFED PORK TENDERLOIN

12 dried apricots
1 1½-lb. large or 2 medium-sized
  pork tenderloins
1 cooking apple

2 tablespoons butter
½ teaspoon salt
dash pepper
¾ cup water

Cooking time: 1 hour
Serves: 4

Soak the apricots in water overnight. Trim the excess fat from the pork tenderloin and split carefully down the center without cutting in half. Drain the apricots. Peel and slice the apple. Arrange the apricots and apple slices inside the tenderloin. Draw the edges together and tie securely with string. Melt the butter in a skillet and brown the meat on all sides. Season with salt and pepper. Add the water, cover, and simmer for 1 hour or until the meat is tender. Remove the string before serving the meat. Slice the tenderloin and serve with a gravy made by thickening the meat juices in the skillet.

SAVORY STEW

2 tablespoons butter
3 onions, sliced
1½ lb. blade or arm steak
1 teaspoon salt
1 teaspoon sugar
1 teaspoon baking soda

¼ cup all-purpose flour
2 cups water
⅓ cup tomato catsup
1 teaspoon Worcestershire sauce
¼ cup plum sauce or mushroom
  catsup

Cooking time: 2½-3 hours
Serves: 4

Melt the butter in a saucepan and sauté the onion until tender and lightly browned. Remove the fat, cut the meat into 1-inch pieces, add to the saucepan, and brown quickly. Mix the salt, sugar, baking soda, and flour to a paste with a little of the cold water. Stir in the sauces and the remaining water and pour the mixture over the meat and onions. Cover the saucepan and simmer for 2½ to 3 hours, until the meat is tender.

STUFFED POT ROAST

3-4 lb. rolled rump
⅓ cup drippings or oil

1 cup water

Cooking time: 2½-3 hours
Serves: 6-8

For stuffing:
1 small onion, chopped
2 tablespoons butter
1 cup fresh bread crumbs

½ teaspoon mixed herbs
½ teaspoon salt
dash pepper

Cut a pocket in the meat. Cook the onion in the butter in a saucepan until tender and lightly browned. Add the bread crumbs, herbs and seasonings and mix together. Lightly press the stuffing into the pocket. Close the opening with meat skewers or by sewing it with a large needle and cotton. Heat the drippings in a large heavy saucepan and brown the meat on all sides. Pour off the fat. Add the water, cover, and cook gently for 2½ to 3 hours, until the meat is tender. Add a little more water if necessary during the cooking. Serve hot with the gravy in the saucepan.

MEAT LOAF

$\frac{3}{4}$ lb. ground beef
$\frac{3}{4}$ lb. sausage meat
2 slices Canadian-style bacon,
   diced
1 cup fresh bread crumbs
1 egg

$\frac{1}{4}$ cup chopped chives
1 teaspoon salt
$\frac{1}{4}$ teaspoon pepper
dry bread crumbs or crushed
   cornflakes for coating
$\frac{1}{3}$-$\frac{1}{2}$ cup drippings or oil

Cooking time: 1 hour
Temperature: 350°
Serves: 4-6

Combine the ground beef, sausage meat, bacon, and bread crumbs with the egg, chives, and seasoning and mix thoroughly. Spread the dry bread crumbs or cornflakes on wax paper. Turn the meat mixture onto the bread crumbs and shape into a sausage approximately 3 inches in diameter. Coat the meat with the bread crumbs. Melt the fat in a covered roasting pan or casserole. Place the loaf in the roasting pan, cover, and cook in a 350° oven for 1 hour. Baste the loaf occasionally during the cooking period. Serve hot or cold.

VEAL AND HAM PIE

$1\frac{1}{4}$ lb. veal stew meat
$\frac{1}{3}$ lb. ham or lean bacon
2 tablespoons butter
2 onions, sliced
1 cup sliced mushrooms
   (optional)

$\frac{1}{4}$ cup cornstarch
salt and pepper
1 quantity Flaky Paste
beaten egg or milk for glazing

Cooking time: $2\frac{1}{2}$-3 hours
Temperature: 450°
   reducing to 375°
Serves: 4

Cut the veal and ham into 1-inch pieces. Melt the butter in a saucepan and sauté the onions and mushrooms until soft but not brown. Add the meat and cover with water. Cover and simmer for 2 to $2\frac{1}{2}$ hours, or until tender. Mix the cornstarch to a smooth paste with a little water, stir into the meat and bring to a boil, stirring continuously. Season to taste with salt and pepper. Pour the meat and gravy into a $2\frac{1}{2}$-pint pie dish with a pie funnel or egg cup (not plastic) in the middle and leave until cold. Roll out the dough (see page 296) on a lightly floured board and cover the pie. Cut a small hole at the top of the pie funnel. Brush the crust with egg or milk. Bake in a 450° oven for 15 minutes than lower the temperature to 375° and bake for a further 15 minutes, until the crust is cooked and goldenbrown and the meat is hot.

VEAL BIRDS

For stuffing:
2 cups fresh bread crumbs
$\frac{1}{4}$ cup finely chopped suet
2 tablespoons chopped parsley
1 teaspoon thyme or mixed herbs

$\frac{1}{2}$ teaspoon grated lemon rind
$\frac{1}{2}$ teaspoon salt
$\frac{1}{4}$ teaspoon pepper
1 egg, beaten

Cooking time: $1\frac{1}{4}$ hours
Temperature: 325°
Serves: 4-6

6 very thin slices veal round
6 tablespoons butter
1 onion, chopped
6 tablespoons all-purpose flour
scant 2 cups chicken stock or

water and chicken bouillon
   cube
salt and pepper
2 tablespoons chopped parsley

Combine all the stuffing ingredients and mix thoroughly. Divide the stuffing into 6 portions and spread on each slice of veal. Roll up and secure with cotton or wooden toothpicks. Heat the butter in a skillet and brown the meat rolls. Place the rolls in an ovenproof casserole. Fry the onion in the butter until soft, stir in the flour, and cook for 1 minute. Add half the stock and heat until thickened, stirring constantly. Add the remaining liquid and stir until boiling. Season to taste with salt and pepper. Pour the sauce over the veal rolls, cover, and cook in a 325° oven for $1\frac{1}{4}$ hours, or until the meat is tender. Remove the cotton or toothpicks before serving, and garnish with chopped parsley.

BRAIN FRITTERS

For batter:
1 cup all-purpose flour
2½ teaspoons baking powder
¼ teaspoon salt

1 egg, beaten
½ cup milk

Serves: 4

4 sets sheep brains
2½ cups water
2 tablespoons vinegar

1 teaspoon salt
oil for frying

To make the batter: Sift the flour, baking powder, and salt into a mixing bowl. Combine the egg and milk. Mix the liquid ingredients into the dry ingredients until smooth to make a thick batter.

To make the fritters: Wash the brains and remove the thin membranes and blood vessels. Soak in cold salted water for 1 hour then rinse. Bring the water, vinegar, and salt to a boil, add the brains, and simmer for 15 minutes. Drain and cover with cold water. Heat the oil to 375° in an electric skillet or until hot enough to brown a 1-inch cube of day-old bread in 60 seconds. Cut each set of brains into 4 to 6 pieces. Coat each piece with batter and place in the hot oil. Fry, turning once, until golden brown and cooked. Drain and serve immediately.

STUFFED HEARTS

For stuffing:
1 onion, chopped
2 tablespoons butter
1½ cups fresh bread crumbs
½ cup diced celery

2 tablespoons chopped parsley
½ teaspoon mixed herbs
salt and pepper

Cooking time: 1½-2 hours
Serves: 4

4 veal hearts
2 tablespoons butter
1½ cups beef stock or water and
   beef bouillon cube

2-3 tablespoons cornstarch
salt and pepper

To make the stuffing: Sauté the onion in the butter until soft but not brown. Combine with the remaining stuffing ingredients and mix thoroughly. Season to taste with salt and pepper.

Wash the hearts. Trim off excess fat and any large blood vessels. If one cavity is wanted for stuffing cut out the wall dividing the two sides of the heart. Dry the cavities with a clean cloth. Fill the hearts with the stuffing and close the opening with small skewers laced together with fine string or sew with coarse cotton. Melt the butter in a saucepan and fry the hearts until brown all over. Add the stock. Cover and simmer for 1½ to 2 hours, or until tender. Mix the cornstarch to a paste with a little cold water, stir into the saucepan, and bring to a boil, stirring continuously. Season to taste with salt and pepper. Remove the string or cotton before serving. Serve hot with gravy or cold with salad.

LIVER LOAF

½ lb. calf, lamb, or pork liver
½ cup boiling water
1 onion, chopped
2 tablespoons butter
4 slices bacon
½ cup sausage meat

1 cup fresh bread crumbs
1 teaspoon Worcestershire sauce
2 teaspoons lemon juice
1 teaspoon celery salt
pepper
1 egg

Cooking time: 45 minutes
Temperature: 375°
Serves: 4-6

Wash the liver and remove the skin and any coarse tubes. Slice the liver then simmer in the boiling water for 5 minutes. Sauté the onion in the butter until tender. Mince the liver, onion, and bacon and mix thoroughly with the remaining ingredients. Press into a greased loaf pan. Cover with aluminum foil and bake in a 375° oven for 45 minutes. Serve hot with Tomato Sauce (see page 59) or serve cold with salad.

SWEETBREAD CROQUETTES

1 lb. veal or lamb sweetbreads
1 onion, finely chopped
½ cup finely chopped mushrooms
¼ cup butter
6 tablespoons all-purpose flour

1 cup milk
salt and pepper
dry bread crumbs and beaten
    egg for coating
oil for frying

Cooking time: 1 hour
Serves: 3-4

Soak the sweetbreads in cold water for 1 hour. Rinse well and place in a saucepan with cold water. Bring slowly to a boil, simmer for 10 minutes, drain, and cover with cold water. When cool, remove the skin and fat. Cover the prepared sweetbreads with salted water, bring to a boil and simmer for 45 to 60 minutes, or until tender. Drain and finely chop the sweetbreads. Fry the onion and mushrooms in the butter in a saucepan until soft but not brown. Stir in the flour and cook gently for 1 minute. Add the milk gradually and stir continuously until boiling. Season to taste with salt and pepper. Mix in the chopped sweetbreads and allow to cool. When cold shape the mixture into croquettes—the number will depend on the size. Roll the croquettes in the bread crumbs, then the egg, and finally the bread crumbs again. Allow to stand for 15 minutes. Heat the oil in a deep skillet to 375° or until hot enough to brown a 1-inch cube of day-old bread in 60 seconds. Fry a few croquettes at a time until golden brown. Drain and serve piping hot.

BEEF TONGUE IN RAISIN SAUCE

1 beef tongue

For sauce:
¼ cup brown sugar
1 teaspoon dry mustard
2 teaspoons cornstarch

¼ cup vinegar
1¾ cups water
¼ cup seedless raisins

Cooking time: about 3¼ hours
    (or 1 hour using
    pressure cooker)
Serves: 4

Wash the tongue thoroughly. Cook by simmering in water for 2½ to 3 hours, or cook in a pressure cooker for 30 to 45 minutes. Drain and cool in cold water. Cut out the undesirable parts of the root end including the very small bones. Remove the skin and any fat. Combine the brown sugar, mustard, and cornstarch. Blend with the vinegar and water. Add the raisins and bring to a boil, stirring continuously. Simmer, uncovered, for 15 minutes until the sauce thickens slightly. Add the tongue, whole or sliced, and cook for 10 to 15 minutes to reheat the meat.

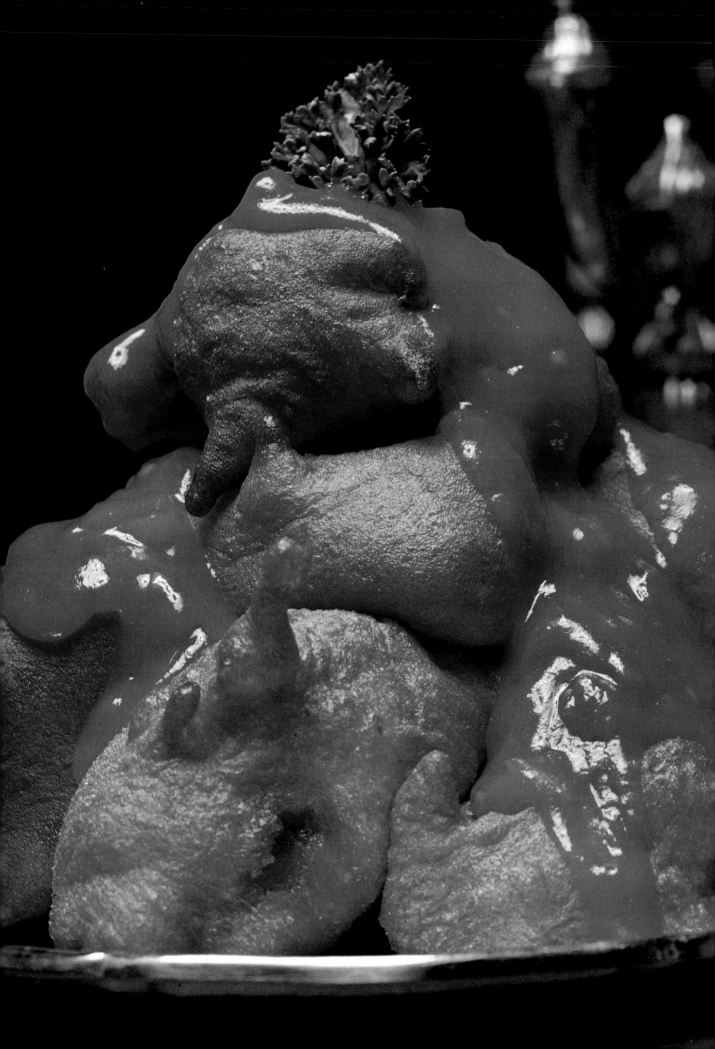

Isabel Horne

Isabel Horne is the principal of *Larnook Domestic Arts Teachers' College* in Melbourne. Isabel has a Diploma of Domestic Arts and is the Founder President of the Home Economics Association of Australia.

Réchauffé Meat Cookery
(or What to do with Leftover Meat)

The French word 'réchauffé' explains this type of dish, as it means 'reheat'. It implies that the food must be heated to the boiling point but must not be recooked. This is essential, as the food value, flavor, and texture of the leftover foods used are spoilt by recooking and the food will become tough, tasteless, and indigestible. Many types of meat may be incorporated into one of these 'reheated' dishes—mutton, beef, veal, poultry, and game—and a wide variety of methods may be used in the making of a réchauffé dish. The food may be reheated in a sauce, in a pie shell, in a batter, in a pancake or an omelet, in a savory custard or a soufflé, as a baked loaf or coated and fried, or as a sauce for pasta. Variations of certain typical national dishes come into this area. When reheating meat in a sauce or gravy, it is advisable to heat the sauce gently first, then add the ground, diced, or sliced meat to the saucepan, to ensure the meat is not over-cooked. A cottage pie is protected by a layer of mashed potato on top. If the food is to be subjected to very high temperatures, as in the cooking of croquettes and noodles, it must be protected by a layer of batter or egg and bread crumbs.

Réchauffé dishes are usually tasty, homely, family fare but certain dishes may suitably be incorporated into a formal dinner menu. It is essential they are prepared with forethought and care.

A FEW POINTS TO REMEMBER

- Give the dish palate appeal—the empty flavor of the leftovers must be overcome.
- Give the dish eye appeal—service and color are important.
- Give the dish a new look and a new name—avoid similarity to the original dish.
  Give the dish a good companion—ensure that flavorsome and attractive accompaniments are served. Salads are good.
  Give the dish a heating through but not a second cooking.
- Give the dish an international flavor.

Be imaginative in your approach to this area of cooking and you will be well rewarded with interesting, tasty, and attractive dishes at the same time as you are practising food economy.

SAVORY PANCAKE

With an Italian flavor.

For pancakes:
1 cup all-purpose flour
salt
1 egg

1¼ cups milk
2 tablespoons soda water
oil for frying

Serves: 4-6

For filling:
1 clove garlic, crushed
¼ cup oil
6-8 scallions, finely chopped
2 large tomatoes, skinned and
    chopped

salt and pepper
¾ cup ground or chopped cold
    meat
1 tablespoon Parmesan cheese
sprig rosemary

For sauce:
1 lb. ripe tomatoes or 1 (16 oz.)
    can tomatoes

salt and pepper
sugar

For garnish:
Mozzarella cheese or grated
    cheese

chopped scallion tops

To make the pancakes: Sift the flour and salt into a mixing bowl. Break the egg into the center. Add the milk gradually to make a smooth batter, beating until bubbles begin to rise. Allow to stand for 30 minutes. Add the soda water just before cooking. To cook, heat the pancake pan and add sufficient oil to coat the bottom. Pour sufficient mixture into the center to cover the bottom thinly and run over the whole pan.
Cook until set, turning once.
To make the filling: Fry the garlic in oil, then remove. Add the scallions (reserve the green tops) and fry lightly. Add the tomatoes with the salt and pepper. Cook until thick. Add the meat, Parmesan cheese, and chopped rosemary. Heat through. To make the sauce: A purée may be made by chopping the tomatoes and reducing them to a pulp by rubbing through a sieve or to a purée in an electric blender. Canned tomatoes may be used for this. Add salt, pepper, and sugar to taste.
To finished the pancake: Have everything hot. Place a pancake on a heatproof dish. Spread a little meat mixture over and cover with a second pancake. Continue to make alternate layers of meat and pancake, using 4 pancakes and ending with a pancake. Pour the tomato sauce over. Garnish the top with slices of Mozzarella or grated cheese. Broil the cheese until golden. Garnish with the chopped scallion tops. Serve very hot, cut into wedges.
Note: Another way of serving: Make 2 very large panckaes. Pile the meat mixture on one, and place the other over it. Cut a cross in the top pancake and roll the 4 corners back. Fill the center with sauce and put grated cheese on top. Broil until golden brown and cut into wedges to serve.

SATAY

The original idea was from the troops of Genghis Khan, so variations are found in many places.

⅓ lb. cold cooked meat
few drops soy sauce
few drops Tabasco sauce
1 teaspoon white vinegar

1 teaspoon oil
1 teaspoon brown sugar
1 clove garlic (optional)

Cooking time: 2 minutes
Serves: 4

Cut the meat into small ½-inch dice, leaving the fat on. Marinate for as long as possible in a mixture of soy sauce, Tabasco sauce, white vinegar, oil, and brown sugar. Crushed garlic may be added if desired. Place on fine skewers. Broil very quickly under a hot broiler. Serve on the skewers accompanied by a variety of well-flavored sauces, such as a combination of:

- peanut butter and white vinegar
- sweet sour pickle with pineapple
- soy and chili sauce
- horseradish relish and sour cream
- puréed mushroom
- tomato paste, cayenne pepper, and crushed garlic.

132

RUMANIAN MOUSSAKA

¼ lb. cold cooked meat (pork,
    lamb, or beef)
½ small onion, finely chopped
½ small green sweet pepper,
    finely chopped
¼ cup oil
2 tablespoons chopped fresh
    herbs
salt and pepper

1 small eggplant or zucchini,
    sliced
2 eggs
1¼ cups milk
¼ cup grated cheese
cayenne pepper
fried chopped onion, tomato,
    and green sweet pepper for
    garnish

Cooking time: 40 minutes
Temperature: 350°
Serves: 4

Grind the meat or chop finely. Fry the onion and sweet pepper lightly in oil. Add to the meat with the herbs and salt and pepper. Sauté the eggplant or zucchini in oil until soft. Place the meat and vegetables in alternate layers in a well greased ovenproof dish, pie dish, or loaf pan. Do not pack hard. Mix the beaten eggs and milk together and add the grated cheese, salt, and cayenne pepper. Pour over the meat and vegetables. Make sure that it goes through the whole mixture by inserting a knife along the sides. Stand the dish in a water bath and cook in a 350° oven for about 40 minutes, or until the custard has set. Remove from the oven and allow to stand a few minutes before turning out onto a heated serving platter. A mixture of chopped onion, tomato, and sweet pepper, fried together in a little oil, may be piled on top for garnish.

Variation: Lines of paprika pepper and dried parsley alternating with Parmesan cheese are another garnish.

Note: Individual moussakas may be made in small ovenproof dishes or ramekins. It may also be served cold with salad. Another method is to cook it in a large skillet as an omelet by mixing the meat and eggplant and pouring the egg mixture over and cooking gently until set.

KROMESKIES

¼ lb. cooked meat (pork, veal,
    lamb)
1 oz. butter
2-3 scallions, chopped
¼ cup all-purpose flour
, cup milk

1 teaspoon chopped parsley
1 teaspoon lemon juice
salt
pepper or cayenne pepper
3 slices bacon
oil for frying

Cooking time: 4-5 minutes
Serves: 2

For fritter batter:
1 cup all-purpose flour
dash salt
2 tablespoons oil

⅔ cup tepid water
1 egg white

Dice the meat finely. Melt the butter and fry the scallions until soft. Stir in the flour, add the milk, and stir until boiling. Add the parsley, lemon juice, salt, and pepper. Cook for 2 minutes, stirring continuously, then add the meat. Set aside to cool.

To make the batter: Sift the flour and salt into a mixing bowl. Pour the oil into the center and gradually add the water, mixing the whole into a smooth batter. Beat until bubbles rise. Whip the egg white to a stiff froth and add just before using the batter.

Dip the bacon into boiling water and leave for 1 minute. Flatten with a knife and cut into 3-inch strips. Put 1 tablespoon of the mixture onto a piece of bacon, then roll into a cork shape. Dip into batter, then deep fry in hot oil. Drain on paper and serve at once accompanied by tomato sauce (see page 59).

INS:
20345
070/66

Paté de Volaille

Paté en Croute

Beurre de Foie

Paté de Canedon
(duc-ling)

Paté de Foie

Paté de Campagne
(country Paté)

Terrine du Chef

Vol au Vents
(HAM)

Paté de Sancerre

Paté Fine Truffé

Paté de Bretagne

Toulousain

Paté Normand

Terrine
(Duck)

Bill May

Bill May learnt about pâtés and terrines by eating them as frequently as possible over many years in France! His skill in making them is revealed by the fact that he now runs a restaurant specializing in charcuterie.

Pâtés and Terrines

Pâté is the name given to any mixture of meats flavored with spices, truffles, wine, brandy, or cognac, and served enclosed in a pastry crust, contained in a terrine, or turned out of a mold. The Romans made pâtés, as did the Greeks before them. Salamis, an island which lies between Athens and Corinth, gave its name to salami, a crudely over-spiced form of pâté encased in a skin.

Terrine means earthenware, from 'terra'—earth. A meat loaf cooked in a terrine may be called a terrine; but it may also be called a pâté in terrine. The answer to the frequent question 'What is the difference between a pâté and a terrine?' must be that there is no clear distinction to be made. The terms are interchangeable. A 'pâté maison', being the pâté of the house, may correctly be called 'terrine du chef'. Good fresh ingredients must be used if a good pâté is to result. There can be no substitute. Pâtés are made from ordinary, unfattened liver, whether of goose, duck, pig, calf, or chicken; from feathered game, quail, pheasants, larks, thrushes; furred game, rabbit, venison, wild boar, and hare; from domestic poultry; and from butcher's meat. They are also made from fish, usually enclosed in pastry and served hot or cold. Most meat is suitable for the production of pâtés and terrines. The meat must be thoroughly fresh and the best of its kind available. The French charcutiers' old joke—the very best lark pâté requires 1 prime lark, 1 prime horse, and seasonings—is a joke of confidence. No matter what one's views are on the use of skylarks for food, the essence of the joke is that larks are used. In Noumea the charcutiers take advantage of local game and make a flying fox pâté. It is said to be delicious. Pâté molds and terrines are available from leading kitchenware stores.

PÂTÉ DE FOIE GRAS

Pâtés are divided into two main orders, those which are served hot and those which are served cold. The most notable pâté, which may be served either hot or cold, is pâté de foie gras. The 'prince' of pâtés is the product of a kind of barbarism. Alexandre Dumas, in his Dictionary of Cuisine, describes the process and makes the comment that 'these animals are submitted to unheard of tortures, worse than those suffered by the early Christians'. The process makes the livers of the geese ten or twelve times larger than nature intended.

HOW TO SERVE PÂTÉS AND TERRINES

All pâtés and terrines may be served as hors d'oeuvre, preferably without fuss—a slice of tomato perhaps, to freshen the palate. Soft chicken liver pâté is used as a substitute for foie gras in certain tournedos dishes. Bolder restauranteurs use truffled pâté for this and others use plain pâté. The firm pâtés and terrines are excellent with salads.

CHICKEN PÂTÉ

1 3-lb. chicken
½ cup brandy
1 tablespoon dried tarragon,
　crushed
salt
freshly ground black pepper
¾ cup finely ground veal
¾ cup finely ground pork

½ cup ground chicken livers
¾ cup finely chopped boiled ham
⅓ cup finely diced salt pork
1 envelope gelatin
1 cup chopped mushrooms
3 cloves garlic, crushed
¼ cup butter
bacon slices

Cooking time:　1½ hours
Temperature:　350°

Remove the breasts from the chicken and cut into slices. Mix the brandy, tarragon, salt, and pepper, add the sliced chicken breast, and put aside to marinate. Bone out the remaining chicken and grind the meat. Add the veal, pork, chicken livers, ham, salt pork and gelatin and mix well. Fry the mushrooms and garlic in the butter and add to the meat mixture. Add the sliced chicken breasts and marinade and stir in until evenly mixed. Line the bottom of a terrine with the bacon slices, fill with the mixture, press down firmly, and top with more bacon slices. Cover with the lid or aluminum foil, place in a pan of water, and cook in a 350° oven for 1½ hours. Allow to cool, then refrigerate for at least 8 hours before either turning out or cutting from the terrine.

CHICKEN LIVER PÂTÉ

½ lb. onions, finely chopped
2 cloves garlic, crushed
½ cup butter
1 lb. fresh chicken livers
3 eggs, hard-cooked and
　chopped

½ cup softened butter
2 tablespoons cognac
salt
freshly ground black pepper
¼ teaspoon ground cloves
½ teaspoon ground mace

Fry the onions and garlic in half the butter until soft. Trim the chicken livers of threads and gall and chop into 1-inch pieces. Add to the cooked onions with the remaining butter and fry slowly until firm but still pink inside. Remove from the heat and stir in the eggs and softened butter. Add the cognac and seasonings and rub through a sieve or blend well in an electric blender. Pot.

LAYER PÂTÉ

For forcemeat:
1 large onion, minced
1 cup finely ground veal
1 cup finely ground pork
¼ cup chopped parsley
¼ teaspoon thyme

bacon slices
ground mace

¼ teaspoon crushed bay leaf
1 envelope gelatin
½ cup brandy
salt
freshly ground black pepper

thin slices veal

Cooking time:　1¼ hours
Temperature:　350°

Put the onion, veal, and pork together into a mixing bowl. Add the herbs, gelatin dissolved in the brandy, salt, and pepper and mix well together. Line the bottom of a mold with bacon slices and cover with a layer of forcemeat. Sprinkle with mace, then repeat the layers of veal and forcemeat, sprinkled with mace, until the mold is full. The forcemeat layers should be thicker than the veal slices. Top with bacon slices, cover with aluminum foil, and stand the mold in a pan of water. Cook in a 350° oven for 1¼ hours. Allow to cool and refrigerate for at least 8 hours before turning out of the mold.
Variation: Leftover turkey and ham may be used instead of ground pork and ground and sliced veal to make a Christmas pâté.

PÂTÉ NORMAND

1 cup finely ground veal
1 cup finely ground pork
½ cup ground pig's liver
⅔ cup chopped chicken liver
⅔ cup chopped pickled pork tongue
½ cup ground pickled pork tongue
¼ cup ground bacon

⅓ cup chopped salt pork
4 cloves garlic, crushed
good dash each ground nutmeg, ground cloves, basil, and marjoram
¼ teaspoon pepper
½ teaspoon salt
1 cup dry sherry
thin slices salt pork

Cooking time: 1½ hours
Temperature: 350°

Thoroughly mix all the ingredients together except the salt pork slices. Line a mold with the salt pork slices. Fill with the mixture and press down firmly. Top with salt pork, cover with aluminum foil, place in a pan of water, and cook in a 350° oven for 1½ hours. Cool, and refrigerate for at least 8 hours before turning out.

PORK LIVER PÂTÉ

1½ lb. pork liver
1½ cups finely ground pork
⅔ cup chopped salt pork
good dash each nutmeg and oregano
¼ teaspoon crushed bay leaf

3 cloves garlic, crushed
2 tablespoons brandy
½ cup dry white wine
dash pepper
bacon slices

Cooking time: 1¼ hours
Temperature: 350°

Mince the pork liver and mix with the pork and salt pork. Add the nutmeg, oregano, bay leaf, garlic, brandy, wine, and pepper and mix thoroughly. Line a terrine with bacon slices, fill with the mixture, and press down firmly. Top with bacon slices, cover with aluminum foil, and cook in a 350° oven for 1¼ hours. Cool, and allow to set in the refrigerator for at least 8 hours before cutting.

POULTRY AND GAME

Johnnie Walker

Johnnie Walker writes a food and wine column, runs two well-known restaurants, and is a founder-member of *The Wine and Food Society of New South Wales.*

Poultry: In this selection of poultry recipes most needs and tastes are catered to. As well as classic and time-tested favorites some unusual and interesting variations are included; also some recipes for what to do with leftovers. With the great popularity nowadays for barbecuing there are also some poultry recipes that can be cooked outdoors.

The question comes up of what wine to serve with various poultry dishes. The answer to this is the wine you like to drink. There would not be so many recipes to choose from if tastes did not vary so much, so we cannot expect everyone to have exactly the same tastes in wine. If uncertain or entertaining guests whose taste you do not know, follow the general rule of serving the same wine used in the cooking of the dish, e.g., for Coq au Vin, a dry red wine is used in the preparation so serve a light to medium bodied dry red wine. In warm and humid climates, choose a rosé to go with duck. Goose, turkey, and pigeon are more often served with dry reds. But whatever wine you choose, as long as you like it and it is in harmony with the dish to be served, go ahead and enjoy it.

CHICKEN

Modern packaging methods have made poultry an everyday item on the menu, a far cry from the times when you had to order in advance or even kill and clean you own!

DRAWING A CHICKEN

If necessary, singe the bird. Make an incision down the length of the neck. Pull out the windpipe and crop. Then cut the neck off close to the body, pulling the skin to one side and leaving a good piece to fold over the back. Place the bird on its back and enlarge the vent opening. Remove the remaining organs carefully and gently through this opening. These consist of the gizzard, intestines, heart, and liver, which has the gall bladder attached to it. Do not break the gall bladder as this makes any part it touches bitter. Remove the lungs, which are the spongy masses lying between the ribs in the hollows of the backbone, and take out the kidneys. Open and clean the gizzard along with the heart, neck, and liver in cold water.

Pandora Roast Wild Duck

TRUSSING A CHICKEN

Cut off the first joint of the legs and press them down close to the sides of the chicken. Fasten with a skewer or tie with string. Secure the wings by running a skewer through the joint of one wing right through the body to the other wing; or tie close to the body with fine string; or fold wings underneath the back.

To truss a fowl for boiling, cut off the whole leg except for the thigh, the end bones of which tuck into the apron. Tie the wings with string close to the body.

JOINTING A CHICKEN

To joint a raw chicken slit the skin round the junction of leg and body and remove the legs. Cut off the wings along with a piece of breast close to the joint. Then cut the breast from the back and cut it in half lengthwise through the bone. If a large chicken, cut in half again crosswise. Trim the back and cut in half. The legs may be cut again at the joint.

CARVING A CHICKEN

The legs are removed by pressing them outward and downward and cutting them off. The wings may be removed by cutting down through the joints along with a portion of breast. The breast is then cut into several thin slices lengthwise, leaving a piece of skin attached to each slice.

A smaller bird is usually divided into 4 pieces. The two legs, and the halved breast and wings, without the back.

Poultry

Cooking time

Stewing chicken—3-8 lb.	Boil 1-2 hours depending on age.
Roasting chicken—3½-5 lb. *Capon—6-8 lb.*	Roast 20 minutes per lb. plus 20 minutes extra, in a 350-375° oven.
Broilers or spring chicken—up to 2⅓ lb.	Roast 1 hour whole or 25-35 minutes jointed, in a 350-375° oven.
Chicken pieces	Fry 10-15 minutes each side.
Pigeons	Roast 25-30 minutes in a 350-375° oven.
Ducklings—1½-2 lb.	Roast 20 minutes per lb. plus 20 minutes extra in a 350-375° oven.
Duck—3-6 lb.	Roast 20-25 minutes per lb. plus 20 minutes extra, in a 350-375° oven.
Goose—10 lb.	Roast 20-25 minutes per lb. plus 20 minutes extra, in a 350-375° oven.
Turkey—8-25 lb.	Roast 20-25 minutes per lb. plus 20 minutes extra for the smaller birds, and 12-15 minutes per lb. plus 20 minutes extra for the larger birds, in a 350-375° oven.

ROAST CHICKEN

1 3-lb. roasting chicken	½ cup butter	Cooking time: 1 hour
salt and pepper	1¼ cups chicken stock	Temperature: 350°
		Serves: 4

Wash and dry the prepared chicken; then rub with salt, pepper, and half the butter. Truss the chicken and place in a greased roasting pan with the remaining butter. Cook in a 350° oven, basting occasionally, for 1 hour, or until tender and golden brown all over. Remove the chicken and keep warm. Add the chicken stock, made from simmering the giblets in water for 30 minutes. Stir in the pan juices and bring to a boil. Strain into a sauce boat and serve with the chicken, bread sauce (see page 59), roast potatoes, and a green vegetable.

Note: The chicken may be stuffed with 2 tablespoons butter and a peeled onion or a bunch of fresh herbs.

CHINESE ROAST CHICKEN

3 cups water	3-4 slices fresh ginger	Cooking time: 45 minutes, and
1 cup soy sauce	1 scallion, chopped	25 minutes to marinate
2 tablespoons sugar	1 teaspoon salt	Temperature: 450°
½ cup dry sherry	1 roasting chicken, about 3-4 lb.	Serves: 4-6

Combine the water, soy sauce, sugar, sherry, ginger, scallion, and salt in a large saucepan and bring slowly to a boil. Place the chicken in the saucepan and boil for 15 minutes. Let the chicken stand or marinate in the mixture for a further 25 minutes, turning once. Remove the chicken and place in a roasting pan in a 450° oven for 30 minutes, until tender and browned all over. Remove and keep warm.

Strain the remaining marinade and add to the pan juices, heat, and pour over the carved chicken before serving.

SPIT ROASTED CHICKEN

1 4-lb. roasting chicken	¼ cup butter	Cooking time: 1¾ hours
salt	Mushroom Stuffing	Temperature: 375°
		Serves: 4-6

Wash, dry, and salt the chicken. Keep the giblets for the stuffing. Rub the cavity of the bird with butter, fill it with Mushroom Stuffing (see page 152), and skewer the opening. Truss the bird. Place the chicken on a rotisserie spit and roast in a 375° oven for 1¾ hours, until it is golden and crisp. Serve with roast potatoes and a green vegetable or a tossed salad.

EAST INDIES BARBECUED CHICKEN

1 2½-lb. broiler	salt	Cooking time: 30 minutes for
oil		sauce; 10-15
		minutes for
		chicken
		Serves: 4-8

For East Indies sauce:
1 onion, finely chopped
1 stalk celery, finely chopped
¼ cup oil
2 cups chicken stock or water
    and chicken bouillon cube
3 medium-sized tomatoes,
    skinned and stewed

¼ apple, peeled and finely
    chopped
3 tablespoons curry powder
½ teaspoon monosodium
    glutamate
salt and pepper

Sauté the onion and celery in the oil until soft and golden. Add the chicken stock, stewed tomatoes, apple, curry powder, monosodium glutamate, and salt and pepper to taste. Simmer for 30 minutes.

Cut the chicken into 8 pieces, brush each piece with oil, and sprinkle with salt. Let the chicken pieces stand for 30 minutes. Grill over glowing coals, basting frequently with East Indies sauce and turning the pieces from time to time, until tender. Serve the barbecued chicken with the sauce and boiled rice, accompanied by chopped fresh pineapple, fruit chutney, and chopped cashew nuts.
Note: The chicken may be broiled under a hot broiler.

CHICKEN AND ORANGE KEBABS

3 oranges	juice of 1 large orange	Cooking time: 10-15 minutes
3-6 slices bacon	¼ cup butter	Serves: 6
1 lb. cooked chicken		
24 small mushroom caps,		

Peel the oranges, remove the pith, and cut into segments. Fry the bacon gently and cut into 1-inch squares. Remove skin and membrane from the chicken and cut the flesh into 1-inch cubes. Thread 6 skewers alternately with orange segments, chicken, cooked mushroom caps and bacon. Brush with a mixture of orange juice and melted butter and grill over hot coals, turning once or twice until lightly browned on all sides. Serve immediately.
Note: The kebabs may be cooked under a broiler.

FRIED MINT CHICKEN

4 cloves garlic, finely chopped	1 teaspoon salt	Cooking time: 30 minutes
½ cup butter	¼ teaspoon pepper	Serves: 4-6
2 2½-lb. broilers	½ cup fresh mint leaves	
1 cup all-purpose flour		

Fry the garlic in the butter until golden; then remove from the pan. Quarter the chickens and dip into seasoned flour. Fry the pieces in the garlic butter until tender. Remove from the heat and add the mint leaves, cover the pan, and let the mixture stand for 3 minutes. Arrange the chicken on a serving platter and serve hot.

Chicken Grand'mère

CHICKEN MARENGO

1 3-lb. frying chicken
salt and pepper
$\frac{1}{4}$ cup oil
2 tablespoons butter
12 mushroom caps
1 clove garlic, crushed

1 teaspoon all-purpose flour
2 large ripe tomatoes, skinned,
    seeded and chopped
$\frac{1}{2}$ cup dry white wine
2 tablespoons tomato paste

Cooking time: 45 minutes
Serves: 4

Cut the chicken into 4 portions. Sprinkle with salt and pepper. Sauté the chicken pieces in a large skillet in the oil and butter until they are golden brown on all sides and almost cooked through. Remove the chicken and keep warm. In a small saucepan simmer the mushroom caps in 1 cup salted water for 5 minutes; drain and reserve the liquid. Add the garlic and flour to the juices left in the skillet and stir over low heat for 1 minute. Add the tomatoes and simmer for a few minutes, then add the wine and $\frac{1}{2}$ cup of the mushroom liquor. Bring to a boil, reduce the heat, and simmer, uncovered, for 15 minutes. Add the tomato paste and salt and pepper to taste. Return the cooked chicken pieces to the pan, add the mushrooms, and simmer all together for 5 minutes. Serve with boiled rice or noodles.

CHICKEN BREASTS WITH BANANA

3 chicken breasts
1$\frac{1}{4}$ cups mashed banana
all-purpose flour

1 egg
1 cup fine fresh bread crumbs
1 cup butter

Cooking time: 15-20 minutes
Temperature: 375°
Serves: 6

Skin the chicken breasts, cut in half, and remove the bones, including the wing tips, but leaving the main wing bones. Put the 6 pieces of prepared breast between 2 sheets of wax paper and beat them thin with the flat side of a cleaver. Put a sixth of the mashed banana on each piece and fold the chicken over the filling to form 6 cutlets of even shape. Dip the cutlets in flour, then in beaten egg, and finally roll them in bread crumbs. Melt the butter in a skillet and fry the chicken until it is golden on the underside. Turn the cutlets over and put them browned side upward in a baking dish with the butter from the skillet. Bake the chicken in a 375° oven for 10 minutes, or until tender.

CHICKEN KIEV MACADAMIA

6 large chicken breasts
salt and pepper
$\frac{3}{4}$ cup chilled butter
3 cloves garlic, halved
1 tablespoon chopped parsley

1 cup all-purpose flour
2 eggs
ground macadamia nuts, cashew
    nuts or fine dry bread crumbs
oil for frying

Cooking time: 15-17 minutes
Serves: 6

Bone the chicken breasts and beat flat with a cleaver. Sprinkle on all sides with salt and pepper and lay them skin side down. In the center of each breast put 2 tablespoons butter, $\frac{1}{2}$ clove garlic, crushed, and $\frac{1}{2}$ teaspoon chopped parsley. Fold the two shorter ends of each breast in toward the center, then overlap the two longer ends to make a tight package. Tie each package securely with string. Roll the breasts in flour seasoned with salt and pepper, dip in beaten egg, and finally roll in ground nuts. If using bread crumbs, dip in beaten egg and bread crumbs twice. Press the nuts or crumbs on firmly and chill the breats for at least 30 minutes, preferably longer. Fry the breasts in deep hot oil (375°) for 5 minutes. Lift them out and gently remove the string. Return the breats to the oil for 10 to 12 minutes, or until cooked. Remove and drain on paper towels. Serve immediately.

CHICKEN SAUTÉ

This recipe is for the basic Chicken Sauté and any number of variations may be made.

1 frying chicken, 3½-4 lb. all-purpose flour 4-6 tablespoons butter salt and pepper	1 cup dry white wine chopped parsley or chives for garnish	Cooking time: 25 minutes Serves: 4

Cut the chicken into 4 joints and dip in flour. Unfloured chicken is more delicate but the flour gives a browner color. Brown the chicken pieces in butter in a large, heavy, deep skillet, turning each piece to color evenly. When browned add salt and pepper and the wine. Lower the heat, cover, and continue cooking until the chicken is tender. Additional flavors may be added during the cooking and the pieces of chicken should be turned two or three times to absorb the added flavors. When the chicken is cooked remove and keep warm. Add a little additional wine if necessary and let the pan juices cook over increased heat for a few minutes. Pour over the chicken and garnish with chopped parsley or chives.

VARIATIONS ON CHICKEN SAUTÉ

Chicken Sauté Paprika: Sauté the chicken as in the above recipe and when the pieces are browned add 2 tablespoons finely chopped onion to the skillet and cook over low heat for 3 to 4 minutes. Season to taste with salt and pepper and add ½ teaspoon thyme and 1 cup dry white wine. Simmer until the chicken is tender. Add a further ½ cup dry white wine and 1 tablespoon paprika pepper and cook slowly for a few minutes. Remove the chicken and reduce the pan juices over high heat. Stir in 1 cup cream. Thicken the sauce with Beurre Manié (see page 59). Adjust the seasoning if necessary. Pour the sauce over the chicken and garnish with a sprinkling of paprika pepper and finely chopped parsley.

Chicken Sauté Mexican: Sauté the chicken. When nearly browned add 2 tablespoons finely chopped onion and cook slowly until the onion and chicken are browned. Season to taste with salt and pepper. Add 1 finely chopped clove garlic and 1 peeled, finely chopped hot chili pepper. Pour over this 1 cup dry white wine and simmer gently until the chicken is tender. Arrange the chicken on a serving platter and pour the pan juices over. Garnish with chopped toasted almonds.

MANGO CHICKEN

1 roasting chicken, about 3½-4 lb. 6 tablespoons butter 2 large onions, thinly sliced 6 slices fresh or canned mango grated nutmeg 3 strips lemon rind	1¼ cups chicken stock salt and pepper juice of 1 lemon ½ cup cream paprika pepper	Cooking time: 1 hour Temperature: 350° Serves: 4

Joint the chicken a few hours before cooking so that the back and trimmings can be made into stock (see page 34). Fry the chicken in half the butter until golden brown. Melt the remaining butter in a saucepan or flameproof casserole and sauté the onion until golden. Add the mango, increase the heat, and cook for 3 to 5 minutes. Add the fried chicken, a little grated nutmeg, lemon rind, chicken stock, and salt and pepper to taste. Cover and cooked in a 350° oven for 1 hour, or until the chicken is tender. Remove the chicken and keep warm. Remove the lemon rind. Add the lemon juice and season to taste. Stir in the cream and allow to come to a gentle simmer. Pour the sauce over the chicken, sprinkle with paprika pepper, and serve with Rice Pilaff (see page 203).

Variation: 2 or 3 peeled, sliced peaches may be used instead of the mango.

ORANGE RICE WITH CHICKEN BREASTS

6 tablespoons butter
2 onions, chopped
2½ cups long-grain rice
2 cups unsweetened orange
    juice, fresh or canned
2 cups water
2 teaspoons grated orange rind
2½ teaspoons salt

1 teaspoon fresh thyme or a dash
    dried thyme
¼ cup butter
½ cup pine nuts or slivered
    almonds
3 small chicken breasts, halved
salt
pepper

Cooking time: 20-25 minutes
Serves: 6

Heat the butter in a saucepan and sauté the onions until soft and golden but not browned. Add the rice and fry, stirring constantly, for 5 minutes, or until the rice is light golden. Add the orange juice, water, orange rind, salt, and thyme. Bring to a boil, stir well, and reduce the heat to a simmer. Cover tightly and simmer for 20 minutes. Turn off the heat and leave the pan covered until serving time.

While the rice is cooking, heat ¼ cup butter in a skillet and lightly fry the pine nuts or almonds until golden. Remove from the skillet. In the same butter, sauté the chicken breasts, seasoned with salt and pepper, until golden brown on all sides and cooked through, about 10 to 15 minutes.

Just before serving, fluff up the rice with a fork. Using a perforated spoon, pile the rice on a heated serving dish. Arrange the chicken breasts on the rice, sprinkle the nuts over, and serve hot.

CHICKEN GRAND' MÈRE

1 4-lb. roasting chicken
Sausage Stuffing
1 slice bacon, diced

½ cup butter
10 small white onions
8 oz. potatoes, peeled and diced

Cooking time: 50 minutes
Temperature: 325°
Serves: 4-6

Fill the chicken with Sausage Stuffing (see page 152). Truss the bird and place it in a large ovenproof earthenware casserole. Add the bacon, butter, and onions. Cover the casserole and cook the chicken in a 325° oven for 30 minutes. Add the potatoes and cook, covered, for 20 minutes longer, or until the chicken is tender. Serve hot from the casserole.

CHICKEN FLORENTINE

1 1½-lb. stewing chicken
1 onion
bouquet garni
salt
½ cup plus 1 tablespoon butter
2 cups mushrooms, chopped
2 green sweet peppers, seeded
    and chopped

1 red sweet pepper, seeded and
    chopped
¼ cup dry sherry
1¼ cups Béchamel Sauce
2 lb. spinach
2 cloves garlic
Parmesan cheese

Cooking time: 1¼ hours
Serves: 4

Prepare the chicken and place in a large saucepan with cold water to cover. Add the onion, bouquet garni, and 1 teaspoon salt, bring to a boil, reduce the heat, and simmer for 1 hour, or until the chicken is tender. Remove the chicken from the stock, remove the meat from the bone, and cut the flesh into 1-inch cubes. Strain the stock and reserve.

In a saucepan melt ½ cup butter and sauté the mushrooms and sweet peppers until tender. Add the cubes of chcicken and the sherry and cook until the sherry has evaporated. Combine with the Béchamel Sauce (see page 50) and keep warm.

Wash the spinach and cook in the reserved chicken stock with the garlic until the spinach is just tender. Drain well and chop finely. Arrange the spinach in the base of a flameproof dish, cover with the chicken mixture, and sprinkle with Parmesan cheese. Dot with the remaining 1 tablespoon butter and place under a hot broiler to brown the sauce, just before serving.
Note: Simple White Sauce (see page 50) may be used instead of Béchamel Sauce.

DUCK À L'ORANGE

Allow 20 minutes per lb. for cooking and 20 minutes extra.

1 duck, 5-6 lb.
salt and pepper
dry white wine
1 tablespoon sugar
1 tablespoon vinegar
1 cup chicken stock or water
  and chicken bouillon cube

juice of 4 oranges
juice of 1 small lemon
$\frac{1}{4}$ cup brandy
orange rind cut into julienne
  strips
orange segments
watercress

Cooking time: 2 hours
Temperature: 400°
  reducing to 350°
Serves: 4

Wipe the duck with a damp cloth and truss. Rub all over with salt and pepper and roast in a 400° oven for 15 minutes. Reduce the temperature to 350° and continue to roast until cooked. Baste every 20 minutes with dry white wine.

In a small pan melt the sugar and vinegar together until it caramelizes. Remove the roasted duck from the oven and keep warm. Remove the excess fat from the roasting pan and add the chicken stock, scraping any

sediment in well. Stir in the orange and lemon juice and the brandy. Finally add the caramelized sugar and vinegar and cook the sauce slowly for 10 minutes. Cut the duck into 4 portions—2 legs, and half the breast with each wing. Arrange the duck on a large heated platter, pour over the sauce, and sprinkle with julienne strips of orange rind. Garnish with orange segments and sprigs of watercress.

DUCK WITH SOUR CHERRIES

(DUCK MONTMORENCY)

1 6-lb. duck
$\frac{1}{2}$ teaspoon celery salt
salt
freshly cracked pepper
$\frac{1}{2}$ cup water
$\frac{1}{2}$ cup butter

$1\frac{1}{2}$ cups chicken stock or water
  and chicken bouillon cube
$\frac{1}{2}$ cup port
$\frac{1}{2}$ cup cherry brandy
$\frac{1}{4}$ cup beurre manié
1 (1 lb. 12 oz.) can sour cherries

Cooking time: 2 hours
Temperature: 400°
  reducing to 350°
Serves: 4-6

Wipe the duck inside and out with a damp cloth. Sprinkle the cavity with celery salt and salt and freshly cracked pepper to taste. Place the duck in a roasting pan, breast side up, and add water to prevent scorching. Cover the breast and legs with a piece of cheesecloth rubbed with butter. Roast the duck in a 400° oven for 30 minutes. Reduce the temperature to 350° and continue to cook the duck until it is tender. Remove the duck to a heated platter. Pour off all the fat from the roasting pan

leaving only the brown sediment, and deglaze the pan with the chicken stock. Add the port and cherry brandy. Blend in the Beurre Manié (see page 59). Put the roasting pan over high heat and bring the sauce to a boil. Cook the sauce, stirring constantly, until it is slightly thick. Drain the cherries, add to the sauce, and heat through. Carve the duck and pour half the sauce over it. Serve the remaining sauce separately in a sauce boat.

MINCED DUCK WITH MADEIRA

2 cups cooked duck
$\frac{1}{2}$ cup Madeira
$\frac{1}{4}$ cup butter
2 tablespoons chopped parsley

juice of $\frac{1}{2}$ lemon
pinch cayenne pepper
salt and pepper

Cooking time: 10 minutes
Serves: 2

Chop the duck finely. If available, mash the cooked liver of the duck and combine it in a chafing dish or skillet with the Madeira, butter, parsley, lemon juice, and cayenne pepper. Season to taste with salt and pepper.

Heat the mixture, blending well, and add the chopped duck. Cook, stirring constantly, just until the duck is heated through. Serve at once on hot buttered toast.

ROAST GOOSE

Allow 20 minutes per lb. for cooking and 20 minutes extra.

1 goose, 8-9 lb.	2 tablespoons butter	Cooking time: 2½-3 hours
Fruit Stuffing	2½ cups stock made from giblets	Temperature: 400°
2 heads red cabbage, about 4 lb.	¼ cup arrowroot or cornstarch	reducing to 350°
1 lb. chestnuts, peeled		

Remove the feet and pinions from the goose and truss neatly to keep the legs and wings near the body. Stuff the goose with prepared Fruit Stuffing (see page 152). Place the goose in a roasting pan and roast in a 400° oven for 30 minutes. Reduce the temperature to 350° and continue to cook for 2 to 2½ hours until tender. Cut the cabbage into small segments, blanch, and braise with the chestnuts in butter and a little stock. When the goose is cooked remove to a serving platter and keep warm. Deglaze the pan with the remaining stock, skim off the fat, and add the arrowroot, blended to a smooth paste with a little cold water. Bring to a boil and strain into a sauce boat. Carve the goose and serve with the cabbage, chestnuts, and gravy.

ROAST TURKEY

Allow 20 minutes per lb. for cooking and 20 minutes extra. The head of a turkey is not usually cut off in trussing, but twisted around one of the wings. However, if purchased pre-packaged the head is usually removed. Truss as for chicken (see page 140).

1 turkey, 10-15 lb.	butter	Cooking time: 4-5 hours
salt	¼ cup all-purpose flour	Temperature: 400°
prepared stuffing	pepper	reducing to 350°
		Serves: 8-12
For stock:		
neck, gizzard, liver, and heart of bird	6 peppercorns	
1 onion, stuck with 10 cloves	3¾ cups water	
1 bay leaf	1 clove garlic (optional)	
½ teaspoon salt	2 stalks celery (optional)	

Wash and dry the turkey and rub the inside well with salt. Fill the body and neck cavity loosely with the prepared stuffing (see page 153). Fold the skin over the neck opening. Truss to secure the legs and wings close to the body. Place the turkey, breast side up, on a rack in a large roasting pan and spread thickly with softened butter. Cover loosely with aluminum foil and roast in a 400° oven for 30 minutes. Reduce the temperature to 350° and continue to roast until tender. Insert a fork in the meatiest part of the leg—if cooked the juices should not be pink. Transfer the turkey to a heated serving platter and keep warm.

Drain off all but ¼ cup fat from the roasting pan. Stir in the flour and cook the roux over a low heat for 1 minute. Gradually add 3 to 3¾ cups stock, stir in the sediment, and bring to a boil, stirring constantly. Simmer for 2 to 3 minutes. Add the mashed cooked turkey liver if available and salt and pepper to taste. Serve with the turkey.

To make the stock: Place all the ingredients in a saucepan with cold water, bring to a boil, and simmer, covered, for 1 hour, or until the liquid is reduced by half. Skim and strain and use as required for the stuffing and gravy.

CARVING A TURKEY

This can be done in the traditional way. Place a fork an inch or two below the breastbone and, slipping the knife under the far wing, make an upward cut as far as you can; then a downward cut through the joint that holds the turkey wing to the body of the turkey; then a straight cut near the neck. The wing should then drop off.

In cutting the leg, make a straight cut through the joint that holds it to the turkey, first cutting away all the strings. Cut an inch or two above the parson's nose, going as far as possible. Now slip the knife behind the joint again. The leg should now fall. Carve the breast meat obliquely.

It is recommended, however, that the meat should be carved straight from the turkey. Carve a slice of the dark leg meat, than a slice across the breast. This will give you the white meat and the stuffing in one slice. Proceed this way and alternate the slices of turkey on the plate, first dark meat and then white meat.

TURKEY WITH HAM AND OLIVES

1 8-lb. turkey
salt and pepper
8 oz. Parma ham, chopped
24 ripe olives
3 cloves garlic, sliced
6 peppercorns, crushed
2 tablespoons ground walnuts

$\frac{1}{2}$ teaspoon ground cloves
$\frac{1}{2}$ teaspoon cinnamon
2 onions, quartered
2 oranges, sliced
3 sprigs parsley
1 bay leaf
$\frac{3}{4}$ cup dry sherry

Cooking time: 2$\frac{1}{2}$ hours
Temperature: 300°
Serves: 6-8

Wash and dry the turkey and rub the body cavity with salt and pepper. Combine the ham with the olives, garlic, and peppercorns and place inside the bird. Skewer and truss the bird and rub the skin with a mixture of ground walnuts, ground cloves, and cinnamon. Wrap the turkey in cheesecloth and tie securely, or wrap securely in greased aluminum foil, and cook in simmering water to cover for approximately 1$\frac{1}{2}$ hours, depending on the age of the bird, until it is almost tender. Remove the wrapping and place the turkey in a baking dish. Add the onions, oranges, parsley sprigs, bay leaf and dry sherry. Cover the dish and cook the bird in a 300° oven for approximately 1 hour, or until it is tender. Remove the turkey, cut into serving pieces, and arrange on a heated serving platter. Strain the sauce in the baking dish and pour it over the bird before serving.

TURKEY FILLETS IN SOUR CREAM

fillets from a 12-lb. turkey
seasoned fine dry bread crumbs
2 eggs
$\frac{1}{4}$ cup water
pinch of salt
butter for frying
2 tablespoons finely chopped
  onion

2 tablespoons finely chopped
  parsley
$\frac{1}{4}$ cup water
1$\frac{1}{4}$ cups sour cream
2 tablespoons all-purpose flour

Cooking time: 1$\frac{1}{4}$-1$\frac{1}{2}$ hours
Temperature: 350°
    reducing to 250°
Serves: 8

Remove the breast meat from a 12-lb. turkey and cut each fillet into 8 equal pieces. Dip the pieces in seasoned fine dry bread crumbs, then in the eggs beaten with $\frac{1}{4}$ cup water and salt, and finally dip again in the crumbs. Brown the fillets on both sides in hot butter and transfer them to a baking dish. Sprinkle the turkey with onion and parsley and add $\frac{1}{4}$ cup water. Pour the sour cream over the fillets, cover the dish, and bake in a 350° oven for 15 minutes. Reduce the temperature to 250° and bake the fillets for 45 minutes, or until they are tender. Remove the cover and increase the heat for the last few minutes of cooking time to crispen. Transfer the turkey to a heated platter. Stir the flour into the sauce in the dish and cook for a few minutes. Strain over the turkey and serve hot.

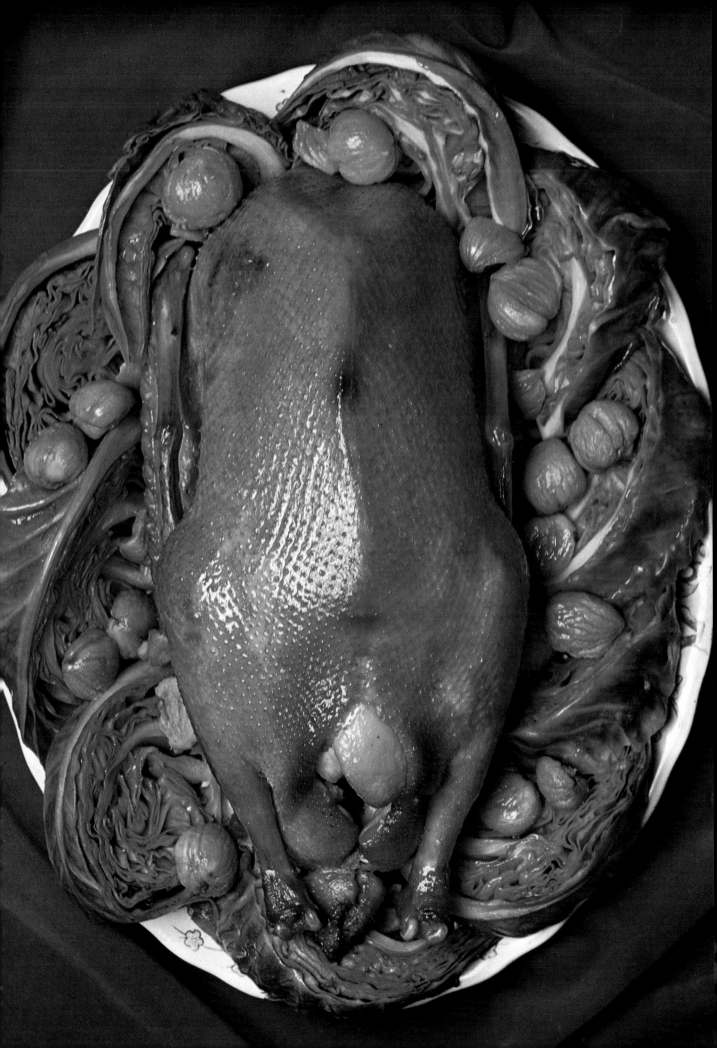

FRUIT STUFFING

For Goose

2½ lb. cooking apples
¼ cup butter

2 tablespoons seedless white
  raisins
2 tablespoons currants

Peel, quarter, and core the apples. Cook for 5 minutes in the butter without allowing the apples to break up. Plump the dried fruits in boiling water for 2 minutes. Drain and dry. Mix the apples and fruit together and use as required.

MUSHROOM STUFFING

For Chicken

2 cups mushrooms, finely
  chopped
6 scallions, finely chopped
⅓ cup chopped parsley
3 slices bacon, diced
chicken giblets, chopped

½ cup chicken stock or water and
  chicken bouillon cube
½ cup dry white wine
salt and pepper
2 egg yolks

Combine the mushrooms, scallions, parsley, and bacon with the chicken giblets. Combine the chicken stock and white wine and add to the mushroom mixture; simmer over low heat until all the moisture is absorbed. Add salt and pepper to taste and bind the stuffing with egg yolks.

SAUSAGE STUFFING

For Chicken

¼ cup butter
¼ cup chopped onion
½ cup sausage meat
1 chicken liver, chopped
7 tablespoons fresh white bread
  crumbs

1 teaspoon finely chopped
  parsley
¼ teaspoon each dried rosemary
  and thyme
salt

Melt the butter in a large skillet and sauté the onion until it is soft and transparent. Stir in the sausage meat, chicken liver, bread crumbs, parsley, rosemary and thyme. Add salt to taste. Cook the mixture, stirring, for 3 minutes.

SAGE AND ONION STUFFING

For Pork and Goose

4-6 onions
¼ cup chopped fresh sage
1 egg, beaten
2 cups fresh white bread crumbs

2 tablespoons butter or beef
  suet, chopped
salt and pepper

Peel the onions and boil in water for 10 minutes. Drain, cool and chop. Mix with the remaining ingredients and season to taste. Use as required to stuff pork or goose.

BALKAN STUFFING

For Turkey

1 onion, finely chopped
¾ cup butter
½ cup blanched slivered almonds
1 cup long-grain rice
stock from the bird

½ cup currants
cooked heart and liver of the bird
extra butter
1 teaspoon chopped dill
1⅓ teaspoon tomato paste

Sauté the onion in the butter until golden. Add the blanched slivered almonds and cook for 3 minutes. Add the rice and cook for a further 5 minutes. Add sufficient stock (see page 149) to cover, add the currants, and simmer, covered, until all the liquid is absorbed. Chop the heart and liver of the bird finely and sauté in butter for 2 to 3 minutes, add the dill and tomato paste, and stir into the rice mixture. Use the stuffing as required.
Note: Sufficient for a 10-lb. turkey.

CHESTNUT AND RICE STUFFING

For Turkey

2⅓ cups long-grain rice
salt
4 onions, chopped
½ cup butter
cooked heart and liver of the bird
½ cup cream
½ cup dry sherry

2 teaspoons fresh tarragon
2 teaspoons fresh thyme
1 teaspoon allspice
juice of 1 lemon
1 lb. raw chestnuts
pepper

Boil the rice in 6¼ cups boiling salted water for 15 minutes and drain well in a colander. Rinse the rice thoroughly under cold running water and place the colander over a pan of simmering water to steam the rice dry. Sauté the onions in butter until golden. Using 2 forks, toss the onions with the rice in a bowl. In the same way, mix in the heart and liver of the bird, previously chopped, also the cream, sherry, tarragon, thyme, allspice, and lemon juice.

Slit the chestnut shells and boil gently in boiling water for 5 minutes; drain. While the nuts are still hot, remove and discard the shells and skins. Place the nuts in boiling water or stock to cover and simmer over low heat for 20 to 30 minutes, or until tender. Drain the nuts, crumble coarsely, and stir into the rice mixture. Season with salt and pepper to taste and chill if possible before use.
Note: Sufficient for a 12 to 15 lb. turkey.

CHEF PAUL'S TURKEY STUFFING

The following quantities are for a 10-lb. bird. Increase or decrease quantities accordingly.

4 oz. veal, finely ground
4 oz. pork, finely ground
4 oz. turkey or chicken liver,
    finely chopped
1 cup all-purpose flour

4 eggs
¼ cup brandy or dry sherry
salt and pepper
mixed herbs to taste, thyme,
    marjoram, sage, bay leaf, etc.

Mix all the ingredients together thoroughly with the desired herbs. Add more flour or bread crumbs if the stuffing is too moist.

Game

A meal featuring some type of game is an out-of-the-ordinary treat to most people, and the stronger flavors of the meat make a pleasant change.

A point to bear in mind when cooking game is that we rarely know the age of the meat we are going to cook. Old, tough game can be tenderized in some cases by marinating. However, cooking times of most game can vary and care needs to be taken in checking regularly during the cooking.

Generally speaking red wines are served with game. However, there are always exceptions — e.g., Rabbit with Tarragon. Dry white wine is an ingredient in this dish and the delicate tarragon flavor calls for something light to drink with it. This is a good example of using the same wine to drink as that used in the recipe. Here again, however, let your own personal taste be the guide.

WILD DUCK

4 wild ducks
dry red wine
bouquet garni
oil
salt and pepper

16 small white onions
6 tablespoons butter
½ cup dry white wine
2 cups mushrooms, sliced

Cooking time: 1-1½ hours
Serves: 4

The wild ducks should be well cleaned and the end feathers singed over a flame. Place in an earthenware or stainless steel bowl and add a bouquet garni. Cover with dry red wine and leave in a cool place for at least 1 day, preferably 2 to 3 days.

When ready to cook, drain the ducks well. Sauté the ducks in hot oil in a large flameproof casserole, turning until seared all over. Pour over the strained marinade and allow to come gently to a boil. Season to taste. Lower the heat, cover, and simmer gently until the ducks

are cooked. The time depends on the age and size of the ducks, about 1 to 1½ hours.

Prepare the small white onions and sauté in butter, turning to soften all over. Do not allow to color. Pour over the dry white wine and gently poach until tender. Do not overcook. Sauté the mushrooms in butter for 5 minutes. Add the onions and mushrooms to the ducks just before serving. If necessary thicken the sauce with a little arrowroot blended with cold water. Serve with small boiled potatoes tossed in butter.

RABBIT WITH PRUNES AND PINE NUTS

2 rabbits, 1½-2 lb. each
½ cup olive oil
2 onions, chopped
4 tomatoes, skinned and chopped
1 bay leaf
2 cloves garlic, crushed

30 blanched, toasted almonds
sprigs of parsley
½ cup water
salt
⅓ cup pine nuts
20 prunes

Cooking time: 1-1¼ hours
Serves: 4-6

Wash and dry the rabbits and cut into serving pieces. Heat the oil in a flameproof casserole or large heavy saucepan. Fry the onions slowly until golden, add the tomatoes and bay leaf, and continue frying for 5 minutes. When the mixture has thickened add the rabbit and simmer, covered, for 30 to 45 minutes.

Crush the garlic, almonds, and parsley with a pestle and mortar and mix in the water; or blend in an electric blender. Add the ground mixture to the rabbit, add salt

to taste, and continue cooking for 30 minutes or until tender. Simmer the pine nuts and prunes in water in separate saucepans. The pine nuts will require 10 to 15 minutes. The cooking time of prunes varies according to size. Drain and add the pine nuts and prunes to the rabbit just before serving.

Note: If added earlier, the pine nuts will not remain white and the prunes will over-sweeten the sauce.

RABBIT WITH TARRAGON

1 young rabbit
seasoned flour
½ cup butter
¾ cup dry white wine

¼ cup fresh tarragon or
1 teaspoon dried tarragon
¼ cup dry white wine

Cooking time: 50 minutes
Temperature: 400°
Serves: 4-6

Skin and clean the rabbit, reserving the liver. Cut into serving pieces and sprinkle lightly with a little seasoned flour. Melt the butter in a large skillet and brown the pieces of rabbit quickly on all sides, being careful not to let the butter burn. Lower the heat, add ¾ cup wine, and cover the pan. Simmer the rabbit gently for about 45 minutes, or until it is tender.

Soak the fresh tarragon leaves or dried tarragon in ¼ cup wine for 30 minutes. Add the flavored wine to the skillet, raise the heat, and turn the pieces of rabbit. Cook for 5 minutes. Remove the rabbit to a heated platter. Pour the sauce over the rabbit. The liver may be sautéed in butter for 5 minutes and added to the sauce sauce just before serving.

JUGGED HARE

1 hare
¼ cup cognac
¼ cup olive oil
salt and pepper
1 onion, thinly sliced
dry red wine
1 cup butter

8 oz. bacon
20 small white onions
¼ cup all-purpose flour
bouquet garni
20 cooked mushrooms
croûtons

Cooking time: 1 hour
Serves: 4-6

If possible, obtain a fresh hare and save the blood and the liver. Cut the hare into serving pieces and place in a bowl with the cognac, oil, a little salt and pepper, and the onion. Cover with dry red wine. Allow to stand in a cool place for several hours, preferably overnight.

Cut the bacon into squares and cook in the butter in a large heavy saucepan. Drain the bacon as soon as it browns and put to one side. Sauté the onions in the butter-bacon drippings mixture, sprinkle with flour, stir, and cook until lightly browned. Drain the hare, add to the onions and fat, and brown well. Add sufficient wine marinade to cover. Add the bouquet garni, cover the pan, and allow to cook gently over low to moderate heat for 40 to 45 minutes. Add the mushrooms and simmer for a further 5 minutes. Remove the hare to a deep warm serving dish. Spoon the mushrooms, reserved bacon, and onions around the hare. Stir the reserved blood and liver into the sauce and cook for 2 to 3 minutes. Strain the sauce over the hare and vegetables. Serve garnished with croûtons.

HARE WITH SOUR CREAM SAUCE

1 saddle of hare larded with
   strips of fat back
1 teaspoon salt
1 teaspoon paprika pepper
flour
½ cup butter
2 cups sour cream
½ cup beef stock or water and

beef bouillon cube
¼ cup vinegar
1 bay leaf
½ teaspoon dried thyme
juice of ½ lemon
2 tablespoons capers
2 tablespoons Beurre Manié

Cooking time: 1-2 hours
Temperature: 350°
Serves: 6

Rub the larded saddle of hare with salt and paprika pepper and sprinkle it generously with flour. Brown on all sides in heated butter in a roasting pan. Pour over the hot sour cream, beef stock, and vinegar. Add the bay leaf and thyme. Roast in a 350° oven for approximately 1 hour, depending on the age of the hare. Baste every 15 minutes. Remove the hare and keep warm. Strain the pan juices and add the lemon juice and capers. Stir in 2 tablespoons Beurre Manié (see page 59). Bring the mixture to a boil and serve separately with the roast hare.

ROAST PARTRIDGE

4 partridges
½ cup butter
4 large croûtes
½ teaspoon cornstarch
½ cup chicken stock or water
   and chicken bouillon cube
For stuffing:

partridge livers, chopped
2 slices bacon, chopped
⅔ cup cooked ham, chopped
1 cup mushrooms, chopped
12 juniper berries
salt and pepper

Cooking time: 50 minutes
Temperature: 350°
Serves: 4

To make the stuffing: Combine the chopped livers of the birds, bacon, ham, mushrooms, and juniper berries and season with salt and pepper.

Prepare the partridges and place the stuffing in the cavities. Secure the openings and place the birds in a roasting pan. Spread with the butter and roast for 50 minutes in a 350° oven, basting occasionally with the pan juices. Place the partridges on croûtes of fried bread on a serving platter and keep warm. Add the cornstarch to the pan juices and stir in the stock. Blend well and simmer for 2 to 3 minutes. Pour a little over each partridge before serving.

ROAST PHEASANT ESPAGNOLE

2 2-lb. pheasants
1½ cups port
salt
¼ cup butter
¼ cup olive oil
3 scallions, finely chopped
2 oz. pâté de foie gras

¼ cup cognac
¼ cup dry sherry
2 teaspoons salt
pinch black pepper
4 chicken livers and 2 pheasant
  livers, finely chopped

Cooking time: 30 minutes
Temperature: 425°

Marinate the cleaned pheasants overnight in the port. Drain the pheasants and reserve the marinade. Place the pheasants in a shallow roasting pan and sprinkle with salt. Brush with half the melted butter. Roast the pheasants in a 425° oven for 15 minutes. Remove the birds from the roasting pan. Remove the breast meat and cut into ½-inch wide strips. Melt the remaining butter in a skillet, add the onions, and cook for 1 minute. Add the pâté de foie gras, cognac and sherry. Ignite. Let the flames die down; then add the wine marinade, salt, pepper and pheasant meat. Simmer for 5 minutes or until the meat is cooked. Remove the pheasant meat to a serving platter and keep warm. Remove the pan from the heat and allow to cool slightly for a minute or two. Stir in the chopped chicken and pheasant livers, reheat for 5 minutes, adjust the seasoning if necessary, and pour the sauce over the pheasant.

Roast Goose

More game

Tui Flower

The cooking of game follows the rules of common sense as applied to cooking any flesh. Young meats may be cooked quickly by roasting or grilling, but older ones need slow, moist cooking. It is therefore important to look for signs of age in birds and animals and when these are recognized the meat should be cooked accordingly. Badly damaged game should not be used. Any storage of game should keep it in good condition before use. Rubbing over with vinegar or soaking in a weak solution of vinegar helps to counter odors. The hanging of game is a matter of personal preference. Few people like game hung until almost high; however, short periods of hanging improve tenderness of flesh and modify the flavor. Game birds are hung before plucking. Most game has little fat on it and what is there is best trimmed off, since it is in the fat that strong flavors are concentrated. Many game birds as well as venison and hare improve with marinating, a process which lessens strong flavors in the flesh and tenderizes older, tougher meat.

The richness of game needs a counter flavor in the accompaniments served with it, and the best ones are those with a sharp tangy taste. Tart fruit jellies or sauces are very popular, spiced fruits and fried apples are also good. Fresh crisp salads also make pleasing contrasts.

PANDORA ROAST WILD DUCK

2 wild ducks	2 slices bacon	Cooking time: 40 minutes
1 apple	1 tablespoon all-purpose flour	Temperature: 400°
1 onion	1 cup giblet stock	Serves: 4-6
salt and pepper		

Dress and truss the ducks, placing a peeled onion in the cavity of one and a peeled apple in the cavity of the other. Rub the surface of each bird lightly with salt and pepper. Place the bacon over the breast of each bird. Place in a 400° oven and roast for 30 minutes. Remove the bacon and brown for 5 minutes, then turn and brown the backs for a few minutes. Lift the birds onto a serving platter and keep warm.

Stir the flour into the pan drippings and heat on top of the cooker. When the mixture froths, gradually add the giblet stock and stir to form a gravy. Bring to a boil, strain, and serve with the carved ducks, accompanied by Bread Sauce (see page 59).

Note: If duck is preferred well done, roast for a longer time at a lower temperature.

To make giblet stock: Simmer the giblets in water with 1 teaspoon salt, 3 peppercorns, and 1 bay leaf, for about an hour, then strain off the liquid and keep until wanted.

ROAST WILD BOAR

Allow 35 minutes per lb. for cooking and 35 minutes extra.

leg or loin of young wild boar	2 apples	Temperature: 350°
oil	2 tablespoons all-purpose flour	
brown sugar	1½ cups vegetable stock	
salt and pepper		

Wild boar is usually skinned while hunting! Wipe the meat well and score through the surface fat. Pour a little oil over the base of the roasting pan and place the joint of pork in it. Brush all over with more oil. Sprinkle with brown sugar, salt, and pepper. Roast in a 350° oven until cooked. Baste frequently with oil during the cooking, using additional oil if the pork is very lean. Thirty to 40 minutes before serving, place the unpeeled apple rings in the roasting pan and turn over. Allow these to brown and turn to the other side. Lift the cooked pork onto a warm serving plate and keep warm. Arrange the apple rings around the pork. Pour off the excess fat. Stir the flour into the pan drippings and cook quickly until frothy. Add 1½ cups vegetable stock and stir to make a gravy. Bring to a boil, strain into a sauce boat, and serve with the pork.

MARINATED ROAST VENISON

Allow 30 minutes per lb. for cooking and 30 minutes extra.

haunch or saddle of venison
2 tablespoons sugar
½ teaspoon ginger
bacon slices to cover
2 tablespoons all-purpose flour
2 tablespoons red currant jelly
For marinade:
2 cups red wine

½ cup oil
½ cup wine vinegar
1 teaspoon salt
1 bay leaf
1 clove garlic, crushed
2 juniper berries
1 onion, sliced

Temperature: 350°

Prepare the marinade by mixing all the ingredients together. Trim and wipe the venison and place in a large bowl. Pour the marinade over the meat and let stand for 24 hours. Turn several times to keep the meat under the liquid during this time. Lift out and pat dry when ready to cook.

Place the venison in a roasting pan and rub over with the sugar and ginger mixed together. Criss-cross the bacon over the top of the meat. Pour ½ cup strained marinade around the meat. Roast in a 350° oven until cooked. Remove the venison to a heated serving dish and keep hot. Stir the flour into the pan and cook quickly for 1 minute, stirring constantly. Strain 1 cup marinade into the pan, stir, and bring to a boil. Stir in the red currant jelly. Serve the gravy with the roast venison.

VENISON ROLLS

6 thin slices venison steak
3 slices fat bacon
½ cup venison scraps or ground
  beef
1 small onion, finely chopped
2 tablespoons oil
1 cup mushrooms, finely chopped

¼ cup fine fresh bread crumbs
salt and pepper to taste
2 tablespoons all-purpose flour
½ cup red wine
1 cup beef stock or water and
  beef-bouillon cube
2 tablespoons tart-flavored jelly

Cooking time: 1 hour
Serves: 6

Beat the venison steak with a cleaver until ¼ inch thick. Cut each bacon slice in half.

Prepare the filling by grinding the scraps of venison, or if not abailable use ground beef. Fry the onion in oil until soft and golden. Add the mushrooms and cook for 1 minute. Add to the meat and stir in the bread crumbs. Season lightly.

Spread a little stuffing on each piece of venison and roll up. Wrap in a bacon strip and secure with either wooden toothpicks or string. Place the rolls side by side in a heavy-based casserole and brown over heat. Turn once and brown the other side. Sprinkle the flour over the meat and add the wine, stock, salt, and pepper. Bring to a boil; then lower the heat and cover. Simmer for 1 hour or until the meat is tender. Lift out the rolls and remove the toothpicks or string. Keep the rolls hot. Stir in the jelly and pour over the rolls.
Serve with hot rice.

VENISON STEW

1 lb. venison
2 onions, sliced
  cup olive oil
1 slice fat bacon, chopped
1 bay leaf
6 peppercorns

2 teaspoons tomato paste
2 cups water
small sprig rosemary
1 clove garlic, crushed
½ cup dry red wine
salt and pepper

Cooking time: 2 hours
Serves: 4

Cut the venison into 1-inch cubes. Fry the onion in hot oil in a large saucepan. Add the bacon and fry. Add the meat, bay leaf, and peppercorns and cook for 2 to 3 minutes until the meat is lightly browned. Add the tomato paste, water, rosemary, garlic, and wine. Season to taste with salt and pepper. Bring to a boil, reduce the heat, and simmer, covered, for 2 hours, stirring occasionally and adding more water if necessary. Test the tenderness of meat by piercing with a fork. Adjust the flavor if necessary and serve.

TANGY BRAISED GAME BIRDS

1 wild duck or pheasant
1 slice bacon, finely chopped
1 onion, finely chopped
2 tablespoons butter
2 tablespoons all-purpose flour
2 cups chicken stock or water
   and chicken bouillon cube

$\frac{1}{4}$ cup white wine
salt and pepper
$\frac{1}{4}$ cup orange juice or red
   currant jelly
10 soaked dried apricots or 10
   button mushrooms
triangles of toast

Cooking time: 1$\frac{1}{4}$ hours
Temperature: 350°
Serves: 3-4

Place the dressed bird in a roasting pan and put in a 350° oven for 20 minutes. Remove the bird and cut into small serving pieces. Fry the bacon and onion in hot butter in a large heavy saucepan. Stir in the flour, then add the stock and wine gradually and stir until the sauce boils. Season with salt and pepper and if wild duck add the orange juice, if pheasant add the red currant jelly. Place the pieces of bird in the sauce and simmer gently until tender, about 45 minutes. Add the apricots to the duck or the mushrooms to the pheasant 10 minutes before serving, and cook gently. Arrange the braised bird with the apricots or mushrooms on a hot plate and boil the sauce rapidly to reduce it by about half. Pour over the the braised birds and serve with small toast triangles.

ROAST GOOSE

Allow 15 to 20 minutes per lb. for cooking and 15 to 20 minutes extra.

1 goose
Sage and Onion Stuffing
salt and pepper

$\frac{1}{4}$ cup all-purpose flour
2 cups giblet stock

Temperature: 400°
   reducing to 350°

Dress the goose. Fill the body cavity with stuffing (see page 152) and truss the bird to keep the wings and legs from springing away from the body. Sprinkle with salt and pepper and place in a roasting pan. Place in a 400° oven and roast for 20 minutes, then lower the temperature to 350° and continue roasting, allowing 15 to 20 minutes per lb. Test when the bird is cooked by waggling the leg. When it moves freely, the goose is cooked. Remove to a heated serving plate and remove the string. Drain off all but about $\frac{1}{4}$ cup of the fat and stir the flour into it. Heat until frothy, then stir in 2 cups giblet stock (see page 158). Bring to a boil. Strain the gravy into a sauce boat. Serve the roast goose with the gravy and Applesauce (see page 59).

BRAISED HARE

1 young hare
$\frac{1}{4}$ cup lemon juice
freshly cracked black pepper
4-5 slices fat bacon
1 onion, sliced
1 carrot, sliced
2 stalks celery, sliced

$\frac{1}{4}$ cup butter
2 tablespoons all-purpose flour
$\frac{1}{2}$ cup red wine
salt
1 sprig parsley
1 sprig thyme
1 bay leaf

Cooking time: 1$\frac{1}{2}$ hours
Serves: 4-5

Cut the hare into serving portions and rub with lemon juice and freshly cracked black pepper. Wrap in the pieces of fat bacon and let stand in a dish for several hours. Sauté the onion, carrot, and celery lightly in hot butter. Stir the flour into the vegetables. Arrange the vegetables on the base of a flameproof casserole. Pour in the wine and season with salt. Tie the parsley, thyme, and bay leaf together to make a bouquet garni and place on the vegetables. Put the bacon-wrapped pieces of hare on the bed of vegetables. Place the lid on the casserole. Cook gently for about 1$\frac{1}{2}$ hours or until the meat is tender.

VEGETABLES

Geraldine Dillon

Geraldine Dillon has her own popular television programme *Fun With Food* in Melbourne. Geraldine studied cookery at the *Emily McPherson College* and the *Cordon Bleu School of Cookery* in London and has studied cookery for the home-maker in her travels throughout America and Europe.

We eat vegetables because they are one of the best sources of vitamins and minerals. Some vegetables, such as peas and beans, are good sources of protein, while roots, stems, leaves, and seeds provide the the body with carbohydrate in the form of starch. Cellulose, which forms the cell walls of plants, is essential for the proper functioning of the digestive organs.

To preserve the food value, the color, and the flavor of vegetables, it is essential that they should be chosen carefully, stored properly, and cooked well.

In this chapter are given some basic methods of cooking vegetables for beginners and, both for them and for the more experienced, I have suggested different ways of preparing and serving vegetables, including the more commonly used and the lesser known varieties. Of course, it is hard to give definite rules for their cooking—there are almost as many schools of thought on this subject as there are varieties of vegetables; however, these methods have been tried and proved successful.

The cooking times which are given are those for the moderately well cooked dish, but, of course, the times may be varied, according to personal taste, as some people prefer vegetables to retain their crispness, whilst others like them very tender.

Many people buy and cook the same few vegetables every week, the only variety being thrust upon them by the change in the seasons. With a little care, proper selection, and a quick reference to the recipes suggested, I feel sure that they will find it easy to introduce into their daily menus refreshing and frequent variety in the choice of vegetables served for the family meal.

A FEW RULES TO REMEMBER

1. In choosing fresh vegetables be sure they are crisp or firm, according to their type, and free from blemishes.
2. Clean them as soon as possible and store in the refrigerator in closed bags, or the vegetable crisper.
3. If the vegetables are unsuitable for storing in the refrigerator, for example, potatoes or onions, place them in a cool, dry, but well ventilated closet, preferably on wire racks.
4. Choose vegetables in season, as they are higher in food value, have a better flavor, and, of course, are cheaper.
5. To retain their food value, prepare vegetables just before cooking.
6. Use as little water as possible when cooking, and boil only until tender—this will retain the color, flavor, and food value. Use the leftover vegetable water for soups, gravies, stock, etc.

Tubers, Bulbs, and Roots	Beets, carrots, chives, garlic, Jerusalem artichokes, leeks, onions, parsnips, potatoes, radishes, scallions, sweet potatoes (yams), swede, turnip
Leaf	Beet tops, Brussels sprouts, cabbage, chicory, greens (collard, kale, mustard greens, turnip tops), lettuce, spinach
Fruit and Flowers	Broccoli, cauliflower, cucumber, eggplant, globe artichokes, marrow squash, squashes, sweet peppers, tomatoes, zucchini
Seeds	Beans (Lima, fava, green), corn, okra, peas
Steam	Asparagus, celeriac (celery root), celery, Swiss chard
Fungi	Mushrooms

GLOBE ARTICHOKE

Cooking time: 30 minutes

The globe artichoke is truly an artichoke, with an outside of overlapping fleshy leaves, a hairy center called the choke, and below the choke the heart, which is also known as the 'fond'. Both the leaves and the heart are edible—the choke is discarded.

To cook: Remove any stalk, wash in salted water, and add the artichokes to a saucepan of boiling salted water. Continue boiling for approximately 45 minutes. The artichoke is cooked when you can remove a leaf easily. Drain thoroughly and serve hot with melted butter.

JERUSALEM ARTICHOKES MORNAY

The Jerusalem artichoke is not a true artichoke. It is a root vegetable and with a nubbly shape.

1½ lb. Jerusalem artichokes	1 teaspoon vinegar	Cooking time: 15 minutes
½ teaspoon lemon juice	1¼ cups Mornay Sauce	Serves: 6
1 teaspoon salt	chopped parsley for garnish	

Scrub and scrape the artichokes, placing them in cold water to which the lemon juice has been added in order to keep them white. Drain the artichokes and place in a saucepan of boiling salted water to cover them. Add the vinegar and simmer for 15 minutes. Drain the artichokes and keep hot. Meanwhile, prepare the Mornay Sauce (see page 51). Serve the artichokes with the Mornay Sauce, and garnish with chopped parsley.
Note: Do not overcook Jerusalem artichokes, as they toughen again with over-cooking.

ASPARAGUS AU BEURRE

1½ lb. asparagus	6 tablespoons butter, melted	Cooking time: 15-20 minutes
1 teaspoon salt		Serves: 6

Trim the asparagus, removing the hard end portion if necessary. Scrape the hard skin from the stalks. Wash, and tie in 3 bundles. Place the bundles, tips upward, in a saucepan containing 1 inch boiling salted water. If this is not possible, place the bundles on their sides in the saucepan. Simmer with the lid on for 15 to 20 minutes, then lift out and drain. Serve with melted butter.

TUSCONIAN GREEN BEANS

2 tablespoons butter
$\frac{1}{4}$ cup dry bread crumbs
$\frac{1}{2}$ teaspoon paprika
$\frac{1}{3}$ cup grated Parmesan cheese

1 lb. green beans, cooked
1 teaspoon butter
salt and pepper

Cooking time: 15 minutes
Serves: 6

Melt the 2 tablespoons butter in a small pan, add the bread crumbs, and stir over medium heat until light golden brown. Blend in the paprika. Remove from the heat, add the Parmesan cheese, and toss until blended. To the hot, cooked green beans, add 1 teaspoon butter and seasonings. Top with the bread crumb mixture. To cook the beans: Place 1 inch water in a saucepan, bring to a boil, add $\frac{1}{2}$ teaspoon salt, and the beans. Bring back to a boil, then simmer for approximately 15 minutes, or until tender.

CREAMED NAVY BEANS

1 lb. navy beans
salt

$\frac{1}{4}$ cup butter
$1\frac{1}{4}$ cups cream

Cooking time: 2-2$\frac{1}{2}$ hours
Serves: 6

The day before the beans are required, cover with boiling water and allow to stand overnight. Drain. Place the beans in a saucepan, cover with fresh cold water, add salt, and bring to a boil. Simmer slowly for 2 to 2$\frac{1}{2}$ hours, or until tender. Drain. Add the butter and return to the heat. Add the cream and simmer gently until thickened, stirring occasionally.

BEETS IN SWEET-SOUR SAUCE

1 cup cooked beets, sliced or
    diced

Serves: 2-3

For sauce:
$\frac{1}{4}$ cup brown sugar
$\frac{1}{2}$ cup water
$\frac{1}{2}$ cup vinegar
salt

2 tablespoons cornstarch
scant $\frac{1}{4}$ cup water
2 tablespoons butter

Place the sugar, water, vinegar, and salt in a saucepan over low heat and dissolve the sugar. In a small bowl, blend the cornstarch with the remaining water. Add a small amount of the hot liquid to the cornstarch, return to the pan, then add the butter. Add the beets and heat through.

BRUSSELS SPROUTS WITH LEMON AND BUTTER

1 lb. Brussels sprouts
$\frac{1}{4}$ cup butter

1 tablespoon lemon juice
$\frac{1}{4}$ cup toasted slivered almonds

Cooking time: 10 minutes
Serves: 4

Remove any wilted leaves from the sprouts and cut a cross in each stem. Wash thoroughly. Place in a pan with sufficient boiling water to cover. Bring back to a boil and simmer covered for 10 minutes, or until just tender. Drain and keep warm. Lightly brown the butter in a saucepan, add the lemon juice, and pour over the sprouts. Sprinkle with the almonds.

BRAISED CABBAGE

1 small cabbage
¼ cup butter
1 small onion, finely chopped

2 slices bacon, finely chopped
1 teaspoon salt
freshly cracked black pepper

Cooking time: 13 minutes
Serves: 6

Trim the cabbage, cut in 4, and wash thoroughly. Cut away the hard stalk and shred the cabbage finely. Melt the butter in a saucepan and fry the onion and bacon for approximately 3 minutes. Add the shredded cabbage, salt, and pepper. Place the lid on the saucepan and simmer for approximately 10 minutes, stirring frequently. Serve at once.

CARROTS VICHY

1 lb. even-sized carrots
⅔ cup water
2 tablespoons butter
salt and pepper

1 teaspoon sugar
chopped parsley
freshly cracked black pepper

Cooking time: 20 minutes
Serves: 4

Wash and prepare the carrots and cut into very thin rounds. Put in a pan with the water and add the butter, seasoning, and sugar. Press a piece of buttered paper down onto the carrots, cover the pan, and cook gently for about 20 minutes, until tender. By this time the liquid should have disappeared and the carrots should have begun to cook gently in the butter and become lightly browned. Sprinkle with parsley and freshly cracked black pepper and serve.

GLAZED CARROTS

1½ lb. carrots
2 tablespoons sugar
¼ cup butter
2½ cups water

1 teaspoon salt
chopped parsley
croûtons

Cooking time: 30 minutes
Serves: 6

Scrape the carrots, and cut into 1½-inch matchstick shapes. Melt the sugar and butter in a saucepan and add the carrots, water, and salt. Bring to a boil and simmer for 15 minutes or until the carrots are cooked. Remove the carrots. Boil the liquid until reduced to one third of the original quantity. Return the carrots to the pan and stir gently to glaze all over. Serve sprinkled with coarsely chopped parsley, and croûtons.

FRENCH FRIED CAULIFLOWER

For sauce:
2 tablespoons butter
¼ cup all-purpose flour
1¼ cups milk
salt and pepper
For fried cauliflower:
1 medium-sized cauliflower
½ cup all-purpose flour

1 egg yolk
salt and pepper
⅓ cup warm water
1 teaspoon butter
2 egg whites
oil for frying
parsley sprigs for garnish

Cooking time: 26 minutes
Serves: 6

To make the sauce: Melt the butter in a small saucepan, remove from the heat, and blend in the flour. Stir until smooth. Add the milk and blend until smooth. Return to the heat, stir constantly until boiling, then cook for 2 minutes. Season with salt and pepper.
To cook the cauliflower: Break the cauliflower into flowerets and cut a slit in the stems. Place in a saucepan with a little boiling salted water. Bring back to a boil, then simmer for 7 to 10 minutes, until barely cooked. Drain and allow to cool.

Dip the cold cauliflower pieces into the hot white sauce and allow to cool. Make a batter with the sieved flour, egg yolk, salt, pepper, and warm water. Stir in the melted butter and the stiffly beaten egg whites. Dip the sauce-covered cauliflower into the batter and deep fry until golden brown. Drain and serve garnished with parsley sprigs.

Eggplant Casserole

BRAISED CELERY

1 bunch celery
3 tablespoons butter
¼ cup all-purpose flour

1¼ cups chicken stock or water
and chicken bouillon cube
salt and pepper

Cooking time: 1¼ hours
Serves: 4

Wash the celery well, removing the leaves, and divide into neat pieces about 3 inches in length. Heat 2 tablespoons of the butter in a saucepan and toss the celery in it for 5 to 10 minutes, until slightly brown on the outside. Remove the celery and keep warm. Melt the remaining butter in the pan and remove from the heat. Stir in the flour. Gradually add the stock. Return to the heat, bring to a boil, stirring continuously, and cook for about 5 minutes, until thick. Then add salt and pepper to taste. Return the celery to the pan and cook over a very low heat, with the lid on, for approximately 1 hour.

CORN ON THE COB WITH BACON

4 corn cobs

8 slices bacon

Cooking time: 12-15 minutes
Serves: 4

Wash the corn cobs, strip off the outer green leaves, and boil in a saucepan with water to cover for about 10 minutes. Drain, wrap around with thin slices of bacon, and broil under a hot broiler until the bacon is cooked. *Note:* The corn will become rather tough if it is boiled too quickly, or for too long.

CUCUMBER

2 cups peeled diced cucumber
2 tablespoons butter

salt and pepper
chopped chives

Cooking time: 6-8 minutes
Serves: 4

Place the diced cucumber in a saucepan of boiling salted water to cover for 2 to 3 minutes. Drain, and return to a pan with a little butter, salt, and pepper. Cover, and cook for 4 to 5 minutes, or until tender. Garnish with finely chopped chives.

EGGPLANT CASSEROLE

3 eggplants
salt
scant ¼ cup oil

1 cup yogurt
¼ cup tomato paste
pepper

Cooking time: 35-40 minutes
Temperature: 350°
Serves: 4

Slice the eggplants without peeling, sprinkle with salt, and leave for 30 minutes to drain. Dry the slices and fry quickly in the oil in a skillet until colored. Place them in an ovenproof casserole as they come from the skillet, layering them with tomato paste and yogurt. Season with pepper. Cover the casserole and bake in a 350° oven for 35 to 40 minutes. Turn out for serving.

BRAISED LETTUCE

2 large heads lettuce
¼ cup butter
1 onion, thinly sliced
1 small carrot, thinly sliced
salt and pepper

3-4 slices bacon
1¼ cups chicken stock or water
and chicken bouillon cube
1 teaspoon tomato paste
chopped parsley for garnish

Cooking time: 40 minutes
Temperature: 350°
Serves: 4

Discard the outside leaves of the lettuce and wash in cold water. Have ready a pan of boiling salted water. Cut each lettuce into quarters, place in the boiling water, and boil for 3 minutes. Remove and plunge into cold water; drain and dry gently with a clean dish towel. Pour the melted butter into a casserole. Place the onion and carrot on top and sprinkle with salt and pepper. Arrange the lettuce on top, season with salt and pepper, and cover with the bacon slices. Mix the stock with the tomato paste and pour over the lettuce, cover with buttered paper, and braise for 40 minutes in a 350° oven. If necessary, add extra stock. Serve hot, sprinkled with chopped parsley.

BAKED STUFFED EGGPLANT

1 eggplant
1 small onion, finely chopped
$\frac{1}{4}$ cup butter
1 cup chopped cooked ham

1 egg
$\frac{1}{4}$ cup grated cheese
$\frac{1}{2}$ cup crushed potato chips

Cooking time: 35 minutes
Temperature: 350°
Serves: 4

Parboil the whole, unpared eggplant for 10 minutes. Cut in half lengthwise. Scoop out the pulp, leaving a 1-inch wall. Cut the pulp in small pieces. Sauté the onion in the butter. Combine with the eggplant pulp, ham, and beaten egg. Fill the shells and top with the cheese and potato chips. Bake in a 350° oven for 25 minutes.

STUFFED GREEN SWEET PEPPERS

4 green sweet peppers
2 tablespoons oil
$\frac{1}{4}$ cup butter
salt and freshly cracked black pepper
generous $\frac{1}{2}$ cup rice
3 cups chicken stock or water

and chicken bouillon cube
$\frac{1}{2}$ onion, finely chopped
$\frac{1}{2}$ cup chopped mushrooms
$\frac{1}{4}$ cup oil
$\frac{1}{2}$ cup finely chopped cooked ham
$\frac{1}{4}$ cup tomato paste
chopped parsley for garnish

Cooking time: 65 minutes
Temperature: 350°
Serves: 4

Remove the tops of the peppers and reserve. Remove the membrane and seeds. Place the peppers in boiling water, add the 2 tablespoons oil, and leave for 5 minutes. Drain well and dry. Place a small piece of butter in each pepper (using half the butter) and season well. Melt the remaining butter in a skillet. Add the rice and fry until golden. Cover with 2 cups of the chicken stock and cook, stirring constantly, until the mixture comes to a boil. Reduce the heat, cover the pan, and cook slowly for 30 minutes, adding a little more chicken stock if necessary. Sauté the onion and mushrooms in the oil and add to the rice mixture. Mix in the ham, season well, and use to stuff the peppers. Replace the pepper caps and place the peppers in a flat ovenproof dish. Blend the tomato paste with the remaining stock, pour over the stuffed peppers, and bake in a 350° oven for 30 to 40 minutes, or until cooked, basting frequently. Sprinkle with chopped parsley.

LEEKS

Cut off the roots and outer leaves and trim green tops, leaving approximately 3 inches. Cut into 1-inch lengths and wash thoroughly. Place in 1 inch boiling salted water, bring back to a boil, and simmer covered for 12 to 15 minutes. Drain, and serve with a Béchamel Sauce (see page 50).

STUFFED MARROW SQUASH

1 large or 2 medium-sized marrow squash
1 onion, finely chopped
$\frac{1}{4}$ cup butter
1 cup thinly sliced mushrooms
$1\frac{1}{2}$ lb. round steak, ground
2 tablespoons chopped chives

2 tablespoons chopped parsley
2 cups fresh white bread crumbs
freshly cracked black pepper
salt
1 egg
brown bread crumbs (optional)
melted butter

Cooking time: $1\frac{1}{2}$ hours
Temperature: 375°
Serves: 6

Peel the marrow squash and remove the ends. Remove all the seeds with a spoon. Fry the onion in the butter for 2 to 3 minutes, add the mushrooms and ground steak, and cook until browned. Remove from the heat. Add the chives, parsley, fresh white bread crumbs, and seasoning. Bind together with the egg. Pack into the shell and secure the ends with wooden toothpicks. Brush with melted butter and, if desired, sprinkle with brown crumbs. Cover with aluminum foil and bake in a 375° oven for $1\frac{1}{2}$ hours, or until soft. Serve in slices, with Tomato Sauce (see page 59).

MUSHROOMS

Wipe the mushrooms, or if very dirty, wash, but do not soak. Do not remove the stems, but trim. Do not peel, unless necessary.

If broiling mushrooms, brush the caps lightly with butter, place them dome side upward and broil for 4 to 5 minutes. Turn the mushrooms over, place a small piece of butter in each, sprinkle with salt, and broil for 2 to 3 minutes.

Sauté sliced mushrooms in a little butter, season well with salt and pepper, add a little lemon juice or cream, and simmer until tender.

STUFFED MUSHROOM CAPS

6 large mushrooms
6 tablespoons butter
red sweet pepper strips for garnish
For stuffing:
2 tablespoons butter
1 small onion, finely chopped
2 tablespoons chopped red

sweet pepper
$\frac{1}{4}$-$\frac{1}{2}$ cup chopped cooked ham
2 tablespoons chopped parsley
salt and pepper
1$\frac{1}{2}$ cups fresh white bread crumbs
$\frac{2}{3}$ cup Béchamel Sauce

Cooking time: 25 minutes
Temperature: 350°
Serves: 6

Prepare the mushrooms and remove the stalks. Chop the stalks finely, and reserve for the stuffing. Arrange the mushroom caps in a greased baking dish, dot with butter, and bake in a 350° oven for 10 minutes. To make the stuffing: Melt the butter in a small saucepan, add the onion, and cook until soft but not brown. Add the sweet pepper, ham, parsley, salt and pepper, chopped mush-room stalks, and bread crumbs. Mix thoroughly and bind together with the Béchamel Sauce (see page 50).

Remove the mushrooms from the oven and cover each mushroom with the prepared stuffing. Return to the oven and bake for a further 15 minutes, or until the mushrooms are tender. Serve hot, garnished with red pepper strips.

PINEAPPLE-STUFFED ONIONS

6 medium-sized onions
1 (15 oz.) can crushed pine-apple, drained

Cooking time: 35-40 minutes
Temperature: 350°
Serves: 6

Peel the onions and cut a small slice off the bottom. Slice approximately $\frac{1}{2}$ inch off the top of each onion. Place in sufficient boiling salted water to cover and cook for 25 to 30 minutes, or until tender. Drain and cool slightly. Remove the center sections of the onions, leaving suffi-cient flesh for them to retain their shape. Fill the onions with heated, crushed pineapple, place in a buttered oven-proof dish, and cook in a 350° oven for 10 to 15 minutes.

CREAMED SPINACH

2 lb. spinach
salt
$\frac{1}{4}$ cup butter

pepper
dash grated nutmeg
$\frac{1}{4}$ cup cream

Cooking time: 15 minutes
Serves: 4

Remove the coarse stems from the spinach leaves. Wash the leaves thoroughly, but do not dry. Cook until tender in $\frac{1}{4}$ cup boiling salted water for 10 to 12 minutes. Drain and press out the water. Rub through a fine sieve or purée in a blender. Melt the butter in a pan, add the spinach, and heat through. Add salt and pepper to taste, the nutmeg, and the cream. Reheat before serving.

GLAZED ONIONS

1 lb. small onions
about 2 tablespoons butter

1 teaspoon sugar
salt and pepper

Cooking time: 15 minutes
Serves: 4

Peel the onions and blanch for 5 to 7 minutes, then drain well. Put in a saucepan with the butter, sugar, and seasoning. Cook gently with the lid on, shaking and stirring from time to time until the onions become tender and well glazed—about 7 to 10 minutes. Care must be taken to cook slowly, or the sugar will scorch. Serve hot.

PEAS FRENCH STYLE

2 tablespoons butter
4 large lettuce leaves
1 onion, sliced
½ teaspoon salt
1 teaspoon sugar
4 parsley stalks

1 slice bacon, chopped
1 lb. fresh peas
⅔ cup water
½ teaspoon all-purpose flour
extra 1 teaspoon butter

Cooking time: 25-30 minutes
Serves: 4

Melt the butter in a saucepan. Shred the lettuce leaves finely and place in the saucepan with the onion, salt, sugar, parsley stalks, bacon and peas. Mix together, then add the water. Bring to a boil, cover, and simmer for 20 to 25 minutes, or until tender. Remove the parsley.

Blend the flour with the extra butter and stir into the peas. Return to the heat, shake the pan gently until the butter and flour mixture has combined with the liquid, and reheat until boiling again. Serve immediately.

GREEN PEAS GRAND'MÈRE

1½ lb. frozen green peas
¼ lb. cooked ham
¼ lb. small pickled white onions
½ cup butter

¼ cup all-purpose flour
1¼ cups chicken stock or water
  and chicken bouillon cube

Cooking time: 30 minutes
Serves: 6

Blanch the peas, and strain. Cut the ham into julienne strips and sauté, with onions, in the butter. Add the flour, and chicken stock, and simmer for 5 minutes. Combine with the peas and onions, and serve hot.

PEAS AND RICE

generous cup long-grain rice
1 onion, sliced
3 tablespoons butter

½ teaspoon salt
½ teaspoon sugar
2¼ cups shelled peas

Cooking time: 20 minutes
Serves: 6

Cook the rice in 8 cups boiling salted water in a large saucepan. Drain and dry. Sauté the onion in 2 tablespoons of the butter until golden. To cook the peas: Place 1 inch water in a saucepan, bring to a boil, and add the salt, sugar, and peas. Bring back to a boil and simmer for 10 to 12 minutes, or until tender.

Drain the peas and fork into the rice with the onion and remaining butter.

BAKED STUFFED POTATOES

6 large even-sized potatoes
salt
¼ cup butter
½ cup hot milk

1 egg (optional)
2 tablespoons chopped chives
  or scallions
¼ cup grated Parmesan cheese

Cooking time: 1½ hours
Temperature: 375°
Serves: 6

Scrub the potatoes and roll in salt. Bake in a 375° oven until tender (about 1½ hours). Cut the top off each potato and scoop out the pulp. Beat with the butter, hot milk, and egg until light and fluffy. Season and flavor with the chopped chives. Pile the mixture back into the potato skins, sprinkle with cheese, and reheat before serving.

CHÂTEAU POTATOES

1 lb. potatoes
about ¼ cup butter
salt

freshly cracked black pepper
chopped parsley for garnish

Cooking time: 20-30 minutes
Serves: 4

Peel and quarter the potatoes and shape to look like large olives, using a potato peeler. Dry the potatoes thoroughly in a clean dish towel after peeling and shaping. Do not soak in water. Heat a large sauté pan, put in the butter, and when hot add the potatoes. Lower the heat and cook slowly for 20 to 30 minutes, shaking the pan gently from time to time. For the first 2 to 3 minutes of cooking, shake the pan gently and continuously to make sure the potatoes are well covered with butter, so they cook evenly. Season lightly during the cooking.

The potatoes when finished should be golden in color and quite soft to touch, but unbroken. Sprinkle with chopped parsley.

Note: Château Potatoes may also be roasted.

FRENCH FRIED POTATOES

6 large potatoes
oil for deep frying

salt

Serves: 6

Peel the potatoes and cut into pieces 2 inches by ½ inch by ½ inch. Stand in a large bowl of ice cold water for at least 30 minutes. Dry the potatoes thoroughly in a clean dish towel. Heat the oil for deep frying until very hot (a 1-inch cube of bread will brown in 1 minute). Place the dry potatoes in the frying basket and lower into the oil. Fry until tender but not browned. Remove the potatoes from the oil and drain. Reserve until just before the time to serve.

Reheat the oil and fry the potatoes until golden, crisp, and slightly puffy. Drain very well, sprinkle with salt, and serve immediately.

Variation:

Shoestring Potatoes: Cut the potatoes into matchstick-shaped pieces; prepare and fry as above.

POTATO CROQUETTES

1 lb. potatoes
1-2 tablespoons butter
1 egg yolk
¼ cup hot milk
salt and pepper

seasoned flour
egg and bread crumbs for
    coating
oil for deep frying

Serves: 4

Cook the peeled potatoes in boiling salted water until tender; drain and dry. Mash with a fork and press through a sieve. Return to the pan. Add the butter, egg yolk, hot milk, and salt and pepper to taste and beat until smoothly blended. Divide into small round or cork-shaped pieces. Roll in seasoned flour, brush with egg, and roll in bread crumbs. Deep fry in hot oil until golden brown.

Note: Potato Croquettes may be made into various shapes.

DUCHESSE POTATOES

6 potatoes
⅓ cup hot milk
4 egg yolks

1½ teaspoons salt
½ teaspoon pepper

Cooking time: 25-30 minutes
Temperature: 350°
Serves: 6

Peel and boil the potatoes, then mash while still warm. (This makes about 5 cups.) Add the milk and the beaten egg yolks. Season with salt and pepper, and beat until smooth and fluffy. (Use an electric mixer or a wooden spoon.) If you have a pastry bag, use a star nozzle, fill the bag with potato, and pipe rosettes onto a greased baking sheet. If not, drop in fluffy spoonfuls onto a greased baking sheet. Place in a 350° oven for 5 to 10 minutes, until tinged with brown.

STUFFED TOMATOES

6 tomatoes
salt
cayenne pepper
2 tablespoons butter
¼ cup all-purpose
⅔ cup chicken stock or milk

¼ cup cold cooked chicken
2 tablespoons cooked ham
   or tongue
white bread crumbs
butter
croûtes, 1-2 inches in diameter

Cooking time: 15 minutes
Temperature: 350°
Serves: 6

Choose even-sized round tomatoes. Cut a slice from the top of each tomato and scoop out the pulp. Turn upside down to drain. Sprinkle the inside with salt and cayenne pepper. Make a panada—melt the butter in a small heavy saucepan, stir in the flour, cook over a low heat for 1 minute, add the stock, and bring to a boil, stirring continuously—this should be a very thick sauce. Add the chicken and ham, cut into ½-inch cubes. Season to taste. Soften the mixture with 2 to 3 tablespoons tomato pulp. Fill the tomato cases with the mixture; cover with bread crumbs and dot with small pieces of butter. Bake in a 350° oven for 10 to 12 minutes. Serve hot on the croutes.

TOMATOES PROVENÇALE

4 medium-sized tomatoes
salt and pepper
2 tablespoons butter

½ cup fresh white bread crumbs
1 clove garlic, crushed

Cooking time: 5-10 minutes
Serves: 4

Cut the tomatoes in half and season the cut surface with salt and pepper. Melt the butter and mix with the bread crumbs, garlic, and salt and pepper. Place one fourth of the mixture on each tomato and cook under a moderately hot broiler until the bread crumbs are golden brown and the tomatoes heated through.

ZUCCHINI

Do not peel the zucchini. Cut off their stems, wash them, and slice diagonally into ¼-inch thick pieces. Blanch in boiling salted water for 2 to 3 minutes, then drain.

    Melt 2 tablespoons butter in a pan and add the zucchini, with salt and pepper. Cover and cook for a few minutes, or until tender, then serve.

Note: Some people like to cook zucchini longer. It is a matter of taste.

ZUCCHINI PROVENÇALE

6 zucchini
1 small onion, chopped
¼ cup butter

1 lb. tomatoes
¾ cup grated cheese
salt and pepper

Cooking time: 15 minutes
Temperature: 350°
Serves: 6

Cut the zucchini into 2-inch slices and sauté, with the onion, in the heated butter for 10 to 15 minutes. Skin the tomatoes, cut into 1-inch slices, and add to the pan with the zucchini. Cook for a few minutes. Grease an ovenproof dish and place in it a layer of tomatoes, followed by a layer of zucchini. Sprinkle between the layers with grated cheese, and salt and pepper. Finish with a layer of tomatoes, sprinkling the top with cheese. Bake in a 350° oven for 45 minutes.

Zucchini Provençale

SALADS

Leone Harrington

Leone Harrington studied at the Auckland Teachers' College, the Tante Marie School of Cookery in England, and Le Cordon Bleu in Paris. She is a cookery journalist and writes regular columns on the subject.

Salads are up to our own creativity. With imagination and thought a gourmet salad can be created. I have listed a few essential steps for you to follow and from these you should be able to develop you own ideas. Salads may be served as an hors d'oeuvre at the beginning of a meal, as an accompaniment to or following the main course, or even as the main course itself. Fruit salads are served as a refreshing dessert.

Always purchase the choicest quality fresh ingredients for salad making. All vegetables used should be young and tender. When marketing, experiment. The leafy salad vegetables add texture and flavor. A mixed green salad should have only two or three varieties of greens in it, e.g. crisp iceberg lettuce with sprays of peppery water-cress, or rougher textured romaine lettuce with sprigs of curly endive. Always serve salads chilled and taste before serving.

Your equipment for salad making should include good quality, sharp, stainless steel knives, one serrated knife for tomatoes, and a screw-top jar for shaking dressings in or a balloon whisk for mixing dressings in the salad bowl. I like to use ceramic, glass, or stainless steel salad bowls as they keep salads cool if chilled before serving.

HOW TO WASH SALAD GREENS

The importance of having perfectly dried and previously crisped greens cannot be over-emphasized, for no matter how perfect a dressing is, it it can be ruined by moisture.

Remove the core from the head of lettuce, lay the head in a colander, and allow a slow flow of cold water to run into the cavity. This will gently loosen and separate the leaves. Carefully wash each leaf under cold running water. Shake free of excess water, dry gently with clean dish towels. Pack loosely in a clean, dry dish towel and roll up lightly or place in an air-tight plastic container, and refrigerate to crispen.

HOW TO TOSS A SALAD

The ritual of tossing salads at the table is a little overplayed. Tossing with salad servers does bruise the delicate greens. Salad may be simply and efficiently tossed in a large mixing bowl in the kitchen. Roll the salad ingredients and dressing lightly and evenly with your hands. Transfer the salad to a chilled salad bowl and bring to the table in glistening triumph.

FRENCH DRESSING

½ teaspoon salt
½ teaspoon freshly cracked
  pepper

3 parts oil
1 part vinegar

Crushed garlic, dry mustard, and chopped herbs may be added. Garlic, mustard, salt, and pepper are first mixed with the oil, then the vinegar is added and all are well mixed. Herbs are added last.

Oils vary. Some people prefer olive, others like safflower or peanut, or perhaps a combination of 2 oils.

We are faced with a large choice of vinegars today — cider, red wine, white wine, and flavored vinegars such as garlic, tarragon, red or white, oregano, basil, or thyme. I prefer lemon juice with some salads, particularly seafood salads. A clove of garlic slivered, put into the oil, and left overnight gives a delicious flavor. Ripe olives covered with olive oil and left overnight or for a few days give a distinctive ripe olive flavor.

ARTICHOKE HEART SALAD

2 cups watercress sprigs
1 head small iceberg lettuce
1 (14½ oz.) can artichoke hearts,
  chilled
½ cup chopped salted almonds

6 scallions, sliced
¼ teaspoon dry mustard
dash sugar
½ cup French dressing, made
  with red wine vinegar

Serves: 6

Trim the watercress, tear the prepared lettuce into small pieces, and place both in a chilled salad bowl. Add the drained artichoke hearts, the almonds, and the scallions. Add the mustard and sugar to the French dressing (see above) and shake well. Drizzle over the salad and roll with clean hands, or toss gently to coat evenly. Serve immediately as a delectable hors d'oeuvre, or with broiled meat.

AVOCADO MOUSSE SALAD

1 large or 2 small avocados, well
  ripened, peeled, and seeded
1 small onion, grated
1 teaspoon salt
freshly cracked black pepper
few drops Worcestershire sauce
2 tablespoons gelatin

½ cup cold water
¼ cup boiling water
¼ cup cream, whipped
¼ cup mayonnaise
lettuce leaves
4-6 radish roses or 2 tomatoes
  for garnish

Serves: 6

Blend the avocados, onion, salt, pepper, and Worcestershire sauce until smooth. Soften the gelatin in ⅓ cup cold water. Add the boiling water, stir until dissolved. Stir in the remaining cold water and cool. When the gelatin mixture is the consistency of egg white, gradually fold in the whipped cream, mayonnaise (see page 55), and avocado mixture. Pour into a mold, previously rinsed with cold water, then chill until set. Invert and unmold onto a chilled plate lined with lettuce leaves. Garnish with radish roses or wedges of tomato. Serve with melba toast (see page 36).

BELGIQUE SPINACH BOWL

2 cups finely shredded spinach
¼ cup finely chopped parsley
3 oranges

2 red-skinned apples
¼ cup French dressing, made
  with lemon juice

Serves: 4

Toss the spinach and parsley in a chilled salad bowl. Peel the oranges, remove the pith, and cut between the membranes into segments with a sharp, serrated knife. Peel and core the apples and slice into rings. Just before serving, combine the fruits with the greens in the salad bowl, pour over the French dressing (see above), toss lightly, and serve immediately. This is delicious with crisply broiled thin pork sausages.

BEAN AND BEET SALAD

2 lb. fresh green beans
salt
½ cup white wine vinegar
½ cup olive oil
½ teaspoon salt
freshly cracked black pepper

1 lb. fresh, small beets
2 tablespoons sugar
½ cup vinegar
4 cloves
1 small head lettuce

Serves: 6

Trim the beans and remove the strings. Cook quickly in ½ inch of boiling, salted water. Drain while the beans are still green and crisp. Arrange in a shallow bowl. Shake the vinegar and oil together, season with salt and pepper, and pour over the beans while still hot. Chill for 1 hour.

Boil the beets in water to cover, with the sugar, until tender. Drain and reserve ½ cup beet water. Remove the outer skin from the beets, arrange them in a shallow dish, and allow to cool. Boil the vinegar, reserved beet water, and cloves for 5 minutes, and pour over the beets. Allow to cool and chill in the refrigerator.

Arrange the prepared lettuce leaves in a large salad bowl. Place the beans in the center. Drain the beets and arrange around the beans. Pour any excess dressing from the beans over the lettuce, and serve immediately.

BEAN SPROUT SALAD

½ cup peanut oil
3 tablespoons cider vinegar
3 tablespoons soy sauce
1 clove garlic, crushed
salt

freshly cracked black pepper
¼ cup finely sliced scallions
¼ cup finely sliced pimento
2 cups bean sprouts
¼ cup sesame seeds, toasted

Serves: 6

In a large salad bowl, whisk together the oil, vinegar, soy sauce, garlic, salt, and pepper. Add the scallions, pimento, bean sprouts, and sesame seeds. Toss gently to coat with the dressing. Chill for 1 to 2 hours before serving. Serve with Oriental food.

CAESAR SALAD

Dressing:
1 clove garlic, cut
1 teaspoon salt
¾ teaspoon freshly cracked
   black pepper
¼ teaspoon dry mustard
¼ teaspoon sugar

1 teaspoon fresh lemon juice
4 anchovy fillets
¼ cup tarragon vinegar
1 cup olive oil
1 raw egg, unbeaten

Serves: 6

For salad:
2 lettuce hearts
2 cloves garlic, thinly sliced
¼ cup olive oil
1 cup croûtons

3 tablespoons finely chopped
   parsley
3 tablespoons freshly grated
   Parmesan cheese

To make the dressing: Rub a salad bowl with the cut clove of garlic. Add the salt, pepper, mustard, sugar, lemon juice, and anchovy fillets and mash well until smooth. Add the vinegar, oil, and egg and stir well with a fork until blended.
To make the salad: Tear the prepared lettuce into small pieces. Cover the garlic with olive oil and leave for at least 30 minutes (overnight if possible). Use the garlic-flavored oil to fry the croûtons until golden on all sides. Drain on paper towels. Stir the dressing in the salad bowl, put the lettuce on top, and sprinkle with parsley. Roll the salad gently from the bottom of the bowl, so that the dressing coats the lettuce evenly. Sprinkle crisp croûtons and Parmesan cheese over and serve immediately.

SWEET PEPPER SALAD

1 green sweet pepper
1 red sweet pepper
2 cups cream-style cottage
   cheese
3 tablespoons finely chopped
parsley
¼ cup finely chopped chives
   or scallions

¼ cup chopped pimento
salt
freshly cracked white pepper
1 head lettuce
½ cup French dressing

Serves: 4-6

Wash and dry the sweet peppers. Cut a slice from each stem end. Remove the seeds and membrane. Combine the cottage cheese, parsley, chives, pimento, salt, and pepper. Spoon into the pepper shells. Wrap in clear plastic and chill overnight, or for at least 1 hour. With a very sharp, thin bladed knife, slice the peppers into ¼-inch thick slices. Tear the prepared lettuce leaves into an open, shallow bowl and toss with French dressing (see page 177). Arrange the pepper slices lightly on top. Serve at once with hot seeded crackers.

For the hot seeded crackers: Select salted, round crackers. Brush with melted butter and sprinkle generously with sesame or poppy seeds. Heat on a baking sheet in a 350° oven until heated through, about 5 minutes.

CELERY SLAW

1 small bunch celery

For dressing:
salt
2 teaspoons sugar
freshly cracked white pepper
½ teaspoon paprika

½ cup grated carrot

½ cup olive oil
3 tablespoons wine vinegar
½ cup sour cream
paprika for garnish

Serves: 6

Detach the stalks of very white, tender celery. Clean thoroughly with a vegetable brush under running water and tear off any coarse membranes. Cut the celery into pieces 1½ inches long and slice lengthwise as finely as possible. Dry in paper towels, then chill. Mix the celery and carrot in a salad bowl, pour the dressing over, toss gently, and sprinkle lightly with more paprika.

To make the dressing: Combine the salt, sugar, pepper, paprika, olive oil, and vinegar. Slowly stir in the sour cream.

CUCUMBER SALAD

3 cucumbers
2 tablespoons salt
2 cloves garlic, cut into slivers
¾ cup cider vinegar

¼ cup sugar
freshly cracked white pepper
2 tablespoons chopped parsley
   or fresh dill

Serves: 4-6

Scrub the cucumber skin free of its waxy coating and dry it. Score with the prongs of a fork. Slice as thinly as possible. The slices should be wafer thin and transparent. Arrange the cucumber slices in a deep bowl and sprinkle with salt. Cover with a small plate to fit inside the bowl and place a heavy weight on top. Stand at room temperature for 2 hours. Place the garlic slivers in the vinegar and allow to stand for at least 30 minutes. Drain away the juice from the cucumbers completely, if necessary squeeze the cucumbers to get them as dry as possible. Combine the garlic-flavored vinegar with the sugar and pepper, and pour over the cucumbers. Taste, and add a little more seasoning if necessary. Cover tightly and chill thoroughly. Before serving, drain off the vinegar and sprinkle the cucumber salad with chopped parsley or dill.

Variations:

Cucumber Sauce: Peel the cucumbers, cut in half lengthwise, and remove the seeds. Slice, stand, drain, and season as for cucumber salad. Purée in an electric blender, and serve as a sauce with fish mousse.

Cucumber in Yogurt: Prepare the cucumber slices as for cucumber salad and combine with 1 carton chilled yogurt. Serve with curry.

Cucumber in Sour Cream: Prepare the cucumber as for cucumber salad and combine with 1 carton chilled sour cream and 1 tablespoon finely chopped mint. Serve with fish mousse or curry.

COLESLAW

1 large or 2 small pineapples
3 cups shredded cabbage
2 carrots, grated
10 scallions, finely sliced
3 red apples, unpeeled and diced
2 tablespoons lemon juice
salt

freshly cracked black pepper
¾ cup sliced celery
1 onion, finely chopped
  (optional)
mayonnaise, or sour cream
  dressing

Serves: 6

For sour cream dressing:
2 teaspoons flour
2 teaspoons sugar
1 teaspoon dry mustard
1 teaspoon salt
dash cayenne pepper

1 egg yolk
⅓ cup cider vinegar
2 tablespoons butter
½ cup sour cream, whipped

Cut the pineapple in half lengthwise. Scoop out the flesh, reserve the shells, and dice the flesh. Combine the pineapple, cabbage, carrot, and scallions. Prepare the apples, and sprinkle with lemon juice. Add the apples to the cabbage with the salt, pepper, celery, and onion. Toss gently to combine. Add sufficient mayonnaise (see page 55) or sour cream dressing to coat, then chill.

Spoon the coleslaw into the pineapple shells and serve. To make the sour cream dressing: In the top of a double boiler combine the flour, sugar, mustard, salt, and cayenne pepper. Beat the egg yolk and cider vinegar, add to the double boiler, and cook over hot water for 7 to 8 minutes, stirring constantly. Stir in the melted butter and allow to cool. Fold the mixture into the sour cream.

GOLD COAST SALAD

4 young, tender spinach leaves
2⅔ cups shelled and de-veined
  cooked shrimp
½ cup French dressing
3 oranges, peeled
1 lb. roast pork, sliced

1 fresh, ripe pineapple, peeled
1 cup cream-style cottage
  cheese
3 tablespoons flaked Brazil nuts,
  toasted

Serves: 4

Line a large dish with torn spinach leaves. Chop the remaining leaves and pile in the center. Marinate the shrimp in the French dressing for 30 minutes. Cut the oranges into slices or segments, cut the sliced pork into strips, and toss together. Remove the 'eyes' from the pineapple and cut into 12 slices, discarding the core.

Drain the shrimp with a slotted spoon, arrange in an outer circle around the spinach leaves. Pile the pork and oranges on top of the leaves in the center. Garnish the platter with pineapple slices, topped with scoops of of cottage cheese, and sprinkle with the flaked, toasted nuts. Serve with mayonnaise (see page 55).

GRAPEFRUIT CUPS

3 large grapefruit
1½ cups seedless green grapes,
  peeled
2 cucumbers, peeled
1 cup mayonnaise

2 avocados, peeled and seeded
lemon juice
freshly cracked white pepper
salt
6 lettuce leaves for serving

Serves: 6

Cut the grapefruit in half in a 'vandyke' shape. Scoop out the flesh from the halves with a grapefruit knife into a bowl. Remove the stem and pith from the grapefruit cups, then wrap and chill them. Add the grapes to the grapefruit sections and chill. Cut the cucumbers into eighths, add to the drained fruit, mix lightly, then

fold in the mayonnaise (see page 55). Cut the avocados into ½-inch cubes, cover with lemon juice, sprinkle with pepper, and salt, and add to the fruit. Spoon into the reserved grapefruit cups and serve on lettuce leaves as an hors d'oeuvre, or with cold roast pork or goose.

GREEN SALAD

1 clove garlic, cut in half
½ head iceberg lettuce
1 romaine lettuce
4 young spinach leaves

3 Belgian endive (optional)
1 green sweet pepper
1½ cups sliced celery

Serves: 6-8

For Green Goddess Dressing:
6 anchovy fillets
¼ cup finely chopped green
    scallion tops
¼ cup finely chopped parsley
¼ cup finely snipped chives

¼ cup tarragon vinegar
1 cup mayonnaise
mustard
salt
freshly cracked black pepper

Rub the salad bowl with garlic. Tear the prepared lettuces and spinach into bite-sized pieces and put into a salad bowl. If using Belgian endive, separate the leaves, trim the stem ends, wash, dry and crisp. Cut into 1-inch pieces. Quarter the pepper, remove the seeds, and membrane, and cut into thin strips. Add the celery to the bowl and toss all together. Cover and chill. When ready to serve add half the Green Goddess Dressing to the salad, and toss gently and thoroughly. Serve the remaining dressing in a small, chilled bowl.

To make the dressing: Chop the anchovy fillets finely and add the scallion tops, parsley, and chives. Add the tarragon vinegar, mayonnaise (see page 55), and mustard, and mix well. Add salt and pepper to taste. Blend well, cover, and seal. Chill for several hours, or better still overnight, to blend the flavors.

WATERCRESS SALAD

6 cups watercress
1 small head lettuce
1 clove garlic, cut
½ cup olive oil
3 tablespoons Vermouth

salt
freshly cracked white pepper
dash sugar
1-1½ teaspoons lemon juice

Serves: 6

Wash and dry the watercress and break into neat sprigs. Wash and dry the lettuce. Lightly pack both the greens into plastic bags, seal, and crisp in the refrigerator until serving time. Rub the salad bowl with garlic. Add the watercress and tear the lettuce into the bowl. Combine the oil and Vermouth, with salt, pepper, sugar, and lemon juice to taste, in a screw-top jar and shake well until blended. Pour over the greens and mix thoroughly with the hands until each leaf is glistening. Serve immediately.

LIMA SALAD

2 cups lima beans
1 onion, thinly sliced
2 cloves garlic
1 teaspoon salt
freshly cracked pepper
olive oil

1 cup green scallion tops
3 tablespoons wine vinegar
2 teaspoons lemon juice
12 whole scallions
pimento-stuffed olives

Serves: 4-6

Soak the lima beans overnight in cold, salted water. Drain. Cover with fresh cold water and simmer gently for about 2 hours, or until tender; drain. Place the scallions in a bowl with the garlic crushed to a pulp with the salt, and cover with olive oil. Allow to stand for 1 hour. Add the lima beans, and scallion tops, finely sliced. Sprinkle with the wine vinegar and lemon juice and toss lightly. Taste and add more lemon juice if necessary. Chill. Tuck scallion curls around the edge of a chilled salad bowl. Spoon the bean salad into the center and garnish with sliced stuffed olives. To make the scallion curls, trim the root and remove the outer leaves of the scallions. Cut the green tops and slice down about 2½ inches to the white part to fringe the ends. Plunge into iced water and chill for 1 hour, or until the ends are curled. Drain and use as required.

Belgique Spinach Bowl, Herbed Tomatoes,
Cucumber Salad, and Avocado Mousse Salad

HOT POTATO SALAD

4 large potatoes, peeled
2 cups diced celery
1 onion, grated
1 teaspoon salt
2 cups water

$\frac{1}{4}$ cup French dressing with herbs
$\frac{1}{2}$ cup mayonnaise
$\frac{1}{2}$ cup sour cream
hard-cooked eggs and tomato
for garnish

Serves: 4-6

Dice the potatoes into $\frac{1}{2}$-inch cubes (there should be about 5 cups). Combine the celery, onion, salt, and water in a large saucepan and bring to a boil. Cover and cook for 20 minutes, or until the potatoes are just tender. Drain and shake gently in the pan over low heat to dry. Pour over the French dressing (see page 177), mix lightly with a fork, and keep hot. Just before serving, mix the mayonnaise (see page 55) with the sour cream and fold into the potato mixture. Spoon into a heated serving dish. Garnish with hard-cooked eggs and tomato wedges. Serve immediately.

RICE AND LITTLE EGG SALAD

2 tomatoes, skinned
4 cups cooked long-grain rice
3 gherkins, finely chopped
1 cup thinly sliced celery

2 cups peas, cooked and drained
$\frac{1}{2}$ cup thinly sliced scallions
$\frac{1}{4}$ cup finely chopped parsley

Serves: 4-6

For dressing:
1 raw egg yolk
$\frac{1}{4}$ cup olive oil
scant $\frac{1}{4}$ cup cider vinegar
2 tablespoons sugar

$\frac{1}{2}$ teaspoon prepared mustard
1 clove garlic, crushed with $\frac{1}{2}$
  teaspoon salt
good dash cayenne pepper

For garnish:
3 eggs, hard-cooked
1 raw egg yolk
salt

freshly cracked white pepper
$\frac{1}{4}$ cup finely chopped parsley

Remove the seeds, drain and dice the tomatoes. Gently toss the rice with the tomatoes, gherkins, celery, peas, scallions, and parsley. Sprinkle the dressing over and gently fold through the rice, then chill. Spoon into a salad bowl, shape lightly into a peak, and serve garnished with the chilled little eggs.
To make the dressing: Beat the egg yolk and gradually add the oil, vinegar, sugar, mustard, garlic, and cayenne pepper.
To make the little egg garnish: Mash the hard-cooked eggs thoroughly. Add the raw egg yolk, salt, and pepper and mix well. Form the mixture into approximately 14 small balls. Poach gently for 2 minutes in simmering water, then drain. Toss the little eggs in parsley, leave until cold, and chill.

HERBED TOMATOES

$1\frac{1}{2}$-2 lb. tomatoes
2 tablespoons sugar
1 cup parsley sprigs, finely
  chopped
1 cup fresh basil leaves, or
  $\frac{1}{4}$ cup dried basil

1 teaspoon salt
$\frac{1}{2}$ teaspoon dry mustard
$\frac{1}{4}$ cup olive oil
2 tablespoons wine vinegar
freshly cracked black pepper

Serves: 4-6

Dip the tomatoes in boiling water, then plunge into cold water and skin them. Keep small tomatoes whole; remove the stem ends. Slice medium or large tomatoes. Arrange the tomatoes in a salad bowl. Sprinkle with the sugar, parsley, and basil. Mix together the salt, mustard, olive oil, vinegar, and pepper. Pour over the tomatoes. Marinate for 2 hours before serving.
Note: If using dried basil, soak in wine vinegar before using in a salad.

SALADE NIÇOISE

This is my adaptation of the famous salad of the Mediterranean.

1 (15 oz.) can tuna or salmon,
   drained
$\frac{3}{4}$ lb. fresh green beans
good dash coriander
$\frac{1}{2}$ lb. small new potatoes

1 cucumber
4 tomatoes, skinned and sliced
$\frac{2}{3}$ cup ripe olives
1 (2 oz.) can flat anchovy fillets

Serves: 4-6

For herb dressing:
$\frac{1}{3}$ cup olive oil
2 tablespoons lemon juice
$\frac{1}{4}$ cup each finely chopped
   parsley and chives
good dash thyme, crumbled

$\frac{1}{2}$ clove garlic
$\frac{1}{4}$ teaspoon salt
dash sugar
freshly cracked black pepper

Break the salmon into chunks, arrange in a chilled glass bowl, cover, and chill. Cook the beans whole, cool, and slice diagonally into $\frac{1}{2}$-inch pieces. Lay on top of the salmon and sprinkle with the coriander. Cook, peel, and slice the new potatoes. Peel, score, and thinly slice the cucumber, arrange in a bowl, sprinkle with salt, and leave for 30 minutes, pressing with a weight to remove excess water. Layer the potatoes, drained cucumber, and tomatoes, on top of the beans. Garnish with plump ripe olives and anchovy fillets. Trickle over the herb dressing.

To make the herb dressing: Combine the oil, lemon juice, parsley, chives, and thyme. Crush the garlic to a pulp with the salt, add to the oil mixture, and season with sugar and pepper to taste. Shake or beat well before using.

POTATO SALAD

1-1$\frac{1}{2}$ lb. potatoes
1 onion, finely chopped
   (optional)

$\frac{2}{3}$-1$\frac{1}{4}$ cups mayonnaise
2 tablespoons finely chopped
   parsley or mint (optional)

Serves: 4-6

Boil the potatoes in their skins. Peel and slice or dice, then add the onion. When cold, mix with enough mayonnaise (see page 55) to moisten. Sprinkle with the parsley or mint before serving.

Variations:
1. Rub the salad bowl with cut garlic—omit the onion.
2. Chopped red sweet pepper with parsley makes an attractive garnish.
3. Crumble $\frac{1}{2}$-$\frac{3}{4}$ cup well-fried bacon over the salad.
4. Fold in 1 cup chopped celery heart, cucumber cubes, or grated carrot, or 2 tablespoons celery seeds.
5. Add 1 cup flaked tuna, salmon, prawns, or lobster.
6. Fold in 3 finely chopped hard-cooked eggs, and $\frac{1}{4}$ cup chopped gherkins or finely chopped chives.
7. Use a French dressing (see page 177), with a little chopped onion added to it, preferably when the potatoes are still warm. Sprinkle with paprika.
8. Substitute yogurt flavored with $\frac{1}{2}$ teaspoon garam masala for the mayonnaise.
9. Fold 1$\frac{1}{2}$ teaspoons curry powder into the mayonnaise.

Note: Garam masala may be obtained from a quality grocery store.

WALDORF SALAD

1 green apple
1 red apple
juice $\frac{1}{2}$ lemon
1 cup finely chopped celery
$\frac{1}{2}$ cup broken walnuts

$\frac{1}{4}$ cup mayonnaise
crisp lettuce leaves
1 red apple, thinly sliced, brushed
   with lemon juice to prevent
   discoloration

Serves: 6

Chill the apples, then core and dice them. Pour the lemon juice over the apples. Combine the apples with the celery, walnuts, and mayonnaise (see page 55). Serve piled into the lettuce leaves. Garnish with slices of red-skinned apple.

FISH SALAD

Raw fish is tenderized and 'cooked' by the citric acid in lemon juice. The flesh becomes opaque during this process.

2 lb. fresh, raw fish (red snapper, fillet of sole, or scallops)

1 cup lemon juice

Serves: 4

For oil and vinegar dressing:
$\frac{1}{2}$ cup finely chopped onion
$\frac{2}{3}$ cup olive oil
$\frac{1}{3}$ cup vinegar

2 teaspoons coarse salt
freshly cracked pepper
crisp lettuce leaves

For coconut cream dressing:
1 cup frozen coconut cream, thawed, or 1 cup coconut milk
salt

freshly cracked white pepper
$\frac{1}{2}$ onion, finely sliced
1 clove garlic, crushed
coconut shells

Bone the fish and cut into 1-inch pieces, about $\frac{1}{2}$-inch thick. Put the fish in an enamel or ceramic bowl. Add the lemon juice. Allow to marinate for approximately $1\frac{1}{2}$ hours. Drain off the juices. At this stage one of the following methods may be followed.
With oil and vinegar: Add the onion to the fish. Blend the olive oil, vinegar, salt, and freshly cracked black pepper to taste. Pour over the fish and onion. Toss lightly and serve in lettuce leaves on individual chilled plates.
With coconut: Mix the coconut cream or coconut milk (see page 420) with the salt, pepper, onion, and garlic and fold into the marinated and drained fish. Spoon into empty halved coconut shells.

SEAFOOD SALAD

1 small crayfish or rock lobster tail
1 lb. jumbo shrimp, cooked, shelled, and de-veined
12 scallops, poached in white wine (optional)
$\frac{1}{2}$ lb. fish fillets, poached and flaked

1 cup French dressing, made with lemon juice
1 cup sour cream or mayonnaise
$\frac{1}{2}$ cup tomato catsup
1 cup finely sliced celery
1 head lettuce
12-16 plump oysters
chopped parsley for garnish

Serves: 6-8

Remove the flesh from the lobster tail, and cut into cubes. Combine the lobster, drained scallops, and flaked fish. Shake the French dressing in a screw-top jar until creamy (see page 177). Pour the dressing over the seafood, cover, and chill. Allow to marinate for 1 hour. Drain the seafood of excess French dressing and remove to a chilled bowl, using a perforated spoon. Mix the sour cream or mayonnaise (see page 55) with the tomato catsup and celery and fold through the seafood. Spoon into a large lettuce-lined salad bowl set over ice, or serve on a bed of finely shredded lettuce in individual, chilled bowls. Top with chilled oysters and sprinkle with finely chopped parsley.

TUNA SALAD

1 (16 oz.) can tuna
1 large dill pickle, chopped
4 scallions, sliced
1 cup peas, cooked
1 red pimento, sliced
$\frac{1}{2}$ cup coarsely broken walnuts

salt
freshly cracked black pepper
$\frac{1}{4}$ cup sour cream
crisp lettuce leaves
2 hard-cooked eggs, finely chopped

Serves: 4

Break the tuna into large chunks and toss with the dill pickle, scallions, peas, pimento, walnuts, and salt and pepper to taste. Add the sour cream and toss lightly.
Spoon into lettuce leaves and sprinkle with the chopped egg.

Gold Coast Salad

TURKEY SALAD

1 clove garlic
1 iceberg lettuce
1 romaine lettuce
1 cup watercress sprigs
1 cup fresh basil leaves
2 avocados peeled, seeded
  and diced

1 cup sliced button mushrooms
1 cup French dressing, made with
  red wine tarragon vinegar
½ cup sliced dill pickle
½ lb. salami, cut into thin strips
½ lb. Swiss cheese, cut into strips
2 lb. cooked turkey, thinly sliced

Serves: 8-10

Rub a salad bowl with the cut clove of garlic and chill. Toss the prepared lettuces, watercress and basil in the bowl, cover, and chill again. Marinate the avocados and mushrooms separately in ¼ cup each of the French dressing (see page 177). Chill for 2 hours. Arrange the avocados, mushrooms, dill pickle, salami, Swiss cheese, and turkey slices over the salad greens. Shake the reserved dressing well, pour over the turkey salad, and toss gently before serving.

CHICKEN AND GRAPE SALAD

This is my own version of the classic Salade Véronique.

4 double chicken breasts
2 stalks celery with leaves,
  roughly chopped
1 onion, sliced
2 tablespoons salt
1½ teaspoons curry powder
2 curry leaves or 1 bay leaf
  (optional)
6 whole peppercorns

5 cups water
1 small head lettuce
4 curly endive leaves
1½ cups cooked ham, cubed
1 lb. seedless green grapes,
  stemmed, washed, and dried
½ lb. seedless green grapes,
  snipped into small clusters

Cooking time: 35 minutes
Serves: 6-8

For dressing:
1 cup mayonnaise
½ cup sour cream
½ cup finely chopped fruit

chutney
2 tablespoons lemon juice
½ teaspoon salt

Rinse the chicken and place in a saucepan with the celery, onion, salt, curry powder, bay leaf and whole peppercorns. Cover with the water, bring to a boil, and simmer for about 35 minutes, or until tender. Drain the chicken, remove the bones and skin, and chill for 3 hours or overnight. Tear the crisped lettuce and endive into bite-sized pieces in a salad bowl. Cover and chill. Cut the chicken into cubes, add the ham, the 1 lb. grapes, and the dressing, and toss gently to mix well. (Flavors improve if the salad is left overnight in a covered container in the refrigerator.) Spoon the chicken salad over the salad greens just before serving. Garnish with the small clusters of chilled green grapes.
To make the dressing: Combine the mayonnaise with the sour cream, chutney, lemon juice, and salt. Chill before using.

AVOCADO-PRAWN SALAD

2 ripe avocados
¼ cup French dressing, garlic
  flavored
12 cooked Pacific prawns

1 (16 oz.) can palm hearts,
  drained and sliced
lettuce

Serves: 4

Cut the avocados in half, scoop out all the flesh, and mash it with a wooden spoon. Add the French dressing (see page 177), and mash to a smooth pulp. Spoon back into the avocado skins. Peel, de-vein, wash, and drain the prawns. Arrange the prawns on the avocados. Garnish with the palm hearts, sliced into rounds about the size of a quarter.

ICED WATERMELON

1 small watermelon
1 papaya, peeled and seeded
2 large oranges
2 large bananas
1 tablespoon lemon juice

1 pineapple
1 cup strawberries
1 cup cherries or black grapes,
    peeled and seeded

Serves: 10-12

For frosting:
$\frac{1}{2}$ lb. cherries with stems joined
    in 2 or 3, or $\frac{1}{2}$ lb. green or
    black grapes, cut into small

clusters
1 lightly beaten egg white
sugar

For syrup for dipping:
1 teaspoon vanilla extract or
    1 teaspoon almond extract
    combined with 1 cup maple
    syrup

or
1$\frac{1}{2}$ teaspoons whiskey or
    1 teaspoon rum combined with
    1 cup maple syrup

Wash and polish the watermelon skin. Mark a decorative pattern on the top third along the length of the melon. With a small, sharp, pointed knife 'vandyke' or scallop the edges. Cut a sliver off the bottom of the melon so it sits firmly. Remove the top of the melon and scoop out the flesh. Remove the seeds and cut the flesh into bite-sized pieces. Wrap and chill the melon shell. Cut the papaya into bite-sized pieces. Peel the oranges, remove the pith, and cut into segments. Peel the bananas, slice diagonally, and brush with lemon juice. Peel the pineapple, remove the 'eyes' with a sharp, pointed knife, cut into thick slices, discard the center core, and cut into bite-sized pieces. Hull the strawberries and wash well. If small, leave whole otherwise cut in half.

Wash the cherries, and remove the stones. Mix the prepared fruits gently in a bowl, cover, and chill.

Spoon the fruits into the chilled melon shell. Place the melon on a large wooden platter, decorated with washed and polished hibiscus, lemon, or banana leaves. Decorate the platter with clusters of frosted cherries or grapes, and surround with small saké cups, or liqueur glasses, filled with one of the dipping syrups. Serve with small forks or wooden toothpicks, for dipping the fruit in syrup before eating.

To frost cherries and grapes: Wash the fruit and pat dry. Brush each with egg white and sprinkle lightly with sifted sugar. Arrange on a wire rack and allow to dry.

PINEAPPLE FRUIT SALAD

1 large ripe pineapple
4 bananas
juice of $\frac{1}{2}$ lemon
$\frac{1}{4}$ cup fresh orange juice
4 oranges
dash salt
1 red-skinned apple, unpeeled
    and diced

1 pear, peeled and diced
1$\frac{1}{2}$ cups seedless small green
    grapes
$\frac{1}{4}$-$\frac{1}{3}$ cup sifted confectioners'
    sugar
1$\frac{1}{4}$ cups cream and sugar for
    serving

Serves: 6-8

Slice the base and top from the pineapple to form a lid. With a long, thin-bladed knife, remove the outer skin from the flesh keeping the skin intact. Remove the cylinder of pineapple flesh. Wrap and chill the shell. Remove the core from the pineapple and cut the flesh into 1-inch chunks. Peel the bananas, slice diagonally, and drench with lemon juice. Combine the pineapple

with the drained bananas and orange juice. Peel the oranges, remove the pith, and cut into segments. Add the salt, apple, pear, and grapes. Chill for 30 minutes. Arrange the pineapple shell on a platter lined with banana or orange leaves. Sprinkle with the confectioners' sugar and spoon the fruits into the pineapple shell. Top with the lid. Serve with whipped, sweetened cream.

GOOSEBERRY AND MELON

Chinese gooseberries are glamorous and nutritious in salads, adding crunch and zing to mixed fruit salads or greens.

1 cantaloupe melon
6 Chinese gooseberries
3 bananas
juice of 1 lemon

$\frac{1}{4}$-$\frac{1}{3}$ cup Cointreau or Grand Marnier
$\frac{1}{4}$ cup sugar
mint sprigs for decoration

Serves: 6-8

Mark the cantaloupe above the halfway mark with a 'scallop' or 'vandyke' line and cut the edge with a small sharp pointed knife. Remove the seeds from the melon and drain. Scoop out the flesh with a large melon baller into a bowl. Wrap the melon shell in clear plastic and chill. Peel the Chinese gooseberries thinly and cut into round slices. Peel the bananas, cut diagonally, and sprinkle with lemon juice. Toss the fruits gently together. Sprinkle the liqueur over. Chill. Just before serving, sprinkle the fruit with sugar and spoon into the reserved melon shell. Decorate with mint sprigs.

SUMMER FRUIT BOWL

1 melon
juice of 1 lemon
$\frac{1}{2}$ cup sugar
1 small pineapple
8 apricots
4 peaches

$\frac{1}{2}$ lb. mulberries
4 bananas
$\frac{1}{2}$ cup Cointreau
1 (16 oz.) can passionfruit
whipped cream or ice cream for serving

Serves: 6-8

Skin the melon and cut into thin slices. Macerate in the lemon juice and half the sugar for 30 minutes. Peel and core the pineapple and cut into chunks. Skin and halve the apricots and quarter the peaches. Wash the mulberries and remove the stems. Skin the bananas and slice diagonally. Combine the prepared fruits and toss gently together with the remaining sugar and the Cointreau. Serve in a bowl, with the passionfruit pulp spooned over. Serve with whipped cream or ice cream.

Summer Fruit Bowl

PASTA AND RICE

Vo Bacon

Vo Bacon, born in America, graduated with a degree in home economics from the University of Nevada in the U.S.A. and is a well-known home economist in industry in Australia. She runs a Cookery School and answers cookery and home management problems on radio and appears on television.

Pasta

Pasta has a long history. The Chinese enjoyed macaroni in various forms as early as 5,000 B.C. Marco Polo gets the credit for bringing it to Italy in the 13th century.

Spirali, lasagne, rigatoni, and vermicelli are only a small part of the pasta parade that has become an everyday part of home cooking. All the hundreds of shapes come under three general classifications:

    solid rod form (such as spaghetti)
    products with a hole (such as macaroni)
    flat shapes (such as noodles).

In addition there are special shapes such as rotini, shell, mafalde, etc. Yet all these shapes are made from basically the same dough, with one exception—egg noodles which have egg solids added.

Pasta is made from durum, a hard amber-colored wheat, mixed with water, kneaded, shaped, and dried. It provides protein and carbohydrates and contains all the nutrients found in wheat. It is a good food and should not be ruined by over-cooking.

TO COOK PASTA

Bring 7 pints salted water to a brisk boil. Add a small amount of pasta at a time. Hold a small amount of long spaghetti near the end and gently lower it into the rapidly boiling water; it softens and curves around the pan as it enters the water. Boil briskly, uncovered, stirring occasionally, until just tender. The Italians call it 'al dente'—the pasta should be firm when bitten between the teeth. Do not over-cook. Drain in a colander. Do not rinse. Serve hot.

FOR DELAYED SERVING

Under-cook the pasta and remove it from the heat. Drain slightly and add a cup or two of cold water. Let it stand until ready to use. Reheat if necessary and drain. When using in salads, cook, drain, and chill the pasta, then rinse it in cold water and drain thoroughly.

SPAGHETTI BOLOGNESE

2 tablespoons butter
½ cup olive oil
½ cup finely chopped bacon or
    lean salt pork
1 onion, finely chopped
1 carrot, finely chopped
1 cup finely ground beef
1 strip lemon rind
½ cup tomato paste
1¼ cups beef stock or water
    and beef bouillon cube

⅔ cup cup dry red or white wine
1 bay leaf
dash nutmeg
½ teaspoon salt
freshly cracked black pepper
1 lb. spaghetti
extra olive oil
Parmesan cheese, for serving

Cooking time: 1 hour
Serves: 6-8

Heat the butter and oil in a saucepan and sauté the bacon, onion, and carrot for 5 minutes. Stir in the ground beef and cook until browned. Add the lemon rind, tomato paste, beef stock, wine, bay leaf, nutmeg, salt and pepper. Bring to a boil and simmer, covered, for 30 minutes, stirring occasionally. Remove the lemon peel, and bay leaf, and simmer, uncovered, for a further 30 minutes.

Cook the spaghetti in boiling, salted water until 'al dente'. Drain and swirl with about 2 tablespoons extra oil. Serve with the sauce spooned into the center and sprinkled with Parmesan cheese.

Note: Butter may be used instead of olive oil for swirling the spaghetti.

SPAGHETTI WITH MEATBALLS

For tomato sauce:
1 (1 lb.) can tomatoes
1 cup tomato catsup
1 (4 oz.) can tomato paste
¼ cup water
¼ cup red wine (optional, use
    more water instead)
For meatballs:
4 slices white bread
2 cups ground chuck or round
    steak
2 tablespoons grated Parmesan
    cheese
2 tablespoons chopped parsley

2 bay leaves, crushed
¼ cup chopped parsley
1 clove garlic, crushed

2 tablespoons grated onion
2 teaspoons salt
¼ teaspoon pepper
¼ teaspoon oregano
1 egg
⅓ cup olive or salad oil

Cooking time: 20 minutes
Serves: 6-8

½ lb. spaghetti

Parmesan cheese, freshly grated,
   for serving

To make the tomato sauce: Combine the tomatoes, tomato catsup, paste, water, wine, bay leaves, parsley, and garlic in a saucepan. Simmer all until thick, stirring occasionally.

To make the meatballs: Place the bread in a small bowl, add enough water to cover, and allow to stand for 2 minutes. Remove the bread and squeeze out any excess water. In a larger bowl, combine the bread with the ground beef, Parmesan cheese, parsley, onion, salt, pepper, oregano, and egg. Mix lightly until thoroughly combined. Shape into small balls. Fry until brown on all sides in the olive oil.

Add the meatballs to the sauce and simmer for 15 to 20 minutes. Meanwhile, cook and drain the spaghetti. Top with the meatballs and sauce and serve with Parmesan cheese.

ITALIAN MARINARA

2 lb. cooked shellfish
(oysters, scallops, prawns,
or rock lobster tails)
1/4 cup olive oil
2 cloves garlic, sliced
1 (1 lb. 13 oz.) can tomatoes,
sieved or puréed

1 1/2 teaspoons salt
1 teaspoon oregano
1 teaspoon chopped parsley
1/4 teaspoon pepper
1/4 cup red wine (optional)
3/4 lb. spaghetti or gemelle
(spiral or corkscrew pasta)

Cooking time: 20 minutes
Serves: 6-8

Shell the fish, wash, and drain. Sauté gently in the medium-hot oil for 5 minutes. Remove from the skillet and keep warm. Add the garlic and sauté until golden. Stir in the tomatoes, salt, oregano, parsley, pepper, and wine. Cook rapidly, uncovered, for 15 minutes or until thickened. Stir occasionally. If the sauce becomes too thick, add 1/4 to 1/2 cup water. Add the shellfish and reheat gently. Meanwhile, cook the spaghetti and drain. Serve immediately with the shellfish sauce.

SPAGHETTI SPRINGTIME

4-6 tomatoes, skinned and
chopped
1/2 lb. cooked hot spaghetti,
drained
1 green sweet pepper, chopped
1/2 cup chopped scallions

1/4 cup chopped ripe olives
salt and pepper to taste
juice of 1/2 lemon
olive oil (about 1/3 cup)
chopped parsley for garnish
Parmesan cheese (optional)

Cooking time: 15-20 minutes
Serves: 6-8

Heat the tomatoes in a saucepan. Stir until hot. Add the hot spaghetti, green pepper, scallions, olives, salt, pepper, and lemon juice. Add enough olive oil to coat the pasta. Toss well.
Sprinkle with parsley. Serve with Parmesan cheese, if desired.

CHICKEN LIVERS SUPREME

1/2 cup olive oil
1/4 cup butter
2 cups finely chopped onion
2 cloves garlic, crushed
1/2 lb. chicken livers, chopped
8 slices bacon, finely chopped
1/2 cup finely chopped parsley

1 green sweet pepper, finely
chopped
1 (1 lb. 13 oz.) can tomatoes
1/3 cup red wine
salt and pepper to taste
1 lb. spaghetti or vermicelli

Cooking time: 35-40 minutes
Serves: 6-8

Heat the olive oil and butter in a skillet. Add the onion and garlic, and sauté until golden. Add the chicken livers and gently sauté for 5 minutes. Add the bacon, parsley, and green pepper. Cover, and simmer for 10 minutes. Stir in the tomatoes, wine, salt, and pepper. Simmer, covered, for 20 minutes, stirring occasionally. Meanwhile, cook the spaghetti until tender, and drain. Serve with the sauce.

VERMICELLI WITH GREEN SAUCE

1/4 cup soft butter
1/4 cup chopped fresh basil
1/4 cup chopped parsley
1 cup softened cream cheese
1/3 cup grated Parmesan cheese
1/4 cup olive oil

1 clove garlic, crushed
3/4 teaspoon freshly cracked
pepper
2/3 cup boiling water
3/4 lb. vermicelli, or thin spaghetti
Parmesan cheese, for serving

Cooking time: 15-20 minutes
Serves: 6-8

In a saucepan, cream together the butter, basil, parsley, cream cheese, Parmesan cheese, oil, garlic, and pepper. Add the boiling water and stir until smoothly combined. Serve over the cooked vermicelli (see page 192), arranged on a warm platter, and sprinkle with Parmesan cheese.

SHELLS WITH CLAM SAUCE

½ lb. pasta shells (maruzze)
¼ cup olive oil
2 cloves garlic, crushed
¼ cup water
1½ teaspoons chopped parsley
½ teaspoon salt

¼ teaspoon oregano
dash pepper
1 cup clams whole or ground
  with liquid
¼ cup butter

Cooking time: 15-20 minutes
Serves: 4-6

Cook and drain the shells (see page 192) just before serving. Heat the oil in a skillet. Add garlic and cook until golden. Slowly stir in the water. Add the parsley, salt, oregano, pepper, and clams with the liquid. Mix well. Heat and add the butter in small quantities. Pour the clam sauce over the shells and serve.

Note: Spirali or gnocchi may be used instead of pasta shells. Other shellfish may be used with the clams.
Variation: To make Shells with Red Clam Sauce, substitute ¾ cup tomato sauce for the clam liquid and omit the butter.

MACARONI SHELLFISH MÒUSSE

1 cup elbow macaroni (cut
  ziti or rigati)
1 tablespoon gelatin
¼ cup cold water
1¼ cups hot water
¼ cup lemon juice
¼ cup sugar

¼ teaspoon salt
4-5 drops Tabasco sauce
2 cups cooked chopped shellfish
  (shrimp or rock lobster tails)
⅔ cup sliced stuffed olives
¼ cup mayonnaise
⅔ cup whipping cream

Cooking time: 20 minutes
Serves: 8-12

Cook the macaroni until tender. Drain. Cool. Soften the gelatin in the cold water. Add the hot water and stir until dissolved. Stir in the lemon juice, sugar, salt, and Tabasco sauce. Chill until partially set (this should be egg-white consistency). Mix with the macaroni, shellfish, olives, and mayonnaise (see page 55). Whip the cream and fold into the mixture. Place in a mold, previously rinsed with cold water. Chill until firm. Serve on a bed of lettuce leaves, accompanied by Horseradish Sauce (see page 361).

Note: Instant macaroni may be used in this recipe.

RICOTTA-STUFFED CANNELLONI WITH TOMATO SAUCE

12 cannelloni
3 cups ricotta or cream
  cheese
2 eggs
¾ cup Parmesan cheese
salt and pepper to taste

dash nutmeg
4-6 large ripe tomatoes,
  skinned and chopped
cup olive oil
¼ cup butter

Cooking time: 35 minutes
Temperature: 350°
Serves: 4-6

Cook the cannelloni according to the directions for cooking pasta (see page 192) and, when still a little firm, add 1 to 2 cups cold water, then set aside until ready to fill.

Mix the ricotta cheese, eggs, and one third of the Parmesan cheese thoroughly. Season to taste with salt, pepper, and nutmeg. Place the prepared tomatoes in a saucepan, and cook, uncovered, to a thick pulp, stirring occasionally. Remove from the heat and stir in the oil gradually.

Drain the cannelloni and fill with the ricotta cheese mixture. Place side by side in a single layer in a buttered shallow baking dish. Pour the tomato sauce around the cannelloni, sprinkle with the remaining Parmesan cheese, and dot with the butter. Bake in a 350° oven until bubbling, about 20 minutes. Serve at once.

Variation: If a different tomato sauce is desired, use the tomato sauce recipe for Spaghetti with Meatballs (see page 194).

*Fettucine all' Alfredo and
Shells with Red Clam Sauce*

LASAGNE NAPOLI

Lasagne itself is thick and hearty, and the sauce is also thick. The dish should be neither soupy nor dry when ready to serve.

$\frac{3}{4}$ lb. lasagne
$\frac{1}{4}$ cup olive or salad oil
1 onion, finely chopped
2 cloves garlic, crushed
2 cups ground steak
1 (4 oz.) can sliced mushrooms
1 cup puréed tomatoes
1 (6 oz.) can tomato paste
1$\frac{1}{2}$ teaspoons oregano or
   marjoram

2$\frac{1}{2}$ teaspoons salt
$\frac{3}{4}$ cup water or red wine
1 egg
1 (10 oz.) package frozen
   spinach, chopped or puréed
1 cup cream-style cottage cheese
$\frac{1}{2}$ cup grated Parmesan cheese
$\frac{1}{2}$ lb. Mozzarella or Cheddar
   cheese

Cooking time: 1$\frac{1}{4}$ hours
Temperature: 350°
Serves: 6-8

Cook the lasagne in boiling water until tender (see page 192). Do not drain the lasagne but leave it in the water until ready for layering. Add 1 to 2 cups cold water and let it stand. This prevents it from sticking together.

Heat 1 tablespoon of the oil in a skillet and fry the onion, garlic, and meat until browned. Stir in the mushrooms, tomatoes, tomato paste, oregano, salt to taste, and water or wine if desired. Simmer for 20 minutes. Meanwhile, blend together the egg, thawed spinach, cottage cheese, Parmesan cheese, remaining oil, and salt. Pour half the meat sauce into an oblong baking dish (13 by 9 inches). Cover with a layer of lasagne. Spread the spinach mixture over the lasagne. Cover with another layer of lasagne and meat sauce. Cover and bake in a 350° oven for 40 to 50 minutes. Cut the Mozzarella or Cheddar cheese into strips. Remove the cover and place strips of cheese on top of the lasagne. Bake until the cheese melts and is bubbly. Serve hot.

BASIC NOODLE DOUGH

(PASTA)

For anyone wanting to try a hand at home-made noodles, here is the recipe.

4 cups all-purpose flour
$\frac{1}{2}$ teaspoon salt

4 medium eggs
approximately $\frac{1}{3}$ cup cold water

Sift the flour and salt together into a large bowl. Make a well in the center. Add the eggs, one at a time, mixing slightly after each addition. Gradually add enough cold water to make a stiff dough. Turn onto a lightly floured surface and knead for 8 to 10 minutes, until the dough is smooth and elastic. Divide into 3 or 4 parts. Roll each part into a wide rectangle, $\frac{1}{8}$ inch thick. Allow to dry for 30 minutes on a clean dish towel on a table, or over the back of a chair.

To cut the paste: Sprinkle each rectangle lightly with flour. Cut with a sharp knife or pastry cutter into the desired shapes. Place on clean dish towels to dry for an hour or so before cooking.

FETTUCINE ALL' ALFREDO

$\frac{1}{2}$ lb. egg noodles, $\frac{1}{4}$ inch wide
   (fettucine)
$\frac{1}{2}$ cup butter
1$\frac{1}{4}$ cups Parmesan cheese
$\frac{1}{4}$ teaspoon salt

dash freshly cracked pepper
1 cup cream
finely chopped parsley
Parmesan cheese, for serving

Cooking time: 20-25 minutes
Serves: 4-6

Cook the noodles in a large saucepan according to the directions on page 192. Meanwhile, melt the butter, then add the Parmesan cheese, salt, pepper, and cream. Cook over a low heat, stirring constantly, until blended. Drain the noodles. Immediately add to the cheese mixture, and toss until the noodles are well coated. Place in a heated serving dish, sprinkle with parsley and Parmesan cheese, and serve at once.

NUTTY MEATBALLS WITH NOODLES

1 cup finely ground chuck steak
$\frac{1}{2}$ cup crisp rice cereal, crushed
$\frac{1}{4}$ cup chopped salted peanuts
2 tablespoons milk
$\frac{1}{2}$ teaspoon salt
dash pepper

2 tablespoons butter
1 ($10\frac{1}{2}$ oz.) can condensed
   cream of mushroom soup
$\frac{1}{4}$ cup milk
$\frac{1}{2}$ lb. curled egg noodles
   (fideline)

Cooking time: see method
Serves: 4-5

Combine together thoroughly the ground steak, crushed cereal, peanuts, milk, salt, and pepper. Shape into 20 small meatballs. Melt the butter in a large saucepan. Add the meatballs, a few at a time. Brown on all sides for 10 minutes. Remove the meatballs. Add the soup and milk to the pan. Mix and heat. Place the browned meatballs in the sauce. Cover, and simmer over low heat for 15 minutes. Meanwhile, cook the noodles and drain. Serve hot with the meatballs and sauce.

RAVIOLI

For filling:
$\frac{1}{4}$ cup olive oil
$1\frac{1}{2}$ cups ground beef or
   shredded chicken
1 cup cooked spinach or
   frozen spinach, thawed

2 eggs
2 tablespoons Parmesan cheese
$\frac{3}{4}$ teaspoon salt
$\frac{1}{4}$ teaspoon pepper

Cooking time: 20 minutes
Yield: 36

1 quantity basic noodle dough
1 quantity tomato sauce

grated Parmesan or Romano
   cheese

To make the filling: Heat the oil in a skillet. Add the meat and cook until browned. Drain the spinach, chop finely, and mix with the beef. Add the beaten eggs, Parmesan cheese, salt, and pepper. Mix well. Set aside until ready to use.

Make the noodle dough (see page 198). Divide the dough into fourths. Roll each fourth into a rectangle $\frac{1}{8}$ inch thick. Cut the dough lengthwise with a cutter into strips 5 inches wide. Alternatively, use ready-to-fill ravioli. Place 2 teaspoons of the filling in the center of each strip $3\frac{1}{2}$ inches apart. Fold each strip in half lengthwise, covering the filling. Seal by pressing the edges together with the prongs of a fork. Press between the mounds of filling and cut with a pastry cutter, sealing the edges with the fork. Add the ravioli gradually, about one third at a time, to a large saucepan of rapidly boiling salted water. Cook until tender (about 20 minutes). Remove with a perforated spoon. Drain well. Place on a warm platter and serve topped with the tomato sauce (see Spaghetti with Meatballs, page 194), and sprinkled with Parmesan or Romano cheese.

GNOCCHI

These Italian dumplings are often made with potatoes, but may be made with semolina or polenta.

3 medium-sized potatoes
   (mature ones)
1 cup all-purpose flour

1 egg
$1\frac{1}{2}$ teaspoons salt
extra flour

Cooking time: 20 minutes
Serves: 4-6

Boil the unpeeled potatoes until tender. Peel them while hot. Place in a mixing bowl, and mash, adding the sifted flour, a little at a time, while the potatoes are hot. Beat until smooth. Turn onto a well-floured board. Knead, working in enough flour to form a smooth, soft, non-sticky dough. Divide the dough into several parts. Roll each into pencil thickness. Cut into $\frac{3}{4}$-inch pieces. With the prongs of a floured fork press each piece so that it curls. Place on wax paper. Sprinkle lightly with flour. Cook immediately, or within 2 hours.

Add the gnocchi, a few at a time, to a large pan of rapidly boiling salted water with a little oil added. Cook for about 5 minutes, or until the gnocchi are tender and come to the surface. Drain and keep warm in a heated bowl until all the gnocchi are cooked.

Serve the gnocchi in tomato sauce (see Spaghetti with Meatballs, page 194) or Bolognese sauce (see page 194) sprinkled with Parmesan cheese. Try it also with a pot roast (see page 125) topped with gravy.

Charmaine Solomon

Charmaine Solomon is a leading food writer and expert on rice and Eastern food. Born in Ceylon, into a family of culinary skill, she combines journalism with good cookery.

Rice

There are literally hundreds of varieties of rice. For the best results in cooking rice, it is important to know what kind of rice to use in various dishes.

- Short-grain rice is suitable for steaming Chinese style, or for Chinese fried rice. It is best for puddings, risotto, or any dish where a creamy result is desired.
- Long-grain rice is required for Indian or Middle Eastern rice dishes such as pilaff, or boiled as an accompaniment to curries.
- Brown rice, prized for its nutritive value and vitamin B content, has more flavor than the polished grains and requires longer cooking. Most recipes using polished rice may be adapted for brown rice, but more liquid will be needed and the cooking time will have to be increased. It has a firmer, more chewy texture than rice that has been polished.
- Basmati, an aromatic table rice grown in Pakistan, is, with its thin, long grains, one of the world's finest varieties of rice. It is practically impossible to cook this rice badly. It always comes up fluffy and separate, and its unique fragrance and flavor makes the addition of other ingredients unnecessary.

TO COOK RICE:

Absorption method: Add 1 cup washed, drained rice to 2 cups boiling water with 1 teaspoon each of salt and butter. Bring to a boil, lower the heat, cover tightly, and cook gently for 15 to 20 minutes. Turn off the heat and allow to stand for 5 minutes before serving.

Most kinds of rice cook perfectly by this method; i.e., 2 cups water for the first cup of rice and 1 cups water for each extra cup of rice, thus: —

1 cup rice	...	...	... 2 cups water
2 cups rice	...	...	... $3\frac{1}{2}$ cups water
3 cups rice	...	...	... 5 cups water
4 cups rice	...	...	... $6\frac{1}{2}$ cups water.

The only exception is brown or natural rice, which needs more than twice the quantity of water. One cup brown rice requires approximately $4\frac{1}{2}$ cups water and takes 1 to $1\frac{1}{4}$ hours to cook.

Water bath method: This method requires a large pan and 8 cups water to each cup of rice. Bring 8 cups water to the boil with 1 level tablespoon salt.

Add 1 cup rice and cook for 12 to 14 minutes, when rice grain pressed between the fingers will feel soft. Drain into a colander and pour hot water through to separate the grains and wash away excess starch. If necessary, keep hot over a pan of simmering water.

Orange Rice with Chicken Breasts, Rice Patties, and Indian Ghee Rice

INDIAN GHEE RICE

4½ cups basmati or long-grain
   rice
½ cup ghee or butter
2 onions, thinly sliced
1 teaspoon turmeric
½ teaspoon saffron
10 cardamom pods, bruised
1 teaspoon peppercorns
4 cloves
3-inch stick cinnamon

7½ cups chicken stock or water
   and chicken bouillon cubes
3 teaspoons salt
¾ cup seedless white raisins
8 eggs, hard-cooked
extra salt
extra turmeric
oil for frying
1½ cups cooked peas
¾ cup blanched almonds

Cooking time: 20 minutes
Serves: 8

Wash the rice, changing the water 3 or 4 times. Put into a large sieve or colander and allow to drain for at least 1 hour. Heat the ghee in a large pan and fry the onion until golden brown. Add the turmeric, saffron, cardamom pods, peppercorns, cloves, and cinnamon. Add the rice and fry for a few minutes, turning it over until all the ghee is absorbed and the rice is golden. Add the hot stock and the salt. Stir well and bring to a boil, turn the heat to very low, and simmer the rice gently. Cover the pan tightly and cook for 15 to 20 minutes. Basmati rice requires only 15 minutes. After 10 minutes, sprinkle the raisins over the rice. Do not stir. At the end of the cooking time, remove the pan from the heat, uncover for a few moments to allow the steam to escape, then replace the lid until ready to serve. The rice will keep warm for at least 30 minutes if left on the side of the cooker in a warm kitchen. Before serving fluff up with a fork and lift the rice carefully onto a heated serving dish, using a perforated metal spoon, to keep the rice grains whole and separate.

While the rice is cooking rub the shelled, hard-cooked eggs with salt and turmeric. Prick the eggs a few times with a fine skewer. (This prevents them from bursting when fried.) Heat a little oil in a skillet and fry the eggs until a golden brown crust forms all over.

Garnish the rice with the hot peas and the almonds, which have been fried in a little butter or ghee until golden. Place whole or halved eggs at intervals around the rice.

CHINESE FRIED RICE

As with many Chinese dishes, this requires only a few minutes of cooking, but a good deal of preparation has to be done first. This may be done early in the day or even the day before, leaving only the final cooking for the last minute.

2¼ cups short-grain rice
½ cup dried mushrooms
1 lb. cooked prawns
1 pair dried Chinese sausages
10 green beans
2 stalks celery
1-inch piece fresh ginger
2 eggs
salt
½ cup peanut oil

¼ cup sesame oil
1 clove garlic, crushed
1 cup chopped scallions
½ cup diced barbecued pork
¼ cup chicken stock or water
   and chicken bouillon cube
¼ cup soy sauce
⅛ teaspoon monosodium
   glutamate

Cooking time: 10 minutes
Serves: 6-8

Cook the rice by the water bath method, drain, and allow to get completely cold. The rice may be cooked a day or two before required and refrigerated if more convenient.

Soak the mushrooms in hot water for 20 minutes. Remove the stems and discard. Cut the mushrooms into thin slices. Shell and de-vein the prawns. Steam the sausages in a colander over boiling water for 5 minutes, then cut into paper-thin diagonal slices. String the beans and celery and cut into very thin diagonal slices. Scrape the skin from the ginger, and grate finely.

Beat the eggs with ¼ teaspoon salt. Heat 2 tablespoons of the peanut oil in a large skillet and fry the eggs to make a large flat pancake. Cut into ½-inch strips and reserve.

Heat the remaining peanut and sesame oils together in a wok or large skillet. Add the ginger and garlic to flavor the oil. Add the mushrooms, prawns, sausages, celery, beans, scallions, and pork. Fry over high heat, tossing with a frying spoon, for 2 to 3 minutes. Add the rice and continue tossing until the rice is heated through. Season well with salt, then sprinkle the stock, soy sauce, and monosodium glutamate, mixed together, over the rice and toss again to mix. Serve hot, garnished with strips of egg.

Note: A wok is a Chinese cooking pan. It has a rounded base and is used for most methods of Chinese cookery. It is obtainable from Chinese stores.

RISOTTO ALLA MILANESE

7½ cups chicken stock or water
  and chicken bouillon cubes
½ cup butter
2 onions, finely chopped
2 cups short-grain rice

½ cup dry white wine
½ teaspoon saffron
½ cup freshly grated Parmesan
  cheese

Cooking time: 45-50 minutes
Serves: 6

Bring the chicken stock to a boil, lower the heat, and keep it simmering gently. In a heavy saucepan melt half the butter, add the onions, and cook until soft and golden, stirring occasionally. Take care they do not brown. Add the rice and cook, stirring, for a few minutes until the grains are coated with butter. Add the wine and cook until it is absorbed, then add 2 cups of the simmering stock. Cook, uncovered, stirring occasionally, until the liquid is almost absorbed then add 2 more cups stock and cook in the same way. Stir the saffron into the remaining stock and simmer for 5 minutes. Add to the rice and cook until the stock is completely absorbed. The rice should be tender and creamy. Gently stir in the remaining butter and the grated cheese with a fork, to avoid crushing the rice grains. Serve at once.

GOLDEN CHICKEN PILAFF

1 3-lb. chicken
1 teaspoon turmeric
2 teaspoons salt
2 tablespoons green masala
  paste
½ cup oil
2 tablespoons butter, or ghee

4 cups hot water
2½ teaspoons salt
2 chicken bouillon cubes
2½ cups long-grain rice
½ cup blanched almonds
½ cup seedless white raisins
3 eggs, hard-cooked

Cooking time: 45-50 minutes
Serves: 6

Cut the chicken into serving pieces and rub with a mixture of half the turmeric, the salt, and the green masala paste. (If green masala paste is difficult to obtain substitute 1 teaspoon each crushed garlic, ginger, and fresh mint.) Allow to stand for 1 hour, or in a refrigerator for several hours. Heat the oil and butter in a skillet, and cook the chicken pieces over medium heat until golden brown, 10 to 15 minutes. Drain on paper towels. Place in an ovenproof dish, cover with aluminum foil, and keep warm in a 250° oven. Pour the oil from the skillet into a cup and reserve. Add 1 cup hot water to the pan, heat, and stir in all the crusty brown pieces from the bottom and sides of the skillet. Add this to the remaining 3 cups hot water, stir in the salt and chicken bouillon cubes, and dissolve.

Put ¼ cup of the oil the chicken was fried in into a saucepan, and heat. Add the remaining turmeric and stir. Add the rice and fry over medium heat until golden, stirring continuously. Add the measured hot liquid. Bring to a boil, then lower the heat, cover tightly, and simmer for 20 minutes. Fry the almonds in the remaining oil. Drain. Fry the raisins and drain. Shell the hard-cooked eggs and halve lengthwise.

When the rice is cooked, uncover and allow the steam to escape for a few minutes, then fluff up with a fork and pile onto a heated serving dish. Arrange the chicken pieces on top, pressing them halfway into the rice. Garnish with the almonds, seedless white raisins and hard-cooked eggs. Serve hot.

BROWN RICE WITH CHEESE

2 tablespoons ghee or butter
¼ cup oil
1½ cups chopped scallions
2¼ cups brown rice
6¼ cups chicken stock or water
  and chicken bouillon cubes

1 teaspoon salt
½ teaspoon freshly cracked
  pepper
½ lb. Swiss cheese, sliced, or
1½ cups grated cheese
parsley sprigs for garnish

Cooking time: 1¼ hours
Serves: 6

Heat the ghee and oil in a pan. Gently fry the scallions (green leaves included) until soft and golden. Add the washed and well-drained rice and fry, stirring continuously, for about 8 minutes. Add the hot stock, salt, and pepper. Stir, cover, and simmer for 1 hour. Turn into a buttered ovenproof dish.

Cover the top of the rice with slices of Swiss cheese, or with grated cheese, and place under a hot broiler, or in a 425° oven until the cheese melts and turns golden. Garnish with parsley sprigs, and serve hot.

RICE PATTIES

1 cup short-grain rice
1 onion, finely chopped
¼ cup butter
3¾ cups chicken stock or water
   and chicken bouillon cubes

2 eggs, beaten
fine bread crumbs
oil for frying
parsley sprigs for garnish

Cooking time: 1 hour
Serves: 6

Cook the rice with the onion cooked in butter, adding the chicken stock in the same way as for Risotto alla Milanese, but omitting the wine, saffron, and cheese. Leave until cool enough to handle, then take large tablespoonfuls of the rice mixture and mold around a filling, which can be one of the following or any other desired. The patties may be molded into oval or round shapes. When all are made, dip into beaten egg, then into bread crumbs. Fry in deep hot oil until golden brown all over and heated through. Drain on paper towels and serve very hot, garnished with fried parsley. The patties may be kept hot in the oven for 10 minutes.
Ham and Prawn Filling: Finely dice ½ cup cooked ham and 1¼ cups cooked prawns, shelled and de-veined. Chop a small onion finely, heat 2 tablespoons butter, and gently fry the onion until soft and golden. Mix with the ham and prawns and season to taste.
Savory Mince Filling: In 2 tablespoons hot oil, fry 1 finely chopped onion and 1 clove crushed garlic. Add 1 cup lean ground beef and stir until the beef changes color. Add ½ teaspoon salt, and pepper to taste. If liked, add ½ cup chopped bacon. Cover, and cook over low heat for about 20 minutes.
Mozzarella Cheese Filling: Cut ¾-inch cubes of Mozzarella cheese, or any other cooking cheese, and enclose in the rice. When the patties are fried the cheese melts slightly and when broken open it separates in long strands. The Italians call these cheese patties 'telephone wires'!

DOLMADES

(STUFFED VINE LEAVES)

16 fresh or canned vine leaves
2 cups lean ground beef
½ cup long-grain rice
2 onions, finely chopped
1 clove garlic, crushed
2 teaspoons salt

½ teaspoon pepper
1 teaspoon dried oregano leaves
2 tablespoons chopped fresh
   mint
2½ cups beef stock or water and
   beef bouillon cube

Cooking time: 1 hour
Serves: 4

If using fresh vine leaves, choose medium-sized leaves that are not too dark in color. Large, dark leaves are tough. Snip off the stems with kitchen scissors, wash well, place in a bowl, and pour boiling water over to soften. If using canned vine leaves in brine, wash in warm water before filling.

To prepare the filling, combine all the remaining ingredients except the stock, mixing thoroughly. Divide the mixture into 16 portions and shape into small sausage shapes. On a wooden board place one leaf at a time, shiny side downwards, and place a portion of meat filling on the leaf, near the stem. Fold over the top of the leaf, then the sides. Roll up, enclosing the meat completely. Pack the rolls close together in a heavy pan in neat rows. If necessary, put a second layer on top of the first. Pour the stock into the pan and cover with the lid. Bring slowly to the simmering point and simmer gently for 45 minutes to 1 hour. Serve hot.

SAFFRON RICE

¼ cup butter
1 large onion, finely chopped
2¼ cups long-grain rice
3½ cups chicken stock or water

   and chicken bouillon cubes
½ teaspoon saffron
2 teaspoons salt
10 whole peppercorns

Cooking time: 25 minutes
Serves: 6

Heat the butter in a saucepan and gently fry the onion until golden. Add the washed and well-drained rice and fry for 2 to 3 minutes, until the grains are coated with butter. Add the hot chicken stock, saffron, salt, and peppercorns. Bring to a boil, then lower the heat, cover tightly, and steam for 20 minutes. Uncover and fluff up the rice gently with a fork. Serve as an accompaniment to fish, poultry, or any kind of meat.

Chicken and Orange Kebabs

205

DESSERTS

Betty Dunleavy

Betty Dunleavy was the Food Editor for two leading Australian magazines for many years before taking up her present position in industry as a Home Service Supervisor.

I love creating desserts, talking about them, and writing about them. I also like to see the look of anticipation—and then satisfaction—on the faces at my table, whether I am serving a quick and easy adaptation from a package or can or a luscious special-occasion masterpiece.

Desserts must be chosen wisely, bearing in mind what is served beforehand. Choose a light dessert to follow a rich main course; if the main course is simple, a richer dessert may follow. Take into consideration the time of year and the fruits in season. There are innumerable delicious desserts that are quick to prepare which are suitable for the family. There are also desserts which require a little more time and thought and therefore you may wish to serve these when guests are expected.

My family feels that a meal is not complete without a dessert—in the summertime a cold refreshing sweet and in the cold of winter months, a hearty steaming pudding.

I have made the variety of desserts in this section as wide as possible to cope with all seasons, including busy days, inventive days, and even days when beating an egg seems a lot of bother.

My suggestion to you is this. Make each recipe, as the occasion demands, just as it is written in the following pages. Then imagine it with different flavors, different custards, sauces, or cream, or even different methods of decoration and serving. The recipes may be altered in these ways to suit your family's or guests' tastes. In this way there should be sufficient dessert ideas to last for a long, long time.

All the recipes are sufficient for a family of five, with an extra helping for the hearty eater or the one with the sweetest tooth.

ALMOND TOFFEE SUNDAE

This attractive variation on the simple junket is ideal for adding interest to the meals of a young family.

$\frac{1}{4}$ lb. almond English toffee
$\frac{1}{4}$ cup sugar
4 teaspoons essence of rennet
  or 2 teaspoons prepared rennet
4 cups warm milk

2-3 bananas
juice of 1 orange or lemon
1 egg white
$\frac{2}{3}$ cup whipping cream
sugar

Serves: 5-6

Crush the almond toffee and sprinkle 1 teaspoonful in the bottom of each sundae glass. Stir the sugar into the warmed milk (about blood heat) and add the rennet, stirring in. Pour into the glasses (each should be three fourths full). Leave at room temperature to coagulate, then chill. Mash the bananas with a fork, add the orange or lemon juice, and fold into the stiffly beaten egg white. Just before serving, top the junket with banana whip, cover with the whipped, sweetened cream, and sprinkle with the remaining crushed toffee.

BERRY FROST

As a change from plain ice cream vary the fruits and serve this often on hot summer days.

2 egg whites
scant $\frac{1}{2}$ cup sugar
1 (14$\frac{1}{2}$ oz.) can evaporated milk
lemon juice

1 package frozen raspberries,
  thawed and drained
2 bananas, mashed
whipped cream for serving

Serves: 5-6

Beat the egg whites and the sugar to a meringue consistency. Whip the thoroughly chilled evaporated milk until thickened and fold it into the meringue, adding lemon juice to taste. Fold in the drained raspberries and the mashed bananas, then spoon into trays and freeze as fast as possible in the refrigerator. Serve decorated with whipped cream.

SPEEDY COFFEE CREAM

This quick and easy dessert may be prepared ahead of time.

1 package vanilla-flavored
  pudding mix
hot-milk coffee
$\frac{1}{3}$ cup Marsala (optional)

1$\frac{1}{4}$ cups cream, lightly whipped
1 (1 lb. 13 oz.) can pear halves
chocolate wafers for serving

Serves: 5-6

Make up the pudding mix according to the directions on the package, using hot-milk coffee instead of the hot milk. Add the Marsala, if used, and fold in the lightly whipped cream. Beat the mixture until thick and foamy. Spoon over 1 or 2 drained pear halves placed in individual dishes, and serve with chocolate wafers.

STAWBERRY SNOW

1 package strawberry instant
  pudding mix
milk

2 egg whites
1 (15$\frac{1}{2}$ oz.) can strawberry pie
  filling

Serves: 5-6

Prepare the instant pudding mix with milk as directed on the package. Beat the egg whites until stiff and lightly fold into the pudding mix. Pile into tall glasses, in alternate layers with the strawberry pie filling, and chill.

RICE TROPICAL

1 cup sugar
1 cup water
2 envelopes gelatin
¼ teaspoon cream of tartar
2 tablespoons lemon juice
1 teaspoon grated lemon rind
1½ cups cooked rice

⅓ cup orange juice
finely grated rind of ½ orange
½ cup sweetened condensed
   milk
2-3 bananas
extra lemon juice

Serves: 5-6

Place the sugar, water, gelatin, and cream of tartar in a pan and boil over medium heat for 10 minutes. Allow to cool and thicken slightly. Stir in the lemon juice and rind and beat until thick and foamy. Combine the rice, orange juice and rind, and condensed milk. Spoon into a large serving dish. Slice the bananas over the top and sprinkle with lemon juice. Top with the thickened marshmallow, and chill before serving.

SHERRIED APRICOTS WITH ALMONDS

1 (1 lb. 13 oz.) can apricots
¾ cup sugar
½ cup sweet sherry

1½-2 pints vanilla ice cream
toasted slivered almonds

Serves: 5-6

Drain the syrup from the apricots. Place in a saucepan with the sugar and cook over low heat until the sugar has dissolved. Bring to a boil and boil until the syrup thickens. Stir in the sherry gradually. Pour the syrup over the apricots, then cool and chill. Serve over portions of ice cream and sprinkle with almond slivers.

SUMMER BERRY PUDDING

1½ lb. soft berry fruit (raspberries,
   strawberries, red currants,
   mulberries, or blueberries)
½ cup water
¾-1 cup sugar, depending
   on fruit

6-8 thin slices bread, crusts
   removed and cut into strips
brandy or kirsch
extra fruit for decorating
whipped cream for serving

Serves: 5-6

Hull and clean the fruit. Stew slowly with the water and sugar in a covered saucepan until the fruit is slightly softened. Line a greased pudding mold with the strips of bread. Half fill the center with the drained fruit and sprinkle with a little brandy or kirsch. Cover with strips of bread. Add the remaining fruit and ¼ cup of the juice, mixed with a little more brandy or kirsch. Cover with a 'lid' of bread strips, then a sheet of aluminum foil and a plate. Put a heavy weight on top of the plate and leave in the refrigerator overnight. To serve, loosen around the edge with a knife and turn out onto a flat plate. Decorate with extra fruit and serve with whipped cream. *Note:* Ladyfingers may be used in place of the strips of bread.

VANITY PRUNE WHIP

2 envelopes gelatin
¼ cup cold water
½ cup hot strong coffee
¼ cup Marsala
dash salt
½ cup sugar

2 squares unsweetened cooking
   chocolate, grated
1 cup cooked, chopped prunes
½ cup coarsely chopped walnuts
1 cup cream, whipped
extra whipped cream and walnuts
   for decoration

Serves: 5-6

Soak the gelatin in the cold water for 5 minutes. Add the coffee, Marsala, salt, sugar, and grated chocolate, and stir until the chocolate is dissolved. Cool until the mixture begins to thicken. Stir in the prunes and walnuts. then carefully fold in the whipped cream. Spoon into dessert or parfait glasses and decorate with whipped cream and walnuts. Chill before serving.

ALL-IN-TOGETHER PUDDING

This pudding is made and cooked all in the one dish! Once you have tried this, it will be sure to become your winter standby.

1 cup chopped dates
1 teaspoon grated lemon rind
2 tablespoons butter or
    margarine chopped
2 cups freshly-made hot strained
    tea
1 egg

1½ cups all-purpose flour, sifted
    with 1½ teaspoons baking
    powder
½ cup brown sugar, firmly packed
½ teaspoon mixed spice
¼ teaspoon salt
extra ½ cup brown sugar

Cooking time: 40-50 minutes
Temperature: 375°
Serves: 5-6

Arrange the dates on the bottom of an 8-inch square cake pan or ovenproof casserole. Add the lemon rind and butter or margarine, and pour half the hot tea over. Stir to melt the butter and soften the dates. Stand aside for 5 minutes. Add the egg, flour, brown sugar, spice, and salt, and beat until thoroughly blended. Scrape the bottom and sides of the pan occasionally while beating. Smooth the batter evenly in the pan. Sprinkle with the extra brown sugar and carefully pour the remaining hot tea over the surface. Bake in a 375° oven for 40 to 50 minutes. Serve warm, with creamy custard.

APPLE PINWHEEL SLICES

½ cup butter or margarine
½ cup sugar
2 egg yolks
¼ cup milk
2 cups all-purpose flour, sifted
    with 2 teaspoons baking
    powder

1 teaspoon cinnamon
2 teaspoons sugar
1 (15 oz.) can apple pie filling
6 tablespoons brown sugar
grated rind of ½ lemon
extra ¼ cup butter

Cooking time: 30-35 minutes
Temperature: 350°
Serves: 5-6

Cream the butter or margarine and sugar together, add the egg yolks and milk, and beat well. Mix in the sifted dry ingredients. Roll out between 2 sheets of wax paper until approximately ¼ inch thick. Spread with the apples mixed with the brown sugar and grated lemon rind. Dot with pieces of extra butter and roll up as for a jelly roll. Place in a buttered shallow pan and slash at intervals almost through. Bake in a 350° oven for 30 to 35 minutes. Serve warm, cut in slices, with cream or custard.

CARAMEL SPONGE DESSERT

This dessert makes a more exciting way of presenting a nutritious baked custard to young families.

6 tablespoons sugar
¼ cup water
2½ cups milk
3 eggs

extra ¼ cup sugar
1 cup soft cake crumbs
vanilla extract
½ cup sugar for meringue

Cooking time: 40-45 minutes
Temperature: 325°
Serves: 5-6

Caramelize the sugar and half the water in a saucepan. Carefully add the remainder of the water and boil over medium heat until the caramel is dissolved. Add the milk and heat. Separate the eggs. Beat the yolks with the extra sugar. Add the hot (not boiling) milk and pour onto the cake crumbs. Flavor with vanilla extract. Pour into a buttered pie dish. Make a meringue with the egg whites and sugar. Place in spoonfuls over the custard mixture. Bake in a 325° oven for 40 to 45 minutes. Serve hot.

CRUSTED PINEAPPLE SLICES

1 large pineapple
½ cup chopped raisins
¼ cup chopped walnuts
2 egg whites

2 teaspoons lemon juice
¾ cup sugar
½ teaspoon grated lemon rind
flaked or shredded coconut

Serves: 5-6

Remove the skin from the pineapple and cut the flesh into rounds, removing the core. Fill the cavity of each slice with a mixture of raisins and walnuts. Combine the lightly beaten egg whites with the lemon juice, sugar, and lemon rind in a heatproof bowl. Beat briskly over boiling water for 5 minutes, then remove from the heat and fold in the coconut. Cool slightly, and pile onto each pineapple slice. Brown the tops lightly under a medium-hot broiler and serve at once.
Variation: Try with peaches or apricots.

CRUNCHY RHUBARB AND APPLE

1 cup cooked apple pulp
2 cups cooked rhubarb
juice of 1 small lemon
1 teaspoon grated lemon rind
2 eggs
1 tablespoon cornstarch

¼ cup corn syrup
scant 2 cups milk
1 teaspoon vanilla extract
½ cup butter or margarine
1¼ cups rolled oats
1 teaspoon mixed spice
6 tablespoons brown sugar

Cooking time: 20 minutes
Temperature: 325°
Serves: 5-6

Combine the apple, rhubarb, lemon juice, and grated lemon rind. Arrange in a greased shallow ovenproof dish. Make a custard with the eggs, cornstarch, corn syrup, and milk. Remove from the heat, add the vanilla extract, and pour the custard over the fruit mixture.

Melt the butter or margarine, add the rolled oats, spice, and brown sugar, and stir over low heat to combine. Spoon over the custard mixture and bake in a 325° oven for 20 minutes. Serve warm or cold.

GOLDEN PUMPKIN PIE

1 quantity Short Crust
2¼ cups mixed dried fruits
½ cup brown sugar, firmly packed
1 teaspoon grated lemon rind
1 green apple, grated
brandy or sweet sherry

2 eggs
¼ teaspoon salt
1 cup evaporated milk
¾ cup cooked mashed pumpkin
whipped cream and walnuts
   for decoration

Cooking time: 40-50 minutes
Temperature: 425°
   reducing to 350°
Serves: 5-6

Line a 9-inch pie plate with the dough and decorate the edge (see page 382). Combine the fruits, one fourth of the brown sugar, the lemon rind, and the apple with 2 to 3 tablespoons brandy or sweet sherry and spoon into the uncooked pie shell. Beat the eggs with the remaining brown sugar and the salt, mix in the evaporated milk and pumpkin, then stir over low heat until warmed but not boiling. Carefully pour over the fruit mixture, place in a 425° oven, and cook for 10 minutes. Reduce the temperature to 350° and cook for a further 30 to 40 minutes, or until the custard is set. Allow to stand for 5 minutes, then prick the surface of the custard with a fork or fine skewer. Sprinkle a little extra brandy or sherry over. When cooled, decorate with whipped cream and walnut pieces.

HONEYED RICE BAKE

1 cup rice	½ cup chopped walnuts	Cooking time: 35-45 minutes
juice and rind of 1 lemon	2 tablespoons butter or margarine	Temperature: 325°
2¾ cups creamy milk	½ teaspoon cinnamon	Serves: 5-6
¾ cup honey	2 eggs, separated	
½ cup seedless white raisins	6 tablespoons sugar	

Place the rice, lemon juice, lemon rind cut in strips, and milk in a saucepan and cook slowly for 15 minutes, stirring occasionally. Heat the honey and combine with the raisins, walnuts, butter, and cinnamon. Remove the lemon rind from the rice and stir in the honey mixture and egg yolks. Spoon into a buttered casserole. Beat the egg whites until stiff, gradually beat in the sugar. Do not overbeat. Spoon onto the rice and bake in a 325° oven for 20 to 30 minutes. Serve warm.

GINGERBREAD PEARS

2 cups all-purpose flour	6 tablespoons butter or margarine	Cooking time: 50-60 minutes
¼ teaspoon salt	¾ cup brown sugar, firmly packed	Temperature: 325°
3 teaspoons ginger	1 large egg	Serves: 5-6
2 teaspoons baking powder	½ cup milk	
½ teaspoon baking soda	¼ cup melted butter	
½ cup molasses or corn syrup	1 (15 oz.) can pear halves	

Sift the flour, salt, ginger, baking powder, and baking soda into a mixing bowl. Place the molasses, butter, and two thirds of the brown sugar into a saucepan and stir over low heat until the sugar is dissolved. Do not overheat. Cool and stir into the dry ingredients. Mix in the egg and warmed milk. Spread the combined remaining brown sugar and melted butter over the bottom of a well-greased oblong cake pan and arrange the drained, sliced pear halves on top. Pour over the gingerbread batter and bake in a 325° oven for 50 to 60 minutes. Cut into squares. Serve warm, with custard or a sauce made from the pear syrup, if desired.

PEACH PRUNE COBBLER

For fruit base:	2 egg yolks	Cooking time: 30-35 minutes
½ cup chopped dried peaches	¼ cup butter or margarine	Temperature: 350°
¼ cup honey	1 dozen prunes, pitted and	Serves: 5-6
½ cup confectioners' sugar	chopped	
¾ cup cream cheese		
¼ cup lemon juice		
For cobbler topping:	1¼ cups all-purpose flour, sifted	
6 tablespoons butter or margarine	with 1¼ teaspoons baking	
6 tablespoons sugar	powder	
¼ cup fruit syrup (from peaches)	2 egg whites	

To make the fruit base: Soak the peaches in hot water to cover for 1 hour, add the honey, and simmer for 20 minutes. Cool. Add the confectioners' sugar gradually to the cream cheese, and beat well. Mix in the lemon juice, egg yolks, softened butter or margarine, and prunes. Arrange the drained, cooked peaches in the bottom of a buttered ovenproof dish and spread the cream cheese mixture over.

To make the cobbler topping: Cream together the butter or margarine and sugar, beat in the fruit syrup, and mix in the sifted flour. Fold in the stiffly beaten egg whites and spread lightly over the fruit base. Bake in a 350° oven for 30 to 35 minutes. Serve with custard or cream.

Variation: Dried apples, apricots, or pears may be substituted for the peaches.

Crusted Pineapple Slices

APRICOT CHEESECAKE

For crumb crust:
½ lb. sweet Graham crackers
½ cup butter

dash nutmeg or cinnamon

Cooking time: 50 minutes
Temperature: 300°
Serves: 5-6

For filling:
2 cups cream cheese
1 cup cottage cheese
1 teaspoon vanilla extract

4 eggs
1 cup sugar
1 (1 lb. 13 oz.) can apricots

For topping:
2 tablespoons sugar
1 teaspoon lemon juice

3 tablespoons cornstarch
½ cup syrup from apricots

To make the crumb crust: Crush the crackers finely. Melt the butter, add to the crushed crackers with the nutmeg or cinnamon, and mix well. Spread over the bottom and sides of an 8-inch spring form pan and press firmly. Refrigerate for about 1 hour.

To make the filling: Press the cheeses through a fine sieve, blend with the vanilla extract, and beat until creamy. Beat the eggs until frothy, then beat in the sugar gradually until the mixture is thick and foamy. Continue beating, while adding the cheese in small portions, mixing each time until smooth. Chop or mash 5 or 6 of the drained apricots and stir into the mixture. Spoon into the crumb crust and press down smoothly. Bake in a 300° oven for 35 to 40 minutes. Allow to cool in the oven with the door ajar.

For the topping: Chop or mash the remainder of the apricots and add the sugar and lemon juice. Blend the cornstarch with the syrup and add to the fruit. Bring to a boil, stirring constantly, then simmer for a few minutes. Cool and spread over the top of the cheesecake. Refrigerate overnight and remove from the pan before serving.

BRANDIED MERINGUE CREAM

4 egg whites
1 cup sugar
3 tablespoons cornstarch
1 cup toasted coarsely chopped
   almonds
2 drops almond extract

½-⅔ cup brandy or liqueur
scant 2 cups whipping cream
2 tablespoons confectioners'
   sugar
½ cup halved and toasted
   almonds, for decoration

Cooking time: 45 minutes
Temperature: 250°
Serves: 5-6

Beat the egg whites until very stiff and dry. Add the sugar gradually, beating well until all the sugar is incorporated. Do not overbeat. Add the cornstarch and fold in the chopped almonds and almond extract. Place in small heaps on greased baking sheets dusted with cornstarch and bake in a 250° oven for 45 minutes. Cool on the sheets. Arrange about one third of the almond meringues, lightly crushed, in the bottoms of individual dessert dishes or brandy balloons. Sprinkle over a little brandy or liqueur. Whip the cream with the confectioners' sugar until soft but thick. Spoon a little of the cream over the meringues and continue to fill the dishes with layers of crushed meringue, sprinkled with brandy, and whipped cream. Decorate with a swirl of cream and the halved, toasted almonds. Chill slightly before serving.

STRAWBERRY CREAM PARFAITS

2 cups good quality cream
   cheese
1¼ cups whipping cream
½ cup sifted confectioners' sugar

2-3 cups strawberries
18 small macaroons
¼ cup sweet sherry

Serves: 5-6

Bring the cream cheese to room temperature and beat until very smooth. Gradually blend in the whipped cream and confectioners' sugar. Fold through about one fourth of the hulled and chopped strawberries and chill well. Crush the macaroons lightly and sprinkle with the sherry. To serve, spoon alternate layers of the cream cheese mixture, macaroon crumbs, and remaining strawberries into parfait glasses. Top with swirls of the cream cheese mixture and a piece of strawberry.

LATTICED CHOCOLATE RUM PIE

1 (14½ oz.) can evaporated milk
2 envelopes gelatin
¾ cup milk
1 cup sugar
dash salt
2 eggs, separated

¼ lb. semi-sweet chocolate
¼ cup rum
1 teaspoon vanilla extract
1 9-inch baked pie shell
1¼ cups whipping cream

Serves: 5-6

Pour the evaporated milk into an ice cube tray, place in the freezer and chill until mushy around the edges. Soften the gelatin in ¼ cup of the milk. Combine three fourths of the sugar with the salt, egg yolks, and softened gelatin in the top of a double boiler and mix well. Cook over boiling water until the mixture thickens slightly, then remove from the heat. Melt half the chocolate and add, beat until smooth, and allow to chill until slightly thickened. Whip the chilled evaporated milk until thick. Fold the whipped milk, rum, and vanilla extract into the chocolate mixture, pour into the baked pie shell (see page 76), and chill thoroughly.

To serve: Whip the cream. Beat the whites until frothy, add the remaining sugar gradually, and continue to beat until soft peaks form. Fold into the whipped cream and spread over the pie. Shave the remaining chocolate into curls and sprinkle over the top of the whipped cream mixture in a lattice pattern.

MACAROON RASPBERRY TORTE

4 egg whites
¾ cup sugar
½ cup finely chopped walnuts
2 tablespoons butter
¼ cup all-purpose flour
cornstarch

1 cup cream
2 tablespoons confectioners' sugar
rum or brandy
3 cups fresh or frozen raspberries
whipped cream for decoration

Cooking time: 15-20 minutes
Temperature: 350°
Serves: 5-6

Whip the egg whites until stiff and gradually add the sugar, beating well after each addition. Fold in the chopped nuts, cooled melted butter, and flour and mix gently. Grease 3 baking sheets and dust lightly with cornstarch. Mark a circle in the middle of each, about 10 inches across, using a saucepan lid as a guide. Divide the mixture equally among the 3 sheets. Spread out and smooth carefully to fill the circles. Bake in a 350° oven for 15 to 20 minutes, until golden brown. Remove, loosen at once with a spatula and lift off the baking sheets. Cool on wire cooling racks. Pour the cream into a bowl and place the bowl over another bowl of broken ice or ice cubes. Beat until slightly thickened, add the confectioners' sugar, flavor with a little rum or brandy and continue beating until stiff. Carefully fold in two thirds of the raspberries. Sandwich the rounds of meringue together with the cream filling. Decorate with the remaining raspberries and extra cream.

MARSHMALLOW MARBLE SQUARES

2½ cups crushed coconut cookies
½ cup butter
sugar
2 cups strawberries
sweet sherry
1 package strawberry-flavored gelatin

1 cup boiling water
½ lb. marshmallows, chopped
⅓ cup milk
1¼ cups whipping cream
whipping cream and extra strawberries, for decoration

Serves: 5-6

Combine the crushed cookies with the melted butter and press firmly over the bottom of a greased 9-inch square cake pan. Chill until firm. Sprinkle a little sugar over the sliced strawberries and allow to stand for 30 minutes. Drain and reserve the juice, adding sufficient sweet sherry to make ½ cup. Dissolve the strawberry gelatin in the boiling water, add the strawberry juice and sherry, and chill until partially set. Combine the marsh-mallows with the milk and stir over low heat until the marshmallows melt. Cool. Whip the cream and fold into the marshmallow mixture. Add the strawberries to the partially set jello, then lightly fold into the marshmallow mixture to give a marbled effect. Pour onto the crumb crust and chill until firm. Cut into squares top with whipped cream, and decorate with extra strawberries before serving.

PARADISE CHIFFON PIE

2 envelopes gelatin
$\frac{1}{4}$ cup cold water
3 bananas
$\frac{1}{4}$ cup lemon juice
1 teaspoon grated lemon rind

3 eggs
$\frac{3}{4}$ cup sugar
$\frac{2}{3}$ cup whipping cream
1 8- or 9-inch baked pie shell
toasted almond halves

Serves: 5-6

Soften the gelatin in the cold water and dissolve over boiling water. Mash the bananas and stir in the lemon juice and rind, egg yolks, and half the sugar. Cook in the top of a double boiler over boiling water, stirring frequently, until the mixture thickens. Remove from the heat, add the dissolved gelatin, and cool. Chill until partially set. Beat the egg whites until stiff and frothy, add the remaining sugar, and beat until thick. Fold into the partially set banana mixture with the whipped cream. Place in the pie shell (see page 76) and chill well. Decorate with almond halves.

PAVLOVA

3 egg whites
$\frac{3}{4}$ cup sugar
$\frac{1}{2}$ teaspoon cornstarch

$\frac{1}{2}$ teaspoon vinegar
$\frac{1}{2}$ teaspoon vanilla extract

Cooking time: $2\frac{1}{2}$ hours
Temperature: 200°
Serves: 6-8

For filling:
$1\frac{1}{4}$ cups whipping cream
2-3 teaspoons confectioners' sugar

$\frac{1}{2}$ teaspoon vanilla extract
1 (1 lb. 13 oz.) can sliced peaches

Whip the egg whites until they are quite stiff. Add the sugar, 1 tablespoon at a time, beating well after each addition. Do not overbeat. Add the cornstarch with the last amount of sugar, then fold in the vinegar and vanilla extract. Draw a 7-inch circle on oiled wax paper placed on a baking sheet. Sprinkle lightly with cornstarch. Spread half the meringue mixture to cover the circle. Place the remaining meringue in a pastry bag with a large plain nozzle and pipe around the edge of the circle to form a wall. Place in a 200° oven for 2 to $2\frac{1}{2}$ hours, until crisp and dry. Open the oven door and cool before removing, then peel away the paper.

Just before serving, spread the whipped cream, flavored with the confectioners' sugar and vanilla extract, over the bottom of the shell and pile the drained peaches over the cream.
Variations: The meringue may be shaped into a cake, dome, or plain pie shell shape as preferred.
Suggested fillings:
Ice cream topped with raspberries.
Fresh fruit salad, sliced canned fruit, or any sliced fresh fruit in season, topped with whipped cream.
Lemon cheese (see page 269), topped with whipped cream.

TORTONI DELIGHTS

These are ideal to serve with coffee and a rum-based liqueur.

$\frac{3}{4}$ cup mixed dried fruit
$\frac{1}{4}$ cup chopped candied cherries
2 bananas, sliced
$\frac{1}{2}$ cup slivered almonds
$\frac{1}{3}$-$\frac{1}{2}$ cup rum
2 egg whites

$\frac{3}{4}$ cup sifted confectioners' sugar
1 cup evaporated milk, chilled
2 tablespoons lemon juice
1 cup semi-sweet chocolate pieces, melted
extra rum, cream, and cherries

Serves: 5-6

Soak the chopped fruit, cherries, bananas, and almonds in the rum overnight. Beat the egg whites until stiff, add the sugar gradually, and beat to form a stiff meringue. Whip the evaporated milk to soft peaks, add the lemon juice, and whip until very stiff. Fold in the chocolate, the meringue, and the fruit mixture. Pile into small paper patty cases and place on a baking sheet sheet. Freeze until firm. Serve 2 or 3 to each person with swirls of rum-flavored whipped cream, topped with whole cherries.

Latticed Chocolate Rum Pie

Crêpes as a Dessert

Phyllis Wright

The batter given for crêpes on page 68 is also used for dessert crêpes or pancakes. If the surrounding crêpe is very fragile, and a well-flavored sweet filling is used, a very delicate dish can be created. A little sugar may be added to the batter if desired.

Crepes Suzette, a most elegant sweet, is supposed to have been named after Princess Suzette. It is said that she created this to serve to Louis XV, with whom she was in love. This recipe has stood the test of centuries. Could we do better than aim to reproduce such as this?

APRICOT AND ORANGE PANCAKES

1 quantity Pancake Batter

For filling:
1½ cups dried apricots
1 cup orange bitter marmalade

1 tablespoon rum
sugar

Serves: 4

For decoration:
2-3 large oranges
orange needle shreds (see

method)

Make the crêpes according to the recipe on page 69.
To make the filling: Wash the apricots thoroughly. Cover with cold water and allow to soak overnight. Transfer the fruit and water to a saucepan and cook gently until soft. Drain off the cooking water and sieve the fruit. Stir in the marmalade and rum and sweeten with a little sugar if too tart. Spread this filling on the cooked crêpes and roll up. Arrange for reheating.
To make the decoration: Orange needle shreds are made with a marmalade shredder or a potato peeler. If using a potato peeler, take 2 or 3 strips of peel from one

orange. Cut these strips into tiny shreds with a sharp knife. Place the shreds in a small pan, cover with cold water, and bring to a boil. Strain under cold running water and drain.
Peel the oranges, removing the outer skin and all pith. Cut the peeled oranges into rounds and place overlapping on the finished dish. Sprinkle with the needle shreds.
Note: If reheating the crêpes in the oven, add the orange slices and shreds just before serving.

NEW YEAR'S EVE PANCAKES

(CRÊPES SAINT SYLVESTRE)

1 quantity Pancake Batter

Serves: 4

For filling:
1 cup mincemeat
2 tablespoons brandy

ice cream
toasted almond halves

Make the pancakes according to the recipe on page 69.
To make the filling: Work the mincemeat with a fork to soften and add brandy to make a spreading consistency. The amount of brandy required will vary according to the mincemeat used. Warm the fruit mixture and spread on the cooked crêpes. Roll up and

arrange on a large platter. Keep warm in a 200° oven. When ready to serve, place a small mound of ice cream on each and sprinkle toasted almonds over.
Variation: As an alternative to using ice cream, warm a little more brandy, pour over the finished dish, and flame.

NUT PANCAKES

1 quantity Pancake Batter   Serves: 4

For filling:
½ cup cream cheese
1 tablespoon lemon juice
½ cup chopped walnuts
sugar (optional)

Make the pancake according to the recipe on page 69. To make the filling: Allow the cheese to come to room temperature. Soften with a wooden spoon and add the lemon juice to make it smooth. Add the walnuts and sugar, if desired. Spread over the cooked crêpes, roll tightly, and arrange in lattice fashion on a serving dish. Keep warm. These may be served with a bowl of fresh strawberries, lightly sprinkled with sugar.
Variation: As an alternative, add a little chopped candied ginger to the filling, when fruit is not served.

MOCHA PANCAKES

1 quantity Pancake Batter   Serves: 4

For filling:
⅓ cup semi-sweet chocolate
   pieces
¼ cup warm black coffee
½ cup unsalted butter
⅔ cup ground almonds
1 tablespoon sugar
crême de menthe (optional)

For the batter: Substitute 2 tablespoons strong black coffee for the 2 tablespoons water mixed with the milk. Then prepare the batter as usual (see page 69) and make the pancakes.
To make the filling: Place the chocolate in a small saucepan, pour on the coffee, and stir over very low heat until smooth. Cream the butter and work in the cooled chocolate. Add the ground almonds and sugar and mix well. Flavor with crême de menthe to taste, if desired.

Spread the filling on the cooked coffee pancakes, roll up and arrange on an ovenproof dish, and reheat very gently. A little extra chopped chocolate may be sprinkled over, before serving.

APPLE AND HONEY PANCAKE GÂTEAU

1 quantity Pancake Batter   Serves: 4

For filling:
1½ lb. cooking apples
½ lemon
cinnamon
sugar
honey
whipping cream

To make the filling: Peel and core the apples and cut into thick slices. Grate the lemon rind and add to the apples with the lemon juice. Set over low heat in a heavy saucepan and allow to soften. Stir occasionally to prevent sticking. When soft, beat with a wooden spoon, add a dash of cinnamon, and, if too tart, sweeten with sugar. Cook the pancakes (see page 69) and leave unfolded.

Place a pancake on a round ovenproof dish and spread first with honey, then a little of the apple mixture. Cover with a second pancake and repeat the layers in this way, ending with an uncovered pancake. Sprinkle a little cinnamon mixed with sugar over the finished dish, and serve with a bowl of whipped cream.

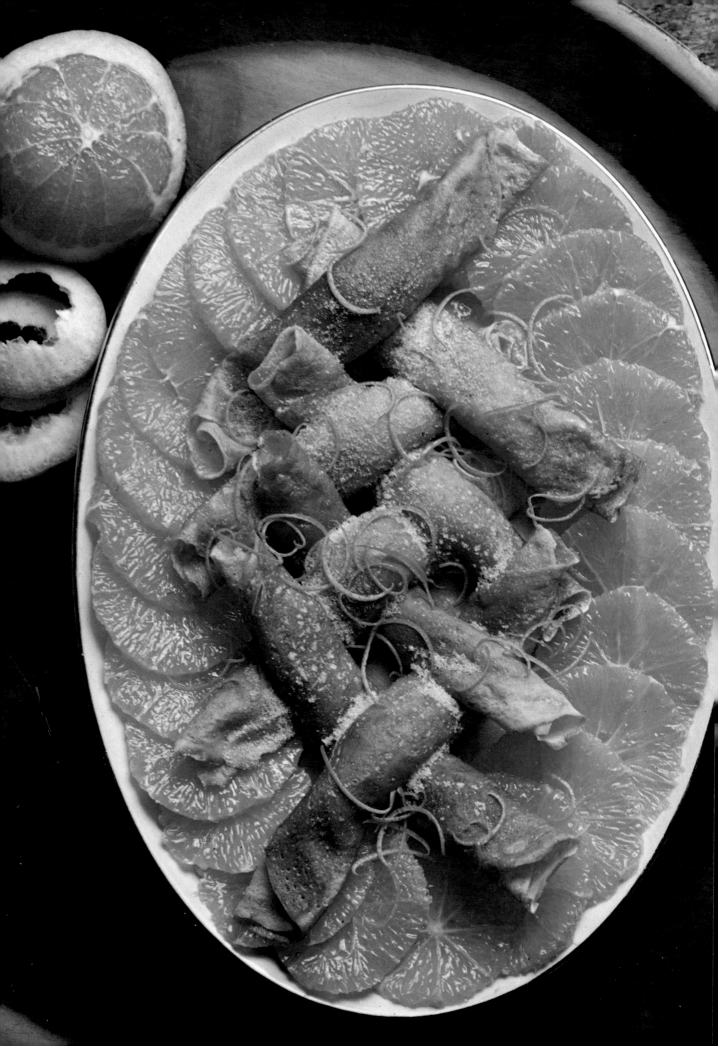

Hot Soufflés and Flans

Eve Knottenbelt

VANILLA SOUFFLÉ

¼ cup butter
⅔ cup sugar
1 vanilla bean or 1 teaspoon
  vanilla extract

1 cup plus 2 tablespoons milk
⅓ cup all-purpose flour
4 egg yolks
5 egg whites

Cooking time: 30 minutes
Temperature: 350°
Serves: 6

Butter the inside of a 6-inch soufflé dish generously, with 1 tablespoon of the butter, and lightly dust with 1 tablespoon of the sugar. Cut a band of wax paper about 7 inches wide and long enough to go round the outside of the dish with a 2-inch overlap. Fold the paper in half lengthwise, butter the top half of one side, and tie round the soufflé dish with string. If using the vanilla bean, put it with the milk in a small saucepan, bring to just below the boiling point, and discard the bean. Melt the remaining butter in a saucepan, add the flour, and cook over gentle heat for 30 seconds. Add the milk and stir continuously until the mixture thickens and boils. Simmer for 5 seconds. Remove from the heat and stir in 6 tablespoons of the sugar and the vanilla extract, if not using the bean. Add the egg yolks, one at a time, beating well after each addition. Beat the egg whites very stiffly until firm peaks are formed. Fold 2 tablespoons egg white into the egg mixture to soften it, then fold in the remaining whites lightly. Bake in the center of a 350° oven for 25 minutes. Sprinkle the top of the soufflé with the remaining sugar and continue cooking for a further 5 minutes. Serve immediately.

VARIATIONS ON VANILLA SOUFFLÉ

Grand Marnier Soufflé

2 oranges
¼ cup Grand Marnier

2 tablespoons Cointreau

Make the soufflé in the same way, adding the grated zest of the oranges and the liqueurs, instead of the vanilla.

Lemon Soufflé

2 lemons

½ cup chopped toasted almonds

Make the soufflé in the same way, adding the grated zest of the lemons, the lemon juice, and the almonds, instead of the vanilla.

Soufflé Rothschild

¼ cup chopped candied fruit
¼ cup brandy or Danziger

Goldwasser
1 cup ripe strawberries

Soak the chopped candied fruit in the brandy overnight. Make the soufflé in the same way, using only half the vanilla flavoring, and adding the candied fruit with the sugar. Add the strawberries to the top of the soufflé when the sugar is sprinkled on top, cutting them in half if they are very large.

Chocolate Soufflé

⅔ cup semi-sweet chocolate
  pieces
½ square unsweetened cooking
  chocolate

1 teaspoon instant coffee
2 tablespoons rum
3 egg yolks

Dissolve the chocolate in   cup cold water over very low heat and add to the mixture in place of the vanilla flavoring. Add the instant coffee and rum at the same time. Otherwise, make as for Vanilla Soufflé.

Apricot and Orange Pancakes

221

Sweet Flans

Although France is often acknowledged as the home of the flan, savory and sweet, it is interesting to read in a seventeenth-century English book of the extensive use of herbs and green vegetables, such as spinach, lettuce, and sorrel, sweetened with honey, used as fillings for sweet pies. Compare these fillings with today's pies of delectable rich egg pie crusts, filled with flavorsome fresh fruits, cream or crème pâtissière, and glazed with syrup flavored with kirsch or brandy.

Sweet flans are now found in many countries of the world, each producing a version of their own. There is apricot flavored with vanilla from Italy, sour cream and caramel from Germany, Bakewell tart from England, and a myriad of fruit flans from France.

The pie crust is one of the simplest to make, and uncooked, freezes very well—a great time-saver for the busy homemaker if the recipe is doubled or trebled.

BAKEWELL TART

For pie crust:

1 cup all-purpose flour	1 egg yolk	Cooking time: 30 minutes
$\frac{1}{4}$ cup butter	1 tablespoon iced water	Temperature: 400°
1 tablespoon sugar	$\frac{1}{2}$ teaspoon vanilla extract	Serves: 4-6
grated rind of 1 lemon		

For filling:

$\frac{1}{4}$ cup strawberry jam	$\frac{1}{4}$ cup butter
2 eggs	$\frac{3}{4}$ cup ground almonds
6 tablespoons sugar	$1\frac{1}{2}$ cups fresh cake crumbs
grated rind and juice of 1 lemon	

To make the pie crust: Sift the flour into a mixing bowl. Add the butter and rub in with the fingertips until the mixture resembles bread crumbs. Add the sugar and lemon rind. Combine the egg yolk, water, and vanilla extract, add to the flour, and mix to a smooth dough. Allow to rest in the refrigerator for 30 minutes. Roll out thinly and line an 8-inch flan ring or pie pan. Trim the edge.

To make the filling: Spread the jam over the bottom of the pie shell. Separate the eggs and beat the yolks with the sugar, lemon rind, and lemon juice until the mixture is creamy. Add the melted butter, ground almonds, and cake crumbs and beat well. Beat the egg whites stiffly and fold into the mixture lightly. Pour into the pie shell and cook in the middle of a 400° oven for about 30 minutes, or until the mixture is set and the top brown.

GRAPE FLAN

For pie crust:

1 cup all-purpose flour	1 egg	Cooking time: 1-1$\frac{1}{4}$ hours
1 teaspoon baking powder	grated rind of 1 lemon	Temperature: 350°
3 tablespoons sugar	6 tablespoons butter	Serves: 4-6

For filling:

1 lb. muscat grapes	6 tablespoons vanilla sugar
3 eggs	$1\frac{1}{4}$ cups cream

To make the pie crust: Sift the flour and baking powder together into a mixing bowl. Beat the sugar and egg until foaming. Add the grated lemon rind. Rub the butter into the flour and mix in the liquid until it forms a soft dough. Chill for 1 hour. Roll out the dough on a lightly floured board and line an 8-inch flan ring or pie pan.
To make the filling: Pick over the grapes, removing any stalks, and wash and drain them well. Arrange the grapes in the unbaked pie shell. Separate the eggs and beat the yolks with the vanilla sugar. Add the cream and mix well. Beat the egg whites stiffly and fold into the egg yolk mixture. Pour over the grapes and bake on the middle shelf of a 350° oven for 1 to 1$\frac{1}{4}$ hours, or until the mixture is set and the top is brown. Chill before serving.

KÄSE KUCHEN

For pie crust:
1 cup all-purpose flour
¼ cup butter
grated rind of 1 lemon

1 egg yolk
2 teaspoons iced water
1 teaspoon lemon juice

Cooking time: 40-50 minutes
Temperature: 350°
Serves: 4-6

For filling:
2 eggs
1¼ cups sour cream
½ cup sugar

3 tablespoons butter
⅓ cup chopped walnuts

To make the pie crust: Sift the flour into a mixing bowl. Add the butter and rub in with the fingertips until the mixture resembles bread crumbs. Add the lemon rind. Mix the egg yolk and water, add to the flour, and mix to a smooth dough with a round-bladed knife. Allow to rest in the refrigerator for 30 minutes. Roll out thinly and line and 8-inch flan ring or pie pan. Trim the edge, line the inside with a layer of greased wax paper, and fill with a layer of dried peas or beans. Cook on the center shelf of a 350° oven for 15 to 20 minutes.

To make the filling: Beat the eggs and sour cream together and heat gently in a saucepan. Place the sugar in the top of a double boiler and allow to dissolve over direct heat. Add the butter and coninue cooking until the mixture is dark golden brown. Place saucepan over boiling water and add the egg and cream mixture, stirring all the time until the caramel is dissolved. Add the walnuts. Pour into the half-cooked pie shell and return to the oven for a further 25 to 30 minutes, or until the mixture is set.

APRICOT FLAN

For pie crust:
1½ cups all-purpose flour
grated rind of 1 lemon
6 tablespoons vanilla sugar
½ cup butter

1 egg yolk
⅓ cup cold water
1 egg white

Cooking time: 30 minutes
Temperature: 400°
reducing to 350°
Serves: 4-6

For filling:
2 lb. fresh apricots or
    1 (1 lb. 13 oz.) can apricots
½ cup sugar

1 cup water
1 teaspoon vanilla extract

For glaze:
syrup from apricots
1 vanilla bean

2 teaspoons lemon juice

To make th pie crust: Sift the flour, add the grated lemon rind and sugar, and rub the butter in with the fingertips until the mixture resembles bread crumbs. Mix the egg yolk and water and blend into the flour with a round-bladed knife, until the mixture forms a soft dough. Knead lightly. Roll out to about ¼-inch thickness and line an 8-inch pie pan or flan ring. Beat the egg white lightly and brush over the bottom of the pie shell. Add the filling and place on the shelf above the center of a 400° oven for 15 minutes. Lower the temperature to

350° and continue cooking for a further 10 to 15 minutes, or until the pie shell is brown. When cool, glaze the apricots with the glaze. Serve the flan chilled.

To make the filling: Cut the apricots in half and simmer until nearly cooked with the sugar, water, and vanilla extra. Drain and arrange attractively in the flan shell. If using the canned variety, drain and reserve the juice.

To make the glaze: Reduce the syrup by one third with the vanilla bean, add the lemon juice, and glaze the apricots, using a small pastry brush.

NORMANDY APPLE FLAN

For pie crust:
1 cup all-purpose flour
¼ cup butter
¼ cup sugar

grated rind of 1 lemon
1 egg yolk
1 tablespoon iced water

Cooking time: 45 minutes
Temperature: 350°
Serves: 4-6

For filling:
1 large cooking apple
⅔ cup cream
3 egg yolks
1 teaspoon cinnamon

¼ cup sugar
3 tablespoons Calvados or
    brandy

To make the pie crust: Sift the flour into a mixing bowl. Add the butter and rub into the flour with the fingertips until the mixture resembles bread crumbs. Add the sugar and lemon rind. Mix the egg yolk and water, add to the flour, and mix to a smooth dough. Allow to rest in the refrigerator for 30 minutes. Roll out thinly and line an 8-inch flan ring or pie pan. Prick the bottom of the shell. Trim the edge and line the inside with a layer of greased wax paper. Fill with a layer of dried peas. Cook on the center shelf of a 350° oven for 15 to 20 minutes.

To make the filling: Peel and core the apples and slice thinly. Arrange them in the pie shell in overlapping circles. Beat the cream, egg yolks, cinnamon, and sugar with the Calvados or brandy, and pour over the apples. Cook on the shelf just above the center of the oven for a further 25 to 30 minutes. Lay a sheet of wax paper over the flan for the last 10 minutes if necessary to prevent over-browning. Serve hot.
Note: This pie may be glazed with warm marmalade before   serving.

STRAWBERRY FLAN

For pie crust:
1 cup all-purpose flour
¼ cup butter
1 tablespoon sugar
¼ cup finely chopped blanched
    almonds

1 egg yolk
2 teaspoons iced water
squeeze lemon juice
½ teaspoon vanilla extract

Cooking time: 30-40 minutes
Temperature: 350°
    reducing to: 300°
Serves: 4-6

For filling:
¾ cup whipping cream
1 tablespoon sugar

1 tablespoon kirsch
2 cups strawberries

For glaze:
⅓ cup red currant jelly
1 teaspoon potato flour or
    cornstarch

1 teaspoon lemon juice
1 tablespoon Kirsch

To make the pastry: Sift the flour into a mixing bowl. Add the butter and rub into the flour with the fingertips until the mixture resembles bread crumbs. Add the sugar and almonds. Mix the egg yolk, water, lemon juice, and vanilla extract, add to the flour, and mix to a smooth dough. Allow to rest in the refrigerator for 30 minutes. Roll out thinly and line an 8-inch flan ring or pie pan. Prick the bottom of the shell. Trim the edge, line the inside with a layer of greased wax paper, and sprinkle with a layer of dried peas. Bake on the center shelf of a 350° oven for 30 to 40 minutes, reducing the heat to 300°

if the pie shell is getting too brown. Cool on a wire cooling rack.
To finish the flan: Whip the cream and flavor with the sugar and kirsch. Cover the bottom of the flan with the whipped cream and arrange the strawberries attractively on top. Bring the red currant jelly to a boil, add the potato flour blended to a smooth paste with a little cold water, and boil for 2 minutes, stirring all the time. Add the lemon juice and kirsch and glaze the fruit while the mixture is hot.

Continental Desserts, Ices, and Ice Creams

Ethel Brice

Ethel Brice combines a career as journalist with that of cook and has collected many exciting recipes in her studies and travels. She has a special flair for Continental cookery.

In the following recipes you will find many fascinating and delicious desserts you can serve to your family or friends. When you want to try something a little different choose a recipe from the Continental dessert section. For something cool, try an ice or an ice cream.

Few people can resist Continental desserts with their rich, beautifully balanced flavors and decorative appearance. They are desserts which every hostess will want to make. At first sight some Continental desserts may seem formidable to the average cook, but there really are no difficultites if the recipes are followed carefully. These beauties come from France, Austria, Hungary, and Germany. Some are light and refreshing fruit desserts flavored with spices, or liqueurs. Some are rich with nuts, butter, eggs, and cream, and are lusciously fattening. Choose serving dishes to complement the dessert as this will enhance its appearance — flat plates for pies, rich gâteaux, and molds, attractive bowls for fruit compotes.

Ices and ice creams are particularly popular in the summer and children love them. Homemade ice cream surpasses any commercially prepared variety and is quite easy to make. By using the freezing compartment of your refrigerator you will be able to make excellent ice cream and sherbets with innumerable varieties. Some homemade ice creams are made from eggs, egg custard, and cream. These are rich in flavor and have a smooth texture. They may have chopped nuts, candied fruits, or fruit purée folded into the basic mixture, or they may be served with a rich fruit, chocolate, or caramel sauce. Make ice cream a day or so in advance if possible, as this gives it a chance to freeze thoroughly and the flavor matures — a big advantage to the busy homemaker who wants to prepare food in advance.

Sherbets, or water ices, have been introduced to America from Italy and France, and make most refreshing summer desserts. It is thought the Arabs and Chinese first made these iced desserts and today they are popular whenever the weather is hot, when refreshing, flavorsome, chilled food is welcome. Serve sherbets and ice cream in chilled sundae or parfait glasses to keep them cool and looking elegant.

Follow these recipes carefully and you will be rewarded with delicious desserts.

Quick Cherry Strudel

CHOCOLATE CHERRY RING

$\frac{1}{4}$ cup candied cherries
2 squares unsweetened cooking
   chocolate
1 tablespoon honey

3 tablespoons mixed chopped
   peel
$\frac{1}{2}$ quantity Short Crust

Cooking time: 30 minutes
Temperature: 425°
   reducing to 350°
Serves: 4-6

Chop the candied cherries and grate the chocolate coarsely. Put the honey, chocolate, candied cherries, and peel into a saucepan and stir over low heat until the chocolate has melted. Roll the dough (see page 299) out into a strip 12 inches long by 6 inches wide. Put the chocolate mixture down the center, moisten the edges of the dough with water, and form into a roll. Shape into a circle on a baking sheet and join the ends together. Brush over with water and make a few small diagonal slits around the top. Bake in a 425° oven for 10 minutes, reduce the temperature to 350°, and bake for another 20 minutes, or until the pastry is crisp and golden.

BRANDIED APPLES

5 apples
butter
2 tablespoons brown sugar
$2\frac{1}{2}$ teaspoons cinnamon

1 tablespoon lemon juice
generous $\frac{1}{4}$ cup brandy
cream for serving

Serves: 5-6

Peel and core the apples and cut into $\frac{1}{4}$-inch slices. Gently fry in butter for 1 minute on each side. Sprinkle with the brown sugar, cinnamon, and lemon juice and continue frying, basting with the liquid in the skillet, until just soft. Warm the brandy, set alight, pour over the apples, and shake the skillet until the flames die down. Serve the apple slices with the juices from the pan, and cream.

MERINGUE AU CHOCOLAT

For meringue:
4 egg whites

1 cup sugar

Cooking time: $1\frac{1}{2}$-2 hours
Temperature: 200°
Serves: 6-8

For filling:
$\frac{1}{2}$ cup sugar
$\frac{3}{4}$ cup hazelnuts
$\frac{1}{2}$ teaspoon vanilla extract
$\frac{1}{2}$ cup semi-sweet chocolate
   pieces
1 cup unsalted butter

2 egg whites
1 cup sifted confectioners' sugar
1 tablespoon rum
whole hazelnuts, toasted, for
   decoration

To make the meringue: Spread a piece of lightly greased aluminum foil on 2 large baking sheets. Beat the egg white until stiff but not dry. Sprinkle in the sugar and beat until very stiff. Fold in the rest of the sugar. Spread the meringue into $4\frac{1}{4}$-inch thick rounds on the sheets. Bake in a 200° oven for $1\frac{1}{2}$ to 2 hours, or until quite dry. Leave in the oven, with the heat turned off, until cold.
To make the filling: Put the sugar into a heavy saucepan and melt over low heat. When it has turned to caramel, add the hazelnuts and vanilla extract and stir lightly to coat the nuts. Quickly pour into a small buttered or oiled pan and allow to set. Melt the chocolate over hot water and cool. Beat the butter until creamy. Beat the egg whites until stiff but not dry and gradually beat in the confectioners' sugar. Beat this meringue into the softened butter, a little at a time. Stir in the cooled chocolate. Crush the hazelnut praline finely and mix into the filling with the rum. Sandwich the meringue rounds together with some of the filling and swirl the rest on top. Decorate the top with a few toasted hazelnuts. Chill for at least 6 hours before cutting.

ORANGE MERINGUES

5 large oranges
15 candied cherries, chopped
sugar to taste
Cointreau

2 egg whites
½ cup sugar
extra sugar

Cooking time: 15 minutes
Temperature: 350°
Serves: 5

Cut about one-third from the top of each orange, carefully remove the flesh, and cut it into pieces. Mix with the candied cherries, sugar to taste, and a sprinkling of Cointreau. Replace in the orange skins. Beat the egg whites until stiff but not dry and gradually beat in the sugar. Continue beating until very stiff. Pile some on top of each orange and dust lightly with sugar. Put into a shallow ovenproof dish, bake in 350° oven for about 15 minutes, or until the meringue is lightly tinted. Serve at once.

PINEAPPLE WITH KÜMMEL

½ medium-sized ripe pineapple
¼ cup clarified butter
¼ cup sugar

⅓ cup Kümmel
⅔ cup cream

Serves: 5

Peel the pineapple and cut into slices or finger-length pieces. Melt the butter in a chafing dish or skillet, add the pineapple, and cook until lightly tinted all over. Sprinkle the sugar over and stir well. Pour the Kümmel over the pineapple, cook for another minute, then pour the cream over, but do not stir. Cook gently to reheat, and serve at once.

QUICK CHERRY STRUDEL

1 (15 oz.) can cherries
¾ cup very finely chopped
  walnuts
¼ cup sugar
grated rind of 3 lemons
1 teaspoon cinnamon

¾ cup soft white bread crumbs
¼ cup butter
½ lb. frozen puff paste
extra butter, melted
confectioners' sugar

Cooking time: 35-40 minutes
Temperature: 425°
  reducing to 375°
Serves: 6

Pit and halve the cherries, put into a sieve, and drain thoroughly. Mix together the walnuts, sugar, lemon rind, cinnamon, and crumbs. Pour the melted butter over and stir to combine.

Put the paste onto a well-floured clean dish towel and roll out to a thin oblong about 14 by 20 inches, having the longer side of the dough nearest to you. Brush over with extra melted butter and spread the crumbs over, leaving a 2-inch margin of dough all around. Arrange the cherries parallel with the longer edge of the dough and near the center. Fold in the sides of the dough and brush the folds with melted butter. Roll up and put on a large, greased baking sheet. Brush all over with melted butter. Bake in a 425° oven for 10 minutes, reduce to 375°, and bake for another 30 minutes, or until golden brown, brushing with melted butter every 10 minutes. Dust with sifted confectioners' sugar and serve warm.

KHOSHAV

¾ cup prunes
1 cup dried apricots
1 cup raisins
½ cup sugar
1 thin strip lemon rind

1 teaspoon allspice
1 teaspoon nutmeg
1-inch piece cinnamon stick
sour cream for serving

Serves: 5

Put the prunes, apricots, and raisins into a mixing bowl, add enough boiling water to cover, and leave overnight. Next day, drain and put into a saucepan with the sugar, lemon rind, spices, cinnamon stick, and enough water to cover. Put the lid on and simmer gently until tender. Cool, remove the lemon rind and cinnamon stick, and transfer to a serving bowl. Chill thoroughly and serve with sour cream.

EGGNOG PIE

½ lb. sweet Graham crackers
½ cup finely chopped walnuts
½ cup butter
1¼ cups milk
4 eggs, separated
⅔ cup sugar

2 tablespoons gelatin
¼ cup hot water
⅔ cup whipping cream
2 tablespoons rum
grated chocolate

Serves: 6

Crush the crackers into fine crumbs and add the walnuts and melted butter. Mix until combined, then press over the bottom and sides of a greased 8-inch spring form pan. Chill while preparing the filling.

Gently heat the milk. Beat the egg yolks lightly with ½ cup of the sugar and slowly stir in the warmed milk. Cook over hot water, stirring constantly, until the custard coats the back of a metal spoon. Sprinkle the gelatin into the hot water and stir until dissolved. Slowly stir into the custard. Chill until thickening, stirring occasionally. Beat the cream and fold ¼ cup of it into the custard with the rum. Beat the egg whites until stiff and gradually beat in the remaining sugar. Gently fold into the custard and pour into the crumb crust. Chill until firm. Remove from the pan and serve topped with the rest of the whipped cream and a sprinkling of grated chocolate.

HUNGARIAN CHESTNUT DESSERT

1 cup unsalted butter
⅔ cup sifted confectioners' sugar
1 (15¾ oz.) can chestnut purée

rum or vanilla extract
⅔ cup whipping cream

Serves: 6-8

For chocolate glaze:
4 squares unsweetened cooking
    chocolate

½ cup sugar
generous ½ cup water
small piece unsalted butter

Dip an 8-inch spring form pan into cold water, and put into the refrigerator at once. Soften the butter a little, then gradually beat in the confectioners' sugar. When light and fluffy, gradually add the chestnut purée, beating well after each addition. Stir in the flavoring. Beat the cream until thick and fold in. Place in the chilled pan, cover with aluminum foil, and chill for 24 hours (in very hot weather, put into the freezer and take out about 1½ hours before serving). Remove from the pan and top with the chocolate glaze just before serving.

To make the chocolate glaze: Chop the chocolate and melt over hot water. Put the sugar and water into a saucepan and bring to a boil, stirring until the sugar has dissolved. Boil until syrupy, then remove from the heat and gradually stir in the chocolate. Add the piece of butter, beat well, cool a little, and pour over the top of the dessert.

MANDEL SULZ

1¼ cups milk
1¼ cups cream
6 tablespoons sugar
generous ½ cup blanched
    almonds

vanilla extract
3 tablespoons gelatin
¼ cup hot water

Serves: 5

For fruit purée:
¾-1 lb. dark red plums, apricots,
    or cherries

sugar
¼ cup dry white wine

Add the milk to the cream, put into a pan with the sugar. Chop the almonds very finely, and add to the milk. Heat gently, stirring until the sugar has dissolved. Stir in the vanilla extract to taste. Dissolve the gelatin in the hot water, and slowly stir into the almond cream. Pour into a lightly oiled mold and chill until firm. Unmold onto a platter and serve.

To make the fruit purée: Gently simmer the fruit in water, with sugar to taste (not too much sugar, as the purée should be slightly tart), until soft. Cool. Purée in an electric blender, or press through a sieve. Stir in the wine, and chill well before serving with the mold.

230

Apricot Gelato and Lemon Ice

APRICOT GELATO

⅓ cup dried apricots
2 tablespoons brandy (optional)
⅔ cup cream

small strip lemon rind
2 egg yolks
⅓ cup sifted confectioners' sugar

Serves: 5

Pour enough boiling water over the apricots to cover and leave for 1 hour. Drain, then simmer in water until soft. Cool. Pour off the water and press the apricots through a coarse sieve, or purée in an electric blender. Stir in the brandy. Put the cream and lemon rind in the top of a double boiler, beat the egg yolks, and add. Stir over hot water until a thick, soft custard is formed. Remove from the heat, put aside to cool, stirring frequently, and then stir in the confectioners' sugar. When cold, strain, and blend with the purée. Transfer to a refrigerator tray, and freeze, stirring the mixture lightly 2 or 3 times.

CASSATA

¼ cup cornstarch
2½ cups milk
¾ cup sugar
vanilla extract
3 egg yolks
dash salt
6 maraschino cherries

¼ cup raisins
2 tablespoons mixed peel
2 teaspoons chopped angelica
2 tablespoons Marsala
½ cup almonds
⅔ cup whipping cream

Serves: 6-8

Blend the cornstarch to a smooth paste with a little of the milk. Add ½ cup of the sugar to the rest of the milk and heat gently. When nearly boiling, add the blended cornstarch, stir until boiling, and simmer for a further 2 to 3 minutes. Remove from the heat, stir in vanilla extract to taste, and cool slightly. Beat the egg yolks and gradually stir into the cooled milk. Return to a low heat and stir for 1 to 2 minutes. Put aside until nearly cold, then pour into refrigerator trays and freeze until firm.

Chop the cherries and raisins, put into a bowl with the chopped peel and angelica, stir in the Marsala, and leave for 30 minutes. Toast the almonds in the oven and chop them. Whip the cream until thickening and gradually beat in the remaining sugar. When thick, mix in the fruit and almonds. Chill well. Allow the frozen custard to soften slightly, spread a layer over the bottom and sides of a mold, and quickly return to the freezer. When firm, put the fruit mixture into the center and cover with the remaining custard. Cover with aluminum foil and freeze until firm.

ICE CREAM PIE

vanilla ice cream
2 eggs, separated
1 egg
¾ cup clear honey
good pinch salt
2 teaspoons instant coffee
  powder

¼ cup evaporated milk
rum or vanilla extract
⅔ cup whipping cream
coarsely chopped toasted
  almonds

Serves: 6

Spread an even ¼-inch thick layer of slightly softened ice cream over the bottom and sides of a chilled, 9-inch pie plate. Quickly put into the freezer. Beat together the egg yolks and the whole egg. Slowly stir in ½ cup of the honey and the salt, coffee powder, and evaporated milk. Cook over hot water, stirring frequently, for 10 to 15 minutes, or until thick. Cool, stir in rum or vanilla extract to taste, and put aside until cold. Beat the egg whites until stiff but not dry and beat in the rest of the honey, adding it in a fine stream. Fold into the cold coffee mixture and then fold in the cream, whipped until thick. Spread over the frozen ice cream, sprinkle chopped almonds over the top, cover with aluminum foil, and freeze again.

HAZELNUT ICE CREAM

1 (6 oz.) can evaporated milk
2 egg yolks
sugar to taste
vanilla extract

1 teaspoon cornstarch
¾ cup hazelnuts, toasted
⅔ cup whipping cream

Serves: 5

Warm the evaporated milk. Beat together the egg yolks and sugar. Gradually stir in the warmed milk and cook over hot water, stirring until the mixture coats the back of the spoon. Add the vanilla extract to taste. Mix the cornstarch with a little water, add, and stir over gently boiling water for 2 minutes. Cover and put aside until cold. Chop the hazelnuts very finely (or put through a nut mill). Stir into the custard. Whip the cream until thick, and fold in. Turn into a refrigerator tray and freeze until firm.

LEMON ICE

¾ cup sugar
2 cups water
½ cup lemon juice

1 teaspoon grated lemon rind
1 egg white
2 tablespoons sugar

Serves: 5

Put the ¾ cup sugar into a saucepan, add the water, and stir gently over low heat until the sugar has dissolved. Stir in the lemon juice and rind and cool. Strain, pour into a refrigerator tray, and freeze, stirring occasionally, until mushy. Transfer to a bowl. Beat the egg white until stiff and gradually beat in the remaining sugar. Fold into the mixture, return to the tray, and freeze.

PEACH SHERBET

⅔ cup sweetened condensed
 milk
2 tablespoons lemon juice
2 tablespoons butter

½ cup water
1 cup mashed, fresh peaches
peach brandy or rum
2 egg whites

Serves: 5

Combine the condensed milk, lemon juice, melted butter, and water. Sprinkle the peaches lightly with peach brandy or rum, mix in, and chill. Beat the egg whites until stiff and fold into the chilled mixture. Put into a refrigerator tray and place in the freezer. When half-frozen, transfer to a chilled bowl and beat until smooth but not melted. Return to the tray and freeze until firm.

FRUIT AND PETITS FOURS

Beverley Sutherland-Smith

Beverley Sutherland-Smith runs a Gourmet Cooking School in Melbourne, Australia. She writes articles for *The Australian Gourmet Magazine* and *The Epicurean* and is the Food master of *The Ladies' Wine and Food Society of Melbourne*.

Dessert Fruits

Very often after a rich meal nothing is more welcome than simple fresh fruit attractively served, and perhaps accompanied by cheese. Today practically any fruit, from the simple apple to the more exotic mango, is available either grown in the States or imported. The dinner table should be completely cleared after the main course, then a set of fruit plates should be laid with the appropriate fruit knives and forks. Dessert fruit served at the end of a dinner must be as perfect and unblemished as possible. It should be washed in gently cold running water and dried on paper towels, and hard-skinned fruit such as apples should be given a polish with a clean, soft cloth.

BRANDIED FRUITS

Recipes for brandied fruits date back hundreds of years and it is a lovely way to enjoy the flavor of short-season fruits all year round as an after dinner delicacy.

The best fruit to brandy is picked on a dry morning after dawn but before the sun has heated the fruit. However this is not always possible as most people do not have their own fruit trees. As long as the fruit is firm, large, and of good quality the finished product will be most successful.

Glass or earthenware containers are the best, for metal must not come in contact with the fruit. Very old recipes recommended that a piece of bladder tied over the top is the best way to seal the jars. Today, instead of the bladder, a piece of thick plastic may be used. Place this over the jars for the first week, while the sugar used to sweeten the fruit dissolves, then seal with a lid. If a metal lid is used be careful it does not come in contact with the brandy. Insert a piece of paper between the brandy and lid as a precaution.

It is difficult to give an exact measurement for the brandy but one point to remember is that the fruit must be well covered by it to avoid fermentation.

BRANDIED KUMQUATS

1 lb. kumquats
1 (26 fluid oz.) bottle brandy

$4\frac{1}{4}$ cups sugar

Wash the kumquats well. Prick each one all over with a darning needle. Place all the ingredients in a large glass jar and leave for 8 days, stirring once a day. Be careful not to break the fruit. The sugar should dissolve at the end of this time, but it takes a little longer in cold weather. Do not store until the sugar is dissolved. Seal the jar and keep in a cool, dark place for 6 months before using.

BRANDIED CHERRIES

rind of 1 orange
4 lb. large cherries

$8\frac{1}{2}$ cups sugar
2 (26 fluid oz.) bottles brandy

Cut the orange rind into very thin strips. Remove the pits from the cherries. Place the fruit in an earthenware crock. Add the sugar. Cover completely with brandy. Stir once a day for 1 week, or until the sugar is completely dissolved. Seal and leave in a cool dark place for 6 weeks before using.

BRANDIED GRAPES

Use only perfect grapes. Divide them into tiny bunches with about 3 grapes in each. Leave the stalks attached. Place gently in a $1\frac{1}{2}$-quart glass jar. Pour over $\frac{3}{4}$ cup sugar and then fill completely to the top with brandy. Seal the jar. Shake the jar occasionally, until the sugar is completely dissolved. Put away in a cool, dark place and keep for 3 months before using.

BRANDIED PEACHES

2 lb. peaches
2 cups sugar

$2\frac{1}{2}$ cups water
$1\frac{1}{2}$ cups brandy

Skin the peaches. Dissolve half the sugar in the water in a saucepan over low heat and poach the peaches in this syrup for 5 minutes. Drain the peaches, cool them, and place in jars. Add the remaining sugar to the syrup, bring to a boil slowly, and boil until thickened and syrupy. Add the brandy to the syrup, cool, pour over the peaches, filling the jars (top up with more brandy if necessary to cover the fruit), and seal. Keep in a cool dark place for 6 weeks before serving.

Elizabeth Callander

Elizabeth Callander has a
Diploma in Household Management, an Associateship in Home
Economics, and is a Bachelor
of Education. Interested in
cookery since childhood, she
has studied food on her travels
round the world and considers
its preparation a rewarding and
enriching art. She is head of the
Home Economics department
at *The Western Australian
Institute of Technology.*

Petits Fours

Petits fours is the name given to miniature fancy cakes and cookies. They may be made from various bases—the classical bases are Genoese sponge cake, fancy cookie mixture, meringue, marzipan, and choux and other rich pastes—and decorated with a variety of creams, icings, jams, and nuts. Petits fours may also include candied, brandied, and fresh fruits coated neatly with a layer of fondant icing, caramel, or rich chocolate. They should be very small, in fact tiny enough to be eaten in one mouthful, as they are usually very rich. They should be uniform in size and if iced or covered with caramel or chocolate they should be served in small paper cases to make them easier to handle.

Petits fours may be served with coffee at the end of a dinner party or at a special function such as a wedding reception, but today they are often served at an afternoon tea or coffee party. When serving them, choose a variety to be served on one plate, some richer than others with a difference in textures and flavors. Make sure your selection has a contrast of soft and crisp, plain and rich. They should also be delicate in design and tasteful in color.

Although many petits fours belong to the field of 'haute cuisine' or 'high class cookery', a careful cook can achieve most successful results by care and attention to every single direction in the recipe. These attractive and popular little cakes and sweetmeats call for neat fingers and a high degree of attention to detail. The icing and decoration of tiny cakes requires careful handling, but the results will be worthwhile. You will find the creative aspects of making petits fours very rewarding as you can make endless attractive and delicious combinations by using different bases, flavorings, ingredients, and designs. In fact with a little care and patience your results will be most professional and will be a delicious finale to your dinner parties. Plan to make a few bases for your petits fours when making up rich cookie mixtures or meringue. These keep well in air-tight containers and may be filled and decorated when required. However, if planning to serve them in quantity at a party it is a good idea to concentrate on one base and add variety with delicious fillings and flavorings, delectable icings, and dainty decorations.

Many of the classical petits fours come from France and therefore have French names. Do not be put off by this but read and follow the recipes carefully stage by stage and you will be highly rewarded with tempting morsels of richness.

PETITS CHOUX AU RHUM

For Choux Paste:
2 tablespoons butter
$\frac{2}{3}$ cup water

$\frac{1}{2}$ cup all-purpose flour
$1\frac{1}{2}$-2 eggs

Cooking time: 25-30 minutes
Temperature: 400°
Yield: 48

For topping:
$\frac{1}{4}$ cup finely chopped blanched
    almonds
$\frac{1}{2}$ cup sugar

$\frac{1}{4}$ cup water
$\frac{1}{8}$ teaspoon cream of tartar

For filling:
$\frac{1}{4}$ cup butter
6 tablespoons all-purpose flour
1 cup milk
$\frac{1}{4}$ cup sugar

1 egg yolk
2 tablespoons cream or
    evaporated milk
1 tablespoon rum

To make the choux paste: Preheat the oven to 400°. Place the butter and water in a small saucepan and heat just to the boiling point. Remove from the heat and quickly mix in the sifted flour. Continue mixing until a smooth paste is formed. Return the mixture to the heat, stirring over low heat until the mixture can be formed into a ball with the spoon. Set aside to cool. Beat the eggs until frothy. When the mixture is only slightly warm, gradually beat in the egg, using sufficient to give a shiny batter which piles softly. Place a $\frac{1}{4}$-inch plain nozzle in a pastry bag and put the paste into the bag. Pipe the paste in small rounds onto a damp baking sheet. Bake just below the middle of the oven for about 30 minutes, until crisp. Remove from the oven and slit the buns open.

To make the topping: Have the chopped nuts spread out on a plate and the shells cool before making the topping. Place the sugar, water, and cream of tartar in a thin bottomed saucepan. Heat slowly until dissolved and then boil rapidly until the syrup becomes pale gold. Remove immediately from the heat. Dip the top of each shell first in the caramel and then into the chopped nuts. Work as quickly as possible. If the caramel thickens it should be gently rewarmed.

To make the filling: Heat the butter in a saucepan until it froths. Add the flour and stir over a low heat until it has a granular appearance. Add half the milk and stir until it makes a smooth paste. Add the remaining liquid gradually whilst stirring over the heat. Bring the mixture to the boiling point stirring continuously. Remove from the heat and stir in the sugar. Beat the egg yolk and cream together. Stir into the thickened mixture. When blended, stir over low heat for 2 minutes. Stir in the rum.

To finish the Petits Choux au Rhum: Place the rum cream in a clean pastry bag and pipe the filling into the shells. Serve in small paper candy cases.

MERINGUE NESTS

For Italian meringue:
$\frac{1}{2}$ lb. lump sugar
$\frac{1}{3}$ cup water
3 egg whites

$\frac{1}{3}$ cup sifted confectioners' sugar
2-3 drops vanilla extract

Cooking time: $1\frac{1}{2}$ hours
Temperature: 200°
    reducing to 150°
Yield: 30

For filling:
fresh strawberries or other fresh
    fruit in season

$1\frac{1}{4}$ cups whipped cream
sugar

To make the Italian meringue: Preheat the oven to 200°. Dissolve the lump sugar in the water over low heat. Boil to 240° (soft ball, see page 327). While the syrup is coming to the required temperature beat the egg whites to the stiff peak stage. When the syrup reaches 240° remove it immediately from the heat and pour it in a steady stream over the stiffly beaten egg whites, beating continuously. Beat until the mixture is smooth, shiny, and thick. Add the vanilla extract. Fold in the confectioners' sugar. Fill a pastry bag with the meringue mixture. Pipe small rings onto an aluminum foil covered baking sheet. Build the edge of each ring up to form a nest. The nests should be just large enough to hold one strawberry. Place in the middle of the oven, immediately reducing the temperature to 150°. Leave to dry out for about $1\frac{1}{2}$ hours. Cool the meringue nests and store in an air-tight tin.

To finish: Wash and hull the strawberries. Chill. Just before serving fill a pastry bag with a star nozzle with whipped cream and pipe a small rose into each nest. Dust the strawberries with sugar and place one in each nest.

LADIES' FINGERS

Yield: 72

Use the basic recipe for Italian meringue (see Meringue Nest, page 239), adding 2 teaspoons instant coffee powder with the confectioners' sugar. Put the mixture in a pastry bag with a fine star nozzle and pipe 2-inch fingers onto an aluminum foil covered baking sheet. Dry out as in the previous recipe. When cold dip each end of the finger into melted chocolate. Leave to dry on a wire cooling rack. Store in an air-tight tin until required.

HAZELNUT HONEY BARS

For cookie dough:
$\frac{3}{4}$ cup hazelnuts
$\frac{1}{2}$ cup butter
$\frac{1}{3}$ cup sugar

$1\frac{1}{4}$ cups all-purpose flour, sifted
honey for filling

Cooking time: 15-20 minutes
Temperature: 300°
Yield: 20

For topping:
$\frac{1}{2}$ egg white

$\frac{1}{2}$ cup sifted confectioners' sugar

To make the cookie dough: Preheat the oven to 300°. Spread the hazelnuts on a baking sheet and place in the oven until brown. Rub the skins off with a cloth and grind the hazelnuts in a grinder with a coarse attachment, or in an electric blender. Cream the butter and sugar. Stir in the ground hazelnuts and sifted flour. Place the dough in the refrigerator for 30 minutes to firm. Divide the dough in half and roll out each section on a lightly floured board to $\frac{1}{8}$-inch thickness. Spread one piece with the topping. Cut the plain dough and the coated dough into bars $2\frac{1}{2}$ inches long and 1 inch wide. Place on a greased baking sheet and cook in the middle of a 300° oven until the cookies are dry underneath, approximately 15 to 20 minutes. Cool and store in an air-tight tin. Just before serving join a plain and a coated finger with honey. To make the topping: Beat the egg white until stiff. Fold in the confectioners' sugar.

COLETTES

For cases:
$\frac{1}{2}$ cup semi-sweet or milk chocolate pieces

24 paper candy cases

Cooking time: 40 minutes
Yield: 24

For filling:
$\frac{1}{2}$ cup ground almonds
1 cup sifted confectioners' sugar
$\frac{1}{4}$ cup hot water

$\frac{1}{2}$ cup unsalted butter
1 egg yolk
1 teaspoon Kirsch

For decoration:
2 tablespoons toasted slivered almonds

To make the cases: Place the chocolate in a heatproof bowl over warm water and work with a spoon until melted. Do not overheat. Line the paper candy cases with melted chocolate by placing $\frac{1}{2}$ teaspoon into each and spreading it with the handle of a teaspoon. Leave to set in the refrigerator.
To make the filling: Spread the ground almonds on a baking sheet and place in a 350° oven until they are toasted to an even golden brown. Stir occasionally. Cool. Dissolve the confectioners' sugar in the hot water.

Set aside to cool.
Beat the butter until soft and creamy. Add the dissolved sugar and beat until blended. Add the egg yolk and the kirsch. Beat well. Fold in the toasted almonds.
To finish: Carefully peel the paper from the chocolate cases. Place a fine star nozzle in a pastry bag and fill with the cream filling. Pipe a rosette to fill each case. Place a sliver of toasted almond in the center to decorate. Store in a sealed container in the refrigerator.

MARZIPAN FOURS

For Genoese:
2 tablespoons unsalted butter
9 tablespoons all-purpose flour

2 eggs
scant $\frac{1}{3}$ cup sugar

Cooking time: 20-30 minutes
Temperature: 350°
Yield: 24 approximately

For Marzipan:
1 cup sugar
$\frac{2}{3}$ cup water
1$\frac{1}{2}$ cups ground almonds
1 egg white

$\frac{1}{2}$-$\frac{2}{3}$ cup sifted confectioners' sugar
vanilla extract
coloring

For finishing:
apricot jam, sieved
red currant jelly

semi-sweet chocolate pieces

To make the Genoese: Preheat the oven to 350°. Place the butter in a china bowl over warm water. Heat until just melted but not oiled. Sift the flour and leave in a warm place to dry. Break the eggs into a mixing bowl and beat until frothy. Beat in half the sugar. Place the bowl over a pan of warm water and gradually beat in the remaining sugar until thick, making sure the mixture only becomes warm. When finished the mixture should be mousse-like; it should support its own weight and retain the marks of the beater. Remove from the heat. Check that the egg mixture, flour, and melted butter are approximately at the same temperature. Add three fourths of the flour by sifting in one fourth at a time and folding with a metal spoon. Add the butter, a little at a time, alternately with the remaining flour. When the butter is incorporated pour at once into a lined, greased, and floured jelly roll pan, 11$\frac{1}{2}$ by 8 inches. Bake in the middle of the oven for 20 to 30 minutes. When cooked the mixture should spring back when lightly touched. Turn the Genoese out to cool. Store in an air-tight tin. Results will be more satisfactory if this cake is made a day in advance of cutting into shape for petits fours.

To make the marzipan: Slowly dissolve the sugar in the water. When all the crystals are dissolved bring the syrup to a boil. Boil to 240° (see page 327). Remove at once from the heat and quickly stir in the ground almonds. Stir in the slightly beaten egg white and cook a moment or two longer over low heat, stirring constantly. Turn the mixture onto a marble slab or plastic board and work it with a spatula until it is cool enough to knead by hand. Use a little confectioners' sugar to reduce sticking. The marzipan firms as it cools so care must be taken to use no more than $\frac{2}{3}$ cup confectioners' sugar. Flavoring and coloring should be worked in while the marzipan is warm. Pastel pinks and greens blend well with the red currant jelly. Wrap in waxed paper and then seal in a plastic bag. Store in an air-tight tin. Results will be more staisfactory if the marzipan is made a day in advance.

To finish the Marzipan Fours: Cut the Genoese into small rounds, approximately 1$\frac{1}{4}$ inches in diameter. Warm the sieved jam and brush the sides of the cakes. Roll the marzipan out to $\frac{3}{16}$-inch thickness, using a little cornstarch on the rolling pin to prevent sticking. Cut strips of marzipan long enough just to meet when wrapped around the sides of the cakes and extending $\frac{1}{4}$ inch above the top of the cakes. Press into place. Gently warm the red currant jelly and when it is liquid pour it on top of the cakes. Melt the chocolate over warm water. Dip the bottoms of the cakes in melted chocolate so that approximately $\frac{3}{16}$-inch of the sides is coated. Stand on aluminum foil until set.

CAKES

Betty Sim

Betty Sim combines an active career as a newspaper cookery editor with a family of three teenagers.

Family Cakes

POINTS FOR SUCCESSFUL CAKE MAKING
CREAMING METHOD
- Cream the butter and sugar until light, white, and fluffy.
- Use fine granulated sugar for a fine-textured cake.
- Beat eggs just until smooth. If overbeaten until frothy, the eggs will become watery.
- Add beaten eggs gradually, beating well after each addition. Sift flour, salt, and raising agent together. Fold this gently into the creamed mixture alternately with the milk until thoroughly mixed.
- Stir in any flavorings and fruit alternately with the flour.
- The final consistency should be a soft dropping consistency. Add more liquid if necessary.

This method is used for butter cakes, small cakes, and rich fruit cakes.

WHIPPED SPONGE METHOD
- Use a spotlessly clean mixing bowl.
- Use fine granulated sugar for a fine-textured cake.
- Sift flour and any other dry ingredients together three times.

METHOD I
- Whip whole eggs with sugar until the mixture is pale lemon colored and thick enough to support its own trail.
- Sift the flour into the mixture and mix with a metal spoon or a plastic spatula using a gentle 'cut-and-fold' action.

Note: If you do not have an electric mixer, use a rotary beater and beat the eggs and sugar over hot water.

METHOD II
- Separate the eggs carefully, making sure there are no specks of yolk in the egg white.
- Beat the egg whites until stiff.
- Add the sugar gradually, whisking continuously until thick and shiny.
- Beat in the egg yolks quickly.
- Sift the flour into the mixture and mix with a metal spoon or a plastic spatula using a gentle 'cut-and-fold' action.

The two variations on this method are used for sponge cakes, jelly rolls, and sponge drops.

Passionfruit Sponge

RUBBING-IN METHOD
- Sift the flour, salt, and raising agents into a clean mixing bowl.
- Cut the fat into small pieces and rub into the flour with the fingertips until the mixture resembles fine bread crumbs.
- Stir in the sugar and other dry ingredients (if used).
- Mix in the egg and milk, beaten together, to form a dough of the required consistency.

This method is used for plain teabreads and nut rolls.

MELTING METHOD
- Sieve all the dry ingredients except raising agents into a clean mixing bowl and stir in the sugar. Make a well in the center.
- Melt the fat and molasses or syrup in a saucepan and pour into the center of the dry ingredients.
- Dissolve the raising agent in milk and add with any beaten egg to the dry ingredients.
- Stir in the center, gradually combining the dry ingredients from the sides of the mixing bowl, as for a batter (see page 68).

This method is used for gingerbread.

COOKING TESTS FOR CAKES
- The times given for baking cakes are approximate.
- Open the oven door carefully, just enough to test the cake quickly.
- The cake should be firm to the touch and slightly shrunken from the sides of the pan when ready. Touch the surface lightly; if the impression of your fingertip remains, the cake is not ready.
- For rich fruit cakes, insert a warm, fine, clean skewer into the center of the cake. It will come out clean if the cake is ready.

Note: All references to baking powder in this book refer to double-acting baking powder.

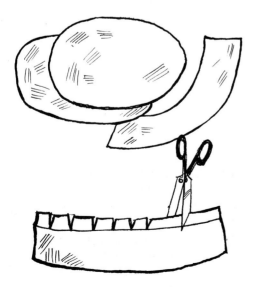

BUTTER CAKE

1 cup butter
generous cup sugar
4 eggs
3 cups all-purpose flour, sifted
with 2½ teaspoons baking
powder
¾ cup milk
1 teaspoon vanilla extract

Cooking time: 1 hour
Temperature: 350°

Line and butter an 8-inch spring form pan and preheat the oven to 350°. Cream the butter and sugar until light, white, and fluffy. Add the beaten eggs, beating well after each addition. Sift the flour and fold in gently, alternately with the milk. Lastly add the vanilla extract. Place the mixture in the prepared pan, smooth the top, and bake for 1 hour, or until cooked. The cake should shrink from the sides of the pan when cooked. Cool on a wire cooling rack.

Variations:
Orange Cake: Add the grated rind and juice of 1 orange with sufficient milk to make up to ¾ cup liquid. Omit the vanilla extract.
Lemon Cake: Replace the vanilla extract with the grated rind of 1 lemon. The best flavor is obtained if the grated lemon rind is creamed with the butter and sugar.
Cherry Cake: Add ½ cup chopped candied cherries when folding in the flour.

LAMINGTONS

For cakes:
1 quantity Butter Cake mixture

For icing:
⅓-½ cup boiling water
2 tablespoons butter
¼ cup cocoa powder
2 cups plus 2 tablespoons sifted
confectioners' sugar
2⅔ cups shredded coconut

Cooking time: 30-35 minutes
Temperature: 350°

Make the basic Butter Cake mixture (see recipe above), place in a greased wax paper lined 11 by 7 inch oblong cake pan, and bake in a 350° oven for 30 to 35 minutes. Cool on a wire cooling rack. Make the cake at least 2 days before needed. Cut the cake into 1½-inch squares. To make the icing: Pour the boiling water over the butter, add the cocoa and mix in, add the sifted confectioners' sugar, and beat well. Stand the bowl of icing over a bowl of hot water. Using a long-pronged fork to hold the squares of cake, dip each piece into the chocolate icing then roll in coconut. Place on a wire cooling rack to set.

LEMON BUTTER CAKE

For lemon butter:
2 tablespoons butter
½ cup sugar
1 egg
1 lemon

Cooking time: 35-45 minutes
Temperature: 375°

For cake:
½ cup butter
¾ cup sugar
1 egg
1½ cups all-purpose flour, sifted
with 1½ teaspoons baking
powder
salt
¼ cup blanched almonds
extra sugar

To make the lemon butter: Place the butter, sugar, beaten egg, and the grated rind and strained juice of the lemon into the top of a double boiler. Place over boiling water and stir with a wooden spoon until thick, about 20 minutes. Cool.
To make the cake: Preheat the oven to 375°. Cream the butter and sugar until light, white, and fluffy. Add the beaten egg and beat well. Stir in the sifted flour and salt.

Knead the mixture lightly and divide in half. Line an 8-inch spring form pan with greased wax paper. Place one half of the dough in the pan and press over the bottom and up the sides. Spread the cooled lemon butter mixture over. Mold the remaining dough into a round and place on top. Decorate with blanched almonds and sprinkle with sugar. Bake for 35 to 45 minutes. Cool on a wire cooling rack.

BUTTERFLY CAKES

¾ cup butter
¾ cup sugar
3 eggs
2 cups all-purpose flour, sifted
    with 2 teaspoons baking
    powder

½ cup milk
jam
whipped cream
confectioners' sugar

Cooking time: 15-20 minutes
Temperature: 400°
Yield: 16 approximately

Preheat the oven to 400°. Butter 16 muffin molds. Cream the butter and sugar until light, white, and fluffy. Add the beaten eggs gradually, beating well after each addition. Gently stir in the sifted flour and the milk. Place 1 tablespoon of the mixture in each muffin cup. Bake for 15 to 20 minutes, until the tops have risen well and are evenly browned. Cool on a wire cooling rack. When the cakes are cool cut a circle from the top of each using a small, sharp knife. Cut the circles in half. Place a small quantity of apricot or raspberry jam on each cake. Cover the jam with 1 teaspoon whipped cream. Replace the half circles to form butterfly wings on top of the cakes. Sprinkle the cakes lightly with sifted confectioners' sugar.

RIVERINA FRUIT CAKES

1 cup butter
generous cup sugar
2 eggs
1 teaspoon baking soda
½ cup boiling water
1 cup chopped pitted dates
1 cup chopped raisins

¾ cup chopped walnuts
2 cups all-purpose flour
1 teaspoon salt
½ teaspoon mixed spice
1 teaspoon cinnamon
1 nutmeg, finely grated

Cooking time: 20 minutes
Temperature: 375°
Yield: 16-18

Preheat the oven to 375°. Cream the butter and sugar until light, white, and fluffy. Add the beaten eggs gradually and beat well. Dissolve the soda in the boiling water. Add to the mixture with the dates, raisins, and walnuts. Sift together the flour, salt, and spices. Fold the sieved dry ingredients into the mixture and fold in gently until thoroughly blended. Place teaspoons of the mixture into buttered muffin molds and bake for 20 minutes, or until cooked. Cool on a wire cooling rack.

APPLE CAKE

½ cup butter
½ cup sugar
2 eggs

1½ cups all-purpose flour, sifted
    with 1½ teaspoons baking
    powder
2 teaspoons cinnamon

Cooking time: 1 hour 10 minutes
Temperature: 375°

For filling:
2 lb. dessert apples
1 cup sugar

½ cup water

For icing:
1 cup sifted confectioners' sugar
2 tablespoons cocoa powder

1 teaspoon butter
1 tablespoon boiling water

To make the filling: Peel, quarter, and core the apples. Cut each quarter into 3 slices. Dissolve the sugar in the water in a large saucepan. Add the apples, cover with a tight lid, and cook gently until the slices are clear but not mushy. This takes about 20 minutes. Set aside to cool. To make the cake: Preheat the oven to 375°. Grease a spring form pan. Cream the butter and sugar until light, white, and fluffy. Add each egg separately, beating well after each addition. Stir in the sifted flour and cinnamon. Allow the dough to stand in the refrigerator for 1 hour. Turn onto a lightly floured board and cut in half. Place one half of the dough in the pan and press over the bottom and up the sides of the pan. Place the apple slices on top. Form the remaining dough in to a round for the lid and place on top of the apples. Make a slit in the center for the steam to escape and bake for about 1 hour 10 minutes. Remove the cake from the oven and allow to cool slightly. Remove from the pan and ice with chocolate icing.
To make the icing: Sift the confectioners' sugar and cocoa powder into a mixing bowl. Add the butter and gradually add the boiling water, 1 teaspoon at a time, stirring continuously until the mixture is smooth. Spread on the apple cake. Serve with whipped cream.

DATE AND NUT CAKE

1 cup chopped pitted dates
1 teaspoon baking soda
¾ cup boiling water
¼ cup butter
½ cup sugar

1 egg
1½ cups all-purpose flour
½ cup chopped walnuts
few drops vanilla extract

Cooking time: 45 minutes or
                 1 hour
Temperature: 350°

Preheat the oven to 350°. Line a loaf pan or an 8-inch spring form pan with greased wax paper. Combine the dates and soda with the boiling water. Leave to cool. Cream the butter and sugar until light, white, and fluffy and mix in the beaten egg. Add the dates, sifted flour, walnuts, and vanilla extract. Pour into the prepared pan and bake for 1 hour if using a loaf pan, and for about 45 minutes if using a spring form pan.

RICH BOILED FRUIT CAKE

8 cups mixed dried fruits
¼ cup corn syrup
⅓ cup rum, sherry, or brandy
¾ cup water
1 cup butter
1 cup, firmly packed, brown
    sugar
5 eggs

3 cups all-purpose flour, sifted
    with 1 teaspoon baking
    powder
¼ teaspoon salt
2 teaspoons mixed spice
¼ teaspoon cinnamon
¼ teaspoon ground nutmeg
½ cup halved blanched almonds

Cooking time: 3½ hours
Temperature: 300°

Place the mixed fruit, corn syrup, and rum, sherry, or brandy with the water in a saucepan. Bring to a boil, stirring occasionally, and simmer for 2 minutes. Pour into a bowl, cover, and allow to stand overnight. Preheat the oven to 300°. Line a 9-inch spring form pan with greased wax paper and 3 layers of brown paper. Cream the butter and brown sugar together well. Add the eggs one at a time, beating well after each addition. Sift the dry ingredients together, then sift half over the boiled fruit mixture. Mix lightly and stir into the creamed mixture. Add the remaining sifted dry ingredients and fold into the mixture. Pour into the prepared pan. Arrange the split blanched almonds in a pattern on the top. Bake for 3½ hours, or until cooked. Remove the cake from the pan, leaving the paper on, and cool on a wire cooling rack.

PASSIONFRUIT SPONGE

For sponge:
4 eggs
¾ cup sugar
¾ cup cornstarch

¼ cup all-purpose flour
1 teaspoon baking powder

Cooking time: 25 minutes
Temperature: 350°
Serves: 8-10

For filling:
1¼ cups whipping cream

For icing:
1 teaspoon melted butter
1 cup sifted confectioners' sugar

1 small can passionfruit

To make the sponge: Preheat the oven to 350°. Grease 2 8-inch layer pans and flour the bases lightly. Separate the eggs and whip the whites until stiff. Add the sugar gradually, beating continuously. Add the egg yolks one at a time and beat again. Sift together the cornstarch, flour, and baking powder 3 times and gently fold into the mixture with a metal spoon. Divide the mixture evenly between the 2 pans. Bake for 20 to 25 minutes. Stand in the pans for 2 to 3 minutes before turning out onto a wire cooling rack, after loosening the sides from the pans with a knife. Cool.

To fill and ice: Place one of the sponges on a serving plate. Spread thickly with whipped cream. Place the second sponge on top. Make the icing by adding the melted butter to the sifted confectioners' sugar. Add the juice and seeds of the passionfruit until the mixture is of a spreading consistency. Spread over the top of the sponge. *Variation:* Crushed strawberries, crushed pineapple, or mashed banana may be substituted for the passionfruit and are equally delicious.

JELLY ROLL

3 eggs

¾ cup sugar

¾ cup all-purpose flour, sifted with ¾ teaspoon baking powder

confectioners' sugar or extra sugar

jelly or Lemon Cheese

Cooking time: 15 minutes

Temperature: 350°

Preheat the oven to 350°. Separate the eggs and whip the whites until stiff. Add the sugar gradually, beating continuously. Add the yolks and mix in thoroughly. Sift the flour, sprinkle onto the mixture, and fold in gently with a metal spoon. Pour into a greased wax paper lined jelly roll pan and bake for 15 minutes. While the jelly roll is cooking sprinkle confectioners' or granulated sugar onto a piece of wax paper. When the roll is cooked turn it out onto the paper, trim off the edges with a sharp knife, spread quickly with warmed jelly or Lemon Cheese (see page 269), and roll up neatly and firmly. Stand the roll on a cooling rack with the join underneath and leave until cool. Sprinkle with more sugar before serving.

MERINGUES

4 egg whites

1 cup sugar

¼ teaspoon cream of tartar

few drops vanilla extract

1¼ cups whipped cream

½ cup crushed fruit

Cooking time: 2 hours

Temperature: Lowest possible setting

Whip the egg whites until stiff. Add the sugar gradually a teaspoon at a time, beating continuously. Fold in the cream of tartar and finally the vanilla extract. Place a plain nozzle into a pastry bag and pipe in small circles onto greased wax paper placed on greased baking sheets. Alternatively, place the meringue mixture in teaspoonfuls on the prepared sheets. Place on the bottom shelf of an oven set as low as possible to dry out for 2 hours. When cool, join together with whipped cream mixed with crushed fruit.

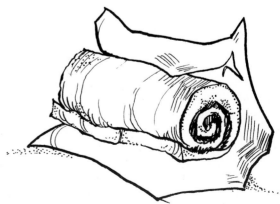

Rosemary Thurston

Rosemary Thurston is interested in the techniques of cookery and combines an active career and busy home life with the light-hearted charm and humor of her Irish ancestors.
She is the cookery expert for a New Zealand women's magazine.

More Family Cakes

An ever-popular cake is the sponge, lavishly filled or topped with flavored, sweetened, whipped cream. The cake may be spread with passionfruit pulp, jam, or lemon honey (lemon cheese) before filling with the cream, or the cream may be decorated with fresh fruit, especially strawberries or sliced Chinese gooseberries.

Fruit cakes of the cut-and-come-again type are good for including in packed lunches or farming afternoon teas. Then there are many variations on the butter cake theme, some with baked-in toppings, others to be left plain or swirled with frosting.

Cake making, like any other cooking, becomes more successful with experience, but here are a few pointers which may be helpful to beginners.

TIPS FOR SUCCESS

- You cannot be exact about baking times because so much depends on the way in which different ovens behave, so baking times in most recipes are to be used as a guide. Generally, if the cake has a cracked top the oven was too hot, or if it takes much longer to be baked than the time indicated, the temperature was too low. In either case, note the difference on the recipe and make the adjustment next time the recipe is used. Or have the local electricity authorities check your oven.

  Spring form pans are good as cakes are so easy to remove from them, particularly those with baked-in toppings. When using one-piece pans, always grease them and as an added precaution against the cake sticking, line with wax paper, shiny side up, cut to fit. This is difficult with a tube pan so line the base only. Recipes to be baked in 7 or 8 inch round cake pans can be baked successfully in an 8-inch tube pan taking about 10 minutes off the time guide.

- To avoid a perfectly baked cake breaking on turning from the pan let it rest for a few minutes in the pan before removal.

Boiled Fruit Cake

251

COCONUT CAKE

1 cup shredded coconut
½ cup milk
1 cup less 2 tablespoons butter
1 cup sugar

2 eggs
1 teaspoon vanilla extract
1¾ cups all-purpose flour
2 teaspoons baking powder

Cooking time: 50 minutes
Temperature: 350°

Combine the coconut and milk and leave to soak for 1 hour. Line a 9- by 3-inch spring form pan with wax paper, grease it, and coat with flour. Preheat the oven to 350°. Cream the butter and sugar until light, white, and fluffy. Beat the eggs and add one third at a time to the creamed mixture, beating well after each addition. Beat in the vanilla extract. Gradually add the coconut mixture. Sift the flour and baking powder and stir into the creamed mixture. Spread into the prepared pan. Bake for 50 minutes. Stand for 5 minutes before turning out onto a wire cooling rack to cool.

COFFEE CAKE

½ cup butter
½ cup sugar
2 eggs
2 tablespoons instant coffee
   powder

1½ cups all-purpose flour
2 teaspoons baking powder
¼ cup milk

Cooking time: 30 minutes
Temperature: 360°

Line an 8-inch spring form pan with greased wax paper. Preheat the oven to 360°. Cream the butter and sugar until light, white, and fluffy. Beat the eggs and add one third at a time to the creamed mixture, beating well after each addition. Add the instant coffee powder and beat well until blended smoothly. Sift the flour and baking powder and add to the creamed mixture alternately with the milk. Spreak into the prepared pan. Bake for 30 minutes. Allow to stand for 5 minutes before turning the cake out onto a wire cooling rack to cool. Frost with coffee-flavored Glacé Icing (see page 268).

MACAROON CAKE

½ cup butter
½ cup sugar
3 egg yolks
1½ cups all-purpose flour

1½ teaspoons baking powder
½ cup milk
1 teaspoon vanilla extract

Cooking time: 45 minutes
Temperature: 350°
Serves: 12

For topping:
3 egg whites
½ cup sugar

1 cup shredded coconut

Line a 9- by 3-inch spring form pan with greased wax paper. Preheat the oven to 350°. Cream the butter and sugar until light, white, and fluffy. Add the egg yolks one at a time, beating well after each addition. Sift the flour and baking powder. Mix the milk and vanilla extract. Add these dry and liquid ingredients alternately to the creamed mixture. Spread into the prepared pan using a spatula.

To make the topping: Whip the egg whites until stiff, then beat in the sugar 2 tablespoons at a time. Stir in the coconut. Spread evenly over the cake in the pan. Bake for 40 to 45 minutes. Let stand for 5 minutes before removing the cake from the pan to cool on a wire cooling rack.

QUEEN CAKES

6 tablespoons butter
¼ cup sugar
¼ cup boiling water
1 egg

1 cup all-purpose flour
1 teaspoon baking powder
½ cup seedless white raisins

Cooking time: 15 minutes
Temperature: 400°

Grease and flour 8 muffin molds. Preheat the oven to 400°. Cream the butter and sugar. Add the boiling water and beat well until blended. Beat the egg; add gradually, beating well after each addition. Sift the flour and baking powder, add the white raisins, and mix. Add the flour mixture to the creamed mixture and stir in gently. Spoon into the prepared muffin molds. Bake for 15 minutes. Remove at once from the molds and cool on a wire cooling rack.

BANANA CAKE

$\frac{1}{2}$ cup butter
scant $\frac{3}{4}$ cup sugar
2 eggs
$\frac{3}{4}$ cup mashed banana
$\frac{1}{4}$ cup warm milk

1 teaspoon baking soda
2 cups all-purpose flour
1 teaspoon baking powder
$\frac{1}{8}$ teaspoon salt

Cooking time: 40 minutes
Temperature: 350°

Line a 9- by 3-inch spring form pan with greased wax paper. Cream the butter and sugar until light, white, and fluffy. Add the beaten eggs gradually, beating well after each addition. Beat in the mashed banana. Combine the warm milk and baking soda and mix into the banana mixture. Sift the flour, baking powder, and salt and stir into the banana mixture. Spread the mixture into the prepared cake pan. Bake for 40 minutes. Let stand for 5 minutes; then turn out onto a wire cooling rack. When cool, ice with Vienna Frosting (see page 269).
Note: Banana must be really well mashed, and over-ripe bananas are the best to use. Sometimes I add $\frac{1}{4}$ teaspoon freshly grated nutmeg to the frosting for an interesting combination of flavors.

ONE EGG CHOCOLATE CAKE

2 tablespoons butter
$\frac{1}{2}$ cup sugar
1 egg
2 tablespoons corn syrup
1 cup all-purpose flour

1 teaspoon baking powder
$\frac{1}{4}$ cup unsweetened cocoa
$\frac{1}{8}$ teaspoon salt
$\frac{1}{2}$ cup milk
$\frac{1}{2}$ teaspoon baking soda

Cooking time: 30 minutes
Temperature: 350°

Preheat oven to 350°. Line an 8-inch round layer pan with greased wax paper. Cream the butter and sugar until light and fluffy. Add the egg and beat well. Beat in the corn syrup. Sift the flour, baking powder, cocoa, and salt. Mix the milk with the baking soda. Stir the sifted dry ingredients and the milk and baking soda alternately into the creamed mixture. Spread the mixture into the prepared cake pan. Bake for 30 minutes. Cool on a wire cooling rack, then frost with Chocolate Frosting (see page 268), or Seven Minute Frosting (see page 269).
Note: For a special occasion, make 2 cakes and layer them with Chocolate Frosting (see page 269) or whipped cream. A little rum added to chocolate icing or chocolate frosting makes the cake even better!

HORSE'S NOSE

3 eggs
$\frac{1}{2}$ cup sugar

3 tablespoons unsweetened
   cocoa
3 tablespoons cornstarch

Cooking time: 15 minutes
Temperature: 375°

For filling:
$1\frac{1}{4}$ cups whipping cream
2 tablespoons confectioners'
   sugar

$\frac{1}{4}$ teaspoon vanilla extract
extra confectioners' sugar

Line a 13- by 9-inch cake pan with wax paper, shiny side up. Grease and flour the paper. Preheat the oven to 375°. Whip the egg whites until stiff. Add the yolks and beat again until thick. Add the sugar 2 tablespoons at a time, beating well between each addition. Sift the cocoa and cornstarch together and fold into the egg mixture. Pour evenly into the prepared pan and bake for 15 minutes.

While the cake is baking, wring a clean dish towel out in cold water. Spread the damp dish towel on a flat surface. When the cake is baked, remove from oven and quickly run a knife around the pan to loosen the cake. Turn the cake at once onto the damp dish towel. Peel the paper off at once. Fold the cake in half lengthwise, placing the cake paper in the fold to keep the two surfaces from sticking. Cool on a wire cooling rack.
To make the filling: Beat the cream and confectioners' sugar together until stiff. Add the vanilla extract. Spread in the fold of the cooled cake. Dust the top of the cake with confectioners' sugar.
Note: You will see why this cake is called Horse's Nose when it is made. Call it Chocolate Foldover if the animal name does not appeal!

SPONGE

3 eggs
½ cup sugar
¾ cup cornstarch
2 tablespoons all-purpose flour

1 teaspoon baking powder
1¼ cups whipping cream
jam or filling
confectioners' sugar

Cooking time: 15 minutes
Temperature: 400°

Grease and flour 2 8-inch round layer pans. Preheat the oven to 400°. Separate the eggs and whip the whites until stiff. Add the yolks and beat again until thick. Beat in the sugar 2 tablespoons at a time. Sift the cornstarch, flour, and baking powder and fold into the beaten eggs and sugar. Divide the mixture between the prepared pans. Bake 15 minutes. Let stand for 3 minutes before turning out onto a wire cooling rack to cool.

Sandwich the sponges with whipped cream, jam, or other filling and sprinkle the top with confectioners' sugar. The cakes may also be served separately with whipped cream on top—easier to eat this way.

SPONGE DROPS

2 eggs
3 tablespoons sugar
3 tablespoons all-purpose flour

2 tablespoons cornstarch
⅛ teaspoon salt
1 teaspoon baking powder

Cooking time: 8 minutes
Temperature: 375°
Yield: 36

For filling:
1¼ cups whipping cream   confectioners' sugar

Cover 2 large baking sheets with greased wax paper, shiny side up. Preheat the oven to 375°. Separate the eggs and whip the whites until thick. Add the yolks and beat again until very thick. Beat in the sugar 2 tablespoons at a time. Sift the flour, cornstarch, salt, and baking powder and fold into the beaten eggs and sugar. Drop the mixture from a teaspoon onto the prepared baking sheets, leaving 1 inch between each drop. Bake for about 8 minutes, or until pale golden brown. Remove at once from the sheets and cool on a wire cooling rack. Store when cool in an air-tight container.

Sandwich in pairs with 2 teaspoons sweetened whipped cream, at least 2 hours before serving.
Note: Sponge Drops, unfilled, keep for weeks in an air-tight tin, so they are good to keep on hand. They can be spread with jam, or Lemon Cheese (see page 269) before filling with whipped cream.

BOILED FRUIT CAKE

¾ cup currants
¾ cup seedless raisins
1 cup seedless white raisins
2 tablespoons candied cherries
3 tablespoons chopped candied
  peel
2 cups cold water

1½ cups butter
3 cups all-purpose flour
1 teaspoon baking powder
3 eggs
1 cup sugar
1 teaspoon almond extract

Cooking time: 2 hours
Temperature: 325°

Place the currants, raisins, white raisins, cherries, and peel in a medium-sized saucepan. Add the cold water. Bring to the boiling point, reduce the heat, and simmer, covered, for 3 minutes. Chop the butter roughly and add to the saucepan, stirring to melt the butter. Cool. Line a 9- by 3-inch spring form pan with greased wax paper. Preheat the oven to 325°. Sift the flour and baking powder. Beat the eggs until thick; then add the sugar ¼ cup at a time, beating well after each addition. Add the fruit mixture to the beaten eggs and sugar. Stir in the sifted flour and baking powder. Stir in the almond extract. Pour into the prepared pan. Bake for 2 hours. Let stand for 10 minutes before turning out onto a wire cooling rack to cool.

Continental Cakes

Ethel Brice

AUSTRIAN ALMOND TORTE

For cake:
4 squares unsweetened cooking
    chocolate
4 eggs, separated

½ cup sugar
1 cup ground almonds

Cooking time: 40 minutes
Temperature: 350°

For decoration:
1 square unsweetened cooking
    chocolate
⅔ cup whipping cream
2 teaspoons sugar

vanilla extract
coarsely chopped toasted
    almonds

To make the cake: Melt the chocolate over hot water, stirring occasionally, and cool. Beat the egg yolks with the sugar until thick and creamy. Slowly beat in the chocolate. Whisk the egg whites until stiff; fold into the chocolate mixture. Sprinkle the ground almonds over the surface, a little at a time, folding in gently after each addition. Pour into a loaf pan approximately 8½ by 4½ by 2½ inches, lined with greased wax paper. Bake for about 40 minutes. Leave in the pan for a few minutes before turning the cake out. Cool on a wire cooling rack.

To decorate the cake: Melt the chocolate over hot water and cool. Whip the cream until thickening, add the sugar, and beat until thick. Stir in vanilla extract to taste. Slowly and carefully stir in the chocolate (the cream must be at room temperature before the chocolate is added). Chill well and then spread all over the cake. Top with the almonds.

Note: Bake the cake the day before it is to be cut.

GÂTEAU AUX CONFITURES

For cake:
¾ cup butter
1 cup sugar
4 eggs
1 teaspoon vanilla extract
1¼ cups all-purpose flour
⅓ cup hot water
½ cup rum

apricot jam
red currant jelly
extra apricot jam, sieved
frosting
red and green candied cherries,
    chopped

Cooking time: 30 minutes
Temperature: 350°

For frosting:
1 egg white
1 teaspoon lemon juice

1 teaspoon rum
about 1 cup confectioners' sugar

To make the cake: Put the butter into a mixing bowl placed in a pan or larger bowl of hot water, and leave until the butter has nearly melted; do not let it get oily. Remove from the hot water and set aside to cool. Gradually beat the sugar into the eggs and beat for 5 minutes. Beat in the vanilla extract. Add the sifted flour and the butter and fold in lightly until just mixed. Pour into 2 greased, lightly floured 8-inch round layer pans and bake for 30 minutes. Cool on a wire cooling rack.

Split each cake in half. Mix the hot water into the rum and sprinkle over 3 of the cake layers. Spread one layer with apricot jam (press through a sieve if it is lumpy) and top with a second layer. Spread red currant jelly over and cover with a third layer. Spread with apricot jam and top with the unsprinkled cake. Cover the cake with warmed, sieved apricot jam, leave for 5 minutes, and then cover with the icing, smoothing on with a knife dipped into hot water. Decorate the top with chopped red and green candied cherries.

To make the icing: Beat together lightly the egg white, lemon juice, and rum. Stir in enough sifted confectioners' sugar to make a spreading consistency.

PRINZREGENTEN TORTE

For cake:
1 cup plus 2 tablespoons butter
1 cup plus 2 tablespoons sugar
4 eggs
1 teaspoon vanilla extract

1¾ cups all-purpose flour
½ cup cornstarch
1 teaspoon baking powder

Cooking time: 7 minutes
Temperature: 350°

For filling:
¼ cup unsweetened cocoa
½ cup cornstarch
⅔ cup sugar
2½ cups milk

½ cup plus 2 tablespoons butter
½ cup plus 2 tablespoons
    unsalted butter

For frosting:
12-14 squares semi-sweet
    chocolate

whipped cream and chocolate

Cut 8 8-inch rounds from wax paper, grease, and place on greased baking sheets.

To make the cake: Cream together the butter and sugar. Beat in the eggs, one at a time, and stir in the vanilla extract. Sift together twice the flour, cornstarch, and baking powder and fold into the mixture. Divide the mixture into 8 equal portions and spread thinly into circles, as evenly as possible, on the wax paper rounds, to within 1½ inches of the edges. Bake for about 7 minutes or until just lightly tinted. Carefully remove each batch as it is done and spread out on a board to cool while the rest are cooking.

When all are cold, join together with the filling. Chill well and cover with the chocolate which has been melted over hot water. Decorate with rosettes of whipped cream and flaked chocolate.

To make the filling: Put the cocoa, cornstarch, and sugar into a mixing bowl and blend to a paste with some of the milk. Bring the remaining milk to the boiling point, add the cornstarch mixture, and stir over moderate heat until thickened. Put aside until lukewarm. Have the butters softened, mix them together, and beat until creamy. Gradually whip into the cornstarch cream. Allow to cool before using.

FRANKFURTHER KRANZ

½ cup less 1 tablespoon butter
scant ¾ cup sugar
2 teaspoon grated lemon rind
3 eggs

1¼ cups all-purpose flour
½ cup cornstarch
2 teaspoons baking powder
sherry

Cooking time: 1 hour
Temperature: 350°

For filling:
½ cup cornstarch
2½ cups milk
thin strip lemon rind
½ cup sugar
dash salt

1 teaspoon vanilla extract
½ cup butter
½ cup unsalted butter
⅔ cup blanched toasted almonds
    for decoration

To make the cake: Cream together the butter, sugar, and lemon rind. Add the beaten eggs gradually, beating in well after each addition. Fold in the flour, cornstarch, and baking powder sifted together. Place in a well-greased, large tube pan or baba mold and bake for 1 hour. Leave until the next day before cutting.

Split the cake horizontally to make 4 layers, sprinkle each with sherry, and join together with some of the filling. Cover with the rest of the filling. Chop the almonds coarsely and sprinkle on the top and sides of the cake.

To make the filling: Mix the cornstarch with 1 cup of the milk. Add the lemon rind, sugar, and salt to the remaining milk and slowly bring to the boiling point. Add the blended cornstarch and stir until boiling. Simmer for 1 minute, stirring constantly. Add the vanilla extract and set aside until tepid, stirring occasionally. Soften the butters a little and then beat together until creamy. Beat in the cream mixture, 2 tablespoons at a time.

Louis Ferguson

Louis Ferguson is a senior cookery lecturer. Born in Scotland and apprenticed there as a chef, Louis believes there is a wealth of delicious food in the different cuisines of the world and aims to reproduce these dishes simply and well.

Gâteaux

These delectable cakes have their origins in Europe and open up a fascinating new field of cooking. There are innumerable ideas for flavoring and decorating these cakes. Gâteaux are rich and offer great scope to the cook because of their decorative appearance. At first sight, the gâteau may seem formidable but with a little care and patience you can achieve excellent results. The highest quality ingredients must be used—fresh butter, eggs, cream, and nuts, with rich fillings and flavorings. They may be served at morning and afternoon tea or coffee parties and may also be included in a dinner menu as the dessert. Individual gâteaux may be made or a large one cut into portions at the table.

The base of a gâteau may be a plain butter cake or sponge flavored with vanilla, chocolate, or coffee. It may have finely chopped nuts or fruits folded through it, or liqueur poured into it after baking. Some gâteaux are layered with jam, almond paste, fresh cream, or butter cream and then decorated with chocolate, praline, candied cherries, chopped nuts, or icing. They are often decorated with butter cream which has been put into a pastry bag with a fancy nozzle. A rich short crust, puff or choux paste, or cookie dough may also be the basis of these cakes, and with the addition of fruits, glazes, and creams is transformed into a gâteau. Again, a baked yeast mixture, soaked in a liqueur or sugar syrup and decorated with fresh or candied fruits, may take the form of a gâteau. Meringue is another mixture which you find in a number of Continental gâteaux.

Some of these gâteaux may appear not to have risen, but in many cases there is no raising agent except air, incorporated through the whipping of egg whites which have then been gently folded through the mixture, or perhaps a very small measure of baking powder. Remember these cakes are very rich and therefore small portions should be served. They will keep moist if covered and kept in a cool place, although any containing fresh cream must be stored in the refrigerator.

It may be necessary to buy some equipment to achieve the best results in this field of cookery, but these items are not expensive and may be collected slowly until you have a number of differently shaped cake pans, pastry bags, and nozzles, which will help you achieve better results.

In the following section you will find some fascinating recipes to try for your family or for your next dinner party.

Schwarzwalder Kirschentorte, Gâteau Suisienne, Gâteau Saint-Honore, and Gâteau Forestière

GÂTEAU MILLE FEUILLES

1¼ quantities Puff Paste
2 tablespoons raspberry jam
¾ cup cream

scant cup sifted confectioners'
   sugar
1 tablespoon cocoa powder

Cooking time: 20 minutes
Temperature: 425°
Serves: 4-6

To prepare the gâteau base: Roll the dough (see page 294) out very thinly to cover a baking sheet approximately 11 by 14 inches. Cut the dough to fit the baking sheet. Divide into three strips 4½ inches wide. Prick the strips with a fork, one all over and the others down the center. Rest in the refrigerator for 1 hour. Bake on the middle shelf of a 425° oven for 20 minutes or until a rich golden brown color. Allow to cool.

To complete the gâteau: Spread the flat strip of dough with jam. Place one hollow-surfaced strip of dough on top, hollow side up. Whip the cream until stiff and pipe down the length of the hollow. Place the other strip of dough on top of the cream, hollow side down. Prepare a firm but spreadable water icing by mixing the confectioners' sugar with cold water. Take a small quantity of the icing and color it with the cocoa powder. Place the chocolate icing in a small paper pastry bag. Spread the white icing over the top of the gâteau. Pipe 6 to 7 chocolate lines down the length of the gâteau. Draw the tip of a skewer or small knife through the icing marking the size of the portions. Draw the skewer in the opposite direction, across each portion, marking the center of the portion. Allow to set and cut into portions.

Note: This is known as feather icing.

GÂTEAU SAINT-HONORÉ

For base:
½ quantity Puff Paste

For choux paste:
6 tablespoons water
2 tablespoons butter
dash salt

½ cup all-purpose flour
2 eggs

Cooking time: 25 minutes
Temperature: 400°
Serves: 5-6

For filling:
3 egg yolks
½ cup sugar
¼ cup all-purpose flour

1¼ cups milk
1 vanilla bean
2 egg whites

For decoration:
¼ lb. lump sugar
¼ cup water
⅔ cup whipping cream

6 red cherries
6 angelica diamonds

To make the base: Roll out the dough (see page 294) to 1/10-inch thickness. Cut out a circle 8 inches in diameter. Prick thoroughly with a fork and allow to rest in the refrigerator for 1 hour.

To make the choux paste: Bring the water, butter, and salt to a boil in a saucepan. Remove from the heat and stir in the flour. Return to the heat and continue stirring until the paste forms a ball and leaves the sides of the saucepan. Cool. Add the beaten eggs, a little at a time, beating well after each addition.

To complete the base: Place the prepared choux paste in a pastry bag with a ½-inch plain nozzle and pipe around the circumference of the puff paste base. Pipe 10 to 12 small blobs of the choux paste onto a lightly greased baking sheet. Bake the sheet of small puffs on the top shelf and the gâteau base on the middle shelf of a 400° oven for 25 to 30 minutes or until dry and crisp.

To make the filling: Cream the egg yolks and sugar. Fold in the flour and mix until smooth. Bring the milk and vanilla bean to a boil. Remove the vanilla bean and, stirring briskly, add the milk to the egg and sugar mixture. When thoroughly mixed return to the saucepan and cook until thick, stirring constantly. Beat the egg whites and fold into the cooled mixture.

To complete the gâteau: Dissolve the loaf sugar in the water in a saucepan and boil until it caramelizes—it turns to an amber color. Placing the small puffs on a skewer or fork, dip them into the caramel and place them around the raised edge of the base. Fill the center with the prepared filling. Decorate with whipped cream, cherries, and angelica.

Note: Leftover scraps of puff paste may be used for the base.

GÂTEAU FORESTIÈRE

1 8-inch Egg Sponge

For champignons:
2 egg whites
scant cup sifted confectioners'
  sugar

1 teaspoon Royal icing
1 teaspoon cocoa powder

Cooking time: 1 hour
Temperature: 200°
Serves: 8

For filling and decoration:
$\frac{1}{4}$ cup crème de cacao
1 quantity Butter Cream
green coloring

$\frac{2}{3}$ cup semi-sweet chocolate
  pieces
1 teaspoon instant coffee powder

To prepare the meringue champignons: Prepare Meringue au Cuite with the egg whites and confectioners' sugar (see page 262). Grease and flour a baking sheet. Place the prepared meringue in a pastry bag with a $\frac{1}{4}$-inch plain nozzle. Pipe 14 to 15 small rounds about $\frac{3}{4}$ inch in diameter, then with the remaining meringue pipe the same number of small mounds with the finishing point drawn upwards. Place the meringues in the lower part of the oven with the temperature at 200°. Allow the meringues to dry out thoroughly; this should take at least 1 hour. When they are ready, smooth down the tops of the rounds by rubbing them lightly on a sieve or the fine side of a grater. Cut the tops off the small pointed mounds, place a spot of Royal Icing (see page 268) on each, and top with a round. The champignons should stand up on their own. When completed. sprinkle lightly with cocoa powder.

To complete the gâteau: Slice the Egg Sponge (see page 262) through the center and sprinkle both slices with the liqueur. Take $\frac{1}{4}$ cup of the Butter Cream (see below), color it green, and set aside. Flavor the remaining cream with one fourth of the chocolate, melted, and the instant coffee. Sandwich the sliced sponge together with a layer of cream ensuring that the bottom of the sponge is on top. Cover the entire sponge with a thin, even, smooth layer of cream. With a knife dipped in hot water, mark the number of desired portions. Place a champignon on each portion and the remaining champignons in the center of the sponge. Allow the remaining chocolate to stand in a warm room for a few minutes and then make some chocolate flakes by drawing a vegetable peeler across the chocolate repeatedly. Let the flakes fall casually over the cake and at the same time prepare sufficient flakes to coat the sides. Place the green cream in a paper pastry bag and cut the end off at an angle for piping leaves. Pipe a neat green leaf at the base of each champignon and a few odd leaves around the champignon group in the center of the gâteau.

GÂTEAU SUCHARD

1 8-inch Chocolate Sponge
1 quantity Butter Cream

$1\frac{2}{3}$ cups semi-sweet or milk
  chocolate pieces
2 tablespoons Royal Icing

To fill and coat the gâteau: Slice the Chocolate Sponge (see page 262) through the center. Flavor the Butter Cream (see Below) with approximately $\frac{1}{2}$ cup melted chocolate. Sandwich the sponge together with a $\frac{1}{2}$-inch layer of cream ensuring that the bottom of the sponge is on top. Cover the top and sides with an even layer of cream and chill until the cream is set and firm. Melt the remaining chocolate in the top of a double boiler over hot water. Place the sponge on a wire cooling rack and quickly coat with melted chocolate. Do not have the chocolate hot and use a knife with a blade 1 inch longer than the diameter of the sponge.

To decorate the gâteau: Place the Royal Icing (see page 268) in a small paper pastry bag and decorate with fine scroll work. The word Suchard may be printed in the center and light scroll work piped around the outer edge.

BUTTER CREAM

$\frac{1}{2}$ quantity Meringue au Cuite

$\frac{3}{4}$ cup butter

Prepare the Meringue au Cuite (see page 262), ensuring that the meringue is both stiff and cool. Cream the butter as lightly as possible and fold in the meringue until smooth.

GÂTEAU SUISIENNE

1 8-inch Egg Sponge
3 cups strawberries
$\frac{1}{4}$ cup sugar

7 tablespoons raspberry jam
1 quantity Meringue au Cuite

Serves: 8

Slice the Egg Sponge (see below) through the center. Select 12 choice berries and set aside. Purée the remaining fruit with the sugar. Spread the fruit purée on the bottom layer of the sponge. Sprinkle the top half of the sponge with a little fruit juice and place on top of the bottom. Cover the surface of the sponge with jam. Place the sponge on an ovenproof plate and pipe fingers of Meringue au Cuite (see below) around the sides. Pipe small shells of meringue around the outer edge on top of the fingers, drawing the points outward. Leave a circle big enough to take the strawberries and fill in the center area with small rosettes of meringue. Brown the meringue under a grill or in a hot oven. Dip the selected strawberries into melted raspberry jam and place them in the space left uncovered by meringue.

SCHWARZWALDER KIRSCHENTORTE

1 8-inch Chocolate Sponge
1 (14 oz.) can sour or black cherries
approximately $\frac{1}{4}$ cup arrowroot
scant 2 cups whipping cream

2 tablespoons kirsch or maraschino
$\frac{2}{3}$ cup semi-sweet chocolate pieces
maraschino cherries for decoration

Serves: 8

Slice the Chocolate Sponge (see below) through twice, making 3 layers. Drain and if necessary pit the cherries. Place the fruit in a pan with a little of the juice and the arrowroot and heat until it thickens to a spreadable consistency. Spread the cherries on the bottom layer of the sponge. Whip the cream and flavor with 1 teaspoon kirsch. Place the second layer of sponge on top of the cherries, sprinkle with kirsch, and cover with a layer of whipped cream. Place the remaining layer of sponge on top and cover the entire sponge with a smooth, even layer of cream. Mark the desired number of portions with a hot, wet knife. Melt the chocolate, spread it thinly on a cold surface, marble preferably, and when the chocolate has just set draw a long, straight-edge knife across the chocolate, pushing forward as you draw through. This should cause the chocolate to roll and flake. Coat the cake, top and sides, with the prepared chocolate. Pipe a rosette of cream on each portion and top with a maraschino cherry.

EGG SPONGE

3 eggs
2 egg yolks
$\frac{1}{2}$ cup sugar

1 cup all-purpose flour, sifted with $\frac{1}{4}$ teaspoon baking powder
$\frac{1}{4}$ cup butter

Cooking time: 20 minutes
Temperature: 375°

Place the eggs, egg yolks, and sugar in a mixing bowl. Whip over hot, but not boiling, water until frothy and warm. Remove from the water and whip until cold. Sift the flour onto the egg and sugar mixture. Carefully and as lightly as possible fold in the flour. When the flour has been mixed in add the melted butter and carefully fold in. Put the mixture into a greased 8-inch flan ring which has been placed on a wax paper lined baking sheet. Bake on the top shelf of 375° oven for 20 to 25 minutes.
Variation: To make a Chocolate Sponge substitute 6 tablespoons cocoa for 6 tablespoons of the flour.

MERINGUE AU CUITE

5 egg whites

$2\frac{1}{4}$ cups sifted confectioners' sugar

Place the egg whites and sifted confectioners' sugar in a china or stainless steel bowl. Place over hot but not boiling water and whip until firm and glossy. Remove from the hot water and whip until firm enough to pipe.

A Wedding Cake

Betty Dunleavy

CLASSIC RICH FRUIT CAKE

A rich fruit cake suitable for Christmas, wedding, birthday, and other celebration cakes. Basic ½ lb. quantity—weight refers to butter weight, not the full weight of the cooked cake.

2¾ cups raisins
1⅓ cups seedless white raisins
⅔ cup dates or prunes
⅓ cup mixed peel
⅔ cup apricots or figs
⅔ cup currants
¼ cup candied cherries
⅔ cup rum, brandy, or sweet sherry
1 cup butter
1 cup brown sugar, firmly packed

} OR 2½ lb. mixed dried fruit

1 teaspoon almond extract
¼ cup maple syrup
4 eggs
½ cup almonds or walnuts, finely chopped
2½ cups all-purpose flour, sifted with 1 teaspoon baking powder
¼ cup cornstarch
2 teaspoons mixed spice
½ teaspoon baking soda
1 teaspoon ground nutmeg

Cooking time: 3½-4 hours
Temperature: 300°
reducing to 250°

Wash, dry, and chop the dried fruits as required, sprinkle with the spirits or sherry, and stand aside for a few hours or overnight. Beat the butter, sugar, almond extract, and syrup together until light and creamy; add the eggs gradually, beating well after each addition. Stir in half the fruit, almonds or walnuts, and the sifted dry ingredients. Add the remainder of the fruit, almonds or walnuts, and the dry ingredients. Spoon the mixture into a prepared 7-inch or 8-inch spring form or square cake pan and press down firmly. Place in a 300° oven and bake for 2½ hours, then reduce the temperature to 250° and bake for a further 1 to 1½ hours.

To prepare the pan: Line the pan with 4 thicknesses of paper, 2 of brown and 2 of white or wax. Care must be taken to miter the corners well so the cooked cake will be of an even shape. Allow the paper to extend 2 to 3 inches above the pan.

QUANTITIES FOR VARIOUS CAKE SIZES

- Half quantities of the above cake mixture, i.e., a ¼-lb. cake spooned into a 5-inch or 6-inch round or square cake pan, requires 2 to 2½ hours in a 300° oven.
- One and a half quantities of the above cake mixture, i.e., a ¾-lb. cake spooned into a 9-inch round or square cake pan, requires 5 to 5½ hours in the coolest position of a 300° oven, reducing after the first 2½ hours to 250°.
- Double quantity of the above cake mixture, i.e., a 1-lb. cake spooned into a 10-inch or 11-inch round or square cake pan, requires 6 to 6½ hours in the coolest position of a 250° oven.
- Three times the quantity of the above cake mixture, i.e., a 1½-lb. cake spooned into a 12-inch round or square cake pan, requires 7 to 7½ hours in the coolest position of a 250° oven.

To avoid over-brown and hardening of the top of the larger cakes, a sheet of paper may be placed over the top for the first 2 to 3 hours of cooking. Leave the cake until cold before turning out and remove all but the last lining paper. Wrap in aluminum foil and store for at least a week before using. Longer storage mellows the flavor.

Note: For extra moistness, a little rum, brandy, or sherry may be brushed over the cake just before wrapping and the process repeated once a week until the cake is required for icing.

Tiered Celebration Cakes

One, two, or three tiered cakes are the most popular. To obtain a balanced effect the size of the cakes must be carefully proportioned.

Suggested sizes:
- One-tier —12 inches in diameter.
- Two-tier —base 11 inches, top 7 inches.
- Three-tier—base 12 inches, middle 9 inches, top 6 inches.

Cake sizes are usually planned to suit the size of the function and the number of slices required. If a large number of slices is needed but only a modest decorated cake is desired, an extra cake (iced but not decorated) may be prepared and presented as cut slices only. Many brides like to keep the top tier of their wedding cake for their first anniversary or perhaps a christening so this must be taken into account when planning the cake quantities.

ALMOND PASTE

3½ cups (1 lb.) sifted
   confectioners' sugar
1-1½ cups ground almonds
2 small or 1 large egg yolk

¼ cup sweet sherry
2-3 teaspoons lemon juice
extra confectioners' sugar
egg white for glazing

Sift the confectioners' sugar, add the ground almonds, and mix well. Add the egg yolks and sherry. Mix to a firm dough with the lemon juice. Turn out onto a pastry board which has been sprinkled with sifted confectioners' sugar and knead lightly. Roll out to the size and shape of the cake. The paste should be approximately ¼ to ⅜ inch thick. Leavel the surface of the cake and brush away any crumbs. Turn upside down onto a board and brush the cake with lightly beaten egg white. This will enable the paste to stick to the cake. Fill in any cracks or unevennesses on the cake with scraps of almond paste to ensure a level surface and contour. Lift the almond paste, either in one whole piece or the top and sides in sections depending on the size of the cake, onto the cake. Mold and smooth into shape, making sure the edges and/or corners are a good shape. Cut away any surplus around the base of the cake to neaten the join at the board. Set aside for at least 2 days to become firm.

FONDANT PASTE

3½ cups (1 lb.) sifted
   confectioners' sugar
1 teaspoon glycerine
2 small or 1 large egg white
2 oz. liquid glucose

extra confectioners' sugar
almond or vanilla extract
pure food coloring
egg white for glazing
cornstarch

Sift the confectioners' sugar into a bowl. Make a well in the center and add the glycerine, egg white, and glucose, which has been heated over boiling water to soften. Stir with a wooden spoon until the mixture is cool, then knead with the hand until all the confectioners' sugar is absorbed. Turn out onto a board which has been lightly sprinkled with extra sifted confectioners' sugar, flavor and color as desired, and knead until smooth and pliable. Cover until ready to use.

Brush the almond paste covered cake lightly with egg white. Use a sprinkling of confectioners' sugar or cornstarch on the board. Roll out the fondant to approximately ¼- to ⅜-inch thickness and large enough barely to cover the cake. Lift onto the cake by rolling around a large rolling pin and unrolling onto the cake. Sprinkle a little cornstarch onto the palms of the hands and smooth the surface and sides, making sure the edges and/or corners are in good shape. Trim the base with a sharp knife to neaten on the board. Allow to set for a few days to dry before decorating.

QUANTITIES FOR VARIOUS CAKE SIZES

Almond Paste
The quantity refers to the amount of confectioners' sugar in the recipe, i.e., 1 lb. Almond Paste is the above mixture.
- One quantity will cover a 6-inch cake.
- One and a half quantities will cover an 8-inch cake.
- Double quantity will cover a 9-inch cake.
- Three quantities will cover an 11-inch cake.
- Three and a half quantities will cover a 12-inch cake.

Fondant Paste
The quantity refers to the amount of confectioners' sugar in the recipe, i.e., 1 lb. Fondant Paste is the recipe as stated above.
- One quantity will cover a 6-inch cake.
- One and a half quantities will cover an 8-inch cake.
- Double quantity will cover a 9-inch cake.
- Three quantities will cover an 11-inch cake.
- Three and a half quantities will cover a 12-inch cake.

These quantities may vary with the depth of the cake or the desired thickness of the Almond or Fondant Paste. Cakes which are to be kept for a long time will keep better with a thicker covering.
Note: Cakes which are not first covered with Almond Paste will need a thicker layer of Fondant so an extra half to one quantity will be required. Alternatively two thin coverings may be used, which will give a smoother, better shape.

Frostings, Icings, and Fillings

Joan Widdowson

Joan Widdowson's forte is cake decorating. She is in charge of the Home Science department of a large technical college in Australia.

The appearance of food is very important and has great bearing on its appeal, whether food for the family or for a special occasion. This is especially so with the presentation of all types of cakes and cookies. Cakes may be iced and decorated elaborately for special occasions such as weddings, birthdays, and christenings, but cakes which your family eat every day are decorated simply. Icings and frostings enable a plain butter cake to be transformed into something suitable to serve to guests. It is important to be neat when decorating cakes and to work out the design to be used before actually starting to frost.

Your choice of frosting depends on the type of cake or cookie to be frosted. Rich fruit, wedding, and birthday cakes are first covered with almond paste and then with fondant paste before decorating. Royal icing is then used for piping and modeling paste is used for molding flowers and other decorations. The period of time between baking and icing is considerably longer than for an ordinary butter or sponge cake. Softer frostings and fillings are made for butter cakes, sponges, and cookies. These may be sandwiched together with jam, fresh cream, or butter cream and covered with a glacé icing or frostings of various flavors. When baking a cake which is to be frosted make sure the surface of the mixture in the cake pan is even. With a butter cake it should be slightly hollowed in the center as they are inclined to rise unevenly, whereas a sponge will rise more evenly. The cake should be completely cool and set before it is frosted. Either stand it on a wire rack or put it on an inverted plate. It is usually a good idea to turn the the cake upside down to frost as it is more likely to have an even bottom. Make sure there are no loose crumbs on the surface. It is advisable to brush the cake over with a thin layer of apricot glaze before covering with a glacé icing. This keeps the cake moist and prevents the cake from absorbing moisture from the icing and therefore making it dull. Use coloring with discretion so that the icing looks palatable and attractive. Use a spatula to spread the icing and decorate immediately with candied cherries, nuts, peel, chocolate, or coconut.

You may choose a soft icing or frosting of the same flavor as the cake, or you may choose one of contrasting flavor and color, such as rum-flavored icing on a chocolate cake.

Intricate designs in icing on special occasion cakes may take time and practice to achieve, but most of the recipes I have given you are for soft frostings which are quick to make, give very pleasing results, and are more enjoyable to eat.

Frostings and Fillings: Chocolate Frosting, Glace or Warm Icing, Seven Minute Frosting, Lemon Cheese, Coffee Vienna Frosting, and Orange and Lemon Fairy Frosting

ROYAL ICING

1½-2 cups sifted confectioners'
    sugar
    (amount varies according to
    size of egg white)

1 teaspoon liquid glucose
1 egg white
4 drops lemon juice or 2 drops
    glacial acetic acid

Sift the confectioners' sugar through a fine sieve. Melt the glucose. Beat the egg white slightly using a wooden spoon; gradually add the confectioners' sugar, beating well. Add the lemon juice and melted glucose and beat until the icing remains in a point when the spoon is drawn up from it. The icing should become glossy and stiff by beating rather than by the addition of extra confectioners' sugar. If white icing is required add a few drops blue food coloring. Cover with a damp cloth until required to prevent the icing drying out and crusting.

Note: A coffee strainer may be used to sieve the confectioners' sugar.

MODELING PASTE

2 tablespoons water
2 teaspoons gelatin
1 teaspoon liquid glucose

scant 2 cups sifted confectioners'
    sugar

Place the water and gelatin in a small saucepan and stir over very low heat until the gelatin dissolves. Add the glucose and dissolve. Remove from the heat. Gradually add half the sifted confectioners' sugar, mixing in well. Place in an air-tight container and leave for several hours —overnight if possible. Knead in the remaining confectioners' sugar until the consistency of the modeling paste resembles a piece of plasticine. Use cornstarch to prevent sticking when rolling out and molding. Extra confectioners' sugar will make the modeling paste too dry. Keep in an air-tight container when not using the paste as it dries out very quickly.

GLACÉ OR WARM ICING

1⅓ cups sifted confectioners'
    sugar
2 tablespoons boiling water

few drops extract (vanilla, lemon,
    coffee, etc.)
coloring

Sift the confectioners' sugar into a small heatproof bowl. Add the boiling water gradually and mix to a smooth paste. Do not add all the water unless necessary. Stir over boiling water for 1 minute. Add essence and colorings as required. Pour the icing quickly over the cake and if necessary smooth the surface with a spatula or a knife dipped in hot water.

Sufficient to cover the top of an 8-inch sponge cake.

Variations:

Chocolate: Add 1 tablespoon cocoa and 1 teaspoon butter.

Mocha: Add 1 tablespoon cocoa and 1 teaspoon butter.
    Use 2 tablespoons strong coffee instead of the water.

Coffee: Add 1 teaspoon instant coffee to the confectioners' sugar.

Spiced: Add ½ teaspoon cinnamon, ½ teaspoon mixed spice, ½ teaspoon nutmeg, and ¼ teaspoon ground cloves to the confectioners' sugar.

CHOCOLATE FROSTING

¼ cup butter
¼ cup water
2 squares unsweetened cooking
    chocolate

2¼ cups sifted confectioners'
    sugar
1 teaspoon vanilla extract

Heat the butter and water, add the chocolate, and heat until it melts. Do not overheat. Gradually add the sifted confectioners' sugar and the vanilla extract; if necessary add a little more water to obtain a spreading consistency.

Variation: Use ¼ cup strong hot coffee instead of water for Mocha Frosting.

SEVEN MINUTE FROSTING

scant cup granulated sugar
1 teaspoon liquid glucose or
  $\frac{1}{2}$ teaspoon cream of tartar

1 egg white
$\frac{1}{4}$ cup water
$\frac{1}{4}$ teaspoon vanilla extract

Place the sugar, glucose or cream of tartar, egg white, and water in the top of a double boiler or in a heatproof bowl over gently boiling water. Beat with a rotary beater over low heat until the mixture is thick enough to hold its shape (approximately 7 minutes). Allow to cool slightly, add the vanilla extract, and spread roughly over the cake. Sufficient to cover a 7-inch layer cake.

Variations:

Pineapple Frosting: Substitute the syrup from canned pineapple for the water. Decorate with candied pineapple.

Creamy Frosting: Substitute $\frac{1}{4}$ cup brown sugar, firmly packed, for $\frac{1}{4}$ cup of the white sugar.

Coconut Frosting: Frost the cake and sprinkle at once with toasted shredded coconut.

Peppermint Frosting: Add a few drops peppermint extract instead of the vanilla extract. Color green or pink.

Marshmallow Frosting: Add 1 cup chopped marshmallows when the mixture is thick.

Chocolate Frosting: Add 3 squares melted unsweetened cooking chocolate just before spreading on the cake.

ORANGE AND LEMON FAIRY FROSTING

1 envelope gelatin
$\frac{1}{4}$ cup water
$\frac{1}{3}$ cup orange juice
2 tablespoons lemon juice

1 egg white
$1\frac{1}{2}$ cups sifted confectioners'
  sugar

Add the gelatin to the water and allow to dissolve over hot water. Leave until cold but not set. Add the strained fruit juice. Beat the egg white until stiff; pour in the gelatin and juice mixture gradually, beating well all the time. Slowly mix in the sifted confectioners' sugar, beating until thick. Spread between the layers and over the top of the cooled cake.

Sufficient for filling and frosting an 8-inch layer cake.

VIENNA FROSTING

scant 2 cups sifted confectioners'
  sugar
$\frac{1}{2}$ cup butter

2 tablespoons sherry
4-5 drops vanilla extract

Cream the butter and add half the confectioners' sugar gradually, beating until creamy and fluffy. Beat in the sherry alternately with the remaining sugar. Stir in the vanilla. Sufficient for a jelly roll or an 8-inch layer cake.

Variations:

Chocolate: Sift 2 tablespoons cocoa powder with the confectioners' sugar.

Orange: Use 2 tablespoons orange juice instead of the sherry and add 1 teaspoon grated orange rind.

Lemon: Use 2 tablespoons lemon juice instead of the sherry and add 1 teaspoon grated lemon rind.

Coffee: Sift in 1 teaspoon instant coffee powder with the confectioners' sugar.

Walnut: Fold in $\frac{1}{4}$ cup finely chopped walnuts.

Liqueur: Use 2 tablespoons of your favorite liqueur instead of the sherry; try crème de menthe or Tia Maria.

LEMON CHEESE

$\frac{1}{4}$ cup butter
2 lemons

yolks of 2 large eggs
$\frac{1}{2}$ cup sugar

Use a double boiler or a heatproof bowl standing in a saucepan of boiling water. Melt the butter in the top of the double boiler or in the bowl, add the grated rind and juice of the lemons, the egg yolks, and the sugar. Stir with a wooden spoon over gently boiling water until the mixture thickens. Allow to cool. Spread between the layers of the cake.

BISCUITS AND COFFEE CAKES

Joan Barbour

Joan Barbour has been a leading home economist in industry for many years. She has a Diploma of Domestic Arts and is now senior home service advisor with the Gas and Fuel Corporation of Victoria, Australia.

Biscuits

The ability to bake a good batch of golden brown biscuits or a high, light sponge is always a test of a good cook. The sponge layer cake recipe appears elsewhere in this book, so let us now consider biscuit baking.

Theories on the best way to make and bake biscuits vary as much as the baked biscuits themselves and ideas differ as to what the appearance and texture of a good biscuit should be.

The following biscuit recipes give the generally accepted ingredient proportions and methods, but in case you would like to experiment with some of the theories for possible improvements to these, I have listed a few, as follows:

TIPS FOR MAKING BISCUITS

- Add 1 to 2 tablespoons sugar to 2 cups flour, even for scones.
- Use confectioners' sugar in place of the granulated sugar for a finer texture.
- Instead of rubbing the butter into the flour, melt it and add to the milk.
- For lighter biscuits, use half milk and half water.
- Ensure the required liquid is always well chilled.
- Handle the dough as little as possible.

Whether to place the biscuits apart or close together on the baking sheet and whether to grease or flour the baking sheet are matters for personal preference, as is the choice between glazing with milk or milk and egg, or leaving them with floury tops.

Whichever way you like your biscuits make them often, for practice makes perfect and a fresh batch of biscuits made especially for your guests is such a pleasant welcoming gesture.

Quick Plain Loaf, Gem Scones, and Scotch Pancakes

PLAIN BISCUITS

2 cups all-purpose flour	2 teaspoons cream of tartar	Cooking time: 12-15 minutes
½ teaspoon salt	2 tablespoons butter or margarine	Temperature: 450°
1 teaspoon baking soda	¾-⅞ cup milk	Yield: 8-10

Sift the flour, salt, baking soda, and cream of tartar into a mixing bowl. Rub the butter into the flour with the fingertips until the mixture resembles fine bread crumbs. Quickly mix in sufficient milk to make a soft dough. Turn the dough onto a lightly floured board and knead lightly until smooth. Roll out to ¾-inch thickness and cut into rounds with a floured cutter. Place the biscuits on a greased baking sheet. Glaze with a little milk and bake in a 450° oven for 12 to 15 minutes. Place the biscuits on a wire cooling rack. When cool break in half and spread with butter or serve with strawberry jam and whipped cream.

Variations:

Fruit Biscuits: Before adding the milk add ½ cup seedless white raisins and 2 tablespoons sugar.

Cheese Biscuits: Before adding the milk add ½ cup grated cheese.

Wholewheat Biscuits: Substitute 1 cup wholewheat flour for 1 cup of the all-purpose flour.

Note: The biscuit dough may also be shaped into a circle, marked into 6 or 8 wedges, and baked in a 450° oven for 20 to 30 minutes.

CHEESE 'N CHUTNEY PINWHEELS

1 quantity Plain Biscuit dough	½ cup grated cheese	Cooking time: 15 minutes
¼ cup chutney		Temperature: 450°

Prepare the biscuit dough (see above) and roll it into a rectangle approximately 14 by 7 inches. Spread the dough with the chutney and sprinkle over the cheese. Moisten one long edge with milk and, starting from the opposite side, roll up firmly into a sausage shape. Cut into 1-inch pieces with a floured knife. Place the biscuits, cut side up, on a well-greased baking sheet and bake in a 450° oven for approximately 15 minutes. Loosen the biscuits with a knife and place on a wire cooling rack. When cool, split and spread with butter.

FRUITY PLAIT

1 quantity Plain Biscuit dough	2 tablespoons, firmly packed, brown sugar	Cooking time: 15-20 minutes
generous cup mixed fruit and nuts	1 tablespoon lemon juice	Temperature: 450°

Prepare the biscuit dough (see above) and roll into a rectangle approximately 13 by 8 inches. Spread the fruit and nut mixture down the center of the dough, leaving a 2-inch margin on each side. Sprinkle with the brown sugar and lemon juice. Cut each margin into 1-inch strips, slanting downward from the fruit in the center. Brush the strips with milk and plait them across the fruit mixture. Lift the plait onto a well-greased baking sheet. Glaze with milk and bake in a 450° oven for 15 to 20 minutes. Lift gently onto a wire cooling rack. When cold, slice and butter.

SCOTCH PANCAKES

1 cup all-purpose flour	1 egg	Yield: 12-16
½ teaspoon baking soda	½ cup milk	
1 teaspoon cream of tartar	2 tablespoons melted butter	
2 tablespoons sugar	(optional)	

Sift the flour into a mixing bowl with the baking soda and cream of tartar and add the sugar. Make a well in the center and add the egg. Add the milk gradually with the melted butter if used, stirring rapidly with a wooden spoon. Mix to a smooth batter. Drop from a spoon onto a lightly greased, heated griddle or skillet. When small bubbles appear on the surface and the underside is lightly browned, turn over and cook the other side. Cool on a clean dish towel on a wire cooling rack. Butter and serve when cold.

QUICK PLAIN LOAF

4 cups all-purpose flour, sifted
    with 4 teaspoons baking
    powder
$\frac{1}{2}$ teaspoon salt
$1\frac{1}{4}$ cups milk

Cooking time: 30-35 minutes
Temperature: 380°

Sift the flour and salt into a mixing bowl. Make a well in the center and add the milk nearly all at once while mixing with a knife to form a fairly moist dough. Turn out immediately onto a lightly floured board and knead to a round about 1 inch thick. Place on a floured baking sheet and bake in a 380° oven for 30 to 35 minutes. Turn onto a wire cooling rack and when cold slice and butter. It should be eaten very fresh.

Variations:

Cheese Loaf: Add $\frac{1}{2}$ cup grated cheese and a dash cayenne pepper to the sifted flour and salt before adding the milk, and sprinkle the loaf with a little more grated cheese before baking.

Fruit Loaf: Add $\frac{1}{2}$ cup mixed dried fruit and 2 table-spoons sugar to the sifted flour and salt before adding the milk.

Orange Loaf: Add the finely grated rind of 1 orange and 2 tablespoons sugar to the sifted flour and salt before adding the milk, and sprinkle the top of the loaf with a little sugar before baking.

POTATO BISCUITS

$\frac{1}{2}$ cup milk
$\frac{1}{2}$ cup water
$\frac{3}{4}$ cup instant potato flakes
1 cup all-purpose flour
2 teaspoons baking powder
dash salt
1 small egg

Cooking time: 15-20 minutes
Temperature: 450°

Heat (but do not boil) the milk and water in a saucepan. Add the potato flakes and mix gently to combine. Spoon the potato into a mixing bowl and sift over it the flour, baking powder, and salt. Mix all together with the beaten egg to form a fairly firm dough. Turn the dough onto a floured board and knead lightly. Roll out to $\frac{3}{4}$-inch thickness and cut into rounds or triangles. Place the biscuits on a greased baking sheet and bake in a 450° oven for 15 to 20 minutes. Turn onto a wire cooling rack and serve warm with butter.

PUMKIN BISCUITS

$\frac{1}{4}$ cup butter or margarine
$\frac{1}{4}$ cup sugar
$\frac{1}{2}$ cup cooked mashed pumpkin
    or other squash
1 egg
$\frac{1}{3}$ cup milk
$2\frac{1}{2}$ cups all-purpose flour, sifted
    with 3 teaspoons baking
    powder

Cooking time: 20 minutes
Temperature: 400°

Cream the butter and sugar. Add the pumpkin and mix well. Add the egg and mix in the milk a little at a time. Add the sifted flour and mix to a soft dough. Turn onto a floured board and knead lightly. Roll out to $\frac{3}{4}$-inch thickness and cut into rounds with a floured cutter. Place the rounds on a greased baking sheet. Glaze with milk and bake in a 400° oven for 20 minutes. Turn onto a wire cooling rack and when cool break open and spread with butter.

GEM SCONES

$\frac{1}{4}$ cup butter
$\frac{1}{2}$ cup sugar
2 eggs
$1\frac{1}{2}$ cups all-purpose flour, sifted
with $1\frac{1}{2}$ teaspoons baking
    powder
dash salt
$\frac{3}{4}$ cup milk

Cooking time: 15 minutes
Temperature: 400°
Yield: 24

While the oven is preheating, put in the ungreased muffin molds to heat.

Cream the butter and sugar together; add the beaten eggs gradually, beating well between each addition. Sift the flour and salt together and add alternately with the milk, folding gently until the batter is of an even consistency. Remove the heated molds from the oven, brush with butter, and half fill with the batter. Bake in a 400° oven for about 15 minutes. Turn onto a wire cooling rack and when cold split and spread with butter.

Betty Dunleavy

BOILED FRUIT LOAF

1 teaspoon mixed spice
½ cup water
3 cups mixed dried fruit, chopped
2 cups chopped nuts
1 cup sweetened condensed

milk
1 cup all-purpose flour
1 teaspoon baking powder
1 egg
1 teaspoon grated lemon rind

Cooking time: 2 hours
Temperature: 325°

Place the spice, water, and mixed fruit in a saucepan and bring to a boil. Simmer for 3 minutes, then allow to cool. Add the chopped nuts and condensed milk. Beat into the sifted flour and baking powder; add the beaten egg and lemon rind. Spoon into a loaf pan lined with greased wax paper and bake in a 325° oven for approximately 2 hours. Cool in the pan and store for for at least 2 to 3 days before using.
Note: Sprinkle a little sherry over the cake while it is still hot for an extra special flavor and moistness.

FRUIT AND WALNUT ROLL

1 cup dried apricots
1⅓ cups raisins
1 cup walnuts
1½ tablespoons lemon juice
2 tablespoons orange juice
½ cup butter or margarine
¾ cup sugar

3 eggs, separated
1 cup shredded coconut
1½ cups all-purpose flour, sifted
    with 1½ teaspoons baking
    powder
½ cup shredded pineapple,
    drained

Cooking time: 1¾ hours
Temperature: 325°

Combine the chopped dried apricots, the raisins, and the walnuts with the fruit juices. Set aside for a few hours to soften the fruit. Cream the butter or margarine and sugar well. Mix in the egg yolks and coconut. Stir in the sifted flour alternately with the soaked fruits and the pineapple. Lightly fold through the stiffly beaten egg whites. Spoon into 2 well-greased large fruit juice cans and cook in a 325° oven for 1¾ hours. Stand in the cans for 30 minutes before turning out. This mixture improves in flavor and texture with keeping.

GINGER COFFEE CAKE

6 tablespoons butter or margarine
½ cup sugar
1 large egg
2 cups all-purpose flour, sifted
    with 2 teaspoons baking
    powder

¼ teaspoon salt
1 cup dry ginger ale
⅓ cup seedless white raisins
⅓ cup chopped mixed candied
    fruit

Cooking time: 1 hour
Temperature: 350°

For topping:
6 tablespoons all-purpose flour
¼ cup, firmly packed, brown
    sugar

2 tablespoons butter
¼ teaspoon ginger

Beat the butter and sugar until creamy; add the beaten egg and then fold in the sifted flour and salt alternately with the ginger ale. Lastly add the white raisins and candied fruit and mix well. Spoon the batter into a 9-inch square pan, greased and lined with greased wax paper. Mix the topping ingredients to a crumbly consistency and sprinkle over the batter. Bake in a 350° oven for 1 hour. Leave in the pan for a few minutes before turning out onto a paper covered cooling rack, then turning back so the crumbly topping is uppermost. Serve cut in slices.

Economical Date and Peanut Roll, Boiled Fruit Loaf, Cheese Biscuit, and Plain Biscuits

ECONOMICAL DATE AND PEANUT ROLL

½ cup butter or margarine
2 cups all-purpose flour
¼ teaspoon ground cloves
1⅓ cups chopped pitted dates

½ cup sugar
¼ cup chopped salted peanuts
1 teaspoon baking powder
1 teaspoon baking soda
⅔ cup milk

Cooking time: 35 minutes
Temperature: 375°

Rub the butter into the sifted flour and ground cloves until the mixture resemble bread crumbs. Mix in the dates, sugar, and peanuts. Dissolve the baking powder and baking soda in the milk. Stir into the dry ingredients. Spoon into a large, well greased fruit juice can. Bake in a 375° oven for 35 to 40 minutes. Cool, slice, butter, and serve.

HONEY LOAF

1½ cups all-purpose flour
1½ teaspoons baking powder
¼ teaspoon salt
½ cup butter or margarine
¾ cup honey
2 eggs

½ cup milk
1 lemon
⅔ cup raisins
½ cup peanuts
extra ¼ cup honey
6 tablespoons sugar

Cooking time: 1¼ or 1¾ hours
Temperature: 325°

Sift the flour, baking powder, and salt into a mixing bowl. Rub in the butter and stir in the warmed honey, beaten eggs, and milk. Fold in the grated rind of the lemon, the chopped raisins, and the peanuts. Pour into 2 small or 2 large loaf pan lined with greased wax paper and bake in a 325° oven for 1¼ or 1¾ hours, depending on the size of the pan. When cooked and still hot brush the combined extra honey and the lemon juice over the top of the cake. Quickly sprinkle with sugar and cool for 10 minutes in the pan. Remove and store for 1 day before slicing and spreading with butter.

SPICY APPLE COFFEE CAKE

3 cups all-purpose flour
3 teaspoons baking powder
dash salt
1 cup sugar
6 tablespoons butter or margarine
1 egg

½ cup milk
1 cup applesauce
⅔ cup seedless white raisins
2 teaspoons cinnamon
melted butter

Cooking time: 55 minutes
Temperature: 350°

Sift the flour, baking powder, and salt with ¾ cup of the sugar. Rub in the butter or margarine with the fingertips and mix to a soft dough with the beaten egg and milk. Turn onto a floured board, knead lightly with well-floured hands, and cut in half. Line a greased 9-inch layer pan with half the mixture; spread with the apple-sauce. Sprinkle with the white raisins, half the cinnamon, and the remaining sugar. Cover with the remaining dough. Glaze with melted butter and sprinkle with the remaining cinnamon. Make a slit in the center for the steam to escape and bake in a 350° oven for 55 minutes.

WHOLEWHEAT BANANA BARS

1½ cups wholewheat all-purpose
   flour
1¼ cups all-purpose flour
2 teaspoons baking powder
6 tablespoons brown sugar
dash salt
1⅓ cups chopped pitted dates

½ cup butter or margarine
¼ cup boiling milk
2 eggs
extra 1 cup milk
3 ripe bananas
¼ cup salted peanuts

Cooking time: 40-45 minutes
Temperature: 325°

Sift the flours, baking powder, sugar, and salt into a mixing bowl and add the dates. Melt the butter or margarine in the boiling milk. Beat the eggs and add the extra milk and the butter and milk mixture. Pour into the dry ingredients, add the mashed bananas, and beat well. Spoon the mixture into 2 well-greased bar pans. Sprinkle with the chopped peanuts and bake in a 325° oven for 40 to 45 minutes. Serve buttered.
Note: As with most banana cakes, this one keeps exceedingly well.

COCONUT FRUIT CAKE

⅔ cup candied pineapple
⅔ cup candied peel
½ cup candied cherries
1 cup blanched slivered almonds
2 tablespoons orange juice
2 tablespoons lemon juice
1⅓ cups shredded coconut
2 tablespoons sherry or brandy
½ cup butter

¾ cup sugar
3 eggs
1½ cups all-purpose flour, sifted
   with 1½ teaspoons baking
   powder
extra ¼ cup orange juice
⅔ cup raisins
extra flour

Cooking time: 2¾ hours
Temperature: 325°

Wash the sugar from the pineapple, peel, and cherries, dry well, and chop into small pieces. Mix well with the slivered almonds and the orange and lemon juice. Allow to stand overnight. Sprinkle the coconut with the sherry or brandy and leave to soak for 30 minutes. Cream the butter and sugar well, add the beaten egg yolks, and then add the soaked coconut. Fold in the sifted flour alternately with the extra orange juice. Add the soaked fruits and nuts and the raisins (lightly dusted with a little flour), then fold in the stiffly beaten egg whites. Turn into an 8-inch spring form pan lined with greased wax paper and bake in a 325° oven for about 2¾ hours. Leave in the pan until cool.

PRIZE-WINNING LIGHT FRUIT CAKE

1 cup butter
½ cup granulated sugar
½ cup, firmly packed, brown
   sugar
grated rind of ½ lemon
5 eggs
2½ cups all-purpose flour

2 teaspoons baking powder
2¼ cups seedless white raisins
½ cup candied cherries chopped
½ cup mixed candied peel,
   chopped
2 tablespoons sherry or brandy

Cooking time: 2-2¼ hours
Temperature: 300°

Line an 8-inch spring form pan with 1 layer of brown and 1 layer of wax paper. Beat the butter with the sugars and lemon rind until very creamy. Add the well-beaten eggs gradually, beating after each addition. Stir in the sifted flour and baking powder alternately with the prepared fruits and the sherry or brandy; mix well. Spoon carefully into the prepared pan to avoid air-holes. Bake in a 300° oven for 2 to 2¼ hours. Cool for 15 minutes before turning out of the pan.
Note: For a more economical light fruit cake use 3 eggs and ½ cup milk.

COOKIES AND BARS

Mary Dunne

Mary Dunne has compiled recipe books and prepared broadcasts and many demonstrations during her career as a dietition and home economist. She now works as the House Service Supervisor for an important national organization.

Cookies

For an in-between-meals snack a cookie or two, especially home-made, is always popular. A full cookie jar is a boon where there is a family.

Cookies may be divided into eight groups according to the method.
1. A soft dough that can be spread or pressed out into a shallow baking pan, then baked and cut into bars while still hot.
2. A soft dough that can be dropped from a spoon on to a baking sheet.
3. A moderately soft dough that can be molded into balls with the hands.
4. A moderately soft dough that can be put through a cookie press.
5. A firm dough which is formed into rolls or bars, then chilled thoroughly in the refrigerator, sliced thinly with a sharp, thin-bladed knife, and baked.
6. A fairly firm dough which is rolled thinly and cut into shapes.
7. A dough made from whipped egg whites, sugar, and coconut or cereal flakes and dropped in small heaps onto a greased baking sheet.
8. Savory biscuit dough; the shortening is rubbed into the flour and the dough rolled very thinly.

HELPFUL HINTS FOR COOKIE MAKING

- It is most important that fresh ingredients be used in cookie making.
- This is specially so with the shortening; only the best quality should be used as the butter or margarine in them gives the biscuits their crispness.
- Most types of cookie are more successful if the softest dough that can be handled is used, and the least amount of flour used for rolling and cutting. Soft doughs are easier to handle if chilled for about 20 to 30 minutes before rolling.
- Chilling the dough gives additional crispness when baked.
- In rolling any dough, turn out on a lightly floured surface, flour the rolling pin, and use only as much pressure as is necessary to roll the dough out into a sheet of the desired thickness.
- Dip the cutter or knife in flour and cut the shapes as close together as possible. Lift the cookies on a broad knife or spatula and place them on a lightly greased baking sheet, allowing a little space between for possible spreading. Shallow pans or sheets should be used as high sides prevent the even distribution of heat necessary to cook and brown the cookies.
- Use 2 teaspoons for placing drop cookies on a baking sheet, one to spoon the mixture, the other to push it off.
- Allow the cookies to cool on the baking sheet before removing unless otherwise stated in the recipe.
- Store cookies in a pottery or glass jar or a tin with a tightly fitting lid.
- Soft cookies may be crispened by placing on an ungreased baking sheet and heating in a 350° oven for 3 to 5 minutes.

Almond Cherry Whirls, Golden Butter Drops, Lemon Blossom Bars, and Coconut Raspberry Dainties

LEMON BLOSSOM BARS

¾ cup butter or margarine
½ cup sifted confectioners' sugar
1½ cups all-purpose flour
½ cup custard powder or
   cornstarch

1 cup sweetened condensed
   milk
½ cup lemon juice
2 eggs
¼ cup sugar
⅓ cup shredded coconut

Cooking time: 30 minutes
Temperature: 350°
Yield: 30

Cream the butter or margarine and confectioners' sugar in a mixing bowl. Gradually work in the flour and custard powder. Press into a greased 9- by 11-inch oblong cake pan and bake in a 350° oven for 15 minutes.

Mix the condensed milk, lemon juice, and egg yolks. Spread on top of the cooked base. Whip the egg whites until stiff; gradually beat in the sugar and fold in the coconut. Spread over the filling and bake for a further 15 minutes. When cold cut into squares or bars.

GOLDEN BUTTER DROPS

½ cup butter or margarine
½ cup sugar
1 egg
1 teaspoon grated orange rind
1 teaspoon grated lemon rind

1¼ cups all-purpose flour, sifted
   with 1 teaspoon baking
   powder
almonds or walnuts

Cooking time: 10-12 minutes
Temperature: 350°
Yield: 36

Melt the butter or margarine in a large saucepan and heat until it becomes light brown in color. Cool, add the sugar, and beat well. Add the egg and the orange and lemon rind and beat again. Add the sifted flour and mix in well. Drop in very small teaspoonfuls onto a greased baking sheet, allowing room for spreading. Place half a blanched almond or a piece of walnut on top of each cookie and bake in a 350° oven for 10 to 12 minutes.

HERMITS

2½ cups all-purpose flour
1 teaspoon baking soda
½ teaspoon mixed spice
½ teaspoon cinnamon
½ cup butter or margarine
6 tablespoons brown sugar,
   firmly packed

½ cup honey
2 eggs
½ cup milk
generous cup mixed dried fruit
1½ tablespoons mixed candied
   peel, finely chopped

Cooking time: 10-15 minutes
Temperature: 375°
Yield: 36

Sift the flour, baking soda, and spices. Cream the butter or margarine, sugar, and honey in a mixing bowl, gradually add the beaten eggs, and mix well. Add the sifted ingredients alternately with the milk, mixed fruit, and mixed peel. Place in teaspoonfuls on a greased baking sheet and bake in a 375° oven for 10 to 15 minutes.

ALMOND CHERRY WHIRLS

1¼ cups all-purpose flour, sifted
   with 1 teaspoon baking
   powder
¼ cup ground almonds
dash salt

¾ cup butter or margarine
⅓ cup sifted confectioners' sugar
almond extract
candied cherries

Cooking time: 12-15 minutes
Temperature: 325°
Yield: 16

Sift the flour, ground almonds, and salt. Cream the butter or margarine and sugar in a mixing bowl. Mix in the sifted ingredients and a few drops almond extract. Beat well until smooth. Using a star nozzle in a pastry bag, pipe rosettes into small paper patty cases. Place a piece of cherry on top of each and place on a baking sheet. Bake in a 325° oven for 12 to 15 minutes.

Colored paper patty cases make these cookies look very attractive.

LEMON FRUIT BARS

½ cup butter or margarine
½ cup sugar
1 egg
1 cup mixed dried fruit

2 cups all-purpose flour, sifted
   with 2 teaspoons baking
   powder
dash salt
blanched almonds

Cooking time: 20 minutes
Temperature: 375°
Yield: 30

For lemon icing:
1 teaspoon butter
2 tablespoons boiling water
2 tablespoons lemon juice

2 cups sifted confectioners'
   sugar
1 teaspoon grated lemon rind

Melt the butter in a large saucepan, add the sugar, and allow the mixture to cool. Add the beaten egg, mixed fruit, and sifted flour and salt. Mix well. Spread in a greased 9- by 11-inch oblong pan and bake in a 375° oven for 20 minutes.

To make the lemon icing: Melt the butter in the boiling water and allow to cool slightly. Add the lemon juice, sifted confectioners' sugar, and lemon rind. Mix to the required consistency. Pour over the cookie slice when cold, and smooth the surface with a knife dipped in hot water. Sprinkle with finely chopped blanched almonds. Serve cut into bars.

COFFEE KISSES

2 cups all-purpose flour, sifted
   with 2 teaspoons baking
   powder
dash salt
½ cup butter or margarine

6 tablespoons sugar
1 egg
1 teaspoon instant coffee
   powder
2 tablespoons hot water

Cooking time: 12-15 minutes
Temperature: 325°
Yield: 36

For coffee cream:
1 teaspoon instant coffee
   powder
2 tablespoons hot water

1⅓ cups sifted confectioners'
   sugar
¼ cup butter

Sift the flour and salt. Cream the butter or margarine and sugar in a mixing bowl and beat in the egg. Dissolve the instant coffee powder in the hot water and add to the mixture alternately with the flour. Mix thoroughly. Pipe through a pastry bag with a plain nozzle onto a greased baking sheet. Bake in a 325° oven for 12 to 15 minutes, allow to cool, then sandwich together with coffee cream.

To make the coffee cream: Dissolve the instant coffee powder in the hot water and allow to cool. Soften the butter and beat to a cream. Gradually beat in the confectioners' sugar and coffee powder.

COCONUT RASPBERRY DAINTIES

1 cup all-purpose flour
6 tablespoons sugar
½ cup butter or margarine

1⅓ cups shredded coconut
1 egg
⅓ cup raspberry jam

Cooking time: 12-15 minutes
Temperature: 350°
Yield: 40 approximately

Sift the flour into a mixing bowl, add the sugar, and rub in the butter or margarine. Stir in the coconut and mix to a firm dough with the beaten egg. Knead lightly then roll out thinly. Cut into rounds with a 2-inch cutter. Remove the centers from half the rounds with a 1-inch cutter. Repeat the rolling and cutting until all the dough is used. Place the cookies on a greased baking sheet, allowing a little room to spread. Bake in a 350° oven for 12 to 15 minutes until golden brown. When cool, spread the rounds with raspberry jam and place a ring on top. A little extra coconut may be sprinkled in the center of each cookie if wished.

CHEESE AND HAM DREAMS

1½ cups all-purpose flour, sifted
   with 1½ teaspoons baking
   powder
½ teaspoon salt
½ teaspoon mustard
dash cayenne pepper

6 tablespoons butter or margarine
1¼ cups finely grated sharp
   cheese
1 egg
1 teaspoon lemon juice
devilled ham spread

Cooking time: 10-12 minutes
Temperature: 350°
Yield: 48

Sift the flour, salt, mustard, and cayenne pepper into a mixing bowl. Rub in the butter or margarine. Add ¾ cup of the cheese. Mix to a firm dough with a little of the beaten egg and the lemon juice. Roll out thinly on a lightly floured board. Cut into various shapes. Brush the tops of the cookies with the remaining egg, then dip the tops into the remaining grated cheese. Place on a greased baking sheet and bake in a 350° oven for 10 to 12 minutes. Allow to cool, then join together with devilled ham spread.

HONEY CHOCOLATE BUBBLES

A favorite with children.

⅔ cup semi-sweet chocolate
   pieces
½ cup butter or margarine
½ cup sugar

¼ cup honey
⅓ cup shredded coconut,
   browned in oven
6 cups crisp rice cereal

Yield: 36

Melt the chocolate in a heatproof bowl over hot water, being careful not to overheat. Place the butter or margarine, sugar, and honey in a saucepan. Dissolve slowly and boil for 3 minutes without stirring. Pour over the rice cereal and coconut and add the melted chocolate. Mix well. Press firmly into a greased 10- by 8-inch oblong cake pan. When cold and quite set cut into squares.

ICE BOX NUTTIES

⅔ cup pitted dates
½ cup walnuts
½ cup butter or margarine
½ cup brown sugar, firmly packed
1 egg

1 teaspoon vanilla extract
2 cups all-purpose flour, sifted
   with 2 teaspoons baking
   powder
dash salt

Cooking time: 10-12 minutes
Temperature: 375°
Yield: 36

Chop the dates and walnuts finely. Cream the butter or margarine and sugar in a mixing bowl and add the beaten egg and vanilla extract. Gradually work in the sifted flour, salt, dates, and walnuts. Divide the mixture into 4 and shape each piece into a roll about 1 inch thick. Wrap securely in wax paper and refrigerate until well chilled. Cut into rounds, place on a greased baking sheet, and bake in a 375° oven for 10 to 12 minutes.

Lemon Fruit Bars, Golden Butter Drops, Coconut Raspberry Dainties, and Coffee Kisses

Rosemary Dempsey

Rosemary Dempsey conducts her own radio program on cookery and demonstrates on television. She has been the cookery editor of *The New Zealand Herald* newspaper for many years.

More Cookies

In the past the home cook used to set aside a day a week to fill the cake and cookie tins. However, today baking is not done on such a grand scale and cooks have been searching for and developing recipes which take less time to prepare and bake.

Cookie dough which is pressed into a pan and after baking is cut into bars, or those baked in small heaps on a baking sheet, are extremely popular as there is no lengthy rolling and cutting to be done. After baking, cool cookies on a wire rack, and the moment they are cool, place them in a tin or jar before they have absorbed any moisture from the air. Cover with a piece of wax paper and a tightly fitting lid. Cookies, if stored correctly, will remain fresh for some time and are very handy for morning and afternoon tea or coffee, suppers, and packed lunches.

Refrigerator cookies have become increasingly popular over the last few years, with the advent of the home freezer and the improvement of the freezing compartment of the normal household refrigerator. The busy housewife can make a large quantity of cookie dough which may be rolled, wrapped, and put into the freezer until the cookies are required. Then the required number are cut off and the dough rewrapped and returned to the freezer. For variety, a number of flavors, chopped nuts, or fruits may be added to the mixture before rolling and freezing.

It is also wise to collect a few recipes for uncooked cookies. These are quick to make and are ideal for the hot summer months when extra cooking is sometimes very tedious and tiring. Although there are innumerable varieties of sweet cookies for sale in every supermarket, no-one could deny the fact that a cookie freshly made at home is truly delicious.

CARAMEL BARS

For base:
6 tablespoons butter
½ cup sugar
2 egg yolks

1½ cups all-purpose flour
1½ teaspoons baking powder

Cooking time: 50 minutes
Temperature: 350°
Yield: 24

For caramel filling:
½ cup sweetened condensed
   milk
½ cup sugar
¼ teaspoon vanilla extract

2 tablespoons butter
1 egg yolk
1 tablespoon corn syrup
3 tablespoons all-purpose flour

For meringue:
3 egg whites

¾ cup sugar

To make the base: Cream the butter and sugar in a mixing bowl. Add the egg yolks and mix well. Add the sifted flour and baking powder and mix well. Press into a greased jelly roll pan.

To make the caramel filling: Combine all the ingredients in a saucepan and stir over low heat until dissolved. Do not allow to boil. Spread over the base.

To make the meringue: Whip the egg whites until stiff but not dry. Gradually add the sugar, beating continuously. Spoon over the caramel. Bake in a 350° oven for 50 minutes. Cut into bars while warm.
Note: If the meringue is becoming too brown, cover with a sheet of wax paper halfway through the cooking period.

CHOCOLATE PEANUT SHORTCAKE

½ cup butter
½ cup sugar
2 egg yolks

2 cups all-purpose flour
1 teaspoon baking powder
apricot jam

Cooking time: 30 minutes
Temperature: 375°
Yield: 30

For topping:
3 squares unsweetened cooking
   chocolate
¾ cup roasted peanuts

¾ cup sugar
2 egg whites

Cream the butter and sugar in a mixing bowl. Add the egg yolks and mix well. Add the sifted flour and baking powder and mix well. Press the mixture into a greased jelly roll pan. Spread with apricot jam, and top with the following mixture.

Melt the chocolate in a heatproof bowl over boiling water and add the remaining ingredients. Stir until the mixture is well blended, then spread over the apricot jam. Bake in a 375° oven for 30 minutes. Cut while hot.

GINGER CRUNCH

½ cup butter
½ cup sugar
1¾ cups all-purpose flour

1 teaspoon baking powder
1 teaspoon ginger

Cooking time: 20-25 minutes
Temperature: 370°
Yield: 24

For icing:
2 tablespoons butter
½ cup sifted confectioners' sugar

2 teaspoons corn syrup
1 teaspoon ginger

Cream the butter and sugar in a mixing bowl. Add the sifted dry ingredients. Mix well and press into a greased 8-inch square pan. Bake in a 370° oven for 20 to 25 minutes.

To make the icing: Put the butter, confectioners' sugar, syrup, and ginger in a saucepan. Heat over low heat until melted then pour over the cookie whilst hot. Cut into slices while still warm.

ANZAC COOKIES

½ cup butter
2 tablespoons corn syrup
1 teaspoon baking soda
¼ cup boiling water

1 cup rolled oats
1 cup shredded coconut
1 cup all-purpose flour
1 cup sugar

Cooking time: 25 minutes
Temperature: 300°
Yield: 40

Melt the butter and corn syrup in a large saucepan over low heat. Add the baking soda mixed with the boiling water. Combine the dry ingredients in a mixing bowl and pour the melted mixture into the center. Mix to a moist but firm consistency. Drop teaspoonfuls of the mixture onto cold greased baking sheets. Bake in a 300° oven for 25 minutes, until golden brown. Cool for a few minutes on the baking sheets before removing to a wire cooling rack.

HOKEY POKEY COOKIES

½ cup butter
½ cup sugar
2 tablespoons corn syrup

2 tablespoons milk
1 teaspoon baking soda
1½ cups all-purpose flour

Cooking time: 10 minutes
Temperature: 325°
Yield: 24

Cream the butter and sugar in a mixing bowl. Warm the syrup and milk in a large saucepan over low heat. Add the baking soda. Beat into the creamed mixture. Fold in the sieved flour. Place in teaspoonfuls, about 2 inches apart, on a cold greased baking sheet. Bake in a 325° oven for 10 minutes. Cool for a few minutes on the baking sheet before removing to a wire cooling rack.

DATE AND WALNUT KISSES

½ cup butter
½ cup sugar
2 eggs
2 cups all-purpose flour

2 teaspoons baking powder
1 tablespoon cocoa powder
1 cup chopped dates
1 cup chopped walnuts

Cooking time: 15 minutes
Temperature: 350°
Yield: 48

Cream the butter and sugar in a mixing bowl. Add the eggs and beat well. Fold in the sifted dry ingredients. Mix in the dates and walnuts. Place in teaspoonfuls on cold greased baking sheets. Bake in 350° oven for about 15 minutes.

PEANUT BUTTER COOKIES

½ cup butter
½ cup sugar
6 tablespoons brown sugar
½ cup peanut butter
1 egg

1¼ cups all-purpose flour
½ teaspoon baking powder
¾ teaspoon baking soda
¼ teaspoon salt

Cooking time: 15 minutes
Temperature: 375°
Yield: 36

Cream the butter, sugars, and peanut butter in a mixing bowl. Add the beaten egg and mix well. Sift and stir in the flour, baking powder, baking soda, and salt. Chill the dough for 15 minutes. Roll into balls the size of large walnuts. Place 3 inches apart on greased baking sheets. Flatten criss-cross fashion with a fork dipped in flour. Bake in a 375° oven for about 15 minutes. Cool for a few minutes on the baking sheets before removing to a cooling rack.

REFRIGERATOR COOKIES

1 cup butter
1⅔ cups sugar
2 eggs
2 teaspoons vanilla extract

3½ cups all-purpose flour
1 teaspoon baking powder
½ teaspoon salt

Cooking time: 10-15 minutes
Temperature: 350°
Yield: 4-5 dozen

Cream the butter and sugar in a mixing bowl, add the eggs and vanilla extract, and beat well. Sift and add the flour, baking powder, and salt. Divide into 5 portions and use as follows:

Coffee: Add 2 teaspoons instant coffee powder, shape into a triangular roll, wrap in wax paper, and chill. Slice ⅛ inch thick and top with an almond.

Coconut and Orange: Add ⅓ cup shredded coconut and ½ teaspoon orange extract. Shape into a roll. Wrap, chill, and slice thinly.

Ginger: Roll, wrap, chill, and slice, topping with a piece of preserved ginger.

Chocolate Pinwheels: Divide the mixture in half. Add 1 tablespoon cocoa powder and ½ teaspoon cinnamon to half the mixture. Shape into a rectangle ¼ inch thick. Shape the other half in to a similar rectangle. Put one rectangle on top of the other, roll up tightly, wrap in wax paper, chill, and slice thinly.

Chocolate Walnut: Add 1 tablespoon cocoa powder and ½ teaspoon cinnamon to half the mixture as for Chocolate Pinwheels. Roll out the chocolate mixture, wrap around the plain mixture, chill, slice, and top each with half a walnut.

Bake in a 350° oven for 10 to 15 minutes.

Note: This cookie dough will keep for months in the freezer if wrapped securely in aluminum foil or plastic. Slice and bake 6, 16, or 60, whenever required for unexpected visitors.

CRISPS

⅞ cup butter
¼ cup sugar
¼ cup sweetened condensed milk

1½ cups all-purpose flour
1 teaspoon baking powder
⅓ cup semi-sweet chocolate pieces

Cooking time: 20 minutes
Temperature: 350°
Yield: 30

Cream the butter and sugar in a mixing bowl. Add the condensed milk and mix well. Sift and add the flour and baking powder. Stir in the chopped chocolate. Roll into small balls. Place on a greased baking sheet. Flatten criss-cross fashion with a fork dipped in flour. Bake in a 350° oven for 20 minutes. Cool for a few minutes on the baking sheet before removing to a cooling rack.

MELTING MOMENTS

⅞ cup butter
⅔ cup sifted confectioners' sugar
1 cup all-purpose flour

scant cup cornstarch
½ teaspoon baking powder

Cooking time: 20 minutes
Temperature: 350°
Yield: 48

Cream the butter and confectioners' sugar in a mixing bowl. Sift and add the flour, cornstarch, and baking powder. Roll into small balls, place on cold greased baking sheets, and flatten each ball slightly with a fork. Alternatively, pipe the dough through a cookie press. Bake in a 350° oven for 20 minutes. When cool, sandwich together with raspberry jam or your favorite frosting.

CHOCOLATE FUDGE COOKIES

½ cup butter
½ cup sugar
1 egg
1 teaspoon vanilla extract

¼ cup cocoa powder
1 cup chopped walnuts
2 tablespoons corn syrup
½ lb. Graham crackers

Yield: 24

Melt the butter in a saucepan, add the sugar, and bring to a boil. Add the well beaten egg, mix well, and add the vanilla extract, cocoa powder, walnuts, corn syrup, and crackers, broken into small pieces. Mix well and press into a greased jelly roll pan. Frost with Chocolate Frosting (see page 268). Cut into bars when cold.

Cream Puffs, Eclairs, and Custard Rings

PASTES AND PIE CRUSTS

Patrick Robinson

Patrick Robinson is a technical college teacher specializing in pastry cooking and cake decorating. Much of his experience has been gained in numerous cake shops, working on wedding, birthday, and special occasion cakes. He later transferred his interest to the catering field and, as chef to a number of catering institutes, gained recognition for his original sweets and decorative buffet pieces.

The ancient Chinese are known to have created the first pastries using only flour and water. These pastries were steamed or fried, and this traditional method of cooking has been carried through to the present day.

The Egyptian Pharaohs some 5,000 years ago placed great importance on pastries, bread, and cakes. So much, in fact, that these delicacies were placed in burial tombs for the 'after life'. Sacrifices to the gods of huge amounts of pastries were made by the rich. The discovery of ancient tombs has revealed these facts, and the remains may be inspected in museums throughout the world.

Pastry making was widely practiced in other Middle Eastern countries, including Syria, Babylon, and Israel, and trading of pastries was carried on between these countries.

In Europe, the Greeks were the first to produce pastries; these were rich in honey and oils. They became specialists, and sold their products in the market places.

The Romans played a very significant part in the development of pastries. A Guild of Roman Bakers was formed in 170 B.C. Later, skilled Italian craftsmen contributed to the development of pastry making, and were taken to France by the nobility to make their delicious goods. This was, no doubt, partly responsible for the magnificent pastry creativity for which the French have been acclaimed. Such masters as Careme, Rouget, and Lesage, to mention but a few, invented masterpieces which aroused much interest and demanded great skill in preparation.

The Germans, Swiss, Austrians, and Dutch have all contributed their specialties, and throughout the world one finds an enormous variety of international pastries being produced in each country.

This section contains a variety of easily produced, attractive, and delectable pastries, incorporating some new ideas in finishing and presentation.

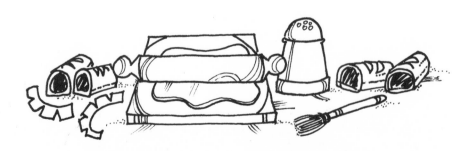

Choux Paste

Choux paste originated in France and is the basis for many delightful sweet and savory variations, such as éclairs, cream puffs, and Gâteau St. Honoré. It is a light, attractive, and easily made paste, made from a cooked dough of water, butter or margarine, and flour. Eggs are then beaten into it.

POINTS FOR SUCCESS
- Cook the mixture in the saucepan until it leaves the sides.
- Beat in the eggs thoroughly.
- Keep the oven door closed for 15 minutes before checking the progress of the baking.
- Cook the paste until quite firm and well dried out.

CHOUX PASTE

1¼ cups water
½ cup butter or margarine
1 tablespoon sugar

1¼ cups all-purpose flour
4 eggs

Place the water, butter, and sugar into a saucepan over medium heat. Sieve the flour onto a piece of wax paper. When the water is boiling and the butter dissolved, quickly pour the flour into the saucepan, stirring rapidly with a wooden spoon. Continue stirring until the mixture forms a smooth soft ball and leaves the sides of the saucepan. Remove from the heat. Allow to cool for 2 minutes. Beat the eggs slightly, add to the mixture one fourth at a time, and beat well until thoroughly absorbed. Continue to beat until a satin-like shine develops. The mixture is now ready for piping.

CHOCOLATE ÉCLAIRS

1 quantity Choux Paste
2½ cups whipping cream

⅔ cup semi-sweet chocolate
    pieces

Cooking time: 20-25 minutes
Temperature: 400°
         reducing to 350°
Yield: 30

To make the éclairs: Preheat the oven to 400°. Lightly grease a baking sheet. Put a ½-inch plain or star nozzle in a pastry bag. Put the Choux Paste into the bag and pipe the éclairs onto the baking sheet. They should be 2 to 3 inches long and 3 inches apart. Sprinkle the éclairs and the tray liberally with water. Bake in a 400° oven for 15 minutes, then reduce the temperature to 350° and bake for a further 5 minutes. Turn the oven off and leave for 5 more minutes if not cooked enough.

The éclairs should be crisp, light, and of an even color. Transfer from the baking sheet to a wire cooling rack. When cool open lengthwise.

To fill, pipe the whipped cream into the éclairs with a star nozzle in a pastry bag. Place the chocolate in the top of a double boiler, melt slowly, and stir well to remove all lumps. Do not overheat. Dip the tops of the éclairs into the chocolate and allow to set.

CREAM PUFFS

1 quantity Choux Paste
2½ cups whipping cream

½ cup sifted confectioners' sugar

Cooking time: 30-35 minutes
Temperature: 400°
         reducing to 350°
Yield: 12

To make the puffs: Preheat the oven to 400°. Lightly grease a baking sheet. Put a ½-inch plain nozzle tube in a pastry bag. Put the Choux Paste into the bag and pipe small pieces about the size of a large walnut onto the baking sheet at least 3 inches apart. Sprinkle the puffs and the tray liberally with water. Cover the puffs with an inverted roasting pan to keep the steam in. Bake for 20 to 25 minutes in a 400° oven, then reduce the temperature to 350° and bake for a further 10 minutes. The puffs should be crisp, light, and of an even color. Remove from the baking sheet to a wire cooling rack. When cool, cut the puffs open across the center.

To fill, whip the cream. Pipe into the puffs and sprinkle heavily with confectioners' sugar.

CUSTARD RINGS

1 quantity Choux Paste

For custard filling:
2½ cups milk
¼ cup sugar
1 tablespoon butter
½ cup cornstarch

3 drops vanilla extract
3 drops yellow coloring
2 large eggs

For decoration:
⅔ cup semi-sweet chocolate
  pieces

½ cup toasted slivered almonds

Cooking time: 20-25 minutes
Temperature: 400°
  reducing to 350°
Yield: 12

To make the rings: Preheat the oven to 400°. Lightly grease a baking sheet. Take a 2-inch pastry cutter, dip the edge in flour, and mark circles on the greased sheet 2 inches apart. Pipe the Choux Paste with a ½-inch plain nozzle in a pastry bag around the edges of the marked rings on the sheet. Sprinkle liberally with water. Bake for 20 minutes in a 400° oven, then reduce the temperature to 350° for 5 minutes. The rings should be crisp, light, and of an even color. Remove from the baking sheet to a wire cooling rack.

To make the custard filling: Place three fourths of the milk, the sugar, and the butter in a saucepan and bring to a boil. Blend the cornstarch with the remaining milk, the vanilla extract, and the yellow coloring. When the milk has boiled lower the heat, pour in the blended cornstarch quickly, and stir rapidly with a whisk or wooden spoon until thickened and smooth. Remove from the heat and cool for 2 minutes. Pour the lightly beaten egg into the custard and mix thoroughly until smooth. To finish the Custard Rings: Slice the Choux Paste rings through the center. Pipe the custard on top of the bases with a ½-inch nozzle. Melt the chocolate in a heatproof bowl or in the top of a double boiler over simmering water, dip the smooth sides of the tops of the rings into the melted chocolate, place on top of the bases, and sprinkle with toasted almonds.

CROQUEMBOUCHE

½ quantity Choux Paste

½ quantity Short Crust

For filling:
½ quantity custard filling or
1¼ cups whipping cream

For decoration:
1 (11 oz.) can mandarin oranges

½ cup candied cherries

For caramel:
¾ cup sugar

1¼ cups water

Cooking time: 30 minutes
Temperature: 400°
  reducing to 375°

To make the Choux Paste puffs: Preheat the oven to 400°. Lightly grease baking sheets. Prepare the Choux Paste and pipe small puffs, the size of small walnuts, approximately 35, onto the sheets. Bake for 10 minutes at 400°. Reduce the temperature to 350° and cook for 5 minutes more. Remove. Cool on wire cooling racks. To make the base: Prepare the Short Crust dough (see page 299). Roll out to ¼ inch thick. Place an 8-inch round plate or saucepan lid on the dough and cut around it with a knife. Prick well with a fork. Place on a cool baking sheet. Rest in the refrigerator for 10 minutes. Bake in a 400° oven until a light straw color. Remove. Cool on a wire cooling rack. To make the filling: Prepare ½ quantity custard filling (see above) or whip the cream. To prepare the decoration: Drain the mandarin oranges and retain the juice. Place the mandarin segments on a wire cooling rack so they drain completely.

To make the caramel: Place the sugar and water in a small saucepan and stir over low heat until the sugar is completely dissolved. Place a lid on the saucepan and boil until a pale golden color. Do not stir during the boiling process. Place the saucepan in a bowl of cold water for approximately 10 seconds, then remove it. Dip the filled puffs into the caramel then arrange them on the Short Crust base in a circle. Continue to build up the layers of puffs, interspersing them with caramel-dipped mandarin segments and cherries.

Mandarin Cream Flan

Puff, Flaky, and Rough Puff Paste

A young baker's apprentice named Claude Gêlée is reputed to be responsible for the accidental discovery of puff paste. It seems he forgot to add the fat when mixing a dough. He wrapped the fat in the dough and to the surprise of all a light, flaky paste resulted. Puff paste is similar to flaky and rough puff paste. A similar process of folding and rolling is used to build up many layers of dough and fat. The main difference is the amount of fat used—in puff paste, equal quantities of fat to flour, in flaky and rough puff paste, three fourths fat to flour. The second difference is in the making of the doughs.

POINTS FOR SUCCESS
- Use firm butter.
- Allow the dough to rest between rollings.
- Bake in a 400° to 450° oven.
- Cover the dough with clear plastic or a damp cloth during the resting periods.
- Roll out with even pressure keeping the ends and sides as square as possible.

PUFF PASTE

2 cups all-purpose flour
good dash salt
1 cup butter or margarine, firm

$\frac{1}{2}$ cup ice cold water
1 teaspoon lemon juice

Sieve the flour and salt into a chilled bowl. Rub 2 tablespoons of the butter into the flour. Make a well in the center of the flour and add the water and lemon juice. Mix with a round bladed knife, drawing in the flour from around the edge until a smooth dough is formed. Place on a lightly floured plate. Make 2 cuts crosswise on the top of the dough and cover with a damp cloth or clear plastic. Rest for 10 minutes in a cool place.

Take the remaining butter and shape into a rectangular block about 4 inches by 2 inches by 1 inch. Roll out the dough to a four-leaf clover shape, leaving a slight rise in the center of the dough. Place the block of butter or margarine in the center and fold over the 4 leaves completely enclosing the butter. Roll the dough into an oblong about 12 by 5 inches. Mark the dough lightly into thirds with a knife. Fold the top third down over the middle third and fold up the bottom third. Give the dough a quarter turn to the left (the folds will then be to right and left) and roll and fold as before. Cover the dough with clear plastic and place in a cool place to rest for 30 minutes. Roll, fold, and turn, as given above, 4 more times. Cover the dough with clear plastic again and rest for 30 minutes in a cool place. Roll, fold, and turn as given above 2 more times. Cover and rest for 15 minutes. Use as required.

PALM LEAVES

1 quantity Puff Paste
1 egg

For decoration:
whipped cream and confectioners'
sugar

dash salt
$\frac{1}{2}$ cup sugar

Cooking time: 14 minutes
Temperature: 425°
Yield: 14-16

Lightly grease a baking sheet. Sprinkle the pastry board with 2 tablespoons of the sugar. Roll out the dough to an oblong 15 by 7 inches. Trim the edges square. Brush the dough with the egg and salt beaten together and sprinkle 2 tablespoons sugar over. Fold the ends into the middle. Brush over with egg and sprinkle with sugar again. Fold in the doubled ends again. Brush over with egg and sprinkle with the remaining 2 tablespoons sugar. Double the dough once more. Cut into slices $\frac{1}{4}$ inch to $\frac{1}{2}$ inch thick. Place on the baking sheet leaving 3 inches between each Palm Leaf. Allow to rest in a cool place for 30 minutes. Bake in a 425° oven for 7 minutes on one side, turn over quickly with a knife, and cook for a further 7 minutes. Remove from the oven and cool on a wire cooling rack.
To decorate: The Palm Leaves may be sandwiched together in pairs with whipped cream and sprinkled with confectioners' sugar. Alternatively they may be frosted with lemon icing.

CHICKEN VOL-AU-VENT

2 quantities Puff Paste
dash salt

1 egg

Cooking time: 25 minutes
Temperature: 425°
    reducing to 350°
Serves: 6-8

For filling:
$\frac{1}{3}$ cup butter
$\frac{2}{3}$ cup all-purpose flour
$\frac{1}{4}$ cup dry white wine
$2\frac{1}{2}$ cups chicken stock or water
   and chicken bouillon cube
salt and pepper

2 drops lemon juice
2 cups diced cooked chicken
1 cup button mushrooms
1 egg yolk
$\frac{1}{4}$ cup cream
parsley sprigs for garnish

Lightly grease a baking sheet. Roll out the dough to a rectangle 17 inches long by 9 inches wide. Cut out an 8-inch circle and place on the baking sheet. Cut out a second 8-inch circle. From the center of this cut out a 5-inch circle and roll it out into a 6-inch circle. Place on the baking sheet and mark in lattice fashion with a knife. Beat the egg and salt together. Brush a thin layer of egg over the first circle of dough, taking care not to let it to run down the edge of the pastry as this will affect the rising. Take the circle of dough with the center removed and place carefully on top of the first circle. Brush egg over the top of the double layer and the latticed circle. Prick the center of the case with a fork several times. Rest the dough for 1 hour in a cool place before baking. Roll out the dough scraps to $\frac{1}{8}$-inch thickness and cut out 18 leaves and 12 crescent shapes using a 2-inch fluted pastry cutter. Decorate the top edge of the vol-au-vent with 12 leaves and the latticed pastry lid with 6

leaves. Brush with egg. Place the crescent shapes on the baking sheet and brush with egg. Bake in a 425° oven for 10 minutes, remove the crescents quickly, and continue the baking for 10 more minutes. Remove the lattice top. Cover the vol-au-vent with wax paper and reduce the oven temperature to 350°. Bake for 5 minutes. Remove and place on a wire cooling rack.
To make the filling: Melt the butter in a small saucepan, add the flour, and cook, stirring, for 2 to 3 minutes. Add the white wine, mix well, and add the hot chicken stock a little at a time, stirring constantly to make a smooth sauce. Cook gently for 10 minutes. Season with salt and pepper. Stir the lemon juice, chicken, and mushrooms. Reheat. Remove from the heat. Mix the egg yolk and cream together and stir into the sauce. Fill the hot vol-au-vent case with the chicken mixture. Arrange the crescents around the base. Place the latticed top on the case. Garnish with parsley.

MATCHES

1 quantity Puff Paste
dash salt
1 egg

2 tablespoons water
$\frac{1}{4}$ cup sugar

Cooking time: 15 minutes
Temperature: 425°
    reducing to 375°
Yield: 16-20

For filling:
$\frac{1}{4}$ cup raspberry jam
scant 2 cups whipping cream
2 tablespoons sugar

confectioners' sugar for
   decoration

Lightly grease a baking sheet. Roll out the dough to an oblong 10 by 6 inches. Trim the edges and cut into 2 pieces, 10 by 3 inches. Cut each strip into 1-inch widths. Brush with the egg and salt, beaten together, sprinkle with the sugar, and place on the sheet. Rest for 30 minutes in a cool place. Bake in a 425° oven for 10 minutes. Reduce the oven temperature to 375° and cook

for a further 5 to 7 minutes. Remove from the oven, cool on a wire cooling rack, and split in half.
   Spread a thin layer of raspberry jam on the bottom half of each bar. Whip the cream and sugar until stiff. Pipe or spread over the jam. Replace the tops and sprinkle with confectioners' sugar.

FLAKY PASTE

2 cups all-purpose flour
dash salt
¾ cup firm butter

½ teaspoon lemon juice
cold water to mix

Sift the flour and salt together into a mixing bowl. Divide the butter into 4 equal portions. Rub 1 portion into the flour with the figertips. Using a round-bladed knife, mix to a pliable soft dough with the lemon juice and cold water. Roll out the dough to an oblong about 12 by 5 inches, keeping the edges straight and the corners square. Brush off the excess flour with a pastry brush. Mark the oblong lightly into thirds with a knife. Place a portion of butter over two thirds of the dough in little pieces. Sprinkle lightly with flour, fold the bottom third of dough up over the middle third, and fold the top third down. Press the edges lightly together with a rolling pin. Give the dough a quarter turn so the folded edges are to right and left.

Roll out and fold as before including another portion of the butter. Cover the dough with clear plastic and chill for 30 minutes. Roll and fold, including the final portion of butter, as before. Cover the dough and chill again for 30 minutes. Roll and fold once more. Use as required.

Note: Equal quantities of butter and lard may be used instead of all butter. Mix both fats together thoroughly before dividing into 4 portions.

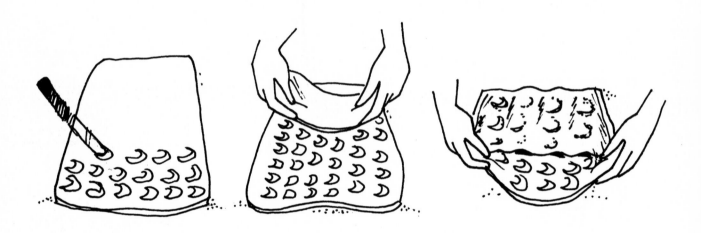

STEAK AND KIDNEY PIE

1 lb. chuck steak
¼ lb. beef or lamb kidney
2 tablespoons drippings or oil
2 onions, chopped
6 tablespoons all-purpose flour

2½ cups water
salt and pepper
1 quantity Flaky Paste
1 egg yolk, beaten with a little
   water, for glazing

Cooking time: 2 hours
Temperature: 425°
Serves: 4-6

Remove any gristle and fat from the meat and cut into 1-inch cubes. Skin and core the kidney and cut into small pieces. Fry the meat in hot drippings or oil in a heavy saucepan until lightly browned. Add the kidney, onion, and flour and cook gently for 5 minutes. Add the water, salt, and pepper and bring to a boil, stirring continuously. Reduce the heat and simmer, covered, until the steak and kidney are tender, about 1½ hours. Place in a pie dish and allow to cool. Roll out the dough (see above) on a lightly floured board until 1 inch larger all around than the top of the pie dish. Cut to fit the pie dish and cut the remaining dough into a strip 1 inch wide. Place the strip on the rim of the pie dish, previously brushed with cold water. Brush the dough rim with cold water and cover with the pie crust. Seal, trim, and decorate the edge. Cut a vent to allow the steam to escape and decorate with a pastry rose and leaves. Brush with the egg glaze and bake in a 425° oven for 20 to 30 minutes. Cover the rose with aluminum foil to prevent burning. Serve hot.

Chicken Vol-au-Vent

SAUSAGE ROLLS

1 quantity Flaky Paste
2 cups sausage meat

egg for glazing

Cooking time: 30 minutes
Temperature: 425°
reducing to 375°
Yield: 24

Divide the dough in half. Roll each half into an oblong 3 by 12 inches. Form the sausage meat into 2 rolls, 12 inches long. Lay the sausage meat down the middle of the dough oblongs. Damp one side of the dough with water, fold the dough over, and press the edges together firmly. Cut each roll into 12 pieces. Glaze the tops of the sausage rolls with beaten egg, place on a baking sheet, and bake in a 425° oven for 15 minutes. Reduce the oven temperature to 375° and bake for a further 10 to 15 minutes.

ROUGH PUFF PASTE

2 cups all-purpose flour
dash salt

$\frac{3}{4}$ cup firm butter
$\frac{1}{2}$ cup water

Sieve the flour and salt into a mixing bowl. Rub 2 tablespoons of the butter into the flour. Cut the remaining butter into 1-inch pieces and mix lightly through the flour. Make a well in the center. Pour the water into the well. Mix in the flour mixture with a round-bladed knife and knead into a dough retaining the pieces of butter through the dough. Cover with clear plastic and rest in the refrigerator for 5 minutes. Place on a floured board and roll the dough out to a rectangle approximately 12 inches long by 5 inches wide. Lightly mark the dough into thirds with a knife, fold the lower third up to cover the middle third, then fold the top third down. Give the dough a quarter turn. Repeat the rolling and folding. Cover with a piece of clear plastic and rest in a cool place for 30 minutes. Repeat the rolling and folding process again and rest for 30 minutes as before. Give the dough one more turn, rolling and folding (making 5 in all), rest for 15 minutes, and then roll out and use as required.

SAVORY CRACKERS

$\frac{1}{2}$ quantity Rough Puff Paste
1 egg
dash salt

2 tablespoons poppy seeds
2 tablespoons sesame seeds

Cooking time: 10-12 minutes
Temperature: 425°
Yield: 48

Lightly grease a baking sheet. Roll out the dough to $\frac{1}{16}$-inch thickness. Prick well with a fork. Beat the egg and salt together and brush over the dough. Cut the dough in half. Sprinkle one half with poppy seeds. Sprinkle the other half with sesame seeds. Cut into small fancy shapes with cookie cutters or a knife. Place on the baking sheet and rest for 30 minutes. Bake the crackers in a 425° oven for 10 to 12 minutes until golden brown. Remove from the sheet and cool on a wire cooling rack. These crackers must be kept in an air-tight container and may be served either plain or as a base for canapés.

CHEESE STRAWS AND RINGS

$\frac{1}{2}$ quantity Rough Puff Paste
1 egg
dash salt

$\frac{1}{2}$ cup finely grated Parmesan
cheese

Cooking time: 10-12 minutes
Temperature: 425°
Yield: 72

Roll out the dough very thinly (about $\frac{1}{16}$-inch thick). Cut out 6 3-inch rounds. Cut out the centers of the rounds using a $2\frac{1}{2}$-inch cutter. Place the rings on a lightly greased baking sheet. Beat the egg and salt together and brush over the surface of the remaining dough. Sprinkle an even covering of cheese over the dough, fold over a third, brush the egg on the dry dough, sprinkle with cheese, then fold the remaining third over. Roll out the dough $\frac{1}{8}$ inch thick, to approximately 10 by 8 inches, trim the edges and ends square, cut into 2 4-inch widths, then cut across into narrow strips. Place on the greased baking sheet with the rings, and allow to rest in the refrigerator for 30 minutes. Bake in a 425° oven for 10 to 12 minutes until light golden brown. Remove from the baking sheet and cool on a wire cooling rack. When cold, arrange the straws in the rings.

Short Crust

Short crust is possibly the most widely used and popular of all pie crusts. It gains its name because of its 'short' eating quality. This shortness is brought about by the choice of fat and the careful mixing of fat and flour. This results in a crust which has great appeal and which may be used as the basis for many dishes, both sweet and salty.

Rich short crust is crisper and richer than plain short crust and is especially good for dessert pies and fruit flans.

POINTS FOR SUCCESS
- Always sieve the flour.
- The fat and water, as well as the utensils, must be cold.
- Handle the ingredients as little and as lightly as possible.
- Do not over-mix the dough or the pastry will be hard and tough.

SHORT CRUST

2 cups all-purpose flour
dash salt
$\frac{1}{4}$ cup butter or margarine

$\frac{1}{4}$ cup lard or shortening
cold water to mix

Sift the flour and salt in a mixing bowl. Rub the fat into the flour lightly, using the fingertips, until the mixture resembles bread crumbs. Using a round-bladed knife, mix to a stiff dough with cold water. Knead lightly.

Note: Butter and margarine add color and flavor to Short Crust; lard helps to make the pastry 'short'. When $\frac{1}{2}$ lb. Short Crust is given in a recipe, this refers to the weight of the flour, i.e., the above recipe.

RICH SHORT CRUST

2 cups all-purpose flour
$\frac{1}{2}$ cup butter
$\frac{1}{4}$ cup sugar

2 egg yolks
cold water to mix

Sieve the flour into a chilled mixing bowl. Add the butter and lightly rub into the flour with the fingertips. When the consistency of fine dry bread crumbs, stir in the sugar and make a well in the center. Add the egg yolk and a little cold water. Mix to a slightly crumbly, stiff dough. The dough is now ready to be kneaded a little. Cover with clear plastic, cool, and rest for 10 minutes in the refrigerator before rolling out.

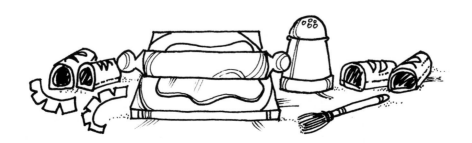

QUICHE

½ quantity Short Crust

For filling:

6 slices bacon	salt
1 small onion, chopped	freshly ground black pepper
⅔ cup milk	½ cup coarsely grated mild cheese
1 egg	1½ tablespoons sliced olives

For garnish:

9 small bacon rolls   parsley sprigs
stuffed olives

Cooking time: 20-25 minutes
Temperature: 400°
    reducing to 350°
Serves: 6-8

Lightly grease a baking sheet. Roll out the dough and line an 8-inch flan ring placed on the baking sheet. Line the pie shell with wax paper and three fourths fill with dried peas or beans. Rest for 10 minutes. Bake in a 400° oven for 10 minutes. Remove the wax paper and dried peas. Return to the oven for 5 minutes. Cool; remove the flan ring from the pie shell.

To make the filling: Cut the bacon into 1-inch pieces and lightly fry for 2 to 3 minutes. Lightly fry the onion in the bacon drippings for 2 minutes. Mix the milk, egg, salt, and pepper together well. Cover the bottom of the pie shell with the bacon. Sprinkle the cheese over, then the olives, and finally the onion. Pour the milk mixture over the top. Bake in a 350° oven for 20 to 25 minutes until set. Cool for 2 to 3 minutes.

To garnish: Lightly broil the bacon rolls and arrange on top of the flan. Cut the stuffed olives in half. Place on the bacon and secure with a wooden toothpick. Garnish with parsley sprigs. Serve hot.

LEMON MERINGUE PIE

½ quantity Short Crust

For lemon filling:

½ cup cornstarch	½ cup sugar
1¼ cups water	yolks of 2 large eggs
2 tablespoons butter	
grated rind and juice of 1 large lemon	

For meringue:

whites of 2 large eggs   ½ cup sugar

Cooking time: 1 hour
Temperature: 400°
    reducing to 300°
Serves: 6

Lightly grease a baking sheet and an 8-inch fluted flan ring. Roll out the dough and line the flan ring placed on the baking sheet. Line the pie shell with a circle of greased wax paper and three fourths fill with dried peas or beans. Rest for 10 minutes. Bake in a 400° oven for 15 minutes. Remove the wax paper and beans and the flan ring. Return the shell to the oven and bake for a further 5 to 10 minutes.

To make the filling: Place the cornstarch, water, butter, lemon rind and juice, and sugar in a saucepan. Beat over moderate heat until boiling, then whip for a further 2 to 3 minutes. Cool slightly. Beat in the egg yolks. Pour into the pie shell.

To make the meringue: Whip the egg whites until stiff. Add half the sugar and whip until stiff again. Gently fold in the remaining sugar. Pile the meringue over the lemon rind and juice, and sugar in a saucepan. Beat pastry all around. Bake in a 300° oven for about 30 minutes until the meringue is golden.

APPLE AMBER

½ quantity Rich Short Crust

For filling:
1 lb. cooking apples	2 eggs
6 tablespoons sugar	¼ cup sugar
1 lemon	extra sugar, candied cherries,
2 tablespoons water	and angelica
3 tablespoons butter	

Cooking time: 1 hour
Temperature: 375°
reducing to 300°
Serves: 4

Lightly grease a 1½-pint pie dish. Roll out the dough to the length of the pie dish and slightly more than twice the depth. Cut the dough in half lengthwise and line the sides of the pie dish. Roll out the leftover dough very thinly and cut out small rounds using a ½-inch plain piping nozzle as a cutter. Damp the edge of the pastry around the pie dish and place the small rounds, overlapping, all around the edge of the pastry as decoration. Place in a cool place to rest for 30 minutes.

Peel, core, and slice the apples thinly. Place the apples, 6 tablespoons sugar, strips of lemon rind, and water in a saucepan. Cover and cook gently until the apples are very soft. Sieve the apples or purée in an electric blender. Add the butter, cut into small pieces, the egg yolks, and the lemon juice and mix well. Brush the pie shell with egg white and pour in the applesauce. Bake in a 375° oven for 30 minutes or until the pastry is crisp and golden.

Whip the egg whites until stiff, fold in the sugar gently, and pile the meringue on top of the apple. Make sure the meringue touches the pastry all round. Sprinkle lightly with extra sugar, decorate with cherries and angelica, and bake in a 300° oven for about 30 minutes, until the meringue is golden.

MANDARIN CREAM FLAN

1 quantity Rich Short Crust

For custard filling:
⅔ cup milk	1½ tablespoons cornstarch
1 tablespoon sugar	2 drops vanilla extract
1 teaspoon butter	2 drops orange extract (optional)
juice and finely grated rind of	2 drops pink coloring
1 small orange	1 egg yolk
¼ cup milk	⅔ cup lemon cheese

For decoration:
⅓ cup semi-sweet chocolate	½ cup sugar
pieces	¼ cup water
18 mandarin segments	⅔ cup whipping cream

Cooking time: 15-18 minutes
Temperature: 400°
Serves: 6-8

Line an 8-inch fluted flan ring with the dough. Line the inside with greased wax paper and one third fill with dried peas or beans. Allow to rest for 10 minutes in a cool place. Bake in a 400° oven for 15 to 18 minutes. Remove and place on a wire cooling rack. After 2 minutes remove the wax paper and dried peas. Cool for a further 5 minutes then carefully remove the flan ring.

To make the filling: Place ⅔ cup milk, the sugar, butter, and orange juice and rind in a saucepan and heat until boiling. Mix ¼ cup milk, the cornstarch extract, coloring, and egg yolk together in a bowl. When the milk is boiling, remove from the heat, pour one third onto the cornstarch mixture, and stir quickly. Pour back into the saucepan and stir quickly until smooth. Reheat, stirring constantly, until boiling. Remove from the heat. Cool for 2 minutes; then add the lemon cheese and mix well. Pour into the cooked pie shell. Spread the mixture level and cool.

To prepare the decoration: Melt the chocolate slowly in a double boiler, pour onto a piece of wax paper on a tray, and spread with a spatula until about ⅛ inch thick. Set in the refrigerator. Cut out 9 1-inch circles, cut in half, and keep in a cool place. Prepare the mandarin segments. Place the sugar and water in a saucepan, cover, bring to a boil, and boil until caramelized (light amber in color). Dip the segments into the caramel using tongs. Put on a greased plate to set. Whip the cream and spread or pipe on top of the custard filling. Arrange the chocolate semicircles and the dipped mandarin segments alternately in 6 rows radiating out from the center. Pipe a rosette of cream in the center.

VIENNESE SHORTBREAD PASTRY

Here is a pastry with delicious 'melt in the mouth' appeal. It is very soft and light when made and is piped through a ½-inch nozzle into a variety of shapes. It is mainly used for fancy shaped cookies which keep extremely well.

⅞ cup butter
½ cup sifted confectioners' sugar
1 egg yolk

2 drops vanilla extract
2 cups all-purpose flour

Lightly grease and flour a baking sheet. Cream the butter and sugar together till white, light, and fluffy. Beat in the egg yolk and the vanilla extract. Warm the flour slightly. Add half the sifted flour, mix in well with a wooden spoon, add the remaining flour, and mix until thoroughly combined. Place the mixture in a large pastry bag fitted with a ½-inch star nozzle and pipe out in the desired shapes.

VIENNESE COOKIES

1 quantity Viennese Shortbread
   Pastry

Cooking time: 10-12 minutes
Temperature: 375°
Yield: 20

To make rosettes: Pipe 2-inch round rosettes on a greased baking sheet. Half a candied cherry may be put in the center of some. Bake in a 375° oven for 10 to 12 minutes until light golden brown. Remove from the sheet. Cool. They may be left plain, sprinkled with confectioners' sugar, or sandwiched together with raspberry jam and whipped cream.

To make fingers: Pipe the mixture onto a greased baking sheet using a large pastry bag and ½-inch star nozzle, in 2½- to 3-inch lengths. Bake in a 375° oven for 10 to 12 minutes. Cool. These may be partly dipped in melted chocolate and allowed to set.

To make rings: Mark a greased and floured baking sheet with a 2-inch round cutter. Pipe with a ½-inch star nozzle on the marked rings. Bake in a 375° oven for 10 to 12 minutes. Cool. To finish, they may be partly dipped in melted chocolate and sprinkled with lightly toasted slivered almonds.

VIENNESE TORTE

½ quantity Viennese Shortbread
   Pastry

Cooking time: 10-12 minutes
Temperature: 375°
Serves: 8-10

For base:
1 8-inch sponge cake
1¼ cups whipped cream
⅓ cup Lemon Cheese

½ cup slivered almonds, lightly
   toasted
confectioners' sugar for sprinkling

Grease and flour a baking sheet and mark a 7½-inch ring on it. Pipe, with a large pastry bag and ½-inch star nozzle, a ring of dough on the inside edge of the marked circle. Pipe 4 lines 1 inch apart and parallel from one side of the ring to the other. Repeat the piping at right angles to the first lines, forming a lattice pattern. Bake in a 375° oven for 10 to 12 minutes until golden brown. Remove from the oven and leave to cool on the baking sheet. To complete the torte: Turn the sponge cake (see page 248), upside-down, cut in half, and spread one half with Lemon Cheese (see page 269), then with a thin layer of cream. Replace the other half on top. Place on a serving plate. Spread cream thickly on top of the sponge, and smooth until level. Carefully lift the cooled lattice pastry circle from the baking sheet and place on top of the cream. Pipe Lemon Cheese into each space between the lattice. Stand the serving plate on an upturned 8-inch cake pan and spread cream around the sides of the torte; press the toasted almonds into the cream. Lightly sprinkle the top with confectioners' sugar. Chill for 30 minutes before serving.

Suet Crust

Suet crust is one of the easiest pie crusts to cook really well. Unlike other pastes suet crust has an artificial raising agent added. This is usually baking powder with all-purpose flour. Suet may be purchased at the meat counter of any store; it must be chopped or grated and all the membranes removed. It is also possible to buy shredded pure suet, in a package.

This dough may be used for both savory and sweet dishes. Meat puddings are usually served from the bowl or mold (wrapped in a white napkin) in which they were steamed or boiled. Fruit puddings are always turned out onto a dish. Serve immediately as the crust does not keep well.

POINTS FOR SUCCESS
- Sift all the dry ingredients together thoroughly.
- Mix grated or chopped suet with a little of the measured flour to keep the pieces separate.
- Never pre-cook pudding fillings. The long slow cooking improves the flavor of fruit fillings and tenderizes the cheaper cuts of meat used for meat puddings. The light, spongy texture of the crust will not be spoiled.
- Keep the water boiling if the pie is being steamed or boiled. If topping up is necessary, use boiling water.

SUET CRUST

2 cups all-purpose flour
1 teaspoon salt
2 teaspoons baking powder
$\frac{3}{4}$ cup shredded suet
approximately $\frac{2}{3}$ cup cold water
to mix

Sift the flour, salt, and baking powder into a bowl, stir in the suet using a round-bladed knife, and mix to a firm dough with cold water. Shape into a ball, cover, and rest for 5 to 10 minutes.

Note: $\frac{1}{2}$ cup of the flour may be replaced by 1 cup fresh white bread crumbs for an extra light and spongy crust, and for a sweet pudding sugar may be added to the flour.

STEAK AND KIDNEY PUDDING

1 quantity Suet Crust
1 lb. stew beef, chuck or blade
$\frac{1}{3}$ lb. beef kidney
2 tablespoons seasoned flour
1 onion, chopped
$\frac{1}{3}$ cup beef stock or water and
beef bouillon cube
parsley for garnish

Cooking time: 3-3½ hours
Serves: 3-4

Knead the dough lightly. Roll two thirds of the dough into a round and line a 6-inch pudding mold.

Wipe the meat and cut into 1-inch cubes. Wash the kidney, remove the core, and cut into small pieces. Toss the meat and kidney in the seasoned flour. Put the meat and onion, mixed together, in the lined pudding mold and add the stock. Roll out the remaining one third of the dough to form a lid, moisten the edge of the dough in the mold, and place the dough lid on top. Cover with greased wax paper and then fasten the cover of the mold securely. Place in a steamer and steam for 3 to 3½ hours. When the pudding is cooked, remove the paper, garnish with a sprig of parsley, and serve.

BLACKBERRY AND APPLE PUDDING

1 quantity Suet Crust
1½ lb. apples, peeled and cored
1⅔ cups blackberries
½ cup sugar
¼ cup water
whipped cream or custard for
serving

Cooking time: 2½-3 hours
Serves: 4

Grease a 6-inch pudding mold. Cut off one third of the dough then roll the remainder into a round and line the pudding mold. Fill the mold with sliced apples and washed blackberries in layers, sprinkling sugar between each layer. Add the water. Roll out the rest of the dough into a round for the top. Damp the edges and press the edges of the lid firmly onto the pudding. Cover with greased wax paper then fasten the lid securely. Steam for 2½ to 3 hours. Serve with cream or custard.

Variation:

Blackberry and Apple Roll: Roll out the dough to an oblong 8 inches wide and ½ inch thick. Damp the edges with water, spread the prepared fruit over, and roll up, pressing the edges together firmly. Place on a greased baking sheet and bake in a 400° oven for 45 to 60 minutes.

*Steak and Kidney Pudding
and Veal and Ham Pie*

LAIT P
DE LA FERME D'ARC
SEINE & MAR
L.NICOLA
PROPRIÉTAIR
22.Rue de Para
PARIS

Hot Water Crust

This pastry gained great popularity in England during Victorian and Edwardian times. It was used for all types of game pies, veal and ham pies, and pork pies. It is just as popular today, for the town of Melton Mowbray in Leicestershire, England is renowned for its pork pies.

The pastry is a very simple one to make and contains only flour, salt, lard, hot water, and egg. The pies which may be made from this pastry are often referred to as raised pies, because of the molding and shaping of the pie shells by hand. Other ways of shaping are by using special hinged, fluted molds and by forming over the base of a jar and supporting with a band of wax paper.

POINTS FOR SUCCESS
- Use the pastry while still warm. Any dough no being used immediately must be kept covered with a clean tea towel in a warm place.
- Knead the dough very thoroughly.
- Make the pies the day before so that they can set properly. During the setting slight contraction occurs between the meat and the top of the pie. This is filled with a jellied stock, making the pies more appealing and appetizing.

HOT WATER CRUST

2½ cups all-purpose flour
1 egg yolk
⅔ cup water

6 tablespoons lard
½ teaspoon salt

Sieve the flour into a warmed bowl. Make a well in the center and add the egg yolk; cover with some of the flour. Heat the water, lard, and salt together in a saucepan until just boiling. Pour immediately into the well and mix with a wooden spoon until the dough is cool enough to handle. Continue to knead the dough with the hands until quite smooth. Shape into a ball, cover, and rest for 10 minutes, keeping warm. The dough is now ready for use.

PORK PIES

For filling:
1 lb. lean pork
3¾ cups water
salt and pepper
1 small carrot

1 stalk celery
1 small onion
dash thyme
1 apple, peeled and thickly sliced

Time: 45 minutes
Temperature: 400°
    reducing to 350°
Yield: 4

1 quantity Hot Water Crust

egg for glazing

For jelly:
1¼ cups pork stock
1 envelope gelatin

seasoning to taste

To prepare the filling: Place the pork with water to cover in a saucepan. Add the seasoning, prepared vegetables, and thyme. Bring to a boil and simmer for 15 minutes. Remove the pork and cut into ½-inch cubes. Strain the remaining liquid.

Divide the prepared dough into 8 pieces, 4 being a little larger. Roll out the larger pieces one at a time and line 4 3-inch deep aluminum foil pie dishes, molding up to the top with the fingers. Fill each pie shell with the diced pork and lay apple slices on top. Roll out the remaining pieces of dough for the pie tops. Brush beaten egg around the edges of the pies, lay the tops on, and seal the edges together with the fingers. Trim with scissors. Press the fingers around the edges to form a fancy edging. Cut 2 slits in the top of each pie and fold back the pastry. Brush with egg. Make 4 decorative leaves and a bud for each pie from leftover dough. Arrange the leaves on the top, around the hole. Place the bud in the center of the leaves. Brush all over with egg glaze. Bake the pies in a 400° oven for 30 minutes or until golden brown, lower the oven temperature to 350°, and bake for a further 15 minutes, covering the pies with wax paper if becoming too brown. Remove from the oven and allow to cool.

To make the jelly: Put the stock and gelatin into a saucepan. Stir until the gelatin has dissolved and season to taste. The jelly should be cooled slightly before using. Remove the bud from the pie carefully with a sharp pointed knife. Pour the jellied stock into each pie with a funnel. Replace the bud. Allow to set before serving.

VEAL AND HAM PIE

For filling:
1 lb. lean veal
3¾ cups water
bouquet garni
dash thyme

½ cup diced ham
salt and pepper
1 or 2 hard-cooked eggs
2 tablespoons veal stock

Cooking time: 1 hour
Temperature: 400°
        reducing to 350°
Serves: 5-6

1 quantity Hot Water Crust

egg for glazing

For jelly:
1¼ cup veal stock
1 envelope gelatin

salt and pepper

To make the filling: Place the veal in the water in a saucepan. Bring to a boil, skim, and add the bouquet garni and thyme. Simmer for 15 minutes. Remove the veal from the water. Cool. Strain the stock and reserve. Cut the veal into ½-inch cubes and mix with the ham, salt, and pepper.

Cut off one third of the dough and reserve for the top. Roll out the remaining piece to a 10-inch circle and heavily flour the bottom of a 5-inch diameter jar. Place the dough over the up-turned jar. Shape by pressing firmly against the sides of the jar. Take a piece of wax paper long enough to wrap around the dough twice and fold it in 3 so it will be ½ inch below the edge of the pie shell. Tie the band of paper around the dough and place all in a cool place until firm. Carefully invert the jar and remove it from the pie shell, giving a slight twist to free it. Place the pie shell on a greased baking sheet. Fill the shell with the meat mixture, putting the hard-cooked egg or eggs in the center of the meat.

Spoon the veal stock over the meat. Roll out the remaining dough to fit the top of the pie. Brush the top edge of the pie with beaten egg, lay the lid on, and press the edges together to seal. Trim off the surplus dough with scissors. Make 2 slits crosswise in the center of the top and fold back the 4 pieces of dough. Roll out leftover scraps of dough and cut out 4 decorative leaves. Brush the folded-back dough with egg. Arrange the leaves on top. Mold a decorative bud from the leftover scraps and place in the center of the leaves. Brush all over with egg. Bake in a 400° oven for 30 minutes, then reduce the oven temperature to 350°. Cover with wax paper if becoming too brown. Bake for a further 30 minutes. (Pies cooked in a hinged mold will require an extra 30 minutes cooking.) Remove the wax paper or mold and cool.

To make the jelly: Follow the same procedure as for the Pork Pies (see page 306), substituting veal stock in place of pork stock. Serve cold.

YEAST COOKERY

Lauma Rungis

Lauma Rungis, born in Latvia, learnt the art of cooking with yeast from her grandmother and mother. She has a Diploma in Food and Nutrition, teaches at a Technical College, and is a caterer specializing in continental cookery.

Yeast is the oldest known leavening agent and the Egyptians are given credit for the accidental discovery of the fermentation process involving yeast. Cooking with yeast is very rewarding because many different buns and teacakes may be produced at the same time from one basic yeast dough. I have been fascinated with yeast doughs and their bakings since my early childhood and I hope to pass on my grandmother's teachings to you in these few lines of advice.

YEAST

Today the easiest form of yeast to use for home breadmaking is a compressed yeast cake. Compressed yeast cake should be light in color without dry dark edges, it should be in large firm pieces and not crumbly, and should have a fresh smell. It may be stored for several weeks in the refrigerator in a tightly covered glass jar or air-tight plastic container but should not be deep frozen as this slows down the activity of the yeast. If compressed yeast is not available, dried yeast may be used and the directions on the package should be followed.

POINTS TO REMEMBER

The two most important things to remember about yeast cookery are:
- The importance of the kneading of a dough.
- The effect of the temperature on a yeast dough.

The dough is kneaded to make the bread light, soft, and finely textured and bread from dough that has not been kneaded sufficiently will be heavy and coarse.

Yeast is very sensitive to temperature. It works best at approximately the same temperature as the human body's temperature (98.4), but it will work at lower temperatures at a slower rate. This means that a yeast dough can be proved (allowed to rise) in a warm place (pleasantly warm to the touch of the hand) in 30 minutes to 1 hour. It will take $1\frac{1}{2}$ to 2 hours to prove or rise in a warm kitchen and it may even be left overnight in a cool place (not the refrigerator), when it should be ready for shaping and baking the following morning.

It is also important to remember that the yeast cell is a living organism which produces the same gas, carbon dioxide, as that produced by a chemical reaction of baking powder. The important difference is that the action of the baking powder takes place inside the oven during baking and the baking powder breads, such as biscuits, rise in the oven. Yeast cells produce the gas during the rising (fermentation) period outside the oven and this means that yeast doughs must be allowed to rise well after shaping and before baking. Very little rising takes place in the hot oven as yeast cells are killed by the high temperature.

Knots, Hazelnut and Strawberry Cake, Spicy Doughnuts, Fruit and Nut Braid, Cinnamon and Currant Fans, and Swedish Tea Ring

PLAIN MILK BREAD DOUGH

4 cups all-purpose flour
1 teaspoon salt
½ oz. compressed yeast or
  ¼ oz. dry yeast

1 tablespoon sugar
1¼ cups milk
¼ cup butter or margarine
extra flour or milk, as required

Sift the flour and salt into a large warm mixing bowl. Make a hollow in the center of the flour. Cream the compressed yeast and sugar. Warm ½ cup of the milk (to body temperature) and add to the yeast and sugar mixture. Mix well. If using dry yeast, add with the sugar to the ½ cup warm milk, and leave until frothy, about 10 minutes. Pour into the hollow. Stir in sufficient of the surrounding flour to make a light, soft batter. Cover the bowl with a cloth and stand in a warm place. Allow to stand till the batter in the center looks spongy and is full of bubbles. Melt the butter, add the rest of the milk, and warm slightly. Pour the milk and butter mixture over the flour and the 'sponge' in the bowl and mix to a soft dough (about the same consistency as a biscuit dough), using extra flour or warm milk as

required. Knead the dough in the bowl until it is smooth and elastic, and leaves the sides of the bowl clean and comes away from the hand. Shape the dough into a ball and press it down in the bottom of the bowl. Sprinkle lightly with flour. Return the bowl to a warm place, cover with a cloth, and allow the dough to rise until it doubles in bulk and a finger imprint on the surface of it disappears quickly. Punch the dough down and knead it lightly again. The dough is now ready for shaping.

Note: A further test for a well-risen dough is to push the floured handle of a wooden spoon into the top of the dough; the hole made should not shrink back or close up quickly.

KNOTS

1 quantity Plain Milk
  Bread Dough
beaten egg for glazing

caraway seeds, poppy seeds,
  or sesame seeds

Cooking time: 10-15 minutes
Temperature: 450°
Yield: 20

Divide the dough into 20 equal portions. Roll each portion, with the hands, on a lightly floured board into a thin round strip (like a thin sausage) and tie it in a knot. Place well apart on a greased baking sheet. Cover with a cloth and allow to rise in a warm place until the

rolls double in size. Glaze with beaten egg, sprinkle with seeds, and bake in a 450° oven for 10 to 15 minutes, or until the rolls are brown top and bottom. Serve warm or cold, with butter.

SESAME CRESCENTS

1 quantity Plain Milk
  Bread Dough
soft butter

beaten egg for glazing
sesame seeds

Cooking time: 10-15 minutes
Temperature: 450°
Yield: 16

Divide the dough in half. Roll each half in a ¼-inch thick circle and spread with soft butter. Cut each circle in 8 wedges. Roll up each wedge from the wider edge toward the point. Stretch slightly and shape into a crescent. Place the crescents well apart on a greased baking sheet. Cover with a cloth and allow to rise in a

warm place until the rolls double in size. Glaze with beaten egg and sprinkle with sesame seeds. Bake in a 450° oven for 10 to 15 minutes, or until the rolls are golden brown top and bottom. Serve warm or cold with butter.

CARAWAY SEED BUNS

1 quantity Plain Milk
  Bread Dough
hard butter

beaten egg for glazing
caraway seeds

Cooking time: 10-15 minutes
Temperature: 450°
Yield: 20

Divide the dough into 20 portions. Roll each portion into a smooth ball. Place on a greased baking sheet, cover with a cloth, and allow to rise until doubled in size. With the floured handle of a wooden spoon make a small hollow in the center of each bun and place a small piece of hard butter into it. Glaze the buns with

the egg glaze and sprinkle with caraway seeds. Bake in a 450° oven for 10 to 15 minutes, or until the buns are golden brown top and bottom.

Note: Sesame or poppy seeds may be substituted for the caraway seeds.

BACON ROLLS

1 quantity Plain Milk
    Bread Dough

beaten egg for glazing

Cooking time: 10-15 minutes
Temperature: 450°
Yield: 24

For filling:
½ lb. bacon
1 small white onion

salt and pepper

Prepare the Plain Milk Bread Dough and allow to rise. To make the filling: Chop the bacon and onion very finely. Place in a dry skillet and fry gently until the onion is tender. Drain well on paper towels and season to taste with salt and pepper. Allow the filling to cool before using.

To make the rolls: Roll out the dough on a lightly floured board into a rectangle ¼ inch thick. Cut into rounds with a floured 3-inch cutter. Place a generous teaspoon of the filling on each round. Fold in half and press the edges tightly to seal well. Stretch slightly and shape into a crescent. Place the rolls with sealed edge down on a greased baking sheet and cover with a cloth. Gather up the leftover pieces of dough. Knead lightly together and roll out and shape as before until all the dough and filling are used up. Allow the rolls to rise in a warm place until they have doubled in size. Glaze with beaten egg and bake in a 450° oven for 10 to 15 minutes, or until the rolls are golden brown top and bottom. Serve warm or cold.

SWEDISH TEA RING

½ quantity Plain Bread Dough
¼ cup butter
1 cup raisins or a mixture of
    dried fruits (larger ones should
    be coarsely chopped)

½ cup sugar
2 teaspoons cinnamon
extra ¼ cup sugar for glazing

Cooking time: 30-35 minutes
Temperature: 400°
    reducing to 350°

Roll the dough into a long narrow rectangle ½ inch thick. Brush with melted butter and sprinkle with a mixture of raisins, sugar, and cinnamon. Starting at one of the long edges, roll the dough up tightly. Stretch slightly and shape into a circle. Tuck one end into the other. Make deep slashes on the outer side of the circle about 2 inches apart. Open up the cuts a little to show the filling. Cover with a cloth and allow to rise in a warm place until doubled in size. Bake in a 400° oven for 15 minutes, reduce the temperature to 350°, and bake for another 15 to 20 minutes, or until the ring is golden brown top and bottom. While hot, glaze with ¼ cup water boiled together for 1 minute with the extra sugar. Serve with butter.

FRUIT AND NUT BRAID

For filling:
½ cup chopped prunes
½ cup chopped dried apricots
¼ cup brandy
½ cup chopped walnuts

½ quantity Plain Milk Bread
    Dough
beaten egg for glazing

1 small cooking apple, peeled,
    cored, and chopped
6 tablespoons sugar
finely grated rind of 1 lemon

extra chopped walnuts and sugar

Cooking time: 40-50 minutes
Temperature: 400°
    reducing to 350°

To make the filling: Soak the chopped prunes and apricots in the brandy for 2 hours. Add the walnuts, apple, sugar, and lemon rind and mix well.

To make the braid: Roll the dough into a rectangle approximately 15 by 12 inches and cut in 3 5-inch wide strips. Place a third of the filling lengthwise down the center of each strip. Fold the long edges over the filling and pinch together tightly. Pinch the ends as well. Place the 3 strips side by side on a greased baking sheet, plait them, and pinch the ends together. Cover with a cloth and allow to rise until double their original size. Brush with beaten egg and sprinkle with extra chopped walnuts mixed with a little sugar. Bake in a 400° oven for 20 minutes, reduce the temperature to 350°, and bake for a further 20 to 30 minutes, or until the braid is golden brown top and bottom. Serve with butter.

CINNAMON AND CURRANT FANS

1 cup currants
¼ cup rum
½ quantity Plain Milk Bread
   Dough

1 small egg, beaten
½ cup sugar mixed with
   2 tablespoons cinnamon
extra sugar for glazing

Cooking time: 15-20 minutes
Temperature: 400°

Soak the currants in the rum for 1 hour and drain. With a floured rolling pin, roll the dough out on a lightly floured board into a rectangle 12 by 10 inches and ½ inch thick. Brush with the beaten egg and sprinkle with the sugar and cinnamon. Sprinkle the currants on top. Roll up the dough tightly, starting from one of the longer edges. Stretch slightly. Cut in 10 thick slices. Slash each slice in 3 without cutting through the bottom of the slice, and place flat on a greased baking sheet. Bend each slice open to resemble a fan. Allow the rolls to rise until doubled in size. Bake in a 400° oven for 15 to 20 minutes. While hot, glaze with the extra sugar boiled for 1 minute with ¼ cup water.

APPLE COFFEE CAKE

For topping:
3 large cooking apples
1 cup water
1 cup sugar
2 cloves

½ quantity Plain Milk Bread
   Dough
1 teaspoon cinnamon mixed with
   2 tablespoons sugar

1 egg
2 tablespoons sugar
2 tablespoons butter

whipped cream and vanilla
sugar for serving

Cooking time: 30 minutes
Temperature: 450°
   reducing to 350°

To make the topping: Peel, quarter, and core the apples. Cut each quarter in 3 slices lengthwise. Bring the water, sugar, and cloves to a boil. Place the apple slices in the boiling syrup, reduce the heat, and simmer gently until the apples are just tender. Remove from the heat and allow the apples to cool in the syrup. Lift the apples from the syrup and drain well.

Beat the egg and sugar; gradually beat in the melted butter.

To make the cake: Press out the dough with floured hands to cover the bottom of a jelly roll pan. Arrange the apple slices in rows on top of the dough. Spread the egg mixture over the apples and allow the cake to rise in a warm place for about 30 minutes, or until it almost fills the pans. Bake in a 450° oven for 10 minutes, reduce the temperature to 350°, and bake for approximately 20 minutes longer, or until the dough is golden brown on the bottom and the apples are browned. Slide the cake onto a wire cooling rack. Sprinkle with the cinnamon and sugar mixture. Allow to cool and cut into squares, triangles, or diamond shapes. Serve with whipped cream, flavored with vanilla sugar.

CREAM CHEESE COFFEE CAKE

½ quantity Plain Milk Bread
   Dough

For topping:
2 cups creamy cottage cheese
finely grated rind of 1 lemon
2 eggs
¼ cup butter, melted

½ cup vanilla sugar
¼ cup cream
2 tablespoons custard powder
⅓ cup seedless white raisins

Cooking time: 50 minutes
Temperature: 450°
   reducing to 350°

To make the topping: Rub the cottage cheese through a sieve. Add all the other ingredients and mix well.

To make the cake: Press out the dough with floured hands to cover the bottom of a jelly roll pan. Spread the filling over the dough. Allow the cake to rise in a warm place for about 30 minutes, or until it almost fills the pan. Bake in a 450° oven for 10 minutes, reduce the oven temperature to 350°, and bake for approximately 40 minutes longer, or until the topping has set. Slide the cake onto a wire cooling rack and allow to cool. Serve cut in small squares.

Bacon Rolls, Latvian Birthday
Cake, and Apple Coffee Cake

RICH YEAST DOUGHS
HOT CROSS BUNS

4 cups all-purpose flour
½ teaspoon salt
¾ oz. compressed yeast or ½ oz. dry yeast
¼ cup sugar
1¼ cups milk
6 tablespoons butter

2 egg yolks
1 teaspoon cinnamon
½ teaspoon mixed spice
1½ cups dried fruit (seedless white raisins, currants, chopped candied pineapple, etc.)

Cooking time: 20 minutes
Temperature: 400°
Yield: 20

For sugar glaze:
¼ cup water boiled with
  ¼ cup sugar for 1 minute

Sift the flour and salt into a warm mixing bowl and make a hollow in the center of the flour. Cream the compressed yeast with 2 tablespoons of the sugar. Warm half the milk and add to the yeast. If using dry yeast, warm half the milk add the yeast and 2 tablespoons of the sugar, and leave until frothy, about 10 minutes. Pour this mixture into the hollow and mix in some of the surrounding flour to make a soft batter. Cover the bowl with a cloth and stand in a warm place till the batter looks spongy and is full of bubbles. Cream the butter with the remaining sugar and beat in the egg yolks. Warm the remaining milk and pour over the flour and sponge in the bowl. Add the creamed butter mixture and mix with the hand to a soft dough, using a little more warm milk if required. Add the spices and dried fruit and knead in the bowl till the dough is smooth and elastic and the fruit starts popping out. Sprinkle the dough with a little flour, cover with a cloth, and stand the bowl in a warm place until the dough has doubled in bulk. Punch the dough down, knead lightly, and turn out onto a floured board. Divide the dough into 20 equal pieces and roll each piece into a smooth ball. Place the balls in a greased roasting pan (12 by 10 inches approximately), 4 balls across and 5 balls along. Cut a cross on top of each. Cover with a cloth and allow to rise in a warm place until the buns have doubled in size and are almost touching. Bake in a 400° oven for 20 minutes, until the buns are golden brown. Turn out onto a cooling rack and while hot brush with the sugar glaze.

SPICY DOUGHNUTS

4 cups all-purpose flour
1 teaspoon salt
1½ oz. compressed yeast or
  ¾ oz. dry yeast
6 tablespoons sugar
⅔ cup milk
7 tablespoons butter
1 egg
2 egg yolks

¼ cup rose water
¾ cup chopped almonds
½ cup sultanas
¼ teaspoon ground cloves
¼ teaspoon ground cardamom
grated rind of 1 lemon
oil for deep frying
confectioners' sugar for
  sprinkling

Sift the flour and salt into a warm mixing bowl and make a hollow in the center of the flour. Cream the compressed yeast with 2 tablespoons of the sugar. Warm the milk and add to the softened yeast. If using dry yeast, warm the milk, add the yeast and 2 tablespoons of the sugar, and leave until frothy, about 10 minutes. Pour into the hollow and mix to a soft batter with some of the surrounding flour. Cover the bowl with a cloth and allow to stand in a warm place until the batter looks spongy and is full of bubbles. Melt the butter. Beat the egg and egg yolks with the rest of the sugar; beat in the melted butter and the rose water. Add the mixture to the flour and the sponge in the bowl and mix with the hand to a soft dough. Add the chopped almonds, seedless white raisins, cloves, cardamom, and lemon rind. Knead in the bowl until the dough is smooth and elastic and the fruit starts popping out. Stand the bowl in a warm place, covered with a cloth, until the dough has doubled in bulk. Punch down and knead lightly. Turn out onto a floured board and roll into a rectangle ½ inch thick. Cut out rounds with a 3-inch cutter, then cut out the centers with a 1½-inch cutter. Place the doughnuts on a floured tray, cover lightly, and stand in a warm place until they are risen and look well rounded. Repeat the process with the leftover dough.

Heat the oil to 375° and deep fry the doughnuts, a few at a time, until golden brown. Drain on paper towels and sprinkle with confectioners' sugar.

HAZELNUT AND STRAWBERRY CAKE

2 cups all-purpose flour
¼ teaspoon salt
½ oz. compressed yeast or
    ¼ oz. dry yeast
2 tablespoons sugar
⅔ cup milk
¼ cup butter

¼ teaspoon ground cardamom
strawberry jam
¼ cup sugar mixed with ½
    teaspoon cinnamon
½ cup finely chopped hazelnuts
whipped cream for serving

Cooking time: 40 minutes
Temperature: 400°
    reducing to 350°

Sift the flour and salt into a warm mixing bowl and make a hollow in the center. Cream the compressed yeast and 1 teaspoon of the sugar. Warm the milk and add to the softened yeast. If using dry yeast, warm the milk, add the yeast and 1 teaspoon of the sugar, and leave until frothy, about 10 minutes. Pour into the hollow and mix to a soft batter with some of the surrounding flour. Cover the bowl with a cloth and stand in a warm place until the batter is spongy and full of bubbles. Cream the butter with the rest of the sugar and add to the flour and the sponge in the bowl. Mix with the hand to a soft dough, using a little more warm milk if required. Add the cardamom and knead well in the bowl until the dough is smooth and elastic and leaves the hand and the sides of the bowl cleanly. Press the dough in the bottom of the bowl, sprinkle with a little flour, cover the bowl with a cloth, and stand in a warm place until the dough doubles in bulk. Punch the dough down and knead lightly. Turn out onto a floured board and divide into 2 pieces. Shape each piece into a smooth sausage. Place one sausage in the bottom of a greased 8-inch tube pan. Make a hollow in the center and fill with strawberry jam. Sprinkle with half the sugar and cinnamon mixture and half the chopped nuts. Cover with the second sausage of dough, spread with strawberry jam, and sprinkle with the remaining sugar and nuts. Stand, covered, in a warm place until the dough rises almost to the top of the pan. Bake in a 400° oven for 20 minutes, reduce the temperature to 350°, and bake for a further 20 minutes. Allow to cool on a wire cooling rack and serve with whipped cream.

LATVIAN BIRTHDAY CAKE

4 cups all-purpose flour
½ teaspoon salt
2 oz. compressed yeast or
    1 oz. dry yeast
2 tablespoons sugar
½ cup milk
6 tablespoons butter
⅓ cup sugar
2 egg yolks
½ cup cream
finely grated rind of 1 lemon
⅓ cup seedless white raisins

⅓ cup currants
⅓ cup chopped candied
    pineapple
½ cup blanched and chopped
    almonds
½ teaspoon ground cardamom
1 teaspoon powdered saffron
beaten egg for glazing
¼ cup blanched and halved
    almonds
confectioners' sugar for sprinkling

Cooking time: 50 minutes
Temperature: 400°
    reducing to 350°

Sift the flour and salt into a warm mixing bowl. Cream the compressed yeast and the 2 tablespoons sugar. Warm the milk and add to the yeast. If using dry yeast, warm the milk and add the yeast and 2 tablespoons sugar. Leave until frothy, about 10 minutes. Make a hollow in the center of the flour and pour in the yeast mixture. Stir sufficient of the surrounding flour into the yeast mixture to make a soft batter. Cover the bowl with a cloth and stand in a warm place until the batter is spongy and full of bubbles. Cream the butter, ⅓ cup sugar, and egg yolks. Warm the cream and add to the flour and sponge together with the butter mixture, lemon rind, white raisins, currants, pineapple, chopped almonds, cardamom, and saffron. Mix with the hand to a firm dough and knead well until the dough is smooth, elastic, and leaves the hand and the sides of the bowl cleanly, and the fruits start popping out of the dough. Place the bowl in a warm place and allow the dough to rise till it doubles in bulk. Punch it down and knead again for about 10 minutes. Allow to rise as before. Turn the dough out onto a floured board. Knead lightly. Pull and twist the dough into a long cylinder. Place on a large greased baking sheet and form into a shape like the letter 'B'. Press the ends down firmly. Cover with a cloth and allow the cake to rise in a warm place until doubled in size. Glaze with beaten egg and press the split almonds over the top of the cake. Bake in a 400° oven for 20 minutes, reduce the temperature to 350°, and bake for a further 30 minutes, or until the cake is golden brown top and bottom. If the almonds brown too much during the baking, cover the cake with a piece of greased wax paper. Slide the cooked cake onto a wire cooling rack, allow to cool slightly, and sprinkle with confectioners' sugar.

Elizabeth Sewell

Danish Pastries

Danish Pastries are called Wienerbrod in Denmark, which means Vienna bread. Wienerbrod originally came from Austria where the making of them has now more or less ceased, so to learn how to make them today, one must go to Denmark.

From the capital of Denmark, Copenhagen, to the smallest village in the country, there is always a 'konditori' or 'bageri' selling these delicious pastries. The shops open very early in the morning and the beautiful aroma of hot pastries wafts into the streets. The children are sent to collect them before breakfast is served and there is always a big selection to choose from. There is a high proportion of butter in the basic dough and many of the pastries have sweet fillings and icings. They are therefore eaten alone, accompanied only by freshly made coffee. Smaller Danish pastries may be included in an afternoon tea party.

After the basic dough has been made, it is rolled out thinly and cut into various shapes, the filling is put in, and the pastries are re-shaped into pinwheels, stars, triangles, rooster combs, and crescents. The Danish baker has a special oven which sprays steam from the top for a few minutes over the pastries. When the steam is turned off the pastries are left to cook in the very hot oven. This process gives Danish pastries their characteristic hard, crisp surface.

Danish pastries are fascinating to make as there are so many varieties. From the basic dough you can make innumerable types. Your family will love them and they will disappear very quickly! Read the recipes carefully and you will find they are not difficult to make.

Elizabeth Sewell studied advanced French and Italian Cookery at Cordon Bleu in London and obtained her diploma. Her experience has covered such widely diverse fields of cookery as managing a restaurant at a ski resort, being hostess at a top restaurant and being the household manager at a University Women's College. As well as being an enthusiastic cook, she is now cookery editor with Paul Hamlyn Pty Ltd (Australia), and has written several cookery books and articles for magazines

Danish Pastries

DANISH PASTRIES

(BASIC RECIPE)

3 cups all-purpose flour	$\frac{1}{4}$ cup sugar
dash salt	$\frac{3}{4}$ cup milk
1 oz. compressed yeast	1 cup butter
1 egg	

Sift the flour and salt into a mixing bowl. Cream the yeast with 1 teaspoonful of the sugar. Add the beaten egg, lukewarm milk, and $\frac{1}{4}$ cup of the butter, melted, to the yeast mixture. Make a well in the flour and add the liquid ingredients slowly. Mix to a smooth dough. Cover and leave at room temperature for 1 hour or until doubled in bulk.

Punch down the dough and turn onto a floured board. Knead lightly. Roll out to an oblong and cover two thirds of the dough with one third of the remaining butter, divided into small pieces. Fold and roll as for Flaky Paste (see page 296). Fold in 3 and roll to an oblong again. Repeat with second quantity of butter, fold, and leave for 15 minutes. Repeat with the last portion of butter, roll out and fold in half. Roll and fold twice more and rest again for 15 minutes. Place dough in a plastic bag and chill for several hours or overnight and use as required.

Almond Filling

$\frac{1}{2}$ cup ground almonds	$\frac{1}{2}$ egg, beaten
3 tablespoons sugar	1-2 drops almond extract

Mix all ingredients together until smooth. Use as required.

Apple Marmalade

1 lb. cooking apples
1 piece lemon rind
6 tablespoons brown sugar,
   firmly packed

Cut apples into quarters, core, and slice (do not peel). Place in a well greased saucepan. Add the lemon rind and cover. Cook over a gentle heat, stirring regularly, until soft. Pass through a sieve or blender.

Return to the rinsed saucepan, add the sugar, and cook over a moderate heat, stirring regularly, until thick. Place in a bowl, cool, and use as required.

Crème Pâtissière

2 egg yolks	$1\frac{1}{4}$ cups milk
$\frac{1}{4}$ cup sugar	1-2 drops vanilla extract
3 tablespoons all-purpose flour	1 egg white
2 tablespoons cornstarch	

Mix the egg yolks with the sugar, flour, and cornstarch to make a smooth paste. (Add a tablespoonful of the milk if necessary.)

Scald the remaining milk and add to the egg yolk mixture, stirring constantly. Add the vanilla extract and return the mixture to the saucepan. Cook gently, stirring constantly, until the Crème Pâtissière thickens.

Beat the egg white until stiff and fold into mixture. Use as required.

Cartwheels

1 quantity Danish Pastry Almond Filling $\frac{1}{3}$ cup raisins	beaten egg for glazing $\frac{1}{4}$ cup flaked almonds	Cooking time: 20-25 minutes Temperature: 400-450°

Roll out the dough to a large oblong, 9 by 14 inches. Spread with Almond Filling and sprinkle with raisins. Roll up as for a jelly roll. Cut in $\frac{1}{4}$-inch slices with a bread knife. Place cut side down on a greased baking sheet. Leave to rise at room temperature for 10 to 20 minutes. Glaze with beaten egg and sprinkle with flaked almonds. Bake for 20 to 25 minutes in a 400-450° oven.

Cream Buns

1 quantity Danish Pastry Apple Marmalade, Almond Filling, or Crème Pâtissière	beaten egg for glazing Glacé Icing	Cooking time: 20-25 minutes Temperature: 400-450°

Roll out the dough to an oblong divisible by 5 inches. Cut into 5-inch squares. Place a teaspoonful of Apple Marmalade, Almond Filling or Crème Pâtissière in the center of each. Fold the 4 corners around the filling. Make sure it is covered completely. Place on a greased baking sheet with the folds facing downward. Press lightly on top. Leave to rise at room temperature for 10 to 20 minutes. Glaze the tops with beaten egg. Bake for 20 to 25 minutes in a 400-450° oven. Frost while still warm with Glacé Icing (see page 268).

Crescents

1 quantity Danish Pastry Almond Filling or Apple	Marmalade beaten egg for glazing	Cooking time: 20-25 minutes Temperature: 400-450°

Roll out the dough to a large round, $\frac{1}{8}$ inch thick. Cut into triangles approximately 3 inches along the bottom. Place a teaspoonful of Almond Filling or Apple Marmalade at the bottom. Roll up loosely from the bottom toward the apex. Shape into crescents. Place on a greased baking sheet. Leave to rise at room temperature for 10 to 20 minutes. Glaze with beaten egg and bake for 20 to 25 minutes in a 400-450° oven.

Pinwheels

1 quantity Danish Pastry Almond Filling or Crème Pâtissière	beaten egg for glazing Glacé Icing	Cooking time: 20-25 minutes Temperature: 400-450°

Roll out the dough to a large oblong, cut into $4\frac{1}{2}$-inch squares. Cut from each corner to within $\frac{1}{2}$ inch of the center. Place a teaspoonful of Almond Filling or Crème Pâtissière in the middle, then take each alternate point to the center. Place on a greased baking sheet. Leave to rise at room temperature for 10 to 20 minutes. Bake for 20 to 25 minutes in a 400-450° oven. Frost while still warm with Glacé Icing (see page 268).

Rooster Combs

1 quantity Danish Pastry Almond Filling	beaten egg for glazing 2 tablespoons sugar	Cooking time: 20-25 minutes Temperature: 400-450°

Roll out the dough to an oblong divisible by 5 inches in length and $3\frac{1}{2}$ inches wide. Place the Almond Filling in a line just below the middle of the length. Brush the bottom edge with beaten egg. Fold over and cut into 5-inch pieces. Make approximately 6 incisions along the 5-inch edge and bend back. Place on a greased baking sheet. Leave at room temperature for 10 to 20 minutes. Glaze with beaten egg and sprinkle with sugar. Bake for 20 to 25 minutes in a 400-450° oven.

BEVERAGES

Sally Hembrow

Sally Hembrow has a weekly television program, 'Living Graciously', a radio program, 'Hot Line to the Oven', and writes a newspaper cookery column. She also conducts private classes in her specially-designed home kitchen.

Just as each year has its variety of seasons so the world of beverages offers us a wide variety of drinks to suit all variations of climate and occasion. In the summer, what could be more refreshing than a long cool drink? You can serve an ice cold lemonade, a fruit punch, or one of the exotic punches or fruit cups containing wine. These are particularly suitable for a festive occasion. Likewise, tomato cocktail is a wonderful way to start a dinner party in the summer. There are many attractive glasses to choose from when serving these summer favorites. Serve them chilled with the addition of ice blocks, sprigs of mint, or thinly sliced citrus fruits or strawberries.

On a winter's evening, what could be more welcoming than a mug of mulled wine, served near an open fire. Later in the evening you can lead your guests into the ritualistic world of coffee with its many tantalizing flavors and haunting aromas. For variety, hot chocolate will warm their hearts. There are many heatproof glasses, china coffee cups, or pottery mugs to choose from when serving your winter favorites.

COFFEE MAKING

The rituals of coffee making are few but important:
1. Keep the coffee maker thoroughly clean and scald with boiling water before use.
2. Select your blend and grind of coffee carefully, paying special attention to flavor. Fresh coffee is the best coffee, so buy in small quantities and store in an air-tight container.
3. Always use freshly drawn water from the cold faucet to avoid foreign tastes and staleness in the water, and bring to a boil before adding the ground coffee. However, never boil coffee as a loss of flavor results.
4. Discover the best timing to suit your flavor preference and blend of coffee, and keep to it. Also test measurements to suit your personal taste.
5. To avoid waste, why not freeze leftover coffee as coffee ice cubes?

PICK-ME-UPS

One authority says the best pick-me-up is to buy a very fresh cabbage and bite big chunks; if you do not agree, try the Eggnog recipe. It should do wonders for you!

Orangeade and Lemonade

LEMONADE

Serves: 2

For syrup:
1 cup sugar
$\frac{2}{3}$ cup water
$\frac{1}{3}$ cup fresh lemon juice
$1\frac{1}{4}$ cups water

mint sprigs
lemon slices
sliced strawberries

Heat the sugar and water slowly in a saucepan. Stir well. Boil for 2 minutes. Cool. Store in the refrigerator. For 2 servings, combine the lemon juice, water, and $\frac{2}{3}$ cup of the chilled sugar syrup. Pour into chilled glasses. Garnish with sprigs of mint, lemon slices, and sliced strawberries.

ORANGEADE

Serves: 4

For syrup:
$\frac{1}{3}$ cup water
$\frac{1}{4}$ cup sugar
$2\frac{1}{2}$ cups orange juice

5 teaspoons lemon juice
$2\frac{1}{2}$ cups soda water
4 sprigs mint, set in ice cubes

Place the water and sugar in a small saucepan. Bring slowly to a boil. Boil slowly for 2 minutes. Remove from the heat. Chill. Mix the sugar syrup, orange juice, lemon juice, and soda water. Pour over the ice cubes in chilled glasses.

GINGER BEER

To make plant:
8 seedless white raisins
juice of 2 lemons
1 teaspoon lemon pulp

4 teaspoons sugar
2 teaspoons ginger
$2\frac{1}{2}$ cups cold water

To feed:
2 teaspoons ginger

4 teaspoons sugar

To make the plant, put the seedless white raisins, lemon juice, lemon pulp, sugar, ginger, and cold water in a screw-top jar. Leave for 2 to 3 days. In warm weather the mixture should then begin to ferment. It will take a little longer in cooler weather. Then, each day for one week, add the ginger and sugar to the jar.

To make ginger beer:
5 cups boiling water
$4\frac{1}{2}$ cups sugar

juice of 4 lemons
9 quarts cold water

Pour the boiling water onto the sugar. Stir until dissolved. Add the lemon juice. Strain into this the ginger beer plant you have made. Use a piece of fine cheesecloth and squeeze the cloth dry. Add the cold water and pour into clean, dry, air-tight bottles. Seal securely. Keep for 3 days before using.

To keep plant alive:
$2\frac{1}{2}$ cups water
2 teaspoons ginger

4 teaspoons sugar

Halve the residue in the cheesecloth. Return to the jar with the water, ginger, and sugar and leave for 1 week. Feed as before.

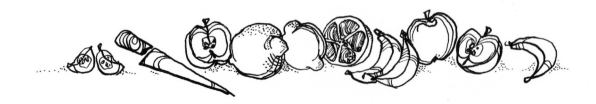

CELEBRATION PUNCH

1¼ cups lemon juice
1¼ cups orange juice
¾ cup sugar syrup
¼ cup grenadine
ice cubes
1¼ cups brandy

fresh fruit salad (pitted fruits
   cut into ½-inch pieces)
bunches of grapes, frozen
3 bottles champagne
block of ice
tonic water

Serves: 20

Place in a punch bowl the lemon juice, orange juice, and sugar syrup (see page 337) mixed with the grenadine. Quarter fill the bowl with ice cubes. Add the brandy and fruit. When ready to serve, add the champagne. Add a block of ice. To break the punch down, add 12 splits of tonic water.

TROPICAL FRUIT PUNCH

1 cup sugar
⅔ cup water
1¼ cups fresh or canned
   pineapple juice
⅔ cup orange juice
1¼ cups grapefruit juice
juice of 1 lemon

5 cups cold weak tea
2½ cups ginger ale
mint sprigs
4 strawberries, finely chopped
⅔ cup finely chopped papaya
1 firm banana, finely chopped
crushed ice

Serves: 14-16

Place the sugar and water in a saucepan over gentle heat. Stir until the sugar is dissolved. Boil for a few minutes. Chill. Add the sugar syrup to the fruit juices and tea. Chill well. Just before serving, add the ginger ale and float the mint and fruits on top of the punch. Add plenty of crushed ice.

PINK BERRY PUNCH

2½ cups sliced rhubarb
1 cup sugar
⅔ cup water
1¼ cups pineapple juice
⅔ cup lemon juice

pink food coloring
cherries, plums, or apricot halves
   set in ice cubes
1 large bottle dry ginger ale

Serves: 8-10

Place the rhubarb, sugar, and water in a saucepan. Cook until the rhubarb is tender. Strain. Add the pineapple and lemon juice. Tint with a few drops of food coloring. Chill well. Before serving pour over the fruited ice cubes. Add the ginger ale.

WHITE WINE CUP

generous 3 cups orange juice
1¼ cups pineapple juice
2½ cups cold water
½ cup sugar
¼ cup grated lemon rind
   (absolutely no pith)
5 cups white wine

2 tablespoons honey
6 cloves
½ teaspoon cinnamon
½ teaspoon nutmeg
scant 2 quarts ginger ale
crushed ice

Serves: 20

Mix all the ingredients except the ginger ale and crushed ice. Allow to stand in the refrigerator for about 3 hours. At serving time, strain, then add the ginger ale and pour over crushed ice.

COLD CIDER CUP

ice cubes
lemon rind
2 pints cider
1 jigger Maraschino

1 jigger Curaçao
1 jigger brandy
soda water

Serves: 6-8

Place the ice cubes and lemon rind in a pitcher. Add the remaining ingredients and soda water, as desired. Serve chilled.

MULLED WINE

2½ cups red wine
juice of ½ lemon
3 cloves

¼ cup sugar
stick cinnamon

Serves: 4

Put the wine into a saucepan. Add the lemon juice, crushed cloves, sugar, and cinnamon. Bring to a boil and simmer for 2 to 3 minutes, stirring all the time. Place a silver spoon in a tumbler and strain in the mixture.

TOMATO COCKTAIL

1 (16 oz.) can tomato juice
salt and pepper to taste
onion salt
celery seeds

1 teaspoon finely chopped
  parsley
lemon wedges

Serves: 2

Combine all the ingredients to taste, except the lemon wedges. Serve in chilled glasses with the lemon wedges.

EGGNOG

1 egg
¼ cup sugar
dash salt

1¼ cups milk
½ teaspoon vanilla extract
freshly grated nutmeg

Serves: 1

Beat the egg until smooth and thick. Beat the sugar and salt into the egg until the sugar is dissolved. Beat in the milk and vanilla extract. Top with a little grated nutmeg. Serve immediately.

*Mocha Milk Shake, Iced
Coffee, and Eggnog*

MOCHA MILK SHAKE

⅓ cup instant coffee powder
¼ cup sugar
2½ cups milk or water
2½ cups chocolate ice cream

⅔ cup cream, whipped and
    sweetened
chocolate shavings (optional)

Serves: 4

Combine the coffee, sugar, and milk. Stir to dissolve. Add the ice cream and stir. Place an ice cube in each of 4 glasses. Pour in the chocolate mixture. Top with fluffs of whipped cream, and shaved semi-sweet chocolate if desired.

ICED COFFEE

½ lb. medium-grind coffee
dash salt
3¾ cups freshly boiled water

5 cups milk
⅔ cup whipping cream
1 egg white

Serves: 6

Put the coffee and salt, into a large jug. Pour over the boiling water. Allow to stand until cool. Strain through a fine strainer. Chill well for a few hours. Just before serving, mix the chilled milk with the coffee. Pour into tall chilled glasses. Whip the cream until fairly stiff. Beat the egg white until stiff. Fold into the cream. Top the coffee with spoonfuls of cream. Serve immediately.

IRISH COFFEE

Irish whiskey is, traditionally, one of the essential ingredients of Irish coffee.

3 tablespoons Irish whiskey
1 teaspoon sugar

1 cup strong hot coffee
whipped cream

Serves: 1

Put the whiskey and sugar into a warmed stemmed glass. Fill the glass to within ½ inch of the brim, with black coffee, hot and strong. Stir well. Top with very thick, or whipped, cream. Do not stir.

HOT COCOA

⅓ cup cocoa powder
6 tablespoons sugar
dash salt

¾ cup water
2¼ cups milk

Serves: 4

Place the cocoa, sugar, salt, and water in a saucepan. Mix well. Bring to a boil over low heat. Boil gently for a few minutes, stirring all the time. Add the milk. Heat thoroughly, but do not boil. Beat with a hand beater until foamy.

CONFECTIONERY

Jean Forward

Jean Forward writes a cookery column for *The Herald*, in Melbourne. Well-known through demonstrations, television and radio cookery talks, she has loved making candy since childhood.

Why make home-made confections when the commercially-produced goods are so cheap and attractive? Well, it is the perfect hobby for a rainy day, very often the first introduction to cookery for youngsters, and also very lucrative for fêtes and fairs. Whether you make a simple batch of toffee or an elaborate Easter egg, you will find a great deal of satisfaction and reward. A candy thermometer makes the job easy, but it is not essential for good results. Here is a guide for you:

Stage	Fahrenheit readings on a candy thermometer	Texture of the syrup when 1 teaspoonful is placed in a glass of cold water.
Soft ball	234—240 degrees	The syrup collects in a mass in the bottom of the glass and can just be gathered together in the fingers.
Firm ball	242—248 degrees	The syrup falls easily into a ball which is firm but still quite pliable.
Hard ball	250—266 degrees	Much firmer than previously, but the ball is still pliable.
Soft crack	270—290 degrees	The syrup separates into hard threads, bendy and not brittle.
Hard crack	300—310 degrees	The syrup makes a crackling sound when it hits the water and the threads are hard and brittle.

TIPS FOR SUCCESS

Liquid glucose or corn syrup prevents mixtures from crystallizing. As a substitute, cream of tartar may be used, 1 teaspoon to each tablespoon of glucose, but it does not give the clear sparkle to taffy which it has when made with glucose.

Always stir sugar and water before they come to a boil but never afterwards for the syrup will crystallize and become sugary. Wash down the inside of the saucepan from time to time with cold water using a small brush. This washes away any grains of undissolved sugar which could cause the whole batch to granulate.

SOFT CARAMELS

¼ cup butter
½ cup sugar
2 tablespoons liquid glucose
⅓ cup water

1 teaspoon vanilla extract
1 cup sweetened condensed
   milk

Melt the butter in a saucepan, add the sugar, glucose, and water, and stir until the sugar is blended. Add the condensed milk and vanilla extract. Cook over low heat, stirring all the time, until the mixture is a pale beige color and begins to leave the sides of the saucepan.

Pour into a greased aluminum foil tray and allow to set. Mark into squares before the mixture is quite cold, and decorate the top with a fork. Wrap in cellophane and seal.

HARD CARAMELS

½ cup butter
1 cup brown sugar, firmly packed

1 cup sweetened condensed
   milk
¼ cup corn syrup

Melt the butter in a saucepan, and add the sugar, condensed milk, and corn syrup. Stir until the sugar is melted. Cook over low heat, stirring all the time, until the mixture is a dark brown and leaves the sides of the

saucepan. Pour into a greased aluminum foil tray and allow to set. Mark into squares before the mixture is quite cold. Wrap in cellophane and seal.

FLOWING CHOCOLATE CARAMELS

1 cup sweetened condensed
   milk

1⅓ cups semi-sweet chocolate
   pieces
½ cup blanched toasted almonds

Place the can of condensed milk in a saucepan with boiling water to cover and boil rapidly for 2½ hours. Allow the can to cool before opening. The milk will be a light caramel color and firm enough to take in teaspoons and roll into balls.

Place the chocolate in the top of a double boiler and melt over hot water. Dip the caramels into the chocolate and place on a sheet of wax paper to cool. Before setting, top with a blanched toasted almond.

BUTTERED BRAZILS

1¼ cups sugar
1¼ cups water
2 tablespoons liquid glucose

1 teaspoon malt vinegar
2 tablespoons butter
2 cups brazil nuts

Place the sugar, water, glucose, and vinegar in a saucepan, heat, and stir until the sugar is dissolved. Add the butter and boil rapidly, without stirring, until the mixture is a rich golden brown, and has reached 310°

(hard crack stage). Drop the brazil nuts into the taffy. Remove them one at a time and place on a greased tray. Allow to cool, then store in air-tight jars.

RICH BUTTERSCOTCH

2 cups sugar
⅔ cup water
½ cup butter

1 teaspoon vinegar
¼ cup liquid glucose

Place the sugar in a saucepan, add the water, and stir over gentle heat until dissolved. Add the butter, vinegar, and glucose and bring to a boil. Cook without stirring until it reaches 280° (soft crack stage), or until a deep

golden brown color. Turn into buttered patty pans and allow to set. Remove from the pans and store in an air-tight jar.

PEANUT BRITTLE

2 cups sugar
½ cup water
¼ cup liquid glucose

1 tablespoon butter
1 teaspoon baking soda
1 cup chopped roasted peanuts

Place the sugar in a saucepan, add the water and glucose, heat, and stir until dissolved. Bring over medium heat to the boiling point. Boil rapidly without stirring until it reaches 280° (soft crack stage) and becomes a deep yellow color. Remove from the heat. Add the melted butter, baking soda, and roasted peanuts. Stir lightly 2 or 3 times, to froth up the mixture, and pour onto a buttered cold surface (marble or stainless steel). As soon as it is cool enough to handle, pull out and stretch thinly until it is almost a wafer of taffy, then turn over and allow to cool. When quite cold, break into bite-sized pieces and store in air-tight jars.

CANDIED APPLES

8-9 small red apples
wooden skewers
2 cups sugar
⅔ cup water

2 tablespoons butter
2 tablespoons liquid glucose
2-3 drops red food coloring

Wash and dry the apples thoroughly and impale them on the skewers. Place the sugar and water in a saucepan and stir over heat until the sugar is dissolved. Add the butter and glucose and cook rapidly, without stirring, until it reaches 300° (hard crack stage). When the mixture stops bubbling, add the red coloring. Stand the saucepan in a large bowl of hot water to prevent the taffy from setting too quickly. Dip the apples into the taffy to coat thoroughly and stand them upright on a tray to set. When cold, wrap in cellophane or wax paper.
Variation: To make Peanut Candied Apples, roll the apples in 1 cup chopped roasted peanuts after dipping into the taffy, and allow to set.

MARSHMALLOWS

1¼ cups sugar
1¼ cups water
2 tablespoons liquid glucose
4 envelopes gelatin
2 egg whites

few drops vanilla extract
toasted shredded coconut, or
  confectioners' sugar mixed
  with cornstarch

Place the sugar and half the water in a large saucepan, bring to a boil, and add the glucose. Cook rapidly until 240° (soft ball stage) is reached. Dissolve the gelatin in the remaining water. Beat the egg whites stiffly and add to the cooled syrup with the vanilla extract and gelatin. Beat in an electric mixer at full speed until the mixture is white and spongy and beginning to set. Pour into a 9-inch square pan which has been previously rinsed with cold water. Stand until quite firm and set. Cut into squares and roll in toasted coconut, or a mixture of equal quantities of sifted confectioners' sugar and cornstarch.
Variations:
Banana Marshmallows: Omit the vanilla extract and add a few drops of lemon juice and banana extract. Color with lemon coloring, and coat in cornstarch and confectioners' sugar.
Strawberry Marshmallows: Omit the vanilla extract and add a few drops of strawberry flavoring and red coloring. Roll in pink-colored coconut.

RAINBOW JELLIES

1 quantity marshmallow
yellow coloring
green coloring
4 envelopes gelatin
1¼ cups water

2 cups sugar
½ teaspoon citric acid
¼ teaspoon cream of tartar
½ teaspoon raspberry extract
red coloring

Make the marshmallow (see page 330) and divide into 2 equal portions. Color one part yellow with a few drops of yellow coloring and pour into a 9-inch square pan, previously rinsed with cold water. Allow to set. Color the remaining portion pale green with a few drops of green coloring and set in a 9-inch square pan. To make the jelly layer, soak the gelatin in half the cold water for 20 minutes. Place the remaining water with the sugar, citric acid, and cream of tartar in a saucepan, bring to a boil, and add the softened gelatin. Cook for 20 minutes. Flavor with raspberry extract and add a few drops of red coloring. Pour into a 9-inch square pan, and set overnight.

The next day, assemble the rainbow jellies. Place one layer of the marshmallow on a board sprinkled with confectioners' sugar, cover with the jelly layer, and then top with the remaining marshmallow. Cut into squares, and toss in confectioners' sugar.

SNOWBALLS

1 cup sugar
4 envelopes gelatin
⅔ cup cold water
2 tablespoons liquid glucose
dash citric acid

1 cup water
1 egg white
⅔ cup semi-sweet chocolate
  pieces
1⅓ cups shredded coconut

Place the sugar in a large saucepan. Soak the gelatin in the cold water. Add the glucose and citric acid to the sugar with the 1 cup water. Heat gently, bring to a boil, and cook without stirring, until 240° (soft ball stage) is reached. Remove from the heat and add the gelatin. Stand in a cool place until barely warm. Beat the egg white and add to the mixture. Beat the mixture with an electric mixer at the highest speed until the mixture is pure white, foamy, and beginning to set. Place in buttered muffin pans, piling high on the top, and allow to set for several hours. Melt the chocolate over hot water. Dip the snowballs into the chocolate and roll in shredded coconut.

Variations:

Rainbows: Remove the snowballs from the muffin pans and roll in multi-colored decorettes.

Kokets: Toast 1 cup shredded coconut in a 350° oven until golden brown, mix into the chocolate coating before dipping the snowballs, and dry on a sheet of wax paper.

Cherry Surprise: Place a drained candied cherry in the center of each muffin pan, pour in the snowball mixture, dip in chocolate, and roll in toasted coconut.

CHOCOLATE EASTER EGGS

Select a special day for making these when the atmosphere is dry and warm, but not too hot.

1-2 cups semi-sweet chocolate
  pieces

1 quantity Royal Icing for
  decoration

Place the chocolate in a small heatproof bowl, stand over a bowl of hot water, and heat until the chocolate reaches a temperature of 85°. Lift the bowl of chocolate from the water and stir until it is quite smooth and very shiny. Heat again over hot water until the chocolate reaches 90°. It is then ready to use for coating the molds.

Bright shiny tin molds are required. Wipe them out with cotton wool or paper tissues to be sure they are perfectly clean. Pour a little of the prepared chocolate into the molds and twist gently to cover the surface. Repeat this several times, until the chocolate is of the thickness desired. Pour off any excess chocolate and turn the mold upside down on a cold surface to set. As the chocolate cools and sets it can be removed easily by pressing the mold at one end. The 2 chocolate halves are joined together to form an egg by touching the edges on a heated metal tray or baking sheet, to melt the chocolate and hold them together. When set, decorate with Royal Icing (see page 268) and tie with a ribbon, if liked.

MARZIPAN

1 cup finely ground almonds
1⅓ cups sifted confectioners'
   sugar

1 egg white
1 teaspoon lemon juice

Mix the ground almonds with the sifted confectioners' sugar and bind together with the egg white and lemon juice. Knead to a smooth dough, wrap in wax paper, and stand for 1 hour before molding into shapes.
Variations:
Marzipan Fingers: Mold into thin finger lengths, dip in melted semi-sweet chocolate, and dry on a sheet of wax paper.
Marzipan Fruits:
Oranges: Form into small balls, about 1 inch across, dip into egg white, and roll in sugar. Allow to dry, then paint with orange food coloring.
Apples: Form into small balls, about 1 inch across, place a clove at each end, to resemble the stalk and blossom ends, allow to dry, then paint with red food coloring.
Pears: Prepare as for apples, pinch one end and shape like a pear, allow to dry, then paint with orange and yellow food coloring.
Bananas: Form into sausage shapes and twist in a half circle; make flat at one end. Allow to dry, paint with yellow food coloring, make streaks with brown coloring, and tip each end with pale green coloring.
Strawberries: Form into round balls, about 1 inch across, pull out to a point at one side, dip in egg white, and roll in sugar. Allow to dry and paint with red food coloring. Make a calyx from a piece of green angelica, and push into the top.

COCONUT ICE

2 cups sugar
1¼ cups water
1⅓ cups shredded coconut

2 tablespoons liquid glucose
pink coloring

Place the sugar and water in a saucepan and bring to a boil. Add the coconut and glucose and boil until the mixture reaches 236° (soft ball stage). Pour into a large mixing bowl and allow to cool slightly. Beat with a wooden spoon until the mixture is cloudy. Pour half the mixture into a foil container and press down evenly. Color the remaining portion with a few drops of pink coloring and place on top of the white mixture; smooth the top. Allow to set, then cut into bars or squares.

CHOCOLATE FUDGE

2 cups sugar
½ cup cocoa powder
1 cup milk

2 tablespoons liquid glucose
2 tablespoons butter
½ teaspoon vanilla extract

Combine the sugar, cocoa, milk, and glucose in a saucepan and stir over low heat until the cocoa is blended. Cook until the mixture reaches 236° (soft ball stage), stirring frequently to prevent scorching. Remove from the heat and pour into a large mixing bowl. Add the butter and stand in a cool place until the mixture is barely warm. Add the vanilla extract and beat rapidly until the mixture is thick and creamy. Pour into a buttered foil container. Mark into squares and allow to set. Store in airtight tins.

CHCOLATE RUM CHERRIES

¾ cup candied cherries
½ cup rum

1⅓ cups semi-sweet chocolate
   pieces

Place the cherries in a screw-top jar and pour in the rum. Stand overnight, shaking occasionally to distribute the rum through the cherries. Next day, drain the cherries carefully and dry on paper towels. Melt the chocolate in the top part of a double boiler over hot water. Dip the cherries into the chocolate and place on a piece of wax paper until set. Store in candy boxes or jars.

Emily Carpenter

Emily Carpenter, Bachelor of Home Science, is a university lecturer. She is responsible for organizing research, teaching, and information programs in food nutrition for the housewife.

In the past, food preservation was essential to life, now it is a matter of choice. The modern homemaker has a wide selection of foods available at all times of the year. Why then is there such widespread interest in this ancient household art? Food which might otherwise go to waste is put to good use. You can create attractive preserves from raw materials and get great pleasure from acting in the best interests of your family.

Homemakers in earlier times had to preserve all kinds of food for out-of-season use. Today, it is no longer merely a question of when to preserve, but also a problem of deciding what should be preserved, which method of preservation to use for each particular food, and how to choose and use your equipment to save time and energy and to give the best results.

Canning

The terms associated with canning must be understood before work can begin. Read this section in conjunction with the guides on canning the various fruits and vegetables (see pages 338-9).

CANNING VOCABULARY

Processing: The application of heat to food to stop enzyme action and to destroy any harmful organisms present. There are two ways of processing, either before or after packing.

Pre-pack processing: Also called the 'open pan' or 'overflow' method. The food is stewed as for table use, ladled into warm sterilized jars, these are filled to overflowing with boiling water, syrup or brine, the rims are wiped with a scalded cloth, and sterilized seals are put on. Use only for fruits and tomatoes, never for vegetables, meat, fish, or convenience foods containing cereals, cheese, bacon, etc.

Advantages: Simple, suitable for small quantities, no processing equipment required.

Disadvantages: Food breaks up as jars are filled. Risk of food spoilage unless handling speedy and hygienic.

Post-pack processing: Food is packed into clean jars, liquid added if needed, jars are closed, and then processed. May be used for fruits and tomatoes, must be used for non-acid foods such as meat, fish, vegetables, and convenience foods.

Advantages: Good appearance; less risk of failure as jars and contents are sterilized together.

Disadvantages: Requires some processing equipment.

Packing methods: With post-pack processing, two packing methods are used.

- Cold pack: Also called 'raw pack'. Food is put into jars, liquid added, jars are covered and processed. Use for foods which might break up if cooked before packing, e.g., berry fruits, tomatoes.
- Hot pack: The food is partly cooked before packing. It shrinks the tissues slightly, and enables more food to be packed into each jar. Use for firm fruits with close textures, e.g., pears, quinces, and vegetables. It scalds or blanches the surface of vegetables and helps preserve a good color.

Processing equipment:

- Oven: An electric oven set at 275°, preferably with thermostatic control, is suitable for processing fruits and tomatoes in glass bottles. Vacuum seal lids cannot be applied before oven

processing as the dry heat may affect the plastic seal. Instead put on a temporary lid (aluminum foil or saucer) while the fruit is in the oven. When ready, the jars are taken one at a time, the temporary lid removed, the jars overflowed, and sealed as described in pre-pack processing. The oven is useful for preserving fruit and tomatoes when no other facilities are available. Do not use for processing non-acid foods (meat, fish, vegetables other than tomatoes, cereals etc.). Cannot be used for processing food in cans.

- Pressure cooker: The use of steam under 10-lb. pressure shortens the processing time by about one third, as the inside temperature is much higher. This is essential for processing non-acid foods in jars or cans. Most fruits cook too quickly under pressure for satisfactory results, although the method may be used at low pressures, e.g., 5 lb., for firm-textured fruits such as pears and quinces. Follow instructions for preserving given in the pressure cooker instruction booklet, as care is needed for successful results.
- Water bath: The filled and sealed jars stand in a container of water which is then heated to the required temperature for the time necessary to preserve the food. Although special preserving outfits are available, some with thermostatic controls, any suitable container can be used, e.g., a preserving pan with improvized lid, a fish kettle, a copper, or a washing machine with a heating element. For small quantities a pressure cooker may be used at normal pressure. Water baths may be used for either quick or slow processing.

Quick Processing: The food, cold or hot packed, is covered with boiling liquid, then the jars are sealed and lowered carefully into the water bath which is almost boiling. The water is raised quickly to a boil and maintained at the boiling point for the required time (see tables 2 and 3 on pages 338-9). It is desirable to have the bath deep enough for the water to cover the jars by at least 1 inch, to prevent loss of liquid from the jars. Otherwise, have a close-fitting lid to ensure the tops of the jars are surrounded by steam and hot air. Use quick processing for fruit, but not vegetables other than tomatoes, or meat or fish. This method is used for processing foods in cans.

Slow Processing: The food is packed raw into the jars, covered with cold liquid, sealed and placed in a cold bath of water which is raised slowly to the

desired temperature, usually below boiling. The time varies according to the food being processed and the temperature being maintained. This is the method usually recommended for fruit by manufacturers of preserving outfits, as it produces a good looking product. With this method, it is not necessary to have jars covered with water to stop liquid being forced out of them. Use slow processing for fruits and tomatoes if desired. Follow manufacturers' recommendations for times and temperatures. Do not use for non-acid foods, which must be processed at temperatures above the boiling point.

Seals: Most modern lids are self-sealing, and the instructions given here refer to this type. They consist of two parts; an inner lid either flat or domed, and an outer screw band. They seal by the creation of a vacuum. When a lid is screwed in place before processing, i.e., for water bath or pressure cooker processing, jars are filled to ½ inch from the top before sealing. During heating, air is driven out of this space. The lid does not seal until the contents of the jar have cooled and contracted, when the vacuum thus created draws the lid closely into contact with the rim. The softened plastic seal on the outer edge of the lid makes an air-tight seal.

The process is slightly different when jars are sealed after processing, as with oven and overflow methods. Here the jar is filled to overflowing, the rim wiped clean, and the scalded lids screwed firmly into place. No air space is left, but as the boiling contents cool they contract, forming a vacuum

which causes the lid to seal hermetically. Domed lids are popular, because they make a loud crack as they are sucked down by the vacuum, and so the number of jars which have sealed can be counted. However, the shock of inversion sometimes lifts the seal from the jar. As flat seals do not invert, they are sometimes more satisfactory. It is important to use self-sealing lids correctly, following the methods outlined here, or the manufacturers' directions. Do not invert jars or tighten screw bands after processing.

Syrups
- Thin: Allow 1 cup sugar to 3 cups water. Use for low calorie or low cost bottled fruits, also for naturally sweet fruits.
- Medium: Allow 1 cup sugar to 2 cups water. Use for most purposes.
- Thick: Allow 1 cup sugar to 1 cup water.

Use for sour fruits or when a luxury product is desired. To make the syrup: Place the sugar in a pan, add the water and bring to a boil. Simmer until the sugar is dissolved. Strain before use.

Honey may replace all or part of the sugar. The flavor and color of the product may be altered if a strongly flavored honey is used. Fruit juices may be substituted for water. Use combinations which add to the flavor or color of the fruit, e.g., raspberry juice for while cherries.

When bottling fruit for diabetics or dieters, use water in place of syrup. Do not add saccharin before processing, as heating develops bitterness. Add saccharin to the fruit just before serving.

Preserved Vegetables

Guide for Canning Fruit

Fruit	Pack	Syrup	Processing Time Boiling Water Bath	Processing Time Oven at 275°
Soft fruit: blackberries, blueberries, currants (black, white, and red), loganberries, mulberries raspberries, thinly sliced rhubarb, strawberries (cover strawberries with boiling syrup and leave overnight before packing and processing)	Cold pack	Boiling, medium to thick syrup depending on tartness of fruit	15 minutes	45 minutes
Small fruit: cherries, gooseberries, grapes, small plums, rhubarb in thick chunks (immature gooseberries will shrivel in strong syrup)	Cold pack	Boiling, medium syrup, may use red juice for cherries, rhubarb	20 minutes	50 minutes
Pit fruit: apples (slices or pulp)	Pre-cook 5-10 minutes depending on firmness	Boiling, medium or thick syrup	15 minutes	45 minutes
pears			25 minutes	55 minutes
quinces	Hot pack		35 minutes	65 minutes
Seed fruit: apricots, nectarines, peaches, large plums	Cold pack	Boiling, medium syrup	30 minutes	60 minutes
Sub-tropical fruit:		Boiling syrup in all cases		
citrus fruit sections	Cold pack	Medium (very little)	20 minutes	50 minutes
figs *Note:* add 2 tablespoons lemon juice to each 1-quart jar of figs.	Hot pack	Thin or medium	40 minutes	not recommended
guavas	Cold or hot pack	Medium	25 minutes Cold pack 20 minutes Hot pack	50-60 minutes
Pineapple	Cold or hot pack	Medium or thick thick	30-35 minutes	60-65 minutes

Canning Vegetables

Most vegetables do not contain enough acid to inhibit the growth of organisms, so that very thorough processing is essential to ensure that preserved vegetables will keep successfully, and pressure canning is the only method recommended as perfectly safe for preserving them. This is in contrast to fruit and tomatoes which require less severe processing, because of their acid content.

To can vegetables: Choose fresh young tender vegetables of high quality. Prepare as for cooking. Blanch in boiling water for a few minutes, then cool quickly. This process scalds the surface of the vegetables, softens the texture slightly, and helps stabilize the vitamin C content and the coloring matter. Pack prepared vegetables firmly into jars, add 1 teaspoon salt to each 1-quart jar, and fill to ½-inch from the rim with boiling water. (Exceptions are peas, beans, and corn which are packed loosely, with 1 inch of head space to allow for expansion.) Seal the jars and process for the required time according to the guide for canning vegetables (see below).

Note:

Cream-style corn: Cut from the cob part way through the kernels and scrape from the cob. Allow 1 part boiling water to 2 parts corn, boil for 3 minutes, and pack loosely in jars, adding ½ teaspoon each salt and sugar to a 1-pint jar.

Whole-kernel corn: Cut the kernels from cob close to the cob, keeping as unbroken as possible. Add water as for cream-style corn, blanch, and proceed as usual.

Important Points:

At altitudes above sea level, the temperature at which water boils will drop because of the lower atmospheric pressure. To ensure that vegetables are processed properly, proceed as follows:

Pressure Cooker Processing: For every 2000 feet above sea level, increase pressure by 1 lb.

Guide for Canning Vegetables

Vegetable (Jars up to 1 quart size unless otherwise stated)	Blanching Time	Processing Time *Pressure Cooker at 10-lb. Pressure*
Asparagus	3 minutes	35 minutes
Beans, green	3 minutes	40 minutes
Beetroot in brine	15 minutes or until tender	40 minutes
Beets in vinegar and water	15 minutes or until tender	30 minutes
Carrots	5 minutes	40 minutes
Corn, cream-style (in 1-pint jars)	3 minutes	110 minutes
Corn, whole kernel	5 minutes	85 minutes
Mushrooms (Button mushrooms in brine)	5 minutes	40 minutes
Peas	3 minutes	50 minutes
Sweet peppers, green or red (Acidify brine with vinegar, 5 ounces per pint)	3 minutes	20 minutes

Setting Test

To test jam, jelly, and marmalade for setting: When drops of jam or jelly falling from the spoon run together to form one drop as it leaves the spoon it is time to test for setting. Drop half a teaspoon of the hot jam or jelly onto a saucer and stand in a cool place. After a few minutes, tip the saucer and the surface of the jam or jelly will wrinkle if it is ready. Alternatively, touch with a fingertip and if a film or skin draws up with it the jam is ready for pouring into clean, dry, warm jars. *Note:* Do not leave small amounts of jam boiling briskly while testing for setting, because they could over-cook and burn in the time the test takes.

FRUIT SALAD JAM

1 lb. apricots
½ lb. peaches
½ lb. pears
½ lb. nectarines

3 bananas
1½ cups crushed pineapple
6 cups sugar

Yield: 5-6 lb.

Prepare all the fruit as for fruit salad. Simmer all except the bananas with the crushed pineapple until cooked but still holding their shape. Add the sliced bananas and sugar, stir until the sugar is dissolved, then boil quickly until the jam will set when tested. Pour into warm jars and cover while hot.

GRAPE AND ORANGE JAM

3 lb. black grapes
1 cup water
6 cups sugar

1 cup chopped raisins
rind and juice of 2 oranges

Yield: 6 lb.

Stem the grapes and cook gently in water until soft and squashy. Strain through a coarse sieve to remove skins and pits and measure the pulp. For each cup of pulp, allow 1 cup sugar. Add the raisins, finely grated orange rind, and orange juice and boil quickly until the jam will set when tested. Pour into warm jars immediately and cover while hot.

MEDLEY JAM

3 lb. plums
1 lb. pears

1 cup water
8 cups sugar

Yield: 6 lb.

A tart variety of dark plum should be selected. The pears should be firm but ripe. Dice the pears and cook slowly with the plums in the water until quite soft and broken in texture. Add the sugar, stir until dissolved, bring to a boil, and cook rapidly until a little will set when tested. Skim off the seeds as they rise. Pour into clean warm jars and cover while hot.
Variations: Many other combinations of fruit can be married together in the same way, and it is a useful way to use small amounts of fruit, e.g., gooseberries and red currants; cherries, red currants, and raspberries.

RASPBERRY JAM

3 lb. raspberries

6 cups sugar

Yield: 5 lb.

Pick over the fruit, removing any leaves, caps, and any damaged fruit. Heat the fruit gently, crushing it to break up the berries and allow the juices to run. As soon as the fruit is soft and broken, add the heated sugar, stir until dissolved, then bring back to a boil, and cook quickly until the jam will set when tested. Cool a little before potting, stirring occasionally to prevent separation into layers. Cover while still hot.

APRICOT CHUTNEY

4 lb. apricots
1 lb. onions
2 cups raisins
2 cups sugar
2½ cups vinegar

1 tablespoon salt
2 teaspoons curry powder
1 teaspoon ginger
½ teaspoon cayenne pepper
  (optional)

Yield: 6 pints

Wash and seed the apricots, removing all blemishes. Place in a pan with the chopped or minced onions and raisins. Add the other ingredients and boil slowly in the uncovered pan for about 1½ hours, or until thick and clear. Pour into clean hot jars and cover while hot. Keep for one month or more before using.

Variations: This recipe can be adapted for many other fruits, e.g., apples, blackberries, gooseberries, plums, peaches, rhubarb. Fruits may be combined or used in conjunction with vegetables, e.g., peach and pear, apple and tomato, beetroot and apple, etc.

Vary spices and dried fruit according to taste. For a darker product, use brown sugar or molasses and include dark brown spices and dried fruit, e.g., cloves, dates. Shallots may replace onions and will give a milder flavor.

MINT RELISH

2 cups cider vinegar
1 cup sugar
1 teaspoon curry powder
1 teaspoon dry mustard
1 teaspoon salt
1 lb. cucumber

1 lb. ripe tomatoes
1 green sweet pepper
½ lb. onions
1 cup raisins
½ cup chopped mint

Yield: 2½ pints

Bring the vinegar to a boil and add the sugar and seasonings. Leave to cool. Peel the cucumber, remove the seeds, and cut the flesh into ¼-inch dice. Sprinkle lightly with salt and leave while preparing the other ingredients. Quarter the tomatoes, remove the seeds, and dice the flesh. Halve the pepper, remove the membrane and seeds, and dice the flesh. Chop the onions finely and the raisins coarsely. Drain the cucumber and add the other prepared vegetables, raisins, and the mint.

Pour the vinegar mixture over, mix well, and pour into sterilized jars. Cover, and stand for at least a week before using.

Variations: If preferred, the vegetables may be ground, covered with the other ingredients, and boiled gently until thick and clear. This gives a consistency more like that of chutney.

Green tomatoes may be used instead of ripe ones. Replace the curry powder with ginger.

PLUM SAUCE

3 lb. dark plums
2 cups brown sugar, firmly
  packed
½ lb. onions, finely chopped
2 tablespoons salt
1 teaspoon ginger

1 teaspoon ground cloves
1 teaspoon peppercorns
¼ teaspoon ground nutmeg
  or mace
2½ cups vinegar

Yield: 3 pints

Simmer the ingredients gently in an open pan until all are tender and mushy. Rub through a sieve to remove the seeds and peppercorns, etc. Return to the pan to boil until the consistency of pouring cream. Pour into sterilized bottles and seal immediately with sterilized caps or corks.

Variations: Other fruits may replace the plums, e.g., apricots, blackberries, gooseberries, peaches, quinces, rhubarb. Apples may be used alone or in combination with other fruits. The spices may be varied to suit the fruit being used, e.g., allspice, cinnamon, cardamom. If a hot sauce is preferred, add ½ teaspoon cayenne pepper or a few chili peppers. The use of cider or wine vinegar gives a pleasant flavor.

PICKLED MUSHROOMS

2 lb. small mushrooms

For spiced vinegar:
2½ cups vinegar
1 onion
2-inch piece cinnamon bark
2-inch piece ginger root, bruised

1 teaspoon allspice berries
½ teaspoon ground nutmeg or
  mace
½ teaspoon peppercorns
1 clove garlic, ·crushed (optional)

Yield: 2½ pints

Choose small mushroom caps for pickling.

Combine all the ingredients for spiced vinegar, bring just to a boil, cover, and let steep for 1 to 2 hours. Meanwhile, peel the mushrooms and remove the stems. When ready, heat the mushrooms gently in the spiced vinegar until they wilt. Pack into small jars, cover with the strained hot vinegar, and seal the jars immediately. Keep for 3 to 4 weeks before using as an hors d'oeuvre or a garnish.

Variations: Other vegetables may be pickled similarly, for instance, cauliflower sprigs, sliced green beans, pickling onions or shallots, diced cucumber (omit the seeds), green tomatoes, green sweet peppers, or a combination of these vegetables. Sprinkle the prepared vegetables with salt, or soak overnight in a brine solution of ⅓ cup salt to 5 cups water. Drain well, pack into jars, cover with cold spiced vinegar, and seal. Keep for several weeks before using.

SPICED BEET PICKLE

4 lb. beets
1 teaspoon cloves
2-inch piece ginger root, bruised
1 teaspoon peppercorns

1 teaspoon mustard seed
2½ cups vinegar
2 tablespoons salt
1 cup sugar

Yield: 7½ pints

Cook the beets·in boiling salted water until tender and the skins will slip off easily. Meanwhile, tie the spices in a cheesecloth bag and simmer with the vinegar, salt, and sugar in a covered pan. When ready, peel the beets, and slice or dice; leave whole if small. Pack into jars, cover with the boiling spiced vinegar, and seal.
Variations: The choice of spices is a matter of taste and may be varied as liked. The sugar may be reduced or

omitted according to preference. Other vegetables may be included, e.g., alternate layers of sliced raw onions and beets or beets and diced fresh cucumber. These vegetables are sprinkled with salt after cutting, to draw out some of the liquid. Drain and rinse before using. To keep these vegetables crisp, cool the spiced vinegar before use.

CANNED TOMATOES

Yield: 20-lb. case tomatoes
fills 12 1-quart jars (whole)
or 10 1-quart jars (tomato
halves)

Tomatoes should be firm and well ripened. To skin tomatoes, put enough for one jar in a muslin bag and dip for 1 to 2 minutes in boiling water. Run a sharp pointed knife around the stem end and the skin should lift off easily. If not, increase the dipping time. Pack whole or in halves, pressing firmly but carefully into the jars, to the top of the shoulders. Add 1 teaspoon salt to each 1-quart jar, fill to ½-inch from the rim with boiling water, seal the jars, and process—boiling water bath for

45 minutes, oven at 275° for 65 minutes.
Note: Tomatoes are the only vegetable which may safely be processed in the oven. To keep whole tomatoes firm for serving in slices, use 1 teaspoon calcium chloride solution instead of salt in the above recipe, otherwise proceed as directed. Calcium chloride solution: Dissolve 2¼ oz. calcium chloride in 2½ cups boiling water. Cool before using.

MARROW SQUASH JAM

3 lb. marrow squash
6 cups sugar

2 lemons
$\frac{1}{4}$ cup chopped preserved ginger

Yield: 5 lb.

Dice the peeled marrow and steam until just tender. Place in a bowl with the sugar, grated rind and juice of the lemons, and the ginger. Heat gently until the sugar is dissolved, then boil until the jam will set when tested. The marrow squash should be transparent and the syrup thick. Pour into clean, hot jars and when cold, seal.

QUINCE JAM

5 lb. quinces
5 pints cold water

10 cups sugar

Yield: 5 lb.

Wash the quinces, but do not peel. Put them whole into a saucepan with a little water. Boil until almost tender, then peel and core them. Put the peel and cores and 5 pints cold water into a preserving pan and simmer for 45 minutes. Strain through a jelly bag, overnight. Do not squeeze. Dice the quinces and cover until needed.

Put the fruit in the juice and bring to a boil, then add the sugar and boil briskly until the jam will set when tested. Allow to cool for about 10 minutes before potting. Before the jam cools in the jars, carefully stir it to keep the pieces of fruit evenly distributed. Seal.

QUICK STRAWBERRY JAM

2 lb. strawberries
6 cups sugar

1 teaspoon tartaric acid

Yield: 4 lb.

The fruit must be ripe but firm. Discard any damaged berries. Hull the berries and wash well. Place in a large saucepan and mash with a potato masher. Add the sugar and bring to a boil. Boil for 5 minutes. Add the tartaric acid and bring to a boil again. Boil for 5 minutes.

It is most important that the time of boiling is measured from when the jam comes to a boil. Pot at once in clean, hot, dry jars. When cold seal with paraffin wax and a cover.

FEIJOA JELLY

This unusual fruit is grown in California and if obtainable makes an excellent jelly.

3 lb. feijoas
water to cover

1 lemon
sugar

Yield: 3 lb.

Small and irregular fruit may be used for jelly, but they must not be damaged.

Wash the fruit well and cut up roughly. Put into a preserving pan and almost cover with water, then simmer for about 45 minutes or until completely pulpy. Strain through a jelly bag overnight; do not squeeze. Measure the juice and put into the pan. Add the juice of the lemon and bring to a boil. Allow 1 cup sugar for each cup of juice and add this when the juice boils. Continue to boil briskly until a little jelly will set when tested. Allow to cool for 5 minutes, then pour into hot, dry jars. Seal when cold.

Apricot Chutney, Spiced Beet
Pickle, and Mint Relish

CAPE GOOSEBERRY JAM

This is another unusual preserve which makes an exciting change.

1¼ lb. cape gooseberries
3 cups sugar

½ lb. cooking apples
1 lemon

Yield: 2 lb.

Remove the cases from the gooseberries before weighing. Put the fruit in a large saucepan and crush with a potato masher. Sprinkle half the sugar over the fruit and leave covered overnight to draw out the juice. Next day add the peeled, cored, and finely chopped apple and bring to a boil. Add the remaining sugar and the juice of the lemon and boil steadily until the jam will set when tested. Pour into warm dry jars and seal when cold.

CHINESE GOOSEBERRY AND ORANGE JAM

2 sweet oranges
1 lemon

3 lb. Chinese gooseberries
6 cups sugar

Yield: 3½ lb.

Peel the rinds thinly from the oranges and lemon, using a potato peeler, to avoid getting any pith. Put these in a cheesecloth bag, loosely tied. Squeeze the juice from the citrus fruits and put in a preserving pan with the peeled and chopped Chinese gooseberries. Put in the cheesecloth bag containing the rind and simmer all together until the fruit is soft. Add the sugar and boil briskly for about 20 minutes, or until the jam will set when tested. Discard the bag of rind and put the jam into hot dry jars. Seal when cold.

PAPAYA AND GINGER JAM

2 lb. papaya, weighed after
    peeling and removal of seeds
3 cups sugar

¼ cup preserved ginger
1 lemon
¼ cup water

Yield: 2½ lb.

Peel the papaya and remove the seeds. Dice the fruit and put into a bowl. Add the sugar and thinly sliced ginger. Cover and leave overnight. Place the fruit mixture in a preserving pan or large saucepan and add the thinly sliced lemon and the water. Bring to a boil and boil briskly until the jam will set when tested. Bottle in clean, hot, dry jars. Seal when cold.

DAMSON CHEESE

3 lb. damson plums
⅔ cup water

sugar

Yield: 3½ lb.

Place the damson plums and water in a saucepan, cover with a lid, and simmer until tender. Press the pulp through a sieve and measure. Allow 1 cup warmed sugar to each cup of pulp, stir until dissolved, then reduce the pulp over heat until thick. Put into hot dry jars and seal.

LEMON CURD

⅓ cup butter
1 cup sugar

2 lemons
6 egg yolks

Yield: 1 lb.

Combine the butter with the sugar and the juice and grated rind of the lemons in the top of a double boiler. Stir over low heat until the butter is melted and the sugar dissolved. Add the egg yolks and cook, stirring constantly, until the mixture is hot (not boiling) and thick. Pour into small, clean, dry jars. Cover with cellophane. In warm climates keep in the refrigerator.

GUAVA JELLY

2½ lb. guavas
½ lb. apples

2 lemons
sugar

Yield: 2½ lb.

Wash the fruit well and cut the apples and lemons into slices. Put into a preserving pan and cover with water. Simmer until the fruit is completely pulpy, about 1 hour. Strain through a jelly bag without squeezing.

Measure the juice, put into a pan, and bring to a boil. Allow 1 cup sugar to each cup juice, adding this when the juice boils. Boil briskly until the jelly will set when tested. Pour into clean hot jars and, when cold, seal.

BLUEBERRY AND APPLE JELLY

1½ lb. blueberries
1½ lb. sliced apples

water
sugar

Yield: Approximately 1 lb. for every 2½ cups juice

Cook the blueberries and apples separately in just enough water to cover, until tender. Strain the fruits overnight through a jelly bag. Do not squeeze. Mix the juices and measure the liquid next day. Bring to a boil.

Add 1½ cups sugar for every cup of liquid. Boil rapidly until the jelly will set when tested. Allow to stand for a few minutes then pour into hot, dry jars. Cover when cold.

JELLY MARMALADE

2 lb. grapefruit
1 lb. lemons

5 pints water
sugar

Yield: 2½ lb.

With a potato peeler take the thin rind from the grapefruit and lemons. Shred this very finely and tie it in cheesecloth muslin loosely. Squeeze the juice from the fruits and retain it. Keep any seeds to soak with the flesh. Roughly chop or grind the flesh and pith of the fruit. Place this and the water with the cheesecloth bag of rind in a bowl and leave to soak overnight. Next day, boil up the soaked pulp in the water with the cheesecloth bag still in it. Add the juice and boil together until the pulp is completely tender. Lift out the bag of rind and reserve.

Strain the remainder through a jelly bag. Do not squeeze, but allow to drip overnight. Measure this liquid and allow 1 cup sugar for every cup of juice. Add the shredded rind and bring the liquid to a boil, then add the sugar. Boil quickly and test after about 20 to 30 minutes to see if the marmalade is at setting stage. If ready, remove from the heat and leave for 15 minutes before potting. Stir well, then pour into hot dry jars. If the peel tends to rise in the jars while the marmalade is still warm, gently stir with a knife. Seal when cold.

MIXED FRUIT MARMALADE

2 grapefruit
2 lemons
2 oranges

5 quarts water
sugar

Yield: 11 lb.

The total weight of the fruit should be about 3 lb.

Wash the fruit well. Cut the fruit up finely and put in a non-metallic container. Cover with the water and soak overnight. Place in a preserving pan and boil for 1 hour. Measure the pulp, return to the pan, and bring

to a boil again. Add 1 cup sugar for every cup of pulp. Boil again, until a little will set when tested. Allow to cool for about 15 minutes before pouring into clean dry jars. When cold, seal.

FIGS IN SYRUP

3 cups water
½ cup vinegar
2½ cups sugar

½ cup preserved ginger
4 lb. figs

Yield: 4 lb.

Put the water, vinegar, sugar, and sliced preserved ginger into a large heavy saucepan and simmer for 30 minutes. Use only firm, undamaged figs. Wipe the figs and trim off the stems. Put the figs into the syrup and simmer very gently for 2 hours. Take care that scorching does not occur towards the end of the time and stir occasionally during the cooking. Pack into clean, hot jars and seal with screw lids. This gives whole figs in a rich syrup. This is not a jam, but may be eaten as jam, or as a dessert fruit.

GUAVA JUICE

This makes a refreshing fruit drink when diluted with water or carbonated water. Sliced lemon or lemon juice may be added to taste.

guavas

sugar

Wash the fruit well and put into a saucepan with water just to cover. Simmer until the fruit is pulpy, then strain off the juice. Measure this and for every 2 cups juice, allow ¾ to 1 cup sugar, depending on the sweetness preferred. Prepare 1-pint preserving jars. Boil the juice and sugar together for 5 minutes. Fill the jars and let them overflow. Place the seals and lids on the jars and screw down.

SQUASH PICKLE

3½ lb. squash
1¼ lb. onions
1 cup chopped green beans
1 cup chopped celery
generous ½ cup salt
5 cups malt vinegar

1 cup sugar
2 tablespoons curry powder
¼ cup dry mustard
1 teaspoon turmeric
½ cup all-purpose flour
1 cup malt vinegar

Yield: 5 lb.

Peel the squash and remove the seeds. Peel the onions and cut into small pieces. Put into a bowl. Put the beans and celery together in another bowl. Sprinkle the salt over the 3 bowls using about ⅓ cup on the squash, and 2 tablespoons each on the other vegetables. Cover and leave overnight. Next day drain through a colander and put all the vegetables, together with the vinegar, sugar, curry powder, mustard, and turmeric, into a preserving pan and boil steadily for 20 minutes. Blend the pickle for a further 5 minutes, stirring frequently. Place in hot dry jars. Seal when cold, preferably with paraffin wax, then a lid. Keep for about 6 weeks to mature before use.

HERBS AND
SPICES

Rosemary Hemphill

Rosemary Hemphill is an expert on the history and cultivation of herbs and spices. She has a flourishing herb garden of her own and puts this to practical use in original and delicious recipes in her kitchen. Rosemary has written four cookery books, three of them on Herbs and Spices.

HERBS AND SPICES

Herbs and spices are the means by which a cook may be inspired to express his or her individuality in a dish, bringing original thoughts and ideas to food. Nearly everyone is able to grow herbs, even if the collection is limited to two or three plants in a sunny window box in a city building. However, if it is not possible to grow or buy fresh herbs, a wide selection of dried herbs is available in most shops.

If you wish to grow only a small number of herbs to begin with, and if space is limited, I would suggest parsley, chives, spearmint, thyme, rosemary, and basil, as six plants with a variety of flavors, which are useful in everyday cooking. When possible, add to your collection balm, borage, chervil, dill, fennel, marjoram, oregano, sage, winter savory, tarragon, and lavender. When planning to grow herbs, start from seed, or buy seedlings and plant them in a well-drained, sunny position, watering them regularly until well established. If growing herbs from seed, sow in the open ground along shallow trenches or in seed boxes, cover lightly with soil, and keep watered until a few inches high and ready to plant out.

Herbs will not grow satisfactorily indoors, but will grow very well in window boxes or in pots of various shapes and sizes on balconies and porches. It is important for them to have fresh air and some sun during the day and for the soil in their containers to be fed with a plant fertilizer occasionally, and to be changed once or twice a year. The correct potting soil for growing plants in containers is available from most nurseries. The most suitable herbs to grow in a restricted space are the small to medium-sized ones, such as sage, small-leaved creeping rosemary, basil, chervil, chives, marjoram, parsley, winter savory, oregano, and thyme. Put mint on its own, as the creeping root system chokes other plants.

In summer, when herbs are growing in abundance, cut them back at intervals and dry the harvested stems. The best way to do this is to hang them upside down in bunches by their stems in an airy, dry place. Some people like to tie a paper bag over the leaves to catch any that may fall and to keep the dust off. Oven drying must be done quickly to be effective and the temperature should not be too hot, otherwise the precious oil in the leaves will evaporate. When the herbs are quite dry and brittle, strip the leaves from the stems and pack them into clean, dry, airtight jars.

With the coming of fall, most herbs which have not been cut back for drying have gone to seed. Some will self-sow either sparsely or liberally, and some not at all, so collect the seed to be sure of next year's crop. Put the collected seed in labeled air-tight envelopes or in labeled screw-top glass jars, and store until spring.

COOKING WITH HERBS

In the following recipes, I have given measurements for fresh herbs when a greater quantity is needed than dried herbs. Remember 1 teaspoon dried herbs substitutes for 2 tablespoons fresh herbs.

ALLSPICE

Allspice is the fruit of a tropical tree native to America and the West Indies, and is also cultivated extensively in Jamaica. The small, sundried berries are sometimes known as pimiento or pimento, as well as allspice. When ground the flavor resembles a combination of cinnamon, juniper, cloves, and nutmeg, hence its name 'allspice'. Whole allspice is used in pickling spice for chutneys and pickles. Ground allspice is used in some commercial spice blends, and as a flavoring for meat dishes, soups, vegetables, spiced seafoods, various cakes, milk puddings, and desserts.

Allspice gives a stimulating tang to the crust and topping of this pie. Elderberries, with their pleasing sharp flavor rather like blackcurrants, go well with apples.

APPLE AND ALLSPICE PIE

For crust:
1½ cups wholewheat all-purpose flour sifted with 1½ teaspoons baking powder
1 teaspoon sugar

1 teaspoon salt
2 teaspoons allspice
½ cup butter or margarine
1 egg, beaten

Cooking time: 30 minutes
Temperature: 350°
Serves: 6

For filling:
1 lb. apples, peeled, cored, and sliced
2-3 sprays ripe elderberries, washed
juice and grated rind of ½ lemon
2 teaspoons all-purpose flour

1 tablespoon sugar
1 egg
⅔ cup milk
1 teaspoon allspice
whipping cream or sour cream for serving

To make the pie crust: Sieve the flour, sugar, salt, and allspice into a mixing bowl. Rub the butter into the flour until the mixture resembles fine bread crumbs. Add the egg, and bind together. Roll the dough out on floured wax paper, turn upside down onto a greased 10-inch pie pan, discard the paper, and press the dough into the pan. Prick all over with a fork.

To make the filling: Place the apples in the pie shell. Pick the elderberries off the stems, and sprinkle among the apples. Add the lemon juice and rind. Combine in a small bowl the flour, sugar, egg, and milk and pour over the apples; sprinkle with allspice. Bake on the middle shelf of a 350° oven for 30 minutes. Serve hot or cold with whipped cream, or sour cream.

ANISE SEED

Anise is an annual plant, native to Middle Eastern countries. It is grown mainly for the licorice-flavored small, oval seeds, which have been used to aid digestion since earliest times. Anise is used in cooking, in medicine, and in the liqueur anisette. The leaves may be used in salads, and as a garnish. The seed flavors breads, rolls, cakes, and cookies, is also used in fruit pies, stewed fruit, cream cheese spreads, milk beverages, puddings, raw vegetable salads, and with cooked vegetables, particularly carrots and cabbage when little or no water is used.

CARROT AND ANISE SEED ASPIC

1 lb. carrots
1 onion
1 green sweet pepper
small jar stuffed olives
7 tablespoons boiling water
3½ envelopes gelatin

1 tablespoon anise seed
2 tablespoons chopped basil
3¾ cups tomato juice
2 tablespoons brown sugar
2 tablespoons white vinegar
salt and pepper

Serves: 4-6

Wash and grate the carrots. Peel and grate the onion. Wash the pepper and chop finely, discarding the seeds. Drain the olives and slice in half. Pour the boiling water onto the gelatin and stir until clear. Combine all the ingredients together in a mixing bowl, then pour into a rinsed mold. Chill until set. Unmold onto a flat dish and surround with sprays of fresh herbs, if available, or lettuce leaves.

Sweet Basil

Bay Leaves

Chives

Mint-Spearmint

Curly-leaved Parsley

Rosemary

Winter Savory

Tarragon

Garden Thyme

BAY LEAF AND BOUQUET GARNI

The bay tree, native to Mediterranean areas, is now grown all over the world. Although it sometimes becomes very large, the bay also makes an attractive small tree if cultivated in a tub, the lateral stems removed, and the top clipped into a neat green ball. The leaves and berries of this tree are rich in an aromatic oil, which in herbal medicine was extracted and used for a variety of complaints. This delicious oil gives the leaves a strong flavor, therefore they should be used sparingly. Pick them straight from the tree or use dried. A bay leaf is a classic ingredient in a bouquet garni for soups, casseroles, and stews, the other herbs usually being a sprig each of thyme, marjoram, and parsley. These should be tied together and removed at the end of cooking. In dried bouquet garni the bay leaves are finely crumbled with the other herbs, so it may go straight into the food. The long simmering softens the herbs, making it unnecessary to remove them. A bay leaf or two can go into soups, stews, and casseroles, into some preserved foods, and when cooking corned beef, salted mutton, pickled pork, tongue, poultry, and fish. Also a bay leaf may be placed on top of a baked milk pudding to give a pleasant, delicate flavor.

BALM

A native of southern Europe, balm was introduced to other regions at a very early period in time. The whole of this lemon-scented plant is fragrant and beneficial, but is not considered valuable enough for culinary purposes to dry in large quantities commercially. Balm was indispensable in the old herb garden. Refreshing teas and healing ointments were made from the leaves and beehives were rubbed with it to prevent the bees from swarming. Grow balm for its flowers to attract bees and for its refreshing leaves to use in cooling summer drinks, wine cups, as a tea, and to mix with ordinary tea; also to flavor fresh fruit salads and fruit puddings.

GOOSEBERRY BALM SHERBET

1 (16 oz.) can gooseberries	1 envelope gelatin	Serves: 4
$\frac{2}{3}$ cup cream	1 tablespoon chopped balm	
2 tablespoons boiling water	4 balm sprigs	

Place the gooseberries and syrup in a blender with the cream. Pour the boiling water onto the gelatin, stir until clear, and add to the other ingredients in the blender. Purée together until pulverized, pour into a mixing bowl, and fold in the chopped balm. Chill in the refrigerator until set. Alternatively, press the gooseberries and syrup through a sieve, add the dissolved gelatin and chopped balm, and chill. Serve in cold sherbet glasses with whipped cream, topped with a sprig of balm.

BASIL

Basil is thought by many to be the most truly fragrant of all culinary herbs. The leaves have a warm, fresh, spicy scent which enhances all types of food. There are several varieties of basil differing widely in appearance, though not much in flavor; a dwarf basil, a purple-leaved variety, and a large-leaved sweet basil which grows to 2 feet high Basil has been used in various parts of the world as a sacred herb, a love-token, and a remedy for many illnesses, including fevers and nervous disorders. In cooking, basil combines particularly well with tomatoes and fish.

BASIL STUFFED SWEET PEPPERS

4 large green or red sweet peppers	$\frac{1}{4}$ cup pine nuts	Cooking time: 30 minutes
3 cups cooked brown rice	salt	Temperature: 350°
4 scallions, finely chopped	freshly cracked black pepper	Serves: 4
12 stuffed olives, sliced	2 teaspoons lemon juice	
$\frac{1}{4}$ cup chopped basil	about $\frac{1}{2}$ cup oil	

Wash the peppers and cut in half, discarding the seeds. Mix together the rice, scallions, olives, basil, pine nuts, salt, pepper, and lemon juice. Fill the halved peppers with the mixture, about $\frac{1}{4}$ cup to each half, and place in a shallow ovenproof dish. Pour a little oil over the rice and the rest around the peppers. Place a sheet of aluminum foil over the top and bake in a 350° oven until the peppers are soft, about 30 minutes. Serve hot for a light lunch with buttered rye bread and wedges of dry, white cheese.

SALAD BURNET

Salad burnet was known and used extensively by the ancient Greeks. The plant is attractive when growing, a series of small, cucumber-flavored leaves on a long soft stem, giving the appearance of one long leaf or spray. The sprays are thickly clustered. The small, raspberry-like flower heads are carried on long, straight stems from the middle of the plant. When young the sprays are used either whole in salads and wine cups, or finely chopped in sandwiches. If using older sprays, the central stem will be tough, so strip off the leaves before using.

CARAWAY SEED

Caraway is a herb native to the Mediterranean. Now growing wild all over Europe, it is a member of the group of aromatic plants known for their digestive properties. The custom of serving roast apples with caraway seed is still kept up in different parts of Britain. In Germany, soups, cabbage dishes, cheeses, and breads are flavored with caraway seeds and in Norway and Sweden a black caraway bread is eaten. Caraway seed may also be used to flavor certain cakes, cookies, some pickles, vegetables, meat, and fish dishes.

VEGETABLE CARAWAY PIE

1 cauliflower
1 green or red sweet pepper
4 eggs, hard-cooked
2 carrots
generous $\frac{1}{3}$ cup whole shelled

almonds
$\frac{1}{4}$ cup butter or margarine
12 scallions
2 tablespoons chopped parsley

Cooking time: 20-30 minutes
Temperature: 350°
Serves: 6

For topping:
$\frac{1}{4}$ cup butter
$\frac{1}{4}$ cup all-purpose flour
$1\frac{1}{4}$ cups milk
1 tablespoon caraway seeds

salt and pepper
1 cup dry bread crumbs
$\frac{1}{2}$ cup grated cheese
2 teaspoons paprika pepper

Wash the cauliflower, break into flowerets, boil in salted water for 5 minutes, and strain. Cut the pepper into strips, discarding the seeds. Shell and quarter the eggs. Wash the carrots and grate coarsely. Brown the almonds in the butter. Wash the scallions and chop finely. Mix all the ingredients together, including the parsley, in a greased ovenproof dish.

To make the topping: Melt the butter in a saucepan, stir in the flour, and add the milk, stirring until thickened. Add the caraway seeds, salt, and pepper. Pour over the vegetables and top with the bread crumbs, cheese, and paprika pepper. Place in a 350° oven for 20 to 30 minutes until heated through and the cheese is melted.

CARDAMOM SEED

This plant originated in India and is valued for the small, hard seeds which are extremely aromatic, having a strong eucalyptus flavor. It is used in Indian cooking, both in curries and in sweet dishes. It is also popular in Scandinavian cookery. Like most of the culinary aromatic seeds, cardamom aids the digestion. As the seed is very hard, it needs to be crushed coarsely, or ground to a powder, before using. Cardamom is marketed in several ways; the whole black seed, the ground seed, and the small, greenish pods in which the seeds grow (this is mainly for cooking with rice for curries). Cardamom seed is an important ingredient in curry powder; it is also used in rice dishes, with squash and sweet potatoes, and in cakes, puddings, and pies. When ground it is delicious in fruit soups and sprinkled on fresh, raw fruit, especially melon slices and ripe pears.

CARDAMOM AND SWEET POTATOES

1 lb. sweet potatoes
juice and grated rind of 1 orange
2 tablespoons honey
1 onion, thinly sliced
salt

2 teaspoons ground cardamom
seed
$\frac{1}{4}$ cup butter or margarine
$\frac{1}{4}$ cup dry bread crumbs

Cooking time: 45 minutes
Temperature: 350°
Serves: 4

Wash and peel the potatoes and slice thinly. Mix the orange juice, grated rind, and honey together. Arrange the potato slices and onion rings in a greased ovenproof dish, pour over the orange and honey mixture, and sprinkle with salt and cardamom. Dot with the butter and sprinkle with bread crumbs. Bake in a 350° oven for 45 minutes. Serve hot.

Pork Casserole with Herb Biscuit Topping

CAYENNE

This red-hot pepper is ground from the small, dried fruit of a species of capsicum, cultivated mainly in the southern zones of the world, the most pungent coming from the island of Zanzibar. An excellent culinary spice, cayenne pepper also has digestive properties. It may replace black pepper in cooking, but as it is extremely hot, use it with care! It is used in cheese dishes, sauces, egg dishes, and with shellfish.

CHEESE AND CAYENNE STRAWS

$\frac{1}{4}$ cup butter
$\frac{1}{2}$ cup flour
$\frac{1}{2}$ cup grated cheese

cayenne pepper
salt

Cooking time: 15 minutes
Temperature: 400°
Serves: 4

Rub the butter, flour, and cheese together and season with cayenne pepper and salt. If the mixture is too stiff, moisten with a little water. Roll out and cut into thin strips which may be twisted or left straight; form 2 or 3 strips into circles. Place carefully on a greased baking sheet and bake in a 400° oven until light brown in color. about 15 minutes. Cool. Fit the cheese straws in bundles into the circles.

PORK CASSEROLE WITH HERB BISCUIT TOPPING

For filling:
1$\frac{3}{4}$ lb. fresh pork picnic shoulder
$\frac{1}{4}$ cup wholewheat all-purpose
  flour
salt and pepper
1 onion, chopped
2 cloves garlic, chopped
$\frac{1}{4}$ cup preserved ginger

6 prunes, pitted
1 bouquet garni (a bay leaf and
  a sprig each of marjoram,
  parsley, and thyme tied
  together), or 2 teaspoons dried
  bouquet garni
1$\frac{1}{4}$ cups red wine

Cooking time: 2$\frac{1}{4}$ hours
Temperature: 300°, increasing
  to 400°
Serves: 4

For herb biscuit topping:
6 tablespoons butter
1$\frac{1}{2}$ cups wholewheat all-purpose
  flour, sifted with 1$\frac{1}{2}$ teaspoons

baking powder
dash salt
$\frac{1}{4}$ cup chopped parsley
cold water to mix

To prepare the filling: Dice the pork and roll in flour, salt, and pepper. Place in a casserole alternately with the other ingredients, the wine last. Put the lid on and cook on the middle shelf of a 300° oven for 2 hours. Remove the lid, take out the bouquet garni if using fresh herbs, place the herb biscuit dough on top, increase the temperature to 400°, and leave to cook for a further 10 to 15 minutes. Serve hot.

To make the biscuit topping: Rub the butter into the flour and salt, add the parsley, and stir in enough cold water to make a stiff dough. Roll out lightly on a floured surface, lift carefully onto the bubbling casserole, and mark into squares with a knife.

CAMOMILE, ENGLISH

The origins of the camomile daisy are obscure; varieties of the plant have grown in a natural state in Europe and North Africa for centuries. The two types which are considered the most beneficial are the English and German camomiles. For tea, only the dried flower-heads are used. These should be picked before noon, then spread out to dry on paper in a cool, shady place. Keep in an air-tight jar when thoroughly dried. Camomile Tea (see page 361) has many uses; as a soothing and healing lotion for styes (strain through a cheesecloth for this), a beautifying lotion for the skin, an aid to digestion and abdominal cramps, a sedative, when sipped steaming hot, and a hair rinse to lighten the hair.

CHIVES

The chive plant is native to northern Europe, and belongs to the same family as the onion, leek, garlic, and scallion. The grass-like leaves have a delicate taste of onion, which goes well with other herbs. Freeze-drying makes it possible for chives to be marketed ready chopped in the dried form. Use chives in dips and spreads, as a garnish for soups and other dishes, with scrambled eggs and omelets, in mayonnaise and sour cream dressings, in mashed potato and potato dishes, and in salads and herb sandwiches.

BAKED CHIVE POTATOES

4 large well-shaped potatoes
2 tablespoons butter or margarine
2 tablespoons coffee cream
salt
freshly cracked pepper
¼ cup chopped chives
½ cup grated cheese

Cooking time: 1¼ hours
Temperature: 350°
Serves: 4

Scrub the potatoes and place on the middle shelf of a 350° oven for approximately 1 hour, or until soft in the center when a skewer is pressed into them. Cut the potatoes in half and carefully scoop out all the white part. Mash this to a cream in a mixing bowl with the butter, cream, salt, and pepper. Add the chives and fill the potato shells with mixture. Top with grated cheese, return to the oven, and bake for a further 15 minutes, or until the cheese has melted. Serve hot.

CLOVES

Whole cloves are the dried flower-buds of an evergreen tree that is native to the Molucca Islands, and is grown today in many hot countries. Aromatic cloves are valued for their medicinal, preservative, and culinary qualities. They are useful both whole and ground. Whole cloves are used in preserves, mulled wines, stewed fruits, soups, meat casseroles, and for flavoring and decorating ham and pork. Ground cloves are an ingredient in curry powder and are included in some soups, spicy sauces, meat dishes, fruit cake, buns, mincemeat, Christmas puddings, and milk puddings.

APPLE PUDDING

1 lb. cooking apples
2 tablespoons lemon juice
5 cloves
¼ cup raisins
¼ cup sugar
whipped cream for serving

Cooking time: 1 hour
Temperature: 350°
Serves: 4-6

For batter:
2 cups all-purpose flour
dash salt
½ cup sugar
2 eggs
2½ cups milk

Peel, core, and slice the apples and sprinkle with the lemon juice. Place in an even layer in a greased 1-quart baking dish. Add the cloves and raisins and sprinkle with the sugar.
To make the batter: Sieve the flour and salt into a mixing bowl. Stir in the sugar. Make a well in the center of the flour, add the eggs, and mix a little flour into the eggs with a wooden spoon. Add half the milk, gradually, stirring in the flour from around the edge, and beat until smooth. Stir in the remaining milk.

Pour the batter over the apple mixture. Bake in a 350° oven for 1 hour. Serve hot with whipped cream.

CURRY POWDER

Curry powder is not one spice, but a blend of many spices which, when combined with food, gives it a unique, aromatic flavor, varying from mild through medium and sweet to very hot, depending on which spices, and how many, are used. Instead of powder, curry paste is sometimes used; this is prepared with moist, spicy ingredients in addition to ground spices. In countries where curries are eaten frequently, each family grinds its own choice of aromatic seeds nearly every day. India, Pakistan, Burma, Ceylon, and Indonesia all have curries varying in strength and flavor. The main solid ingredient in a curry dish may be chicken, rabbit, meat, fish, shellfish, vegetables, or hard-cooked eggs. Curry powder may also be used to flavor dips and spreads, certain soups, cream dressings, scrambled eggs, and omelets.

CURRIED MAYONNAISE FOR POTATO SALAD

1¼ cups mayonnaise
1 tablespoon finely chopped
   scallions
1 tablespoon sweet chutney
1-2 teaspoons curry powder

(depending on strength)
salt
1 lb. potatoes, cooked and diced
1 tablespoon chopped parsley,
   coriander, chervil, or dill

Serves: 4-6

Pour the mayonnaise into a mixing bowl and stir in the scallions and chutney. Add the curry powder gradually, tasting for desired strength. Add the salt. Pour the curried mayonnaise over the potatoes. Add the parsley, toss gently, and chill before serving.

GARLIC

Garlic is so old that its country of origin is not certain. Its uses are recorded in legend and history. The ancient Greeks and Romans consumed large quantities of garlic. Throughout the ages it has been distinguished for its antiseptic properties, both internally and externally. Garlic bulbs are available from stores; each bulb is made up of separate sections called cloves, each covered by a thin skin which is peeled off before using. Garlic is also marketed dried in several ways, crushed to a fine powder, or mixed with salt as a flavoring. Garlic is also shredded into fine, dehydrated chips, which may be reconstituted in liquid. Use in French dressing, butter for spreads, sauces, dips, and meat dishes, with tomatoes and egg-plant, in pickles, salads, and seafoods, and for garlic bread.

GARLIC BREAD

1 long French loaf
2 cloves garlic

1 cup butter

Cooking time: 10-15 minutes
Temperature: 400°
Serves: 8-12

You will probably have to cut the loaf in half as there are not many ovens long enough to hold an unbroken French loaf. With a sharp knife, cut the bread in slices almost to the bottom, being careful not to sever the slices. Peel and crush the garlic and mash thoroughly into the butter. Spread the garlic butter generously on both sides of the bread slices. Wrap loosely in aluminum foil and place in a 400° oven for 10 to 15 minutes, until the bread is crisp and golden. Serve hot, each person tearing off his own slice.

Carrot and Anise Seed Aspic

HERB SANDWICHES

Fresh, green, chopped herbs make delicious refreshing fillings for sandwiches. Brown or wholewheat bread, spread with butter or margarine, is recommended. To help bring out the flavor of the herbs, spread a film of peanut butter, cottage cheese, or cream cheese on the buttered bread. Pick the herbs, wash well, strip the leaves from the stems (except for herbs with very soft stems like salad burnet), and chop finely. These sandwiches may be made in advance, wrapped in aluminum foil, and refrigerated or deep frozen. Allow time for the sandwiches to thaw. Serve with morning or afternoon tea or coffee, or as an accompaniment to soups, entrées, or light luncheon and supper dishes.

Mixed Herbs: Pick several sprays of parsley, chives, marjoram, salad burnet, and tarragon, two leaves of eau-de-cologne mint, and one sage leaf, and chop all together. The dominant herb is tarragon, the others are complementary. Instead of tarragon, use another strong aromatic herb like rosemary, basil, or oregano. Eau-de-cologne mint and sage have strong flavors and are excellent when used sparingly with other herbs.

Chives and Cottage Cheese: Spread buttered bread with 2 tablespoons chopped chives and $\frac{1}{2}$ cup cottage or cream cheese mixed together.

Marjoram and Cottage Cheese: Spread buttered bread with cottage or cream cheese, and lay on top unchopped marjoram leaves, which are soft and pleasant to eat whole.

Borage and Peanut Butter: Spread buttered bread with peanut butter, heap with chopped young borage leaves, and season with salt and pepper (borage tastes slightly like oysters). It is important to mince or chop these leaves finely as they have a rough surface.

Salad Burnet and Peanut Butter: Spread buttered bread with peanut butter and top with chopped salad burnet, which has a fresh cucumber flavor.

The following sandwiches are better if made shortly before serving. Do not freeze them.

Basil and Tomato: Lay slices of tomato on buttered bread, sprinkle with salt, pepper, and sugar, and add chopped basil.

Dill and Cucumber: Lay thin slices of cucumber, peeled or unpeeled, on buttered bread, sprinkle with salt and pepper, and add chopped dill.

Chervil and Egg: Make scrambled egg and add chopped chervil. Spread when cold on buttered bread.

Lovage and Grated Apple: Mix chopped lovage leaves with grated apple, a little lemon juice and honey, and salt and pepper. Lay between lettuce leaves on buttered bread.

HERB TEAS

A tea made from the leaves or flowers of certain herbs makes a pleasing after-dinner drink for those who do not drink coffee. There are times when herb teas may be taken more frequently, for instance peppermint tea helps a cold and is excellent to drink three times a day. Dried elder flowers, an old remedy for a fever, may be added to the teapot with the peppermint. Many herb teas, or infusions, are excellent lotions for the skin, giving it a natural, soft bloom. The infusion must be cooled first, and then lightly applied to the face with soaked pads of cotton wool. Elder flower tea, for example, is excellent for sunburn and freckles.

The best known herb and flower teas are made with peppermint leaves, thyme leaves, sage leaves, lemon verbena leaves, nettle leaves, camomile flowers, lime flowers, elder flowers, and borage flowers.

Most leaves for herb teas are dried first, although they can be picked and used fresh from the garden. Flowers for tea are nearly always dried. Keep a separate teapot for herb teas, and when using the dried leaves, put 1 to 2 teaspoons into the pot and pour in boiling water, allow to infuse for 3 to 4 minutes, then strain into cups. Do not add milk. Lemon, honey, or orange flower water are suggested flavorings. If picking fresh herbs for tea, allow a greater quantity than the dried and infuse for several minutes longer. For flower teas, bring a small saucepan of water to a boil, then add a small handful of dried flowers, put the lid on, and simmer for 1 minute. Allow the tea to stnad for a few minutes longer, then strain and flavor as desired.

PEPPERMINT TEA

Serves: 2

For dried peppermint leaves: Put 2 teaspoons leaves into a teapot, pour boiling water onto the leaves, cover, and infuse for 3 to 4 minutes. Strain into cups. If wished, sweeten with honey and flavor with lemon.

For fresh peppermint leaves: Pick a small handful of peppermint (about 4 stalks 4 inches long), wash them, and put in a teapot. Pour boiling water onto the leaves, cover, and infuse for 5 to 7 minutes. Strain into cups and flavor as desired.

CAMOMILE TEA

Serves: 2

Measure 2 cups of water into a saucepan (preferably enamel or glass) and bring to a boil. Sprinkle 2 teaspoons dried camomile flowers into the water, put on the lid, and simmer for 1 minute. Remove from the heat and leave covered for another 2 to 3 minutes so the valuable extract is not lost. Strain into cups and flavor as for Peppermint Tea.

HORSERADISH

This herb has been cultivated for thousands of years and is thought to have come from Eastern Europe. Both the root and leaves of horseradish were used as a medicine during the Middle Ages, and as a condiment in Denmark and Germany. Nowadays, the pungently hot root is still used in cooking. When grated and mixed with a sauce, it is an excellent accompaniment to meat, especially beef and pork. Fresh horseradish roots are difficult to obtain so they are dried and ground to a powder, or finely grated and dried. When soaked in cream and vinegar for a little time, the dried, grated horseradish reconstitutes, making a delicious sauce, with both flavor and texture. Use a pinch of fresh or dried grated horseradish, or powdered horseradish, in vegetale juice, seafood cocktails, sour cream dressings, and dips.

HORSERADISH SAUCE

Serves: 4

2 teaspoons dried grated
   horseradish
1 tablespoon white vinegar
$\frac{1}{4}$ teaspoon salt
dash pepper
$\frac{1}{4}$ teaspoon sugar
1 teaspoon French mustard
$\frac{2}{3}$ cup whipped cream

Mix all the ingredients together. Serve chilled.

Note: If using fresh horseradish, use double quantity.

MACE AND NUTMEG

Mace and nutmeg are grouped together because they are both part of one fruit from the same tree, which grows in the Molucca Islands, Ceylon, Sumatra, and Malaya. When ripe, the green fruit splits open revealing the different sections. Beneath the outer covering is a scarlet network or aril, which when dried is known as mace; within this lacy covering is the nutmeg. The flavors of mace and nutmeg are very similar, mace being stronger. Mace may be marketed whole, when it is known as a 'blade' of mace, but more frequently it is ground to a golden powder. Nutmeg is usually ground to a dark, brown powder, but the hard, dried seed may be kept in a small jar and grated when required. Ground nutmeg has long been recognized for its soothing effect on the digestive system. Use mace and nutmeg sprinkled on eggnogs, baked milk puddings, custards, soups, and creamed mushrooms, use with sweet potatoes, carrots, and eggplant, in sauces, cheese dishes, egg dishes, and fish dishes, with game, veal, pork, and lamb, in fruit cakes, and fruit puddings.

NUTMEG BANANA CUSTARD

Serves: 4

2 inches vanilla bean or 1
   teaspoon vanilla extract
2 cups milk
2 egg yolks
1 egg
2 tablespoons sugar
2 tablespoons butter, cut into
   pieces
3 ripe bananas, cut into rings
1 tablespoon nutmeg
whipping cream for serving

Split the vanilla bean and place in a saucepan with the milk. Heat together slowly, then stand on one side just before the milk boils. Remove the vanilla bean. (Alternatively put the vanilla extract into the milk and heat in the same way.) Beat the egg yolks and egg with the sugar, pour a little of the milk onto them, and return to the saucepan. Add the butter. Beat over low heat with a rotary beater until thick. Remove the saucepan from the heat and beat a little longer. Pour into a jug and allow to cool. When cold, pour into a serving dish over the bananas. Chill. Coat with nutmeg and serve with whipped cream.

Variation: Oranges peeled and cut into segments may be used instead of bananas.

DILL SEED AND DILL LEAVES

The dill plant, native to southern Europe, found its way many centuries ago to colder parts and the name we now know it by comes from the Norse word 'dilla' meaning 'to lull'. Dill water, made from boiling down the seeds, was given to babies to soothe them in early Saxon times, as it is today, and occurs in the 10th-century vocabulary of Alfric, Archbishop of Canterbury. Both the fragrant green leaves and the stronger tasting seeds are excellent for cooking. Use chopped green leaves, fresh or dried, to flavor soups, salads, fish, chicken, scrambled eggs, and vegetables. Dill seed is used when preparing dill cucumbers, is sprinkled on breads, rolls, and apple pie, used with veal, pork, and kidneys, and goes well in all cabbage dishes.

DILL, CUCUMBER, AND GRAPE SALAD

1 large cucumber
2 teaspoons salt
$\frac{1}{2}$ lb. seedless green grapes
2 teaspoons dill seeds

1 tablespoon finely chopped
  fresh dill leaves (if available)
$1\frac{1}{4}$ cups sour cream
freshly cracked pepper

Serves: 4-6

Wash the cucumber and slice thinly into a bowl, leaving on the peel; sprinkle with salt. Cover and leave for 30 minutes, then drain off the excess liquid. Pick the washed grapes carefully off the bunch so that there are no stems attached and mix with the cucumber. Add the dill seed, chopped dill leaves, sour cream, pepper, and more salt to taste if necessary. Chill before serving with cold chicken.

FENNEL SEED

Fennel is native to Mediterranean countries, but long ago it was taken to other lands by the Romans and today grows in most parts of the world. Fennel is mentioned in the early Anglo-Saxon herbals, it was regarded as one of the nine sacred herbs. Among its ancient uses was the restoration of eyesight and fennel essence was used 'to make those more lean that are too fat'. There is a tall variety of fennel which grows wild along roadsides; the taste of the leaves is rather strong and not as pleasant as the cultivated plant, Florence fennel, which is smaller, bushier, and has a swollen bulbous stem like celery. All parts of this herb are useful. Slice the broad, greenish-white stems thinly and toss in French dressing, add them to green salads, and serve with cheese. The leaves are traditionally an accompaniment to fish. Fennel seed gives an aromatic taste to pork, liver, and kidneys, it goes into breads and cakes, on top of rolls and fruit pies, and into pickles, chutneys, sauces, salads, cheese mixtures, spreads, and some curry powders.

PEAR AND FENNEL SEED CHUTNEY

$2\frac{1}{2}$ lb. pears
1 green apple
1 lb. onions
2 cups sugar
2 cups white vinegar

1 cup seeded raisins
2 tablespoons fennel seed
1 teaspoon cumin
1 teaspoon salt

Cooking time: 1 hour

Peel, core, and chop the pears and apple and chop the onions. Put all the ingredients into a heavy saucepan and bring to a boil, lower the heat, and simmer until the mixture thickens and is syrupy, about 1 hour. Stir during the cooking to prevent the chutney sticking. Seal in jars when cold.
Variation: Peaches or plums may be used instead of pears.

FENUGREEK

This plant is native to the eastern shores of the Mediterranean, and is also cultivated in India and Africa. The seed of the plant is used in cookery, in the blending of all good curry powders, and in some chutneys and relishes. The seeds are small, hard, and angular, lemon-colored, aromatic, and rather bitter. They have been highly esteemed through the ages by the Egyptians, Greeks, and Romans for medicinal and culinary purposes. In Egypt, the seeds are allowed to sprout, and then eaten.

Gooseberry Balm Sherbet

MINT

Mint is yet another herb native to the Mediterranean, which has been growing naturally for thousands of years in other countries. There are several types of mint varying greatly in appearance and flavor, e.g., applemint, curly mint, eau-de-cologne mint, peppermint, spearmint, and pennyroyal. Applemint is excellent to use along with spearmint; curly mint has rather coarse leaves and tastes very like spearmint, and may be used instead of it; eau-de-cologne mint is delicious in summer drinks and a leaf or two improves herb sandwiches and salads; peppermint has many medicinal qualities which make it highly esteemed for a herb tea. Amongst other virtues, mint was believed by the ancients to prevent the coagulation of milk. Use mint in a sharp sauce for lamb, in a mint jelly, in iced tea, cold summer drinks, fruit salads, and green salad, with peas, eggplant, squash, and new potatoes, and in meat, poultry, or fish dishes when milk, cream, or yogurt is used.

MINT AND GRAPEFRUIT JELLY

1 cup mint leaves
1½ cups grapefruit juice, fresh
   or canned
2 cups sugar
green coloring
1½ oz. pectin powder

Chop the mint leaves, put with the grapefruit juice and sugar into a saucepan, and bring to a boil. Remove from the heat and allow to stand for 10 to 15 minutes with the lid on. Add a few drops of green coloring and the pectin. Return to the heat, stir, and bring to a boil again; boil for 1 minute, stirring all the time. Remove any scum and pour into clean warm jars immediately as the jelly sets very quickly. Keep in the refrigerator and use within 10 days. Serve with hot or cold meat.

ROSEMARY

Rosemary is thought to have originated from the Mediterranean. It is one of the oldest known herbs, and is referred to in the early Saxon herbal, the 'Leech Book of Bald'. There are perhaps more mystical and sacred legends surrounding this herb than any other. Rosemary was believed by the ancients to strengthen the memory, hence the saying 'rosemary for remembrance'. This herb goes into the making of high quality shampoos and hair tonics, the oil from the plant having a stimulating action on the hair roots. Rosemary tea is a good remedy for headaches and indigestion. The vital, pungent flavor of rosemary, either fresh or dried, gives a delicious fragrance to food. A whole sprig may be used to flavor roast or boiled meat, but when mixing rosemary into food, always chop or crumble the spiky leaves first. Use rosemary in liver pâté, pea soup, spinach soup, casseroles, and stews, with boiled or roast lamb, veal, pork, and beef, in white sauce with boiled onions, in many Italian and Greek dishes, and in biscuits.

LAMB SHANKS ROSEMARY

4 lamb shanks
¼ cup all-purpose flour
2 cloves garlic, chopped
1 onion, chopped
1 sweet pepper, chopped
1 tablespoon rosemary, chopped

6 juniper berries, lightly crushed
1 teaspoon black peppercorns
2 teaspoons grated lemon rind
2 tablespoons tomato paste
1⅔ cups dry white wine

Cooking time: 2 hours
Temperature: 300°
Serves: 4

Roll the shanks in flour and place in a casserole with the other ingredients. Cover with the lid and bake in a 300° oven for 2 hours. Add a little water during the cooking if necessary. Serve hot with boiled rice.

364

OREGANO

The wild marjoram, known as oregano, is native to the Mediterranean, and is widely used in cooking in these regions. Oregano grows extremely well in sunny, dry conditions. It does not thrive in colder climates. The plant resembles its relative marjoram, except that the leaves are coarser and far more pungent, and it even looks hardier when growing. Use oregano in tomato dishes, in Italian and Greek dishes, and whenever a robust flavor is desired. It goes well with many vegetables, including eggplant, sweet pepper, zucchini, squash, and onions, and in soups, salads, meatballs, meat loaves, and highly seasoned sauces. It is this herb, with garlic, which goes into Veal Pizzaiola.

VEAL PIZZAIOLA

2 lb. veal steaks
¼ cup oil
1½ lb. tomatoes, skinned and chopped

2-3 cloves garlic, chopped
2 tablespoons chopped oregano
salt and pepper

Cooking time: 1 hour
Serves: 4

Cut the veal into serving portions. Heat the oil in a large skillet, add the veal, tomatoes, garlic, oregano, salt, and pepper, and simmer over medium heat for about 1 hour, or until the veal is tender. Remove the veal from the sauce, keep hot, and simmer the tomato mixture a little longer. Replace the veal in the skillet with the tomatoes to heat through. Serve with the rich sauce poured over the veal steaks.

PAPRIKA

Paprika comes from a red sweet pepper, native to central America and cultivated today in different parts of Europe and the United States. The best paprika pepper is said to come from Hungary. The flavor and color of this mild fragrant pepper varies widely, and after drying, it is ground and sometimes blended with other peppers of the same family differing in degrees of pungency. The highest quality paprika pepper comes from fruit which has been carefully graded, with all stalks and stems removed. A good paprika should be dark red in color (exposure to bright light for some time causes fading) and it should have a warm, pungent scent. The vitamin C content is very high. Paprika pepper is not hot so it may be used quite freely in cooking and for garnishing. Use as a garnish for savories, dips, and spreads, sprinkle on pale-colored salads, stir into cream sauces, cheese dishes, and egg dishes. It goes into Hungarian goulash, veal paprika, chicken paprika, and some fish dishes.

SALMON PAPRIKA

For an entrée, luncheon, or supper dish

¼ cup butter or margarine
6 tablespoons all-purpose flour
1 tablespoon paprika
2½ cups milk
salt and pepper

1 (15 oz.) can red salmon
7 tablespoons dry bread crumbs
extra butter
lemon slices

Cooking time: 15 minutes
Temperature: 350°
Serves: 4

Melt the butter in a saucepan and stir in the flour and paprika. Gradually add the milk, stirring constantly until the sauce has thickened and is smooth. Season to taste with salt and pepper. Drain and flake the fish, discarding the bones, and stir into the sauce. Pour into buttered scallop shells, or a buttered ovenproof dish. Top with the bread crumbs and dot with butter. Brown in a 350° oven for 15 minutes. Serve hot with slices of lemon and Herb Sandwiches (see page 360).

PARSLEY

Parsley has been known all over the world for so many centuries that its origins are obscure; however, most records agree that it first came from Sardinia. There are several varieties, all excellent to grow and use. Curly-leaved parsley sprigs make an attractive garnish for food; Italian parsley, which has a larger, less crinkled leaf, and is a bigger plant, is useful in cooking. Parsley contains iron and vitamin B and is good for kidney and liver ailments. It is said that ancient warriors fed their chariot horses with the leaves. If you have plenty of fresh parsley, fry a large bunch of curly sprays to go with cooked fish. Make a nourishing and delicious parsley soup or parsley jelly to eat with cooked meat. Use parsley, fresh or dried, as a garnish for most dishes, in a bouquet garni for soups, casseroles, and stews, in scrambled egg, mashed potatoes, white sauce, omelets, and pasta dishes, and with creamed brains, fish, poultry, and rabbit.

PARSLEY SOUP

This is an excellent, nourishing soup, rich in vitamins.

1 large bunch parsley	1 onion, chopped	Cooking time: 45-60 minutes
1 lb. potatoes	2 tablespoons salt	Serves: 4-6
½ head lettuce	5 pints water	

Wash the parsley, remove the stems, reserve a little for garnishing, and cut the rest up coarsely. Peel and wash the potatoes; cut into small chunks. Wash the lettuce, discard any discolored leaves, and chop roughly. Put all the ingredients into a large saucepan with the salt and water and bring to a boil. Simmer, covered, for 45 to 60 minutes. Press the soup through a sieve, or purée in a blender. Return to the saucepan to keep hot. Garnish with the reserved parsley, very finely chopped, and serve hot. In summer chill the soup and add a spoonful of cream to each portion.

PEPPER

Pepper, both black and white, is the fruit of a climbing vine, native to the East Indies, and cultivated in India, Sumatra, and Indonesia. The fruit, or berries, are picked when they are red and not quite ripe, then dried, when they become black and wrinkled—these are black peppercorns. For white pepper, the dark outer husk is removed, leaving the light, smooth core, which is milder in flavor. Both white and black pepper may be bought either whole, cracked, or ground to a fine powder. Many people like to grind their own pepper at the table in a pepper mill, using either whole black or white peppercorns. Cracked black or white peppercorns are used for flavoring and garnishing. The ground black pepper is usually kept for flavoring food during cooking, while the ground white pepper is put in shakers for the table. Pepper has been highly prized throughout the centuries for its value as a food preservative, and at times has been used as currency instead of gold or silver. Drop a few whole peppercorns into soups, stews, and casseroles, or when boiling salted pork, mutton, or beef. Use in pickles, spice vinegars, and sauces. Cracked peppercorns give character to steak 'au poivre' (see page 450). Ground pepper is a universal seasoning, and is an ingredient in most curry powders.

PEPPER STEAK WITH ARTICHOKE HEARTS

2 lb. beef tenderloin	2 tablespoons lemon juice	Serves: 4
oil	1 teaspoon French mustard	
2 tablespoons cracked black peppercorns	1 teaspoon tarragon	
coarse salt	salt	
½ cup butter or margarine	1 (7 oz.) can artichoke hearts	

Trim the steak and cut into serving portions. Brush with oil, press the cracked peppercorns into each side, and sprinkle with coarse salt, freshly ground, if possible. (If you cannot buy pepper already cracked, place whole peppercorns between folded wax paper and bang with the blunt side of a steak mallet, or a rolling pin, until the pepper resembles coarse bread crumbs.) Broil the steaks, place in a warm serving dish, and keep warm. Melt the butter, add the lemon juice, French mustard, tarragon, salt to taste, and the artichoke hearts, cut in half. Allow the artichokes to heat through and pour over the steak. Serve hot.

Crab Mousse and Caviar with Herb Sandwiches

TARRAGON

Tarragon is native to Europe and parts of Asia. There are two accepted culinary types, French tarragon and Russian tarragon. The leaves have a delicate, aromatic taste which is prized by cooks because it suits certain food to perfection. Its uses in the kitchen are many, and if the dried leaves are from France, they may even be better, and are certainly equal, in flavor to the fresh herb. Use in Hollandaise, Béarnaise, and Tartar Sauce, also in sour cream sauces, mayonnaise, and French dressing, in chicken stuffing, either with bread crumbs or by itself, fricasseéd chicken, and chicken livers, in egg dishes, fish dishes, and salads.

TARRAGON CHICKEN WITH MUSHROOM

1 roasting chicken, 3-3½ lb.
¼ cup tarragon leaves
salt and pepper

For mushroom gravy:
½ lb. mushrooms
1 tablespoon cornstarch

1¼ cups milk
butter

salt
cayenne pepper

Cooking time: 1¾ hours
Temperature: 350°
Serves: 4

Wash the chicken, put the tarragon leaves into the cavity, and sprinkle with salt and pepper. Place the bird in a saucepan, add the milk, and simmer, covered, for 15 minutes. Remove the chicken carefully and reserve the milk. Place the bird in a roasting pan with a little butter and cover with buttered paper. Bake in a 350° oven for 1½ hours, basting occasionally. When the chicken is cooked, place on a serving dish and keep hot.
To make the mushroom gravy: Wash the mushrooms, peel if necessary, and slice thinly. Place the roasting pan with the chicken drippings over heat, add the mushrooms, and stir until cooked, adding a little more butter if necessary. Pour in the reserved milk, having blended some of it with the cornstarch. Add the blended cornstarch, bring to a boil stirring continuously, and flavor with salt and cayenne pepper. Serve hot in a sauce boat with the chicken.

SESAME SEED

These small, pearly seeds come from the pod of a herb grown in many parts of the world. The sesame plant is thought to have originated in Afghanistan. Cleopatra used rich sesame oil as a skin food. The oil has been used in medicine, for light, and in food. The most famous association is probably with Ali Baba's magic words: 'Open sesame!' A cream made from the seeds goes into halva, a delicious confection made popular by Greek, Egyptian, and Syrian people. Nourishing sesame meal, made from the ground seed, is excellent for vegetarian diets. The flavor of sesame seed is brought out when cooked, so sprinkle on cookies or a sauce dish before baking, mix into a dough before rolling out, and fry seeds lightly in butter, or dry fry until colored, before mixing into mashed potato, a tossed salad, or a fruit salad. Sprinkle browned seeds on cooked fish and creamed chicken.

FROSTED SESAME MELON

1 honeydew melon
1 cup cottage cheese
1 tablespoon honey
1 teaspoon lemon juice
¼ cup sesame seeds

1 egg white
⅔-¾ cup shredded coconut
scented geranium leaves (if
    available) or lettuce leaves

Serves: 4-6

Peel the melon, slice off the top, and scoop out the seeds. In a mixing bowl blend together until creamy the cottage cheese, honey, and lemon juice. Toast the sesame seeds in a dry skillet over gentle heat, tossing until golden brown. Stir into the cheese mixture, then press into the melon cavity and secure the top with wooden toothpicks.
With a pastry brush, coat the melon all over with lightly beaten egg white, then carefully roll in the coconut until the melon is frosted all over. Chill in the refrigerator. To serve, cut the melon into rings and place each one on a large, scented geranium leaf, or a lettuce leaf.

THYME

Thyme originally came from Mediterranean countries. There are numerous varieties flourishing in a wild state, all with a fragrant perfume. Although it might look scraggy, thyme has more scent and grows better in harsh, hot conditions on rocky ground. The name 'thyme' is said to have come from the Greek 'thumus', 'courage', and the herb was regarded as an emblem of bravery for centuries. Thyme has many curative properties, having been used as a remedy for whooping cough, colic, and fever. Garden thyme is the species most often used in flavoring; it goes with sage and marjoram in mixed herbs, and with a bay leaf, marjoram, and parsley makes a bouquet garni. Use thyme in soups, with onions, zucchini, and beans, in stuffed eggplant and sweet peppers, with lamb, beef, pork, veal, liver, and sauces, in poultry stuffings, with fish and shellfish, in cheese dishes, and in herb dumplings.

CRAB MOUSSE AND CAVIAR

$1\frac{1}{4}$ cups mayonnaise
$1\frac{1}{4}$ cups whipping cream
1 tablespoon thyme
salt
dash cayenne pepper
1 lb. crab meat

2 tablespoons boiling water
1 envelope gelatin
$\frac{1}{4}$ cup red or black caviar
sprays of fresh herbs
lettuce or endive leaves

Serves: 4

Blended the mayonnaise (see page 55) and cream together in a mixing bowl and add the thyme, salt, and cayenne pepper. Flank the crab meat and fold into the other ingredients. Pour the boiling water onto the gelatin, stir until clear, and combine with the crab mixture. Pour into a mold previously rinsed with cold water. Chill in the refrigerator until set. Unmold onto a serving plate, place the caviar on top of the mousse, and surround with sprays of fresh herbs, including thyme, or with salad greens. Serve with Herb Sandwiches (see page 360).

VANILLA BEAN

This strongly-scented bean comes from a climbing orchid native to central America. The golden flowers eventually turn to seed pods about 6 inches long, which, when dried, are black and shiny like licorice, and thin and flat like green beans. There are liquid synthetic extracts on the market which smell very like the true vanilla extract, but there is really nothing quite as delicious as the rich, penetrating perfume of vanilla beans. Only a little is needed for flavoring. Cut 2 inches off the bean, slit down the center, and infuse in hot milk or cream for a few minutes. Remove the bean and use the liquid in ice cream, cold milk puddings, or cake mixtures. When making a baked milk pudding, put the bean in during the cooking time and remove later. The piece of vanilla bean may be used two or three times. After use, wash and store in a lidded container, such as a sugar canister where it remains dry and clean and scents the sugar.

VANILLA CREAMED RICE PUDDING

2 tablespoons short-grain rice
$2\frac{1}{2}$ cups milk
1 tablespoon sugar

1 teaspoon butter
2 inches vanilla bean
2 teaspoons nutmeg

Cooking time: $2\text{-}2\frac{1}{2}$ hours
Temperature: 300°
Serves: 4

Stir the rice, milk, and sugar together in a buttered oven-proof dish. Add the vanilla bean. Sprinkle the top with nutmeg. Place on the middle shelf of a 300° oven and cook for 2 to $2\frac{1}{2}$ hours. Stir the pudding gently once or twice during the cooking, slipping a spoon under the skin to do so. Serve hot or cold. When serving cold, remove the skin and sprinkle the top with sugar and more nutmeg. When convenient, take out the vanilla bean, wash and dry it, and store in a jar of sugar until used again.

FAMILY FARE

Joyce Allen

Joyce Allen is the cookery editor for an Australian daily newspaper. She has a Home Science Teachers Certificate. Her experience in industry and in planning food programs, combined with her role as wife and mother, gives her an understanding of the problems of the home-maker seeking to provide appetizing, balanced family meals on a limited income.

This chapter is planned for those who run a home and cook for a family. Good eating is one of the most important features of daily family life. Every mother likes to gather her family around an attractive table to enjoy a delicious meal. However, the art of cooking for a family requires a little care and thought. The task of working out daily menus for the family should not be confusing for the housewife. She has to keep in mind all the time the foods that are actually available and in season, the foods that are essential to the health of her family, the food her family likes, and the money she has to spend.

In selecting and testing recipes for Family Fare I have chosen a selection of simply prepared dishes, both meat dishes and desserts, which provide delicious food for the family meal. Many of the recipes are basic family favorites with the addition of a few interesting ingredients to give you some new, exciting ideas. I have tried to use ingredients that are readily available on most kitchen shelves. Some of the recipes are economical for the budget-minded housewife. I have also included some light tasty dishes which are ideal to serve for weekend family lunches or suppers, and many of these dishes can be prepared in advance. A few recipes are for special family occasions when you may have some visitors to join your family meal. Many of the dishes can also be served at a special luncheon when you have to prepare something ahead, with a minimum of last-minute fuss.

FAMILY MENUS

The housewife has to plan and serve a well-balanced diet, according to the likes and dislikes of her family. A great deal can be accomplished with a little though and roundabout methods. For instance, vegetables which are refused by the children may be eaten with enjoyment when they form part of a soup or broth, or are served in a salad. Milk which is refused as a drink may be enjoyed in a dessert.

The home-maker must also think about the color and texture of the food she serves to her family. Appearance counts a good deal in the enjoyment of a good meal. For example, steamed fish, boiled potatoes, and haricot beans have an unappetizing off-white color-scheme, but if the same fish is broiled and served with creamed potatoes and green peas or tomatoes, it will have a very different appeal. The following are some suggested menus for family meals for the four seasons of the year. I hope these plans give you lots of ideas for family meals and help you to plan your shopping list.

Tasty Roast Beef, Potatoes, Pumpkin, and Brussels Sprouts

371

Spring Menus

SUNDAY	MONDAY	TUESDAY	WEDNESDAY	THURSDAY	FRIDAY	SATURDAY
Tasty Roast Beef Potatoes Pumpkin Brussels Sprouts Refrigerator Cheesecake	Ham Slices with Cheese Topping Potatoes Corn Tomatoes Normandy Apple Flan	Sweet and Sour Veal Rice Zucchini Lemon Foam Dessert	Boiled Ham with Cabbage New Potatoes Lima or Fava Quick Cherry Strudel	Baked Shanks Potatoes Cauliflower Beans Pineapple Flummery	Macaroni and Fish Pie Green Beans Tomatoes Fresh Fruit	Pea Soup Spanish Omelet Green Salad Cheese
Delicious Crumbed Chicken with Cream Sauce Peas New Potatoes Latticed Chocolate Rum Pie	Lamb Fry and Bacon Potatoes Tomatoes Beans Nut Pancakes	Barbecued Pork Chops Potatoes Peas Fresh Fruit	Fricassée of Veal with Mushrooms Potatoes Tomatoes Green Salad Grape Flan	Spaghetti Bolognese Green Salad Dutch Apple Cake	Sea Trout Meunière French Fried Tomatoes Quick Flummery	Scotch Eggs Tomato Sauce Potatoes Green Salad Cheese
Rack of Lamb Potatoes Spinach Peas Pavlova	Haricot Stew French Fried Potatoes Green Salad Cheese Fresh Fruit	Pork Chop Suey Rice Fruit Salad Ice Cream	Braised Lamb Tongues Potatoes Tomatoes Spinach Gooseberry Balm Sherbet	Savory Stew Potatoes Carrots Peas Caramel Queen Pudding	Tuna Salad New Potatoes Pineapple Delight	Ham and Onion Flan Green Salad Fresh Fruit
Roast Stuffed Breast of Veal Potatoes Beans Apricot Gelato	Satay Carrots Lima or Fava Beans Stewed Fruit Ice Cream	Pork Casserole with Herb Biscuit Topping Red Cabbage Nutmeg Banana Custard	Nutty Meatballs with Noodles Green Salad Lemon Delicious Pudding	Sauté of Kidney Rice Zucchini Peach Prune Cobbler	Seashore Créole Rice Peas Cheese	Egg and Potato Pie Peas Tomatoes Fresh Fruit

Summer Menus

SUNDAY	MONDAY	TUESDAY	WEDNESDAY	THURSDAY	FRIDAY	SATURDAY
Stuffed Fresh Pork Arm Roast Potatoes Pumpkin Peas Delicious Ice Cream	Fricassée of Pork Potatoes Onions Beans Almond Toffee Sundae	Brawn New Potatoes Tomatoes Green Salad Pain Perdu	Mixed Grill Potatoes Cauliflower Vanity Prune Whip	Sweet and Sour Pork Rice Peas Zucchini Apricot Flan	Crunchy Cod Fingers French Fried Potatoes Tomatoes Ripple Ice Cream	Scalloped Corn and Carrots Green Salad Fresh Fruit
Roast Loin of Veal Potatoes Carrots Green Salad Orange Angel Pie	Savory Meatballs Spaghetti Tomato Sauce Ice Cream	Delicious Lamb Chops New Potatoes Peas Strawberry Flummery	Kromeskies Rice Tomatoes Coleslaw Caramel Custard	Liver Loaf Green Salad Sherried Apricots with Almonds	Savory Poached Fish Green Salad Rice Tropical	Chicken and Grape Salad French Fried Potatoes Fruit Salad
Marinated Roast Lamb Potatoes Peas Zucchini Summer Berry Pudding	Cold Lamb French Fried Potatoes Green Salad Speedy Coffee Cream	Meat Loaf Green Salad Ice Cream with Caramel Sauce	Beef Curry Rice Khoshav	Lamb Leg Steaks with Apricots Potatoes Ratatouille Eggnog Pie	Smoked Fish Salad Stewed Fruit Custard	Parsley Soup Scrambled Egg Fresh Fruit
Roast Chicken Potatoes Peas Carrots Paradise Chiffon Pie	Chicken and Orange Kebabs Potatoes Green Salad Berry Frost	Sweet Pepper Salad Garlic Bread Melon with Ice Cream	Dolmades Rice Strawberry Snow	Beef Tongue in Raisin Sauce Sweet Potatoes Peas Chocolate Ice Cream Roll	Soused Trout Green Salad Tangy Fruit Marshmallow	Corn and Ham Flan French Fried Potatoes Tomatoes Fresh Fruit

Fall Menus

SUNDAY	MONDAY	TUESDAY	WEDNESDAY	THURSDAY	FRIDAY	SATURDAY
Roast Leg of Lamb Potatoes Quinces Beans Loganberry Soufflé	Savory Pancake Tomatoes Stewed Fruit	Pork and Paprika Casserole Rice Brococoli Caramel Queen Pudding	Ground Beef and Noodle Casserole Green Salad Lemon Marshmallow Fruit Salad	Chicken with Mushrooms Potatoes Beans Lemon Ice	Herb Baked Trout Potatoes Peas Tomatoes Apple and Lemon Crunch	Creamed Corn Ham 'n' Eggs Garlic Bread Green Salad Fresh Fruit
Roast Leg of Pork Applesauce Potatoes Carrots Peas Lemon Meringue Pie	Cock-a-Leekie Apple and Allspice Pie Cheese	Lamb Kebabs Banana Rice Apricot and Orange Pancakes	Veal and Ham Pie Potatoes Onions Spinach Quick Mix Steamed Pudding	Brown Stew Potatoes Pumpkin Cauliflower Pears with Sour Cream	Oyster Stuffed Sole Potatoes Tomatoes Upside-down Pudding	Minestrone Soup Cheese SoufflF Green Salad Fresh Fruit
Roast Beef Potatoes Pumpkin Cauliflower Apple Pie	Moussaka Rice Stewed Fruit	Rabbit with Prunes and Pine Nuts Potatoes Zucchini Instant Creamy Mincemeat Pie	Fried Rice with Chicken Tomatoes Apricot Gelato	Pickled Pork with Sautéed Potatoes Cabbage Carrots Pineapple Sherbet	Grilled Whiting Tartar Sauce French Fried Potatoes Green Salad Bakewell Tart	Pumpkin Soup Egg, Bacon, and Pea Pie Tomatoes Fresh Fruit
Roast Leg of Lamb Potatoes Parsnips Spinach Caramel Custard	Rice Patties Tomatoes Zucchini Apricot Cream	Crumbed Lamb Chops Potatoes Eggplant Sago Cream Fluff	Beef Olives Potatoes Parsnips Carrots Apple Pie	Lasagne Green Salad Chocolate Mousse	Sweet and Sour Tuna Rice Stewed Fruit	Hamburgers French Fried Potatoes Green Salad Cheese Fresh Fruit

Winter Menus

SUNDAY	MONDAY	TUESDAY	WEDNESDAY	THURSDAY	FRIDAY	SATURDAY
Crown Roast of Pork Applesauce Potatoes Broccoli Pumpkin Black-Eyed Susan Pie	Bortsch Gingerbread Pears Cheese	Favorite Meat Pie Potatoes Glazed Carrots Pineapple Sherbet	Rabbit with Tarragon Potatoes Onions Beans Mince Roly-Poly	Osso Bucco Rice Pilaff Crunchy Rhubarb and Apple	Deep Fried Mullet Tartar Sauce Potatoes Carrots Crusted Pineapple Slices	Vegetable Broth Bacon and Cheese Pie Coleslaw Fresh Fruit
Pot Roast Stuffed Steak Potatoes Carrots Brussels Sprouts Baked Cheesecake	Lamb Stew Potatoes Broccoli All-in-Together Pudding	Devilled Meatballs on Noodles Green Salad Baked Apple Dumplings	Stuffed Hearts Potatoes Cabbage Caramel Sponge Dessert	Steak and Kidney Pie Potatoes Beans Vanilla Creamed Rice Pudding	Baked Snapper Potatoes Carrots Peas Upside-Down Pudding	Cream of Lentil Soup Quiche Lorraine Fresh Fruit
Roast Leg of Lamb Potatoes Cabbage Carrots Coconut Fruit Pie	Satay Rice Tomatoes Chocolate Cherry Ring	Grilled Lamb Chops Potatoes Cabbage Apple Amber	Curried Steak Rice Beans Fresh Fruit	Boiled Beef Potatoes Carrots Blackberry and Apple Pudding	Braised Fish Potatoes Tomatoes Celery Plum Pudding	Potato Soup Cheese and Tomato Flan Stewed Fruit
Standing Rib Roast of Beef Yorkshire Pudding Potatoes Brussels Sprouts Chocolate Pudding with Chocolate Sauce	Moussaka Rice Stewed Fruit	Steak with Prunes Potatoes Broccoli Golden Pumpkin Pie	Veal Goulash Noodles Broccoli Apple and Honey Pancake Gâteau	Kidneys Sauté Potatoes Carrots Peas Turnips Raspberry Fool	Tomato Soup Broiled Mullet Potatoes Beans Lemon Delicious Pudding Honeyed Rice Bake	Cream of Carrot Soup Packaged Chops Coleslaw Cheese Fresh Fruit

POTATO SOUP

¼ cup drippings or lard
2 lb. potatoes, peeled and sliced
2 onions, chopped
2 stalks celery, chopped
5 cups chicken stock or water

and chicken bouillon cubes
bouquet garni
⅔ cup milk
salt and pepper
grated nutmeg

Cooking time: 45-50 minutes
Serves: 4-6

Melt the drippings in a large heavy saucepan. Add the potatoes, onions, and celery. Put a lid on the pan and cook over low heat for 10 minutes, shaking the pan gently occasionally. Heat the stock until boiling; add to the vegetables with the bouquet garni. Simmer gently for about 30 minutes, until the vegetables are tender.

Remove the bouquet garni, cool, and rub through a sieve or purée in a blender. Return the purée to a clean saucepan, reheat, and add the milk, salt, pepper, and nutmeg to taste. Serve hot.
Variation: For Cream of Potato Soup, use cream instead of milk.

VEGETABLE BROTH

3 tablespoons butter
1 carrot, chopped
1 onion, chopped
1 parsnip, chopped
2 stalks celery, chopped

¼ cup all-purpose flour
5 cups beef stock or water and
  beef bouillon cubes
chopped parsley

Cooking time: 40 minutes
Serves: 6

Melt the butter in a large saucepan. Add the vegetables and fry lightly without browning. Sprinkle with the flour and cook, stirring constantly, until the flour is lightly browned. Add the stock and simmer gently for 30 minutes. Sprinkle with chopped parsley before serving.

TASTY ROAST BEEF

2 teaspoons instant coffee
  powder
2 teaspoons dry mustard
¼ cup all-purpose flour
1 teaspoon salt

¼ teaspoon black pepper
1 teaspoon brown sugar
3-4 lb. rolled rib of beef
drippings
vegetables

Cooking time: 1½-2 hours
Temperature: 400°
  reducing to 350°
Serves: 6

Mix together the coffee, mustard, flour, salt, pepper, and brown sugar and rub all over the meat, using a skewer to force some down into the center of the joint. Heat the drippings in a roasting pan, put the meat in, and place in a 400° oven to sear the outside. Turn after 5 minutes. Reduce the heat to 350° and roast until cooked to taste, basting occasionally.

Parboil the potatoes and pumpkin, etc., for 10 minutes, drain well, and place around the roast beef 45 minutes before the end of the cooking time. When the meat is cooked, place on a heated serving dish and keep warm. Drain the vegetables on absorbent paper towels and keep them warm. Drain off the drippings and make the gravy (see page 52). Serve the roast beef with gravy, roast vegetables, and a green vegetable.
Note: If quinces are in season, they make a delicious accompaniment to roast beef. Peel, core, and slice into the same size as the other vegetables to be roasted. Parboil, drain well, and roast with the meat, turning once or twice to brown evenly.

Rack of Lamb

CURRIED STEAK

2 lb. chuck steak
walnut-sized piece ginger root
1 large cooking apple
$\frac{1}{4}$ cup oil
1 large onion, chopped
1 clove garlic, crushed (optional)
1 cup sliced celery
1 cup carrot rings
2 tablespoons brown sugar
2 tablespoons curry powder

2 teaspoons salt
$\frac{1}{4}$ teaspoon pepper
1 cup beef stock or water and
  beef bouillon cube
2 tablespoons lemon juice
finely grated rind of 1 lemon
3 cloves
$\frac{1}{2}$-1 cup seedless white raisins
$\frac{1}{4}$ cup cornstarch

Cooking time: 2$\frac{1}{2}$ hours
Serves: 5-6

Cut the meat into 1- to 1$\frac{1}{2}$-inch cubes. Chop the ginger finely. Peel, core, and chop the apple. Heat the oil in a large saucepan, add the prepared vegetables and sugar, and sauté until browned. Add the curry powder, salt, and pepper, sauté for a few minutes, and add the prepared meat, stock, lemon juice, rind, and cloves. Cover and bring to the boiling point. Reduce the heat and simmer gently for 2 hours. Add the washed raisins and continue to cook slowly until the meat is tender, about 30 minutes longer. Taste and adjust the flavor. Blend the cornstarch to a smooth paste with a little cold water, add to the curry, and stir gently until thickened. Serve the curry with boiled rice.

STEAK WITH PRUNES

This is one of those valuable dishes that can be prepared early in the day, then just placed in the oven to bake when required. Good for family fare or for entertaining.

2 lb. chuck steak
$\frac{1}{4}$ cup all-purpose flour
2 teaspoons salt
freshly cracked pepper
2 tablespoons brown sugar
1$\frac{1}{3}$ cups prunes

1 large onion, finely chopped
2 teaspoons soy sauce
2 tablespoons vinegar
2 tablespoons meat or fruit sauce
$\frac{3}{4}$ cup water

Cooking time: 2 hours
Temperature: 325°
Serves: 5-6

Cut the steak into 1-inch pieces. Mix the flour, salt, pepper, and sugar in a clean paper bag, add the meat, and shake together until coated. Pit the prunes. Place layers of meat, onions, and prunes in a casserole, finishing with meat. Mix the soy sauce, vinegar, meat or fruit sauce, and water and pour over the contents of the casserole. Cover with a piece of aluminum foil, then a lid. Bake in a 325° oven for 2 hours, or until cooked.

VEAL GOULASH

2 lb. veal shoulder
1 tablespoon paprika pepper
2 teaspoons salt
$\frac{1}{4}$ teaspoon pepper
$\frac{1}{4}$ cup cornstarch
$\frac{1}{4}$ cup oil
2 large onions, chopped
1 teaspoon sugar

2 large tomatoes, skinned and
  chopped
$\frac{1}{2}$ teaspoon chili powder
$\frac{1}{2}$ teaspoon caraway seeds
  (optional)
bouquet garni
1 large red sweet pepper
monosodium glutamate

Cooking time: 2 hours
Serves: 5-6

Cut the veal into 1-inch cubes. In a clean paper bag, mix the paprika pepper, salt, pepper, and cornstarch. Add the veal and shake together until coated. Heat the oil in a large saucepan, sauté the veal until browned, cooking in 2 or 3 lots, then remove. Add the onions, sprinkle with the sugar, and fry gently until golden brown. Add the tomatoes, chili powder, and caraway seeds. Stir in the meat; add the bouquet garni. Cover and simmer gently over low heat until cooked, about 2 hours. Add the chopped, seeded red sweet pepper and a shake of monosodium glutamate during the last 30 minutes. Remove the bouquet garni. Taste and adjust the flavor if necessary, before serving.

Note: The tomatoes usually add sufficient liquid for cooking, but if necessary a little water may be added—but not too much.

SWEET AND SOUR VEAL

Serves: 5-6

2 lb. veal steak or boned veal
   shoulder
1 teaspoon monosodium
   glutamate
1 teaspoon paprika pepper
2 tablespoons sherry

$\frac{1}{4}$ cup cornstarch
$\frac{1}{4}$ cup all-purpose flour
salt and pepper
2 eggs
oil for frying

For sauce:
1$\frac{1}{2}$ cups water
2 chicken bouillon cubes
walnut-sized piece ginger root
$\frac{1}{2}$ cup pineapple syrup
$\frac{3}{4}$ cup vinegar
$\frac{3}{4}$ cup brown sugar
2 tablespoons soy sauce
freshly cracked pepper

salt
2 stalks celery
1 large red sweet pepper
1 cup carrot strips
6 scallions
1 (15 oz.) can pineapple pieces
$\frac{1}{4}$ cup cornstarch

Cut the veal into 1-inch cubes. Place in a large mixing bowl and sprinkle with the monosodium glutamate, paprika pepper, and sherry. Cover and leave to stand for 30 minutes, turning over a couple of times. Sift the cornstarch, flour, salt, and pepper into a mixing bowl. Break the eggs into a well in the center and mix in the flour, beating to a smooth batter. Dip pieces of the veal in the batter, drain against the side of the bowl, and deep fry in hot oil until cooked and browned. Continue until all the veal is cooked and keep warm.

To make the sauce: Put the water and bouillon cubes in a large skillet or saucepan. Add the ginger, peeled and finely chopped, pineapple syrup (drained from the pineapple pieces), vinegar, brown sugar, soy sauce, pepper, and salt. Simmer for 10 minutes. Taste and adjust the flavor if necessary. Add the veal and simmer for 15 minutes. Prepare the vegetables. Strip the celery and slice diagonally into $\frac{1}{4}$-inch slices. Remove the seeds from the pepper and cut it into strips. Scrape the carrot, cut into strips, parboil for a few minutes, and drain. Strip the scallions and slice into $\frac{1}{2}$-inch pieces. Cut the drained pineapple pieces in half. Add the vegetables and pineapple to the veal, increase the heat, cover, and cook until thoroughly hot, stirring occasionally. Add the cornstarch blended to a smooth paste with a little cold water. Stir until thickened. Serve with boiled rice.

Note: Pork may be substituted for the veal, or use half veal and half pork. When frying pork, cook until nearly tender, then reheat the oil and fry for a few more minutes until crisp.

PORK CHOP SUEY

Serves: 5-6

2 lb. pork
dash oil
monosodium glutamate
1 large green or red sweet
   pepper
2 stalks celery
6 scallions
2-3 cups button mushrooms

$\frac{1}{4}$ cup cornstarch
2 teaspoons soy sauce
2 tablespoons vinegar
1 teaspoon brown sugar
freshly cracked pepper
2 cups chicken stock or water
   and chicken bouillon cube

Cut the pork evenly into $\frac{3}{4}$-inch pieces. Heat a little oil in a skillet, add half the pork, fry until cooked and brown, remove, add the remaining pork, and cook in the same way. Place the cooked pork in a large mixing bowl, sprinkle with monosodium glutamate, toss together, cover, and leave. Prepare the vegetables. Remove the seeds from the pepper and cut it into slivers, slice the celery diagonally, and strip and chop the scallions. Wash and drain the mushrooms, peel if necessary, and slice vertically, making them into little 'umbrellas'. Pour $\frac{1}{4}$ cup oil into the skillet, add the prepared pepper, celery, and scallions, sauté until they steam well, add the prepared mushrooms, continue to cook only until thoroughly heated, and remove from the skillet. Blend the cornstarch with the soy sauce, vinegar, sugar, pepper, and stock, add to the skillet, and stir until boiled and thickened. Taste and adjust the flavor as liked. Add the pork, cover, and simmer for about 15 minutes. Increase the heat, add the vegetables, and heat only until very hot, gently mixing together as they heat. Serve with boiled rice.

BARBECUED PORK CHOPS

5 pork loin chops
2 tablespoons vinegar
$\frac{1}{4}$ cup tomato catsup
$\frac{1}{4}$ cup thick fruit or meat sauce
2 teaspoons soy sauce

$\frac{1}{4}$ cup oil
1 large onion, chopped
2 tablespoons brown sugar
2 tablespoons cornstarch
$\frac{3}{4}$ cup water

Cooking time: 45 minutes
Serves: 5

Place the chops in a shallow dish. Mix together the vinegar, tomato catsup, thick fruit or meat sauce, and soy sauce and spoon over the chops. Cover, and leave in the refrigerator for 2 to 3 hours. Heat the oil in a large skillet, add the onion and brown sugar, and fry until browned.

Stir in the cornstarch and add the water, chops, and liquid (marinade) from the dish. Cover and simmer until the chops are tender, about 45 minutes, turning and basting occasionally. Take care that the liquid does not evaporate too much; if necessary add a little more water.

CRUMBED LAMB CHOPS

4 or 8 rib chops
$\frac{1}{4}$ cup all-purpose flour
1 teaspoon salt
$\frac{1}{4}$ teaspoon pepper

$\frac{1}{2}$ teaspoon cinnamon
1 egg
fine dry bread crumbs

Cooking time: 40 minutes
Temperature: 375°
Serves: 4

Filling 1:
canned paste such as devilled
  ham, chicken and veal, liver
  sausage, etc.

Filling 2:
1$\frac{1}{2}$ cups soft bread crumbs
$\frac{1}{4}$ cup grated onion
$\frac{1}{4}$ cup tomato sauce or catsup

2 tablespoons chopped parsley
salt and pepper
grated lemon rind

Filling 3:
prepared mustard

chopped cooked ham

Remove any excess gristle and fat from the chops. Using a sharp knife, cut a pocket in each chop. Spread the inside with the selected filling:
1. Spread the selected paste inside each pocket.
2. Mix the bread crumbs with the onion, tomato sauce, parsley, pepper, salt, and lemon rind. Add a little more sauce if necessary just to bind together. Divide the stuffing among the chops and spread inside the pockets.
3. Spread the inside of the pockets thinly with the prepared mustard and cover with chopped ham.

When the chops are filled, press the edges together. Mix together the flour, salt, pepper, and cinnamon. Dip the chops into the seasoned flour, then into beaten egg, then in crumbs, pressing the crumbs firmly on with a knife. Bake or fry the chops until cooked.

To bake the chops: Heat 6 tablespoons butter or oil in a baking dish. Arrange the chops in the dish and bake in a 375° oven, turning once, for about 40 minutes or until cooked.

To fry the chops: Shallow fry in heated oil until cooked, turning once. Drain them on paper towels before serving.

A tasty sauce to serve with the chops is gravy (see page 52), with a little sherry and finely chopped cooked ham added just before serving.

Boiled Beef

DELICIOUS LAMB CHOPS

4 boneless lamb shoulder chops,
  cut thickly
1 onion, finely chopped
½ cup black currant jelly

finely grated rind and juice of
  1 lemon
2 tablespoons meat or fruit sauce
2 tablespoons tomato catsup
½ cup water

Cooking time: 30-40 minutes
Serves: 4

Cut the fat around the chops in a few places. Heat the skillet, add the chops, and cook until well browned on both sides, turning frequently. Remove from the skillet. Sauté the onion until lightly browned. Add the black currant jelly, lemon rind and juice, sauces, and water. Heat until blended, then replace the chops. Cover and simmer until cooked, about 30 to 40 minutes, turning once or twice. If the sauce is not thick enough, uncover during the last 10 minutes of the cooking time.

LAMB KEBABS

1 4-lb. leg of lamb, boned
¼ cup tomato sauce
¼ cup thick meat or fruit sauce
2 tablespoons vinegar
2 tablespoons soy sauce

2 tablespoons oil
2 tablespoons brown sugar
juice of 1 onion
freshly cracked pepper
3 bacon slices

Serves: 6

Cut the lamb into 1-inch cubes. Mix together the remaining ingredients except the bacon. Put the lamb in a dish with a lid, pour the mixed sauces over, and mix together so all the pieces of meat are coated. Leave for at least 4 hours in the refrigerator. This tenderizes the lamb and also gives it a delicious flavor. Cut the bacon into 1-inch pieces. Spear the lamb cubes onto skewers, putting a piece of bacon between each. Heat the broiler and broil the kebabs until they are cooked, turning frequently.
Variations: Spear a selection of vegetables onto skewers and broil with the lamb. Try tomato quarters, pineapple wedges, small onions, mushrooms, or corn cobs boiled, then cut into 1-inch rings and speared on skewers. Brush the vegetables with melted butter before broiling.
Note: The quantity of lamb on a whole leg will be too much for 6 people. Spear the quantity required for kebabs and put the remainder back into the refrigerator in the marinade. For the next night's meal, add sufficient lamb chops and bake slowly in the oven for a delicious casserole.

CRUMBED CHICKEN WITH CREAM SAUCE

8-10 chicken pieces
dash monosodium glutamate
freshly cracked pepper

For sauce:
½ cup dry white wine
1 onion, chopped
1 sprig each sage, marjoram,
  thyme
6 peppercorns

⅔ cup sour cream
6 tablespoons butter
2 cups fine dry bread crumbs

3 scallions, sliced
1 bay leaf
strip lemon rind
⅔ cup sour cream
monosodium glutamate

Cooking time: 40-50 minutes
Temperature: 375°
Serves: 5

Rinse the chicken pieces and dry with paper towels. Sprinkle with monosodium glutamate and pepper. Arrange the pieces in a single layer in a shallow dish. Spread with sour cream. Cover and refrigerate for at least 4 to 5 hours (over night if possible), turning once or twice and brushing the cream evenly over the pieces. Mix the melted butter with the bread crumbs. Dip the chicken pieces in the crumbs, making sure they are well coated. Arrange in an ovenproof dish and cover with buttered aluminum foil. Bake in a 375° oven until cooked and golden brown, about 40 to 50 minutes, turning once during the cooking time. Serve the crumbed chicken with Cream Sauce (optional).
To make the sauce: Put the wine in a small saucepan and add the onion, washed herbs, peppercorns, scallions, bay leaf, and lemon rind. Cover, bring to a boil and simmer gently for 5 minutes. Uncover, increase the heat, and boil until reduced by half. Strain and return to a clean saucepan. Stir in the sour cream and a good shake of monosodium glutamate. Taste and add more salt and pepper if necessary. Heat gently without boiling and serve with the chicken.

CHICKEN WITH MUSHROOMS

This is an excellent dish to choose when it is necessary to prepare a meal the day before. The chicken may be cooked and the stock prepared and chilled. The final preparation will then take only a short time just before cooking.

1 stewing chicken, 3-3½ lb.
1 large onion, chopped
1 bay leaf
bouquet garni
6 peppercorns
2 teaspoons salt

2 cups mushrooms
¼ cup fat from the stock
6 tablespoons all-purpose flour
2 cups chicken stock
salt and pepper

Cooking time: 2 hours 40 minutes
Temperature: 325°
Serves: 5-6

Cook the chicken for 1½ hours or until tender in water to cover, with the onion, bay leaf, bouquet garni, peppercorns, and salt. When cooked, remove the chicken and cool until it can be handled. Remove the flesh from the bones, replace the bones in the saucepan, and boil for 30 minutes longer. Strain the stock and cool by standing in a bowl of ice so the fat will set on top. Cut the chicken into neat pieces. Wash and drain the mushrooms. If necessary peel. If large, break off the stems. Slice the mushrooms vertically to form 'umbrellas'. If the stems are removed, cut into ½-inch pieces. Remove the chicken fat from the top of the stock and heat ¼ cup in a saucepan. Stir in the flour, cook for 1 minute, add the stock, and stir until it boils and thickens. Add salt and pepper to taste. Arrange layers of chicken, mushrooms, and sauce in an ovenproof dish. Cover and bake in a 325° oven for about 40 minutes.

FRIED RICE WITH CHICKEN

1 chicken, 2½-3 lb.
1 large onion, chopped
bouquet garni
6 peppercorns
2 teaspoons salt
2 slices bacon
¼ cup butter
1¼ cups rice
½ cup vermicelli

2 eggs
freshly cracked black pepper
2½ cups chicken stock
1 cup chopped celery
1 large red sweet pepper, chopped
6 scallions
soy sauce (optional)

Cooking time: Chicken: 1½ hours
Rice: 25 minutes
Serves: 5-6

Wash the chicken, place in a saucepan, and add warm water barely to cover. Add the onion, bouquet garni, peppercorns, and salt, cover, and cook gently until tender, about 1½ hours. Remove the chicken and allow to cool. Remove the flesh from the bones, replace the bones in the stock, and boil for 15 minutes with the lid off. Strain the stock and measure 2½ cups. Cut the bacon into 1-inch pieces, place in a large saucepan with the butter, and heat until the butter melts. Add the rice and vermicelli and sauté until browned. Push the rice to one side. Tilt the pan and add the eggs beaten with salt and pepper. Cook until set, then remove, cut into strips, and reserve. Add the chicken stock to the rice. Cover and boil until just cooked, about 15 minutes (do not overcook). Add the celery, red pepper, scallions, chicken, and egg. Taste and adjust the flavor if necessary. Add a little soy sauce to taste if desired. Cover and heat through, occasionally turning the ingredients over with a turner.

CREAMED CORN, HAM, 'N' EGGS

½ cup butter
1 large onion, finely chopped
1 (1 lb.) can creamed corn
¼-½ lb. cooked ham

3-4 eggs, hard-cooked
3 slices bread
2 tablespoons oil

Cooking time: 20 minutes
Temperature: 350°
Serves: 4-5

Melt half the butter, sauté the onion until cooked but not browned, and add the corn. Cut the ham into small pieces; slice the eggs and add to the corn. Lightly fold together so the eggs are not broken too much. Place in buttered ovenproof individual serving dishes, or one large dish. Cover with a lid or aluminum foil and heat in a 350° oven for 20 minutes. Prepare croûtons from the bread and fry in oil and the remaining butter: drain well. Sprinkle the croûtons over the corn, ham, and eggs before serving.

FAVORITE MEAT PIE

2 lb. chuck steak
¼ cup oil
2 onions, chopped
½ cup chopped celery
½ cup chopped carrot
2 cups beef stock or water and
   beef bouillon cube
2 teaspoons salt

¼ teaspoon freshly cracked
   black pepper
¼ teaspoon ground nutmeg
1 teaspoon meat extract
  (optional)
6 tablespoons all-purpose flour
¾ quantity Short Crust
beaten egg for glazing

Cooking time: 2½ hours
Temperature: 375°
Serves: 5

Cut the steak into 1-inch cubes. Heat the oil in a large saucepan and fry the steak in about 3 lots until browned; remove. Fry the onions until browned, add the celery and carrot, and cook for a few minutes. Replace the meat, add the stock, cover, and simmer gently for 1 hour. Add the salt, pepper, and nutmeg and simmer for a further 1 hour, until cooked. Blend the meat extract and flour to a smooth paste with a little cold water, add to the saucepan, and allow to thicken. Taste and adjust the flavor. Place the meat in a 1-quart pie dish, place an egg cup in the center, add sufficient gravy to come within 1 inch of the top, and reserve the remainder for serving. Make the pie crust (see page 299). Roll out the dough on a lightly floured board to 1 inch larger all around than the top of the pie dish. Cut off a ½-inch wide strip and place it on the edge of the dish, which has previously been brushed with water. Wet the strip of dough, lift the remaining dough on, easing it gently. (If stretched it will shrink in cooking.) Press the edges together, trim, and decorate with a knife. Glaze the pastry with beaten egg. Roll out any scraps of dough, make a rose and leaves, and place on the pie. With a knife or skewer, make a few holes in the crust for the steam to escape. Bake in a 375° oven for 25 minutes, or until cooked.

Variation: Add 2 lamb kidneys or ½ beef kidney to the steak. Wash well, trim, skin, and chop the kidney into small pieces.

CHEESE AND TOMATO FLAN

½ quantity Short Crust

For filling:
1½ cups grated sharp cheese
1 onion, finely chopped
2 teaspoons chopped fresh
   oregano or ½ teaspoon dried
   oregano
¼ lb. salami, thinly sliced

1 (5 oz.) can tomato paste
⅓ cup water
½ teaspoon salt
freshly cracked pepper
1 egg
stuffed olives or anchovies

Cooking time: 25-30 minutes
Temperature: 400°
   reducing to 375°
Serves: 5-6

Roll out the dough (see page 299) and line an 8- to 9-inch flan ring.

To make the filling: Sprinkle half of the cheese into the prepared pie shell and sprinkle with the onion and oregano. Cut each salami slice into 4 pieces and arrange over the top. Mix the tomato paste, water, salt, and pepper and spoon over evenly. Beat the egg, spoon over all, then sprinkle with the remaining cheese. Decorate with sliced olives or anchovies. Place the flan in a 400° oven, reduce the heat to 375° immediately, and bake until cooked and set, about 25 to 30 minutes. Leave for a few minutes before removing the flan ring. Slide the flan on to a flat serving dish.

Note: A useful tip—if liked, cut a piece of cardboard in a circle about 1 inch larger than the diameter of the flan ring. Cover with aluminum foil. Place on a baking sheet and place the ring on this before filling. Later it will act as a serving plate and save any accidents when lifting.

*Favorite Meat Pie, Creamed Potatoes,
Glazed Carrots, and Pineapple Sherbet*

BACON AND CHEESE PIE

1 quantity Short Crust

For filling:
8 slices bacon
2 teaspoons dry mustard
$\frac{1}{4}$ teaspoon pepper
salt
2 tomatoes, skinned and sliced

1 cup coarsely grated sharp
  cheese
1 egg, beaten
milk for glazing

Cooking time: 30-35
Temperature: 400°
Serves: 5-6

Prepare the dough (see page 299). Cut the dough into 2 pieces, one larger than the other. Roll out the larger portion on a lightly floured board and line a round 9-inch pie pan.

To make the filling: Cut the bacon into small pieces. Mix the mustard, pepper, and salt. Place half of the bacon and sliced tomatoes, a sprinkle of salt, then half of the cheese in the pan. Sprinkle over half the mustard mixture. Repeat the layers. Beat the egg and spoon over the pie. Roll out the reserved dough and cover the pie. Seal and trim the edges. Pinch a frill or mark the edges with a teaspoon. Glaze the top with milk. Knead any scraps of dough together, roll out thinly, and cut into leaves. Mark and glaze them and arrange on the pie. Make a depression in the center of the pie and add a dough rose. Bake in a 400° oven for about 30 to 35 minutes until cooked.

MACARONI AND FISH PIE

2 cups macaroni
1 large onion, sliced
1$\frac{1}{2}$ lb. cod or snapper fillets
salt and pepper
juice and rind of 1 lemon
$\frac{1}{4}$ cup butter or margarine
$\frac{1}{2}$ cup all-purpose flour

dash nutmeg
2$\frac{1}{2}$ cups milk
1 cup grated sharp cheese
2 eggs, hard-cooked
coarsely grated cheese
corn or wheat flakes

Cooking time: 20 minutes
Temperature: 350°
Serves: 4-5

Boil the macaroni in plenty of boiling salted water with the onion. When cooked, drain and remove the onion. Steam the fish fillets, sprinkled with the salt, pepper, and juice and rind of the lemon, on a buttered plate, covered with a lid, over hot water. Flake the fish roughly, remove the skin and bones, and reserve any liquid remaining. Melt the butter in a saucepan, add the flour, nutmeg, salt, and pepper, and cook for 1 minute over low heat. Add the milk and any liquid from the fish. Increase the heat, stir the sauce until it boils and thickens, then add the 1 cup cheese. Season to taste. Grease an ovenproof casserole well with butter. Put half the macaroni in the bottom; cover with half of the fish and half of the sauce. Cover with the remaining macaroni and add the sliced hard-cooked eggs and remaining fish. Spoon the sauce over the top. Sprinkle with coarsely grated cheese and corn or wheat flakes. Bake in a 350° oven until the pie is hot and the top crisp, about 20 minutes.

BRAWN

1 lb. beef shank
1 breast of veal
$\frac{1}{2}$ lb. lean salt pork
6 peppercorns
3 cloves

$\frac{1}{4}$ teaspoon mace
bouquet garni
2 tablespoons vinegar
2 envelopes gelatin

Cooking time: 2$\frac{1}{2}$-3 hours

Chop the meats roughly. Place all the meat in a large saucepan and barely cover with water. Add the peppercorns, cloves, mace, bouquet garni, and vinegar, cover, and bring to a boil. Simmer gently until cooked, about 2$\frac{1}{2}$ to 3 hours. Drain and reserve the stock. Cut the meat up evenly, removing the bones, if any. Soak the gelatin in $\frac{1}{4}$ cup water. Strain the stock. Measure 2$\frac{1}{2}$ cups back into the saucepan. Taste and adjust the flavor of the stock if necessary. Add the soaked gelatin and bring to a boil. Mix in the prepared meat and place in a mold previously rinsed with cold water. Cool, then chill in the refrigerator until set.

APPLE AND LEMON CRUNCH

For lemon sauce:
$\frac{1}{2}$ cup sugar
$\frac{1}{4}$ cup cornstarch
grated rind of 1 lemon
1 cup water

1 egg, beaten
2 tablespoons butter
$\frac{1}{4}$ cup lemon juice

Cooking time: 35 minutes
Temperature: 350°
Serves: 5-6

For crunch mixture:
$\frac{1}{2}$ cup butter or margarine
$\frac{3}{4}$ cup brown sugar, firmly packed
$\frac{3}{4}$ cup all-purpose flour
dash salt
2 teaspoons cinnamon
1 cup shredded coconut

1 cup crisp rice cereal
1 (15 oz.) can apple pie filling
dash cloves
whipping cream or custard
   for serving

To make the lemon sauce: Blend the sugar, cornstarch, and lemon rind with the water in a saucepan. Cook, stirring until thickened. Remove from the heat, add a little to the beaten egg, return to the saucepan, and cook until thickened. Remove from the heat and add the butter and lemon juice.

To make the crunch mixture: Cream the butter and brown sugar; add the sifted flour, salt, and cinnamon.

Add the coconut and rice cereal and mix together lightly but thoroughly. Butter an ovenproof dish and sprinkle in half the crumb mixture. Cover with the apple and sprinkle lightly with the cloves. Cover with the lemon sauce and top with the remaining crumb mixture. Bake in a 350° oven for about 35 minutes, until cooked and the top is crisp. Serve while still warm with whipped cream or custard.

BLACK-EYED SUSAN PIE

1 quantity Rich Short Crust
sugar for glazing

whipping cream or ice cream
   for serving

Cooking time: 25 minutes
Temperature: 400°
   reducing to 350°
Serves: 6-8

For filling:
2 (15 oz.) cans apple pie filling
$\frac{1}{4}$ teaspoon cloves
$\frac{1}{2}$ cup sugar

finely grated rind of 1 lemon
2 tablespoons cornstarch
12 prunes for decoration

To make the filling: Empty the apple into a mixing bowl, mix with the cloves, sugar, lemon rind, and cornstarch, and leave to stand while making the pie crust.

Make the pie crust (see page 299) and knead until smooth on a lightly floured board. Cut into 2 portions, one a little larger. Roll out the larger piece and line a round 9-inch pie pan. Place the filling in the pie shell, spreading evenly. Roll out the scraps of dough and cut

into $\frac{1}{2}$-inch strips. Glaze with water and sprinkle lightly with sugar. Place on the pie in a lattice fashion. Trim and decorate the edges. Arrange half a prune in alternate apple squares. Place in a 400° oven, reduce to 350° immediately, and bake until cooked and browned, about 25 minutes. Serve while still warm with whipped cream or ice cream.

LEMON DELICIOUS PUDDING

$\frac{1}{4}$ cup butter
$\frac{3}{4}$ cup sugar
3 eggs, separated
$\frac{1}{3}$ cup flour

rind of 1 lemon
juice of 2 lemons
$1\frac{1}{2}$ cups milk

Cooking time: 35 minutes
Temperature: 350°
Serves: 4-5

Cream the butter and $\frac{1}{2}$ cup of the sugar, add the egg yolks, and beat well. Add the sifted flour, lemon rind, and juice. Add the milk slowly to the creamed mixture, stirring well. Beat the egg whites with the remaining

sugar until stiff, fold into the mixture, and put into a well-greased ovenproof casserole or pie dish. Stand the dish in a larger dish with water. Bake in a 350° oven for 35 minutes. Serve warm or cold.

BAKED CHEESECAKE

For pie crust:
2 cups all-purpose flour, sifted
   with $\frac{1}{2}$ teaspoon baking
   powder
dash salt

$\frac{1}{4}$ cup confectioners' sugar
$\frac{1}{2}$ cup butter
$\frac{1}{3}$ cup cold water or milk

Cooking time: 40-50 minutes
Temperature: 375°
   reducing to 350°
Serves: 8-10

For filling:
1 lb. cream cheese
finely grated rind of 1 lemon
$\frac{1}{4}$ cup lemon juice
$\frac{1}{4}$ cup all-purpose flour
dash salt
$\frac{2}{3}$ cup sugar
2 large eggs

$\frac{2}{3}$ cup sour cream or coffee
   cream
$\frac{1}{2}$ cup seedless white raisins or
   raisins
whipped cream for serving
   (optional)

To make the crust: Sift the flour, salt, and confectioners' sugar into a mixing bowl. Cut the butter into the flour with a knife and coat with flour. Rub the butter into the flour until the mixture resembles bread crumbs. Add the water or milk and mix to a stiff dough. Wrap and chill.

To make the filling: Beat the cream cheese with the lemon rind and juice until smooth. Add the flour, salt, and half the sugar and beat in, add 1 egg, beat until mixed, then beat in the second egg and remaining sugar. Add the cream and raisins to the mixture, beating only until mixed in.

Roll out one thrid of the dough and line the bottom of a greased 8-inch spring form pan. Roll out half of the remaining dough and line the sides of the pan, molding the dough together so the shell is in one piece. Carefully pour the prepared filling into the pie shell (if you pour it over to the back of a tablespoon it will not damage the dough). Roll out the remaining dough into a circle, prick with a fork, and carefully place over the cheese filling. Press the edges of the dough together. Place in a 375° oven, reduce the heat to 350° immediately, and bake until cooked and golden brown, about 40 to 50 minutes. To test, insert a skewer into the cheesecake; if set the skewer will come out clean. Serve the cheesecake while still warm, or cold if preferred, with whipped cream.

CHOCOLATE PUDDING

$\frac{1}{4}$ cup butter or margarine
$\frac{1}{4}$ cup sugar
2 tablespoons boiling water
1 large egg
$\frac{1}{2}$ teaspoon vanilla extract
$\frac{1}{3}$ cup cocoa powder

hot water
raspberry jam
1 cup all-purpose flour, sifted
   with 1 teaspoon baking
   powder
dash salt

Cooking time: 20 minutes
Temperature: 350°
Serves: 5

Cream the butter, sugar, and boiling water well, add the egg and vanilla extract, and beat in thoroughly. Put the cocoa into a cup, make up to $\frac{1}{2}$ cup with hot water, mix together until blended, and cool. Grease 5 custard cups well and put a generous teaspoon jam in the bottom of each. Sift the flour and salt, then sift into the creamed mixture. Add the cocoa mixture and mix all until blended. Divide the mixture among the prepared molds. Have a skillet heated with about $\frac{3}{4}$ inch water. Place the molds in (no need to cover with paper), cover with a lid, and cook for 20 minutes. Turn out and serve hot with Chocolate Sauce.

CHOCOLATE SAUCE

$\frac{1}{4}$ cup cornstarch
$\frac{1}{4}$ cup cocoa powder
$\frac{1}{4}$ cup sugar
dash salt

$1\frac{1}{2}$ cups hot water
2 tablespoons butter
$\frac{1}{2}$ teaspoon vanilla extract

Mix the cornstarch, cocoa, sugar, and salt in a small saucepan. Add sufficient of the hot water to blend, then add the remaining water. Stir over heat until it boils and thickens, then mix in the butter and vanilla extract. Serve hot, poured over the Chocolate Pudding.

Devilled Meatballs on Noodles, Green Salad, and Baked Apple Dumplings

PLUM PUDDING

¼ cup butter or margarine
¼ cup brown sugar, firmly packed
1 cup milk
12 dates, pitted and chopped
½ cup seedless white raisins
¼ cup currants
¼ cup mixed candied peel, chopped
finely grated rind of 1 orange or lemon

1 teaspoon baking soda
1 cup all-purpose flour, sifted with 1 teaspoon baking powder
2 teaspoons mixed spice or cinnamon
dash salt
custard, whipping cream, or ice cream for serving

Cooking time: 2 hours
Serves: 5-6

Well grease a 1½-quart pudding mold and line the bottom with greased wax paper. Put the butter, sugar, and milk into a saucepan, add the chopped dates, white raisins, currants, peel, and lemon or orange rind, and bring to a boil. Remove from the heat, add the baking soda, and allow to foam. Sift in the flour, spice, and salt, and mix lightly until blended. Empty into the prepared bowl. Cover with the lid and steam for 2 hours. Turn out and serve with custard, whipped cream, or ice cream.
Note: If any is left, it is delicious buttered for a packed lunch the next day.

MINCE ROLY-POLY

¾ quantity Short Crust

For filling:
¼ cup raisins
¼ cup seedless white raisins
¼ cup currants
¼ cup chopped mixed candied peel

1 apple
¼ cup brown sugar, firmly packed
1 teaspoon mixed spice
finely grated rind and juice of 1 lemon

Cooking time: 35 minutes
Temperature: 375°
Serves: 5-6

For syrup:
⅓ cup brown sugar, firmly packed
¼ cup margarine or butter
1 cup hot water

custard or whipping cream for serving

To make the filling: Mix together the raisins, seedless white raisins, currants, and peel. Peel the apple, coarsely grate into the fruit, and add the sugar, mixed spice, and lemon rind and juice.

Make the dough (see page 299) and roll out to an oblong about 10 by 12 inches. Cover with the filling. Roll up and place in a greased, oblong, ovenproof dish; prick with a fork.

Boil the syrup ingredients together and spoon around and over the roll. Bake in a 375° oven for 35 minutes, or until cooked. Serve warm with custard or whipped cream.

STRAWBERRY FLUMMERY

2 envelopes gelatin
½ cup cold water
¼ cup all-purpose flour
1 cup sugar
½ cup orange juice

2 tablespoons lemon juice
1 cup hot water
½ cup crushed strawberries
whipped cream or ice cream for serving

Serves: 5

Put the gelatin to soak in the cold water. Mix the flour and sugar in a saucepan and add sufficient orange juice to blend to a smooth paste. Add the remaining orange juice, the lemon juice, and the hot water. Stir over heat until it boils and thickens. Add the soaked gelatin and stir until dissolved. Cool, then empty into a mixing bowl and chill until it is starting to thicken. Beat well until very thick, and at least doubled in volume. Add the strawberries and beat well again. Empty into a serving bowl and chill until set. Serve with whipped cream or ice cream topped with a few whole strawberries.

UPSIDE-DOWN PUDDING

This is a most adaptable dessert. If the oven is in use for dinner, bake it, but if not, then use your electric skillet, as the result will be equally good.

$\frac{1}{4}$ cup butter or margarine
$\frac{1}{3}$ cup brown sugar, firmly packed

a selection of dried apricots,
    prunes, pineapple, cherries,
    chopped walnuts or almonds

Cooking time: 30 or 40 minutes
Temperature: 350°, 420° in
    electric skillet
Serves: 5-6

For the cake mixture:
$\frac{1}{4}$ cup butter or margarine
$\frac{1}{2}$ cup white or brown sugar
1 large egg
1 teaspoon vanilla extract
$1\frac{1}{4}$ cups all-purpose flour, sifted

with $1\frac{1}{2}$ teaspoons baking
    powder
$\frac{1}{3}$ cup milk
whipped cream or ice cream for
    serving (optional)

Line the bottom of a well-greased 8-inch spring form pan with greased wax paper. Beat the butter and brown sugar until well mixed and spread on the bottom and a little way up the sides of the pan. Arrange the prepared selected fruit and nuts in a pattern on top of the butter and sugar.

To make the cake mixture: Cream the butter and sugar, add the egg and vanilla extract, and beat well together. Sift the flour and salt and stir half into the creamed mixture. Add the milk, then the remaining flour, and mix until smooth. Carefully spread in the prepared pan. Cook in one of the following ways:

In the oven: Bake in a 350° oven for about 30 minutes or until cooked. Leave for a few minutes, then turn out onto a serving dish and remove the paper.

In the skillet: Heat the skillet with an asbestos mat in place and covered with the lid. Place the pudding on the mat. Cover with the lid and leave until cooked, about 40 to 45 minutes. Turn out as directed. Serve either warm or cold, with whipped cream or ice cream if desired.

CHOCOLATE ICE CREAM ROLL

4 large eggs, separated
$\frac{1}{2}$ cup sugar
dash salt
$\frac{1}{4}$ cup cornstarch
$\frac{1}{4}$ cup cocoa powder
3 tablespoons rum or Marsala
1 quart vanilla or coffee ice

cream
$\frac{1}{2}$ cup semi-sweet chocolate
    pieces
$\frac{2}{3}$ cup coffee cream
$\frac{1}{2}$ teaspoon vanilla extract
chopped walnuts
extra chocolate

Cooking time: 15-20 minutes
Temperature: 350°
Serves: 6-8

Grease a 10- by 14-inch oblong cake pan and line with greased wax paper or aluminum foil. Beat the egg yolks and half the sugar together. Add the salt to the egg whites, beat until stiff, add the remaining sugar, and beat until dissolved. Fold the meringue into the egg yolk mixture. Sift the cornstarch and cocoa together and sift gently on top of the mixture. Pour the rum or Marsala around the edge and fold all together lightly. Spread mixture evenly in the pan. Place in a 350° oven and bake until cooked, about 15 to 20 minutes. Turn onto a clean, damp, dish towel and roll up, then unroll and re-roll without the dish towel. Leave until quite cold. Have the ice cream slightly soft. Spread quickly on the unrolled cake and roll up. Wrap in clear plastic wrap or aluminum foil. Freeze until the ice cream sets (preferably overnight).

Put the chocolate in a bowl, stand in hot (not boiling) water over heat until melted, add the cream, and stir to blend. Cool and add the vanilla extract. Stand in a bowl of ice. Beat until thick, then quickly spread over the roll, roughing with a fork. Sprinkle with chopped walnuts and grate a little extra chocolate over. Wrap and freeze until required.

ICE CREAM

2 eggs, separated
$\frac{1}{2}$ cup sugar
$\frac{2}{3}$ cup whipping cream

$\frac{1}{3}$ cup orange juice, grapefruit
    juice, or strong coffee

Serves: 6

Whip the egg whites until stiff, gradually add the sugar, and beat until dissolved. Add the egg yolks and beat until thoroughly mixed. Whip the cream until thick but not stiff and fold into the egg mixture with the fruit juice or coffee. Put into a refrigerator tray. Freeze quickly until set. Serve with Caramel Sauce.

CARAMEL SAUCE

1 cup sugar
¼ cup cold water
½ cup hot water

1 can sweetened condensed
  milk
1 teaspoon vanilla extract
1 tablespoon corn syrup

Place the sugar and cold water in a small saucepan. Place over low heat and stir until nearly boiling and the sugar is dissolved. Wipe the sides of the saucepan free of sugar grains. Increase the heat and boil until the sauce turns a caramel color. Quickly remove from the heat and slowly add the hot water. Return to the heat until the syrup dissolves. Remove from the heat and add the condensed milk, vanilla extract, and corn syrup. Bottle and store in the refrigerator until required.

Note: It is a good idea to make up a double quantity of this sauce and store it in the refrigerator to serve with ice cream.

CARAMEL CUSTARD

½ cup sugar
2½ cups milk
3 eggs

1 teaspoon vanilla extract
dash salt

Cooking time: 20-30 minutes
Temperature: 350°, 260° in
             electric skillet
Serves: 6

Heat the sugar in a small saucepan over medium heat until it caramelizes. Watch continuously and move the saucepan around so the caramel colors evenly. Remove from the heat. Carefully pour half the milk down the side of the saucepan (it foams up quickly). Put back over low heat until all the caramel dissolves in the milk. Remove from the heat. Beat the eggs, stir in the remaining milk, vanilla extract, and salt, add the caramel mixture, and mix together. Grease 6 custard cups and pour in sufficient custard to come within about ½ inch of the top. Place in a baking pan with about ¾-inch depth of water and bake in a 350° oven until set, about 20 to 30 minutes. Alternatively, put the same depth of water into an electric skillet. Set the temperature to 260°, place the molds in, cover, and cook until set, 20 to 30 minutes. Leave standing for about 5 minutes, then turn out and serve hot. If preferred cold, leave in the molds, refrigerate and turn out when required.

LEMON FOAM DESSERT

2 large lemons
1 cup sugar
2 cups water

½ cup cornstarch
2 egg whites
dash salt

Serves: 4-5

Wash the lemons. Using a potato peeler, very finely peel the rind from both and squeeze out the juice. Place the rind and juice in a saucepan with the sugar and water. Bring slowly to a boil, stirring until the sugar dissolves. Blend the cornstarch to a smooth paste with a little cold water, add to the contents of the saucepan, and stir over heat until boiling and thickened. Remove from the heat and take out the lemon rind. Stand in a bowl of ice until cooled. Whip the egg whites stiffly with the salt. Beat the cooled mixture with a rotary beater until smooth, fold in the stiffly beaten egg whites, and place in a serving bowl. Chill until serving time. Serve with custard made with the remaining egg yolks.

CUSTARD

¼ cup sugar
2 tablespoons cornstarch
2 egg yolks
2 cups milk

about 6 peach leaves or piece
  finely peeled lemon rind
vanilla extract (optional)

Mix the sugar, cornstarch, and egg yolks in a small saucepan with sufficient of the measured milk to mix. Add the remaining milk, with the washed peach leaves or lemon rind. Bring just to a boil, stirring continuously until thickened. Remove from the heat and take out the peach leaves or lemon rind. Taste and add a little vanilla extract if liked. Pour into a serving jug or bowl. Cover the top with a piece of clear plastic wrap. Chill until serving time.

Refrigerator Cheesecake

ORANGE ANGEL PIE

For meringue shell:
3 egg whites
dash salt

¼ teaspoon cream of tartar
¾ cup sugar

Cooking time: 1½ hours
Temperature: 250°
Serves: 6-8

For filling:
2 envelopes gelatin
½ cup water
finely grated rind of 2 oranges
1 cup orange juice
2 tablespoons lemon juice
4 egg yolks
dash salt

½ cup sugar
⅔ cup whipping cream
1 egg white
whipped cream and 1 (11 oz.)
  can mandarin oranges for
  serving

To make the meringue shell: Whip the egg whites stiffly with the salt and cream of tartar. Gradually add the sugar, beating well until dissolved. Spread the meringue evenly over the bottom and sides of a greased, round, 9-inch pie pan, piling the sides up a little above the edge and making a slight well in the center. Dry out in a 250° oven until set and slightly tinted, about 1½ hours. Turn off the heat and leave the pie in the oven for a further 30 minutes. Cool.

To make the filling: Soak the gelatin in water. Put the orange rind and juice, lemon juice, egg yolks, salt, and half the sugar in a small saucepan; heat together stirring continuously until mixed. Add the soaked gelatin. Stir over low heat or in the top part of a double boiler over hot water until slightly thickened. Remove from the heat, cool, then stand in a bowl of ice until beginning to thicken. Beat until smooth. Whip the cream until thick. Whip the egg white until stiff and beat in the remaining sugar. Fold the cream and whipped egg white into the orange mixture and place in the cooled meringue shell. Cover with clear plastic and refrigerate overnight. Decorate with whipped cream and drained mandarin oranges.

PEARS WITH SOUR CREAM

1 cup water
1 cup water
finely grated rind and juice of
  1 lemon
walnut-sized piece ginger root

6 cloves
6 firm, slightly under-ripe pears
1¼ cups sour cream
3 tablespoons brown sugar
nutmeg

Serves: 6

Make a syrup by gently heating the water, sugar, lemon rind and juice, chopped ginger, and cloves in a shallow saucepan or skillet. Heat slowly until boiling. Peel the pears, cut in half, and remove the cores. Place the pears in the syrup, reduce the heat, and poach gently until tender but of good shape. Remove carefully with a per-forated spoon and arrange in a shallow ovenproof serving dish; cool. Spoon the sour cream over and sprinkle with brown sugar and nutmeg. Place under a hot broiler, at least 3 inches from the heat. Broil until the sugar bubbles a little. Cool, then place in the refrigerator; if possible leave until the next day before serving.

PINEAPPLE SHERBET

1 (15 oz.) can crushed pineapple
1 envelope gelatin
2 tablespoons water
¼ cup lemon juice
½ cup cold milk

2 egg whites
¼ cup sugar
Crème de Menthe or sugared
  mint sprigs for serving

Serves: 5-6

Drain the pineapple and reserve ½ cup fruit pulp. Dissolve the gelatin in water. Put the remaining pineapple pulp with the pineapple juice and lemon juice in a blender and purée. Add the dissolved gelatin and the milk and mix until blended. Place in a refrigerator tray and freeze until set. Whip the egg whites stiffly, add the sugar gradually, and beat until dissolved. Place the frozen mixture in a mixing bowl, beat well, then fold in the whipped egg whites. Empty into the refrigerator tray and freeze until quite set. Serve topped with the reserved pineapple pulp and a drizzle of Crème de Menthe or a sugared mint sprig.

REFRIGERATOR CHEESECAKE

This is ideal for a special Sunday family lunch.

For crumb crust:
½ lb. Graham crackers
½ cup butter

2 teaspoons cinnamon

Cooking time: 8 minutes
Temperature: 350°
Serves: 10-12

For filling:
2 envelopes gelatin
¼ cup lemon juice
1½ cups cream cheese
finely grated rind of 2 lemons
3 eggs, separated
½ cup sugar

dash salt
1¼ cups whipping cream or sour
  cream
whipped cream and strawberries
  or pineapple for decoration

To make the crumb crust: Crush the crackers finely. Melt the butter, add the crackers and cinnamon, and mix well. Grease the bottom and sides of an 8-inch spring form pan. Press and mold the cracker dough over the bottom and sides of the pan to make a firm crust. Bake in a 350° oven for 8 minutes, then cool and chill in the refrigerator.

To make the filling: Add the gelatin to the lemon juice, stand in hot water, and heat until dissolved; cool a little. Beat the cream cheese with the lemon rind and add the egg yolks, half the sugar, and the dissolved gelatin. Beat well until the mixture is smooth. Beat the cream until thick. Whip the egg whites and salt until stiff; beat in the remaining sugar gradually, as for a meringue. Fold the cream cheese mixture, cream, and meringue lightly but thoroughly together. Carefully place into the prepared crumb crust shell. Chill until set. Serve topped with whipped cream. If liked, decorate with strawberries or pineapple.

SAGO CREAM FLUFF

⅓ cup sago
2½ cups milk
finely peeled rind of 1 lemon
6 tablespoons sugar

3 eggs, separated
dash salt
½ teaspoon vanilla extract
stewed fruit for serving

Serves: 4-5

Wash and drain the sago. Put in a saucepan with the milk, lemon rind, and ¼ cup of the sugar. Allow to stand for 30 minutes. Stir over heat until nearly boiling, reduce the heat, cover, and cook slowly, stirring occasionally, until the sago is quite cooked, about 15 minutes. Beat the egg yolks with the salt, add a little sago mixture, return to the saucepan, and stir until thickened a little more. Remove from the heat, take out the lemon rind, and leave until cool. Whip the egg whites stiffly, add the vanilla extract and remaining sugar and beat in, and fold into the sago mixture. Empty into a serving bowl and chill until serving time. Serve with stewed fruit.

Note: If in season, try washing 3 or 4 young peach leaves and use in place of the lemon peel. They give a delicious, slightly almond flavor. Use the same idea for egg custards.

QUICK FLUMMERY

I always store a can of evaporated milk in the refrigerator for this type of sweet. This is ideal to make if you only have a short time for preparation, as it is quickly made, and even 30 minutes in the refrigerator will set it enough to serve.

1 (12 oz.) can evaporated milk
½ cup sugar
2 envelopes gelatin
¼ cup water

½ cup orange juice
½ cup crushed strawberries
whipping cream or ice cream
  for serving

Serves: 5-6

Chill the evaporated milk overnight in the refrigerator. Empty the milk into a large mixing bowl and add the sugar. Add the gelatin to the water and dissolve it by standing in boiling water. Remove from the heat, add the orange juice, and mix together. Beat the milk mixture for a few minutes, add the orange mixture, and beat until thick and fluffy. Add the strawberries and beat again until very thick. Place in a serving bowl and chill until set. Serve with cream or ice cream, topped with a few whole strawberries.

Variation: Pineapple Flummery. Replace the orange juice with the juice drained from 1(15 oz.) can crushed pineapple, and use ¾ cup drained crushed pineapple in place of the strawberries.

Alison Holst

Alison Holst has written two cookery books, written for magazines, made regular television appearances and radio broadcasts, and given popular live cookery demonstrations. Alison has a Bachelor of Home Science degree and feels that her active life with two children and many visitors, on a limited budget, makes her well aware of the catering problems of the busy homemaker.

More Family Fare

Every housewife tries to provide interesting, nutritious, and economical meals for her family, and with good ingredients and an open mind, she generally succeeds.

Milk, cream, butter, cheese, eggs, seafood, fruit, vegetables, and a variety of interesting breads play a large part in family diets. These products are essential, for with large families to cater to and youngsters' hearty appetites to satisfy, the average housewife must base her meal planning on the keynote of economy. Do not, however, be led into believing that meals prepared with simple ingredients must be dull and uninteresting. With the wide range of herbs and spices, along with sauces and flavorings, available today, meals are not only a pleasure and delight to prepare, but also a never-ending source of adventure.

The following recipes use different flavors to their greatest advantage, and will bring a gleam of pleasure to your family's faces as they tuck into an exciting new range of family meals!

Crunchy Cod Fingers, French Fried Potatoes,
Baked Tomatoes, and Ripple Ice Cream

395

CREAM OF LENTIL SOUP

½ cup lentils
½-¾ cup sliced carrots
½ cup chopped onions
½ cup sliced celery
2 cups water
2 chicken bouillon cubes

2 tablespoons butter
2 tablespoons all-purpose flour
2 cups milk
3 bacon slices, cooked and
  chopped

Cooking time: 45 minutes
Serves: 4-5

Soak the lentils in cold water to cover overnight. Drain and place with the other vegetables in a medium-sized saucepan with a tight-fitting lid. Add the water and simmer for 30 minutes. Add the bouillon cubes and simmer for 15 minutes longer, or until the lentils are soft and the carrots tender. Cool. Purée the mixture in a blender or press through a sieve. Melt the butter, add the flour, then the milk one third at a time. Stir well and boil between additions. Gradually add the hot puréed vegetables to the hot sauce, stirring constantly. Heat to the boiling point. Dilute with more milk if desired. Adjust the seasoning. Serve immediately, topped with the chopped bacon.

Note: Replace some of the butter with bacon drippings if desired.

CRUNCHY COD FINGERS

1¼-1½ lb. cod fillets or other
  inexpensive, soft-fleshed fish
½ teaspoon curry powder
¼ teaspoon celery salt
¼ teaspoon onion or garlic salt

1 teaspoon water
½ cup all-purpose flour
1 egg
1 cup fine dry bread crumbs

Cooking time: 4-6 minutes
Serves: 4

Lie the fillets skin side down. Feel where the bones are and cut them out carefully. Cut the boned fillets into fingers about 3 inches by ½ by ½. Mix the seasonings with the water. Add the egg and beat to mix well. Coat the fingers with flour, then egg, then bread crumbs. Shallow fry for 2 to 3 minutes on each side in hot fat (about 380°). Do not overcook. Serve with baked tomatoes, French fried potatoes, or a green salad.

Note: The coating becomes firmer on standing. Fingers may be coated, covered, and refrigerated for several hours before cooking.

DEVILLED MEATBALLS ON NOODLES

1½ lb. ground beef
2 eggs
½ cup fine dry bread crumbs
¼ cup milk
1 teaspoon salt
½ teaspoon dried mixed herbs
¼ cup oil or drippings
½ cup finely chopped onion
½-1 cup coarsely grated apple

¼-½ cup chutney
1½ cups hot water
2 beef bouillon cubes
2 tablespoons brown sugar
2 tablespoons soy sauce
2 tablespoons cornstarch
¾ lb. egg noodles or spaghetti
¼ cup butter

Cooking time: 20-30 minutes
Serves: 6-8

Mix together the ground beef, eggs, bread crumbs, milk, salt, and herbs. Shape into very small balls with damp hands, making 40 to 60 balls. Heat the oil in a large skillet and cook 20 to 30 balls at a time. Rotate the pan constantly to keep the balls from sticking or flattening during cooking. As soon as the meatballs are brown (3 to 5 minutes), remove and drain them.

Pour off all but about 3 tablespoons of fat from the skillet. Fry the onion in this until tender. Add the grated apple, chutney, hot water and beef bouillon cubes, brown sugar, and soy sauce. Thicken the gravy with the cornstarch, blended to a thin paste with cold water. Add the meatballs and reheat in the sauce. Cook the noodles according to the directions on the package. Toss the drained noodles in butter. Serve the meatballs on top of the buttered noodles.

SHRIMP-STUFFED SOLE

4 4-oz. sole or flounder fillets

For stuffing:
2 tablespoons chopped onion
2 tablespoons butter
1 cup soft bread crumbs
½ teaspoon salt

pepper
dash nutmeg
½ cup peeled, chopped shrimp

For sauce:
2 tablespoons butter
3 tablespoons all-purpose flour

1 cup milk

For topping:
2 tablespoons butter
1 cup soft bread crumbs
¼ teaspoon salt
¼ cup finely grated Cheddar

or Parmesan cheese
lemon and parsley sprigs for
garnish

Cooking time: 40-45 minutes
Temperature: 350°
Serves: 4

Wipe the fillets of fish with a damp cloth and lay them skin side up on a plate or board.

To make the stuffing: Fry the chopped onion in the butter until tender and transparent but not brown. Add the remaining ingredients for the stuffing, mix well, then place half of the mixture on the center of each fillet. Fold the top and bottom of the fillet over and place the fillets, ends underneath, in a greased ovenproof dish (one layer deep).

To make the sauce: Melt the butter, add the flour, then stir in the milk ½ cup at a time, boiling and stirring well between additions. Pour the sauce evenly over the fillets.

To make the topping: Melt the butter, remove from the heat, and add the remaining ingredients. Sprinkle thickly and evenly over the fillets.

Bake, uncovered, in a 350° oven for 40 to 45 minutes, until the topping is golden brown and the fillets cooked through. Garnish with lemon and parsley.

GROUND BEEF AND NOODLE CASSEROLE

⅓-½ lb. egg noodles
2 tablespoons oil or drippings
1 lb. ground beef
1 clove garlic, finely chopped
2 beef bouillon cubes
2 cups water
½ cup tomato catsup

¼ teaspoon dried mixed herbs
¼ cup cornstarch
salt, pepper, and sugar to taste
1-1½ cups grated sharp Cheddar
cheese
½ teaspoon paprika pepper

Cooking time: 1¼ hours
Temperature: 350°
Serves: 4-6

Cook the noodles in boiling salted water until tender but not soft. Drain and rinse. Melt the oil or drippings in a large skillet and brown the ground beef and garlic. Stir frequently during the cooking. Dissolve the beef bouillon cubes in the water and add to the browned meat. Add the tomato catsup and herbs, cover, and simmer for 15 minutes. Thicken with the cornstarch blended with a little cold water. Taste and season carefully.

Put half the cooked noodles in an ovenproof dish. Cover with half the meat, then half the cheese. Repeat the layers with the remaining ingredients. Sprinkle the top layer of cheese with paprika pepper. Cover tightly. Bake in a 350° oven for 1 hour. Serve with a green salad or a cooked green vegetable.

LAMB LEG STEAKS WITH APRICOTS

4 lamb leg steaks
¼ cup all purpose flour for
   coating
1 tablespoon drippings
⅓ cup dried apricots
¾ cup water
2 tablespoons brown sugar

½ teaspoon curry powder
½ teaspoon dry mustard
½ teaspoon ginger
1 tablespoon all-purpose flour
2 tablespoons vinegar
¼ cup tomato catsup

Trim away any fat from the steaks, coat with flour, and brown them on both sides in drippings in a skillet. Drain on paper towels and arrange them one layer deep in an ovenproof dish. Add the dried apricots, chopped or whole, to the water in a small saucepan. Simmer, covered, for 10 minutes. Mix the remaining ingredients in a small mixing bowl. Pour enough hot water from the apricots onto them to make a thin smooth paste. Pour this mixture back into the saucepan with the apricots and bring to a boil, stirring constantly. Pour over the chops, cover tightly, and bake in a 325° oven for about 2 hours. Turn the chops occasionally during the cooking, so all parts of them come in contact with the liquid. There should be 4 to 5 tablespoons liquid for serving. Add extra liquid during the cooking if the lid is not tightly fitting.

Before serving the chops, drain off the liquid and remove any fat. Pour the fat-free liquid back over the chops. Serve the chops with mashed potatoes, cabbage, and pumpkin, or with baked potatoes, mashed turnip, and green peas.

PORK AND PAPRIKA CASSEROLE

1½ lb. lean pork arm or blade
   steaks
1 cup thickly sliced onion
½-1 cup mushrooms, sliced
¼ cup finely chopped green
   sweet pepper or celery

2-3 tablespoons paprika pepper
2 beef bouillon cubes
1 cup hot water
arrowroot or cornstarch to
   thicken
chopped parlsey

Cooking time: 1½-2 hours
Temperature: 350°
Serves: 4-6

Cut the pork into 1-inch cubes, discarding the bone. Mix the pork, onion, mushrooms, and green pepper or celery in a deep ovenproof dish. Add the paprika pepper (the larger amount gives a better color). Add the bouillon cubes dissolved in the water. Cover tightly and cook in a 350° oven for 1½ hours. Do not overcook. Thicken the casserole with a thin arrowroot or cornstarch paste. Sprinkle with chopped parsley. Serve on buttered rice, or with baked potatoes and a green vegetable.

EGG, BACON, AND PEA PIE

¾ quantity Short Crust

For filling:
6-8 slices bacon
5-6 eggs

1 cup cooked peas
salt and pepper

Cooking time: 35-45 minutes
Temperature: 400°
   reducing to 350°
Serves: 4-6

Make the paste (see page 299), cover, and chill for at least 15 minutes. Roll out thinly into 2 circles 10 to 12 inches in diameter. Handle the dough carefully to avoid stretching it. Line a 9-inch pie pan with one circle. Trim the edges.

To make the filling: Fry or bake the bacon until cooked. Cut into pieces about 1 inch square. Put one third of the bacon into the uncooked pie shell. Break in 3 eggs, add another third of the bacon, the drained peas, and salt and pepper. Add the remaining eggs and bacon. Break one egg and reserve part of it for glazing the top of the pie. Brush the edge of the pie with cold water. Put the upper crust in place. Fold the edge of the top crust under the edge of the bottom crust. Decorate or flute the edges. Cut 2 or 3 holes in the crust to let the steam escape during the cooking. Glaze the top with the reserved beaten egg. Bake in the middle of a 400° oven for 15 minutes, or until the pastry starts browning, reduce the heat to 350°, and bake for a further 20 to 30 minutes, until the filling is firm. Serve hot or cold.

*Pork and Paprika Casserole, Buttered Rice,
Broccoli and Caramel Queen Pudding*

EGG AND POTATO PIE

3 cups sliced cooked potato
3 hard-cooked eggs
3-4 slices bacon, chopped
$\frac{1}{2}$ cup finely grated cheese
3 tablespoons butter
3 tablespoons all-purpose flour

$\frac{1}{2}$ teaspoon mustard
$\frac{1}{2}$ teaspoon salt
$\frac{1}{2}$ teaspoon celery salt
$1\frac{1}{2}$ cups milk
1 cup soft bread crumbs and 2
   tablespoons butter for topping

Cooking time: 30-45 minutes
Temperature: 375°
Serves: 4-5

Prepare the potato, eggs, bacon, and cheese. Melt the butter in a saucepan, add the flour, mustard, salt, and celery salt, and mix well. Add the milk in 3 lots, boiling and stirring between additions. Place half the sliced potato in a greased ovenproof dish. Add half the eggs, bacon, and cheese and cover with half the sauce. Repeat with remaining ingredients.

To make buttered crumbs for the topping, melt the butter, remove from the heat, and toss the crumbs in it. Sprinkle over the sauce. Bake uncovered in a 375° oven for 30 to 45 minutes, depending on the shape of the dish. Serve hot.

Note: The bacon may be cooked first if desired, and the bacon drippings used with the butter in the sauce. Fresh or dried herbs may be added for extra flavor.

SCALLOPED CORN AND CARROTS

$\frac{1}{3}$ cup butter
1 cup chopped onion
$\frac{1}{4}$ cup all-purpose flour
$\frac{1}{2}$-1 teaspoon curry powder
1 teaspoon salt
1 teaspoon sugar
1 cup milk or milk and liquid
   from corn

1 cup corn, cooked or canned
1 cup carrots, diced and cooked
1 tablespoon butter
1 cup stale bread, diced in
   $\frac{1}{4}$-inch cubes

Cooking time: 30-45 minutes
Temperature: 375°
Serves: 4-6

Melt $\frac{1}{4}$ cup butter in a saucepan, add the chopped onion, stir, cover, and cook gently for 5 minutes until tender but not browned. Add the flour, curry powder, salt, and sugar. Add the liquid in 3 lots, boiling and stirring well between additions. Fold the corn and carrots into the cooked sauce. Place in an ovenproof dish. Melt the remaining butter. Remove from the heat and toss the bread cubes in it. Sprinkle the buttered bread cubes over the vegetables. Bake uncovered in a 375° oven for 30 to 45 minutes. Serve with broiled meat and a green vegetable or salad.

Note: This dish may be prepared in advance, and reheated when needed.

BAKED APPLE DUMPLINGS

1 quantity Short Crust

For caramel sauce:
1 tablespoon butter
$\frac{1}{4}$ cup brown sugar, firmly packed

2 large apples

1 cup water

Cooking time: 45 minutes
Temperature: 400°
Serves: 4

Make the paste (see page 299). Press into a ball and chill for at least 15 minutes. Roll out thinly to a 16- to 18-inch square. Cut into 4 small squares.

Peel and core the apples. Cut each in half and place a half, cut side down, in the middle of each dough square. Dampen the edges of the dough with a little cold water and bring the 4 corners together. Pinch the edges together tightly, fluting or folding them to look attractive. Grease a large shallow ovenproof dish and stand the 4 dumplings on it. Bake, uncovered, in a 400° oven for 15 minutes, then pour the hot sauce over (made by heating together the butter, brown sugar, and water). Baste after the apples have cooked for 15 minutes longer. If the sauce evaporates too quickly, add a little boiling water toward the end of the cooking time. Serve after the dumplings have cooked for 45 minutes. Spoon the sauce over the apples for serving.

Note: If the sauce thickens too much it becomes taffy-like as it cools.

CARAMEL QUEEN PUDDING

½ cup sugar
2 cups milk
¼ teaspoon salt
2 egg yolks
½ teaspoon vanilla extract
1 cup coarsely crumbled stale

bread
¼ cup apricot, raspberry, or
    strawberry jam
2 egg whites
dash salt
cream for serving

Cooking time: 1-1¼ hours
Temperature: 325°
    increasing to 350°
Serves: 4

Place half of the sugar in a medium-sized heavy-bottomed saucepan, over moderate heat. Do not stir, but tilt the saucepan occasionally to heat the sugar evenly. As the sugar caramelizes shake the saucepan; lower the heat if necessary. Leave over the heat until the sugar is completely liquid and golden in color. Remove from the heat and cool slightly. Add the milk and salt and heat gently, stirring constantly, until the caramel dissolves in the milk.

Combine the salt, egg yolks, and vanilla extract in an ovenproof dish. Pour the hot milk onto this, then stir in the crumbled bread. Stand the dish in a roasting pan of hot water and bake uncovered in a 325° oven for 45 to 60 minutes, or until the center of the custard feels firm. Remove from the oven and spread with jam. Whip the egg whites and salt till foamy. Add the remaining sugar and beat until peaks form with tops which curl over. (Do not overbeat.) Pile the meringue on the custard. Bake in a 350° oven until the meringue browns. Serve warm with coffee cream.

COCONUT FRUIT PIE

1 quantity Puff, Flaky, or Short
    Crust Paste
4-5 tablespoons raspberry,
    strawberry, or apricot jam
½ cup seedless white raisins or
    currants
½ cup butter

1 cup sugar
2 eggs
2 cups shredded coconut
¼ teaspoon vanilla or almond
    extract
cream for serving

Cooking time: 25-35 minutes
Temperature: 400°
    reducing to 350°
Serves: 4-6

Roll the dough (see page 294) out thinly to fit a 9-inch square pan or 9-inch pie pan. Spread the jam evenly over the dough. Sprinkle the fruit over the jam. Soften the butter in a mixing bowl. Add the sugar and eggs and beat for 30 seconds with a wooden spoon. Add the coconut and flavoring. Mix well and pour over the fruit, spreading the mixture as evenly as possible. Bake in a 400° oven for 10 minutes, then reduce the temperature to 350° and bake for a further 15 to 25 minutes, until the coconut topping is evenly browned and the center feels firm. Do not overcook. Serve warm with cream.

Note: Leftover pie can be cut into small pieces when cold, and kept for 2 to 3 days.

RIPPLE ICE CREAM

2 egg whites
¼ cup sugar
2 egg yolks
2 tablespoons water
1 cup whipping cream

¼-½ cup sweetened crushed
    berries, or ¼-⅓ cup grated
    semi-sweet chocolate, or
    ½ teaspoon vanilla extract
    or other flavoring

Serves: 4-6

Set the refrigerator to the coldest setting. Whip the egg whites to a stiff foam, add half the sugar, and beat until the peaks stand upright. In another bowl, beat the egg yolks with the water until thick, then beat in the remaining sugar. In a third bowl, beat the chilled cream until thick. Fold the 3 mixtures together. Mix in the flavoring, enough to give a ripple effect. Freeze immediately. Cover the container as soon as the mixture is solid.

Note: This ice cream does not need a second beating.

CONVENIENCE FOODS

Margery Westaway

Margery Westaway is a well known home economist in industry. She has a Professional Certificate in Homecraft and has combined a busy career life successfully with a family life.

Modern convenience foods, whether they be canned, dried, or frozen, may quickly be transformed to suit any menu.

Fifty years ago every home had a pantry which was stocked by the housewife with jars of home preserved fruits, jams, chutneys, pickles, and sauces. These were proudly displayed, as her ability as a home-maker was often judged by the quality and quantity of the preserves which filled the shelves. For many years pantries have been out of fashion but, once again, they are now being built into the latest houses. How different are the foods stored in these pantries! The shelves are mainly stocked with a wide variety of high-quality canned and packaged foods.

Many kitchens have a freezer, giving an even wider choice of foods, ready cooked and needing only to be thawed or heated to provide a family snack, an entrée, a dessert, or even a meal of several courses. The modern refrigerator makes it possible to keep frozen foods always on hand. Foods that once were limited to a short season are now available all the year around.

The busy housewife should put some thought into the selection of these convenience foods and she will be amazed at the variety of dishes she will be able to produce. Building up a good stock can be interesting and fun. When marketing, collect a few items each time and you will be able to produce meals quickly for impromptu parties and unexpected guests. When considering convenience foods include items such as rice, pastas, and instant mashed potato, canned meats and fish, salad dressings, and sauces. Evaporated milk and cream may be handy and there are many canned fruits and preserves to choose from. Include a few packaged cake and pudding mixes. Frozen meats, fish, pastry, bread, and vegetables may be kept in the freezing compartment of your refrigerator and ice cream is helpful when preparing desserts. The imaginative housewife can combine two or three convenience foods to create in minutes, dishes that once took hours to prepare.

In this chapter I have also included a dinner party menu with recipes which can be prepared quickly from convenience foods kept on your store shelves and in the refrigerator.

Brampton Burgers and Instant Creamy Mincemeat Pie

BRAMPTON BURGERS

1 package frozen hamburgers (4)	$\frac{1}{4}$ lb. frozen baby carrots	Cooking time: 10 minutes
2 tablespoons oil	$\frac{1}{4}$ lb. frozen green beans	Serves: 4
$\frac{1}{3}$ cup chopped onion	$\frac{1}{2}$ cup pineapple tidbits, canned	
2 tablespoons tomato paste	or fresh	
2 chicken bouillon cubes,	1 teaspoon sugar	
crumbled	1 teaspoon vinegar	
$\frac{1}{4}$ cup water		

Broil or fry the hamburgers according to the directions on the package, and keep them hot. Heat the oil in a small saucepan and fry the onion without browning for 2 minutes. Add all of the remaining ingredients except the vinegar, bring to a boil, cover, and cook over low to moderate heat for 6 to 8 minutes until the vegetables are tender, stirring occasionally. Add the vinegar and adjust seasoning to taste. Serve the burgers topped with the vegetable sauce.

Note: This colorful tangy vegetable sauce may be served with other meats such as fried chicken, veal, or sausages.

CHEESE AND PINEAPPLE REFRESHER

1 (15 oz.) can pineapple slices	$\frac{1}{3}$ cup chopped cucumber	Cooking time: 5 minutes
4 lettuce leaves	(optional)	Serves: 4
1 cup cottage cheese or	$\frac{1}{4}$ cup chopped walnuts or	
cream cheese	almonds	
1 tablespoon honey	parsley sprigs or chopped nuts	
	for garnish	

Chill and drain the pineapple and place one slice on each lettuce leaf. Chop the remaining pineapple and mix with the cottage cheese, honey, cucumber if desired, and nuts. A little pineapple juice may be added if desired. Mix well and serve on the pineapple slices. Garnish with parsley or chopped nuts.

Note: If using a processed cream cheese that is very rich, serve smaller quantities on the pineapple slices.
Variation: This flavored cottage cheese may be served on wholewheat crackers as a snack, or used to stuff prunes or canned pears or peaches as an hors d'oeuvre.

CHICKEN AND MUSHROOM VOLS-AU-VENT

2 chicken bouillon cubes	1 (8 oz.) can mushrooms	Cooking time: 15-20 minutes
$\frac{1}{4}$ cup sour cream	4 individual ready-baked	Temperature: 350°
1 (16 oz.) can macaroni chicken	vol-au-vent cases	Serves: 4
supreme		

Crumble the bouillon cubes and mix with the sour cream. Add the macaroni chicken supreme and drained mushrooms. Stir to combine, and place in the vol-au-vent cases. Place on a baking sheet and bake in a 350° oven for 15 to 20 minutes.

Note: If macaroni chicken supreme is not available, use an equal quantity (2 cups) of canned or fresh cooked chicken in $1\frac{1}{4}$ cups white sauce.

HAM AND ASPARAGUS ROLLS

1 (14 oz.) can asparagus spears	$\frac{1}{4}$ cup cornstarch	Cooking time: 25-30 minutes
1 (4 oz.) package ham slices	1 cup milk	Temperature: 350°
1 (16 oz.) can cream of chicken	2 tablespoons butter or margarine	Serves: 4
soup	$1\frac{1}{2}$ cups fresh bread crumbs	

Roll 2 or 3 spears of asparagus in each slice of ham and place in an ovenproof dish. Heat the soup in a saucepan; blend the cornstarch with the milk and stir into the soup. Stir until boiling, simmer for 1 minute, and pour over the ham rolls. Melt the butter, mix with the bread crumbs, and sprinkle on top of the sauce. Bake in a 350° oven for 25 to 30 minutes.

CONTINENTAL PILAFF

7 tablespoons oil
1 cup plus 2 tablespoons
   long-grain rice
$\frac{1}{2}$ cup hopped onion
5 chicken bouillon cubes
$\frac{1}{3}$ cup tomato paste
2 cups water

$\frac{1}{2}$ lb. frozen chicken livers,
   chopped
2 oz. canned or packaged ham
   or bacon
$\frac{1}{4}$ cup almonds, fried or baked
$\frac{1}{4}$ cup chopped scallions

Cooking time: 35-40 minutes
Temperature: 350°
Serves: 4-5

Heat $\frac{1}{2}$ cup of the oil in a skillet and slowly cook the rice and onions until lightly browned. Mix the crumbled bouillon cubes with the tomato paste and water, pour over the rice, and stir until boiling. Transfer to a casserole, cover and place in a 350° oven. Cook for 35 to 40 minutes until all the liquid is absorbed and the rice is tender. Heat the remaining oil, fry the chicken livers and chopped ham or bacon for 3 to 4 minutes, and stir through the cooked rice. Adjust seasoning and top with the almonds and scallions.

Variations: A package of chicken noodle soup may be used instead of chicken bouillon cubes, using $2\frac{1}{2}$ cups water instead of 2 cups.

CURRIED VEGETABLES

1 cup plus 2 tablespoons
   long-grain rice
$\frac{1}{3}$ cup frozen cauliflower
$\frac{1}{3}$ cup frozen green beans
$\frac{1}{3}$ cup frozen baby carrots
$\frac{1}{3}$ cup fruit chutney

1 (16 oz.) can vegetable soup
1 cup water
$\frac{1}{3}$ cup oil
1 tablespoon curry powder
1 (10 oz.) can red kidney beans,
   drained

Cooking time: 15 minutes
Serves: 4

Cook the rice in plenty of boiling salted water for 15 minutes and drain. While the rice is cooking, place the cauliflower, green beans, and carrots in a saucepan of boiling water, bring back to a boil, simmer for 1 minute, and drain. Place the chutney, soup, and water in a saucepan and bring to a boil, stirring occasionally. Heat the oil in a skillet and fry the curry powder for 2 minutes, then add the drained vegetables and fry for a further 2 minutes, add the kidney beans and heated soup, bring to a boil, and simmer for 1 minute. Serve the curried vegetables over the hot drained rice.

Variations: Any of the following ingredients may be added:
1 sliced banana, $\frac{1}{2}$ cup seedless white raisins or raisins, $\frac{1}{4}$ cup shredded coconut, $\frac{1}{4}$ cup cashew nuts.

SUMMERTIME SALMON AND RICE

$\frac{1}{4}$ cup blanched almonds
$\frac{1}{4}$ cup vegetable oil
1 small green sweet pepper,
   chopped
1 (10 oz.) can whole kernel corn
4 cups cold cooked rice

$\frac{1}{4}$ cup chopped scallions
salt
pepper
1 (8 oz.) can red salmon
12 stuffed olives

Cooking time: 15 minutes
Serves: 4-5

For dressing:
$\frac{1}{2}$ cup tomato catsup
$\frac{1}{2}$ cup mayonnaise

1 (4 oz.) can cream or
$\frac{1}{2}$ cup fresh cream

Split the almonds and cut into quarters. Heat the oil in a medium-sized saucepan and gently cook the almonds until golden brown. Lift from the oil. Remove the saucepan from the heat, add to the remaining oil the sweet pepper, drained corn, rice, and scallions, and season to taste with salt and pepper. Drain the salmon, remove the bones and stir gently through the rice with the almonds and halved olives. Chill before serving, accompanied by the dressing.

To make the dressing: Mix the tomato catsup, mayonnaise, and cream together. Chill before serving.

Note: This quickly-made seafood dressing has many uses. It is suitable for seafood cocktails and may be served with avocados.

SWEET AND SOUR TUNA

¼ cup butter
½ cup all-purpose flour
1¼ cups milk
1 (15 oz.) can pineapple tidbits
1 (10 oz.) can whole kernel corn
1 teaspoon salt

dash pepper
2 tablespoons sugar
¼ cup vinegar
1 (7 oz.) can tuna
¼ cup chopped scallions

Cooking time: 10-15 minutes
Serves: 4-5

Melt the butter in a medium-sized saucepan, add the flour, and stir over low heat for 1 minute. Remove from the heat. Blend in the milk and stir over heat until boiling. Drain the pineapple, add the juice to the sauce and stir until smooth, then add the pineapple tidbits, drained corn, salt, pepper, sugar, vinegar, drained and flaked tuna, and scallions. Bring slowly to a boil, stirring occasionally. Simmer for 2 minutes. Adjust seasoings if necessary. Serve with croûtons, or boiled rice.

CORN AND HAM FLAN

¾ lb. pie crust mix

For filling:
2 tablespoons butter
¼ cup chopped onion
1 (10 oz.) can whole kernel corn
1 tablespoon chopped parsley
3 eggs
1 teaspoon salt

dash pepper
1 cup evaporated milk
2 oz. canned or packaged ham
  or bacon
⅙ lb. sharp cheese

Cooking time: 30-35 minutes
Temperature: 375°
Serves: 6

To make the flan: Prepare the pie crust mix according to the directions on the package. Roll out the dough on a lightly floured board and line an 8-inch flan ring or a round 8-inch pie plate. Brush the pie shell with a little egg white.
To make the filling: Melt the butter in a small saucepan and cook the onion slowly without browning for 2 minutes. Mix the onion with the drained corn and the parsley and spread over the pie shell. Beat the eggs lightly with the salt and pepper. Heat the evaporated milk until lukewarm, mix with the eggs, and pour over the sweet corn. Top with slices of ham or bacon and thin slices of cheese. Bake in a 375° oven for 30 to 35 minutes, or until the crust is golden brown and the filling is set in the center.

QUICK-MIX STEAMED PUDDING

1 package chocolate cake mix
1 egg

¾ cup milk

Cooking time: 1½ hours
Serves: 8

Prepare the cake mix with the egg and milk or water, according to directions on the' package. Pour into a greased 2- to 2½-quart pudding mold and cover with a lid, foil, or greased double wax paper. Place the mold in a saucepan of boiling water and keep the level of the water half way up the mold during cooking. Steam for 1½ hours. Unmold the pudding while hot and serve with cream, ice cream, chocolate sauce, or custard.

Note: When cooking for smaller numbers, make up the the whole cake mix as directed, but pour only half the cake batter into 1½-quart mold and steam for 1 hour. Alternatively, fill individual molds and steam for 20 to 25 minutes. Bake the remaining cake batter in a greased 7-inch layer cake pan in a 350° oven for 25 to 30 minutes.

Variations: Any flavored cake mix may be used.
Golden Steamed Pudding: Place ¼ cup corn or maple syrup in the bottom of the pudding mold before adding a yellow cake batter.
Upside-down Pudding: Mix 2 tablespoons softened or melted butter with ¼ cup brown sugar and spread in the bottom of a pudding mold, and add a slice of pineapple, some soaked dried apricots, some canided cherries, or some blanched almonds before adding a yellow cake batter.
Fruit Mince Pudding: Add ½ cup all-purpose flour sifted with ½ teaspoon baking powder when mixing the cake. Stir in 1 cup mincemeat before pouring into the pudding mold.

An Impromptu Meal: Asparagus Rolls Supreme, Tuna Aurora, Buttered Vegetables, Potato Crisps and Tangy Fruit Marshmellow

LEMON MARSHMALLOW FRUIT SALAD

1 package lemon pie filling
1¼ cups water
1 (4 oz.) can cream or ½ cup
   fresh cream
1 cup marshmallows, halved

1 (15 oz.) can fruit salad
mint leaves and candied cherries
   for decoration

Serves: 4-5

Empty the pie filling into a small saucepan and blend in the water. Stir constantly over medium heat until the mixture boils and thickens. Allow the mixture to become quite cold then fold in the cream, marshmallows, and drained fruit salad. Spoon the mixture into a glass serving bowl or individual dishes, and chill in the refrigerator. Decorate with fresh mint leaves and candied

cherries before serving.

Note: These directions for making the pie filling may differ from those on the package. Egg yolks are not necessary in this dessert.

This dessert may be made the day before it is required, in fact the flavor is even better when it is stored overnight in the refrigerator.

PINEAPPLE DELIGHT

1 egg
¼ cup sugar
1 cup evaporated milk
1 small can crushed pineapple

1 package lemon-flavored
   jello
1 cup water

Serves: 4

Beat the egg and sugar together in a mixing bowl and add the evaporated milk and crushed pineapple. Dissolve the jello in the water over low heat, stirring constantly. Remove the saucepan from the heat and immediately add the beaten egg and milk to the hot jello. Stir until combined and pour into a serving dish or individual glass

dishes. Place in the refrigerator to chill and serve with cream or ice cream.

Variation: Orange or pineapple jello may be used instead of lemon. Other flavors of jello may be used with appropriate fruit in place of pineapple.

INSTANT CREAMY MINCEMEAT PIE

1 7-inch cooked pie shell
1 cup mincemeat
1 package vanilla instant dessert

scant 2 cups milk
whipped cream, candied cherries,
   nuts, or angelica for decoration

Serves: 4-5

Spread the bottom of the pie shell with the mincemeat. Prepare the instant dessert with milk according to the directions on the package and pour immediately into the pie shell over the mincemeat. Place in the refrigerator to chill. Before serving, the pie may be decorated with cream, cherries, nuts, or angelica.

Note: This dessert is made in less than 5 minutes from convenience foods from the store cupboard, but is a delightful combination of flavors and textures. It is suitable for a family meal or, when decorated as suggested, may be served at a buffet party.

PINEAPPLE UPSIDE-DOWN PUDDING

6 tablespoons brown sugar
3 tablespoons butter or margarine
1 (15 oz.) can pineapple slices
6 candied cherries or almonds or
   prunes

1 package orange, lemon, or
   vanilla cake mix
1 egg
¾ cup milk

Cooking time: 45-50 minutes
Temperature: 350°
Serves: 6

Mix the sugar with the softened or melted butter and spread in the bottom of a well greased 8-inch spring form pan. Arrange the drained pineapple slices over the sugar and butter, placing cherries, almonds, or pitted prunes in between the pineapple slices. Make up the cake mix

with the egg and milk or water, according to the directions, and spread over the pineapple in the pan. Bake in a 350° oven for 45 to 50 minutes. Remove from the oven and allow to stand for 2 to 3 minutes before turning upside-down on a serving plate. May be served hot or cold.

IMPROMPTU MEAL FOR SIX PEOPLE

A carefully planned and well stocked store cupboard will enable you to greet those unexpected guests with a smile, confident in the knowledge that you can prepare a meal in a matter of minutes.

ASPARAGUS ROLLS SUPREME

sliced bread
1 (14 oz.) can asparagus spears
butter or margarine

olives or parsley sprigs for
    garnish

Cooking time: 10 minutes
Temperature: 400°
Serves: 6

For sauce:
1 (16 oz.) can cream of chicken
    soup
2 tablespoons cornstarch

1 cup milk
salt and pepper

Cut the crusts from the bread, place a spear of asparagus on each slice, roll up tightly, and secure with wooden toothpicks. Brush the rolls lightly with softened or melted butter, place on a baking sheet, and bake in a 400° oven for 10 minutes or until lightly browned but not baked hard.

To make the sauce: Heat the soup in a small saucepan. Blend the cornstarch with the milk, add to the soup, and stir constantly until boiling. Simmer for 1 minute. Add the salt and pepper to taste before serving.

To serve, place the rolls in a heated dish and remove the picks. Pour the sauce over the rolls, garnish with chopped olives or parsley, and serve hot.

TUNA AURORA

$\frac{1}{3}$ lb. noodles or spaghetti
1 (16 oz.) can tomato soup
1 (15 oz.) can pineapple tidbits

$\frac{1}{2}$ cup sliced green sweet pepper
    or 1 cup frozen green beans
1 (1 lb. 4 oz.) can tuna, drained

Cooking time: 20-25 minutes
Temperature: 350°
Serves: 6

Cook the noodles in plenty of boiling salted water for the time stated on the package. Heat the tomato soup, pineapple tidbits and juice, and sweet pepper or beans in a large saucepan; stir until boiling. Add the drained cooked noodles and bring back to a boil. Place the tuna in a large casserole, pour over the hot contents of the saucepan, cover, and bake in a 350° oven for 20 to 25 minutes. Serve with buttered vegetables and potato straws or chips if desired.

TANGY FRUIT MARSHMALLOW

2 envelopes gelatin
$\frac{1}{4}$ cup boiling water
1 (10 oz.) can mandarin oranges
$\frac{1}{4}$ cup sliced banana
$\frac{1}{4}$ cup concentrated orange juice
$\frac{1}{4}$ cup preserved lemon juice

    or juice of 1 lemon
3 egg whites
$\frac{1}{2}$ cup sugar
whipped cream and almonds,
    or lemon or orange rind
    for decoration

Serves: 6

Dissolve the gelatin in boiling water. Drain the mandarins and chop half the segments into small pieces. Place all mandarins in a mixing bowl with the sliced banana. Place 1 teaspoon of the orange juice in each of 6 individual serving glasses. Pour the remaining orange juice and the lemon juice over the fruit in the mixing bowl. Beat the whites until stiff and heat in the sugar. Stir in the fruits, juices, and dissolved gelatin. Mix well and place in the 6 individual glasses. Place in the refrigerator to chill. Top with whipped cream and almonds or finely grated lemon or orange rind for decoration.

Note: This quickly made dessert is glamorous enough for any dinner party when served in champagne glasses. If using glasses with hollow stems it will be necessary to increase the quantity of concentrated juice placed in the glasses.

Variations: In place of mandarins use tinned papaya or fruit salad, well drained, or 2 red-skinned apples, grated without peeling.

INTERNATIONAL COOKERY

Margaret Fulton

Margaret Fulton is Cookery Editor of the popular Australian magazine *Woman's Day*, and through this medium her recipes go into over half a million homes every week. She is the author of the best-selling *Margaret Fulton Cookbook* and has also written the *Woman's Day Cookbook*. A Scot by birth, Margaret Fulton brings to the culinary scene not only her background of good, wholesome Scottish food but a flair for entertaining and international cuisine. She travels abroad every year collecting new exciting recipes and adapts these in her inimitable style so that every housewife can follow them easily.

The advantage of being an expert in any field is that people know what to show you when you visit their country. I am invited to the leading restaurants and the homes of the best cooks. Chefs and home cooks alike take pleasure in sharing their recipes with me. In this chapter on International Cookery I have planned a typical meal for a variety of nations, ranging from Europe to the East, followed by recipes for you to try for yourselves.

PACIFIC ISLANDS COOKERY

'An island feast!' Magic words that conjure up visions of moonlight on the sea, waving palms, a return to native life and tribal customs, sitting island fashion around the exotic tropical food that adds to the color and beauty of the setting.

Throughout this menu you will find that coconut milk is used for flavoring and richness. This is because coconuts are so plentiful in the islands. The white meat of fresh coconuts is grated and the milk is extracted and used in every course from soups and appetizers through to desserts.

In Tahiti, fish is 'cooked' in lime juice. It is marinated in the juice until the fish becomes opaque, then served with a rich coconut cream dressing flavored with garlic. Coconut milk is used in the curry sauce for the chicken and coconut appears again in Tahitian-style ice cream.

Tahitian Coconut Ice Cream

An Island Luau

Limed Fish

Laulaus with Curry Sauce

Boiled Rice

Tahitian Coconut Ice Cream

LIMED FISH

2 lb. bream fillets or any firm
  white fish fillets
juice of 4 limes or lemons
1 clove garlic, crushed
½-¾ cup Coconut Cream

sliced hard-cooked eggs
onion rings
cucumber cubes
sliced tomato for garnish

Serves: 6

Remove all skin and bones from the fish and cut into ½-inch dice. Put into a glass or earthenware bowl and pour the lime juice over. Cover and chill for at least 3 hours, turning with a wooden spoon from time to time. Avoid using metal spoons or utensils for this dish. The lime juice will turn the fish white and opaque and it will look and taste like cooked fish.

Take the fish from the bowl and squeeze out all the juice. Mix the garlic with the Coconut Cream (see page 420) and spoon over the fish. Serve in sea shells garnished with egg, onion, cucumber, and tomato. This dish makes a delicious luncheon salad. In Tahiti it is always served with baked breadfruit and baked bananas. Crusty bread may be used as a substitute.

Variation: For a fish cocktail serve in cocktail glasses or grapefruit shells.

LAULAUS WITH CURRY SAUCE

4 whole chicken breasts or
  2 2½-lb. roasting chickens
all-purpose flour
¼ cup butter
2 tablespoons oil

For sauce:
3 tablespoons butter
1 large onion, finely chopped
1 clove garlic, crushed
2 tablespoons finely chopped
  fresh ginger

spinach leaves
1 small onion, finely chopped
salt and pepper
¼ cup light soy sauce
corn husks or aluminum foil

2 tablespoons curry powder
½ teaspoon brown sugar
2 tablespoons all-purpose flour
3¾ cups Coconut Milk
salt

Cooking time: 1½ hours
Serves: 6

Bone the chicken breasts and cut into quarters. If using whole chickens cut into small pieces removing all bones and include some breast meat in each package. Coat the chicken lightly with flour. Heat the butter and oil in a skillet and sauté the chicken until golden, turning once. Wash the spinach and wrap a few pieces of browned chicken in each leaf. Add a little onion, salt and pepper to taste, and a sprinkling of soy sauce. Cross 2 corn husks, place the spinach-wrapped chicken in the center, and pull the end of the husks over and tie with string. Steam in a steamer or colander, covered, over simmering water, for 1½ hours. Remove the string and serve hot with boiled rice (see page 201) and a bowl of curry sauce.

To make the sauce: Melt the butter; add the onion, garlic, and ginger. Sauté until light golden. Add the curry powder and sugar. Mix well and stir in the flour. Gradually add the Coconut Milk (see page 420), stirring constantly. Bring to a boil and season with salt to taste.

Note: Two spinach leaves may be used to wrap the chicken if no corn husks are available, or use dried bamboo leaves which are sold at some Chinese grocery stores. They must be blanched in boiling water before use. Thin strips of the leaves are used for tying the bundles. Or use aluminum foil to make the packages.

TAHITIAN COCONUT ICE CREAM

1¼ cups whipping cream
⅓ cup confectioners' sugar
1 teaspoon vanilla extract

2 egg whites
3 tablespoons toasted shredded
coconut

Serves: 6

For sauce:
2 tablespoons chopped candied
pineapple
2 tablespoons chopped candied
apricots

½ cup rum

Whip the cream very lightly. Add the confectioners' sugar and vanilla to the cream. Whip the egg whites until stiff and fold lightly and thoroughly in to the cream. Pour into refrigerator trays and freeze until firm around the edges. Remove from the refrigerator and soften in a bowl, fold in the toasted coconut, return to the trays, and freeze until firm. To serve, spoon the ice cream into serving dishes. Combine the sauce ingredients and heat gently. This may be done in a small saucepan over a table burner, or on the stove and brought to the table. Set a match to the sauce and stir it until the flames are about to die down, then ladle over the ice cream.

CHINESE COOKERY

Chinese cookery enjoys the reputation along with French cooking of being the most subtle and delicious in the world. The Chinese are both fastidious and discerning about food. Confucius is reported to have spoken against eating anything over-cooked, under-cooked, crookedly cut, served without the right sauce, or not in season—that was twenty-five centuries ago, and these principles still apply today.

The technique of cooking Chinese style may be applied to almost any ingredients. Preparation takes time because the food is often cut into small pieces, all the same size. The actual cooking time is brief and once you practice with a few dishes it is surprising how easy it is to cook Chinese meals at home.

Chinese menus are usually planned on a basis of each dish making 4 portions. On this basis it is better not to increase the quantity of food in each recipe but to add another dish if cooking for more people.

Plain boiled rice always accompanies Chinese meals. Chinese fried rice may also be served. A simple fruit compote of canned Chinese lychees and mandarin sections would complete this meal.

A Chinese Menu

Prawn Chow Mein

Crisp Skin Duck

Braised Chicken with Green Sweet Peppers

Boiled Rice

Chinese Fried Rice

Compote of Lychees and Mandarins

PRAWN CHOW MEIN

½ lb. egg noodles
7 tablespoons peanut oil
oil for deep frying
1 lb. green prawns
1 tablespoon Chinese wine or
   dry sherry
½ teaspoon salt

For seasonings:
2 teaspoons Chinese wine or
   dry sherry
½ teaspoon salt

1 teaspoon cornstarch
1 stalk celery
¾ cup dried mushrooms, soaked
   in warm water for 20 minutes
10 water chestnuts or 1 onion
1 cup snow peas or 1-inch pieces
   green beans

½ teaspoon sugar
1 teaspoon soy sauce

Serves: 4

Drop the noodle bundles into boiling salted water and when they begin to soften separate with a chopstick or fork. Do not crowd. When tender, about 8 to 10 minutes, drain well and rinse under running water. Place on a tray covered with paper towels. (Sprinkle with 2 tablespoons peanut oil to prevent sticking.) Deep fry handfuls of noodles separately, turning once to crisp and brown both sides. Drain.

Halve the prawns and remove the black vein. Sprinkle with the wine, salt, and cornstarch and let stand for 5 minutes. Slice the celery, drained mushrooms (discard stems), and water chestnuts. Heat 2 tablespoons oil and sauté the vegetables for 2 minutes. Remove. Add another 3 tablespoons oil to the pan and sauté the prawns until the color changes. Return the vegetables and mix well; then add the seasonings, mixed together. Cook for 2 minutes. Serve hot on the crisp fried noodles.

Note: If using cooked prawns, add to the vegetables with the seasonings and cook just long enough to heat through.

CRISP SKIN DUCK

1 3-lb. young duck
2 tablespoons salt
1 tablespoon sugar
1 teaspoon red food coloring
2 cloves star anise
small piece green ginger
1 small clove garlic

4 dried mushrooms, soaked in
   warm water for 20 minutes
1 egg
⅓ cup cornstarch
oil for deep frying
salt and coarsely cracked black
   pepper

Cooking time: 1-1½ hours
Serves: 4

Rub the duck with a mixture of salt, sugar, and red food coloring. Steam with the star anise, ginger, peeled garlic, and mushrooms for 1 to 1½ hours, or until the duck is tender. Allow to cool, then remove the duck, brush with beaten egg, and dip into the cornstarch. Deep fry the duck in hot oil until the skin is crisp, about 15 minutes, basting with the oil while cooking. To serve, chop into bite-sized pieces and arrange on a heated serving dish, skin side upward. Serve with a mixture of equal quantities of salt and coarsely cracked pepper. Serve with boiled or fried rice (see page 202).

Note: When steaming duck, place on a rack or in a perforated basket so the duck sits well above the water.

BRAISED CHICKEN WITH GREEN SWEET PEPPERS

1 tablespoon dry sherry
1 tablespoon cornstarch
1 lb. chicken breasts

For seasonings:
1 tablespoon dry sherry
1½ teaspoons salt

7 tablespoons oil
2 green sweet peppers, cut into
   shreds

pinch monosodium glutamate

Cooking time: 8 minutes
Serves: 4

Mix together the sherry and cornstarch. Add the finely shredded chicken and marinate for 5 minutes. Heat 2 tablespoon oil and sauté the pepper shreds for 2 minutes. Remove to a platter. Heat the remaining oil and sauté the chicken until it turns white. Add the peppers and seasonings, which have been mixed together. Mix well and serve hot.

While the Japanese cuisine is not well known in the Western world it deserves special attention because of its unique qualities.

The primary element of Japanese food is the absolute freshness of ingredients. Seafood dishes star, for example Sashimi, the delectable preparation of raw fish. There is the internationally popular method of frying fresh fish, prawns, shrimp or vegetables in Tempura batter and seasoning with Tempura sauce. And there are Sushi, often served as appetizers, delicately vinegar-flavored rice molded into individual bite-sized shapes with shrimp, raw fish, cucumber, or smoked salmon.

As a first course barbecued chicken and chicken livers comes to the table as Yakitori. The light, delicate, steamed custard, Chawan-mushi, would be a good second course. This dish seems to be a favorite with all visitors to Japan and it is easy to make at home.

Sukiyaki is one of the best known Japanese dishes; it is a kind of fondue that you cook at the table. Thin strips of beef, noodles, fresh vegetables, and chunks of bean curd are simmered in a light, sweet stock and eaten as they cook. Electric skillets and table top cooking apparatus have simplified the cooking of this dish in the Western world.

Try Japanese dishes one by one. Sukiyaki followed by a bowl of rice is a good start and is a meal in itself. Graduate to the preparation of a complete meal after practice of individual dishes, or serve Yakitori or Chawan-mushi as a first course to any national food.

A Japanese Menu

Yakitori

Chawan-mushi

Sukiyaki

Boiled Rice

YAKITORI

1½ lb. chicken breasts
½ lb. chicken livers

⅓ cup vegetable oil
24 10-inch bamboo skewers

Cooking time: 8-10 minutes
Serves: 4-6

For marinade:
¼ cup sugar
⅓ cup soy sauce
¼ cup mirin (sweet saké)
  or sweet sherry

½ cup cocktail or barbecue sauce

For Gomo-shio:
2 tablespoons table salt

¼ cup toasted sesame seeds

Cut the chicken and chicken livers into ¾-inch squares. Sauté in oil over a medium heat for 4 to 5 minutes. Combine the ingredients for the marinade, add to the pan, and continue to cook for a further 3 to 4 minutes. Place 3 to 4 pieces of chicken and chicken livers on bamboo skewers. If necessary, reheat under a hot broiler or over hot coals in a hibachi before serving. Serve with a barbecue sauce or Gomo-shio made by combining the salt and sesame seeds. Serve as a first course, or, if required for a main course, with fluffy boiled rice (see page 201). Serve 6 as a first course or 4 as a main course.
Note: A hibachi is a Japanese portable barbecue.

CHAWAN-MUSHI

¼ lb. chicken breast
1½ teaspoons soy sauce
2 oz. fish
salt
6 small dried mushrooms
few green beans

6 eggs
1 teaspoon salt
1½ teaspoons dry sherry
dash monosodium glutamate
6 cups soup stock
6 small prawns

Cooking time: 25 minutes
Serves: 6

For soup stock:
1 piece dried seaweed 2 inches
    square

6 cups water
½ oz. shaved bonito

Dice the chicken, sprinkle with soy sauce, and allow to stand for 5 minutes. Cut the fish into 6 slices and sprinkle with salt. Soak the mushrooms in warm water for 20 minutes and slice the beans thinly. Beat the eggs lightly. Add the salt, sherry, and monosodium glutamate to the cooled soup stock and mix with the eggs. Strain and pour into lidded soup cups with the chicken, prawns, fish, and quartered mushrooms. Place in a steamer and steam over gently boiling water over medium heat for 25 minutes (or use an electric skillet with ½ inch water). Garnish with beans just before removing from the cooker. Serve hot.

Note: If soup cups are not available, custard cups may be used. Aluminum foil can replace lids.
To make the soup stock: Wipe the dried seaweed with a wet cloth, put into a pan with the water, and bring to a boil. Remove the seaweed just before the stock reaches the boiling point, reduce the heat to moderate, add the bonito, and turn the heat off just before the liquid boils. Leave until the shavings settle, then strain.
Note: Dried seaweed and bonito are available from Chinese grocery stores. Packaged Japanese soup stock prepared according to the directions on the package may be used instead of seaweed and bonito.

SUKIYAKI

1½-2 lb. beef tenderloin or sirloin
    tip, cut into ⅛-inch thick slices
½ lb. bean curd, broiled until
    golden (optional)
¾ lb. transparent noodles, boiled
    for 1-2 minutes and cut into
    2-inch lengths
10 scallions, cut diagonally into
    2-inch lengths
½ lb. Chinese or Savoy cabbage,

    cut into 3-inch strips
6 dried mushrooms, soaked in
    warm water for 20 minutes
    and drained
suet to grease pan
¼ cup soy sauce
2 tablespoons saké or dry sherry
1 tablespoon sugar
½ cup soup stock
pinch monosodium glutamate

Serves: 6

Arrange the steak, bean curd, noodles, and vegetables on a tray. Grease the pan with the piece of suet and heat. Put in some of the beef, piece by piece, and brown lightly. Add the bean curd, noodles, scallions, cabbage, and mushrooms. Combine the soy sauce, sherry, sugar, soup stock, and monosodium glutamate and sprinkle over the ingredients in the pan. Cook over medium heat. Serve

and eat while the Sukiyaki is cooking, adding more ingredients as food is removed. Use gentle heat to prevent over-cooking. Serve with boiled rice (see page 201).
Note: Japanese soup stock may be bought from most large food halls in department stores or from Chinese gorcery stores. Ask for dried soup powder in packages. Alternatively use chicken bouillon cubes.

India is a vast country and its food varies from region to region. It is a common mistake to think that all Indian food is hot. Spicy, yes, but not always hot. In fact, there are many curries in which chili powder or pepper (the only hot ingredients) do not feature at all.

However, the subtle spicing of curries is a peculiarly Eastern art and there are not many people, regardless of their nationality, who do not appreciate a really good curry. A curry meal is exotic and yet very simple to prepare. Rice, either plain boiled or cooked with spices, is always served with the curries. An important part of of the meal is the selection of accompaniments or sambals. A most suitable dessert would be a well chilled salad of fresh fruit (see page 191).

An Indian Meal

Beef Curry

Chicken Curry

Ghee Rice

Accompaniments

Fresh Fruit Salad

BEEF CURRY

2 large onions
2-inch piece fresh ginger
3-4 cloves garlic
6 tablespoons ghee
7 tablespoons curry powder
1 teaspoon turmeric

2 teaspoons black mustard seeds
  (optional)
2 teaspoons salt
2 tablespoons vinegar
3 lb. blade steak
2 fresh chili peppers
3 ripe tomatoes

Cooking time: 2 hours
Serves: 6-8

Finely chop the onions, peel and grate the ginger, and crush the garlic; heat the ghee in a saucepan and gently fry until golden. Add the curry powder, turmeric, and mustard seeds and fry gently over low heat for 2 to 3 minutes. Add the salt and vinegar and stir well. Cut the steak into 1-inch cubes, add to the curry mixture and fry, stirring to coat the meat well. Add the seeded chili pepper and the chopped tomatoes. Cover the pan and simmer on very low heat for about 2 hours. Serve with with accompaniments. If the gravy is too thin when the meat is tender, cook over high heat, uncovered, until reduced.

CHICKEN CURRY

2 onions
2 cloves garlic
1-inch piece fresh ginger
¼ cup ghee
¼ cup curry powder
2 large ripe tomatoes
2 teaspoons paprika pepper
2 cloves

3-inch stick cinnamon
2 cups Coconut Milk
2 teaspoons salt
2 fresh chili peppers
1 stewing chicken, 3½-4 lb.
¼ cup cream or sour cream
2 tablespoons chopped fresh
  mint

Cooking time: 1¼ hours
Serves: 4-6

Finely chop the onions, crush the garlic, and grate the ginger; cook gently in the hot ghee in a saucepan until beginning to turn golden. Add the curry powder and cook for 3 to 4 minutes. Add the skinned, seeded, and diced tomatoes, paprika pepper, cloves, cinnamon, Coconut Milk (see page 420), salt, and seeded chili peppers. Simmer, covered, for about 15 minutes, then add the chicken cut into serving pieces and simmer for 45 minutes to 1 hour, until the chicken is tender. Remove the chili peppers. Add the cream and mint. Heat through and serve with accompaniments.

Lomo con Jerez (Loin of Pork with Sherry)

GHEE RICE

$\frac{1}{4}$ cup ghee
1 onion
good pinch saffron
$\frac{1}{2}$ teaspoon turmeric
2$\frac{1}{4}$ cups long-grain rice
8 peppercorns
2 cloves
4 cardamom pods

3-inch stick cinnamon
3$\frac{1}{2}$ cups chicken stock or water
   and bouillon cubes
2 teaspoons salt
$\frac{1}{2}$ cup sultanas
1 cup cooked peas
$\frac{1}{2}$ cup lightly fried almonds

Cooking time: 25 minutes
Serves: 6

Heat the ghee in a saucepan and fry half the finely sliced onion until golden brown, then add the saffron and turmeric. Stir well for a minute. Add the rice and fry for a few minutes, stirring until it is golden in color. Add the spices, stock, salt and remaining onion. Stir well and bring to a boil. Reduce the heat to very low, cover, and steam gently for 20 to 25 minutes. After 15 minutes sprinkle the sultanas over the rice but do not stir. When cooked remove from heat and keep covered until ready to serve. A few minutes before serving uncover the pan to allow the steam to escape. Fluff up with a fork and lift the rice onto a serving dish with a slotted spoon to prevent mashing the grains. Garnish with peas and almonds.

ACCOMPANIMENTS

A selection of accompaniments with varying flavors and textures is an important part of an Indian curry meal. There is generally at least one hot sambal, one piquant sambal, a sweet or cooling accompaniment such as fresh fruit, and a crisp one such as poppadums or fried dried fish.

Tomato and Onion Sambal: Skin and dice 3 firm red tomatoes and combine with 1 onion, finely chopped, 1 clove garlic, crushed, $\frac{1}{4}$ cup oil, 2 tablespoons vinegar or lemon juice, a dash hot pepper (Tabasco) sauce, chili powder, and salt to taste. Toss lightly to mix and serve well chilled.

Bombay Duck: A misleading name. This is actually dried, salted fish. Though it is a favorite accompaniment to curry and rice, it is an acquired taste as it is rather pungent. Fry in hot oil until crisp and golden, then drain on paper towels. This may be done ahead of time and the 'ducks' kept crisp in an air-tight container.

Poppadums: These fine lentil wafers are fried for a few seconds in deep, hot oil. The oil should be hot enough to make the poppadums swell and curl as soon as they are dropped in. If the oil is not hot enough, the poppadums will be oily and tough. Fry one at a time and drain on paper towels.

Fresh Pineapple: Peel the pineapple and remove the hard core. Cut into $\frac{1}{2}$-inch cubes. Sprinkle lightly with salt and, if liked, a little chili powder. Chill and serve sprinkled with chopped mint.

COCONUT MILK

Put 3 cups shredded coconut into a saucepan, pour 3 cups milk over, and bring slowly to a boil. Allow to cool to lukewarm. Put into a blender and blend at high speed for 2 to 3 minutes. Strain. If no blender is available, knead the coconut well when cool enough to handle and strain through a fine strainer, pressing well to extract as much milk as possible. This is the first extract or thick milk. Repeat the process with the same coconut and 3 more cups milk. This will give thinner milk, which will still have a good flavor.

COCONUT CREAM

Make as above, using half cream, half milk. Leave in the refrigerator overnight and spoon off the creamy top to use as Coconut Cream. The remaining Coconut Milk is excellent for curries.

The flavor of Spanish food epitomizes the spirit of that warm, sunny country, its colorful people, its Flamenco music and dancing, its gaiety and pathos.

It sings with the richness of golden olive oil, the perfumes of saffron and other spices, the tartness of sun-ripened tomatoes and pimientos. There are many dishes that come to mind when I recall the meals I have enjoyed in Spain. Among them is that refreshing iced soup, Gazpacho (see page 47), the wonderful shellfish, and that superb combination of rice, seafood, saffron, garlic, and chicken which is the prize of Valencia—the famous Paella (see page 93).

For this menu I have chosen other dishes, just as typically Spanish but perhaps not so well known. Delicate almond soup, a pork loin roast deliciously spiced and basted with sherry, and an unusual dessert, Fried Cream.

A Spanish Menu

Almond Soup

Lomo Con Jerez
(Loin of Pork with Sherry)

Crema Frita
(Fried Cream)

ALMOND SOUP

1 cup shelled blanched almonds
5 cups milk
1 onion, finely chopped
1 celery heart, finely chopped
2 tablespoons butter

2 tablespoons all-purpose flour
cayenne pepper, ground mace, and salt to taste
½ cup toasted almond slivers

Cooking time: 15 minutes
Serves: 6

Put the almonds through the fine blade of a food grinder. Simmer in 2 cups of milk with the onion and celery. Make a roux with the butter and flour and add the remaining milk gradually. Mix this into the first mixture and cook in a double boiler, stirring, until of the thickness of cream soup. Season with cayenne pepper, mace, and salt. Top each portion with toasted almond slivers. May be served hot or well chilled.

LOMO CON JEREZ

(LOIN OF PORK WITH SHERRY)

1 pork loin roast, 5-6 lb.
2½ teaspoons salt
½ teaspoon freshly cracked black pepper
½ teaspoon cumin

½ teaspoon powdered saffron
2 cloves garlic, crushed
¼ cup finely chopped parsley
¼ cup olive oil
2 cups medium dry sherry

Cooking time: 2½-3 hours
Temperature: 400°
   reducing to 350°
Serves: 6

Have the butcher trim the fat and tie the loin. Rub with a mixture of the salt, pepper, cumin, saffron, garlic, and parsley. Let stand for 2 hours.

Heat the oil in a deep roasting pan or Dutch oven. Brown the pork in it on all sides, then roast in a 400° oven for 30 minutes. Pour off the fat and add the sherry. Continue to roast in a 350° oven for a further 2 to 2½ hours, or until the pork is tender and well done, basting frequently. Serve hot with Saffron Rice (see page 205).

CREMA FRITA

(FRIED CREAM)

4 egg yolks
½ cup sugar
½ cup all-purpose flour
2½ cups milk, scalded
¼ cup sweet sherry

1 teaspoon vanilla extract
1 egg, beaten
½ cup dry bread crumbs
6 tablespoons butter
confectioners' sugar

Serves: 6

Beat the egg yolks in a saucepan. Blend the sugar and flour, add to the egg yolks, and mix until smooth. Gradually add the hot milk, stirring constantly to prevent curdling. Add the sherry and cook over very gentle heat, stirring constantly, until the mixture is very thick. Stir in the vanilla extract and pour the custard into an oblong cake pan approximately 10 by 6 inches which has been rinsed with cold water. Chill until firm. Cut the custard into squares, dip in the beaten egg and then in the bread crumbs, and brown in hot butter. Serve hot, sprinkled with confectioners' sugar.

ITALIAN COOKERY

Variety is the spice of life and anyone who visits Italy is immediately struck by the great variety and many contrasts in architecture, dress, and food as he travels north or south.

Italian antipasto is famous. It may be as simple as a selection of peppery salami, green or ripe olives, crisp radishes or scallions. On the other hand it could be an elaborate arrangement of luxury foods in a variety of sauces.

For simple meals the antipasto often gives way to soup or macaroni, but seldom does pasta take the place of a main dish of poultry, meat, or fish. Next comes the cheese and fruit course, or a light dessert.

The suggested meal could be served as a luncheon or dinner—it would be the main meal of the day. Remember the Chianti!

An Italian Luncheon or Dinner

Stracciatella

Lasagne

Green Salad

Zabaglione Soufflés

STRACCIATELLA

(ROMAN EGG DROP SOUP)

3 eggs
2 tablespoons grated Romano
cheese

2 tablespoons finely chopped
parsley
6 cups chicken stock or water
and chicken bouillon cubes

Cooking time: 5 minutes
Serves: 6

Beat the eggs thoroughly and stir in the cheese and parsley. Bring the stock to a boil. Stir in the egg mixture and simmer the soup for a few seconds, or until the eggs cook. Serve immediately. The egg will appear as little flakes in the soup.

Leeks a la Grecque and Kotopoulo me Lemono (Chicken with Lemon)

LASAGNE

¼ cup olive oil
1 cup ground beef
1 cup ground pork
1 onion, finely chopped
1 clove garlic, chopped
1 teaspoon chopped parsley
1 (8 oz.) can tomato paste
scant 2 cups water

½ teaspoon salt
½ teaspoon pepper
½ lb. lasagne
½ lb. Mozzarella cheese, sliced
  thinly
½ lb. ricotta cheese
¼ cup grated Romano cheese

Cooking time: 2 hours
Temperature: 350°
Serves: 6

Heat the oil in a saucepan, add the beef and pork, and brown with the onion, garlic, and parsley. Stir in the tomato paste, water, salt, and pepper and simmer for 1½ hours. Meanwhile bring a large saucepan of water to a boil and add 1½ teaspoons salt and the lasagne, broken in half. Boil for 20 minutes, stirring constantly to prevent the pasta sticking, until tender. Drain.

In a greased casserole about 2 inches deep, arrange alternate layers of lasagne, sauce, Mozzarella cheese, and ricotta cheese. Repeat the layers until the lasagne is all used, ending with ricotta cheese. Sprinkle with grated Romano cheese and bake in a 350° oven for 25 to 30 minutes.

ZABAGLIONE SOUFFLÉS

1½ envelopes gelatin
6 tablespoons water
3 eggs, separated

½ cup sugar
½ cup Marsala or sweet sherry

Serves: 6

Sprinkle the gelatin onto the water and allow to soften for 3 minutes. Dissolve over hot water. In the top part of a double boiler or in a heatproof bowl, beat the egg yolks with a rotary beater. Add half the sugar and beat until thick and pale in color. Add the gelatin and beat well. Gradually beat in the Marsala. Place the pan over simmering water and continue to beat until the mixture foams and begins to thicken. Be careful not to over-cook. Cool, then chill until beginning to set. Whip the egg whites until stiff, gradually whip in the remaining sugar, and then fold into the egg yolk mixture. Spoon into tall glasses and serve cold. If liked, serve with a ladyfinger or macaroon cookie.

GREEK COOKERY

Ancient Greeks had a word for a lover of good food—epicure—and even today Greek food reaches epicurean heights.

Greek dishes abound in seafood from the Mediterranean waters, lamb, and olives. You will also find chicken, rice, and pasta featuring. The food is neither oily nor hotly spiced, yet it is varied and interesting. The flavors and seasonings are subtle, egg and lemon combining in many delicate sauces. Feta, the creamy white goats' cheese, ricotta, and cottage cheese find their way into salads, pasta dishes, and pastries, and combined with sun-ripened olives make a simple antipasto or even a simple meal when accompanied by coarse crusty bread. Desserts, cakes, and pastries are sweet and syrupy in the Turkish manner.

A Greek Menu

Leeks â la Grecque

Kotopoulo me Lemono
(Chicken with Lemon)

Halva

424

LEEKS À LA GRECQUE

6 medium-sized leeks
2 tablespoons fresh chopped
   tarragon or 1 teaspoon dried
   tarragon
2 tablespoons lemon juice
1 clove garlic, crushed
2 tablespoons finely chopped
   parsley

1 tomato, skinned and seeded
pinch thyme
salt and freshly cracked black
   pepper
1 bay leaf
$\frac{1}{4}$ cup olive oil
1 cup water

Cooking time: 10-15 minutes
Serves: 6

Cut the tops off the leeks, leaving 2 inches of green tops. Wash thoroughly to remove any grit. If the leeks are large, halve lengthwise. Put all the ingredients into a heavy saucepan or flameproof casserole. (A flat stainless steel or earthenware pan is best.) Cover and bring to a boil. Lower the heat and simmer gently for about 10 minutes until the leeks are tender but firm. Allow to cool, then chill.

KOTOPOULO ME LEMONO

(CHICKEN WITH LEMON)

1 4-lb. stewing chicken
1 lemon
salt and pepper
2 carrots, sliced
2 medium-sized onions, sliced
3 stalks celery, sliced

2 cups mushrooms
$\frac{1}{4}$ cup butter
$\frac{2}{3}$ cup dry sherry
1 cup blanched almonds
1 egg
7 tablespoons cream

Cooking time: $1\frac{1}{2}$-3 hours
Serves: 6

Rub the chicken all over with half the lemon and season well with plenty of salt and pepper. Put the other half of the lemon inside the chicken and tie the legs together. In a large pan, bring enough water to a boil to cover the chicken. Add the chicken, carrots, onions, and celery. Simmer until the chicken is tender, about $1\frac{1}{4}$-$1\frac{1}{2}$ hours. If the bird is an old stewing hen it will take 3 hours. In this case do not add the vegetables until the last hour of the cooking time. Put the chicken onto a serving dish and keep warm. Reserve $1\frac{1}{4}$ cups chicken stock. Slice the mushrooms and gently cook in butter until softened. Add the reserved chicken stock, the sherry, and the almonds and heat gently. Beat the egg and cream, blend in some of the hot stock gradually, then pour into the saucepan and stir over a gentle heat until the sauce thickens. Do not allow the mixture to boil. Taste and add more salt and pepper if necessary. Pour over the chicken and serve.

HALVA

$\frac{3}{4}$ cup unsalted butter
1 cup sugar
4 eggs

1 cup chopped blanched almonds
$2\frac{1}{3}$ cups semolina
1 teaspoon cinnamon

Cooking time: 35-40 minutes
Temperature: 350°
Serves: 6

For syrup:
generous 2 cups sugar
1 3-inch stick cinnamon

4 cups water
2 tablespoons lemon juice

Cream the butter until softened and gradually beat in the sugar. Add the eggs, one at a time, beating well after each. Stir in the almonds and blend thoroughly. Put the semolina into a bowl, add the cinnamon, then the almond mixture. Brush a 9-inch square cake pan with melted butter. Spread the batter evenly in the pan and bake in a 350° oven for 35 to 40 minutes. Pour the cooled syrup over and leave until cold. Serve cut into squares. To make the syrup: Heat the sugar, cinnamon stick, and water until the sugar dissolves. Bring to a boil and cook until it becomes a fairly thick syrup; stir in the lemon juice. Cool.

There is perhaps no other country in the world where food and wine have such a romantic setting and it is hard not to think of Wiener Schnitzel and Sachertorte other than to the strains of a Strauss waltz.

A typical Austrian meal would be filling indeed. The first course would be soup with noodles or dumplings and fresh rolls, then fish with a rich sauce and boiled potatoes. This would be followed by meat with salad and/or a selection of vegetables, then chicken, then a rich sweet and cakes, coffee, and liqueurs. The food is so delicious and the atmosphere so gay that it is possible to get through such a meal.

The selected menu shows the lighter side of Austrian cooking. The soup relies on a good basic stock, the veal and sauerkraut may be accompanied by a small portion of boiled potatoes. Serve the Linzertorte warm with whipped cream; it is equally good cold and served with coffee.

An Austrian Dinner

Tyrolean Horseradish Soup

Stuffed Loin of Veal

Sauerkraut and Apples

Linzertorte

TYROLEAN HORSERADISH SOUP

5 cups beef
  consommé
salt and pepper

$\frac{1}{4}$ cup freshly grated horseradish
  or prepared horseradish relish

Bring the consommé to a boil. Add the salt and pepper to taste and the horseradish. Serve immediately.

Note: Canned beef consommé or water and beef bouillon cubes may be used for the soup base.

STUFFED LOIN OF VEAL

1 2$\frac{1}{2}$-lb. veal loin roast
grated rind and juice of 1 lemon
4 mushrooms, chopped
1 cup fine white bread crumbs
2 tablespoons chopped parsley
1 cup chopped bacon

4 anchovy fillets
salt and pepper
1 egg yolk
$\frac{1}{2}$ cup butter
1 cup chicken stock or water
  and chicken bouillon cube

Cooking time: 1$\frac{1}{2}$ hours
Temperature: 375°
Serves: 6

Have the butcher remove the bones and skin from the loin. Rub over with the lemon juice. Combine the mushrooms and bread crumbs with the parsley, lemon rind, bacon, and the mashed anchovy fillets. Season with salt and pepper and moisten with the egg yolk. If not moist enough add a little milk. Spread the stuffing over the veal and roll up. Tie with string or use skewers to hold it together. Brown well on all sides in the melted butter in a large heavy flameproof casserole. Pour the stock over and roast in a 375° oven until tender. Do not cover, and allow 35 minutes to each pound. Turn the veal several times during the cooking and baste with the stock. Serve the juices from the casserole as a sauce.

SAUERKRAUT AND APPLES

Cooking time:　30 minutes
Serves:　　　　6

A simple way to prepare this dish is to simmer 1 (2 lb.) can sauerkraut in water for 10 minutes. Pour off the water. Lightly fry 2 peeled, chopped apples with $\frac{1}{4}$ cup diced bacon for a few minutes. Add 1 chopped onion, cook a further 5 minutes, add the sauerkraut, and simmer gently for 10 minutes. Season to taste.

LINZERTORTE

1 cup all-purpose flour
$\frac{1}{4}$ cup sugar
1 tablespoon cocoa powder
$\frac{1}{2}$ teaspoon cinnamon
$\frac{1}{2}$ teaspoon baking powder
pinch ground cloves (optional)
pinch salt

1 cup ground almonds
$\frac{1}{2}$ cup butter
milk or Kirsch
$1\frac{1}{2}$ cups jam, raspberry, currant,
　or strawberry
egg for glazing
whipped cream

Cooking time:　40 minutes
Temperature:　375°
Serves:　　　　6-8

Sift all the dry ingredients except the almonds into a mixing bowl. Add the almonds. Rub in the butter. Add milk or Kirsch if required to make a dry dough. Knead only until combined. Rest the dough in the refrigerator for 30 minutes. Roll out two thirds of the mixture and press onto the bottom of an 8-inch greased spring form pan. Spread the jam on top. Roll out the remaining dough, cut into $\frac{1}{2}$-inch strips, and arrange cross wise on top, using the last one as an edging around the side of the cake. Press down lightly. Chill again. Brush with beaten egg and bake in a 375° oven for 35 to 40 minutes. Allow to cool in the pan. Serve with whipped cream.

Variation: Decorate the Linzertorte with raspberries and sifted confectioners' sugar and serve with a bowl of fresh raspberries.

RUSSIAN COOKERY

Most people think of Russian food as exotic—mounds of caviar with the tiny, freshly made yeast buckwheat pancakes known as Blinis, Bortsch with sour cream, and Stroganoff, which now appear on menus throughout the world. Sour cream, or smetana as it is known in Russia, is an ingredient that gives Russian food a distinct character of its own. Cooked beet served hot or cold in a sauce of sour cream and grated horseradish shows what sour cream can do for a simple vegetable.

The selected Russian menu includes three simple dishes which may easily be made at home. The cherry soup would be made in Russia with fresh fruit when available, the stroganoff is an unusual but authentic recipe with grated raw onion added to the dish just before it is served. The dessert is perhaps a less well known version of the great classic, Strawberries à la Romanoff, and one which is also authentic. There is a simpler version of Strawberries Romanoff which simply combines sugared strawberries with Curaçao topped with whipped cream.

A Russian Luncheon

Cherry Soup

Beef Stroganoff

Strawberries à la Romanoff

428

CHERRY SOUP

1 (16 oz.) jar sour cherries
3¾ cups water
3-4 cardamom pods, pounded
¼ cup sugar

1 lemon
2 tablespoons cornstarch
chopped parsley

Cooking time: 15 minutes
Serves: 6

Heat the cherries in their syrup with the water, cardamom, sugar, and the thinly peeled rind of the lemon. Simmer gently for 10 minutes. Rub through a sieve. Blend the cornstarch in a little cold water to a smooth paste, gradually add to the fruit purée, and bring to the simmering point, stirring. Cook for about 5 minutes, stirring all the time until the soup has thickened and has a translucent appearance. Stir in the juice of the lemon. Serve cold, sprinkled with chopped parsley.

BEEF STROGANOFF

2 lb. beef tenderloin
salt and pepper
¼ cup butter

¼ cup tomato paste
⅔ cup sour cream
2 tablespoons grated onion

Cooking time: 15 minutes
Serves: 6

Cut the beef into thin strips, 1½ inches long and ¼ inch wide. Sprinkle well with salt and pepper and let stand for 2 hours in a cool place or in the refrigerator.

Heat a skillet, add the butter, and fry the pieces of beef until just colored. Add the tomato paste and sour cream; heat gently or cook in a double boiler over hot water for 10 to 15 minutes. Taste for seasoning and just before serving add the grated onion. Serve at once with a side dish of boiled rice or potato balls and thin slices of dark bread generously buttered, or with crisp potato straws.

STRAWBERRIES À LA ROMANOFF

1 cup whipping cream
1¼ pints vanilla ice cream
2 lb. strawberries

sugar
1 liqueur glass Cointreau

Serves: 6

Whip the cream until stiff. Soften the ice cream slightly, and fold in the cream. Put into freezer trays and freeze until firm. Wash and hull the strawberries and add sugar to taste, reserving a few strawberries for decoration. Chill. Before serving add the Cointreau to the strawberries. Soften the ice cream and fold in the strawberries. Decorate with a few reserved strawberries and serve at once.

GERMAN COOKERY

Germany has given its food to many parts of the world. There is hardly a delicatessen that does not show the influence of at least a dozen delicacies of German origin, the great array of sausages, the sauerkraut, the herring, and of course, the heavenly Rhine wines. Not only the hamburger and frankfurter have German origins, but the famous jelly or Berlin doughnut is known to many a Berliner as 'Pfannkuchen'.

In a country that boasts a soup for every day of the year, be assured the German housewife is not only a good but a careful cook.

For the selected menu the Rollmop Salad illustrates the heartiness of many German dishes. The dessert course features the famous black cherries of Germany that are preserved and sent to all areas of the globe.

A German Menu

Rollmop Salad

German Sour Chicken

Black Cherry Soufflé

ROLLMOP SALAD

4 rollmops
⅔ cup salad dressing or sour cream
1 teaspoon sugar
¼ teaspoon dry mustard
2 tablespoons white wine
salt and pepper

2 large boiled potatoes
1 small cooked beet
few crisp lettuce leaves
1 red apple, cut into cubes
4 dill pickles, sliced
6 scallions

Serves: 6

Cut the rollmops into strips. Mix the salad dressing with the sugar, mustard, and wine. Season to taste with salt and pepper. Dice the potatoes and beet and fold into the dressing. Place the lettuce leaves on a flat platter with the potato and beet and top with the rollmops. Arrange the apple cubes, slices of dill pickle, and finely sliced scallion around the sides.

GERMAN SOUR CHICKEN

4 lb. chicken pieces
⅓ cup vinegar
2½ cups water
1 bay leaf
3 cloves

¼ teaspoon grated nutmeg
1 onion, sliced
salt and pepper
⅔ cup sour cream

Cooking time: 50-60 minutes
Serves: 6

Put the chicken pieces into a saucepan with the vinegar and water. Add the bay leaf, cloves, nutmeg, onion, salt, and pepper. Cover and simmer gently until the chicken is tender, about 30 minutes. Remove the bay leaf and cloves. Add the sour cream, stirring until blended. Simmer gently for a further 10 minutes over very low heat. Serve with boiled new potatoes and a green vegetable.

BLACK CHERRY SOUFFLÉ

3 tablespoons butter
2 tablespoons all-purpose flour
1 cup milk
¼ teaspoon salt
½ cup sugar

1 (16 oz.) jar pitted black cherries
4 egg yolks, slightly beaten
5 egg whites
1-2 teaspoons arrowroot

Cooking time: 40 minutes
Temperature: 375°
    reducing to 350°
Serves: 6

Brush a soufflé dish well with butter and sprinkle with sugar. Melt the butter in a saucepan, stir in the flour, and cook for 1 minute. Remove from the heat and gradually add the milk, stirring constantly. Mix in the salt and sugar. Return to the heat and cook, stirring constantly, until the sauce is thick and smooth. Cool. Add the drained pitted cherries and the egg yolks and mix well. Beat the egg whites stiffly and gently fold into the mixture. Pour into the prepared soufflé dish. Stand the dish in a pan of hot water and bake in 375° oven for 15 minutes. Reduce the heat to 350° and cook for a further 25 minutes. Serve immediately with a sauce made by heating the cherry syrup blended with arrowroot, stirring continuously until thickened.

No Scandinavian meal would be complete without a fish dish. This could be in the form of a salad or a tempting hors d'oeuvre, using one of the many types of herring, salted, smoked, or in vinegar, or the delectable shrimp, smoked salmon, or fresh fish.

Denmark produces some of the finest ham and bacon in the world; it also produces excellent pork, and the Danes have a 'way' with pork. The main dish in this menu is pork done in the Danish manner with prunes. This may be served with mashed potatoes, or if liked, Danish Sugar Browned Potatoes.

A Finnish dessert makes a perfect finish to this Scandinavian meal.

A Scandinavian Meal

Fiskepudding
(Fish Pudding with Hollandaise Sauce)

Plommonspackad Fläskkarre
(Pork Stuffed with Prunes)

Sugar Browned Potatoes

Mansikkalumi
(Strawberry Snow)

FISKEPUDDING

(FISH PUDDING)

1 lb. raw white fish (flounder, haddock, or snapper)
½ cup butter
few drops anchovy extract
1 teaspoon salt
freshly ground pepper
3 eggs
6 tablespoons all-purpose flour

2 cups milk
2 cups cream
brown bread crumbs and butter to coat mold
parsley sprigs, sliced cucumber, and shrimp or prawns for garnish

Cooking time: 1-1½ hours
Temperature: 300°
Serves: 6

Remove any bones and skin from the fish. Put it twice through a grinder. Put the fish in a large bowl and add the butter and anchovy extract. Pound and work well together. Add the salt and pepper, then the slightly beaten eggs and flour alternately. Gradually add the milk and cream, beating in well. If the mixture starts to curdle place the bowl over simmering water and heat until smooth. Grease a 1-quart mold (it may be a pudding bowl, a loaf pan, or a ring mold) and coat with the bread crumbs. Spoon in the fish mixture (it should come three fourths of the way up the sides of the mold), cover with wax paper, and stand the mold in a roasting pan of boiling water. Bake in a 300° oven for 1 to 1½ hours. To test if done, insert a thin-bladed knife; if it comes out clean the pudding is cooked. Turn out very carefully. Garnish with parsley, thin slices of cucumber, and fresh or canned shrimp or prawns. Serve with Hollandaise Sauce (see page 56).

PLOMMONSPACKAD FLÄSKKARRE

(PORK STUFFED WITH PRUNES)

15 prunes
1 boned pork loin roast, 3-3½ lb.
2 teaspoons salt

½ teaspoon ginger
½ teaspoon freshly cracked
    pepper

Cooking time: 1½-2 hours
Temperature: 350°
Serves: 6

Soak the prunes overnight in water and simmer gently until tender, about 5 minutes. Drain and reserve 1 cup juice. Split the prunes in half and remove the pits. Flatten the meat. Mix the salt, ginger, and pepper and rub into the meat. Lay the prunes on top. Roll up the meat and tie with string. Brown all over in an ovenproof casserole over direct heat, using a little oil if there is little fat on the meat. Add the prune juice. Cover and bake in a 350° oven for 1½ hours, basting from time to time, until tender. Put the pork on a serving dish and remove the string. Carve in slices and serve with Applesauce (see page 59) or cooked prunes and red cabbage. Serve the pan juices separately.

SUGAR BROWNED POTOTES

Serves: 6

Boil small potatoes in the usual way. Then, for 2 lb. potatoes, melt 3 tablespoons butter and 3 tablespoons sugar in a heavy pan and turn the potatoes in this mixture until they have a rich brown crust.

MANSIKKALUMI

(STRAWBERRY SNOW)

2 envelopes gelatin
¼ cup water
2 cups crushed strawberries
4 egg whites

½ cup sugar
1 cup whipping cream
extra whole strawberries for
    decoration

Serves: 6

Sprinkle the gelatin over the water and allow to soften for 5 minutes. Heat 1 cup crushed strawberries to the boiling point, add the gelatin, and stir until dissolved. Chill until the mixture begins to set around the edges of the bowl. Whip the egg whites until soft peaks form and gradually whip in the sugar. Fold into the strawberry mixture, then add the remaining strawberries and whipped cream. Serve immediately in individual glass dishes and decorate each with the whole strawberries.

Note: This dessert may also be served frozen. Pour the mixture into freezer trays and freeze.

COOKERY OF THE NETHERLANDS AND BELGIUM

Dutch cooking is very characteristic and national. The generous use of rice and spices is a reminder of her colonial days in tropical areas. Nutmeg is used freely to flavor potatoes, spinach, turnips, soups, cheese dishes, meats, and cakes.

Exotic Rijstafel, a Javanese feast of rice, beef, pork, fish, chicken, pickled vegetables, and sambals, is so closely associated with Holland that it often appears on international menus as Dutch. A simpler dish, but also originating in the Dutch East Indies, now Indonesia, is Nasi Goreng—very popular with Dutch families.

In Holland and Belgium the youngest and most tender vegetables are grown in the fertile soil. A visitor cannot help but be impressed by the care with which they are both grown and cooked.

Meat dishes are not served every day, nor is meat served in large quantities, but the Dutch way of pot roasting has led to the heavy demand for Dutch ovens, the heavy cast iron pots that cook turkey, chicken, and other whole joints to perfection.

Haringsla
(Herring Salad)

Carbonnade à la Flamande
(Flemish Carbonnade)

Dutch Apple Cake

HARINGSLA

(HERRING SALAD)

2 large raw salt herring or
   canned pickled herring
2 cooking apples
1 cooked beet
1 head lettuce
6 new potatoes

$\frac{1}{4}$ cup olive oil
$\frac{1}{3}$ cup vinegar
salt and pepper
2 eggs, hard-cooked
2 sweet pickled cucumbers
3 pickled onions

Carefully remove the bones and skin from the fish. Cut the fillets into small pieces. Peel, core, and finely chop the apples. Peel and dice the beet. Wash and dry the lettuce, then shred the leaves. Boil the potatoes in their skins; peel and dice them. Mix all these ingredients together in a bowl. Whip the oil and vinegar together until well blended and season with salt and freshly cracked black pepper to taste. Sprinkle over the salad ingredients and toss gently. Arrange in a salad bowl. Garnish with sliced hard-cooked eggs, sliced cucumber, onions.

CARBONNADE À LA FLAMANDE

(FLEMISH CARBONNADE)

all-purpose flour
salt and pepper
2 lb. chuck steak
$\frac{1}{4}$ cup oil
6 onions, sliced

1 clove garlic, finely chopped
1$\frac{1}{4}$ cups beer
2 tablespoons chopped parsley
1 bay leaf
$\frac{1}{4}$ teaspoon thyme

Cooking time: 1$\frac{1}{4}$ hours
Serves: 6

Season the flour with salt and freshly cracked black pepper. Cut the steak into 1-inch cubes and coat with the seasoned flour. Heat the oil in a heavy saucepan or flameproof casserole, add the onion and garlic, and cook until tender but not brown. Remove the onion and garlic and reserve. Dust the excess flour from the meat, add to the pan, and brown well on all sides, adding a little more oil if necessary. Return the onions to the pan and add the remaining ingredients. Cover and cook over low heat until the meat is tender, about 1$\frac{1}{4}$ hours. Serve hot with boiled potatoes.

Variation: Carbonnade may also be finished with rounds of crustry French bread spread with French or German mustard. These are pushed below the surface of the carbonnade to soak with the gravy and are baked for the last 15 to 20 minutes of the cooking time.

Moules à la Provençale

DUTCH APPLE CAKE

For pie crust:
¾ cup butter
1¾ cups all-purpose flour
6 tablespoons sugar
1 egg yolk

For filling:
5-6 large cooking apples
½ cup sugar
¾ cup red currant jelly

1 tablespoon iced water finely
    grated rind of 1 large lemon
whipping cream for serving
few drops vanilla extract

cinnamon
¼ cup blanched slivered almonds

Cooking time: 35-40 minutes
Temperature: 400°
    reducing to 350°
Serves: 6

To make the pie crust: Cream the butter and mix in the flour, sugar, egg yolk, water, lemon rind, and vanilla extract. Blend the mixture with the hands until smooth. Chill for 30 minutes. Divide into 2 portions, one slightly larger than the other. Press the larger portion into the bottom and sides of a greased 8-inch spring form pan. Chill while preparing the filling.

To make the filling: Peel the apples and cut into thin slices, sprinkle with sugar, and gently mix in the red currant jelly. Spoon into the pie shell. Roll out the remaining dough on a lightly floured board to ¼-inch thickness. Cut into strips and arrange over the apples in a lattice design. Sprinkle the strips with cinnamon and the visible apples with slivered almonds. Bake in a 400° oven for 15 minutes. Reduce the temperature to 350° and bake for a further 20 to 25 minutes, until the apples are tender and the pastry is golden. Cool and remove from the spring form pan. Serve warm with whipped cream flavored with a little vanilla extract.

SWISS COOKERY

Switzerland is a gourmet's paradise where quality is very much in evidence. In hotels and restaurants the food is international but always prepared to perfection, for Switerland is the home of training schools for hotel and restaurant cookery. Many of the world's great hoteliers and chefs began their life work in Switerland.

Behind the international hotel there is simpler fare, but standards remain at the same high level. Rich cream,

milk, and butter are used freely. The Swiss are masters of the art of cooking. Veal and chicken dishes are outstanding, excellent wine is used in cookery. and the cheeses of Switzerland need no introduction.

If you lean towards the picturesque, good food, and good wine you could not do better than go to Switzerland; if that is out of the question, cook the Swiss way.

A Swiss Meal

Rosti und Geschnitzeltes

(Fried Potatoes and Shredded Veal in Cream Sauce)

Savarin

436

GESCHNITZELTES
(SHREDDED VEAL IN CREAM SAUCE)

1½ lb. thin veal steaks
2 tablespoons all-purpose flour
2 tablespoons butter
1 onion, finely chopped
1 clove garlic, finely chopped

salt and pepper
1 teaspoon paprika pepper
7 tablespoons red wine
2 tablespoons tomato paste
⅔ cup cream

Cooking time: 25-30 minutes
Serves: 6

Cut the veal into thin strips and sprinkle with the flour. Heat the butter in a heavy skillet and add the veal. Fry quickly, turning constantly. As soon as the veal starts to color, add the onion and garlic. Season with salt, freshly cracked pepper, and paprika pepper. Pour in the wine and add the tomato paste. Lastly stir in the cream. Cover and simmer for 25 to 30 minutes.

ROSTI
(SWISS FRIED POTATOES)

6 large potatoes
¼ cup butter or 2 tablespoons
  butter and 2 tablespoons
  shortening

1 onion, finely chopped, or
  3 slices bacon (optional)
salt and pepper

Serves: 6

Scrub the potatoes and boil in their skins until barely tender; drain and peel immediately. Cut into thin slices. Heat the butter (or a mixture of butter and shortening, which gives the best results) in a heavy skillet, add the potato slices and (if used) the onion or bacon, cut into dice, and season with salt and pepper. Fry over high heat, turning the potatoes occasionally to brown on all sides. Lower the heat, press the potatoes firmly into the pan, and fry slowly for a few minutes until a golden crust forms underneath. Cover and cook gently until tender, about 5 to 10 minutes. To serve, turn into a plate so that the brown crust is uppermost. Serve at once.

SAVARIN

½ cup milk
½ cake compressed yeast or
  ¼ oz. dry yeast
2 egg yolks
¼ cup sugar
1 whole egg

¼ cup unsalted butter
few drops vanilla extract
1¾ cups all-purpose flour
slivered almonds and candied
  fruits, for decorating (optional)
whipped cream, for serving

Cooking time: 25-30 minutes
Temperature: 400°
Serves: 8-10

For syrup:
1¼ cups water
1 cup sugar

few drops vanilla extract
⅓ cup Kirsch

For apricot glaze:
½ cup apricot jam

2 tablespoons water

Scald the milk, cool to lukewarm, and add the yeast, stirring until smooth. If using dry yeast, allow to stand for about 10 minutes, until frothy. Beat the egg yolks until thick and gradually add the sugar. Beat in the whole egg vigorously. Melt the butter and add to the egg mixture while still slightly warm. Add the vanilla extract. Stir in the milk and yeast mixture and beat in the sifted flour, adding more if necessary to make a medium-stiff batter. Beat vigorously by hand. Put in a clean, greased bowl, cover with a cloth, and put in a warm place to rise for 2 hours. Pour into 2 greased 7-inch savarin molds or tube pans and leave to rise again in a warm place until double in volume. Bake in a 400° oven for 25 to 30 minutes. While still hot, pour over the syrup. Allow to stand until the syrup is absorbed. Turn out onto a serving platter and brush all over with apricot glaze. Decorate with almonds and, if liked, candied fruits. Fill the center with whipped cream.

To make the syrup: Combine the water, sugar, and vanilla extract in a saucepan. Bring to a boil and simmer for 10 minutes. Add the Kirsch.

To make the apricot glaze: Heat the jam with the water until boiling. Press through a sieve and use to brush over the savarin.

Note: Savarins freeze well and if only one is required cool the second cake (do not pour the syrup over), wrap in aluminum foil, and freeze. To reheat, put in a 300° oven for 10 to 12 minutes until warm, then pour over hot syrup and glaze.

FRENCH COOKERY

The fabled food of France has earned for that country a reputation second to none among lovers of good food. It is here that chefs are honored on a par with learned doctors and other professional men, and no wonder. They too have spent years learning their art.

The average French woman too has the approach of an artist—an artist in love. Whether it is delicately flavored sauce rich with cream, or simple peasant food with a strong smell of garlic, each dish the French housewife makes is given as much care as if it were intended for a royal banquet—or a lover.

In France, the quality of the raw ingredients is all-important and food is treated with the respect it deserves. This menu is typically French provincial and features the mussels which are so plentiful along the coast, simply steamed then drenched in garlic butter, roast lamb with vegetables, and a dessert so simple yet utterly delicious that it is known throughout the world as French Toast.

A French Provincial Meal

Moules à la Provençale
(Mussels with Garlic)

Pré-salé à la Bretonne
(Roast Leg of Lamb with Garlic)

Pain Perdu
(French Toast)

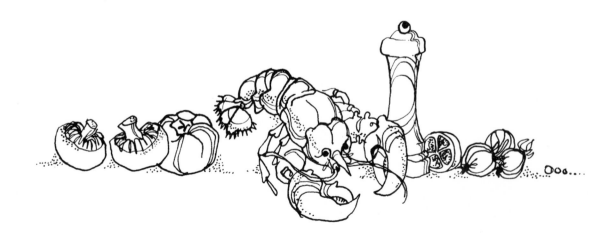

MOULES À LA PROVENÇALE

(MUSSELS WITH GARLIC)

6 quarts mussels
1 cup butter
salt and pepper

2 cloves garlic, finely chopped
¼ cup chopped parsley
fine dry bread crumbs

Serves: 6

Scrub the mussels well and wash under running cold water. Steam open the mussels by shaking them in a deep pan over high heat. Keep the mussels on the lower shell and arrange on a platter. Melt the butter and add the salt, pepper, garlic, and parsley. Drizzle the butter over the mussels. Sprinkle with bread crumbs and place under a preheated hot broiler until brown. Serve at once.

PRÉ-SALÉ À LA BRETONNE

(ROAST LEG OF LAMB WITH GARLIC)

1 leg of lamb, 3½-4 lb.
4 cloves garlic, quartered
salt and pepper
6 artichoke hearts (optional)
juice of 1 lemon
butter
2 lb. fresh green peas

1 lettuce heart
2-3 small onions
2 lumps sugar
⅓ cup cream
chopped parsley and sprigs of
  watercress for garnish

Cooking time: 2 hours
Temperature: 400°
  reducing to 350°
Serves: 6

Wipe the leg of lamb and trim off the excess fat. With a small pointed knife make incisions in the lamb at intervals and insert ¼ clove garlic in each cut. Season with salt and pepper and cook in a 400° oven for 20 minutes, then reduce the temperature to 350°, and roast for a further 1¼ to 1¾ hours, allowing 25 minutes to the pound.

Trim the artichoke hearts and rub with lemon juice to prevent discoloration. Poach in lightly salted water until almost done, then drain and simmer gently in melted butter in a covered saucepan. Shell the peas and place in a saucepan with a little water, salt, pepper, the lettuce heart, onions, and sugar lumps. Cook gently until tender and almost all the moisture has evaporated. Drain off any remaining liquid, remove the lettuce and onions, and add a generous lump of butter to the pan. Shake over heat until the butter melts, then add the cream and shake the pan to mix. Slice the leg of lamb in even slices and arrange them on a hot platter. Skim the fat from the pan juices and pour the juices over the meat. Garnish the platter with artichoke hearts and mounds of green peas, sprinkled with chopped parsley. Place a small bunch of watercress at each end of the platter.

PAIN PERDU

(FRENCH TOAST)

6 thick slices day-old bread
1¼ cups milk
¼ cup sugar
½ teaspoon vanilla extract
2 tablespoons Grand Marnier
  (optional)

2 eggs, beaten
all-purpose flour
clarified butter for frying
sugar for serving

Serves: 6

Soak the slices of bread in the milk sweetened with the sugar and flavored with the vanilla and Grand Marnier. Dip the soaked bread into the beaten eggs, then into flour. Shake off the excess flour and fry the bread in hot clarified butter until golden brown on both sides, turning once. Sprinkle generously with sugar and serve hot.

WINE AND FOOD

Wines

Len Evans

Len Evans has written three books on wine, writes regularly for magazines, and is a wine merchant, vigneron, and restauranteur.

John Stanford is a graduate of the Oenology School, Roseworthy College, in Adelaide, Australia, and is the Federal Manager of The Australian Wine Bureau.

Frank Margan writes a regular wine and food column, and owns a vineyard himself. In addition to his journalistic activities he has written a book on wine.

Wine is a contradiction. In its simplest form wine is nothing more than a drink. It is the juice of fermented mashed grapes—that's all. It is also incredibly complex in its nuances, flavors, characteristics, and conditions. Of all the alcholic beverages it has inspired more poets, consoled more kings, brought joy to more lives than any other drink. If only the wine and food snob could remember that once in a while he would enjoy it more. There are hundreds of different types and styles throughout the world, ranging from the vin ordinaire bought in French supermarkets from a tap under which you put your own old bottle, to the great claret and Burgundy vintages; throughout the world different circumstances and traditions have evolved all sorts and shades of wine.

The Germans long ago found that the Riesling, Sylvaner, and Traminer grapes produced fragrant flowery wines of great finesse and style along their Rhine, Moselle, and Nahe rivers. They also found that they could not make quality red wine because of the intemperate climate. So they concentrate on their quality whites. The French, a parochial nation, make wonderful wines, red and white, still and sparkling, but hundreds of years ago decided which areas were best for which wines. In Portugal, the marvellous black-red wines of the Douro valley, originally fortified with brandy spirit to preserve them—a practice which has long since become an integral part of their manufacture—are regarded as supreme, though some very pleasant light wines are also made. Spain, too, makes many styles of wine, though the climate is considered ideal for the production of various sherries and dessert wines.

From either side of the Rhine, from Germany and from Alsace in France, come delicious fragrant white wines—Hocks, Moselles, Rieslings, Sylvaners—which, though ranging from light and dry to very luscious and fruity, are all similar in style and have as their distinguishing characteristic a uniquely fresh, delicate, and fruity flavor and bouquet. The labels on German bottles appear very complicated but in fact they are quite explicit. First comes the name of the village or district, then the vintage and variety of grape, then, on some of the finest wines, the state of the grape when it was picked, e.g., Spätlese, gathered late so they yield a sweeter, richer juice.

France, though second to Italy in the actual quantity of wine produced, is generally held to produce the largest number of really great wines. From the Bordeaux area (clarets) and from Burgundy come the world's finest wines, both whites and reds, but the Loire further north produces some excellent white wines, very suitable for fish (e.g., Muscadet), some reds, and the popular Rosé d'Anjou; the Rhône produces among others the famous Châteauneuf-du-Pape; and from the northern plains comes of course the genuine champagne.

Italy produces the largest output of wine of any country, but, as in France, a great deal of it is vin ordinaire which does not travel and which is drunk young and rough on the actual site of its making. Chianti is the Italian wine which everyone knows, and several Italian wines rejoice in curious names, such as Lacrima Christi, Est! Est! Est!, and Inferno. From Sicily comes the famous dessert wine Marsala.

Spain and Portugal, and the island of Madeira, are the homes of more great fortified wines—sherry, port, and Madeira. Wines of similar type are made elsewhere, and some are excellent, but nothing can equal a true sherry for flavor and texture.

Other wine-growing regions of the world produce many distinguished wines — Austria, Czechoslovakia, Cyprus, Hungary, Rumania, and Switzerland in Europe; South Africa; and more recently but now producing many excellent wines, Australia and New Zealand, and California, which supplies the States with a great deal of good table wine. Many of these wines are made from the same grapes and in the same style as the great French and German wines, but differences in climate, soil, altitude, and method of production give them their own distinctive development so that the wines have their own character.

COOKING WITH WINE

Under the section Service of Wine there is useful guidance on what wines to serve with what dishes and how to serve them; the other way to use wine to complement food is to cook with it. Meat and fish is tenderized and given a delicious flavor by being marinated in wine and spices, stews and casseroles are made into haute cuisine dishes when cooked in wine, and there are many delicious desserts which use fortified wines to give them their special rich taste. A most spectacular way to use alcohol is to flambé, for example, the Christmas pudding, Crêpes Suzette, steaks, and numerous fruit desserts. When you cook with wine remember that although the alcohol is mostly evaporated the basic quality and essence is what remains and gives the dish its flavor, so while of course you would not use a vintage claret for cooking, the wine used should be sound and of reasonable quality. If you are not drinking a very expensive wine it is a good idea to use some of it in the cooking; this way you will ensure that the food and wine complement each other to perfection. For cooking with red wine a full-bodied wine such as a Beaujolais or a Chianti is ideal, for white a fairly strong not too dry wine is best, e.g., a Graves or Chablis. Sweeter white wines are used for some desserts, for instance a Sauternes for syllabub and possets.

Sherry, port, Marsala, and Madeira are all used in cooking as well as unfortified wines. They give a rich, full-bodied flavor to meat, poultry, and desserts. Sherry and Madeira are good in soups as a last minute addition before serving, Marsala is of course an essential ingredient of Zabaglione.

Many puddings and desserts are enhanced by the use of liqueurs—Cointreau, Curaçao, or Grand Marnier (all orange-flavored), Kirsch, apricot brandy, Tia Maria (coffee), Crème de Menthe, and Green Chartreuse or Bénédictine (herb-flavored)—and Kirsch, as well as being the perfect accompaniment to fruits such as pineapple, is the essential ingredient in a Swiss cheese fondue. Finally, rum and brandy have many uses in the kitchen. Rum is a splendid flavoring for cakes and puddings, and excellent for flaming. Brandy, the most useful spirit in the kitchen, has a natural affinity with many kinds of food. It is used as a preservative in such recipes as peaches in brandy, as well as a flavoring ingredient in many desserts and meat dishes.

Wine once opened does not keep very long as exposure to the air turns it sour quickly. However, if you pour leftover wine into a smaller bottle to reduce the airspace, and cork it up firmly or use a screw-top lid, it will keep for several days and will be excellent to use in cooking. White wines keep better in the refrigerator, red wines should be kept in a cool place and a very little brandy or sherry added helps preserve them for a few days.

441

PACIFIC PRAWNS WITH ROSEMARY

⅓ cup olive oil
1½ quarts fresh Pacific prawns, unpeeled
6 cloves garlic, finely chopped
6-8 stalks fresh rosemary

1 teaspoon salt
½ teaspoon freshly ground black pepper
½ cup dry white wine
2 tablespoons chopped parsley

Cooking time: 30 minutes
Serves: 6

Heat the oil in a skillet and sauté the unpeeled prawns and garlic for 5 to 10 minutes. Strip the rosemary leaves from the stalks and add with the salt and pepper. Sauté for a further 5 minutes. Add the wine and parsley and simmer for 10 minutes. Serve on a heated serving dish and pour over the remaining juice. Serve with white wine.

PERSIAN CARPET EGGS

(SHERRIED EGGS)

rind of 1 orange
12 eggs
¾ cup dry sherry (fino)
¼ cup Grand Marnier
¼ cup tomato paste

½ cup cream
¼ teaspoon saffron
½ teaspoon paprika pepper
¼ cup butter

Serves: 6

Slice the orange rind very finely. Place all the ingredients except the butter in a mixing bowl and beat until evenly combined. Heat the butter in a large saucepan, pour in the mixture, and cook over a low heat, stirring occasionally, as for scrambled eggs (see page 63) until the eggs are cooked. Serve with white wine.

PIGEONS AND PEAS IN RED WINE

6 squabs
1½ cups chicken stock or water and chicken bouillon cube
1⅔ cups soft red wine
6 thick slices Canadian-style bacon

1 cup butter
½ cup brandy
1 cup all-purpose flour
salt and pepper
bouquet garni
1½ cups fresh shelled peas

Cooking time: 45 minutes-1 hour
Serves: 6

Remove the pigeon livers, gizzards, etc., and chop finely. Place in an electric blender with the chicken stock and wine and blend thoroughly. Dice the bacon. Melt the butter in a heavy saucepan and brown the birds thoroughly. Flame in a little brandy. Remove. Add the bacon and brown. Remove. Stir in the flour and cook lightly for 1 minute over low heat. Add the chicken stock and wine mixture, salt and pepper, and bouquet garni and simmer for 5 minutes. Add the birds, bacon, and peas. Cook for a further 30 minutes, or until the birds are tender. Serve hot with red wine.

The Vineyard

WHITE WINE RATATOUILLE

¼ cup olive oil
2 cloves crushed garlic
1 lb. eggplant, thinly sliced
2 lb. tomatoes, thinly sliced
1 lb. zucchini, thinly sliced

4 green or red sweet peppers
   seeded and thinly sliced
salt and pepper
1⅔ cups old white wine

Cooking time: 1 hour
Serves: 6

Heat the oil and garlic in a large skillet and brown the vegetables in turn, cooking quickly and transferring to a deep, heavy saucepan or flameproof casserole when browned. When all are browned, pour the oil over them, season with salt and pepper, pour over the wine, and simmer over low heat for 1 hour. Do not sitr. Serve hot as a vegetable accompaniment or cold as an hors d'oeuvre. Serve with white or red wine.

MANGOES IN CHAMPAGNE

3 mangoes
3 tablespoons yellow Chartreuse

1 (26 fluid oz.) bottle brut
   champagne

Serves: 6

Peel and slice the mangoes and place in 6 parfait or tulip glasses. Sprinkle with 1 tablespoon yellow chartreuse per glass and place in the refrigerator to chill well. Chill the champagne. Remove the glasses from the refrigerator after 1 hour. Uncork the ice-cold champagne and top up each glass. Serve at once with champagne.

444

CELERY AND CHEESE APPETIZERS

¾ cup grated Roquefort or
  Danish Blue cheese
2 tablespoons butter, softened

1 tablespoon coffee cream
1 tablespoon brandy
4 stalks crisp celery

Yield: 12

Blend the grated cheese with the softened butter and cream until smooth, then beat until fluffy. Beat in the brandy. Place the mixture in a pastry bag with a plain or star nozzle and pipe along the hollows of the washed celery stalks. Cut the filled stalks into 1-inch pieces and serve as an appetizer with pre-dinner drinks, or at a party.

CRAB PERNOD

3 egg yolks
⅔ cup cream
salt and pepper
ground nutmeg
2 tablespoons anis (e.g., Pernod)

2 tablespoons butter
1 small clove garlic, crushed
¼ cup white wine
1 cup crab meat
chopped parsley for garnish

Cooking time: 10-15 minutes
Serves: 4

Make a sauce in the top of a double boiler by stirring the lightly beaten egg yolks with the cream over hot water. Season lightly with salt, pepper, and a dash of nutmeg. Stir in a quarter of the Pernod, cover, and leave standing over hot water, stirring every few minutes. Melt the butter in a saucepan and fry the garlic for 1 to 2 minutes: Reduce the heat, add the white wine, remaining Pernod, and crab meat, and simmer gently for 2 minutes. Remove from the heat and add the pan juices and crab slowly to the cream sauce, stirring gently. Serve hot in small bowls garnished with a sprinkling of finely chopped parsley. Serve with white wine.

SALTIMBOCCA

Veal is very delicate and in this dish the ham and cheese in the center must be cooked through without overcooking the veal. Mozzarella cheese gives the best flavoring.

4 slices veal steak
¼ cup butter
2 cloves garlic
4 thin slices proscuitto or
  Parma ham
⅔ cup sweet Vermouth

4 slices Mozzarella, Romano, or
  Provolone cheese
¼ cup white wine
1 teaspoon cornstarch
2 tablespoons capers, chopped

Cooking time: 5-10 minutes
Serves: 4

Flatten the veal steaks with a meat mallet (or rolling pin) and trim to oblongs 8 by 4 inches. Heat a heavy skillet, melt the butter, and fry the garlic for 1 to 2 minutes. Sear each slice of veal on both sides for 5 to 10 seconds and remove from the skillet. Place the ham on a plate, pour ¼ cup of the sweet Vermouth over, and then lay the ham on the veal. Place a slice of cheese, 4 by 4 inches, on one end of each steak, fold the veal and ham over, and secure the ends and sides with wooden toothpicks. Return the veal to the garlic butter over medium heat, add the remaining sweet Vermouth, cover, and cook gently for 3 to 5 minutes on each side, according to the thickness of the slices. Remove the veal and keep hot. Pour the white wine into the skillet and stir over low heat. Sprinkle the cornstarch over, stir in the cream and capers, and heat gently until thickened. Pour over the veal slices and serve hot, garnished with beans or broccoli. Serve with white wine.

PEPPERED STEAK

(STEAK AU POIVRE)

4 beef tenderloin steaks, 2 inches
    thick
1 clove garlic
salt

white or black peppercorns
$\frac{1}{4}$ cup butter
$\frac{1}{2}$ cup brandy
$\frac{2}{3}$ cup cream

Cooking time: 10-15 minutes
Serves: 4

Trim the steaks and shape neatly. Cut the end off a juicy clove of garlic and rub the steaks all over with it. Sprinkle each piece with salt and rub well in. Crush the peppercorns coarsely in a mortar or in a small bowl with the back of a spoon. Press and pat the pepper into the surface of the meat in a thin layer, top, bottom, and sides. Heat a heavy skillet and melt the butter. When the butter stops frothing, sear the steaks on all sides until plump and rare with expanded juices. (Use a pair of tongs to turn and seal each piece all over). Press the pepper back into the surface if it crumbles off. Pour the brandy over, ignite, and burn out. Remove the steaks and keep hot without allowing them to overheat. Raise the glaze on the pan with a small dash of brandy, stir in the cream, taste, and adjust the flavor if necessary; reduce the heat and stir for 3 to 4 minutes until the residual juices have blended.

RARE ROAST RUMP OF BEEF

1 6-lb. piece standing rump
salt
freshly ground pepper
garlic

2 tablespoons butter
2 tablespoons oil
$\frac{2}{3}$-$1\frac{1}{4}$ cups red wine

Cooking time: 2 hours
Temperature: 475˘
   reducing to 325ˆ
Serves: 8

Preheat the oven to 475°. Rub the surface of the meat with salt and ground pepper. Spike the surface with slices of garlic. Fry 2 cloves chopped garlic in the butter and oil for 1 minute and brush onto the surface of the meat. Place the meat on a rack in a roasting pan, lean side up, and cook in a 475° oven for 10 minutes. Remove, turn fat side up, brush with the remaining garlic butter and oil, and return to the oven. Reduce the oven temperature to 325° and cook for a further 1$\frac{3}{4}$ hours. Remove the meat and place on a heated serving dish, keep warm in a low oven, and allow to set for 10 minutes. (This setting makes the meat easier to carve.) Drain off all but 2 tablespoons fat from the roasting pan. Add the wine, place over low heat, and stir in the pan juices. Serve with green vegetables, small new potatoes, and Horseradish Sauce (see page 361) or English mustard. Serve with red wine.

Mangoes in Champagne

Service of Wine
Frank Margan

Wine, in all its various types, can be used in many ways. There are certain formalities that should be followed in serving certain wines but the great experience in wine is to become so familar with it, so involved, that your imagination comes into play, and you can then use wine in many interesting and exciting ways.

WINE GLASSES

The eye appeal of wine is very important. What your eye sees in food and wine has a great deal to do with your subsequent palate enjoyment. Wine glasses should always be in clear glass and they should always be clean and sparkling bright. Wine has magnificent color, be it white or red. The ideal wine glass has a stem to keep the fingers away from the bowl so that you avoid marking the glass and avoid obscuring the color of the wine. The same reasoning is behind the opposition to colored glasses or cut crystal glasses for wine. Colored glass hides the natural color of the wine and the winemaker's years of effort to get brilliant color in his product are nullified. Cut glass has the effect of refracting or bending the light passing through it and so preventing a full appreciation of the brilliance of the color of the wine.

THE APPETIZER WINES

The appetizer wines, a group which includes the sherry and Vermouth range, are more restricted in use than most other wines because they are designed to fill a specific purpose. They are supposed to refresh the mouth and liven the taste buds in preparation for the food that is to follow, and hence their name 'appetizer'. Dry sherries are served before a meal. They may be chilled or not, depending on your taste. There are purists who say sherry should not be chilled but one should remember that sherry is consumed in its birthplace, Spain, at a mean temperature of less than 65° and to get your sherry at this temperature in the height of a hot summer may mean chilling it.

TABLE WINES

Serve good quality red wines and white wines in clean, clear-stemmed glasses. Serve about 4 fluid ounces red or white wine per person in a glass of about 6-fluid-ounce capacity.

White wines should be served chilled but not too cold. Twenty minutes in the refrigerator will bring the temperature down to about 55° or 58° and it should not be any colder than this. If there is any rule about the chilling of white wine it is simply that the better the white wine the less it should be chilled. A rare, top class, aged bottle of dry white wine might even be best when served at room temperature.

The ideal way of chilling a white wine is to put it into an ice bucket half an hour before it is to be served, with the cork removed so the chilling process in the bucket associated with the passage of warm air over the open top of the wine has the effect of liberating the bouquet.

Red wine should be served at room temperature or around 65° or slightly above.

Leave a fairly large gap between the surface of the wine and the rim of the glass so that the bouquet of the wine is caught up in the space and presented to your nose at its best.

If you get a wine in a glass that is too cold for you, simply place the palms of your hands around the glass and warm it gently in this way for a couple of minutes.

There is no real rule about serving white wines with white meat or red wines with red meat. Drink what you like best but at the same time try to get the best possible taste sensation from the combination of your wine and your food. Often this combination brings in the rule of white with white and red with red. With a plain roast chicken a dry white wine of the hock style makes the ideal accompaniment because the wine flavor is delicate and light and the chicken is delicate and light. With a baron of beef serve a full-bodied Burgundy. With chicken cacciatori, with its rich sauce of tomatoes, onions, garlic, and spices, a light claret is the best type of wine to serve.

Strive for a combination of flavors, never allowing the flavor of the wine to overwhelm the flavor of the food and vice versa. The best way of achieving this is to serve the same wine at the table as that used in cooking the food. The better the wine you use in your food, the better the dish will be. And the better the wine the happier the cook!

CHAMPAGNE

Champagne, the king of drinks, should be the best you can get and the drier, it is, the better. It should be served by itself in the tall, elegant, slender, inverted cone that is the French flûte. It is the ideal champagne glass and keeps the bubbles in the wine longer.

Champagne should always be well chilled. Champagne is at its most magnificent at the beginning of the meal as an aperitif or as a party starter, giving a quick lift and a happy, relaxed feeling on just one glass.

DESSERT WINES

Here the word dessert means the traditional nuts, fruits, and confections served at the very end of a formal dinner. The most famous of these wines are port and Madeira, and they are, as their name indicates, served with the traditional dessert at the end of the meal, generally in small 2-fluid-ounce glasses. They may also be served as a warming drink throughout a cold winter's evening.

BRANDY

Brandy, the spirit of wine, comes in many forms. As a cognac, rich and brown, heavy and smooth in the mouth, it should be served at the end of a meal in a brandy balloon with a narrow mouth so that the great scents of the drink can be trapped and savored. It is not necessary to warm the glass and indeed glass warming can be overdone so the alcohol is driven out of the brandy. The heat of the hand is generally enough to warm the brandy to the point where its bouquet is liberated. Brandy is high in spirit and the spirit burns quite beautifully with a blue flame. Try this at the dinner table if you have before you a cup of good hot coffee. Warm the coffee spoon in the coffee then put brandy into the spoon, light it, and turn the spoon into the coffee. The brandy will burn on top of the coffee— a most spectacular sight, especially with the lights turned low—and the coffee will taste the better for it.

MIXED DRINKS AND REFRESHERS WITH WINE

In mixing wine drinks one of the best ways of making them attractive is the use of ice and the correct glasses. The proper glass is perhaps one of the few rules that you should try and follow in serving wines. Use plenty of ice in mixed drinks because it adds sparkle, tinkle, and glamor. Put the ice in the glass first, and pour the drink over it. Do not use ice that is well crushed unless all your ingredients are very chilled, otherwise the crushed ice will melt and water down your drink. Chunky ice looks best in a highball glass with a thick solid bottom which is an ideal glass for serving mixed drinks with wine. A tip is to frost the glass by wetting the outside and putting it into the freezer for 20 minutes. This adds eye appeal especially in summer.

- There is a type of sherry with a high sugar content which is inclined to have a depressing effect on the palate so that it is not an appetizer wine. This is the full-bodied type called Oloroso. I find the best way to serve sweet sherry and Vermouth is to mix it with soda and ice in a long glass, a simple, refreshing drink at any time of day.

- Sweet sherry can also be 'tricked up' to make some extraordinarily good drinks. For instance, in a highball glass pour 2 fluid ounces sweet sherry over ice, add a couple of drops of bitters and the juice of half an orange, add a thin slice of orange for decoration, and top the glass up with soda.

- A good hot wine drink is made by heating wine with honey and cinnamon. A cup of honey, a stick and a half of cinnamon, and a half flagon (40 fluid ounces) of either red or white wine, warmed, with 2 fluid ounces brandy added just before serving, makes a delicious, relaxing, and very warming drink on a winter's night. It is very satisfying and easy to make. The only thing to guard against is overheating the wine so the alcohol is driven off. The wine should not be boiling but just hot enough to drink in comfortable sips.

- To make a spritzer pour 3 fluid ounces dry white wine over ice in a tall glass and top up with soda. If the drink is for someone with a sweet tooth then use lemonade rather than soda to get that sweet touch.

- Hook, line, and sinker is the same mixture with a dash of lime juice added, making it a little more luscious to taste and very thirst-quenching in hot weather.

- The Anglo-Saxon Sangria is 3 fluid ounces red wine poured over ice in a highball glass, the juice of half an orange squeezed in, a long twist of the orange peel to decorate the glass, all topped up with soda or lemonade according to taste.

STORAGE OF WINE

Where do you store wine? If you have no cellar under the house and no room to make one you can keep all the wine you need for your immediate requirements in a cupboard in the kitchen, as long as it is away from the cooker or any other source of heat. A cupboard that is little used is best, for wine in storage likes to be kept in the dark, to be kept quiet and free from vibration, to have a fairly even tempeature anywhere between 55° and 70°, and to be out of a draft and away from any strong odor. In your kitchen cupboard your little cellar of wine is available for service at the table or for use in the kitchen. There need be only one bottle each of a dry sherry, a sweet or medium-dry sherry, and your favorite Vermouth, and a bottle of port and a bottle of Madeira for those end of meal pleasures; and in addition, a few bottles of your favorite red and white wines. You might have four bottles of white and two of red in the summer and four of red and two of white in the winter as a minimum. One bottle of a fortified wine is sufficient as they do not improve in the bottle and only take up space. However, build up your stock of red wines and white wines to as high as you can let them go! Now for some cooking...

SHERRIED OLIVES

1 (8 oz.) can or jar pitted olives   dry sherry

Drain the olives and put in a screw-top jar which holds 2½ cups. Add enough sherry to cover completely. Cover and let stand overnight. Drain the olives and serve with a salad or as an appetizer. The remaining sherry may be used to flavor meat or fish. Serve with an appetizer wine.

Variations: Add 1 clove garlic, sliced, a few fennel seeds, oregano or basil, or a dash of Tabasco sauce.

SPAGHETTI MONTANARA

1 clove garlic, crushed
2 tablespoons oil
2 tablespoons butter
1 onion, finely chopped
¼ lb. lean salt pork, diced

⅔ cup dry white wine
1 lb. tomatoes, chopped
1 sprig basil
1 lb. spaghetti
¼ lb. Gruyère cheese, diced

Serves: 4-5

Fry the garlic in the oil and butter until golden. Remove the garlic from the pan and fry the onion and salt pork until the onion is soft. Add the white wine and allow to evaporate. Add the tomatoes and basil leaves and cook for 10 to 12 minutes, stirring frequently. Cook the spaghetti in boiling salted water, drain, and add to the sauce. Sprinkle with Gruyère cheese and serve immediately. Serve with white wine.

VEAL CHOPS PARMESAN

4 veal kidney chops
juice of 1 lemon
salt
freshly ground black pepper

6 tablespoons butter
flour
grated Parmesan cheese
¾ cup dry white wine

Cooking time: 30-40 minutes
Serves: 4

Sprinkle the chops on both sides with lemon juice and rub in the salt and pepper. Brush with 2 tablespoons melted butter and sprinkle with flour. Sprinkle the chops liberally with the cheese. Allow to stand for a few minutes then turn the chops over and coat the second side in the same way. Allow the chops to stand for about 1 hour in the refrigerator until the coating is set. Sauté the chops quickly in a heavy skillet in the remaining butter until browned on both sides. Pour the wine around the chops, cover, and simmer slowly for 30 to 40 minutes. Serve hot. Serve with white wine.

SYLLABUB

¾ cup sugar
2 cups Sauternes

3¾ cups whipping cream
ground or grated nutmeg

Serves: 4

Mix together the sugar, Sauternes, and cream and beat until frothy. Serve with a sprinkling of nutmeg.

Peppered Steak

John Buck

SMOKED EEL AND TOMATO SOUFFLÉ

½ lb. smoked eel, skinned and boned
2 tablespoons butter
¼ cup all-purpose flour

1 cup tomato pulp
salt and black pepper
¼ cup white wine
4 egg yolks
5 egg whites

Cooking time: 25-30 minutes
Temperature: 400°
reducing to 375°
Serves: 4

Prepare a soufflé dish. Finely chop the eel. Melt the butter in a saucepan. Stir in the flour. Add the tomato pulp and stir until the mixture thickens. Season with salt and pepper and remove from the heat. Add the wine and beat in the egg yolks slowly, one at a time, and finally add the eel. In a separate bowl whip the egg whites until stiff. Stir a large spoonful of the egg whites into the sauce to lighten it. Fold in the rest of the egg whites quickly. Place in the prepared soufflé dish and place in the middle of a 400° oven. Reduce the temperature to 375° and bake for 25 to 30 minutes. Serve immediately with white wine —a Riesling.

FISH IN WINE

1 lb. white fish fillets
½ cup fresh white bread crumbs
dash tarragon
½ cup sliced mushrooms
1 onion, thinly sliced

¼ cup chopped parsley
1 teaspoon grated lemon rind
1 egg
⅔ cup dry white wine

Cooking time: 20 minutes
Temperature: 350°
Serves: 4

Place half the fish fillets in a baking dish. Mix the bread crumbs, tarragon, mushrooms, onions, parsley, and lemon rind with the egg. Place the mixture on top of the fish fillets and put the remaining fillets on top. Secure with wooden toothpicks. Pour the white wine over and bake in a 350° oven for 20 minutes. Serve accompanied by a full-bodied dry white wine, such as Chablis.

DUCKLING WITH ORANGE AND SWEET PEPPER

1 3-lb. duck
3 tablespoons butter
1 sprig fresh thyme
1 bay leaf
2 parsley stalks
2 onions, thinly sliced
salt
¼ teaspoon freshly ground white pepper

⅔ cup dry red wine
1¼ cups chicken stock or water and chicken bouillon cube
1 large orange
1 large red sweet pepper
2 teaspoons arrowroot
paprika pepper
1 teaspoon chopped parsley

Cooking time: 1½ hours
Temperature: 375°
Serves: 4

Prepare the duck, place 1 tablespoon butter and the herbs inside, and truss it. Rub over with a little butter. Fry the onion in the remaining butter. Place the duck and onions in a casserole with the salt and white pepper. Heat the wine, flambé it, and pour over the duck along with the stock. Braise gently in a 375° oven without the lid for about 1½ hours, basting every 15 minutes. While the duck is cooking, blanch the orange for 5 minutes, cut in half, and slice finely. Blanch and shred the pepper. Add the orange slices and shredded pepper to the duck for the final 30 minutes of cooking. Take out the duck, carve, and keep hot. Strain the gravy and reduce to taste, then thicken slightly with the arrowroot blended with a little cold water. Add paprika pepper to taste and pour the gravy over the duck. Sprinkle with the chopped parsley, and serve with baked potatoes and a tossed green salad. Serve with red wine.

TROUT IN CHAMPAGNE SAUCE

4 trout
2 shallots
⅓ cup butter

salt and pepper
½ bottle champagne
few sprigs chervil

Cooking time: 6 minutes
Serves: 4

Clean, wash, and dry the trout well. Peel and chop the shallots. Melt the butter in a skillet, add the shallots, then almost at once add the trout. Cook over high heat for 5 to 6 minutes, turning once and shaking the skillet from time to time. The fish should be golden brown. Remove the fish from the skillet, season with salt and pepper, and keep warm.

Discard the butter and shallots, then heat the champagne in the skillet. Do not allow to boil. Pour over the trout, garnish with chopped chervil, and serve at once, accompanied by a chilled champagne.

COD STEAKS IN WHITE WINE

2 tablespoons butter
1 onion, finely chopped
4 tomatoes, skinned and seeded
1 tablespoon chopped parsley
½ cup dry white wine

⅓ cup water
salt and pepper to taste
4 cod steaks
½ quantity Beurre Manié
parsley sprigs, for garnishing

Cooking time: 20-25 minutes
Serves: 4

Melt the butter in a skillet and cook the onion gently until soft but not browned. Add the tomatoes, parsley, white wine, water, and salt and pepper to taste and bring to a boil. Place the cod steaks on top of the vegetables, cover the skillet, and cook over very low heat for 20 minutes.

To serve, remove the fish from the skillet and arrange on a heated serving dish; keep warm. Add the Beurre Manié (see page 59) to the skillet in small pieces, stirring constantly until the sauce thickens. Pour the sauce over the cod steaks, garnish with parsley sprigs, and serve with mashed potatoes.

VITELLO TONNATO

8 anchovy fillets
¼ cup milk
2 carrots, peeled
1 rolled breast of veal, about
    2½ lb.
6 dill pickles, halved lengthwise
1 onion, peeled and sliced
For sauce:
1 (7 oz.) can tuna fish
2 anchovy fillets
¼ cup veal stock
4 egg yolks
For garnish:
3 tablespoons capers

1 stalk celery, sliced
juice and thinly pared rind of
    ½ lemon
⅔ cup dry white wine
¼ cup olive oil
1¼ cups cold water

2 cups olive oil
¼ cup lemon juice
salt

3 pickled onions

Cooking time: 2 hours
Serves: 6

Soak the anchovy fillets in the milk for 10 minutes to remove the excess salt. Drain, discarding the milk. Slice one carrot and cut the other into strips. Make small incisions in the veal and insert the anchovy fillets. Tie the strips of carrot and dill pickle onto the veal with string. Place the veal in a large flameproof casserole or heavy saucepan with the onion, carrot, and celery. Add the lemon juice and rind, wine, olive oil, and water. Cover the casserole, place over medium heat, and simmer for about 2 hours, or until the veal is tender. Remove the casserole from the heat, take out the veal, and remove and discard the string, dill pickles, and carrot. Place the veal in a bowl, strain the stock over it, and leave to cool. Discard the vegetables. When cold, boil the stock in a small saucepan over high heat until reduced to about ⅓ cup. To make the sauce: Drain the oil from the tuna and pound the fish with the anchovy fillets to a paste. Mix in ¼ cup of the reserved stock and press through a fine sieve. Place the egg yolks in a bowl or a blender. Add the olive oil gradually, beating constantly until a thick mayonnaise is formed. Add the lemon juice and gradually stir in the tuna paste. The sauce should be a thick pouring consistency. Add the remaining veal stock if it is too thick. Add salt to taste.

To serve: Thinly slice the veal and arrange on a serving platter. Coat with some of the sauce and serve the rest in in a sauce boat. Garnish with the capers and pickled onions.

453

BEEF À LA MODE

3 lb. rolled rump roast
salt
freshly cracked black pepper
2 tablespoons drippings or lard
1½ cups red wine
1-2 veal knuckles
¼ lb. pork fat back, diced
1½ cups stock or water and
  bouillon cubes

bay leaf, thyme, and parsley,
  tied together
1 clove garlic, peeled
3 tablespoons brandy
1 lb. carrots, peeled and sliced
1 lb. small onions, peeled
1 tablespoon cornstarch

Cooking time: 4 hours
Temperature: 275°
Serves: 8

Rub the meat with salt and pepper. Heat the drippings in a heavy casserole and brown the meat on all sides. Spoon off surplus drippings. Add the red wine and boil rapidly for a few minutes, then add the veal knuckle, diced fat back, stock, herbs, garlic, and brandy. Cover with wax paper and the lid, and cook in a 275° oven for 2½ hours. Turn the meat over, add the carrots and onions, and cook for a further 1½ hours, until the meat is very tender. Remove the meat from the casserole and place on a heated serving platter. Surround with the drained carrots and onions and keep warm. Strain the juices into a small saucepan and skim off any surplus fat. Boil rapidly until reduced to about 2½ cups, then stir in the cornstarch, blended with a little cold water, and stir until smooth and thickened. Taste and adjust seasoning. Pour a little of the gravy over the meat and vegetables and serve the remainder in a sauce boat.

BEEF IN RED WINE

4 lb. chuck steak
dry red wine
bouquet garni
4 onions, sliced
¾ cup butter

salt and pepper
20 small onions
1 cup dry white wine
½ lb. mushrooms
chopped parsley, for garnish

Cooking time: 2 hours
Serves: 4-6

Cut the beef into 1-inch cubes and place in an earthenware or stainless steel bowl. Cover with dry red wine and add the bouquet garni. Leave to marinate in a cool place for 24 hours.

When ready to cook, drain the beef, reserving the marinade. Sauté the sliced onions in one third of the butter in a heavy flameproof casserole until golden. Add the beef and brown for 10 minutes. Pour over the reserved marinade and season to taste with salt and pepper. Bring to a boil, cover, lower the heat, and simmer until the beef is tender, about 1½ to 2 hours. Sauté the small onions whole in the remaining butter until they begin to soften, but do not allow them to color. Pour over the white wine and allow the onions to poach gently, turning once or twice, until they are cooked. Add to the beef with the mushrooms 5 minutes before serving. Serve sprinkled with chopped parsley.

PORK CHOPS IN CIDER

6 pork loin chops
3 tablespoons butter
1 large onion, chopped
1 large cooking apple, peeled,
  cored, and chopped

scant 2 cups cider
salt
pepper
parsley sprigs, for garnishing

Cooking time: 55 minutes
Temperature: 350°
Serves: 6

Sauté the chops in the butter in a skillet for 5 minutes, turning once to brown both sides. Remove from the skillet and place in a heavy ovenproof casserole. In the same butter, sauté the chopped onion and apple together for 5 minutes and add to the pork. Pour over the cider and cook in a 350° oven for 45 minutes, or until the chops are tender. Serve with boiled rice, a vegetable such as zucchini, and garnished with parsley sprigs.

COQ AU VIN

1 frying chicken, 2½-3 lb.
¼ cup butter
4 small onions
4 slices Canadian bacon, diced
¼ cup brandy
1⅔ cups red wine

1¼ cups chicken stock or water
 and chicken bouillon cube
salt and pepper
2 cloves garlic, crushed
bouquet garni
2 cups button mushrooms
beurre manié

Cooking time: 1 hour
Serves: 4

Cut the chicken into serving pieces. Melt the butter in a flameproof casserole and fry the onions and bacon until golden brown. Remove the onions and bacon and in the remaining fat fry the pieces of chicken to a light golden color on all sides. Pour the warmed brandy over the chicken, ignite, and flame. Add the red wine, chicken stock, salt and pepper to taste, garlic, and bouquet garni. Bring to a boil, return the onions and bacon, and add the whole mushrooms. Cover the casserole, reduce the heat, and simmer gently for 40 minutes, or until the chicken is tender. Thicken with beurre manié (see page 59). Remove the bouquet garni and adjust the flavor if necessary. Serve with either fluffy white rice or small new potatoes.

Note: Coq au Vin may also be cooked in a 325° oven for 40 minutes, or until tender.

CHEESE FONDUE

1½ cups dry white wine
1 clove garlic
4 cups grated Emmenthal or
 Gruyère cheese

1 tablespoon cornstarch
3 tablespoons Kirsch
freshly cracked black pepper
freshly ground nutmeg

Cooking time: 10-12 minutes
Serves: 4

Heat the wine in a fondue dish or heavy flameproof casserole. Chop the garlic finely and add to the wine, bring to a boil, and boil for 5 minutes. Cool the wine(it must not be boiling when you add the cheese or the cheese may go stringy), then add the cheese gradually, stirring all the time and waiting until each lot is absorbed before adding the next. Bring to just below the boiling point, by which time the cheese will all have melted. Blend the cornstarch with a little wine or some of the Kirsch and stir in. Add the Kirsch, pepper, and nutmeg to taste and transfer the pan to the fondue stand. Keep the fondue gently bubbling over the spirt stove, turning the flame down as the diners eat the fondue. Serve with cubes of crusty French bread on long forks. The diners dip bread cubes into the cheese. In Switzerland many people consider the chewy cheese left at the bottom the pan after all the sauce has been eaten to be the most delectable part of the dish.

TRIFLE

leftover sponge, yellow, or
 layer cake
¼ cup raspberry or strawberry
 jam
¼ cup sherry
2 cups fresh raspberries, or 1
 (12 oz.) can fruit cocktail,
 drained

1 quantity Vanilla Custard Sauce
1¼ cups whipping cream
¼ cup blanched, slivered almonds
2 tablespoons candied cherries
12 miniature macaroons

Serves: 4

Spread the leftover sponge cake with jam and place in the bottom of a glass serving bowl. Pour over the sherry and leave to soak into the sponge cake for a few minutes. Place the raspberries or fruit cocktail on top of the cake and cover with the Vanilla Custard Sauce (see page 61). Cover with a plate to prevent a skin from forming on the custard and leave until the custard is quite cold. Whip the cream until thick and spread over the custard. Some of it may be placed in a pastry bag with a star nozzle and piped around the edges. Decorate the trifle with almonds and candied cherries and stand the macaroons around the edge of the bowl.

CRÈME DE MENTHE ICE CREAM

2 eggs, separated
½ cup sifted confectioners' sugar

2 tablespoons Crème de Menthe
⅔ cup whipping cream

Serves: 4

Beat the egg whites until stiff, then beat in the confectioners' sugar gradually. Beat the egg yolks and Crème de Menthe together in a second bowl, then beat into the egg white mixture a little at a time. Whip the cream lightly and fold it into the egg white mixture. Place in a freezer tray, cover, and freeze. This ice needs no beating during the freezing. Serve with wafers or crisp plain cookies.

PINEAPPLE WITH KIRSCH

1 medium-sized pineapple
¼ cup Kirsch

⅔ cup whipping cream

Serves: 5

Peel the pineapple, which should be ripe and juicy, cut into rounds, and remove the eyes, reserving any juice. Place the slices in individual dishes. Mix the juice with the Kirsch and pour over the pineapple slices. Leave the pineapple in a cool place for 30 minutes so the fruit soaks up the liqueur flavor. Just before serving, whip the cream and pile on top of the pineapple slices.

Note: This makes a delicious and refreshing dessert after a heavy meal.

GOURMET RECIPES

'To bring together and to serve all who believe that a right understanding of Wine and Food is an essential part of personal contentment and health and that an intelligent approach to the pleasures and problems of the table offers far greater rewards than the mere satisfaction of appetite.' This is only one of the aims and objects of a gourmet! The Oxford dictionary says a gourmet is a connoisseur of table delicacies, especially wine. This definition often fills people with awe, but this should not be the case.

In this chapter of our book we have asked a number of leading gourmet groups, who are interested in good food and wine, to prepare a menu fit for a gourmet. Their recipes follow each menu, and informed wine selections are given for each menu.

These menus will give you some tempting ideas for your dinner parties. They are different but practical. They allow you to prepare parts of the menu in advance so you can relax with your guests. Enjoy making some of these truly delicious, memorable dinners.

Duckling with Orange and
Sweet Pepper

Menu	**Wines**
Caviar Mousse	*A dry champagne*
Rock Lobster Tails Bev-Jo	*A full-flavored white Burgundy*
Lamb à la Président	*A light dry Bordeaux*
Soubise Sauce	
Green Salad	
Orange Joy	*A fruity-flavored Riesling*
Coffee	*A vintage port*

CAVIAR MOUSSE

3 oz. caviar
½ pint whipped cream
juice of 1 lemon
3 tablespoons mayonnaise

2 drops Tabasco sauce
1 teaspoon grated onion
1 envelope gelatin

Serves: 6

Combine together the caviar, whipped cream, lemon juice, mayonnaise (see page 55), Tabasco sauce, and onion. Dissolve the gelatin in ¼ cup hot water. Cool and mix gently with the other ingredients. Place the mixture in a mold previously rinsed with cold water (a fish-shaped mold is excellent). Set in the refrigerator. When firm, turn out gently onto a serving platter. Serve with thin slices of toast.

ROCK LOBSTER TAILS BEV-JO

6 rock lobster tails
seasoned flour

clarified butter for frying

Serves: 6

For sauce:
¾ cup white wine
¼ cup hot water
2 teaspoons tomato paste
2 scallions, chopped

2 tablespoons chopped parsley
    stalks
dash Tabasco sauce
salt and pepper

Remove the meat carefully in one piece from the lobster tails. Cut the meat into round pieces ½ inch thick; these are known as medallions. Dip the medallions in seasoned flour and sauté gently in clarified butter. Drain on paper towels.

To make sauce: Mix together all the ingredients in a large shallow saucepan. Cook the lobster gently in the sauce for 5 minutes. Arrange the lobster on a serving dish, pour the sauce over, and serve immediately.

LAMB À LA PRÉSIDENT

1 loin of lamb consisting of
    10 chops
6 tablespoons butter
salt and pepper

For pea purée:
2 tablespoons butter
1 white onion, finely chopped
2 tablespoons chopped parsley
2 lettuce leaves

pea purée
1½ quantities Puff Paste
1 egg beaten with 2 tablespoons
    cream

2 lb. fresh peas
2 teaspoons salt
2 teaspoons sugar
2 egg yolks

Cooking time: 1 hour
Temperature: 425°
   reducing to 350°
Serves: 5-6

Have your butcher bone the loin of lamb. Remove any fatty pieces and cut off the flap, leaving a long piece of tender meat. Brown the meat on all sides in hot butter and leave to cool. Season the lamb well with salt and pepper. Spread the top of the lamb with a thick layer of the pea purée. Roll the dough (see page 294) out thinly to an oblong large enough to cover the lamb. Place the lamb on one end of the dough, wrap the dough over to enclose the meat, and seal the edges with a little egg and cream glaze. Brush the dough with egg and cream glaze. Prick the top to allow the steam to escape. Place on a greased baking sheet and chill for at least 1 hour. Bake in

a 425° oven for 10 minutes, then reduce the temperature to 350° and cook for a further 50 minutes. Allow to stand for 5 minutes before carving. Serve in thick slices accompanied by Soubise Sauce (see page 51).

To make the pea purée: Melt the butter in a saucepan, add the onion, parsley, and lettuce leaves torn into small pieces, and sauté until the onion is soft. Shell the peas and add to the pan. Add the salt, sugar, and water to cover and cook for 20 minutes or until the peas are tender. Drain, cool, and press through a sieve or purée in an electric blender. Stir in the egg yolks and allow to cool before using.

ORANGE JOY

12 large navel oranges
1½ cups sugar
¼ cup corn syrup

1½ cups water
red culinary coloring
juice of 2 lemons

Serves: 6

Remove the rind in long slices from 4 oranges. Remove all of the pith from these slices and cut the rind lengthwise into very thin julienne strips. Using a stainless steel knife with a serrated edge, peel and remove the pith from the remaining oranges. Remove any white membrane. Cut the oranges into segments between the membrane and place in a bowl.

Place the julienne strips in a saucepan with 2 cups water. Cover and bring to a boil. Drain and set the rind aside. Place the sugar, syrup, 1½ cups water, and a few

drops red coloring in a saucepan over heat. Be sparing with the coloring for the color should be a light, delicate pink, not a deep red. Bring to a boil, stirring to dissolve the sugar. Cook for 10 minutes. Add the peel and cook for a further 15 minutes. The syrup should be very slightly thickened. Add the lemon juice. Pour the hot syrup over the orange quarters, cover, and when cool, refrigerate overnight. Next day, arrange the orange segments with the syrup attractively in a crystal bowl.

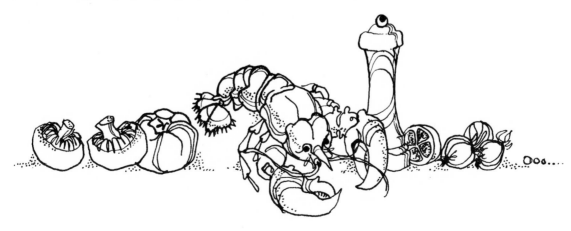

Menu	Wines
Snapper with White Wine	*A light Riesling or white Burgundy*
Chicken Livers Paysanne	*A rosé*
Carpet Bag Steak *Grilled Tomatoes* *Garlic Bread* *Green Salad*	*A full-flavored aromatic Bordeaux*
Citrus Soufflé	*A champagne*
Coffee	*Follow with a brandy to be sipped and savored!*

SNAPPER WITH WHITE WINE

1 3½-lb. snapper
1 cup thinly sliced mushrooms
1 onion, thinly sliced
salt and pepper
1 bay leaf

dash thyme
1 cup fresh bread crumbs
¼ cup butter
¾ cup dry white wine
2 limes or lemons

Cooking time: 40 minutes
Temperature: 350°
Serves: 6

Clean the snapper and place in a flat buttered ovenproof dish. Cover with the mushrooms and onion and season with salt and pepper. Add the bay leaf and sprinkle with the thyme and bread crumbs. Dot the snapper with butter and cover with the wine. Bake in a 350° oven for 40 minutes, or until the fish is tender. Serve with lime or lemon juice.

CHICKEN LIVERS PAYSANNE

1 onion, chopped
¼ cup butter
1½ lb. chicken livers, chopped
1 teaspoon marjoram
2 teaspoons chopped parsley

⅓ cup red wine
1 cup sour cream
salt and pepper
boiled rice

Serves: 6-8

Sauté the onion in the butter. Add the chicken livers and cook for 5 minutes. Add the marjoram, parsley, wine, sour cream, and salt and pepper to taste. Simmer for 5 minutes and serve with hot boiled rice.

CARPET BAG STEAK

4 lb. beef in 1 piece, tenderloin,
   sirloin tip, or rump
$\frac{1}{4}$ cup butter
12-18 oysters
1 cup chopped mushrooms
3 cups fresh white bread crumbs

2 tablespoons chopped parsley
grated rind of $\frac{1}{2}$ lemon
salt
pepper
paprika pepper
1 egg

Cooking time: 1-1$\frac{1}{2}$ hours
Temperature: 375°
Serves: 6-8

Trim the meat and cut small pockets in it, one for each person. Heat the butter in a saucepan and gently fry the oysters and mushrooms for 5 minutes. Transfer to a mixing bowl and mix in the bread crumbs, parsley, lemon rind, and seasonings. Beat the egg and stir into the mixture. Place the stuffing in the pockets in the meat and either sew or skewer the edges together. Roast in a 375° oven for 1 to 1$\frac{1}{2}$ hours, depending on the cut of meat.

Serve with a green salad, broiled or baked tomatoes, topped with grated Parmesan cheese and garnished with parsley, and garlic bread (see page 358).

CITRUS SOUFFLÉ

4 eggs, separated
$\frac{2}{3}$ cup sugar
1 tablespoon each grated lemon
   and orange rind
$\frac{1}{4}$ cup each orange and lemon
   juice

1$\frac{1}{2}$ envelopes gelatin softened
   in $\frac{1}{4}$ cup orange juice
1 cup evaporated milk, chilled
   icy cold
finely chopped walnuts or
   hazelnuts

Serves: 6-8

Beat the egg yolks, gradually adding the sugar, until very thick and creamy, about 5 minutes. Add the fruit rind and juice and beat for a further minute. Dissolve the gelatin in $\frac{1}{4}$ cup orange juice over hot water, cool to body temperature, and stir into the egg mixture. Chill until partially set. Whip the icy cold evaporated milk until stiff, then beat in the gelatin mixture. Fold in the stiffly beaten egg whites lightly. Pour into a prepared 6-inch soufflé dish, with a 2-inch wetted waxpaper collar. Chill until set. Remove the paper collar carefully. Press the nuts into the sides and decorate as desired.

RILLETTES OF PORK

Rillettes can be kept for some weeks in the refrigerator, but should be removed several hours before serving in order to soften.

1½ lb. boneless shoulder butt	bouquet garni	Cooking time: 4 hours
½ lb. fat back	¼ pint water	Temperature: 250°
salt	pepper	Serves: 12
2 cloves garlic, crushed		

Rub the meat well with salt and leave to stand for 4 hours. Cut into 1-inch pieces and place in a heavy earthenware or an enamelled cast iron casserole with the garlic and bouquet garni. Add the water, season with pepper, and cook in a 250° oven for 4 hours.

Drain the meat and reserve the fat. Place the meat in a mixing bowl and beat slowly with an electric beater until the meat fibers separate. Pack the meat loosely in jars and fill with the reserved fat. Allow to cool. Cover with aluminum foil. Serve rillettes in large slices on individual plates with lightly toasted brown bread (unbuttered) on which to spread it.

Note: It is impractical to make very small quantities of rillettes, but the surplus not required for the meal can be stored indefinitely. Rillettes are both aromatic and filling.

FILLETS OF TROUT GRENOBLOISE

6 trout fillets	clarified butter	Cooking time: 10 minutes
seasoned flour	¼ cup capers	Serves: 6

For sauce:
1 lemon	2 teaspoons Worcestershire
½ cup butter	sauce

Trim and wipe the trout fillets. Dip into seasoned flour. Heat the clarified butter in a heavy skillet, large enough to take all the fish at one time, or use 2 pans (the fish should all be cooked at once). When the butter is hot but not smoking, place in the fish, flesh side down, and fry until the fillets are crisp underneath. Turn the fillets over, lower the heat, and cook for a further 5 minutes on the other side. Remove the fillets and place on a heated serving platter, sprinkle with diced lemon and capers, and cover with the Grenobloise (brown butter) sauce. To make the sauce: Peel the lemon and cut the flesh into ¼-inch dice, discarding the seeds and pith. Heat the butter in a skillet until it foams. When a light brown sediment appears and the foam subsides, remove from the heat and add the Worcestershire sauce (stand back!), and the juice that has drained from the diced lemon. Set aside in a warm place.

ROAST BEEF TENDERLOIN WITH SAUCE VALOIS

The temperature and weight given in this recipe will produce rare beef. In general, for rare beef, allow 15 minutes per lb. and 15 minutes over, for medium beef, allow 20 minutes per lb. and 20 minutes over.

1 3-lb. piece beef tenderloin

8 slices bacon

Cooking time: 1 hour
Temperature: 400°
Serves: 6

For sauce:
1 cup dry white wine
2 tablespoons wine vinegar
8 shallots, chopped
12 peppercorns, coarsely cracked
1 teaspoon chervil
1 teaspoon tarragon

1 cup clarified butter
3 egg yolks
½ teaspoon salt
2 tablespoons chopped parsley
2 tablespoons chopped chives

Trim the beef of all surface fat and tendons. Cover with the bacon. Alternatively, if a larding needle is available, cut some of the bacon into thin strips and lard the joint instead. Place the beef on a rack in a roasting pan and roast in a 400° oven for 1 hour, or until a temperature of 130° is reached on a meat thermometer stuck into the thickest part of the beef.

To make the sauce: Place the wine, vinegar, shallots, peppercorns, chervil, and tarragon in a saucepan. Reduce the liquid over gentle heat until it has evaporated and reduced to one fourth of the original volume. Strain through a fine sieve or cheesecloth. Melt the butter. Beat half the wine liquor with the egg yolks and salt over gentle heat until the mixture thickens. Remove from the heat and add the melted butter slowly, beating continuously with a whisk. The sauce will thicken. If further thinning is required, add more wine liquor to taste. Just before serving, add the finely chopped parsley and chives. Keep warm in the top of a double boiler or stand the pan in a larger pan of hot, not boiling water.

To serve, carve the beef into 6 portions and spoon some of the sauce over each portion. The remainder of the sauce may be served from a sauce boat. Serve with little potatoes, potroasted in their jackets in a little butter, artichoke hearts, and asparagus tips.

ICED ORANGES IN BRANDY

6 large juicy oranges
¼ cup sugar

1 cup brandy
1 cup chopped dates (optional)

Serves: 6

Stand the oranges on a plate and remove the rind and white pith, using a stainless steel knife with a serrated edge. Cut the oranges into segments, removing the membrane. Place on a deep plate with any orange juice and sprinkle with the sugar and brandy. Allow to stand for at least 2 hours in the refrigerator. To serve, divide the orange slices among 6 individual serving plates, spoon the juice over, and sprinkle with chopped dates if desired.

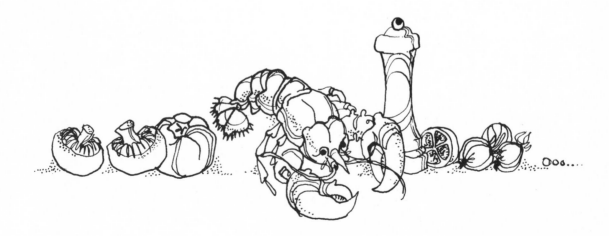

Crayfish Bev-Jo

Menu	Wines
Chilled Cucumber Soup	*A crisp aromatic young Rhine Riesling*
Dodine of Duck	*A light aromatic dry red*
Green Salad	
Cheese	
Raspberry Fool	*A dry champagne*
Coffee	*A tawny port*

CHILLED CUCUMBER SOUP

3 cucumbers
¼ cup butter
1 leek, sliced
bay leaf
2 tablespoons all-purpose flour
3 cups chicken stock
1 teaspoon salt

1¼ cups cream
juice of 1 lemon
1 teaspoon finely chopped dill
  or mint
pepper
⅔ cup sour cream for serving

Cooking time: 1 hour
Serves: 12

Peel 2 cucumbers and slice thinly. Sauté in the butter in a saucepan with the sliced leek and bay leaf for 20 minutes, or until tender but not browned. Stir in the flour. Add the chicken stock (see page 34) and salt and simmer covered for 30 minutes. Cool and press through a sieve or purée in an electric blender. Chill. Peel the remaining cucumber, remove the seeds, and grate the flesh. Stir into the purée with the cream, lemon juice, and dill or mint. Season to taste with salt and pepper. Chill in the refrigerator for at least 30 minutes.

Serve in chilled soup cups with a fluff of sour cream on top of each portion.

DODINE OF DUCK

1 5-lb. duck
1 teaspoon salt
¼ teaspoon pepper
⅛ teaspoon allspice

⅓ cup armagnac or good brandy
½ cup extra armagnac or Madeira
watercress

Cooking time: 2 hours
Temperature: 350°
Serves: 12

For stuffing:
1 lb. finely ground lean pork
1 lb. finely ground veal
6 chicken livers, chopped
⅓ cup Chablis or dry white wine

2 eggs
1 teaspoon salt
3 large truffles, chopped
⅛ cup Madeira or truffle liquor

To bone the duck: Cut off the wing tips and first wing joint. With a sharp filleting knife, slit the duck down the belly and work the knife along the rib cage to the backbone, cutting against the bones. Detach the leg and shoulder joints from the rib cage then, carefully, again working against the bone, bone out the leg bones, except for the small leg bone, and bone the upper joint of the wing. Remove as much of the solid fat as possible.

Place the boned duck in a shallow dish and sprinkle with the salt, pepper, allspice, and armagnac. Place in the refrigerator and marinate for several hours or overnight.

To make the stuffing: Mix all the ingredients together until evenly combined. Spread the duck out on a board, skin side down, and spread the entire surface with the stuffing. Fold the neckskin over the filling, fold the sides over, re-forming the duck neatly, and sew up the skin. Place the duck in a greased roasting pan and cook in a 350° oven for 2 hours, or until the meat is cooked. Remove the duck to a heated serving platter. Pour off all fat from the pan, leaving the pan juices. Add ½ cup armagnac or Madeira and cook over heat, stirring continuously until it boils. Strain over the duck and serve garnished with watercress.

Note: Mushrooms may be used in place of truffles.

RASPBERRY FOOL

3 lb. raspberries
1¼ cups water
1 cup sugar
1¼ cups whipping cream

1 quantity Vanilla Custard Sauce
⅔ cup whipped cream for
  decoration

Serves: 12

Clean the raspberries and remove the stems; wash them and put in a large saucepan with the water and sugar. Stew the raspberries until soft, cool, then rub through a sieve or puree in an electric blender. Whip the cream and mix with the custard (see page 61) and raspberry purée.

Serve in a glass bowl or in individual glasses. Decorate with whipped cream.
Note: Frozen raspberries or fresh loganberries may be used instead of fresh raspberries.

MUSHROOM SOUFFLÉ

6 tablespoons butter
1 scallion, chopped
1½ lb. mushrooms, finely chopped
6 tablespoons all-purpose flour
1 cup milk

1 teaspoon salt
dash cayenne pepper
½ teaspoon grated nutmeg
4 egg yolks
5 egg whites

Cooking time: 35 minutes
Temperature: 375°
Serves: 6

Melt 2 tablespoons of the butter in a saucepan and gently fry the chopped scallion until soft but not brown. Add the mushrooms and cook slowly for 10 minutes.

In another saucepan, melt the remaining butter, stir in the flour, and cook over low heat for 1 minute or until the flour just starts to turn golden. Add the heated milk and bring to a boil over medium heat, stirring continuously with a wooden spoon or whipping with a wire balloon whisk. Mix in the salt, pepper, nutmeg, and mushroom mixture. Cool. Stir in the slightly beaten egg yolks. Whip the egg whites until stiff but not too dry and fold gently into the sauce. Place in a buttered soufflé dish or deep ovenproof dish and bake in a 375° oven for 35 minutes, or until the soufflé is cooked. Serve immediately.

FROGS' LEGS

24 frogs' legs
2½ cups fish stock
2½ cups white wine

1 quantity White Sauce
⅔ cup cream

Serves: 6

Poach the frogs' legs in a mixture of the fish stock (see recipe for Bouillabaisse, page 43) and white wine, for 10 minutes, or until tender. Remove and keep warm. Make the White Sauce (see page 50), substituting the poaching liquor for the milk. Season to taste and stir in the cream. Add the frogs' legs and reheat gently before serving.

Roast Beef Tenderloin with
Sauce Valois

NOIX DE VEAU À LA REBOUX

2 1-lb. noix de veau	½ quantity Espagnole Sauce	Cooking time: 40 minutes
2 veal kidneys	1-2 cups dry bread crumbs	Temperature: 350°
¼ cup butter	½ quantity Madeira Sauce	Serves: 6

The noix of veal is the rump cut lengthwise, and is a cut commonly used in France. You will have to have your butcher prepare it specially for you. Trim the nuts of veal into neat shapes. Roast in a 350° oven for 20 minutes. Remove from the oven and slice thinly.

Sauté the kidneys in butter until they seize up. Slice thinly. Combine half the Espagnole Sauce (see page 52) with the sliced kidneys. Spread between the veal slices and reform the veal to its original shape. Coat the veal with the remaining sauce and sprinkle with bread crumbs. Return the veal to a 350° oven and cook for a further 15 minutes, or until cooked and the crumbs are golden. Serve hot with Madeira Sauce (see page 54).

PEACHES À L'AURORE

6 ripe peaches	½ cup sugar	Serves: 6
1¼ cups water	¼-½ cup Kirsch	

For strawberry mousse:
2 cups small strawberries	2½ cups whipping cream
generous cup sugar	

Dip the peaches into boiling water then into iced water and remove the skins. Place the water and sugar in a large shallow saucepan and heat until the sugar is dissolved. Add Kirsch to taste. Poach the peaches gently until soft and leave to cool in the syrup.

To make the strawberry mousse: Rub the strawberries through a sieve or purée in an electric blender. Add the sugar and whipped cream and mix until evenly combined. Place the mousse in the freezer to set. Remove 10 minutes before serving and whip with an electric mixer.

To serve, drain the peaches and arrange on top of the strawberry mousse.

Menu

Tarator Soup

Fish a l'Orange

Roast Stuffed Lamb
Rice

Chocolate Cheesecake

Coffee

Wines

A dry sherry

A fresh crisp light Hock

A crisp aromatic light dry red

TARATOR SOUP

2 cucumbers
$\frac{3}{4}$ cup French dressing
1$\frac{1}{4}$ quarts yogurt
$\frac{1}{4}$ cup chopped mint
salt
white pepper

Serves: 8

Peel the cucumber and cut the flesh into very small dice. Combine the French dressing (see page 177) with the yogurt. Add the diced cucumber and chopped mint and season to taste with salt and pepper. Chill thoroughly before serving.

FISH À L'ORANGE

6-8 halibut steaks, about 2 lb. altogether
seasoned flour
2 eggs, beaten
2 cups white dry bread crumbs
1 clove garlic, crushed
olive oil for frying
$\frac{1}{2}$ cup French dressing
$\frac{1}{2}$ cup orange juice
2 extra tablespoons orange juice
1 teaspoon grated orange rind
1 quantity Hollandaise Sauce
orange segments and avocado slices for garnish

Serves: 6-8

Remove the skin and bones from the halibut steaks. Dip in the seasoned flour, then in the beaten egg and the bread crumbs. Press the bread crumbs on firmly. Fry the garlic in the olive oil, add the fish, and fry over a low heat until cooked; the fish should be a clear white right through the center. Remove the fish and place in a serving dish. Pour the French dressing (see page 177) and orange juice over. Cover with aluminum foil and refrigerate for 3 to 4 hours.

Combine the 2 tablespoons orange juice and the orange rind with the Hollandaise Sauce (see page 56). Serve the fish chilled with the sauce spooned on top and garnished with orange segments and avocado slices.

ROAST STUFFED LAMB

1 4-lb. leg of lamb
1 clove garlic

For stuffing:
2 tablespoons butter
1 onion, finely chopped
1 clove garlic, crushed
2 slices bacon, chopped
$\frac{2}{3}$ cup chopped dried apricots

2 tablespoons brown sugar
salt and pepper

$\frac{1}{2}$ teaspoon ginger
1 egg
$\frac{1}{4}$ cup fresh white bread crumbs
salt and pepper

Cooking time: $1\frac{1}{2}$-2 hours
Temperature: 350°
Serves: 6-8

Have the butcher bone the leg of lamb.

To make the stuffing: Melt the butter in a saucepan and fry the onion, garlic, and bacon until the onion is soft. Remove from the heat and add the apricots and ginger. Stir in the beaten egg and bread crumbs and season to taste with salt and pepper.

Fill the pocket in the lamb with the stuffing and seal each end with a piece of aluminum foil. Rub a cut clove of garlic over the lamb and sprinkle with the brown sugar and salt and pepper. Place on a rack in a roasting pan with $1\frac{1}{4}$ cups water in the pan. Cook in a 350° oven for $1\frac{1}{2}$ to 2 hours, or until tender, turning over to brown all sides. Remove the lamb and keep warm.

To make the gravy, pour off all but 2 tablespoons of the pan juices. Place over medium heat, add the flour, and stir until browned. Add the chicken stock (see page 34) and red wine and stir until the gravy boils. Strain into a warm gravy boat.

Serve the lamb on a bed of boiled rice accompanied by a vegetable (e.g., zucchini) and the gravy.

CHOCOLATE CHEESECAKE

For crumb crust:
$\frac{1}{2}$ lb. Graham crackers

7-8 tablespoons butter

For filling:
1 cup semi-sweet chocolate
  pieces
1 cup cottage cheese
$\frac{1}{2}$ cup sugar
1 teaspoon vanilla extract

2 eggs, separated
$1\frac{1}{4}$ cups whipping cream
$\frac{3}{4}$ cup chopped walnuts
$\frac{2}{3}$ cup whipped cream for serving

Cooking time: 15 minutes
Temperature: 325°
Serves: 8

Crush the crackers between 2 sheets of wax paper or in a plastic bag with a rolling pin. Combine with the melted butter. Press onto and mold over the bottom and sides of a 9-inch spring form pan. Bake in a 325° oven for 10 to 15 minutes. Remove and allow to cool.

To make the filling: Melt the chocolate in a bowl over hot water. Combine the cottage cheese with the sugar and vanilla extract. Beat in the egg yolks. Add the melted chocolate and mix until smooth. Whip the cream and fold into the mixture. Finally, beat the egg whites and fold into the mixture with the walnuts, reserving $\frac{1}{4}$ cup for deocration. Pour the mixture into the prepared crumb crust. Chill thoroughly until set. Remove from the pan and decorate with the extra whipped cream and the reserved walnuts before serving.

Menu	**Wines**
Vichyssoise	*A light dry sherry*
Asparagus Hollandaise	*A delicate full-flavored young white Burgundy*
Whitebait Fritters	
Salmis of Duck *Potatoes Dauphinoise* *Orange Salad*	*A crisp aromatic Bordeaux*
Coffee Gâteau	*A smooth fruity Sauternes*
Coffee	

Note: For Vichyssoise recipe see page 47.

ASPARAGUS HOLLANDAISE

1½ lb. asparagus   1 quantity Hollandaise Sauce   Serves: 6

Stand the bundles of asparagus in a large saucepan with the tips at the top. Add the salt and 2 inches of water. Allow to cook for 15 minutes with the lid on tightly. Drain well. Arrange the asparagus on individual plates, keeping all the tips at the same end. Pour the Hollandaise (see page 56) over the tips only and serve immediately.

WHITEBAIT FRITTERS

1½ lb. whitebait   salt and pepper   Serves: 6
2 eggs   olive oil
3 tablespoons all-purpose flour   lemon wedges for serving

Place the whitebait in a wire strainer, wash thoroughly, then pour 5 cups boiling water over them. Mix the egg yolks and flour to a smooth paste, adding a little water if too stiff. Beat the egg whites until stiff, add salt and pepper, and fold in the whitebait. Heat the olive oil in a heavy deep pan and add the fritter mixture gently from a tablespoon. Turn over after a few minutes. Drain on paper towels. Serve with wedges of lemon.

SALMIS OF DUCK

1 4-lb. duck
salt and pepper
6 slices bacon
$\frac{1}{4}$ cup all-purpose flour
1 tablespoon brown sugar
1 cup chicken stock
1 onion, chopped
juice of $\frac{1}{2}$ lemon

grated rind of $\frac{1}{2}$ lemon
$\frac{1}{2}$ cup red wine
$\frac{1}{4}$ cup Cointreau
$\frac{1}{8}$ teaspoon oregano
$\frac{1}{4}$ teaspoon basil
dash cinnamon, cloves, nutmeg
    thyme, and sage

Cooking time: 3 hours
Temperature: 350°
Serves: 6

Sprinkle the duck with salt and pepper and place the bacon slices over the breast. Wrap in aluminum foil. Cook in a 350° oven for approximately 2 hours. Remove and carve the meat into small pieces. Pour off the fat from the juices in the pan, leaving about 2 tablespoons, and add the flour, salt, pepper, and brown sugar. Stir and cook until brown. Stir in the chicken stock (see page 34), chopped onion, lemon juice and rind, red wine, Cointreau, oregano, basil, cinnamon, cloves, nutmeg, thyme, and sage and bring to a boil. Place the pieces of duck in an ovenproof dish and pour the sauce over. Cover with aluminum foil. Cook in a 350° oven for 1 hour and serve hot.

POTATOES DAUPHINOISE

2 lb. potatoes
1 clove garlic
$\frac{1}{4}$ cup butter
salt and pepper

grated nutmeg
$2\frac{1}{2}$ cups cream
$\frac{1}{2}$-1 cup grated Gruyère cheese

Cooking time: $1\frac{1}{2}$-2 hours
Temperature: 300°
  increasing to 425°
Serves: 6

Peel the potatoes and slice into thin even rounds. Rinse in cold water and shake dry in a clean dish towel. Place in layers in a shallow earthenware dish which has been rubbed with the cut garlic clove and well buttered. Season with salt and pepper and grated nutmeg. Pour the cream over the potatoes and top with small pieces of butter and the grated cheese. Cook in a 300° oven for $1\frac{1}{2}$ to 2 hours. During the last few minutes, increase the oven temperature to 425° to get a fine golden crust on the potatoes. Serve hot.

COFFEE GÂTEAU

sponge fingers or leftover cake
sherry or brandy
3 envelopes gelatin
6 tablespoons water
5 egg yolks
3 tablespoons sugar

$2\frac{1}{2}$ cups milk
3 tablespoons instant coffee
    powder
$1\frac{1}{4}$ cups whipping cream
whipped cream, walnuts, and
    grated chocolate, for decorating

Serves: 6

Line a mold with sponge fingers or cake and sprinkle well with sherry or brandy. Sprinkle the gelatin over the water and leave to soak. Beat the egg yolks and sugar until thick and creamy. Warm the milk slightly and add the coffee powder, stirring well to dissolve. Blend well with the egg yolks and sugar and strain back into the pan. Return to the heat and thicken the custard, without letting it boil and stirring constantly. Strain into a bowl. Dissolve the gelatin in the water over low heat and add to the custard. Set aside until cool and beginning to set. Whip the cream lightly and fold into the mixture. Pour into the sponge lined mold and place in the refrigerator to set for several hours. When set, turn out onto a serving plate, cover with whipped cream, and decorate with walnuts and grated chocolate.

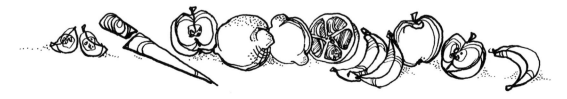

EDITOR'S CHOICE

Anne Marshall

Anne Marshall has a Diploma in Home Economics from the Gloucester Training College of Domestic Science, England, where she specialized in advanced cookery and nutrition. Anne has taught cookery to students and housewives and has worked in the food industry on both sides of the world.

This section of our cookery book is called Editor's Choice and it contains a selection of some of my favorite dishes. Nearly every aspect of cookery has been covered in this book already by many enthusiastic cooks and it is important that this enthusiasm for good food and wine is conveyed to you.

Cooking should draw people together, not separate them into experts and 'those who are less experienced'. In order to cook well you have to understand certain things about food and the development of flavor, which is surely one of the most important points of good cookery. Imagine the delicious, mouth-watering smell of frying onions. Did you know that onions contain some sugar? While frying onions you are in fact caramelizing the sugar content which gives you a delicious flavor and a rich, golden color. This is why the recipes for so many tasty, flavorsome casseroles, stews, braises, soups, and sauces start off with—'Sauté the onions until golden brown'. The fat used for frying or sautéeing is often a mixture of butter and oil. This is ideal for the butter gives a delicious flavor to the dish and the oil gives a crispness to the frying food as well as preventing the butter from burning. The natural flavors of meat and fish can be truly delicious in the form of tender spring lamb or rich, full-flavored beef, or freshly caught, sweet, juicy prawns, but in certain made-up dishes, such as casseroles, soufflés and flans, or pasta and rice dishes, these flavors are definitely enhanced by the addition of certain flavorsome vegetables, herbs and spices, tomato paste, wine, cream, or rich stock or sauce. Again compare the flavor of a simple basic white sauce with the flavor of a Béchamel sauce in which vegetables and herbs are first infused in the milk. A little extra time and effect is necessary but the delicious flavor is worth it, for sauces are used in so many other tasty dishes. Similarly, in the chapters on hors d'oeuvres and salads the cold foods are invariably served with refreshing, tangy French dressing or rich creamy mayonnaise which adds delicious additional flavor.

Remember that as well as experimenting with flavoring ingredients in your cookery, you should ensure the flavors of each dish and each course of a meal complement one another. So to round off the book, I am giving you four menus with some delicious recipes which are full of flavor, for the four seasons of the year. I hope you will try them and enjoy them.

Cheese Blintzes

Pork Casserole
Potatoes
Braised Red Cabbage

Chocolate Mousse

CHEESE BLINTZES

A blintz is a filled pancake, usually made with wholewheat flour.

For batter:
1 cup wholewheat all-purpose flour
2 tablespoons butter

3 eggs
1¼ cups milk
clarified butter for frying

Cooking time: 15 minutes
Temperature: 400°
Serves: 6

For filling:
1 cup cottage cheese
¼ cup sour cream
salt and pepper
¼ teaspoon paprika pepper

dash cayenne pepper
1¼ cups sour cream and 1 finely chopped onion for serving

To make the batter: Place the flour in a mixing bowl and make a well in the center. Add the melted butter, eggs, and half the milk and beat until smooth. Stir in the remaining milk.

To make the filling: Mix together the cottage cheese, sour cream, and seasonings and beat well.

Melt a small piece of clarified butter in a small skillet or pancake pan, over a farily high heat. Pour in about ¼ cup batter, tilting the pan to coat the bottom (see page 69).

Cook the pancake until golden brown underneath (2 to 3 minutes), loosen with a spatula, turn over, and cook until the other side is golden. Turn out carefully and keep warm. When all the blintzes are cooked, place a little filling on each, fold the sides over, and roll up. Place in a greased ovenproof dish and bake in a 400° oven for 10 minutes. Serve hot, topped with sour cream and chopped onion.

PORK CASSEROLE

1½-2 lb. tenderloin or lean leg of pork
¼ cup lard
1 onion, chopped
juice of ½ lemon
bay leaf
1½-2 teaspoons salt
freshly ground black pepper
1¼ cups red wine

½ cup all-purpose flour
1 cup water
1 chicken bouillon cube
1 cup sliced mushrooms
2 cloves garlic, crushed
2 tablespoons butter
⅔ cup white wine
1¼ cups sour cream

Cooking time: 30 or 40 minutes
Serves: 6

Slice the tenderloin thinly, or cut the leg meat into 1-inch cubes. Melt the lard in a large saucepan or flameproof casserole and gently fry the onions for 5 minutes. Add the pork, lemon juice, bay leaf, salt, pepper, and half the red wine, cover, and cook gently for 15 minutes. Lift the pork out. Add the flour to the pan and cook over a medium heat, stirring continuously, for 1 to 2 minutes. Add the water, chicken bouillon cube, and remaining red wine and bring to a boil, stirring continuously. Sauté the mushrooms and crushed garlic in a saucepan in melted butter for 2 to 3 minutes. Add the white wine, cover, and simmer gently for 10 minutes. Return the pork to the pan, add the mushroom mixture, and simmer, covered, until the pork is tender (about 5 minutes for tenderloin and 15 minutes for leg meat). Taste and adjust the seasoning if necessary. Add the sour cream and reheat without boiling. Serve hot with creamed potatoes and Braised Red Cabbage.

Note: This recipe is ideal for a buffet party as it can be eaten with a fork.

Coffee Gâteau

BRAISED RED CABBAGE

½ head medium-sized red
  cabbage
2 tablespoons butter
1 onion, sliced
2 apples, peeled, cored, and
  sliced

⅓ cup wine vinegar
⅓ cup water
2 tablespoons sugar
2 teaspoons salt
freshly ground black pepper

Cooking time: 1½ hours
Temperature: 325°
Serves: 6

Wash the red cabbage, remove the stalk, and shred finely. Place the cabbage in a large saucepan of boiling water, bring back to a boil, and boil for 1 minute. Drain well.

Melt the butter in a saucepan and fry the onion until soft but not browned. Add the sliced apples and cook for a further 2 minutes. Place a layer of cabbage in a greased ovenproof casserole. Cover with a layer of the onion and apple mixture. Continue the layers, sprinkling with wine vinegar, water, sugar, salt, and pepper between each layer. Place a piece of buttered paper over and cover with the lid. Cook in a 325° oven for 1½ hours, or until the cabbage is tender. Serve hot.

CHOCOLATE MOUSSE

Rich and delicious

1⅓ cups semi-sweet chocolate
  pieces
⅓ cup black coffee or water
1 tablespoon butter

2 tablespoons brandy or rum
  (optional)
4 eggs
1¼ cups whipping cream

Serves: 6

Melt the chocolate in the top of a double boiler or in a heatproof bowl over gently boiling water. Remove from the heat and stir in the butter and brandy or rum, if desired. Separate the eggs and add the yolks one at a time to the warm chocolate mixture, stirring continuously. Whip the whites until stiff and stir into the chocolate mixture. Pour the mousse into small mousse pots, or small individual glass dessert dishes, and place in the refrigerator until set. Serve with a little cream poured over the surface, or whip the cream and pipe a large rosette onto each mousse, using a pastry bag with a ½-inch star nozzle.

Summer Menu

Melon in Port

Summer Chicken and Pork
Rice
Lettuce and Lychee Salad

Loganberry Soufflé

MELON IN PORT

1 large or 2 small canteloupe
  melons

¼ cup sugar
1½ cups port

Serves: 6

Cut the melon in half and remove the seeds. Scoop out the flesh with a melon baller and place in individual serving dishes. Sprinkle with sugar and pour over the port. Allow to stand for at least 30 minutes and chill before serving.

Note: The melon may be cut into wedges for service if you do not have a melon baller.

SUMMER CHICKEN AND PORK

1 2-lb. chicken
1 lb. pork chops or leg of pork
⅓ cup oil
1 large onion, chopped
2 cloves garlic, crushed
3 tomatoes, skinned and chopped

½ teaspoon ground chili pepper
⅓ cup sesame seeds
1 cup chicken stock or water and
   chicken bouillon cube
¼ cup soy sauce
1½ cups peas, cooked or frozen

Cooking time: 1 hour
Serves: 6

Joint the chicken, remove the meat from the bone, and cut into 1-inch pieces. Remove the fat from the pork and cut into 1-inch cubes. Heat the oil in a large heavy saucepan and fry the chicken and pork until browned, about 5 to 10 minutes. Lift the chicken and pork out. Add the onion and garlic to the pan and sauté until golden. Add the tomatoes, reduce the heat, and simmer for 5 minutes. Return the meat to the pan and add the chili pepper,

sesame seeds, chicken stock, and soy sauce. Cover the pan. Bring to the simmering point and simmer gently for 30 minutes. Add the peas and cook for a further 5 minutes or until the meat is tender. Serve hot with boiled rice.

Note: Lamb may be substituted for the chicken.

LETTUCE AND LYCHEE SALAD

1 head lettuce
1 (20 oz.) can lychees
½ cup French dressing made with
   tarragon vinegar and a dash
   dry mustard

Serves: 6

Prepare the lettuce, dry well, and crispen in the refrigerator. Drain the lychees and cut into segments. Tear the lettuce into a chilled salad bowl, add the lychees, and

toss with the French dressing (see page 177) just before serving.

LOGANBERRY SOUFFLÈ

3 eggs
⅓ cup sugar
1 cup loganberry juice
2 envelopes gelatin

1¼ cups whipping cream
½ cup loganberries
whipped cream and extra
   loganberries for decoration

Serves: 6

Tie a band of double wax paper, or single wax paper with a layer of aluminum foil, around the outside of a china soufflé dish, to stand 2 to 3 inches above the dish.

Separate the eggs and beat the egg yolks, sugar, and ⅔ cup loganberry juice in a heatproof bowl over boiling water until thick and light. Dissolve the gelatin in the remaining ⅓ cup loganberry juice and stir quickly into the beaten mixture. Both mixtures should be at body temperature to combine smoothly and to prevent the soufflé separating.

Whip the cream and fold into the mixture with the loganberries. Whip the egg whites until stiff and gently

fold into the mixture, using a tablespoon or a plastic spatula. Pour into the prepared soufflé dish and place in the refrigerator to set.

When set, remove the paper carefully, unrolling from the soufflé and easing it off with a clean knife dipped in cold water. Decorate the top of the soufflé with swirls of whipped cream and extra loganberries.

Note: The loganberries may be soaked in Maraschino or Kirsch liqueur before adding to the soufflé mixture. Canned loganberries or fresh, stewed loganberries may be used.

Tasty Pineapple Spareribs

Lobster Thermidor
Potato Straws
Peas

Apricot Cream
Shortbread Fingers

TASTY PINEAPPLE SPARERIBS

3 lb. pork spareribs
1½ cups cider vinegar
1 cup cornstarch
¼ cup molasses
¼ cup soy sauce

1 cup oil
1 (15 oz.) can pineapple pieces
¾ cup water
¼ cup sugar
1 green sweet pepper

Cooking time: 45 minutes
Serves: 6

Cut the spareribs into individual ribs. Bring a large saucepan of water to a boil. Add ½ cup vinegar and the spareribs, bring back to a boil, and boil for 15 minutes. Drain. Mix together the cornstarch, molasses, and soy sauce in a mixing bowl and dip the spareribs into the mixture. Heat the oil in a skillet and fry the spareribs until brown. Remove the meat and drain well. Drain the pineapple. Reserve ¾ cup pineapple juice and bring to a boil in a clean skillet with the water, sugar, and remaining vinegar. Add the spareribs, cover, and simmer gently for 25 minutes, turning the ribs frequently. Add the pineapple pieces and green sweet pepper, seeded and cut into julienne strips, and cook for a further 5 minutes. Serve hot.

Note: Spareribs are eaten with the fingers.

LOBSTER THERMIDOR

3 medium-sized cooked lobsters
¼ cup butter
1 small onion, finely chopped
½ cup chopped mushrooms
6 tablespoons all-purpose flour
scant 2 cups milk
¼ teaspoon dry mustard
¼ teaspoon celery salt
1 teaspoon salt

dash cayenne pepper
⅔ cup cream
2 egg yolks
¼ cup dry sherry
2 teaspoons lemon juice
½-¾ cup grated cheese
lemon slices and parsley sprigs
    for garnish

Serves: 6

For buttered bread crumbs:
¼ cup butter

1 cup fresh bread crumbs

Remove the claws and cut the lobsters in half lengthwise. Remove the lobster meat, discard the intestinal vein, and cut the meat into 1-inch cubes. Wash, dry, and reserve the shells. Melt the butter in a saucepan and gently fry the onion and mushrooms for 2 to 3 minutes. Stir in the flour and cook over low heat for 1 minute. Add the milk and bring to a boil over medium heat, stirring continuously. Add the mustard, celery salt, salt, and cayenne pepper. Stir in the cream, egg yolks, sherry, lemon juice, and lobster meat. Heat through and place the mixture in the shells. Sprinkle with the grated cheese and buttered bread crumbs. Place under a heated broiler until golden brown. Serve hot garnished with lemon slices and parsley and accompanied by potato straws (see page 173) and peas.

To make the buttered bread crumbs: Melt the butter in a saucepan, add the bread crumbs, and fry, stirring continuously, until golden brown.

APRICOT CREAM

1 cup dried apricots or 1 lb.
fresh or canned apricots
sugar

1¼ cups whipping cream
2 envelopes gelatin

Serves: 6

If using dried apricots, soak in cold water overnight. Drain. Place in a saucepan with 1¼ cups fresh water and stew, covered, until tender. If using fresh apricots, stew gently with 1¼ cups water in a covered saucepan until tender. Cool and drain the apricots and retain the juice. Press the apricots through a sieve or purée in an electric blender. Make the purée up to 1¼ cups with apricot juice. Add sugar to taste. Whip the cream and mix gently with the fruit purée until smoothly combined. Dissolve the gelatin in ⅓ cup fruit juice then stir into the mixture. Pour the mixture into a mold, previously rinsed with cold water, and place in the refrigerator to set. Turn out onto a serving platter and serve accompanied by Shortbread Fingers.

SHORTBREAD FINGERS

1¼ cups all-purpose flour
⅓ cup rice flour

6 tablespoons sugar
⅔ cup butter

Cooking time: 20-25 minutes
Temperature: 300°
Yield: 16-18

Sieve the flour, rice flour, and sugar into a mixing bowl. Add the butter and knead and squeeze it into the dry ingredients, using one hand only, until that mixture is combined to a smooth, stiff dough. Roll the dough out on a lightly floured surface to a 6 by 10 inch oblong, using gentle even pressure with a lightly floured rolling pin. Cut down the center of the oblong, trim the edges, and cut across into fingers. Place the fingers on a greased baking sheet, prick well, and place in the refrigerator to rest for at least 30 minutes. Bake in a 300° oven for 20 to 25 minutes until light golden. Allow to set on the baking sheet before removing to a wire cooling rack. Store in an air-tight container.

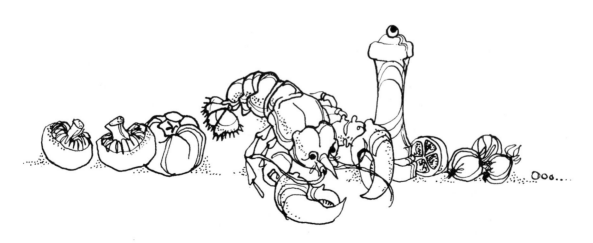

Stuffed Zucchini

Beef Tenderloin Dubarry
Potato Cake
Green Salad

Grapefruit Cheesecake

STUFFED ZUCCHINI

9 medium-sized zucchini
2 tablespoons olive oil
1 onion, chopped
1 clove garlic, crushed
$\frac{1}{4}$-$\frac{1}{2}$ cup chopped cooked ham
$\frac{1}{2}$ cup chopped mushrooms
$\frac{1}{4}$ cup tomato paste

rind and juice of 1 lemon
$\frac{1}{2}$ teaspoon tarragon
$\frac{1}{2}$ teaspoon salt
freshly ground black pepper
sliced tomato, $\frac{2}{3}$ cup sour cream,
    and finely chopped scallions
    for serving

Cooking time: 20 minutes
Temperature: 350°
Serves: 6

Wash the zucchini and cut in half lengthwise. Scoop out the seeds and pulp with a teaspoon leaving a $\frac{1}{4}$-inch thick shell: reserve the pulp. Place the zucchini shells in a pan of boiling water and boil for 1 to 2 minutes; remove and drain well. Heat the oil in a saucepan and fry the onion and garlic until soft and golden. Remove from the heat and stir in the ham, mushrooms, tomato paste, grated lemon rind and lemon juice, tarragon, and reserved zucchini pulp. Add salt and pepper to taste. Place the zucchini in a greased baking dish and cook in a 350° oven for 20 minutes or until the zucchini are tender. Serve hot on individual plates with a slice of tomato topped with sour cream and sprinkled with chopped scallions.

BEEF TENDERLOIN DUBARRY

A delicious combination of roast beef and cheese

1 2$\frac{1}{2}$-lb. beef tenderloin
salt
freshly ground black pepper
5 slices bacon

1 medium-sized cauliflower
$\frac{1}{2}$ cup grated Parmesan or
    Gruyère cheese
parsley sprigs for garnish

Cooking time: 35-45 minutes
Temperature: 400°
Serves: 6

For sauce:
2$\frac{1}{2}$ cups White Sauce
$\frac{2}{3}$ cup chicken stock or
    vegetable water

$\frac{1}{2}$ cup grated Parmesan or
    Gruyère cheese

Trim any fat off the beef tenderloin. Sprinkle the beef with salt and pepper and rub into the meat. Place the meat on a piece of greased aluminum foil. Cut the bacon slices into 4-inch strips and lay overlapping over the beef. Wrap the beef up loosely in the foil and place in a roasting pan. Roast in a 400° oven for 15 to 20 minutes. Unwrap the foil, and continue to cook the beef to required taste, rare, meidum, or well cooked, testing with a skewer or fork. Place on a heated serving dish and keep warm. Meanwhile, prepare the cauliflower and cut into flowerets. Boil the cauliflower in a pan of boiling salted water for 10 minutes or until tender but not soft or broken. Drain well and place around the cooked beef. Coat the beef and cauliflower with cheese sauce and sprinkle with the re-maining $\frac{1}{2}$ cup Parmesan cheese. Place under a hot broiler or return to a hot oven until the sauce is golden. Serve hot, garnished with parsley and accompanied by a green salad.
To make the sauce: Make 2$\frac{1}{2}$ cups White Sauce (see page 50) and stir in the chicken stock or vegetable water. Heat gently until reduced by one fourth. Stir in the cheese and cook gently until melted. Taste and adjust the seasoning if necessary.

Note: Beef Tenderloin Dubarry may be served placed on top of a Potato Cake, see following recipe.

POTATO CAKE

Potatoes cooked in this way have a delicious natural nutty flavor.

1½ lb. potaotes	salt	Cooking time: 45 minutes
3 tablespoons butter	white pepper	Temperature: 425°
		Serves: 6

Peel the potatoes and cut into julienne strips. Dry well in a clean dish towel. Rub the butter over the bottom and sides of a small heavy skillet or a 7-inch layer pan. Place the potatoes in the pan and season with salt and pepper. Cover with a layer of buttered paper and cook over a medium heat for 10 to 15 minutes or until the potatoes begin to turn golden underneath. Transfer to a 425° oven and cook for a further 30 minutes, or until cooked. Test with a knife. Turn out, bottom side up, like a cake, and arrange the meat on top. Serve hot.

GRAPEFRUIT CHEESECAKE

A refreshing cheesecake with a tangy flavor

For crumb crust:
½ lb. Graham crackers
1 teaspoon cinnamon
1 teaspoon nutmeg

¼ teaspoon ground cloves
6 tablespoons butter

Serves: 8-10

For filling:
2 grapefruit
2 eggs
¾ cup sugar
2 envelopes gelatin
1½ cups cream cheese

rind and juice of 1 lemon
1¼ cups whipping cream
⅔ cup whipped cream for
   decoration

To prepare the crumb crust: Place the crackers in a clean plastic bag and crush with a rolling pin. Place in a mixing bowl with the ground spices and melted butter. Mix until combined and spread and mold over the bottom and sides of a well-greased 8-inch spring form pan. Chill in the refrigerator until set.

To make the filling: Grate sufficient of the grapefruit rind to fill 1 teaspoon. Peel the grapefruit, using a serrated knife, over a plate to retain the juice. Remove all white pith and cut the grapefruit into segments. Reserve 8 to 10 segments for decoration and chop the remainder of the fruit. Reserve ½ cup grapefruit juice.

Separate 1 egg and place the yolk in the top of a double boiler with the remaining egg and the sugar. Beat over gently boiling water until thick and creamy; cool. Dissolve the gelatin in half the measured grapefruit juice. Cool and stir into the egg mixture. Both mixtures should be at body temperature to combine smoothly. Sieve the cream cheese and mix with the chopped grapefruit, remaining grapefruit juice, and rind and juice of the lemon. Mix with the egg mixture. Whip the cream and fold into the mixture. Whip the egg white until stiff and fold into the mixture. Pour the filling into the prepared crumb shell and place in the refrigerator until set.

To serve, remove carefully from the pan and decorate with swirls of whipped cream and grapefruit segments.

Noix de Veau a la Reboux

CONVERSIONS

The following pages explain how to convert the American Standard measures used in this book to Imperial and metric measures. Tables of equivalents are given and also useful lists of some common culinary terms and names of equipment.

CONVERTING AMERICAN VOLUME MEASURES TO IMPERIAL WEIGHTS AND MEASURES

The great difference between the American and Imperial systems of culinary measurement is that Americans measure by volume for both liquids and solids, while the British measure by weight for solids and use volume only for liquids and for very small amounts of solids where absolute accuracy is not vital. As the density of individual ingredients varies enormously, an exhaustive list of commonly used ingredients and their weight equivalents follows. If you check against this list to find out what 1 cup of the given ingredient weighs, you will very easily be able to convert the quantities in this book into pounds and ounces. It must be noted that an American Standard cup is a standard measure holding 8 fluid ounces and all the measures in this book use this cup. For a detailed list of the capacity of cups and tablespoons see page 16. The American pint is 16 fluid ounces, or 2 cups, while the Imperial pint is 20 fluid ounces, or $2\frac{1}{2}$ cups.

LIQUIDS

American	Imperial
1 teaspoon	1 teaspoon
1 tablespoon	1 tablespoon
2 tablespoons	$1\frac{1}{2}$ tablespoons
3 tablespoons	2 tablespoons
4 tablespoons ($\frac{1}{4}$ cup)	3 tablespoons
5 tablespoons ($\frac{1}{3}$ cup)	4 tablespoons
6 tablespoons	5 tablespoons
7 tablespoons	$5\frac{1}{2}$ tablespoons
8 tablespoons ($\frac{1}{2}$ cup)	6 tablespoons
$\frac{2}{3}$ cup	$\frac{1}{4}$ pint (5 fluid ounces)
$1\frac{1}{4}$ cups	$\frac{1}{2}$ pint (10 fluid ounces)
scant 2 cups (15 fluid ounces)	$\frac{3}{4}$ pint
2 cups (16 fluid ounces)	generous $\frac{3}{4}$ pint
$2\frac{1}{2}$ cups	1 pint
3 cups	$1\frac{1}{5}$ pints
4 cups (2 pints, 1 quart)	$1\frac{1}{2}$ pints
$4\frac{1}{2}$ cups	$1\frac{3}{4}$ pints
5 cups	2 pints
3 pints ($1\frac{1}{2}$ quarts)	$2\frac{1}{2}$ pints
4 pints (2 quarts)	$3\frac{1}{4}$ pints
6 pints	5 pints

SOLIDS

Ingredient	American		Imperial
basics			
flour	1	cup	4 ounces
	$\frac{1}{4}$	cup	1 ounce
	2	tablespoons	$\frac{1}{2}$ ounce
cornflour	1	cup	$4\frac{1}{2}$ ounces
	$\frac{1}{4}$	cup	1 ounce
sugar	1	cup	8 ounces
	$\frac{1}{4}$	cup	2 ounces
	2	tablespoons	1 ounce
icing sugar, sifted	1	cup	$4\frac{1}{2}$ ounces
	$\frac{1}{4}$	cup	1 ounce
butter, margarine, lard, dirpping	1	cup	8 ounces
	$\frac{1}{4}$	cup	2 ounces
	2	tablespoons	1 ounce
suet, shredded	1	cup	5 ounces
cheese, grated	1	cup	4 ounces
	$\frac{1}{4}$	cup	1 ounce
cheese, cottage	1	cup	8 ounces
cereals			
pearl barley	1	cup	7 ounces
tapioca	1	cup	6 ounces
cornmeal	1	cup	5 ounces
cracked wheat	1	cup	$4\frac{1}{2}$ ounces
semolina	1	cup	6 ounces
ground rice	1	cup	6 ounces
fresh soft breadcrumbs, cake crumbs	1	cup	2 ounces
dried breadcrumbs	1	cup	4 ounces
biscuit crumbs	$\frac{3}{4}$	cup	2 ounces
rice crispies	1	cup	1 ounce
long-grain rice	1	cup	7 ounces
rolled oats	1	cup	$3\frac{1}{2}$ ounces
oatmeal	1	cup	6 ounces
split peas, lentils	1	cup	8 ounces
dried chick peas	1	cup	7 ounces

vegetables

chopped cooked spinach	1 cup	7½ ounces
sliced or button mushrooms	1 cup	3-4 ounces
shelled peas	¾ cup	4 ounces
bean sprouts	1 cup	2 ounces
blackcurrants, redcurrants	1 cup	4 ounces
bilberries	1 cup	4 ounces
raspberries	1 cup	5 ounces
strawberries, whole	1 cup	5 ounces
strawberries, crushed	1 cup	6 ounces

preserves

jam, jelly, marmalade	1 cup	11-12 ounces
clear honey, golden syrup, molasses, black treacle	1 cup	12 ounces
corn syrup, maple syrup	1 cup	11 ounces

dried fruit and nuts

raisins, currants, sultanas, chopped candied peel	1 cup	5-6 ounces
stoned dates	1 cup	6½ ounces
glacé cherries	1 cup	8 ounces
prunes, unsoaked	1 cup	6 ounces
dried apricots	1 cup	5-6 ounces
halved shelled walnuts	1 cup	4 ounces
pine nuts	1 cup	3-4 ounces
whole shelled almonds	1 cup	5 ounces
blanched slivered almonds	1 cup	4 ounces
whole shelled peanuts	1 cup	7 ounces
chopped nuts (most kinds)	1 cup	4 ounces
ground almonds	1 cup	4 ounces
desiccated coconut	1 cup	3 ounces

miscellaneous

minced raw meat	1 cup	8 ounces
chopped cooked meat (ham, beef)	1 cup	6 ounces
curry powder	1 cup	2 ounces
stoned olives	1 cup	5-6 ounces
instant coffee powder	1 cup	2 ounces
tomato purée	¼ cup	2¾ ounces (smallest can)
gelatine	1 envelope	¼ ounce
	1 tablespoon	¼ ounce
peeled prawns	1 cup	6 ounces
caviar	¼ cup	2 ounces
semi-sweet chocolate pieces	1 cup	6 ounces
unsweetened cooking chocolate	1 square	1 ounce
condensed milk	1 cup	1 (14 ounce) can

SUBSTITUTES

American	British
all-purpose flour	plain flour
bacon	streaky bacon
bacon, Canadian style	lean or back bacon
baking powder, double-acting	baking powder
cooking chocolate, semi-sweet	plain choclate or chocolate Meunier
cooking chocolate, unsweetened	Baker's unsweetened cooking chocolate
corn syrup, maple syrup	golden syrup
cream, coffee	single cream
cream, whipping	double cream
Graham crackers	digestive biscuits
lima beans, fava beans	broad beans
marrow squash	vegetable marrow
molasses	black treacle
navy beans	haricot beans
shredded coconut	desiccated coconut
shrimp, jumbo	Dublin Bay prawns or scampi
sugar, brown	soft brown sugar
sugar (granulated)	granulated or castor sugar

NAMES OF INGREDIENTS

American	British
baking soda	bicarbonate of soda
beet	beetroot
blueberries	bilberries
bouillon cube	stock cube
candied cherries	glacé cherries
candied fruits	crystallized fruits

American	British
chicory	curly endive
chili pepper	chilli pepper
coffee cake	tea cake, teabread
confectioners' sugar	icing sugar
cornstarch	cornflour
cracker crumbs	biscuit crumbs
endive, Belgian	chicory
fruit-flavored gelatin	flavored jelly packets
ground rice	rice flour
lettuce, iceberg	Webb's Wonder lettuce
saltines	savoury biscuits
scallions	spring onions
seedless white raisins	sultanas
sweet pepper, green or red	pepper or capsicum, green or red
vanilla bean	vanilla pod
vanilla extract	vanilla essence
zucchini	courgettes

TERMS AND EQUIPMENT

American	British
baking sheet	baking tray
batter	pancake batter or cake mixture
biscuit	scone
broil	grill
candy	sweet
cookie	biscuit
cookie cutter	biscuit/pastry cutter
cookie press	biscuit press
custard cups	dariole moulds
dough	bread dough or raw pastry
frosting	icing
grind, ground	mince, minced
layer pan	sandwich cake tin
jelly roll pan	Swiss roll tin
muffin pans	patty tins, bun tins
pancake turner	fish slice
paper towels	kitchen paper
pastry bag	piping bag
pie	pie, tart, flan
pie crust	pastry
pie pan, plate	flan ring, flan dish, tart plate
pie shell	pastry case
pudding mold	pudding basin or metal mould with clip-on lid
punch down dough	knock back dough
pit	stone, seed, pip
skillet	frying pan
spring form pan	deep cake tin, loose-bottomed preferably
tube pan	ring mould
wax paper	greaseproof paper

CUTS OF MEAT

In The United States retail cuts of meat are not the same as those sold in Britain. The following list gives a suitable alternative, as close in price and style as possible, for occasions when a recipe in this book calls for a cut not available in British shops. American meat cutters prepare quite a number of boned and rolled or otherwise prepared joints which are not normally prepared by British butchers; unboned joints may be substituted allowing more weights.

	American	British
beef	stew meat	stewing steak
	ground beef	mince
	blade or arm steak	braising steak
	corned beef	silverside or brisket
	rolled rump roast or standing rump	sirloin or topside
	standing rib roast	rib, back or fore
	tenderloin	fillet
veal	round steaks	thin slices from top of leg (escalopes)
lamb	leg steak, arm chop, blade chop	chump chop
	loin chop	loin chop
	rib chop	cutlet
pork	fat back	pork fat or fat belly
	lean salt pork	salt belly
	fresh picnic shoulder, blade, Boston butt	hand and spring, lean unsalted belly
	arm steak, blade steak	chump chop
	loin chop	loin chop
	rib chop	neck chop
	tenderloin	fillet
ham	ham slice	gammon steak
	bacon	streaky bacon

492   *Carpet Bag Steak*

Canadian bacon	lean bacon
smoked picnic shoulder	forehock, slipper

OVEN TEMPERATURES

All oven temperatures in this book are given in degrees Fahrenheit. The table gives conversions to the Celsius scale and Gas Mark.

Fahrenheit	Celsius	Gas Mark
225	110	$\frac{1}{4}$
250	130	$\frac{1}{2}$
275	140	1
300	150	2
325	170	3
350	180	4
375	190	5
400	200	6
425	220	7
450	230	8
475	240	9

CONVERSION TO METRIC MEASURES

In converting to metric measures it is easiest and most convenient to work in units of 25 grams. It will be seen from the tables that this sometimes gives a noticeably smaller or larger amount than the original quantity in the recipe. Where the difference is sufficiently great to alter the proportions of a recipe substantially, the liquid measurements should be adjusted slightly.

Ounces and fluid ounces	Grams and Millilitres to nearest whole figure	Recommended equivalent in Grams and Millilitres
1	28	25
2	57	50
3	85	75
4	113	125
5	142	150
6	170	175
7	198	200
8	226	225
9	255	250
10	283	275
11	311	300
12	340	350
13	368	375
14	396	400
15	428	425
16	456	450
17	484	475
18	512	500
19	541	550
20	569	575

There are 1000 grams in a kilogram and 1000 millilitres (10 decilitres) in a litre. Using the above table as a guide, it can be seen that 8 ounces ($\frac{1}{2}$ lb.) equals 225 grams, 1 lb. equals 450 grams, 2 lb. is 900 grams, etc. Liquid conversions are equally simple: $\frac{1}{4}$ pint (5 fluid ounces) is 150 millilitres ($1\frac{1}{2}$ decilitres), $\frac{1}{2}$ pint is 275 millilitres, 1 pint is 575 millilitres.
When converting from American measures the following will be helpful:

American	Metric
1 cup	scant $\frac{1}{4}$ litre (225 millilitres)
2 cups (1 pint)	$4\frac{1}{2}$ decilitres (450 millilitres)
$4\frac{1}{2}$ cups	1 litre
10 cups (5 pints)	$2\frac{1}{4}$ litres

ACKNOWLEDGMENTS

The editor would like to
thank the following for their
help and co-operation in the
preparation of this book:
Air New Zealand
Allowrie Products
Ansett Airlines of Australia
Corning Glass Works
Crown Crystal Glass
Fowlers Vacola Manufacturing Co Ltd.
Har-V-Sales (Tupperware)
Hemphill's Herbs and Spices Pty. Ltd.
Incorporated Agencies Pty. Ltd.
Kenwood Peerless Pty. Ltd.
Master Foods of Australia Pty. Ltd.
Raco Corporation Pty. Ltd.
Salter Geo. and Co. Pty. Ltd.
Trans-Australia Airlines
Tulloch's Vineyard
Wine Bureau

Glossary

Acidify: To add lemon juice or vinegar to water, a sauce, or cooked dish.

Antipasto: Italian, 'before the pasta'. Appetizer of assorted vegetables, fish, or cold cuts of meat.

Aspic: The culinary name for calves' feet jelly, or jelly made with bones of meat, fish, or poultry. May be made from commercial aspic.

Au gratin: Food baked in a shallow ovenproof gratin dish, sprinkled with bread crumbs, covered with sauce dotted with butter, and browned in the oven or under the broiler until a crisp gratin coating forms. Often contains cheese, but not essential.

Bain-marie: A French kitchen utensil designed to keep liquids at simmering point without coming to a boil. It consists of a saucepan standing in a larger pan which is filled with boiling water. A bain-marie is a great help in keeping sauces, stews, and soups hot without over-cooking. In domestic kitchens, a double boiler can do double duty as a bain-marie.

Bake: To cook by dry heat in the oven. This term is usually used only for breads, cakes, biscuits, pies, cookies and pastries,

Baste: To pour or spoon liquid over food as it cooks to moisten and flavor it.

Batter: A mixture of flour and some liquid, beaten together, it is thin enough to coat food, pour, or be dropped from a spoon. Also cake batter, uncooked cake.

Beat: To mix with a spoon, spatula, whisk, rotary beater, or electric mixer; to make a mixture smooth and light by enclosing air.

Beurre manié: Equal quantities of butter and flour kneaded together and added bit by bit to a stew, casserole, or sauce to thicken it.

Blanch: To heat in boiling water or steam. This can be done for several reasons: (1) to loosen outer skins of fruit, nuts, or vegetables; (2) to whiten sweetbreads, veal, or chicken; (3) to remove excess salt or bitter flavor from bacon, ham, Brussels sprouts, turnips, endive, etc; (4) to prepare fruits and vegetables for canning, freezing, or preserving.

Blend: To mix two or more ingredients thoroughly, usually a powdered ingredient and a liquid mixed to a smooth paste using a wooden spoon.

Boil: To bring to the boiling point and keep there, to cook in liquid which is boiling.

Boiling point: The temperature at which bubbles rise continually and break over the entire surface of a liquid—212° at sea level.

Bone: To remove the bones from fish, chicken poultry, or game.

Bouillon: A clear soup, usually made from beef.

Bouquet garni: A bunch or 'faggot' of culinary herbs, used to flavor stews, casseroles, and sauces. Usually consists of sprigs of parsley, thyme, marjoram, rosemary, a bay leaf, peppercorns, and cloves, tied in cheesecloth.

Buttermilk: A fermented milk product from which fat has been removed in the process of churning.

Braise: To simmer gently in a covered casserole on a layer of mirepoix, in a small amount of liquid.

Broil: See grill.

Caramelize: To melt sugar in a small heavy saucepan, until it is a golden brown syrup.

Chaudfroid: A jellied white sauce made of butter, flour, chicken stock, egg yolks, cream, and gelatin. Used to give a shiny white glaze to fish, chicken, ham, etc.

Canapé: A small piece of bread, pastry, biscuit, or cookie topped with meat, fish, or cheese and served as a cocktail tidbit.

Chill: To place in the refrigerator or other cold place until cold.

Chop: To cut into very small pieces with a sharp knife or a chopper.

Chowder: A soup, usually using fish, clams, or vegetables, made with milk.

Clarify:
1. To clear a stock or broth by adding slightly beaten egg whites and crushed egg shells and bringing to a boil. The stock is cooled and strained before using.
2. To cleanse fat drippings for deep frying by adding water and melting very gently. When cool the clean fat is removed and the sediment is left at the bottom.
3. To melt salted butter and drain the oil off the salty sediment.

Cool: To allow to stand at room temperature until no longer warm to the touch.

Coat: To cover entire surface with a mixture such as seasoned flour, bread crumbs, batter, or to cover vegetables with sauce.

Coddle: To cook slowly and gently in water just below the boiling point.

Compote: Fruits stewed in syrup and served as a dessert.

Consommé: A clear soup made usually with beef with an intensive flavor.

Court bouillon: The liquid in which fish, poultry, or meat is cooked to give added flavor. A simple court bouillon consists of water to which you have added 1 bay leaf, 2 stalks celery, 1 onion, 2 carrots, and salt and freshly ground black pepper to taste. Other additives: wine, vinegar, stock, olive oil, garlic, shallots, cloves, etc.

Cream: To cream butter and sugar by beating with a wooden spoon or an electric mixer until light, white, and fluffy like whipped cream.

Crêpe: A very thin pancake served with a rich salty or sweet filling.

Croûton: Fried or toasted cubes of bread used as a garnish or topping or accompaniment to soup.

Cut in: To combine fat and dry ingredients with two knives, scissor-fashion, or with a pastry blender, when making pastry.

Deep fry: To cook in deep hot fat or oil which covers the food, until crisp and golden.

Devil: To cook food by combining it with a highly seasoned hot sauce which contains Worcestershire sauce and mustard.

Dice: To cut into small even cubes.

Disjoint: To cut poultry, game, or small animals into serving pieces by dividing at the joint.

Dissolve: To mix a dry ingredient with liquid until it is absorbed.

Dredge: To coat food with a fine ingredient by dusting, sprinkling, or rolling the food in flour, cornstarch, cornmeal, sugar, confectioners' sugar, etc.

Drippings: The residue left in the pan after meat or poultry is cooked, usually including fat.

Dust: To sprinkle lightly as with flour or sugar.

Entrée: A single made-up dish, served before the main course of roast meat or game or poultry.

Escallop: See scallop. To bake food with liquid, usually white sauce, with a covering of bread crumbs and sometimes cheese.

Fillet: 1. Fish cut off the bone lengthwise. 2. To cut meat or fish to use in cooking.

Fish fumet: A highly concentrated fish stock, made by reducing well-flavored fish stock. Used to poach fish, fish fillets, or fish steaks, and flavor sauces.

Flake: To break into small pieces with a fork.

Flame: To spoon alcohol over food and ignite.

Fold in: To add other ingredients to a mixture which has been beaten until light and fluffy, using a plastic spatula or tablespoon with a light cut and fold movement so the air is not lost.

Fricassée: A stew made from white meats and vegetables and served in a thickened sauce.

Fry: To cook in a little fat or oil in a frying pan.

Fondue: A dish of Swiss origin cooked in a special pan over a flame at the table.

Frosting: A thick mixture of sugar and other ingredients used to frost a cake.

Garnish: To decorate food, usually with something edible.

Glaze: A thin coating of beaten egg, syrup, or aspic which is brushed over pie crusts (beaten egg), fruits (syrup) or cooked fish, ham, tongue, chicken, etc. (aspic).

Grate: To rub a food against a grater to form small particles.

Gelatin: A protein substance found in the connective tissue of bones of animals.

Grease: To rub lightly with butter, margarine, oil, or fat.

Grill: To cook by direct heat such as an open fire. Today, by charcoal, gas, or electricity.

Homogenize: To process a food, such as milk, so that fats are completely integrated and will not separate.

Julienne: Cut into fine strips the length of a matchstick.

Knead: To work dough with hands until it is of the desired elasticity or consistency.

Lard: 1. Common cooking fat obtained by melting down pork fat. 2. The strips can be threaded with a larding needle, or inserted in cuts made in the meat.

Lardons: Strips of fat or bacon used as above.

Liaison: To thicken a sauce, gravy, or stew; 1. by the addition of flour, cornstarch, arrowroot, rice flour, potato flour, or a beurre manié (flour and butter); 2. by stirring in egg yolk, cream, or, in the case of certain dishes of poultry or game, blood.

Macédoine: 1. A mixture of raw or cooked fruit for a fruit salad. 2. A mixture of cooked diced vegetables, often garnished with a cream sauce, mayonnaise, or aspic, and served as an hors d'oeuvre, salad, or as a garnish.

Marinade: Usually a mixture of an oil, acid, and seasonings in which food is marinated to give it more flavor and to soften the tissues of tough food.

Marinate: To let food stand in a marinade.

Mask: To cover cooked food with sauce.

Mocha: A combination of coffee and chocolate flavors.

Monosodium glutamate: A crystalline chemical product added to food to intensify the natural flavor.

Mince: To reduce to very small particles with a mincer, chopper, or knife.

Mirepoix: Diced carrots, onion, celery (usually bacon or ham), simmered in butter until soft. Used to add flavor to dishes of meat, poultry, and fish.

Oven fry: To cook meat, fish, or poultry in fat in the oven, uncovered, basting food with fat from time to time.

Parboil: To boil until partially cooked.

Pare or peel:
1. To cut off outside skin or covering of a fruit or vegetable with a knife or vegetable peeler.
2. To peel fruits such as oranges or bananas without using a knife.

Parfait: A frozen dessert made with whipped cream usually layered with a syrup, or a fruit, in a tall narrow glass.

Pasteurize: To destroy certain micro-organisms by holding at a temperature of 140° to 180° for a stated length of time.

Pâté: A highly seasoned meat paste, usually served as a hors d'oeuvre.

Petit four: A small cake usually iced on top and sides and delicately decorated.

Pit: To remove pit, stone, or seed, as from cherries.

Poach: To cook gently in simmering liquid.

Port wine cheese: A semi hard, blue-veined, well matured cheese, usually Stilton, that has port wine poured on to it and is left until the wine has soaked right into the cheese.

Pound: To reduce to very small particles, or a paste, with a mortar and pestle.

Praline: A confection made by preparing a syrup and adding nuts.

Preheat: To have oven or cooking appliance at desired temperature before putting in food.

Purée: To press through a fine sieve or put in a food blender to produce a smooth thick mixture.

Ragoût: A stew made from regular-sized pieces of meat, poultry, or fish, sautéed in fat until brown and then simmered with stock, meat juices, or water, or a combination of these, until tender.

Ramekin: Individual baking dish.

Reduce: To cook a sauce over a high heat, uncovered, until it is reduced by evaporation to the desired consistency. This culinary process improves both flavor and appearance.

Roast: To cook meat by direct heat on a spit or in the oven, although 'baking' would be a better term, for when meat is cooked in a closed area (oven) vapor accumulates and changes texture and flavor of true roast.

Roux: A mixture of fat and flour cooked slowly over a low heat used as a foundation for sauces, soups, and thick gravies.

Sauté: To fry lightly in a small amount of hot fat or oil, shaking the pan or turning food frequently during cooking, usually until the fat or oil is absorbed.

Scald: To heat to temperature just below the boiling point, with small bubbles rising occasionally to the surface.

Score: To make evenly spaced, shallow slits or cuts with a knife on the surface of food.

Shred: To cut into thin pieces.

Simmer: To cook in liquid just below the boiling point, with small bubbles rising occasionally to the surface.

Skim: To remove foam, fat, or solid substance from the surface of a cooking, or cooked mixture.

Sliver: To cut in long, thin pieces.

Sour cream: A cultured, commercial product, usually 18% butterfat content. Used as a topping for vegetables and fruit, in sauces, gravies, and meat dishes.

Steam: To cook food in vapor rising from boiling water.

Stew: A long slow method of cooking in a covered pan in a small amount of liquid, usually to tenderize tough meat.

Stir: To mix with a spoon with a circular motion.

Stock: A liquid containing the flavors, extracts, and nutrients of the bones, meat, fish, or vegetables in which it is cooked.

Tamarind juice: Made by soaking dried tamarind fruit in hot water for 20 minutes, pressing through a sieve to make a purée, and then diluting the purée with water to a pouring consistency.

Timbale: Individual baked custards made with minced fish, poultry, or vegetables.

Torte: A rich cake made with crumbs and eggs, containing fruit and nuts.

Toss: To mix lightly, especially salad of fresh greens, using a fork and spoon.

Index